The Letter to the Ephesians

The New International Commentary on the New Testament

General Editors

NED B. STONEHOUSE
(1946–1962)

F. F. BRUCE
(1962–1990)

GORDON D. FEE
(1990–2012)

JOEL B. GREEN
(2013–)

The Letter to the
EPHESIANS

Lynn H. Cohick

William B. Eerdmans Publishing Company
Grand Rapids, Michigan

Wm. B. Eerdmans Publishing Co.
4035 Park East Court SE, Grand Rapids, Michigan 49546
www.eerdmans.com

© 2020 Lynn H. Cohick
All rights reserved
Published 2020
Printed in the United States of America

26 25   3 4 5 6 7

ISBN 978-0-8028-6842-8

Library of Congress Cataloging-in-Publication Data

Names: Cohick, Lynn H., author.
Title: The letter to the Ephesians / Lynn H. Cohick.
Description: Grand Rapids, Michigan : William B. Eerdmans Publishing Company, 2020. | Series: The new international commentary on the New Testament | Includes bibliographical references and index. | Summary: "A commentary on the book of Ephesians, including both close textual reading and engagement with relevant scholarly debates"—Provided by publisher.
Identifiers: LCCN 2020012152 | ISBN 9780802868428 (hardcover)
Subjects: LCSH: Bible. Ephesians—Commentaries. | Bible. Ephesians—Criticism, Textual.
Classification: LCC BS2695.53 .C645 2020 | DDC 227/.5077—dc23
LC record available at https://lccn.loc.gov/2020012152

Unless otherwise noted, Scripture quotations are taken from the Holy Bible, New International Version™, NIV™. Copyright 1973, 1978, 1984, 2011 by Biblica, Inc. Used with permission of Biblica and Zondervan. All rights reserved worldwide.

The "New International Version" is a trademark registered in the European Union Intellectual Property Office (EUIPO) and United States Patent and Trademark Office by Biblica, Inc. The "NIV," "Biblica," "International Bible Society," and the Biblica Logo are trademarks registered in the United States Patent and Trademark Office by Biblica, Inc. Used with permission.

To Maria Sisley McTarnaghan and Christopher Scott Harrison

Contents

List of Excursuses — xi
General Editor's Preface — xiii
Author's Preface — xv
Abbreviations — xvii
Bibliography — xix

INTRODUCTION — 1
  I. AUTHORSHIP — 3
    A. Authorship Question Unpacked — 3
    B. Ephesians as Deutero-Pauline — 4
      1. Theology — 5
      2. Literary Style — 8
      3. Historical Circumstances — 9
      4. Relationship between Ephesians and Colossians — 12
    C. Pseudepigraphy in the Ancient World — 15
    D. Genuine or Forgery — 19
    E. Secretaries and Letter Writing in the Ancient World — 23
    F. Conclusions on the Pseudepigraphic Paul and Ephesians — 24
  II. RECIPIENTS — 25
    A. Textual Evidence for the Omission of "in Ephesus" — 26
    B. Evaluation of the Evidence — 28
  III. OCCASION FOR WRITING EPHESIANS — 30

Contents

IV. Purpose of Ephesians	32
V. First-Century Ephesus	34
A. Cult of Artemis	34
B. Imperial Cult	36
C. Magic and Powers in Ephesus	40
D. Judaism in Ephesus	42
E. Ephesus and Paul's Visit (Acts 19)	43
VI. Date and Provenance of Ephesians	45
A. Ephesus	45
B. Rome	47
VII. Structure of Ephesians	47
A. Analysis of Letter	48
B. Outline of Letter	52
VIII. Outline of the Commentary	53
IX. Theology of Ephesians	55
A. Paul's Use of the Old Testament	55
B. Christology or Theology?	57
C. God the Father	61
D. God the Spirit	62
E. The Lord Jesus Christ	63
1. Jesus Christ as Son of the Father	63
2. Christ	63
3. Lord	64
4. Christ Our Peace	66
F. Trinitarian Language in Ephesians	66
G. The Church in Ephesians	67
H. Mystery of the Gospel and the Church	70
X. The New Perspective on Paul and Ephesians	71

Text and Commentary

	77
I. Paul's Opening Greeting (1:1–2)	77
II. Theological Explication of the Gospel (1:3–3:21)	83

Contents

    A. Eulogy and Prayer (1:3–23) — 83
        1. Thanksgiving to God through Christ (1:3–14) — 83
            Thematic Outline of 1:3–14 — 88
            a. Adopted by the Father (1:3–6) — 88
            b. Redeemed by the Son (1:7–12) — 102
            c. Sealed by the Holy Spirit (1:13–14) — 111
        2. God's Work through Christ's Rule over All Things (1:15–23) — 113
            a. Prayer for the Ephesians (1:15–19) — 115
            b. God Raised and Exalted Christ (1:20–23) — 122
    B. The Riches of His Grace (2:1–22) — 139
        1. God's Grace Rescues Humanity (2:1–10) — 140
            a. Human Plight in the Present Age (2:1–3) — 142
            b. God's Actions in Christ for Believers (2:4–7) — 150
            c. God's Gift of Grace (2:8–10) — 156
        2. Christ Is Our Peace (2:11–22) — 171
            a. Gentiles Far from God (2:11–13) — 175
            b. Christ Creates One New People (2:14–18) — 181
            c. Christ Builds His Church (2:19–22) — 195
    C. Mystery of Salvation Revealed (3:1–21) — 200
        1. Digression Concerning the Revealed Mystery (3:1–13) — 201
            a. Paul's Insight into the Mystery (3:1–5) — 204
            b. Mystery of Gentile Participation in Christ (3:6–7) — 212
            c. Paul's Suffering for Gentiles' Glory (3:8–13) — 214
        2. Prayer to Be Established in Christ's Love (3:14–21) — 226
            a. Paul Prays to the Father of All (3:14–15) — 227
            b. Paul Prays for Christ's Love (3:16–19) — 230
            c. Paul Glorifies the Father (3:20–21) — 235
III. EXHORTATION TO HOLY LIVING (4:1–6:20) — 238
    A. Walk Worthy of Your Calling (4:1–32) — 241
        1. Unity in One Spirit, One Lord, One Father (4:1–6) — 243
        2. Christ's Gift to the Church (4:7–16) — 254
            a. Christ Ascended and Descended (4:7–10) — 255
            b. Christ's Body Grows to Fullness (4:11–16) — 264

Contents

      3. Put on the New Self (4:17–24)   277
      4. Speak Truth with Compassion (4:25–32)   289
   B. Walk as Christ Walked (5:1–21)   305
      1. Follow God's Example (5:1–2)   305
      2. Inherit the Kingdom (5:3–6)   312
      3. Darkness and Light (5:7–14)   324
      4. Be Filled with the Holy Spirit (5:15–21)   333
   C. The Household Codes (5:21–6:9)   348
      1. Wife and Husband (5:21–33)   348
         a. Instructions to Wives (5:21–24)   350
         b. Instructions to Husbands (5:25–33)   359
      2. Children and Parents (6:1–4)   373
      3. Slaves and Masters (6:5–9)   385
   D. Armor of God (6:10–20)   407
      1. Be Strong in the Lord (6:10–13)   409
      2. Put on God's Armor (6:14–17)   415
      3. Pray in the Spirit (6:18–20)   427
IV. Final Greetings (6:21–24)   433

Index of Subjects   439
Index of Authors   449
Index of Scripture and Other Ancient Texts   455

List of Excursuses

Ephesians 1:3–14 and Its Relationship to the Epistle	87
"In Christ"	91
The Meaning of *Kephalē*	130
"Body" Metaphors in the Ancient World	135
Christian Anti-Judaism	168
Supersessionism	189
Paul's Arrest in Jerusalem	206
"Faith in Christ" or "the Faithfulness of Christ"	221
Imitate God as Beloved Children	310
The Household Codes in the Ancient World	342
Principle of Reciprocity	369
Children in the Greco-Roman World	376
Slavery and Interpretation of the Household Codes Today	385
Slavery in the Ancient World	391
Military Images and Metaphors in Paul's Letters	425

General Editor's Preface

As Acts tells the story, the Lord choreographed an encounter between Philip and an Ethiopian eunuch on the road from Jerusalem to Gaza. This Ethiopian, who had a copy of at least some of the Scriptures, was reading from the prophet Isaiah. Hearing him read, Philip inquired, "Are you really grasping the significance of what you are reading?" (NRSV). The Ethiopian responded, "How can I, unless someone guides me?" The result was that Philip shared the good news about Jesus with him, and the Ethiopian was baptized as a new Christ-follower (Acts 8:26–40).

It is difficult to imagine a more pressing mandate for the work of a commentary than this: to come alongside readers of Scripture in order to lead them so that they can grasp the significance of what they read—and to do so in ways that are not only informative but transformative. This has been and remains the aim of the New International Commentary on the New Testament. The interpretive work on display in this volume—and, indeed, in this commentary series—can find no better raison d'être and serve no better ambition.

What distinguishes such a commentary?

First and foremost, we are concerned with the text of Scripture. It does not mean that we are not concerned with the history of scholarship and scholarly debate. It means, rather, that we strive to provide a commentary on the text and not on the scholarly debate. It means that the centerpiece of our work is a readable guide for readers of these texts, with references to critical issues and literature, as well as interaction with them, all found in our plentiful footnotes. Nor does it mean that we eschew certain critical methods or require that each contributor follow a certain approach. Rather, we take up whatever methods and pursue whatever approaches assist our work of making plain the significance of these texts.

Second, we self-consciously locate ourselves as Christ-followers who read Scripture in the service of the church and its mission in the world. Reading in the service of the church does not guarantee a particular kind of interpretation—say, one that is supportive of the church in all times and places or that merely parrots what the church wants to say. The history of interpretation demonstrates that, at times, the Scriptures speak a needed prophetic word of challenge, calling the church back to its vocation as the church. And at other times, the Scriptures speak a word of encouragement, reminding the church of its identity as a people who follow a crucified Messiah and serve a God who will vindicate God's ways and God's people.

We also recognize that, although the Scriptures are best read and understood through prayerful study and in the context of the church's worship, our reading of them cannot be separated from the world that the church engages in mission. C. S. Lewis rightly noted that what we see is determined in part by where we are standing, and the world in which we stand presses us with questions that cannot help but inform our interpretive work.

It is not enough to talk about what God *once said*, for we need to hear again and again what the Spirit, through the Scriptures, *is now saying* to the church. Accordingly, we inquire into the theological significance of what we read and into how this message might take root in the lives of God's people.

Finally, the New International Commentary on the New Testament is written above all for pastors, teachers, and students. That is, our work is located in that place between the more critical commentaries, with their lines of untranslated Greek and Aramaic and Latin, and the homiletical commentaries that seek to work out how a text might speak to congregations. Our hope is that those preparing to teach and preach God's word will find in these pages the guide they need, and that those learning the work of exegesis will find here an exemplar worth emulating.

Author's Preface

Ephesians has been a rich source for my studies of women in the early church, family life in the ancient world, and Jew/gentile relations. Thus, I was quite eager to accept the invitation to work through the entire epistle, exploring its theology and vision of the faithful life. However, two concerns gave me pause. First, this volume would partially "replace" that of F. F. Bruce, a distinguished scholar whose work shaped biblical studies in the twentieth century. I wondered that I should be asked to fill such shoes. Second, numerous questions surrounding the authorship and audience of the letter, the vast secondary literature, the complex and inflammatory "household codes"—these weighty realities presented formidable challenges. But as I entered the literary world of the epistle, as I explored its theological claims, and as I pondered its expansive vision of salvation, I was exceedingly grateful for the opportunity to drink deeply from this well.

I began this project with a plan to withhold judgment on authorship questions until I had written the body of the commentary. But I soon realized that many interpretative questions hinged on whether the author could be reliably identified as the apostle Paul. I shifted my approach to explore the topic of authorship alongside a close reading of the Greek text. My conclusion, that Paul is the author, shapes my assessment of the epistle's meaning and purpose. I use Paul's other letters throughout this commentary as points of comparison to further elucidate his objectives in Ephesians. I locate the epistle within the first generation of believers, when the band of Jesus followers were led primarily by Jews, and the gentile converts were growing in number. And I draw on the book of Acts to provide historical context of Paul's missionary efforts within Greco-Roman cities.

Concluding that Paul is responsible for the epistle, however, was only part of the challenge. A second, related question surfaced, namely, why did Paul write Ephesians? While the epistle lacks the drama of the Corinthian correspondence or the emotion of Galatians, it provides a richly developed picture of salvation at the cosmic and the mundane levels. I highlight the language of Father, Son, and Holy Spirit that Paul uses to describe and celebrate the salvation in Christ that created the church, his body.

Author's Preface

I have used the NIV (2011) translation and commented on its interpretive decisions on a few occasions. I include numerous excursuses to expand on an aspect of the biblical text, a theological trajectory from the text, or a summary of historical, social, and cultural settings. I hope to provide readers with a map of the theological, historical, and literary landscape so that they can explore the rich topography of Ephesians in their own ecclesial communities.

I am grateful to Trevor Thompson, senior acquisitions editor, for his excellent editorial work and his efficient shepherding of the process. I am indebted to Joel Green's editorial oversight throughout this project. His wise counsel deepened my analysis of the biblical text, and his spot-on critique of my argument made this work stronger. I could not have persevered without the encouragement of Scot McKnight, author of the Colossians and the Philemon commentaries in this series. Scot's unswerving belief in me and this project provided the much-needed motivation to stay the course. I began this project as a New Testament professor at Wheaton College (IL), where I had the opportunity to teach Ephesians frequently as part of the Pauline corpus. The interaction with Wheaton College students widened and sharpened my views, and I remain indebted to their insights. I continued writing as I held the post of interim Dean of Humanities and Theological Studies. I am grateful to the Wheaton community, and especially my colleagues Michael Graves, Keith Johnson, Amy Peeler, and George Kalantzis, for their answers to my too-frequent questions and their encouragement along the way. With much of the work done, I moved to take up the position of Provost/Dean of Denver Seminary. I am grateful to President Mark Young, who made financial resources available for research assistants and celebrated my progress toward completion. I could not have managed without excellent assistants over the years, and my heartfelt thanks extends to Caleb Friedeman, Courtney Zboncak, Julie N. Dykes, and Jennay Wilson.

I am blessed by the encouragement I received from my parents and children. Above all, I am grateful for my husband's love and encouragement in writing this commentary. Jim Cohick, thank you for exemplifying to me and our children the humble heart of Christ, the godly love of a father, and the passionate desire to honor God in all things.

From my childhood, I have treasured the friendship of Maria Sisley McTarnaghan. I address her parents as aunt and uncle, and she is as close as a cousin, even sister, to me. In the years that I have been writing this commentary, we have watched our children graduate, marry, and set out on their own. She has offered unfailing support and generous love, always seasoned with humor and a smile. Alongside her support, my brother, Christopher S. Harrison, has been the ballast in the turbulent seas that make up life's changes and growth. Both Maria and Chris live Eph 4:2, and I am eternally grateful for their witness in my life. This work is dedicated to them.

Abbreviations

ABD	*Anchor Bible Dictionary*. Edited by David Noel Freedman. 6 vols. New York: Doubleday, 1992.
ANF	*Ante-Nicene Fathers*
ANRW	*Aufstieg und Niedergang der römischen Welt: Geschichte und Kultur Roms im Spiegel der neueren Forschung*, part 2: *Principat*. Edited by Hildegard Temporini and Wolfgang Haase. Berlin: de Gruyter, 1972–.
BDAG	Frederick W. Danker, Walter Bauer, William F. Arndt, and F. Wilbur Gingrich. *Greek-English Lexicon of the New Testament and Other Early Christian Literature*. 3rd edition. Chicago: University of Chicago Press, 2000.
DPL	*Dictionary of Paul and His Letters*. Edited by Gerald F. Hawthorne and Ralph P. Martin. Downers Grove, IL: InterVarsity Press, 1993.
EDB	*Eerdmans Dictionary of the Bible*. Edited by David Noel Freedman. Grand Rapids: Eerdmans, 2000.
ESV	English Standard Version
HCSB	Holman Christian Standard Bible
JSNTSup	Journal for the Study of the New Testament Supplement Series
KJV	King James Version
L&N	*Greek-English Lexicon of the New Testament: Based on Semantic Domains*. Edited by Johannes P. Louw and Eugene A. Nida. New York: United Bible Societies, 1989.
LSJ	*A Greek-English Lexicon*. Edited by Henry George Liddell, Robert Scott, and Henry Stuart Jones. Oxford: Clarendon, 1996.
LXX	Septuagint
MT	Masoretic Text
NASB	New American Standard Bible
NICNT	New International Commentary on the New Testament

Abbreviations

NIV	New International Version
NPNF[1]	*Nicene and Post-Nicene Fathers*, series 1
NPNF[2]	*Nicene and Post-Nicene Fathers*, series 2
NRSV	New Revised Standard Version
NTS	*New Testament Studies*
PG	Patrologia Graeca. Edited by Jacques-Paul Migne. 162 vols. Paris, 1857–86.
TNIV	Today's New International Version
WUNT	Wissenschaftliche Untersuchungen zum Neuen Testament

Bibliography

I. COMMENTARIES

These commentaries are cited by last name, volume number where appropriate, and page.

Arnold, Clinton E. *Ephesians*. Zondervan Exegetical Commentary on the New Testament. Grand Rapids: Zondervan, 2010.
Barth, Markus. *Ephesians*. 2 vols. Anchor Yale Bible 34. Garden City, NY: Doubleday, 1974.
Best, Ernest. *A Critical and Exegetical Commentary on Ephesians*. International Critical Commentary. Edinburgh: T&T Clark, 1998.
Bock, Darrell L. *Ephesians: An Introduction and Commentary*. Tyndale New Testament Commentaries. Downers Grove, IL: IVP Academic, 2019.
Bruce, F. F. *The Epistles to the Colossians, to Philemon, and to the Ephesians*. NICNT. Grand Rapids: Eerdmans, 1984.
Cohick, Lynn H. *Ephesians*. New Covenant Commentary Series. Eugene, OR: Cascade, 2010.
Conzelmann, Hans. "Der Brief an die Epheser." Pages 86–124 in *Die Briefe an die Galater, Epheser, Philipper, Kolosser, Thessalonicher und Philemon*. Das Neue Testament Deutsch 8. Edited by J. Becker, H. Conzelmann, and G. Friedrich. Göttingen: Vandenhoeck & Ruprecht, 1976.
Eadie, John. *A Commentary on the Greek Text of the Epistle of Paul to the Ephesians*. 2nd edition. Edinburgh: T&T Clark, 1883. Reprinted Grand Rapids: Baker, 1979.
Fowl, Stephen E. *Ephesians*. New Testament Library. Louisville: Westminster John Knox, 2012.
Heine, Ronald E. *Commentaries of Origen and Jerome on St. Paul's Epistle to the Ephesians*. Oxford Early Christian Studies. Oxford: Oxford University Press, 2002.

Bibliography

Hoehner, Harold W. *Ephesians: An Exegetical Commentary*. Grand Rapids: Baker Academic, 2002.

Larkin, William J. *Ephesians: A Handbook on the Greek Text*. Waco, TX: Baylor University Press, 2009.

Lincoln, Andrew T. *Ephesians*. Word Biblical Commentary 42. Grand Rapids: Zondervan, 1990.

MacDonald, Margaret Y. *Colossians and Ephesians*. Sacra Pagina 17. Collegeville, MN: Liturgical Press, 2000.

Merkle, Benjamin L. *Ephesians*. Exegetical Guide to the Greek New Testament. Nashville: B&H Academic, 2016.

Morris, Leon. *Expository Reflections on the Letter to the Ephesians*. Grand Rapids: Baker, 1994.

Muddiman, John. *The Epistle to the Ephesians*. Black's New Testament Commentaries. New York: Continuum, 2001.

Perkins, Pheme. *Ephesians*. Abingdon New Testament Commentaries. Nashville: Abingdon, 1997.

Roberts, Mark D. *Ephesians*. Story of God Bible Commentary. Grand Rapids: Zondervan, 2016.

Salmond, S. D. F. *The Epistle to the Ephesians*. Expositor's Greek Testament 3. Edited by W. Robertson Nicoll. London: Hodder & Stoughton, 1903.

Schlier, Heinrich. *Der Brief an die Epheser: Ein Kommentar*. Düsseldorf: Patmos, 1957.

Schnackenburg, Rudolf. *The Epistle to the Ephesians: A Commentary*. Translated by H. Heron. Edinburgh: T&T Clark, 1991.

Schüssler Fiorenza, Elisabeth. *Ephesians*. Wisdom Commentary. Wilmington, DE: Glazier, 2017.

Snodgrass, Klyne. *Ephesians*. NIV Application Commentary. Grand Rapids: Zondervan, 1996.

Speyr, Adrienne von. *Der Epheserbrief*. Einsiedeln: Johannes-Verlag, 1983. English: *The Letter to the Ephesians*. Translated by Adrian Walker. San Francisco: Ignatius, 1996.

Thielman, Frank. *Ephesians*. Baker Exegetical Commentary on the New Testament. Grand Rapids: Baker Academic, 2010.

Witherington, Ben, III. *The Letters to Philemon, the Colossians, and the Ephesians: A Socio-Rhetorical Commentary on the Captivity Epistles*. Grand Rapids: Eerdmans, 2007.

Yoder Neufeld, Thomas R. *Ephesians*. Believers Church Bible Commentary. Scottsdale, PA: Herald, 2002.

II. ANCIENT SOURCES

Ammianus Marcellinus. *The Later Roman Empire (A.D. 354–378)*. Translated by Walter Hamilton. Introduction and notes by Andrew Wallace-Hadrill. London: Penguin, 1986.
Athanasius. *De synodis* 2.27, Anathema 26. *Select Works and Letters of Athanasius, Bishop of Alexandria*. Edited by A. Robertson. NPNF² 4. Edited by Philip Schaff and Henry Wace. Reprinted Grand Rapids: Eerdmans, 1980.
Augustine. *The Works of Saint Augustine: A Translation for the 21st Century, Sermons III/18 (273–305A) on the Saints*. Translated by Edmund Hill. New York: New City Press, 1994.
Cyril of Alexandria. *De recta fide ad Arcadiam et Marinam*.
Dio Chrysostom. *On Covetousness* in *Discourses 12–30*. Translated by J. W. Cohoon. Loeb Classical Library 339. Cambridge: Harvard University Press, 1939.
Erasmus. *Collected Works of Erasmus*, vol. 43: *Paraphrases on the Epistles to the Corinthians, Ephesians, Philippians, Colossians, and Thessalonians*. Edited by Robert D. Sider. Toronto: University of Toronto Press, 2009.
Josephus. *The Jewish War*. Translated by G. A. Williamson. Revised by E. Mary Smallwood. London: Penguin, 1981.
Julian of Norwich. *Showings: Authoritative Text, Contexts, Criticism*. Edited by Denise Nowakowski Baker. Norton Critical Edition. New York: Norton, 2005.
Julian of Norwich. *Showings*. Translated by Edmund Colledge and James Walsh. Classics of Western Spirituality. Mahwah, NJ: Paulist Press, 1978.
Lutz, Cora E., ed. *Musonius Rufus: "The Roman Socrates."* Yale Classical Studies 10. New Haven: Yale University Press, 1947.
Plutarch. *Moralia*. Translated by W. C. Helmbold. 16 vols. Cambridge: Harvard University Press, 1970.

III. GENERAL BIBLIOGRAPHY

Abernethy, Andrew. *The Book of Isaiah and God's Kingdom: A Theological-Thematic Approach to the Book of Isaiah*. New Studies in Biblical Theology 40. Downers Grove, IL: IVP Academic, 2016.
Allen, John A. "The 'In Christ' Formula in Ephesians." *NTS* 5 (1958–59): 54–62.
Anderson, Gary A. *Charity: The Place of the Poor in the Biblical Tradition*. New Haven: Yale University Press, 2013.
———. *Sin: A History*. New Haven: Yale University Press, 2009.
Arnold, Clinton E. *Ephesians: Power and Magic—the Concept of Power in Ephe-

sians in Light of Its Historical Setting. Society for New Testament Study Monograph 63. Cambridge: Cambridge University Press, 1989.

Aune, David E. "Magic in Early Christianity." *ANRW* 23.1.1507–57.

Ayres, Lewis. *Augustine and the Trinity*. Cambridge: Cambridge University Press, 2010.

———. *Nicaea and Its Legacy: An Approach to Fourth-Century Trinitarian Theology*. Oxford: Oxford University Press, 2004.

Bachmann, Michael, and Johannes Woyke, eds. *Lutherische und neue Paulusperspektive: Beiträge zu einem Schlüsselproblem der gegenwärtigen exegetischen Diskussion*. WUNT 182. Tübingen: Mohr Siebeck, 2005.

Bailey, Kenneth E. *Paul through Mediterranean Eyes: Cultural Studies in 1 Corinthians*. Downers Grove, IL: InterVarsity Press, 2011.

Balch, David L. *Let Wives Be Submissive: The Domestic Code in 1 Peter*. Society of Biblical Literature Monograph Series 26. Chico, CA: Scholars Press, 1981.

Bales, William. "The Descent of Christ in Ephesians 4:9." *Catholic Biblical Quarterly* 72 (2010): 84–100.

Banks, Robert. "'Walking' as a Metaphor of the Christian Life: The Origins of a Significant Pauline Usage." Pages 303–13 in *Perspectives on Language and Text: Essays and Poems in Honor of Francis I. Andersen's Sixtieth Birthday July 29, 1985*. Edited by Edgar W. Conrad and Edward G. Newing. Winona Lake, IN: Eisenbrauns, 1987.

Barclay, John M. G. *Jews in the Mediterranean Diaspora: From Alexander to Trajan*. Berkeley: University of California Press, 1999.

———. *Paul and the Gift*. Grand Rapids: Eerdmans, 2015.

———. "Paul, Philemon, and the Dilemma of Christian Slave-Ownership." *NTS* 37 (1991): 161–86.

———. "Paul, the Gift, and the Battle over Gentile Circumcision: Revisiting the Logic of Galatians." *Australian Biblical Review* 58 (2010): 36–56.

———. "Pure Grace? Paul's Distinctive Jewish Theology of Gift." *Studia Theologica: Nordic Journal of Theology* 68 (2014): 4–20.

———. "Under Grace: The Christ-Gift and the Construction of a Christian *Habitus*." Pages 59–76 in *Apocalyptic Paul: Cosmos and Anthropos in Romans 5–8*. Edited by Beverly Roberts Gaventa. Waco, TX: Baylor University Press, 2013.

Barth, Karl. *Church Dogmatics*, vol. 4.3.2: *The Doctrine of Reconciliation*. Edited by G. W. Bromiley and T. F. Torrance. Translated by G. W. Bromiley. Edinburgh: T&T Clark, 1962.

Barth, Markus. *Israel und die Kirche im Brief des Paulus an die Epheser*. Munich: Kaiser, 1959.

———. *The People of God*. JSNTSup 5. Sheffield: JSOT Press, 1983. Revised English edition of *Paulus—Apostat oder Apostel*. Regensburg: Pustet, 1997.

Barton, Carlin. *Roman Honor: The Fire in the Bones*. Berkeley: University of California Press, 2001.

Bauckham, Richard. *God Crucified: Monotheism and Christology in the New Testament*. Grand Rapids: Eerdmans, 1998.

Baum, Armin D. "Content and Form: Authorship Attribution and Pseudonymity in Ancient Speeches, Letters, Lectures, and Translations: A Rejoinder to Bart Ehrman." *Journal of Biblical Literature* 136.2 (2017): 381–403.

———. *Pseudepigraphie und literarische Fälschung im frühen Christentum*. WUNT 138. Tübingen: Mohr Siebeck, 2001.

———. "Semantic Variation within the *Corpus Paulinum*: Linguistic Considerations Concerning the Richer Vocabulary of the Pastoral Epistles." *Tyndale Bulletin* 59 (2008): 271–92.

Baur, Ferdinand Christian. *Paul the Apostle of Jesus Christ: His Life and Works, His Epistles and Teachings*. Reprinted Peabody, MA: Hendrickson, 2003. Original: *Paulus, der Apostel Jesu Christi*, 1845.

———. *Die sogenannten Pastoralbriefe des Apostels Paulus aufs neue kritisch untersucht*. Stuttgart: Cotta, 1835.

Beard, Mary, John North, and Simon Price. *Religions of Rome*, vol. 1: *A History*. Cambridge: Cambridge University Press, 1998.

Beilby, James, and Paul R. Eddy, eds. *The Nature of Atonement: Four Views*. Downers Grove, IL: IVP Academic, 2006.

Bell, Richard H. "Faith in Christ: Some Exegetical and Theological Reflections on Philippians 3:9 and Ephesians 3:12." Pages 111–25 in *The Faith of Jesus Christ*. Edited by Michael F. Bird and Preston M. Sprinkle. Peabody, MA: Hendrickson, 2009.

Berger, K. "Hellenistische Gattungen im Neuen Testament." *ANRW* 2.25.2: 1031–1432, 1831–85.

Berrin, Shani. "Qumran *Pesharim*." Pages 110–33 in *Biblical Interpretation at Qumran*. Edited by Matthias Henze. Grand Rapids: Eerdmans, 2005.

Best, Ernest. "Ephesians i.1." Pages 29–41 in *Text and Interpretation: Studies in the New Testament Presented to Matthew Black*. Edited by Ernest Best and Robert McLean Wilson. Cambridge: Cambridge University Press, 1979.

———. "Ephesians 4:28: Thieves in the Church." *Irish Biblical Studies* 14 (1992): 2–9.

———. "Recipients and Title of the Letter to the Ephesians: Why and When the Designation 'Ephesians'?" *ANRW* 2.25.4 (1987): 3247–79.

———. "Who Used Whom? The Relationship of Ephesians and Colossians." *NTS* 43 (1997): 72–96.

Betsworth, Sharon. *Children in Early Christian Narratives*. London: Bloomsbury T&T Clark, 2015.

Betz, Hans Dieter, ed. *The Greek Magical Papyri in Translation*, vol. 1: *Text*. Chicago: University of Chicago Press, 1986.

Bibliography

Billings, J. Todd. "Undying Love." *First Things* 248 (December 2014): 45–49.

———. *Union with Christ: Reframing Theology and Ministry for the Church*. Grand Rapids: Baker Academic, 2011.

Bird, Michael F. *An Anomalous Jew: Paul among Jews, Greeks, and Romans*. Grand Rapids: Eerdmans, 2016.

———. *Jesus and the Origins of the Gentile Mission*. London: T&T Clark, 2007.

———. "Reassessing a Rhetorical Approach to Paul's Letters." *Expository Times* 119.9 (2008): 374–79.

Bird, Michael F., and Preston M. Sprinkle, eds. *The Faith of Jesus Christ: Exegetical, Biblical, and Theological Studies*. Peabody, MA: Hendrickson, 2009.

Bird, Michael F., et al., eds. *How God Became Jesus: The Real Origins of Belief in Jesus' Divine Nature*. Grand Rapids: Zondervan, 2014.

Bishop, M. C., and J. C. N. Coulston. *Roman Military Equipment from the Punic Wars to the Fall of Rome*. London: Batsford, 1993.

Blaising, C. A. "Dispensation, Dispensationalism." Pages 248–49 in *Evangelical Dictionary of Theology*. Edited by Daniel J. Treier. 3rd edition. Grand Rapids: Baker Academic, 2017.

Boersma, Hans. *Violence, Hospitality, and the Cross: Reappropriating the Atonement Tradition*. Grand Rapids: Baker Academic, 2004.

Bohak, Gideon. *Ancient Jewish Magic: A History*. Cambridge: Cambridge University Press, 2008.

Bonhoeffer, Dietrich. *The Cost of Discipleship*. New York: Touchstone, 1995. Original: *Nachfolge*. Munich: Kaiser, 1937.

Braaten, Carl E., and Robert W. Jenson, eds. *In One Body through the Cross: The Princeton Proposal for Christian Unity*. Grand Rapids: Eerdmans, 2003.

Bradley, Keith R. *Discovering the Roman Family: Studies in Roman Social History*. Oxford: Oxford University Press, 1991.

———. "Images of Childhood." Pages 183–96 in *Plutarch's Advice to the Bride and Groom and a Consolation to His Wife*. Edited by Sarah B. Pomeroy. Oxford: Oxford University Press, 1999.

———. "Sacrificing the Family: Christian Martyrs and Their Kin." Pages 104–25 in *Apuleius and Antonine Rome: Historical Essays*. Toronto: University of Toronto Press, 2012.

Brannon, M. Jeff. *The Heavenlies in Ephesians: A Lexical, Exegetical, and Conceptual Analysis*. London: T&T Clark, 2011.

Braund, Susanna. *Seneca: De Clementia, Edited with Text, Translation, and Commentary*. Oxford: Oxford University Press, 2009.

Braxton, Brad Ronnell. *No Longer Slaves: Galatians and African American Experience*. Collegeville, MN: Liturgical Press, 2002.

Buell, Denise Kimber. "Challenges and Strategies for Speaking about Ethnicity in the New Testament and New Testament Studies." *Svensk exegetisk årsbok* 79 (2014): 33–51.

---. *Why This New Race: Ethnic Reasoning in Early Christianity*. New York: Columbia University Press, 2005.

Bultmann, Rudolf. *Primitive Christianity in Its Contemporary Setting*. Translated by R. H. Fuller. London: Thames & Hudson, 1956. Translation of *Das Urchristentum im Rahmen der antiken Religionen*. Zürich: Artemis-Verlag, 1949.

---. "The Significance of the Old Testament for Christian Faith." Pages 8–35 in *The Old Testament and Christian Faith: A Theological Discussion*. Edited and translated by Bernard W. Anderson. New York: Harper & Row, 1963.

---. *Theology of the New Testament*. 2 vols. Translated by Kendrick Grobel. Waco, TX: Baylor University Press, 2007. Originally New York: Scribner, 1951–55.

Burke, Trevor J. *Family Matters: A Socio-Historical Study of Kinship Metaphors in 1 Thessalonians*. London: T&T Clark, 2003.

Burkert, Walter. *Ancient Mystery Cults*. Cambridge: Harvard University Press, 1987.

Burnette, Samuel D. "The Kingdom in First Corinthians: Reevaluating an Underestimated Pauline Theme." PhD diss., Southern Baptist Theological Seminary, 2016.

Calvin, John. *Institutes of the Christian Religion*. 2 vols. Translated by Ford Lewis Battles. Edited by John T. McNeill. Library of Christian Classics. Philadelphia: Westminster, 1960.

---. "The Thirty First Sermon, Which Is the Eleventh on the Fourth Chapter." Pages 447–60 in *Sermons on the Epistle to the Ephesians*. Translated by Arthur Golding. Original: 1562. 1577. Reprinted Edinburgh: Banner of Truth, 1973.

Campbell, Constantine R. *Basics of Verbal Aspect in Biblical Greek*. Grand Rapids: Zondervan, 2008.

---. *Paul and Union with Christ: An Exegetical and Theological Study*. Grand Rapids: Zondervan, 2012.

Campbell, Douglas. *Framing Paul: An Epistolary Biography*. Grand Rapids: Eerdmans, 2014.

---. *The Quest for Paul's Gospel: A Suggested Strategy*. London: T&T Clark, 2005.

Canavan, Rosemary. *Clothing the Body of Christ at Colossae: A Visual Construction of Identity*. WUNT 334. Tübingen: Mohr Siebeck, 2012.

Capes, David B. *The Divine Christ: Paul, the Lord Jesus, and the Scriptures of Israel*. Grand Rapids: Baker Academic, 2018.

Carr, Wesley. *Angels and Principalities: The Background, Meaning, and Development of the Pauline Phrase hai archai kai hai exousiai*. Society for New Testament Study Monograph 42. Cambridge: Cambridge University Press, 1981.

Carroll, Maureen. *Infancy and Earliest Childhood in the Roman World: "A Fragment of Time."* Oxford: Oxford University Press, 2018.

Bibliography

Carson, D. A., Peter T. O'Brien, and Mark A. Seifrid, eds. *Justification and Variegated Judaism*. Vol. 1: *The Complexities of Second Temple Judaism*. Grand Rapids: Baker Academic, 2001.

Cartledge, Paul Anthony. "Slavery." Page 1415 in *The Oxford Classical Dictionary*. 3rd edition. Edited by Simon Hornblower and Antony Spawforth. Oxford: Oxford University Press, 1996.

Carver, W. O. *Ephesians: The Glory of God in the Christian Calling*. Reprinted Nashville: Broadman, 1979.

Cassidy, Richard J. *Paul in Chains: Roman Imprisonment and the Letters of St. Paul*. New York: Crossroad, 2001.

Casson, Lionel. *Travel in the Ancient World*. Baltimore: Johns Hopkins University Press, 1994.

Cervin, Richard. "Does Κεφαλή Mean 'Source' or 'Authority Over' in Greek Literature? A Rebuttal." *Trinity Journal* 10 (1989): 85–112.

Chapman, Stephen B. "Saul/Paul: Onomastics, Typology, and Christian Scripture." Pages 214–43 in *The Word Leaps the Gap: Essays on Scripture and Theology in Honor of Richard B. Hays*. Edited by J. Ross Wagner, C. Kavin Rowe, and A. Katherine Grieb. Grand Rapids: Eerdmans, 2008.

Chester, Stephen J. *Reading Paul with the Reformers: Reconciling Old and New Perspectives*. Grand Rapids: Eerdmans, 2017.

Childs, Brevard S. *The New Testament as Canon: An Introduction*. Philadelphia: Fortress, 1985.

Classen, Carl Joachim. *Rhetorical Criticism of the New Testament*. WUNT 128. Tübingen: Mohr Siebeck, 2000.

Cleland, Liza, Glenys Davies, and Lloyd Llewellyn-Jones. *Greek and Roman Dress from A to Z*. New York: Routledge, 2007.

Cohen, Shaye J. D. *The Beginnings of Jewishness: Boundaries, Varieties, Uncertainties*. Berkeley: University of California Press, 1999.

———. "Judaism and Jewishness." Pages 513–15 in *Jewish Annotated New Testament*. Edited by Amy-Jill Levine and Marc Zvi Brettler. Oxford: Oxford University Press, 2011.

Cohick, Lynn H. "The Gospel as God's Gift: Good News from Ephesians 1:1–3:12." Pages 150–72 in *Is the Gospel Good News?* Edited by Stanley E. Porter and Hughson T. Ong. Eugene, OR: Pickwick, 2018.

———. "Jews and Christians." Pages 68–83 in *The Routledge Companion to Early Christian Thought*. Edited by D. Jeffrey Bingham. New York: Routledge, 2010.

———. "The New Perspective and the Christian Life in Paul's Letter to the Ephesians." Pages 19–45 in *The Apostle Paul and the Christian Life: Ethical and Missional Implications of the New Perspective*. Edited by Scot McKnight and Joseph B. Modica. Grand Rapids: Baker Academic, 2016.

———. *Philippians*. Story of God Bible Commentary. Grand Rapids: Zondervan, 2013.

———. "Poverty and Its Causes in the Early Church." Pages 16–27 in *Poverty in the Early Church and Today: A Conversation*. Edited by Steve Walton and Hannah Swithinbank. London: T&T Clark, 2019.

———. "Women, Children, and Families in the Roman World." Pages 179–88 in *The World of the New Testament: Cultural, Social, and Historical Contexts*. Edited by Joel B. Green and Lee Martin McDonald. Grand Rapids: Baker Academic, 2013.

———. *Women in the World of the Earliest Christians: Illuminating Ancient Ways of Life*. Grand Rapids: Baker Academic, 2009.

Cole, Spencer. *Cicero and the Deification of Rome*. Cambridge: Cambridge University Press, 2014.

Conzelmann, Hans. *1 Corinthians: A Commentary on the First Epistle to the Corinthians*. Hermeneia. Philadelphia: Fortress, 1990.

Cortez, Marc. *Christological Anthropology in Historical Perspective: Ancient and Contemporary Approaches to Theological Anthropology*. Grand Rapids: Zondervan, 2016.

Couenhoven, Jesse. *Predestination: A Guide for the Perplexed*. London: T&T Clark, 2018.

Cranfield, C. E. B. *A Critical and Exegetical Commentary on the Epistle to the Romans*. International Critical Commentary. Edinburgh: T&T Clark, 1975.

Crook, Zeba A. *Reconceptualising Conversion*. Beihefte zur Zeitschrift für die neutestamentliche Wissenschaft 130. Berlin: de Gruyter, 2004.

Czajkowski, Kimberley. *Localized Law: The Babatha and Salome Komaise Archive*. Oxford Studies in Roman Society and Law. Oxford: Oxford University Press, 2017.

Dahl, Nils A. "Adresse und Proömium des Epheserbriefes." *Theologische Zeitschrift* 7 (1951): 241–64.

Darko, Daniel K. "Adopted Siblings in the Household of God: Kinship Lexemes in the Social Identity Construction of Ephesians." Pages 333–46 in *The T&T Clark Handbook to Social Identity in the New Testament*. Edited by J. Brian Tucker and Coleman A. Baker. London: Bloomsbury T&T Clark, 2014.

Dawson, Gerrit Scott. *Jesus Ascended: The Meaning of Christ's Continuing Incarnation*. London: T&T Clark, 2004.

De Boer, Willis Peter. *The Imitation of Paul: An Exegetical Study*. Reprinted Eugene: Wipf & Stock, 2016.

De Ste. Croix, G. E. M. *The Class Struggle in the Ancient Greek World: From the Archaic Age to the Arab Conquest*. Ithaca: Cornell University Press, 1981.

Deissmann, Adolf. "Ephesia Grammata." Pages 121–24 in *Abhandlung zur Semitischen Religionskunde und Sprachwissenschaft*. Edited by W. Frankenberg and F. Küchler. Beihefte zur Zeitschrift für die alttestamentliche Wissenschaft 33. Giessen: Töpelmann, 1918.

———. *Paul: A Study in Social and Religious History*. Translated by William E. Wilson. 2nd edition. London: Hodder & Stoughton, 1926.

DeSilva, David A. *Honor, Patronage, Kinship, and Purity: Unlocking New Testament Culture*. Downers Grove, IL: InterVarsity Press, 2000.

———. "How Greek Was the Author of 'Hebrews'?" Pages 629–49 in *Christian Origins and Greco-Roman Culture: Social and Literary Contexts for the New Testament*. Edited by Stanley E. Porter and Andrew W. Pitts. Early Christianity in Its Hellenistic Context 1. Leiden: Brill, 2013.

Dibelius, M. *Der Brief des Jakobus*. Kritisch-exegetischer Kommentar über das Neue Testament 15. Göttingen: Vandenhoeck & Ruprecht, 1964.

Dickie, Matthew W. *Magic and Magicians in the Greco-Roman World*. New York: Routledge, 2001.

Donelson, Lewis R. *Pseudepigraphy and Ethical Argument in the Pastoral Epistles*. Hermeneutische Untersuchungen zur Theologie 22. Tübingen: Mohr Siebeck, 1986. Reprinted Eugene, OR: Wipf & Stock, 2015.

Doty, William G. *Letters in Primitive Christianity*. Philadelphia: Fortress, 1973. Reprinted Eugene, OR: Wipf & Stock, 2014.

Dunn, James D. G. *Christology in the Making: A New Testament Inquiry into the Origins of the Doctrine of the Incarnation*. 2nd edition. Grand Rapids: Eerdmans, 1996.

———. *Did the First Christians Worship Jesus? The New Testament Evidence*. Louisville: Westminster John Knox, 2010.

———. *The New Perspective on Paul*. WUNT 185. Tübingen: Mohr Siebeck, 2005. Revised edition Grand Rapids: Eerdmans, 2008.

———. "The New Perspective on Paul." *Bulletin of the John Rylands University Library of Manchester* 65 (1983): 95–122.

———. "A New Perspective on the New Perspective on Paul." *Early Christianity* 4.2 (2013): 157–82.

———. *Romans 9–16*. Word Biblical Commentary 38B. Grand Rapids: Zondervan, 1988.

———. *The Theology of Paul the Apostle*. Grand Rapids: Eerdmans, 1998.

Dyson, Stephen L. "Native Revolts in the Roman Empire." *Historia* 20 (1971): 239–74.

Eastman, Susan Grove. *Paul and the Person: Reframing Paul's Anthropology*. Grand Rapids: Eerdmans, 2017.

Ehrman, Bart D. *Forged: Writing in the Name of God—Why the Bible's Authors Are Not Who We Think They Are*. New York: HarperOne, 2011.

———. *Forgery and Counter-forgery: The Use of Literary Deceit in Early Christian Polemics*. Oxford: Oxford University Press, 2013.

———. *How Jesus Became God: The Exaltation of a Jewish Preacher from Galilee*. San Francisco: HarperCollins, 2014.

Elliott, Neil, and Mark Reasoner, eds. *Documents and Images for the Study of Paul*. Minneapolis: Fortress, 2011.

Emery, Gilles. *The Trinitarian Theology of St Thomas Aquinas*. Translated by Francesca Aran Murphy. Oxford, Oxford University Press, 2007.

Fee, Gordon D. *The First and Second Letters to the Thessalonians*. NICNT. Grand Rapids: Eerdmans, 2009.

———. *The First Epistle to the Corinthians*. NICNT. Grand Rapids: Eerdmans, 1987.

———. *Jesus the Lord according to Paul the Apostle: A Concise Introduction*. Grand Rapids: Baker Academic, 2018.

———. *Pauline Christology: An Exegetical-Theological Study*. Peabody, MA: Hendrickson, 2007.

———. *Paul, the Spirit, and the People of God*. Peabody, MA: Hendrickson, 1996.

Feldman, Louis H. *Jew and Gentile in the Ancient World: Attitudes and Interactions from Alexander to Justinian*. Princeton: Princeton University Press, 1993.

Fitzmyer, Joseph A. *Romans: A New Translation with Introduction and Commentary*. Anchor Yale Bible 33. New York: Doubleday, 1993.

Foster, Paul. "The First Contribution to the Πίστις Χριστοῦ Debate: A Study of Ephesians 3:12." *Journal for the Study of the New Testament* 85 (2002): 75–96.

———. "Πιστις Χριστου Terminology in Philippians and Ephesians." Pages 99–109 in *The Faith of Jesus Christ*. Edited by Michael F. Bird and Preston M. Sprinkle. Peabody, MA: Hendrickson, 2009.

Foster, Robert L. "Reoriented to the Cosmos: Cosmology and Theology in Ephesians through Philemon." Pages 107–24 in *Cosmology and New Testament Theology*. Edited by Jonathan T. Pennington and Sean M. McDonough. London: T&T Clark, 2008.

Fowl, Stephen E. *Engaging Scripture: A Model for Theological Interpretation*. Malden, MA: Blackwell, 1998. Reprinted Eugene, OR: Wipf & Stock, 2008.

Fredriksen, Paula. "The Birth of Christianity and the Origins of Christian Anti-Judaism." Pages 8–30 in *Jesus, Judaism, and Christian Anti-Judaism: Reading the New Testament after the Holocaust*. Edited by Paula Fredriksen and Adele Reinhartz. Louisville: Westminster John Knox, 2002.

Frier, Bruce W., and Thomas A. J. McGinn. *A Casebook on Roman Family Law*. American Philological Association: Classical Resources Series. Oxford: Oxford University Press, 2004.

Frymer-Kensky, Tikva, David Novak, Peter Ochs, and Michael Signer. "*Dabru Emet*: A Jewish Statement on Christian and Christianity." *New York Times*, September 10, 2000.

Gager, John G. *The Origins of Anti-Semitism: Attitudes towards Judaism in Pagan and Christian Antiquity*. Oxford: Oxford University Press, 1985.

———. "Paul, the Apostle of Judaism." Pages 56–76 in *Jesus, Judaism, and Christian Anti-Judaism: Reading the New Testament after the Holocaust*. Edited by Paula Fredriksen and Adele Reinhartz. Louisville: Westminster John Knox, 2002.

———. *Reinventing Paul*. Oxford: Oxford University Press, 2000.

———. *Who Made Early Christianity? The Jewish Lives of the Apostle Paul*. New York: Columbia University Press, 2015.

Galinsky, Karl. "The Cult of the Roman Emperor: Uniter or Divider?" Pages 1–22 in *Rome and Religion: A Cross-Disciplinary Dialogue on the Imperial Cult*. Edited by Jeffrey Brodd and Jonathan L. Reed. Atlanta: SBL, 2011.

Garland, David E. *1 Corinthians*. Baker Exegetical Commentary on the New Testament. Grand Rapids: Baker Academic, 2003.

Garnsey, Peter. *Food and Society in Classical Antiquity*. Cambridge: Cambridge University Press, 1999.

———. *Ideas of Slavery from Aristotle to Augustine*. Cambridge: Cambridge University Press, 1996.

Garnsey, Peter, and Richard Saller. *The Roman Empire: Economy, Society, and Culture*. Berkeley: University of California Press, 1987.

Gaston, Lloyd. *Paul and the Torah*. Vancouver: University of British Columbia Press, 1987.

Gaventa, Beverly Roberts. *Our Mother Saint Paul*. Louisville: Westminster John Knox, 2007.

Gaventa, Beverly Roberts, ed. *Apocalyptic Paul: Cosmos and Anthropos in Romans 5–8*. Waco, TX: Baylor University Press, 2013.

Gerdmar, Anders. *Roots of Theological Anti-Semitism: German Biblical Interpretation and the Jews, from Herder and Semler to Kittel and Bultmann*. Leiden: Brill, 2009.

Glancy, Jennifer A. *Slavery as Moral Problem: In the Early Church and Today*. Minneapolis: Fortress, 2011.

———. *Slavery in Early Christianity*. Oxford: Oxford University Press, 2002.

Goguel, Maurice. "Esquisse d'une solution nouvelle du problème de l'épître aux Éphésiens." *Revue de l'histoire et de des relgions* 111 (1935): 254–84; 112 (1936): 73–99.

Gombis, Timothy G. *The Drama of Ephesians: Participating in the Triumph of God*. Downers Grove, IL: IVP Academic, 2010.

———. "Ephesians 3:2–13: Pointless Digression, or Epitome of the Triumph of God in Christ?" *Westminster Theological Journal* 66 (2004): 313–23.

Goodman, Martin. *Mission and Conversion: Proselytizing in the Religious History of the Roman Empire*. Oxford: Clarendon Press, 1994.

———. *The Ruling Class in Judaea: The Origins of the Jewish Revolt against Rome A.D. 66–70*. Cambridge: Cambridge University Press, 1987.

Goodspeed, Edgar J. *The Formation of the New Testament*. Chicago: University of Chicago Press, 1926.

———. *The Key to Ephesians*. Chicago: University of Chicago Press, 1956.

———. *The Meaning of Ephesians*. Chicago: University of Chicago Press, 1933. Reprinted Eugene OR: Wipf & Stock, 2012.

Gorman, Michael J. *Becoming the Gospel: Paul, Participation, and Mission*. Grand Rapids: Eerdmans, 2015.

———. *Cruciformity: Paul's Narrative Spirituality of the Cross*. Grand Rapids: Eerdmans, 2001.

———. *Inhabiting the Cruciform God: Kenosis, Justification, and Theosis in Paul's Narrative Soteriology*. Grand Rapids: Eerdmans, 2009.

———. *Participating in Christ: Explorations in Paul's Theology and Spirituality*. Grand Rapids: Baker Academic, 2019.

———. "Romans and the Participationist Perspective." Pages 59–79 in *Preaching Romans: Four Perspectives*. Edited by Scot McKnight and Joseph B. Modica. Grand Rapids: Eerdmans, 2019.

Gradel, Ittai. *Emperor Worship and Roman Religion*. Oxford: Oxford University Press, 2002.

Graf, Fritz. "Ephesia Grammata." Page 1023 in vol. 4 of *Brill's New Pauly: Encyclopaedia of the Ancient World*. Edited by Hubert Cancik, Helmuth Schneider, Christine F. Salazar. Leiden: Brill, 2004.

Graves, Michael W. *Jerome's Hebrew Philology: A Study Based on His Commentary on Jeremiah*. Supplements to Vigiliae Christianae 90. Leiden: Brill, 2007.

———. "The Literary Quality of Scripture as Seen by the Early Church." *Tyndale Bulletin* 61.2 (2010): 173–78.

Green, Joel B. *Conversion in Luke-Acts: Divine Action, Human Cognition, and the People of God*. Grand Rapids: Baker Academic, 2015.

———. *The Gospel of Luke*. NICNT. Grand Rapids: Eerdmans, 1997.

Grindheim, Sigurd. "A Deutero-Pauline Mystery? Ecclesiology in Colossians and Ephesians." Pages 173–95 in *Paul and Pseudepigraphy*. Edited by Stanley E. Porter and Gregory P. Fewster. Pauline Studies 8. Leiden: Brill, 2013.

Grossman, Maxine. "Ephesians." Pages 345–53 in *Jewish Annotated New Testament*. Edited by Amy-Jill Levine and Marc Zvi Brettler. Oxford: Oxford University Press, 2011.

Grubbs, Judith Evans. "Infant Exposure and Infanticide." Pages 83–107 in *The Oxford Handbook of Childhood and Education in the Classical World*. Edited by Judith Evans Grubbs and Tim Parkin with Roslynne Bell. Oxford: Oxford University Press, 2013.

———. "Promoting Pietas through Roman Law." Pages 377–92 in *A Companion to Families in the Greek and Roman Worlds*. Edited by Beryl Rawson. London: Wiley-Blackwell, 2010.

Grudem, Wayne. "Does *Kephalē* ('Head') Mean 'Source' or 'Authority Over' in

Greek Literature? A Survey of 2,336 Examples." *Trinity Journal* 6 (1985): 38–59.

———. "The Meaning of *Kephalē* ('Head'): An Evaluation of New Evidence, Real and Alleged." *Journal of the Evangelical Theology Study* 44 (2001): 25–65.

Gruen, Erich S. *Diaspora: Jews amidst Greeks and Romans*. Cambridge: Harvard University Press, 2002.

———. *Heritage and Hellenism: The Reinvention of Jewish Tradition*. Berkeley: University of California Press, 1998.

Gundry-Volf, Judith M. "The Least and the Greatest: Children in the New Testament." Pages 29–60 in *The Child in Christian Thought*. Edited by Marcia J. Bunge. Grand Rapids: Eerdmans, 2001.

Habinek, Thomas. "*Imago suae vitae*: Seneca's Life and Career." Pages 3–32 in *Brill's Companion to Seneca: Philosopher and Dramatist*. Edited by Andreas Heil and Gregor Damschen with Mario Waida. Leiden: Brill, 2014.

Harnack, Adolf von. "Das Alte Testament in den Paulinischen Briefen und in den Paulinischen Gemeinden." *Sitzungsberichte der Preussischen Akademie der Wissenschaften* (1928): 124–41.

Harrill, J. Albert. *Slaves in the New Testament: Literary, Social, and Moral Dimensions*. Minneapolis: Fortress, 2006.

Harris, W. Hall, III. *The Descent of Christ: Ephesians 4:7–11 and Traditional Hebrew Imagery*. Arbeiten zur Geschichte des antiken Judentums und des Urchristentums 32. Leiden: Brill, 1996.

Harrison, James R. *Paul's Language of Grace in Its Graeco-Roman Context*. WUNT 2/172. Tübingen: Mohr Siebeck, 2003.

Harvey, Brian K., ed. and trans. *Daily Life in Ancient Rome: A Sourcebook*. Indianapolis: Hackett, 2016.

Haufe, Günter. "Reich Gottes bei Paulus und in der Jesustradition." *NTS* 31 (1985): 467–72.

Hays, Richard B. *The Conversion of the Imagination: Paul as Interpreter of Israel's Scripture*. Grand Rapids: Eerdmans, 2005.

———. *Echoes of Scripture in the Letters of Paul*. New Haven: Yale University Press, 1989.

———. *The Faith of Jesus Christ: An Investigation of the Narrative Substructure of Galatians 3:1–4:11*. Society of Biblical Literature Dissertation Series 56. Chico: Scholars Press, 1983. 2nd edition: *The Faith of Christ: The Narrative Substructure of Galatians 3:1–4:11*. Biblical Resource 56. Grand Rapids: Eerdmans, 2002.

———. *The Moral Vision of the New Testament: Community, Cross, New Creation; A Contemporary Introduction to New Testament Ethics*. San Francisco: HarperSanFrancisco, 1996.

———. "What Is 'Real Participation in Christ'? A Dialogue with E. P. Sanders on Pauline Soteriology." Pages 336–51 in *Redefining First-Century Jewish and Christian Identities: Essays in Honor of Ed Parish Sanders*. Edited by Fabian E. Udoh et al. Notre Dame: University of Notre Dame Press, 2008.

Heffernan, Thomas J. *The Passion of Perpetua and Felicity*. Oxford: Oxford University Press, 2012.

Heil, John Paul. *Ephesians: Empowerment to Walk in Love for the Unity of All in Christ*. SBL Studies in Biblical Literature 13. Atlanta: SBL, 2007.

———. "Ephesians 5:18b: 'But Be Filled in the Spirit.'" *Catholic Biblical Quarterly* 69 (2007): 506–16.

Heim, Erin M. *Adoption in Galatians and Romans: Contemporary Metaphor Theories and the Pauline Huiothesia Metaphors*. Biblical Interpretations 153. Leiden: Brill, 2017.

Helgeland, John, Robert Daly, and J. Patout Burns, eds. *Christians and the Military: The Early Experience*. Philadelphia: Fortress, 1985.

Hemer, Colin J. *Book of Acts in the Setting of Hellenistic History*. Winona Lake, IN: Eisenbrauns, 1990.

Hengel, Martin. "Christology and New Testament Chronology: A Problem in the History of Earliest Christianity." Pages 30–47 in *Between Jesus and Paul: Studies in the History of Earliest Christianity*. Translated by John Bowden. London: SCM, 1983.

———. *Judaism and Hellenism: Studies in Their Encounter in Palestine in the Early Hellenistic Period*. Translated by John Bowden. 2 vols. Philadelphia: Fortress, 1974.

———. *The Son of God: The Origin of Christology and the History of Jewish-Hellenistic Religion*. Translated by John Bowden. London: SCM, 1975.

Hering, James P. *The Colossian and Ephesian Haustafeln in Theological Contexts: An Analysis of Their Origins, Relationships, and Message*. New York: Peter Lang, 2007.

Heschel, Susannah. *The Aryan Jesus: Christian Theologians and the Bible in Nazi Germany*. Princeton: Princeton University Press, 2008.

Hezser, Catherine. *Jewish Slavery in Antiquity*. Oxford: Oxford University Press, 2005.

Hill, Wesley. *Paul and the Trinity: Persons, Relations, and the Pauline Letters*. Grand Rapids: Eerdmans, 2015.

Hoag, Gary G. *Wealth in Ancient Ephesus and the First Letter to Timothy: Fresh Insights from Ephesiaca by Xenophon of Ephesus*. Bulletin for Biblical Research Supplement 11. Winona Lake, IN: Eisenbrauns, 2015.

Hobbes, Thomas. *Leviathan*. London: Dent, 1914.

Hobbs, Raymond. "The Language of Warfare in the New Testament." Pages 259–73 in *Modelling Early Christianity: Social Scientific Studies of the New Testament in Its Context*. Edited by Philip F. Esler. London: Routledge, 1995.

Hodge, Caroline Johnson. *If Sons, Then Heirs: A Study of Kinship and Ethnicity in the Letters of Paul*. Oxford: Oxford University Press, 2007.

Hood, Jason B. *Imitating God in Christ: Recapturing a Biblical Pattern.* Downers Grove, IL: IVP Academic, 2013.

Horgan, Maurya P. *Pesharim: Qumran Interpretations of Biblical Books.* Catholic Biblical Quarterly Monograph Series 8. Washington, DC: Catholic Biblical Association of America, 1979.

Hoss, Stefanie. "The Roman Military Belt." Pages 29–44 in *Wearing the Cloak: Dressing the Soldier in Roman Times.* Edited by Marie-Louise Nosch. Ancient Textiles Series 10. Oxford: Oxbow, 2012.

Hübner, Hans. "Zur gegenwärtigen Diskussion über die Theologie des Paulus." *Jahrbuch für Biblische Theologie* 7 (1992): 399–413.

Hughes, Frank Witt. *Early Christian Rhetoric and 2 Thessalonians.* JSNTSup 30. Sheffield: Sheffield Academic, 1989.

Hüneburg, Martin. "Paulus versus Paulus: Der Epheserbrief als Korrektur des Kolosserbriefes." Pages 387–409 in *Pseudepigraphie und Verfasserfiktion in frühchristlichen Briefen.* Edited by J. Frey et al. WUNT 246. Tübingen: Mohr Siebeck, 2009.

Hurtado, Larry W. *God in New Testament Theology.* Nashville: Abingdon, 2010.

———. *Lord Jesus Christ: Devotion to Jesus in Earliest Christianity.* Grand Rapids: Eerdmans, 2003.

———. *One God, One Lord: Early Christian Devotion and Ancient Jewish Monotheism.* 2nd edition. London: T&T Clark, 1998.

Huskinson, Janet. "Representing Women on Roman Sarcophagi." Pages 11–31 in *The Material Culture of Sex, Procreation, and Marriage in Premodern Europe.* Edited by Anne L. McClanan and Karen Rosoff Encarnación. New York: Palgrave, 2002.

Isaac, Benjamin. *The Invention of Racism in Classical Antiquity.* Princeton: Princeton University Press, 2004.

Jeal, Roy R. *Integrating Theology and Ethics in Ephesians: The Ethos of Communication.* Studies in Bible and Early Christianity 43. Lewiston, NY: Mellon, 2000.

Joshel, Sandra R. "Slavery and Roman Literary Culture." Pages 214–40 in *The Ancient Mediterranean World.* Vol. 1 of *The Cambridge World History of Slavery.* Edited by Keith Bradley and Paul Cartledge. Cambridge: Cambridge University Press, 2011.

———. *Slavery in the Roman World.* Cambridge Introduction to Roman Civilization. Cambridge: Cambridge University Press, 2010.

Karaman, Elif Hilal. *Ephesian Women in Greco-Roman and Early Christian Perspective.* WUNT 474. Tübingen: Mohr Siebeck, 2018.

Käsemann, Ernst. "Epheserbrief." Pages 517–20 in vol. 2 of *Religion in Geschichte und Gegenwart.* Edited by Kurt Galling. 3rd edition. Tübingen: Mohr Siebeck, 1958.

———. "Ephesians and Acts." Pages 288–97 in *Studies in Luke-Acts*. Edited by Leander E. Keck and J. Louis Martyn. London: SPCK, 1968.

———. "Paul and Early Catholicism." Pages 236–51 in *New Testament Questions of Today*. Philadelphia: Fortress, 1967. Reprinted London: SCM, 1969.

Keating, James F., and Thomas Joseph White, eds. *Divine Impassibility and the Mystery of Human Suffering*. Grand Rapids: Eerdmans, 2009.

Keener, Craig S. *Acts: An Exegetical Commentary*. 4 vols. Grand Rapids: Baker Academic, 2012.

———. *Paul, Women, and Wives: Marriage and Women's Ministry in the Letters of Paul*. Peabody, MA: Hendrickson, 1992.

Kelly, J. N. D. *Jerome: His Life, Writings, and Controversies*. Peabody, MA: Hendrickson, 1998.

Kennedy, George A., trans. *Progymnasmata: Greek Textbooks of Prose Composition and Rhetoric*. Leiden: Brill, 2003.

Kenny, Anthony. *A Stylometric Study of the New Testament*. Oxford: Clarendon, 1986.

Klaiber, Walter. *Rechtfertigung und Gemeinde: Eine Untersuchung zum paulinischen Kirchenverständnis*. Göttingen: Vandenhoeck & Ruprecht, 1982.

Klauck, Hans-Josef. *Ancient Letters and the New Testament: A Guide to Context and Exegesis*. Translated by Daniel P. Bailey. Waco, TX: Baylor University Press, 2006.

Klawans, Jonathan. *Josephus and the Theologies of Ancient Judaism*. Oxford: Oxford University Press, 2012.

Knox, John. *Philemon among the Letters of Paul: A New View of Its Place and Importance*. New York: Abingdon, 1963.

Kraemer, Ross S., ed. *Women's Religions in the Greco-Roman World: A Sourcebook*. Oxford: Oxford University Press, 2004.

Kreitzer, Larry J. "'Crude Language' and 'Shameful Things Done in Secret' (Ephesians 5.4, 12): Allusions to the Cult of Demeter/Cybele in Hierapolis?" *Journal for the Study of the New Testament* 71 (1998): 51–77.

Krentz, Edgar. "Paul, Games, and the Military." Pages 344–83 in *Paul in the Greco-Roman World: A Handbook*. Edited by J. Paul Sampley. Harrisburg, PA: Trinity, 2003.

Laes, Christian. *Children in the Roman Empire: Outsiders Within*. Cambridge: Cambridge University Press, 2011.

Lakoff, George, and Mark Johnson. *Metaphors We Live By*. Chicago: University of Chicago Press, 1980.

Lang, T. J. *Mystery and the Making of a Christian Historical Consciousness: From Paul to the Second Century*. Berlin: de Gruyter, 2015.

Langmuir, Gavin L. *History, Religion, and Antisemitism*. Los Angeles: University of California Press, 1990.

Bibliography

Lau, Te-Li. *The Politics of Peace: Ephesians, Dio Chrysostom, and the Confucian Four Books*. Supplements to Novum Testamentum 133. Leiden: Brill, 2010.

Lee-Barnewall, Michelle. "Turning ΚΕΦΑΛΗ on Its Head: The Rhetoric of Reversal in Ephesians 5:21–33." Pages 599–614 in *Christian Origins and Greco-Roman Culture: Social and Literary Contexts for the New Testament*. Edited by Stanley E. Porter and Andrew W. Pitts. Leiden: Brill, 2013.

Lee, Chee-Chiew. *The Blessing of Abraham, the Spirit, and Justification in Galatians: Their Relationship and Significance in Understanding Paul's Theology*. Eugene, OR: Pickwick, 2013.

Lefkowitz, Mary R., and Maureen B. Fant, eds. *Women's Life in Greece and Rome: A Source Book in Translation*. 4th edition. Baltimore: Johns Hopkins University Press, 2016.

Levin, Carole. *The Heart and Stomach of a King: Elizabeth I and the Politics of Sex and Power*. 2nd edition. Philadelphia: University of Pennsylvania Press, 2013.

Levine, Amy-Jill. "Bearing False Witness: Common Errors Made about Early Judaism." Pages 760–63 in *The Jewish Annotated New Testament*. 2nd edition. Edited by Amy-Jill Levine and Marc Zvi Brettler. Oxford: Oxford University Press, 2011.

———. *The Misunderstood Jew: The Church and the Scandal of the Jewish Jesus*. San Francisco: HarperSanFrancisco, 2006.

Levinskaya, Irina. *The Book of Acts in Its Diaspora Setting*. The Book of Acts in Its First Century Setting 5. Grand Rapids: Eerdmans, 1996.

Leyerle, Blake. "Children and 'the Child' in Early Christianity." Pages 559–79 in *The Oxford Handbook of Childhood and Education in the Classical World*. Edited by Judith Evans Grubbs and Tim Parkin. Oxford: Oxford University Press, 2013.

Lietzmann, H. *An die Römer*. Handbuch zum Neuen Testament 8. Tübingen: Mohr Siebeck, 1971.

Lieu, Judith, John North, and Tessa Rajak, eds. *The Jews among Pagans and Christians in the Roman Empire*. New York: Routledge, 1992.

Lightfoot, J. B. *Biblical Essays*. London: Macmillan, 1893. Reprinted Grand Rapids: Baker, 1979.

Lincoln, Andrew T. "The Church and Israel in Ephesians 2." *Catholic Biblical Quarterly* 49 (1987): 605–24.

Lindemann, Andreas. *Die Aufhebung der Zeit: Geschichtsverständnis und Eschatologie im Epheserbrief*. Studien zum Neuen Testament 12. Edited by Günter Klein, Willi Marxsen, and Wolfgang Schrage. Gütersloh: Gütersloher Verlagshaus, 1975.

Linebaugh, Jonathan. *God, Grace, and Righteousness in Wisdom of Solomon and Paul's Letter to the Romans*. Leiden: Brill, 2013.

Longenecker, Bruce W. *Remember the Poor: Paul, Poverty, and the Greco-Roman World*. Grand Rapids: Eerdmans, 2010.

Longenecker, Richard N. *Biblical Exegesis in the Apostolic Period*. 2nd edition. Grand Rapids: Eerdmans, 1999.

Longman, Tremper, III, and Daniel G. Reid. *God Is a Warrior*. Grand Rapids: Zondervan, 1995.

Lyons, George. "Church and Holiness in Ephesians." Pages 238–56 in *Holiness and Ecclesiology in the New Testament*. Edited by Kent E. Brower and Andy Johnson. Grand Rapids, Eerdmans, 2007.

MacDonald, Margaret Y. *The Power of Children: The Construction of Families in the Greco-Roman World*. Waco, TX: Baylor University Press, 2014.

Maier, Harry O. *Picturing Paul in Empire: Imperial Image, Text, and Persuasion in Colossians, Ephesians and the Pastoral Epistles*. London: Bloomsbury T&T Clark, 2013.

Malherbe, Abraham J. *Paul and the Popular Philosophers*. Minneapolis: Fortress, 1989. Reprinted 2006.

Martín-Asensio, Gustavo. *Transitivity-Based Foregrounding in the Acts of the Apostles: A Functional-Grammatical Approach to the Lukan Perspective*. JSNTSup 202. Sheffield: Sheffield Academic Press, 2000.

Martin, Dale B. *The Corinthian Body*. New Haven: Yale University Press, 1995.

Martin, Ralph P. "An Epistle in Search of a Life-Setting." *Expository Times* 79 (1968): 296–302.

———. *Reconciliation: A Study of Paul's Theology*. Revised edition. Eugene, OR: Wipf & Stock, 1997.

Mathewson, David L. "The Abused Present." *Bulletin for Biblical Research* 23.3 (2013): 343–63.

———. "Being Filled with the Spirit." Pages 85–87 in *Devotions on the Greek New Testament: 52 Reflections to Inspire and Instruct*. Edited by J. Scott Duvall and Verlyn D. Verbrugge. Grand Rapids: Zondervan, 2012.

Mathewson, David L., and Elodie Ballantine Emig, *Intermediate Greek Grammar: Syntax for Students of the New Testament*. Grand Rapids: Baker Academic, 2016.

Matlock, R. Barry. "Detheologizing the ΠΙΣΤΙΣ ΧΡΙΣΤΟΥ Debate: Cautionary Remarks from a Lexical Semantic Perspective." *Novum Testamentum* 42 (2000): 1–23.

Mattingly, Harold. *Augustus to Vitellus*. Vol. 1 of *Coins from the Roman Empire in the British Museum*. London: British Museum, 1965. Originally 1923.

McCaulley, Esau D. *Sharing in the Son's Inheritance: Davidic Messianism and Paul's Worldwide Interpretation of the Abrahamic Land Promise in Galatians*. Library of New Testament Studies 608. London: T&T Clark, 2019.

McKnight, Scot. *Colossians*. NICNT. Grand Rapids: Eerdmans, 2018.

———. *Jesus and His Death: Historiography, the Historical Jesus, and Atonement Theory*. Waco, TX: Baylor University Press, 2005.

———. *Kingdom Conspiracy: Returning to the Radical Mission of the Local Church*. Grand Rapids: Brazos, 2014.

———. *Philemon*. NICNT. Grand Rapids: Eerdmans, 2017.

McNeel, Jennifer Houston. *Paul as Infant and Nursing Mother: Metaphor, Rhetoric, and Identity in 1 Thessalonians 2:5–8*. Atlanta: SBL, 2014.

Metzger, Bruce M. "Literary Forgeries and Canonical Pseudepigrapha." *Journal of Biblical Literature* 91.1 (1972): 3–24.

Mickelsen, Berkeley, and Alvera Mickelsen, "What Does *Kephalē* Mean in the New Testament?" Pages 97–110 in *Women, Authority, and the Bible*. Edited by Alvera Mickelsen. Downers Grove, IL: InterVarsity Press, 1986.

Mitton, C. Leslie. *The Epistle to the Ephesians: Its Authorship, Origin, and Purpose*. Oxford: Clarendon, 1951. Reprinted Eugene, OR: Wipf & Stock, 2002.

Morris, Leon L. *Atonement: Its Meaning and Significance*. Leicester: InterVarsity Press, 1983.

Mott, Stephen Charles. "The Power of Giving and Receiving: Reciprocity in Hellenistic Benevolence." Pages 60–72 in *Current Issues in Biblical and Patristic Interpretation: Studies in Honor of Merrill C. Tenney Presented by His Former Students*. Edited by Gerald F. Hawthorne. Grand Rapids: Eerdmans, 1975.

Moulton, J. H. *Prolegomena*. Vol. 1 of *A Grammar of New Testament Greek*. Edinburgh: T&T Clark, 1908.

Mouritsen, Henrik. *The Freedman in the Roman World*. Cambridge: Cambridge University Press, 2011.

Moxnes, Halvor, ed. *Constructing Early Christian Families: Family as Social Reality and Metaphor*. London: Routledge, 1997.

Murray, John. *Redemption—Accomplished and Applied*. Grand Rapids: Eerdmans, 1955.

Nanos, Mark D. *Reading Paul within Judaism: Collected Essays of Mark D. Nanos*, vol. 1. Eugene, OR: Cascade, 2017.

Nanos, Mark D., and Magnus Zetterholm. *Paul within Judaism: Restoring the First-Century Context to the Apostle*. Minneapolis: Fortress, 2015.

Nasrallah, Laura Salah. *Christian Responses to Roman Art and Architecture: The Second Century Church amid the Spaces of Empire*. Cambridge: Cambridge University Press, 2010.

Nirenberg, David. *Anti-Judaism: The Western Tradition*. New York: Norton, 2013.

Noll, Mark. *The Civil War as a Theological Crisis*. Chapel Hill: University of North Carolina Press, 2006.

Nostra Aetate. The Declaration on the Relation of the Church with Non-Christian Religions of the Second Vatican Council. October 28, 1965.

Novak, David. *Jewish-Christian Dialogue: A Jewish Justification*. Oxford: Oxford University Press, 1989.

Novenson, Matthew V. *Christ among the Messiahs: Christ Language in Paul and Messiah Language in Ancient Judaism*. Oxford: Oxford University Press, 2012.

Nussbaum, Martha C. "The Incomplete Feminism of Musonius Rufus, Platonist, Stoic, and Roman." Pages 283–325 in *The Sleep of Reason: Erotic Experience and Sexual Ethics in Ancient Greece*. Edited by Martha C. Nussbaum and Juha Sihvola. Chicago: University of Chicago Press, 2002.

Ophir, Adi, and Ishay Rosen-Zvi. *Goy: Israel's Multiple Others and the Birth of the Gentile*. Oxford: Oxford University Press, 2018.

Orr, Peter. *Christ Absent and Present: A Study in Pauline Christology*. WUNT 354. Tübingen: Mohr Siebeck, 2014.

Osgood, Josiah. *Turia: A Roman Woman's Civil War*. Oxford: Oxford University Press, 2014.

Osiek, Carolyn, and Margaret Y. MacDonald with Janet H. Tulloch. *A Woman's Place: House Churches in Earliest Christianity*. Minneapolis: Fortress, 2006.

Overfield, P. D. "*Pleroma*: A Study in Content and Context." *NTS* 25 (1975): 384–96.

Patterson, Orlando. *Slavery and Social Death: A Comparative Study*. Cambridge: Harvard University Press, 1982.

Pervo, Richard I. *Acts: A Commentary*. Hermeneia. Minneapolis: Fortress, 2009.

Pitts, Andrew W. "Philosophical and Epistolary Contexts for Pauline Paraenesis." Pages 269–306 in *Paul and the Ancient Letter Form*. Edited by Stanley E. Porter and Sean A. Adams. Leiden: Brill, 2010.

Pokorný, Petr. *Der Epheserbrief und die Gnosis: Die Bedeutung des Haupt-Glieder-Gedankens in der entstehenden Kirche*. Berlin: Evangelische Verlagsanstalt, 1965.

Pollard, Elizabeth Ann. "Magic Accusations against Women in Tacitus' *Annals*." Pages 183–218 in *Daughters of Hecate*. Edited by Kimberly Stratton and Dayna Kalleres. New York: Oxford University Press, 2014.

———. "Magic Accusations against Women in the Greco-Roman World from the First through the Fifth Centuries C.E." PhD diss., University of Pennsylvania, 2001.

Porter, Stanley E. "'Ἴστε Γινώσκοντες in Ephesians 5,5: Does Chiasm Solve a Problem?" *Zeitschrift für die neutestamentliche Wissenschaft* 81 (1990): 270–76.

———. "Paul, Virtues, Vices, and Household Codes." Pages 369–90 in vol. 2 of *Paul in the Greco-Roman World: A Handbook*. Revised edition. Edited by J. Paul Sampley. London: Bloomsbury T&T Clark, 2016.

Porter, Stanley E., and Bryan R. Dyer. "Oral Texts? A Reassessment of the Oral Rhetorical Nature of Paul's Letters in Light of Recent Studies." *Journal of the Evangelical Theology Study* 55.2 (2012): 323–41.

Preisendanz, Karl. *Papyri graecae magicae: Die griechischen Zauberpapyri*. 3 vols. Berlin: Teubner, 1928–42. Second revised. Stuttgart: Heinrichs, 1973–74.

Price, S. R. F. *Rituals and Power: The Roman Imperial Cult in Asia Minor*. Cambridge: Cambridge University Press, 1984.

Ramelli, Ilaria L. E. *Social Justice and the Legitimacy of Slavery: The Role of Philosophical Asceticism from Ancient Judaism to Late Antiquity*. Oxford: Oxford University Press, 2016.

Rapske, Brian M. *The Book of Acts and Paul in Roman Custody*. The Book of Acts in Its First Century Setting 3. Grand Rapids: Eerdmans, 1994.

———. "Prison, Prisoner." Pages 827–30 in *Dictionary of New Testament Background*. Edited by Craig A. Evans and Stanley E. Porter. Downers Grove, IL: InterVarsity Press, 2000.

Reece, Steve. *Paul's Large Letters: Paul's Autographic Subscriptions in the Light of Ancient Epistolary Conventions*. Library of New Testament Studies 561. London: T&T Clark, 2017.

Rese, M. "Die Vorzüge Israels in Röm. 9,4f. und Eph. 2,12." *Theologische Zeitschrift* 31 (1975): 211–22.

Rhee, Helen. *Loving the Poor, Saving the Rich: Wealth, Poverty, and Early Christian Formation*. Grand Rapids: Baker Academic, 2012.

Richards, E. Randolph. *Paul and First-Century Letter Writing: Secretaries, Composition, and Collection*. Downers Grove, IL: InterVarsity Press, 2004.

———. "Will the Real Author Please Stand Up?" Pages 113–36 in *Come Let Us Reason: New Essays in Christian Apologetics*. Edited by Paul Copan and William Lane Craig. Nashville: B&H Academic, 2012.

Richardson, Neil. *Paul's Language about God*. JSNTSup 99. Sheffield: Sheffield Academic Press, 1994.

Richlin, Amy. *The Garden of Priapus: Sexuality and Aggression in Roman Humor*. Revised edition. Oxford: Oxford University Press, 1992.

Rist, M. "Pseudepigraphy and the Early Christians." Pages 75–91 in *Studies in New Testament and Early Christian Literature: Essays in Honor of A. P. Wikgren*. Supplements to Novum Testamentum 33. Edited by David E. Aune. Leiden: Brill, 1972.

Roberts, J. H. "Belydenisuitsprake as Pauliniese breifoorgange." *Hervormde Teologiese Studies* 44 (1988): 81–97.

Robertson, A. T. *A Grammar of the Greek New Testament in the Light of Historical Research*. Nashville: Broadman, 1934.

Robertson, Paul M. *Paul's Letters and Contemporary Greco-Roman Literature: Theorizing a New Taxonomy*. Supplements to Novum Testamentum 167. Leiden: Brill, 2016.

Robinson, John A. T. *The Body: A Study in Pauline Theology*. London: SCM, 1952.

Rogers, Guy MacLean. *The Mysteries of Artemis of Ephesos: Cult, Polis, and Change in the Graeco-Roman World*. New Haven: Yale University Press, 2012.

Roon, A. van. *The Authenticity of Ephesians.* Leiden: Brill, 1974.
Rosenmeyer, Patricia A. *Ancient Epistolary Fictions: The Letter in Greek Literature.* Cambridge: Cambridge University Press, 2001.
Rosner, Brian S. *Greed as Idolatry: The Origin and Meaning of a Pauline Metaphor.* Grand Rapids: Eerdmans, 2007.
Roth, Ulrike. "Paul and Slavery: Economic Perspectives." Pages 155–82 in *Paul and Economics*, edited by Raymond Pickett and Thomas R. Blanton IV. Minneapolis: Fortress, 2017.
Rowe, C. Kavin. *Early Narrative Christology: The Lord in the Gospel of Luke.* Grand Rapids: Baker Academic, 2009.
Ruden, Sarah. *Paul among the People: The Apostle Reinterpreted and Reimagined in His Own Time.* New York: Pantheon, 2010.
Ruether, Rosemary Radford. *Faith and Fratricide: The Theological Roots of Anti-Semitism.* New York: Seabury, 1974. Reprinted Eugene, OR: Wipf & Stock, 1997.
Runge, Steven E. *Discourse Grammar of the Greek New Testament: A Practical Introduction for Teaching and Exegesis.* Peabody, MA: Hendrickson, 2010.
Russell, D. A. *Criticism in Antiquity.* London: Duckworth, 1981.
Rutledge, Fleming. *The Crucifixion: Understanding the Death of Jesus Christ.* Grand Rapids: Eerdmans, 2015.
Saller, Richard P. "*Pater Familias, Mater Familias,* and the Gendered Semantics of the Roman Household." *Classical Philology* 94 (1999): 182–97.
Sanders, E. P. *Judaism: Practice and Belief, 63 BCE–66 CE.* Minneapolis: Fortress, 1992. Reprinted 2016.
———. *Paul and Palestinian Judaism: A Comparison of Patterns of Religion.* 40th anniversary edition. Minneapolis: Fortress, 2017.
Scheidel, Walter, Ian Morris, and Richard Saller, eds. *The Cambridge Economic History of the Greco-Roman World.* Cambridge: Cambridge University Press, 2007.
Schenck, Kenneth. "2 Corinthians and the Πίστις Χριστοῦ Debate." *Catholic Biblical Quarterly* 70 (2008): 524–37.
Schlier, Heinrich. *Christus und die Kirche im Epheserbrief.* Beiträge zur historischen Theologie 6. Tübingen: Mohr Siebeck, 1930.
Schweitzer, Albert. *The Mysticism of Paul the Apostle.* Translated by W. Montgomery. London: Black, 1930. Reprinted Baltimore: Johns Hopkins University Press, 1998.
Schweizer, E. *Das Leben des Herrn in der Gemeinde und ihren Diensten.* Zürich: EVZ, 1946.
Seierstad, Asne. *The Bookseller of Kabul.* Translated by Ingrid Christophersen. Boston: Little, Brown, 2003.
Selderhuis, Herman J. *John Calvin: A Pilgrim's Life.* Translated by Albert Gootjes. Downers Grove, IL: InterVarsity Press, 2009.

Sellin, Gerhard. "Epheserbrief." Pages 1343–47 in vol. 2 of *Religion in Geschichte und Gegenwart*. Edited by Hans Dieter Betz. 4th edition. Tübingen: Mohr Siebeck, 1999.

Severy, Beth. *Augustus and the Family at the Birth of the Roman Empire*. New York: Routledge, 2004.

Sharkey, Sarah Borden. *An Aristotelian Feminism*. Switzerland: Springer, 2016.

Sherwood, Aaron. "Paul's Imprisonment as the Glory of the *Ethnē*: A Discourse Analysis of Ephesians 3:1–13." *Bulletin for Biblical Research* 22.1 (2012): 97–111.

Shogren, Gary Steven. "The Pauline Proclamation of the Kingdom of God and the Kingdom of Christ within its New Testament Setting." PhD diss., University of Aberdeen, 1986.

———. "'The Wicked Will Not Inherit the Kingdom of God': A Pauline Warning and the Hermeneutics of Liberation Theology and of Brian McLaren." *Trinity Journal* 31 (2010): 95–113.

Sigismund-Nielsen, Hanne. "Vibia Perpetua—An Indecent Woman." Pages 103–17 in *Perpetua's Passions: Multidisciplinary Approaches to the Passio Perpetuae et Felicitatis*. Edited by Jan N. Bremmer and Marco Formisano. Oxford: Oxford University Press, 2012.

Smith, Julien. *Christ the Ideal King: Cultural Context, Rhetorical Strategy, and the Power of Divine Monarchy in Ephesians*. WUNT 313. Tübingen: Mohr Siebeck, 2011.

Smith, Nicholas D. "Aristotle's Theory of Natural Slavery." *Phoenix* 37 (1983): 109–22.

Snowden, Frank M., Jr. *Blacks in Antiquity: Ethiopians in the Greco-Roman Experience*. Cambridge: Harvard University Press, 1970.

Son, Sang-Won (Aaron). "The Church as 'One New Man': Ecclesiology and Anthropology in Ephesians." *Southwestern Journal of Theology* 52.1 (2009): 18–31.

Soskice, Janet Martin. *The Kindness of God: Metaphor, Gender. and Religious Language*. Oxford: Oxford University Press, 2007.

Soulen, R. Kendall. *God of Israel and Christian Theology*. Minneapolis: Fortress, 1996.

Speyer, W. *Die literarische Fälschung im heidnischen und christlichen Altertum: Ein Versuch ihrer Deutung*. Handbuch der Altertumswissenschaft. Munich: Beck, 1971.

Stacey, Peter. "Senecan Political Thought from the Middle Ages to Early Modernity." Pages 289–302 in *The Cambridge Companion to Seneca*. Edited by Shadi Bartsch and Alessandro Schiesaro. Cambridge: Cambridge University Press, 2015.

Starling, David. *Not My People: Gentiles as Exiles in Pauline Hermeneutics*. Beihefte zur Zeitschrift für die neutestamentliche Wissenschaft 184. Berlin: de Gruyter, 2011.

Stec, David M. *The Targum of Psalms*. Aramaic Bible 16. Collegeville, MN: Liturgical Press, 2004.

Stegemann, Hartmut, and Eileen Schuller, eds.; Carol Newsom, trans. *Qumran Cave 1*, vol. 3: *1QHodayot^a*. Discoveries in the Judaean Desert 40. Oxford: Clarendon, 2009.

Stendahl, Krister. "The Apostle Paul and the Introspective Conscience of the West." *Harvard Theological Review* 56.3 (1963): 199–215.

———. *Paul among Jews and Gentiles, and Other Essays*. Philadelphia: Fortress, 1976.

Stirewalt, M. Luther, Jr. *Studies in Ancient Greek Epistolography*. SBL Resources for Biblical Studies 27. Atlanta: Scholars Press, 1993.

Stowe, Harriet Beecher. *Uncle Tom's Cabin*. Hartford, CT: Worthington, 1901.

Stowers, Stanley K. *Letter Writing in Greco-Roman Antiquity*. Philadelphia: Westminster, 1986.

———. *A Rereading of Romans: Justice, Jews, and Gentiles*. New Haven: Yale University Press, 1994.

Strelan, Rick. *Paul, Artemis, and the Jews in Ephesus*. Berlin: de Gruyter, 1996.

Strobel, Regula. "Der Beihilfe beschuldigt: Christliche Theologie auf der Anklagebank." *Feministisch theologische Zeitschrift* 9 (1993): 3–6.

Suh, Robert H. "The Use of Ezekiel 37 in Ephesians 2." *Journal of the Evangelical Theology Study* 50.4 (2007): 715–33.

Swartley, Willard M. "Peace." Pages 354–60 in *The Westminster Theological Wordbook of the Bible*. Edited by Donald E. Gowan. Louisville: Westminster John Knox, 2003.

Tanner, Kathryn. *Christ the Key*. Cambridge: Cambridge University Press, 2010.

———. *Jesus, Humanity, and the Trinity: A Brief Systematic Theology*. Minneapolis: Fortress, 2001.

Taylor, Lily Ross. *The Divinity of the Roman Emperor*. Middletown, CT: American Philological Association, 1931.

Tellbe, Mikael. *Christ-Believers in Ephesus: A Textual Analysis of Early Christian Identity Formation in Local Perspective*. WUNT 242. Tübingen: Mohr Siebeck, 2009.

Thate, Michael J., Kevin J. Vanhoozer, and Constantine R. Campbell, eds. *"In Christ" in Paul: Explorations in Paul's Theology of Union and Participation*. Tübingen: Mohr Siebeck, 2014. Reprinted Grand Rapids: Eerdmans, 2018.

Thiselton, Anthony C. *The First Epistle to the Corinthians*. New International Greek Testament Commentary. Grand Rapids: Eerdmans, 2000.

Thomas, Matthew J. "Origen on Paul's Authorship of Hebrews." *NTS* 65 (2019): 598–609.

Thompson, James W. *The Church according to Paul: Rediscovering the Community Conformed to Christ*. Grand Rapids: Baker Academic, 2014.
Thompson, Marianne Meye. *The Promise of the Father: Jesus and God in the New Testament*. Louisville: Westminster John Knox, 2000.
Thorsen, Don. "*Prima Gratia, Prima Fide*, and *Prima Scriptura*: Reforming Protestant Principles." Pages 201–24 in *The Continuing Relevance of Wesleyan Theology: Essays in Honor of Laurence W. Wood*. Edited by Nathan Crawford. Eugene, OR: Pickwick, 2011.
Towner, Philip H. *The Letters to Timothy and Titus*. NICNT. Grand Rapids: Eerdmans, 2006.
Trebilco, Paul R. *The Early Christians in Ephesus from Paul to Ignatius*. Tübingen: Mohr Siebeck, 2004; Grand Rapids: Eerdmans, 2007.
———. "Engaging—or Not Engaging—the City: Reading 1 and 2 Timothy and the Johannine Letters in the City of Ephesus." Pages 160–86 in *The Urban World and the First Christians*. Edited by Steve Walton, Paul R. Trebilco, and David W. J. Gill. Grand Rapids: Eerdmans, 2017.
Tutu, Desmond. Address at His Enthronement as Anglican Archbishop of Cape Town. September 7, 1986.
Uzzi, Jeannine Diddle. "The Power of Parenthood in Official Roman Art." Pages 61–81 in *Constructions of Childhood in Ancient Greece and Italy*. Edited by Ada Cohen and Jeremy B. Rutter. Hesperia Supplement 41. Princeton: American School of Classical Studies in Athens, 2007.
Vickers, Jason E. "Wesley's Theological Emphases." Pages 190–206 in *The Cambridge Companion to John Wesley*. Edited by Randy L. Maddox and Jason E. Vickers. Cambridge: Cambridge University Press, 2010.
Volf, Miroslav. *Exclusion and Embrace: A Theological Exploration of Identity, Otherness, and Reconciliation*. Nashville: Abingdon, 1996.
Vout, Caroline. *Power and Eroticism in Imperial Rome*. Cambridge: Cambridge University Press, 2007.
Wainwright, Arthur William. *The Trinity in the New Testament*. London: SPCK, 1962.
Wallace, Daniel B. *Greek Grammar: Beyond the Basics; An Exegetical Syntax of the New Testament*. Grand Rapids: Zondervan, 1996.
Wansink, Craig S. *Chained in Christ: The Experience and Rhetoric of Paul's Imprisonments*. JSNTSup 130. Sheffield: Sheffield Academic, 1996.
Wassen, Cecilia. *Women in the Damascus Document*. Atlanta: Scholars Press, 2005.
Watson, Francis. *Paul, Judaism, and the Gentiles: Beyond the New Perspective*. Revised edition. Grand Rapids: Eerdmans, 2007.
———. "The Triune Divine Identity: Reflections on Pauline God-Language, in Disagreement with J. D. G. Dunn." *Journal for the Study of the New Testament* 23.80 (March 2001): 99–124.

Bibliography

Weima, Jeffrey A. D. *1–2 Thessalonians*. Baker Exegetical Commentary on the New Testament. Grand Rapids: Baker Academic, 2014.

———. *Paul the Ancient Letter Writer: An Introduction to Epistolary Analysis*. Grand Rapids: Baker Academic, 2016.

Westerholm, Stephen. *Perspectives Old and New: The "Lutheran" Paul and His Critics*. Grand Rapids: Eerdmans, 2003.

Westfall, Cynthia Long. *Paul and Gender: Reclaiming the Apostle's Vision for Men and Women in Christ*. Grand Rapids: Baker Academic, 2016.

———. "'This Is a Great Metaphor!' Reciprocity in the Ephesians Household Code." Pages 561–98 in *Christian Origins and Greco-Roman Culture: Social and Literary Contexts for the New Testament*. Edited by Stanley E. Porter and Andrew W. Pitts. Leiden: Brill, 2013.

Wheatley, Alan B. *Patronage in Early Christianity: Its Use and Transformation from Jesus to Paul of Samosata*. Princeton Theological Monograph Series 160. Eugene, OR: Pickwick, 2011.

Wilder, Terry L. *Pseudonymity, the New Testament, and Deception: An Inquiry into Intention and Reception*. Lanham, MD: University Press of America, 2004.

Williams, Margaret H. *The Jews among the Greeks and Romans: A Diaspora Sourcebook*. Baltimore: Johns Hopkins University Press, 1998.

Willitts, Joel. "Conclusion." Pages 315–19 in *Introduction to Messianic Judaism: Its Ecclesial Context and Biblical Foundations*. Edited by David Rudolph and Joel Willitts. Grand Rapids: Zondervan, 2013.

Winer, G. B. *A Grammar of the Idiom of the New Testament, Prepared as a Solid Basis for the Interpretation of the New Testament*. 7th edition. Revised by G. Lünemann. Andover: Draper, 1881.

Wink, Walter. *Naming the Powers: The Language of Power in the New Testament*. Philadelphia: Fortress, 1984.

———. *The Powers That Be: Theology for a New Millennium*. New York: Doubleday, 1998.

Wistrand, E. *The So-called Laudatio Turiae: Introduction, Text, Translation, Commentary*. Studia Graeca et Latina Gothoburgensia 34. Göteborg: Acta Universitatis Gothoburgensis, 1976.

Witherington, Ben, III. *Conflict and Community in Corinth: A Socio-Rhetorical Commentary on 1 and 2 Corinthians*. Grand Rapids: Eerdmans, 1995.

———. *Jesus, Paul, and the End of the World: A Comparative Study in New Testament Eschatology*. Downers Grove, IL: InterVarsity Press, 1992.

Wright, Christopher J. H. *The Mission of God's People: A Biblical Theology for the Church's Mission*. Grand Rapids: Zondervan, 2010.

Wright, N. T. *The New Testament and the People of God*. Minneapolis: Fortress, 1992.

———. *Paul and His Recent Interpreters*. Minneapolis: Fortress, 2015.

BIBLIOGRAPHY

———. *Paul and the Faithfulness of God*. 2 vols. Minneapolis: Fortress, 2013.
———. *Paul: In Fresh Perspective*. Minneapolis: Fortress, 2005.
Yinger, Kent L. *The New Perspective on Paul: An Introduction*. Eugene, OR: Cascade, 2011.
Yoder Neufeld, Thomas R. *Put on the Armour of God: The Divine Warrior from Isaiah to Ephesians*. JSNTSup 140. Sheffield: Sheffield Academic Press, 1997.
Yong, Amos. *In the Days of Caesar: Pentecostalism and Political Theology*. Grand Rapids: Eerdmans, 2010.

Introduction

The letter to the Ephesians soars to celestial heights in its depiction of God's powerful grace and pauses over familial and community relationships common in the first century. The epistle offers a spatial map of the cosmos to locate God the Father, Christ the Lord, and the Holy Spirit as well as the believers' position. Ephesians narrates a plot that begins before the creation of the world, continues with God's redemption of his people from sin and the creation of a new people in Christ, and promises eternal fellowship with God and fellow believers. It picks up the story of two human groups, Jews and gentiles, labeled by their nearness or distance from God and characterized as devout or idolaters. The climax of the narrative is the revealing of God's mystery, the Messiah who establishes the kingdom of Christ and of God (5:5), who redeems sinners for God, and who creates a new people in himself, the body of Christ. The story has two remaining chapters. The penultimate one is being written by the church now, as believers mature and are transformed by the work of Christ. This chapter takes place on two planes: the spiritual realm, with its powers and authorities, as well as the mundane world of commerce, marriage, family—the stuff of our mortal existence. Evil vies for power and influence, but God prevails, for Christ has been raised, and the Spirit's seal is immutable. The final chapter of this redemption story celebrates the fully realized kingdom of God, wherein Christ brings all things to unity in himself.

    The letter's argument begins with a lengthy summary of the historical unfolding of God's plan of salvation through the work of Jesus Christ. The goal of the plan is to produce adopted children who are holy and blameless, who are both Jew and gentile by birth. Chapter one continues that the salvation plan also is victorious over the forces of evil and introduces an image of the church as Christ's body. Chapter two spotlights gentile inclusion into God's family, from two vantage points. First, gentiles are described as moving from the realm of the prince of the kingdom of the air, to the throne of

Introduction

God, where the Son is seated at the Father's right hand. Second, gentiles are described as distant from the commonwealth of Israel, the people of God. Christ, "our peace" (2:14), draws them in and creates a new humanity. This new family is also being built into God's temple, where the Holy Spirit lives. At this point, Paul digresses in chapter three to explain his role in the salvation plan, as one who has been given grace to proclaim the mystery of salvation. He follows with a prayer and doxology, before proceeding to offer a lengthy paraenetic section.

In these last three chapters, Paul offers several striking images that address Christian lifestyle and maturity. First, he promotes the unity of the church and its growth through the gifts given it by Christ. Next, he speaks of believers participating in Christ's life, putting on Christ, to live a truth-filled and righteous life. Believers are to keep their tongue from evil and hurtful words and to uplift the community life of believers. Paul continues in this vein in chapter five, contrasting believers who walk in love and light with "gentiles" who walk in darkness and have no share in God's kingdom. The church is animated by the Holy Spirit as it worships together. The household relationships of the first century (wife/husband, children/parents, slave/owner) are addressed through the work of Christ. The conclusion of the letter implores believers to put on the armor of God, to stand fast against the spiritual forces that seek them harm.

We might summarize the contents of the epistle as "indicative/imperative." The first three chapters offer descriptions of who believers are in Christ, and the second half of the epistle presents the implications and ramifications of this testimony. The first three chapters explicate the cosmic reality of God's definitive victory in Christ and Christ's ultimate work in unifying the universe, and the second half addresses the proper behavior necessary to stand firm during the final days of darkness's reign. The first three chapters explain how by faith in Christ, Jews are joined with gentiles into one family. This new, united humanity is now summoned to a holy life, to mature and grow together as members of Christ's body. While there is much truth to this description of the epistle's structure, it can also be misleading to rest a theological paradigm on a grammatical construction.[1] Paul's argument is better understood as a tapestry that weaves threads of past, present, and future realities of salvation history as they pertain to believers' lives in fellowship with Christ. Being "in Christ" connects the present and the future and brings fact and potential together to create a holy people unto God.

---

1. Stanley Porter, "Holiness, Sanctification," *DPL* 401.

I. AUTHORSHIP

The theological statements within Ephesians can be difficult to understand, if sweepingly magnificent in places. The majority of the recipients are recognizable as pagans living in the latter half of the first century who convert to follow Christ and the gospel message. The newly formed community addressed in the letter shares commonalities with other communities identified as believers in the Lord Jesus Christ. Questions arise, however, about whether Paul wrote the epistle. Unpacking this tangled ball of string includes isolating presuppositions and explaining authorship in the ancient world. A quick review of how we got to this point launches our discussion.

A. AUTHORSHIP QUESTION UNPACKED

Within New Testament studies today, Ephesians is often deemed deutero-Pauline, or one of the "disputed" letters.[2] The *Hauptbriefe* or "genuine" Pauline letters include Romans, 1 and 2 Corinthians, and Galatians. Paul wrote these directly with the aid of a secretary. (I will say more about the secretary's role below.) Philippians, 1 Thessalonians, and Philemon are usually determined to be genuinely Pauline.[3] The authorship of Colossians and 2 Thessalonians might be questioned. Ephesians and the Pastoral Epistles are often judged as non-Pauline.

In the late eighteenth century, F. C. Baur cast doubts on the genuineness of Ephesians, prompted in part by his overarching theory about the early church.[4] This reconstruction argued for two factions within the church: Peter and his Jewish Christianity over against Paul, representing gentile Christian-

---

2. Hoehner, 9–20, offers a chart listing 279 scholars and 390 of their works and finds that up until 1960 more scholars favored Pauline authorship and that only between 1971–90 did 58 percent of scholars deny Pauline authorship.

3. Bart Ehrman, *Forged: Writing in the Name of God—Why the Bible's Authors Are Not Who We Think They Are* (New York: HarperOne, 2011), 92–93, includes Philippians, 1 Thessalonians, and Philemon, to make seven authentic Pauline letters.

4. Ferdinand Christian Baur, *Paul the Apostle of Jesus Christ: His Life and Works, His Epistles and Teachings* (reprinted Peabody, MA: Hendrickson, 2003 [German original: *Paulus, der Apostel Jesu Christi*, 1845]. Baur, the father of the Tübingen school, argued that only Romans, 1 and 2 Corinthians, and Galatians were authentically Pauline. He used Hegel's dialectic as a grid to understand the early church, claiming sharp divisions between the Jewish wing of the church under Peter and the gentile church led by Paul. Baur's anti-Judaism permeated his theory, as seen in this quotation from p. 263 of his commentary: "The chief reason why their Judaistic position was so narrow was just their natural incapacity to raise themselves from the lower state of religious consciousness to a higher and freer one."

ity. More recently, German Protestant scholars such as Käsemann, Lindemann, and Conzelmann viewed Ephesians as evidence for a "deutero-Pauline development towards the 'catholicism' of second-century Christianity. They argued for the letter's emphasis on the universal Church and the succession of ministries from the apostles, as well as its loss of eschatological expectations."[5] Currently, some scholars a priori conclude that certain key doctrines, such as justification by faith in Jesus Christ or apocalyptic views, epitomize Paul's message; therefore, they dispute Pauline authorship of those letters lacking such language or topics. Moreover, they suggest that the writing style and grammar of Ephesians are too dissimilar from the undisputed letters to be authentically Paul. These objections assume a normative "Paul" held as a measuring stick against Ephesians.

To address this complex landscape, I will first sketch the specific arguments used to label Ephesians as deutero-Pauline and offer counterarguments. Second, I will describe the category of pseudepigraphy, the label often applied to the disputed letters. The texts belonging to this category of ancient documents were written by a person other than the one named as author in the document. Pseudepigraphy is contrasted with forgery, in that pseudepigraphy is not intended to deceive readers, but rather entertain them. The forged document, by contrast, deceives readers in hopes of gain. By setting aside the element of deception, the theory goes, pseudepigraphy was acceptable within the early church. Looking at the available ancient evidence helps us decide whether the label "pseudepigraphic" best describes Ephesians. If such a classification does not fit (and I do not think it does), then how are we to best explain the distinctive aspects of this epistle vis-à-vis the other Pauline letters? To answer this question, I explore the duties of a secretary and examine the role of Paul's coauthors to help explain certain distinctive attributes within Ephesians.[6]

B. EPHESIANS AS DEUTERO-PAULINE

Those promoting the deutero-Pauline label for Ephesians use four basic criteria: (1) theology; (2) grammar, vocabulary, and syntax; (3) historical circumstances; and (4) relationship to Colossians. The author of the non-Pauline text

---

5. Muddiman, 14. See Conzelmann; Andreas Lindemann, *Die Aufhebung der Zeit: Geschichtsverständnis und Eschatologie im Epheserbrief*, Studien zum Neuen Testament 12 (Gütersloh: Gütersloher Verlagshaus, 1975); E. Käsemann, "Epheserbrief," in *Religion in Geschichte und Gegenwart*, ed. Kurt Galling, 3rd ed. (Tübingen: Mohr Siebeck, 1958), 2:517–20.

6. Scholars who hold to Pauline authorship include Barth, 36–50; Thielman, 1–5; Arnold, 46–50; Bruce, 240; and Hoehner, 2–61.

is said to be one of Paul's disciples, carrying on the apostle's teaching for a new day. Ephesians might have been a circular letter or a cover letter introducing the Pauline collection.[7]

1. Theology

The first argument contends that the theological content of Ephesians is far enough removed from that expressed in the accepted letters to be classified as non-Pauline. For example, Romans and Galatians emphasize justification by faith over against works of the law. Ephesians, however, speaks of salvation by grace through faith (2:5, 8) and mentions "not by works" (2:9) once, with no additional clause "of the law." Romans, Galatians, and the Corinthian correspondence underline the cross as fundamental for forgiveness of sins, while Ephesians emphasizes the cross as bringing together Jew and gentile in Christ. Again, the four genuine epistles feature the future fulfillment of salvation, while Ephesians stresses its accomplishment at this time (2:5-6). Ephesians highlights reconciliation between Jew and gentile in Christ, rather than reconciliation to God, which is typical of the undisputed letters. Ephesians' picture of the universal church contrasts with the local congregations emphasized in the Corinthian and Philippian letters. This is evident in the shared language of "mystery" and "the body of Christ," which is distinctly developed in Ephesians as gentiles united with Jews in the church.[8] Finally, the Ephesians' household codes are determined to be at odds with Paul's call for celibacy in 1 Cor 7.[9]

Yet to each of the arguments that Ephesians falls outside Paul's theological boundaries, one can offer a counterreading. For example, Paul's use of "mystery" in his epistles ranges from a description of Israel's hardening and gentile inclusion (Rom 11:25-26) to the cross as God's wisdom (1 Cor 2:1, 7), to its use as a synonym of Paul's preaching (1 Cor 4:1; Col 4:3-4), to the change that happens at the resurrection of the body (1 Cor 15:51), to Christ himself as God's wisdom (Col 1:27), and to the believers' hope of glory (2:2). To this expansive use of "mystery" we might include Paul's use of the term in

---

7. Ephesians serving as a cover letter is promoted by E. J. Goodspeed, *The Key to Ephesians* (Chicago: University of Chicago Press, 1956), xii–xiv. The circular-letter theory is promoted by J. B. Lightfoot, *Biblical Essays* (London: Macmillan, 1893; reprinted Grand Rapids: Baker, 1979), 392–93; Bruce, 249–50. For a counterargument, see Perkins, 17–19.

8. M. Rese, "Die Vorzüge Israels in Röm. 9,4f. und Eph. 2,12," *Theologische Zeitschrift* 31 (1975): 211–22, argues against Pauline authorship because the epistle shifts to the church the distinctiveness and particularity of Israel.

9. Perkins, 20–32, offers an excellent summary of the differences between Ephesians and the undisputed letters.

Introduction

Ephesians as a synonym of the apostle's preaching (6:19) and as summarizing the gentile inclusion by Christ into God's people (3:3–9); this latter example is similar to Paul's declaration to the Romans that this mystery is now revealed so that gentiles might come to faith (Rom 16:25–26). My point is that Paul shows a range of usages for "mystery" within the undisputed letters, and its use in Ephesians does not stand outside those conventional meanings.[10]

To take up another example, Paul addresses the church universal in his opening lines to the Corinthians and reminds them of their baptism into one Spirit (1 Cor 1:2; 12:7–14). Paul does not indicate that the spiritual gifts distributed to the body of Christ occur in each local community; indeed, it would be highly unlikely that each local group had an apostle (1 Cor 12:27–31). Romans and Galatians have language about believers being children of Abraham, an image that stretches beyond the local congregation. Paul speaks of the church as "the Israel of God" in his closing blessing to the Galatians (6:16). In sum, the local church and the church universal exist side by side in Paul's letters, as both entities together express Paul's understanding of the body of Christ.

To the charge that Ephesians expresses a realized or overrealized eschatology, I would point to Paul's declaration to the Corinthians that "now is the day of salvation" (2 Cor 6:2), alluding to Isa 49:8, now accomplished in part in Paul's ministry. Paul declares to the Romans that they are justified and also glorified (Rom 8:30). This language presents a picture similar to that of Ephesians, which stresses that believers who by grace *have been* saved are seated now with the exalted Christ (Eph 2:5–6). Paul shows flexibility within the undisputed letters, evidenced by 2 Corinthians, which speaks of being "naked," perhaps a reference to the soul's existing for a time without a body (5:2–4), while 1 Corinthians celebrates the resurrection of the body at the sounding trumpet (15:52).[11] Barth identifies as eschatological elements within Ephesians the not-yet-inserted capstone, Christ (2:20–22), and the growing body (church) toward its head, Christ (4:15–16).[12]

Although it is true that Paul does not speak about justification by faith and God's righteousness in Ephesians, it is also the case that Paul

---

10. Sigurd Grindheim, "A Deutero-Pauline Mystery? Ecclesiology in Colossians and Ephesians," in *Paul and Pseudepigraphy*, ed. Stanley E. Porter and Gregory P. Fewster, Pauline Studies 8 (Leiden: Brill, 2013), 173, concludes that "while Colossians and Ephesians show clear traces of a later development . . . this development represents a complex reapplication of familiar Pauline terms and themes in a way that is consistent with the logic of the apostle's earlier letters." For an opposite conclusion, see Perkins, 22–23.

11. See E. Randolph Richards, "Will the Real Author Please Stand Up?," in *Come Let Us Reason: New Essays in Christian Apologetics*, ed. Paul Copan and William Lane Craig (Nashville: B&H Academic, 2012), 116n13.

12. Markus Barth, *The People of God*, JSNTSup 5 (Sheffield: JSOT Press, 1983), 47; rev. English ed. of *Paulus—Apostat oder Apostel* (Regensburg: Pustet, 1997).

uses the term "righteousness" only once in 1 Corinthians (and not at all in the Thessalonian correspondence) to describe Christ who became for us God's wisdom, righteousness, holiness, and redemption (1 Cor 1:30; see Eph 4:24; 5:9; 6:14). Yet the Corinthian correspondence is not disqualified as Pauline.

Finally, Paul answers the Corinthians' questions about the proper role of sex in marriage and related concerns such as marriage between a believer and nonbeliever and the advisability of virginity and celibacy. None of those concerns surface in Ephesians, which instead promotes unity and oneness within the community. Marriage serves as one example of such unity, as demonstrated by Paul's reflection on Genesis and its proclamation of the married couple as "one flesh" (5:25–33). The attention to virginity in 1 Corinthians, then, is tied tightly to their particular questions, and the epistle genre is adept at targeting specific questions, as well as presenting broad and general information.

We must also point to the similarities between Ephesians and the undisputed letters. These include the use of Old Testament quotations and allusions, coupled with an emphasis on the ancient narrative of salvation laid out in Israel's Scriptures. The emphasis on God as creator, the need for forgiveness of sins, and the full redemption in Christ through his death and resurrection ground the letter's discussion of the church. Again, church as a body or the temple of God are elastic images found in the so-called genuine letters. Ephesians shares with Romans a general presentation of the gospel message with a lack of contextual specificity.[13] The claims that Ephesians promotes only a realized eschatology fail to consider fully the apocalyptic emphasis on this present age of darkness and the need for God's armor to stand fast against the principalities and powers at war with those who walk in the light (Eph 1:10, 21; 2:7; 4:30; see also Gal 1:4; 1 Thess 5:8). Important topics such as the kingdom of God (Rom 14:17; 1 Cor 6:9; Gal 5:21; Eph 5:5), the inheritance of the saints (Rom 4:13–14; Gal 3:29–4:7; Eph 1:14), and the church as a body or temple (Rom 12:4–5; 1 Cor 3:16; 12:12–27; 2 Cor 6:16; Eph 1:22–23; 2:15, 21; 5:30) are similarly represented across the letters. In sum, the theological variations between Ephesians and the undisputed letters are no different in kind or degree than those we find between the undisputed letters.

---

13. Douglas Campbell, *Framing Paul: An Epistolary Biography* (Grand Rapids: Eerdmans, 2014), 310, continues: "Romans had a highly practical and specific exigence for which its sets of generalized discussions proved necessary," that is, Paul's eventual arrival in Rome. He concludes that Ephesians has such a context, namely, shaping their identity as converts (315).

Introduction

2. Literary Style

The second category focuses on the literary characteristics of Ephesians. The argument against Pauline authorship contends that, while the prescript and postscript follow general Pauline patterns, the body of the letter is better described as a theological treatise or an "epistolary sermon."[14] The letter has a high number of lengthy sentences composed of multiple subordinate clauses. For example, Eph 1:3–14 is a single sentence in Greek (see also 1:15–23; 2:1–7; 3:1–7; 4:11–16; 6:14–20). The widespread use of synonyms and the expansive use of genitive phrases, excessive parallelism, and amplification characterize this letter's literary style. This slows the tempo of the text compared to the brisk pace typical of Paul's letters. Throughout the epistle we find grammatical ambiguities, which will be covered in the commentary.[15] We observe distinct phrases such as "in the heavenly realms" (1:3, 20; 2:6; 3:10; 6:12) that are typically expressed as "in heaven" (2 Cor 5:1; Phil 3:20; see also Col 1:16, 20).

A statistical or stylometric analysis might resolve the issue, if it distinguishes Paul's words from traditional material and quotations in the text and takes account of the occasional nature of Paul's letters. The statistical approach must also work with a large enough sample size, and most agree that the *Hauptbriefe* do not meet this criterion. Rather than focusing on *hapax legomena* (words used in only one letter), Anthony Kenny focuses on conjunctions (such as "and" and "but") and subordinate clauses that might reveal an author's style.[16] He concludes that there is both great diversity and commonality among all thirteen letters attributed to Paul. Romans, Philippians, and 2 Timothy, composed without a cosender, were closest to what is often seen as the center of Paul's thought. Ephesians falls in the middle of the range. First Corinthians is farthest from this center; perhaps this is due to the influence of the cosender, Sosthenes. When Ephesians is compared to Galatians, the results are surprising. Each letter contains about the same number of *hapax legomena*.[17] Alongside stylometric data, we find in the undisputed

---

14. Roy R. Jeal, *Integrating Theology and Ethics in Ephesians: The Ethos of Communication*, Studies in Bible and Early Christianity 43 (Lewiston, NY: Mellon, 2000), 39, 43–51. Jeal writes: "Ephesians corresponds with 'sermon' by having a distinct paraenetic concern in chapters 4–6, yet without explaining the relationship between the behavior it calls for and the theological conceptions that it contains in chapter 1–3" (50–51). See also Lincoln, xxxiv–xl, for a summary of arguments.

15. Thielman, 6, lists several lexical ambiguities, especially from Eph 1–2.

16. Anthony Kenny, *A Stylometric Study of the New Testament* (Oxford: Clarendon, 1986), 99–100. See also Armin Baum, "Semantic Variation within the *Corpus Paulinum*: Linguistic Considerations Concerning the Richer Vocabulary of the Pastoral Epistles," *Tyndale Bulletin* 59 (2008): 271–92.

17. Hoehner, 24. Forty-one terms out of 2,429 in Ephesians; 35 terms (31 without

letters examples of lengthy sentences (1 Cor 1:4–8; Phil 1:3–7) and ambiguous grammar and syntax (Rom 5:12–18; 2 Cor 2:12–7:7).[18]

Ancient authors drew on traditional material as they explained and defended their positions. For example, Paul offers the church's traditional, succinct summary of the gospel as he presents his teachings on resurrection to the Corinthians (1 Cor 15:1–8; see also Rom 10:9; Phil 2:6–11). Authors might also quote their opponents' positions; Paul does so in several places (e.g., 1 Cor 6:12; 10:23). New Testament authors drew on Scripture, sometimes by directly quoting it, other times with allusions and echoes. Ancient authors reused and repurposed their work, evidenced in Cicero's work in several places.[19] We see these options on display in Ephesians. Paul used traditional material in his quotation of what is possibly a hymn (5:14) and a confession (4:4–6) and in his citation of and allusions to Scripture (1:22; 4:8; 5:31; 6:2). These materials will show up as stylistic differences, but that should not be counted as data determining the authorship question.

3. Historical Circumstances

The third general complaint against Pauline authorship is the claim that the historical situation that prompted Ephesians is too vaguely sketched to have come from Paul's pen. There are no impending crises, no specific travel plans, no greetings to specific persons. We have no warnings against false teachers, no answers to questions asked by the congregation. Although Acts tells us that Paul spent a good deal of time in Ephesus (Acts 19:8–10), this letter speaks to those who "heard" about him, not to those who know him personally. The letter addresses a general group of gentiles who have converted to the gospel, but does not speak to Jewish believers, although presumably there are a number of them in the local congregation.[20] Rather

---

proper names) out of 2,220 words in Galatians. Only in Galatians does Paul speak of "the present evil age" or "the fruit of the Spirit" or point to "the marks of Jesus," but these distinctive phrases are not cited to dispute Pauline authorship (Gal 1:4; 5:22; 6:17).

18. Thielman, 11.

19. Cicero, *Letters to Family* 12.4.1; 10.28.1; see also Ignatius, *To the Philadelphians* 11.2: "In their love the brethren of Troas wish to be remembered. It is from here that I send this letter through the kindness of Burrus, who, as a testimonial of honor, was sent by the Ephesians and Smyrnaeans to accompany me"; *To the Smyrnaeans* 12.1: "In their affection the brethren at Troas wish to be remembered to you. It is from here that I send this letter through the kindness of Burrus, whom you conjointly with your brethren, the Ephesians, commissioned to accompany me." For a general discussion, see Richards, "Will the Real Author Please Stand Up?," 123.

20. Campbell, *Framing Paul*, 310, 337. He argues that "Ephesians" should be identified as the letter to the Laodiceans mentioned in Col 4:16.

INTRODUCTION

than exhibiting tension between Jews and gentiles, this church appears as an integrated community.

The lack of specific historical information, or the vagueness about the church's situation, however, could equally apply to Romans, a letter no one disputes as genuinely Paul. The stated purpose of Romans, to introduce Paul to the Roman believers, should hardly take fifteen chapters of dense theology. Like Ephesians, Romans also provides an extensive explanation of the gospel before applying its message to practical expressions. Paul's emphasis on gentile inclusion into the family of God draws on his reading of Isaiah and his eschatological outlook, highlighting the image of those near and far being brought together in fulfillment of the prophet's vision. This emphasis is not neatly placed in a local or universal category, but fits better in a prophetic and eschatological category, and the latter two are typical Pauline emphases. Nor should we conclude that the oneness of Jew and gentile emphasized in Ephesians has been accomplished on the ground, as it were. The passage points to a result of Christ's work on the cross; alongside forgiveness of sins we have unity as one new humanity (1:7; 2:15).

Moreover, there is historical specificity within the epistle as it relates to Paul's situation in at least four areas. First, Paul addresses the overwhelming influence of the Artemis cult and temple. Artemis dominated the religious landscape, literally, in Ephesus. Her temple welcomed many pilgrims, and the city identified itself with the goddess at a deep level. Paul's emphasis in Ephesians on the superiority of Christ over all powers and authorities meets the claims of Artemis devotees head on.[21] Moreover, the imperial cult played an oversized role as the city vied for influence among its neighbors in Asia Minor. The cult promoted the imperial family as worthy leaders appointed by the gods. Paul's rejoinder in Ephesians stresses that all things are under Christ's feet and he has the eternal victory over all authorities (1:21–22).[22]

Second, Paul claims to be in chains. Few today doubt that the apostle endured imprisonments as he remarks to the Corinthians and Philippians (2 Cor 11:23–28; Phil 1:13; see also Col 4:3; Phlm 1, 9). Some suggest that the notes about Paul's chains comprise a leitmotif necessary to provide verisimilitude to the pseudepigraphic work.[23] I find this notion at odds with the position that the pseudepigraphic author's motive was to honor Paul. It is not merely Paul's voice, but his testimony as a martyr, that is packed into

---

21. Thielman, 20. For more on Artemis, see introduction, p. 34, above.
22. Thielman, 21–23.
23. Lincoln writes: "Certainly someone writing in Paul's name is calculated to increase his readers' favor and trust by digressing about the suffering apostle's ministry on their behalf" (xliv). To my mind, there is little distance between "calculated" and "hoodwinked." See also Fowl, 15n15.

the phrase "in chains."[24] Why would a faithful Christian take upon himself or herself the high honor of incipient martyrdom as a literary device? Another theory speculates that an imprisonment motif provides the counternarrative in the face of imperial Rome. Paul's identity and that of the church drew on Jesus's death at Rome's hand and his subsequent resurrection. Social memory is formed by creating a shared past and future to address present needs. Individual biographies are woven into the communal memory, and this past is made active through rituals and moral actions that build the community's identity.[25] The mention of chains was the pseudepigraphic author's reinforcement of the church's identity. While this theory offers a helpful explanation of social identity, it does not demonstrate that the "in chains" reference is pseudepigraphic.

Third, Paul remarks that the Ephesians have "heard" of him, when one would expect, based on Acts, that they "know" him (3:2; see also 1:15). It is possible that Paul's remarks refer primarily to his current predicament—he is in chains. His point, then, is that the Ephesians should not be discouraged by his imprisonment (3:13). This seems unlikely, however, given that Paul spent just under three years in the city during his third missionary journey.[26] Yet if one takes into account that Paul has been away from the city for about seven years, four of those as a prisoner of Rome, then perhaps he could not be certain that he would know a majority of the congregation. It is also possible that the city itself had a few house churches, some of whom were not connected with Paul's ministry. From Acts, we learn that Ephesus had a Jewish Christian group taught by Apollos (18:24–26). When Paul visited Ephesus, he met believers who knew only John's baptism, a detail that suggests they were Jews (19:1–7).[27] Paul preached in the synagogue, then left with fellow believers to teach in the market (19:8–10). We do not know whether the group led

---

24. Richard J. Cassidy, *Paul in Chains: Roman Imprisonment and the Letters of St. Paul* (New York: Crossroad, 2001), 87–89.

25. Harry O. Maier, *Picturing Paul in Empire: Imperial Image, Text, and Persuasion in Colossians, Ephesians, and the Pastoral Epistles* (London: T&T Clark, 2013), 64–66, addresses collective memory in Colossians, concluding: "By reminding its audience of his chains, the letter binds both author and audience into a shared past established by the death, resurrection and enthronement of Christ, a past made active by means of a continuing putting to death of the self in the present (3.5)" (66).

26. If Paul wrote this letter before his third missionary journey, then this problem goes away. Campbell, *Framing Paul*, 329, suggests that Ephesians (Laodiceans) and Colossians were written about 50–52 CE. The ancient church figure Theodore of Mopsuestia suggests that Ephesians was written before Paul's visit to the city; see Thielman, 16n29.

27. It is unlikely that these twelve men were discipled by Apollos; see Paul Trebilco, *The Early Christians in Ephesus from Paul to Ignatius* (Grand Rapids: Eerdmans, 2007; Tübingen: Mohr Siebeck, 2004), 122.

by Apollos remained in the synagogue or left but did not join Paul's group.[28] Similarly, Paul speaks about several factions that grew up in Corinth, one that claimed Apollos as their leader, another that professed Paul. However, Apollos and Paul were not at odds with each other (1 Cor 3:6; 16:12). In Ephesus, there might have been a few house churches distinguished as primarily Jewish or gentile, churches that had little contact but no animosity toward each other. Paul's letter would remind these groups of their identity as a single entity, Christ's body, the church.

Finally, to the claim that Eph 2:11–22 testifies to a community of unified Jews and gentiles, and thus represents a generation after Paul, I offer two responses. First, there is little evidence that the early-second-century church exemplified a unity of Jew and gentile. More likely, Jewish communities who followed Jesus slowly disappeared with the rise of rabbinic Judaism and the growth of the gentile church.[29] Second, Paul describes in 2:11–22 what is true in light of Christ's redemption. He presents the results of Christ's work as making a new people, a new body of which he is the head. The Ephesian community is clearly not unified in all things, for Paul speaks about striving for unity in the Spirit and keeping the bond of peace (4:3). Paul makes a similar argument in Galatians, that Jews and Greeks, slave and free, and male and female are all one in Christ. This claim addresses God's work in Christ, even as the churches must walk in the Spirit and in the freedom they have in Christ (Gal 5:1, 16).[30]

4. Relationship between Ephesians and Colossians

A final complaint against Pauline authorship revolves around the complicated relationship between Ephesians and Colossians. Ephesians' similarity with Colossians suggests to some that the author of Ephesians borrowed from Colossians to create this letter. The facts are compelling: 34 percent of the terms in Colossians are found in Ephesians (26.5 percent of Ephesians' language is found in Colossians). The recommendation of Tychicus, at twenty-nine words, is found verbatim in both (Eph 6:21–22; Col 4:7–8).[31] The

---

28. Trebilco, *Early Christians in Ephesus*, 153.

29. Lynn H. Cohick, "Jews and Christians," in *The Routledge Companion to Early Christian Thought*, ed. D. Jeffrey Bingham (New York: Routledge, 2010), 68–83.

30. Michael J. Gorman, *Becoming the Gospel: Paul, Participation, and Mission* (Grand Rapids: Eerdmans, 2015), 184, comments on Eph 2:14: "This is the 'indicative' of the gospel—that which God has done, that which is. The indicative carries within it an 'imperative'—that which now needs to be."

31. Lincoln, xlviii. He offers a useful and extensive discussion of the many parallels (xlviii–lviii). See, e.g., Eph 4:1–2 with Col 3:12; Eph 5:19–6:9 with Col 3:16–25.

Authorship

purpose of this transcription could be that the author of Ephesians desired readers to remark on its similarity with Colossians and conclude the apostle wrote both letters.[32] Even more, the overall style and themes are similar in the two epistles. For example, the recipients are identified as both "saints" and as "faithful"; nowhere else are these descriptors used together. Again, the characteristics of Christ found in the exaltation of the cosmic Christ in Colossians (1:15–20) have close parallels in the thanksgiving offered in Ephesians (1:20–23). Finally, the sentences are long and complex in both letters. Moreover, and a bit ironically, Ephesians' differences from Colossians serve as grounds to argue its pseudo-Pauline authorship. The author of Ephesians uses new vocabulary ("heavenly places" and "reconcile") or new uses for the same terms. Yet no consistent pattern emerges in the alleged borrowing.[33]

Nowhere is the overlap between Colossians and Ephesians more apparent than in the household codes. Much of the language is similar, if not verbatim, between the household codes in these two letters.[34] Similarities with Colossians include a paraenetic section preceding the household code and a basic framework of the ordering of the three pairs.[35] In contrast, 1 Peter speaks first to slaves, but does not mention owners, and then addresses wives/husbands, and does not consider the parent/child pair. Ephesians and Colossians have an extended discussion to slaves and owners, yet Ephesians greatly expands the section on marriage. The basic argument for pseudepigraphic authorship is that the author of Ephesians built the household codes on the Colossians framework. As such, the reader can do a bit of redaction criticism to discern the theological and paraenetic emphases within Ephesians.

However, the differences are also instructive, as a redaction-critical approach reveals. Colossians emphasizes Christ as head and supreme Lord worthy of all honor and obedience, and his disciples as servants. Paul takes advantage of the common understanding of the slave's subservient role to make his point about serving Christ. Paul then turns the hierarchical structure

---

32. Muddiman, 8. He also observes an alternative, namely that Paul or a scribe wrote both as the two epistles were written and delivered at the same time.

33. Muddiman, 10, observes that it is "by no means as obvious as many more recent scholars have assumed, that the relationship of Colossians and Ephesians is one of direct literary dependence and always and in every case of the latter upon the former." He continues that those who see Ephesians as dependent on Colossians bolster their argument by claiming Ephesians also draws on other Pauline letters. This approach has the ironic outcome that "in some places Ephesians *appears more Pauline* than Colossians."

34. James P. Hering, *The Colossian and Ephesian Haustafeln in Theological Contexts: An Analysis of Their Origins, Relationships, and Message* (New York: Peter Lang, 2007), 154, finds "an intricate literary relationship between the two forms."

35. Dionysius of Halicarnassus, *Roman Antiquities* 2.26.1–4, discusses the same three pairs in the same order as we find in Colossians and Ephesians.

upside down by undercutting the owners' right of domination over his or her slaves. Paul retains this teaching in Ephesians and adds an extensive discussion on marriage that illustrates Christ's union with the church, a leitmotif of the epistle. The unique phrase "out of fear/reverence for Christ" echoes in this passage, as the title "Christ" is used seven times (5:23, 24, 25, 29, 32; 6:5, 6). Additionally, Ephesians includes a transitional sentence introducing the household codes that provides the interpretive key for the reader, namely, that mutual submission out of reverence for Christ must be the lens through which these household codes are read.[36] Paul removes the negative charge to husbands to not be harsh with their wives (Col 3:19) and replaces it with an extensive, positive command to love their wives (Eph 5:25–33). Paul links a wife's submission to the church's submission so that she serves as a role model for all believers.

The similarities to Colossians need not lead one to conclude that Ephesians was written by someone other than Paul, for several reasons. First, the verbatim lines at the letters' closing can be explained more simply as a secretary copying the letter carrier's description, an ordinary and efficient use of time and material. Again, why copy the name Tychicus out of the several used by Colossians, since this man is unknown in other letters?[37] This would be an odd sentence to commit to memory, particularly while not holding onto anything else, such as the poetic description of the cosmic Christ (Col 1:15–20). Second, the comparisons often are general.[38] The structures do not line up, as Ephesians includes a second prayer (3:14–19) and omits the exaltation of Christ (Col 1:15–20) but speaks of Christ our peace (2:14–18). Most telling, Ephesians omits the central argument in Colossians (2:1–3:4) and greatly expands the household codes. These differences lead some to argue that the author of Ephesians also drew from the undisputed letters;[39] however, this

---

36. Hering, *Colossian and Ephesian Haustafeln*, 155, remarks: "The author, citing mutual submission in the fear of Christ, sets a distinct and intentional measure of regulating the mandates along intra-human and reciprocal, yet Christ-directed lines."

37. C. Leslie Mitton, *The Epistle to the Ephesians: Its Authorship, Origin, and Purpose* (Oxford: Clarendon, 1951; reprinted Eugene, OR: Wipf & Stock, 2002), 268, argues that the author of Ephesians consulted Tychicus, who approved the pseudepigraphic letter. Muddiman, 297, rightly questions whether Tychicus would have assented to what was clearly fictitious.

38. Muddiman, vii (see also 9–10), rightly concludes that a comparison of alleged parallels reveals an "astonishing variety" and that "the same basic idea may be freely expressed in quite different phraseology: in places Colossians has the neater or more evocative formulation, but almost as often the Ephesians version is better." He continues, unpersuasively in my view, that the canonical Ephesians is built with fragments from an earlier letter Paul wrote from an Ephesian prison to the Laodiceans, with additions by an editor who created the letter sent by Paul from Rome (298).

39. Lincoln, lvi–lviii.

stance faces the hurdle of having Ephesians sound more like Paul than the apparently authentic Colossians.[40]

Third, the similarities and differences do not clearly show that Ephesians relied on Colossians. There is no intrinsic or disinterested way to demonstrate priority. Solid arguments can be made for Ephesians serving as the model for Colossians, and vice versa.[41] The situation is further nuanced when we consider the possibilities that the letters employ traditional, creedal, and liturgical language and that a single author repeated general, common language in two letters written at about the same time. The oral character of tradition and liturgy helps explain how these two letters can share similar language and yet not reflect extensive verbatim expressions. Likely, Paul's work with the secretary reflects the nuances of preaching a sermon to different audiences.[42] Lincoln, who holds that a later author composed Ephesians based on Paul's Colossians, concludes that this writer "has immersed himself in his source material to such an extent that it has become part of his way of thinking."[43] Better to conclude that the similarities and nuanced distinctions reveal a single author's theological range.[44]

C. PSEUDEPIGRAPHY IN THE ANCIENT WORLD

Those who suggest Paul did not write Ephesians generally point to the ancient category of pseudepigraphic letters to explain its differences from the undisputed letters.[45] Pseudepigraphy describes a work written by someone other than the named author. By contrast, the label "anonymous" refers to the author's name not being attached to the text. In antiquity, some originally anonymous texts were later ascribed to leading thinkers. Pseudepigraphic letters claim as their author a leading figure of the past, a great teacher or philosopher, such as Plato or Diogenes.[46] These letters honored his teaching

---

40. Muddiman, 10.
41. Muddiman, 9. Campbell, *Framing Paul*, 318–23, argues that Ephesians (which he identifies as the "Letter to the Laodiceans" mentioned in Col 4:16) was drafted first, then urgent news came from Colossae that required a hasty letter dispatched that carried similar themes and addressed the emergency. Lincoln, l, states that "the far more obvious hypothesis is that Colossians served as the basis for Ephesians." Ernest Best, "Who Used Whom? The Relationship of Ephesians and Colossians," *NTS* 43 (1997): 72–96, argues for the priority of Ephesians.
42. Roberts, 8.
43. Lincoln, lv.
44. Scot McKnight, *Colossians*, NICNT (Grand Rapids: Eerdmans, 2018), 17, draws the same conclusion.
45. Cohick, 19–24.
46. Pseudepigraphy should be distinguished from pseudonymity, which has a ficti-

before a new audience. They were typically addressed to an individual, who was also a well-known figure. The letters included historical details, perhaps to increase the entertainment value.[47] They emphasized imitation of the ancient worthy, incorporating personal details to motivate readers to emulate their good deeds.[48] These letters could be read in conjunction with the philosophers' major works. The letters circulated as a collection, not individually. The pseudepigraphic epistolary evidence from the first and second centuries CE suggests that many of the letters were produced in a school setting.

Pythagoras's works are an example of pseudepigraphy. This sixth-century BCE philosopher was reputed to have written little; much of his work survives because his disciples wrote his ideas. The second-century CE Neoplatonist Porphyry explains that of the 280 works attributed to Pythagoras, 200 were published by his students under their master's name, while 80 were written by the philosopher directly. Porphyry is content to label all 280 works as from Pythagoras.[49] The fourth-century CE text *Letters of Paul and Seneca* could be an example of a Christian pseudepigraphic work written for entertainment[50] or to promote Paul's status by linking him with a venerable philosopher of his day, thereby securing Seneca's good name within Christian circles.[51] At the heart of this literary category is the modern conviction that these letters were *not* deceptive.[52]

---

tious author's name attached, a nom de plume. George Eliot is the pen name of Mary Anne Evans, for example.

47. Patricia A. Rosenmeyer, *Ancient Epistolary Fictions: The Letter in Greek Literature* (Cambridge: Cambridge University Press, 2001), 198–99, writes: "The goal of the pseudonymous epistolographer was thus to work the bare bones of a biography into a compelling life story. He was both scholar and creative artist, researching historical materials in order to define the bounds of the tradition, and using his imagination to elaborate creatively and dramatically on that tradition." Thielman, 1, identifies such collections as "innocent fictions."

48. Maier, *Picturing Paul in Empire*, 32, labels Ephesians as a "kind of epistolary *prosopopeia*" that "helps one avoid largely anachronistic debates concerning authenticity, forgery and dissimulation" as the writer "plays" Paul in addressing an audience with content the writer wishes to convey.

49. Armin Baum, "Content and Form: Authorship Attribution and Pseudonymity in Ancient Speeches, Letters, Lectures, and Translations: A Rejoinder to Bart Ehrman," *Journal of Biblical Literature* 136.2 (2017): 393, concludes that Porphyry indicates he finds legitimate the students' editing of their teacher's words: "Porphyry did not demand that these edited books be regarded as authentic only if they contained the exact words of Pythagoras."

50. Thielman, 2, argues: "Their form as an exchange of correspondence may have been intended to signal that they were not authentic documents but edifying fabrications."

51. Bart Ehrman, *Forgery and Counter-forgery: The Use of Literary Deceit in Early Christian Polemics* (Oxford: Oxford University Press, 2013), 527, suggests that these letters bolstered Seneca's profile among Latin Christian writers such as Jerome.

52. F. C. Baur launched this view in *Die sogenannten Pastoralbriefe des Apostels Paulus aufs neue kritisch untersucht* (Stuttgart: Cotta, 1835). W. Speyer, *Die literarische Fälschung*

Accusations of forgery would be brought, however, if a person in the first or second century wrote in Cicero's or Seneca's name, for he or she clearly intended either to benefit at the expense of the great orator and philosopher or to destroy their reputations by misrepresenting their ideas. For example, the second-century CE physician Galen decries the forged production of his works. He recounts a debate in a bookshop about the authenticity of a copy of his book. After reading only a few lines, a man who claimed to be knowledgeable of Galen's work tosses the document aside as an inferior forgery.[53] Galen speaks of writing many of his texts based on lectures he delivered, and the clever reader distinguished both the false style and content of the document.[54] The person who wrote the forgery probably gained financially, and Galen was frustrated that such a poor document had his good name attached.[55] Did Paul face a similar situation with the Thessalonians? In 2 Thess 2:2 Paul worries that a false message about the day of the Lord is circulating among believers and that this teaching allegedly comes from him. The biblical text is unclear as to whether the believers have received a letter purportedly from Paul or whether his actual letter has been wrongly interpreted. The second option is more likely, as Paul continues to warn the Thessalonians against false teaching and deceptive claims about his gospel (2:3, 15).[56]

Typically, scholars who hold Ephesians to be pseudepigraphic distinguish this category from forgery, because the actual authors' motives in producing pseudepigraphic letters were judged to be honorable inasmuch they promoted Paul's teachings or ethics fairly.[57] Some locate Ephesians' authority

---

im heidnischen und christlichen Altertum: Ein Versuch ihrer Deutung, Handbuch der Altertumswissenschaft (Munich: Beck, 1971), offers a detailed bibliography up to 1970 on the literature.

53. See Bruce M. Metzger, "Literary Forgeries and Canonical Pseudepigrapha," *Journal of Biblical Literature* 91.1 (1972): 6.

54. Galen of Pergamum, *De libris propriis* in *Scripta Minora* 2.91.1–93.16.

55. Diogenes Laertius (*Lives* 10.3) wrote that the Stoic Diotimus wrote fifty obscene letters in his opponent Epicurus's name, attempting to ruin his reputation. Quintilian, *Institutio oratoria* 7.2.24, lamented the practice of the court stenographers to publish his orations as their own work, based on their court records.

56. Jeffrey A. D. Weima, *1–2 Thessalonians*, Baker Exegetical Commentary on the New Testament (Grand Rapids: Baker Academic, 2014), 504–6. See also Gordon D. Fee, *The First and Second Letters to the Thessalonians*, NICNT (Grand Rapids: Eerdmans, 2009), 271–77. Alternatively, Frank Witt Hughes, *Early Christian Rhetoric and 2 Thessalonians*, JSNTSup 30 (Sheffield: Sheffield Academic, 1989), 91–95, argues (unpersuasively in my view) that Colossians and Ephesians are the false letters referred to by the pseudepigraphic author of 2 Thessalonians.

57. Determining the motives of an author, then and now, is not a simple matter; see Terry L. Wilder, *Pseudonymity, the New Testament, and Deception: An Inquiry into Intention and Reception* (Lanham, MD: University Press of America, 2004), 100–101. See also Hans-

in its canonical standing; therefore, conclusions about its authorship carry less weight and are relevant mainly in efforts to build Paul's biography or the epistle's provenance.[58] No suspicion is attached to differences from the genuine letters, because all share canonical authority.

A close comparison with the Pauline corpus, however, demonstrates significant differences with the pseudepigraphic letters of the first century. First, pseudepigraphic letters had as their implied author someone who had been deceased for hundreds of years. Living figures or those recently deceased were not considered acceptable subjects for pseudepigraphic epistles. Second, pseudepigraphic letters circulated as a collection. In contrast, each of Paul's epistles was sent to a single congregation, even if the letter was later shared with a nearby community (Col 4:16). Third, many pseudepigraphic letters had no sender's name, for the corpus itself included the attributed name. In the collection of Paul's letters, each letter retains the sender's name. Fourth, while the pseudepigraphic letters offered personal or historical details, there is no attempt to create or maintain a relationship with the readers. Paul's letters, however, include personal information as a way to connect with his congregations. Fifth, the pseudepigraphic letters tended to be shorter than the New Testament letters (perhaps the length of Philemon), and the content was quite general. The differences add up to the conclusion that pseudepigraphy is not a category into which Paul's letters would easily fit.

A variation on the question of pseudepigraphy was brought forward by E. J. Goodspeed in 1926.[59] He suggested that Ephesians was a cover letter for the newly collected letters of Paul, a collection created by an eager devotee who traced the missionary journeys in Acts to find Paul's other letters.[60] For numerous and solid reasons, his specific theory has persuaded few.[61] How-

---

Josef Klauck, *Ancient Letters and the New Testament: A Guide to Context and Exegesis*, trans. Daniel P. Bailey (Waco, TX: Baylor University Press, 2006). Armin D. Baum, *Pseudepigraphie und literarische Fälschung im frühen Christentum*, WUNT 138 (Tübingen: Mohr Siebeck, 2001), 51–63, concludes that students could affix their teacher's name to writings produced by the students, but they were to publish their own ideas under their own names, not that of their famous instructor.

58. Brevard S. Childs, *The New Testament as Canon: An Introduction* (Philadelphia: Fortress, 1985), 51–52, argues that the authority of the biblical text comes from its status as canon, not its authorship.

59. E. J. Goodspeed, *The Formation of the New Testament* (Chicago: University of Chicago Press, 1926), 28.

60. John Knox, *Philemon among the Letters of Paul: A New View of Its Place and Importance* (New York: Abingdon, 1963), 85–92, argues that Onesimus was the collector of Paul's letters, and Goodspeed was persuaded by this refinement of his theory (*Key to Ephesians*, xiv–xvi).

61. Muddiman, 12–14, discusses Goodspeed's theory that Ephesians was a pseudonymous cover letter for the newly collected letters of Paul. He argues that this theory encour-

ever, the general thrust of his argument has had "a broad impact on how Ephesians has been understood."[62] Douglas Campbell argues that the canonical Ephesians is Paul's letter to the Laodiceans, mentioned in Col 4:16. He argues that both epistles were composed while Paul was imprisoned in 50 CE, primarily with an "oral process of composition . . . in which one deeply reflective and carefully memorized text [Ephesians/Laodiceans] has filtered through into another compositional 'performance.'"[63] Campbell concludes: "According to our frame, Laodiceans was written during an incarceration in 50 CE, while Paul was returning to the Aegean from a critical meeting in Jerusalem that took place in turn on the heels of a dramatic confrontation in Syrian Antioch over the status of Paul's pagan converts."[64]

D. GENUINE OR FORGERY

If the category of pseudepigraphy does not fit for Ephesians, must we thus conclude it is a forgery?[65] The answer is yes if one accepts the arguments that Ephesians is too dissimilar to Paul's undisputed letters to be genuine.[66] Bart Ehrman argues that many of the New Testament works are forgeries; however, he does not resolve why the early church would accept those forgeries as authoritative, yet speak out against the general practices of forgery and lying.[67] Ehrman describes Ephesians as a "counterforgery" (*Gegenfälschung*),

---

ages "scholars to amass a whole battery of evidence against the authenticity of Ephesians." See also Best, 66, for a critique.

62. MacDonald, 16. She concludes that "it is no exaggeration to say that Ephesians constitutes the first interpretation of and guide to Pauline tradition in light of the disappearance of Paul." Muddiman, 20, suggests a composite letter from a genuine letter of Paul to which has been added material by an editor, using "almost equal proportions Pauline and non-Pauline vocabulary, style, forms, settings, purposes and theology." He points to Maurice Goguel, "Esquisse d'une solution nouvelle du problème de l'épître aux Éphésiens," *Revue de l'histoire et des religions* 111 (1935): 254–84; 112 (1936): 73–99, who suggests a similar solution.

63. Campbell, *Framing Paul*, 323, 337. He adds that "prison literature is often a fundamentally oral process, committed to writing at later stages and in fragile ways" (323).

64. Campbell, *Framing Paul*, 329. He contends that his theory addresses the arguments for pseudepigraphy by placing the epistle before Romans, 1 and 2 Corinthians, and Galatians and by linking it closely in a specific manner with Colossians (326–32).

65. For a brief discussion on Plato's "noble falsehood" and why it is not directly applicable to the authorship question, see Cohick, 24–25.

66. Ehrman, *Forgery and Counter-forgery*, 27–31, pinpoints the desire to deceive as central to forgeries. He also identifies polemics as a typical context for forgeries. Wilder, *Pseudonymity*, 82–99, discusses the key role that authorial intention plays in determining whether a text is pseudepigraphic or a forgery.

67. Lewis R. Donelson, *Pseudepigraphy and Ethical Argument in the Pastoral Epis-*

Introduction

a category describing those works that refute forgeries.[68] Ehrman argues that polemics drove the production of forgeries in the early centuries of the early church.[69] We turn now to examine the ancient conversation about forgeries.

The ancient world, from classical Athens to fifth-century CE Rome, promoted literary analysis and rhetorical criticism. Important for our purposes, they distinguished between the work's content or ideas and its rhetorical forms, which could be modified to fit the occasion.[70] This mindset is far from our modern dictum, "the medium is the message." Instead, the ancient Greco-Roman elite culture viewed rhetoric as clothing that dressed the body to fit the occasion. Rhetoricians, orators, and philosophers energetically debated a given composition's style in part to establish their extensive knowledge of rhetoric and Greek and Latin literature. They discussed authorship questions as a means to showing their breadth of literary knowledge and their rhetorical acumen.[71]

This separation of content and rhetorical form resulted in authors striving to present their ideas with rhetorical flair suitable to the audience and occasion. Josephus employed scribes to express his thoughts on the Jewish revolt in elegant Greek, and he is clear that he authored his historical volumes.[72] Over two hundred years later, Jerome informs us that Pope

---

tles, Hermeneutische Untersuchungen zur Theologie 22 (Tübingen: Mohr Siebeck, 1986; reprinted Eugene, OR: Wipf & Stock, 2015), 11, rightly concludes after examining Greek and Latin works that "no one ever seems to have accepted a document as religiously and philosophically prescriptive which was known to be forged." See also Muddiman, viii, who asks: "If the author wanted simply to promote the legacy of Paul in the post-Pauline period, would not forging a letter in his name be a very odd way of going about it?"

68. Ehrman, *Forgery and Counter-forgery*, 190; see also 183: "If Colossians was forged—as it almost certainly was—there can be no thought of Paul himself imitating it in another piece of correspondence." See also Martin Hüneburg, "Paulus versus Paulus: Der Epheserbrief als Korrektur des Kolosserbriefes," in *Pseudepigraphie und Verfasserfiktion in frühchristlichen Briefen*, ed. J. Frey et al., WUNT 246 (Tübingen: Mohr Siebeck, 2009), 387–409.

69. Ehrman, *Forgery and Counter-forgery*, 151. Before him, M. Rist, "Pseudepigraphy and the Early Christians," in *Studies in New Testament and Early Christian Literature: Essays in Honor of A. P. Wikgren*, ed. David Edward Aune, Supplements to Novum Testamentum 33 (Leiden: Brill, 1972), 89, concludes that nine of the New Testament works are attributed correctly. See also Donelson, *Pseudepigraphy and Ethical Argument*, 17, who states that "doctrinal correctness" was the primary means of discerning authentic from forged texts.

70. D. A. Russell, *Criticism in Antiquity* (London: Duckworth, 1981), 4, writes about the centrality of this distinction: "A process of 'invention' precedes the process of expression, and there is thus a sharp distinction between content [*to logomenon*] and verbal form [*lexis*]."

71. Contra Schüssler Fiorenza, lxiii: "The ancients did not consistently judge borrowing a well-known person's title and writing in the person's name as negative."

72. Josephus, *Against Apion* 1.9 §50: "Then, in the leisure that Rome afforded me, with

Damasus "spoke no words but mine," as Jerome praised his own excellent command of both Latin and Greek. Yet Jerome recognized that Pope Damasus was the *author* of these speeches and missives because their ideas and authority were located in the pope himself.[73] Both Jerome's and Josephus's comments reveal the conviction that authorship is centered in ideas, not the rhetorical form those ideas took.[74] Relatedly, early Christians acknowledged Scripture's inadequate literary style and sought to explain it as an expression of the biblical author's humility or as a vehicle to reach the common person. In the fourth century, scholars such as Ambrose, Augustine, and Jerome began defending Scripture's unique literary qualities as befitting its sacred nature.[75]

Origen's discussion of the authorship of Hebrews provides a useful window into the ancient view of authorship and authority. Origen observes (rightly) that Hebrews' style is elevated compared to Paul's thirteen letters. He also concludes that the content aligns with Paul's thought and thus has no quarrel with those in the church who claim that Paul himself wrote the epistle. His own view is that Hebrews expresses the thoughts of Paul by someone who worked closely with the apostle. Origen is content to declare that only God knows who wrote Hebrews.[76] That said, when he cites Hebrews, he attributes the epistle to Paul.[77] His comments reveal that the ancient readers detected stylistic differences in the Greek texts, but determined the authorship question primarily on the basis of the text's content.[78]

---

all my materials in readiness, and with the aid of some assistants [συνεργοῖς] for the sake of the Greek, at last I committed to writing my narrative of the events" (translation by Henry St. J. Thackeray in Loeb Classical Library).

73. Jerome, *Letters* 45.3. Unlike his fellow pagan grammarians, Jerome placed great emphasis on the text's meaning. See Michael W. Graves, *Jerome's Hebrew Philology: A Study Based on His Commentary on Jeremiah*, Supplements to Vigiliae Christianae 90 (Leiden: Brill, 2007), 73–75. See also J. N. D. Kelly, *Jerome: His Life, Writings, and Controversies* (Peabody, MA: Hendrickson, 1998), 82, who, citing Jerome, *Apology* 2, 20, claims that Pope Damasus "entrusted him [Jerome] with 'the dictation [i.e., drafting] of letters on church affairs.'"

74. Juvenal, *Satire* 7.230–31, mocks the excesses of such activities demanded of teachers.

75. Ambrose, *Epistles* 21, explains that biblical authors wrote in agreement with grace, for God is above rhetoric rules; nevertheless, one finds rhetoric in the biblical texts. See Michael W. Graves, "The Literary Quality of Scripture as Seen by the Early Church," *Tyndale Bulletin* 61.2 (2010): 173–78.

76. Origen's remarks are preserved in Eusebius, *Ecclesiastical History* 6.25.11–14.

77. Origen, *First Principles* 3.1.10; 3.2.4, 5; 4.1.24; *Against Celsus* 7.29; *Commentary on Job* 2.6; 10.11. See also Matthew J. Thomas, "Origen on Paul's Authorship of Hebrews," *NTS* 65 (2019): 608–9.

78. Clement of Alexandria postulates that Paul wrote Hebrews in the Hebrew lan-

Introduction

Jerome's work on the questions of authorship and authenticity supports and develops Origen's remarks. He demonstrates his education in typical fashion in his comments, as he discusses the literary style and content of different texts. These observations indicate that Jerome's view of authorship did not demand that the apostle's exact terms were used. What mattered was that the content fit the named author.[79] Jerome, following Origen, describes the complex theology in Ephesians as Paul's way to combat the paganism and magic prevalent in Ephesus, equipping believers for the battle against powers and principalities.[80] Erasmus, writing in 1519, discusses Ephesians' authorship: "Certainly, the style differs so much from the other Epistles of Paul, that it could seem to be the work of another person did not the heart and soul of the Pauline mind assert clearly his claim to this letter."[81]

The ancient evidence suggests that polemics are behind much of the ancient Christian discussion about forgery and authorship. However, the evidence also reveals that scholars in the ancient world focused primarily on a text's content when determining authorship and did not expect or require that the words in the document come directly from the mouth or pen of the attributed author. If the content matched the author's known works, then the document in question was assumed to be authentic, even if the style differed from other works. But if the style was consistent, and the content was at odds with known teachings, the document was dismissed as forged. The style variations within an author's corpus could be explained by the use of secretaries. A closer look at the mechanics of writing in the ancient world offers another way to explain at least the literary differences that stretch across the Pauline corpus.

---

guage and Luke translated it into Greek. Luke refrained from identifying the epistle's author because the "Hebrews" were suspicious of Paul. See Eusebius, *Ecclesiastical History* 6.14.2–3.

79. Baum, "Content and Form," 385. Baum highlights Jerome's theory on translation within the New Testament, wherein he explains that the evangelists captured the meaning of the Hebrew as they translated into Greek. Jerome claims to do the same in his translation work and thus believes he is no falsifier of the text or a fabricator of doctrine; *Epistle* 57.5.1 (Corpus Scriptorum Ecclesiasticorum Latinorum 54.513.9–10; translation from *NPNF²* 6:115); 57.7.1–5; 57.9.7.

80. Jerome, *Commentary on Ephesians*, preface, book 1.

81. Erasmus, *Collected Works of Erasmus*, vol. 43: *Paraphrases on the Epistles to the Corinthians, Ephesians, Philippians, Colossians, and Thessalonians*, ed. Robert D. Sider (Toronto: University of Toronto Press, 2009), 300n12.

E. SECRETARIES AND LETTER WRITING IN THE ANCIENT WORLD

Paul used secretaries (*amanuenses*) in writing his letters, as did most people in the ancient world. One of Paul's scribes, Tertius, identifies himself to the Romans (16:22). In some ways, the secretarial pools of the 1950s, with their shorthand and typing skills, mimic the ancient world's amanuenses. Many educated people in the ancient world could read but did not have the skills to produce an elegantly scripted document. Paul likely included himself in this number, as his note to the Corinthians indicates (1 Cor 16:21; see also Gal 6:11; Phlm 19). Josephus acknowledges his coworkers, who helped him express his thoughts in polished Greek. These scribes are what we might call today ghostwriters.[82]

The secretary held a skilled position that included an ability to write shorthand and take dictation. It is an open question as to whether the secretary wrote word-for-word what Paul dictated or produced a paraphrase based on Paul's instructions. Paul might have made changes to the draft, and the secretary then produced a final copy, to which Paul might add a personal note, for example, "I, Paul, write this greeting in my own hand" (1 Cor 16:21; see also Gal 6:11; Col 4:18; 2 Thess 3:17; Phlm 19).[83] The secretary might produce a copy in case the letter was damaged in route. Cicero planned for just this eventuality. When his letter to Julius Caesar got wet, he averted disaster by handing the letter carrier a copy of that letter.[84] Cicero kept copies of his letters[85] and might have shared the same letter between his friends.[86] This practice would likely be followed by Paul.[87]

An interesting feature of several of Paul's letters, although not Ephesians, is the mention of cosenders. Paul names Sosthenes, Silas, and Timothy. The practice of coauthoring a letter was rare in Paul's day and thus invites

---

82. Richards, "Will the Real Author Please Stand Up?," 119.

83. Steve Reece, *Paul's Large Letters: Paul's Autographic Subscriptions in the Light of Ancient Epistolary Conventions*, Library of New Testament Studies 561 (London: T&T Clark, 2017), 9, observes that Paul's personal statements follow the typical custom of attaching a personal statement. These comments were included to add weight to the letter's authority and alleviate concerns about forgery, as well as further the relationship between sender and recipient.

84. Cicero, *Letters to Quintus* 2.12.4.

85. Cicero, *Letters to Family* 7.25.1.

86. Cicero, *Letters to Atticus* 3.9.

87. Campbell, *Framing Paul*, 284: "Paul evidently kept copies of his letters; the letters circulated through multiple congregations (see Col 4:16); and copies seem to have been made and studied in these locations."

interpretation. Are the cosenders also coauthors?[88] Did these coworkers have a hand in the actual writing, were they active discussion partners shaping the letter's content, or were they merely acknowledged by Paul because they were known to the recipients? How might we determine their level of participation? Perhaps their presence is suggestive of Paul's collaborative leadership.[89] Their position alongside Paul's name where one expects an author's name encourages the view that these individuals contributed to the letter in significant ways. For example, the distinct vocabulary of 1 Corinthians may be related to contributions of its unique cosender, Sosthenes.[90] Yet the repetition of "I" (Paul) in the cosent letters cautions against insisting that the cosenders were also coauthors. The circumstances surrounding each letter, including Paul's imprisonments, probably altered the level of participation of the cosenders. Paul's reference to cosenders at the very least seeks to persuade the recipients that his gospel message is shared by the likes of Sosthenes or Timothy; therefore, Paul is not simply giving a courteous nod to some on his ministry team.[91]

F. CONCLUSIONS ON THE PSEUDEPIGRAPHIC PAUL AND EPHESIANS

Behind claims of forgery or pseudepigraphy rests the conviction that we can know with certainty which epistles are genuine. Can we really determine that? On what basis? The reasoning becomes circular, as we first posit what is essential to Paul—for example, language of justification or apocalyptic worldview—and then compare each letter based on the few that match the preestablished criteria. Distinguishing Paul's gospel message from later developments can be based on a priori assessments about the range of the author's theological reach and the pace and scope of the church's development

---

88. Eight of the thirteen letters attributed to Paul include cosenders. Ephesians, along with Romans and Galatians and the Pastorals, do not have specific cosenders. Jeffrey A. D. Weima, *Paul the Ancient Letter Writer: An Introduction to Epistolary Analysis* (Grand Rapids: Baker Academic, 2016), 27, discusses Cicero, *Letters to Atticus* 11.5.1, wherein he remarks on his friend's coauthored letters and those written only by Atticus.

89. E. Randolph Richards, *Paul and First-Century Letter Writing: Secretaries, Composition, and Collection* (Downers Grove, IL: InterVarsity Press, 2004), 32–36.

90. Kenny, *Stylometric Study of the New Testament*, 99–100. Weima, *Paul the Ancient Letter Writer*, 27, counters that Paul uses "I" extensively in the epistle, thus challenging the notion that Sosthenes had a voice in the letter.

91. Weima, *Paul the Ancient Letter Writer*, 29–30, offers several examples, including Timothy, who was with Paul when the latter wrote Romans, but is not mentioned as a cosender (see Rom 1:1; 16:21).

in its early decades. Evaluations assume a "Paul" untouched by his coauthors' influence, or church tradition, or his secretaries. Such a "Paul" is more of a scholarly construct at odds with what we know about letter writing and authorship discussions in the ancient world.[92] I argue that the preponderance of evidence for Pauline authorship overcomes the arguments against his authorship.[93]

II. RECIPIENTS

From the letter itself, we can draw a few general conclusions about the recipients of this letter. First, Paul encourages them not to be disheartened by his imprisonment. He explains how this challenging situation is their "glory" (3:13). Paul draws this remarkable conclusion from his understanding of his calling as God's gift of grace. The calling empowered Paul to offer the gospel of Christ to gentiles, and in executing this call, Paul finds himself in chains.

Second, the recipients are primarily gentiles. Paul uses "we" and "you" as he unfolds his argument, stating that "you followed the ways of this world" (2:2), "you . . . are Gentiles by birth" (2:11). Paul clearly distinguishes between gentiles who have darkened understanding and are ignorant of God's ways (4:17–18) and those who are now brought near to God through Christ (2:17–18). The recipients are gentiles who formerly practiced paganism and now follow Christ, but have not accepted the Jewish rites of circumcision, food laws, Sabbath rest, and other identity markers of Second Temple Judaism.[94] The book of Acts indicates that a Jewish Christian community grew in

---

92. N. T. Wright, *Paul and the Faithfulness of God* (Minneapolis: Fortress, 2016), 1:61, assumes that Ephesians is "highly likely to be Pauline" and thus uses the epistle as evidence of Paul's thought.

93. For a brief summary of the argument that Ephesians is authentic, see Te-Li Lau, *The Politics of Peace: Ephesians, Dio Chrysostom, and the Confucian Four Books*, Supplements to Novum Testamentum 133 (Leiden: Brill, 2010), 22–24. Bock, *Ephesians*, 20, asks, "how much difference is enough to point to an author separate from Paul? The call is admittedly hard to pin down, yet nothing in what we have discussed points clearly to a distinct author more than to Paul working with his own thought."

94. Schüssler Fiorenza, lxiv–lxvii, identifies the recipients as Jewish Messianists. She rightly cautions that when the "parting of the ways" between Jews and Christians occurred is a matter of debate, and she warns against anachronistically imposing later understanding of Judaism and Christianity back into Paul's day. Nevertheless, her assertion fails to take full measure of Paul's claim that in Christ Jew and gentile become one new humanity (2:15). The gentile leaves behind paganism, not to become a Jew, but to become a follower of Jesus Messiah.

Introduction

Ephesus under Apollos's care (18:24–26), but it remained for Paul to focus on the gentiles (19:8–10). However, Paul quotes and alludes to Jewish Scripture throughout Ephesians, suggesting at the very least that the recipients viewed these texts as authoritative in their communities.

Third, there are hints that particular gentile cultural practices or pagan beliefs continued to influence the community. It may be that at least some Ephesians were listening to an alternative message and drawn to practices that Paul considered sexually immoral and greedy (5:6). And perhaps the congregation needed reassurance of God's surpassing power over all authorities of the universe. This fear was widespread throughout the pagan population, and based on Acts 19, it seems to have had a special hold in Ephesus.

In sum, the internal evidence from the letter itself points to a gentile audience that has left its pagan ways to follow Christ, but has yet to fully comprehend the magnitude of their exalted position as God's children and to fully embrace a holy lifestyle. The internal evidence does not rule out Pauline authorship or an Ephesus provenance; however, it does not strengthen these claims either.

A. TEXTUAL EVIDENCE FOR THE OMISSION OF "IN EPHESUS"

The absence of the phrase "in Ephesus" (1:1) in some early manuscripts calls into question the recipients' identity as the church in Ephesus.[95] The oldest source, P46, a third-century Alexandrian uncial, does not include "in Ephesus" in the opening verse. The text of P46 reads: "To the saints who are and to believers in Christ Jesus."[96] However, the superscription of P46 identifies the epistle as to the Ephesians. The fourth-century Alexandrian codices Sinaiticus and Vaticanus also omit "in Ephesus," but like P46 they include "to the Ephesians" in the superscription.[97] These two later codices vary slightly from P46, the oldest source.[98] Origen worked from a manuscript that did

---

95. Ernest Best, "Ephesians i.1," in *Text and Interpretation: Studies in the New Testament Presented to Matthew Black*, ed. Ernest Best and Robert McLean Wilson (Cambridge: Cambridge University Press, 1979), 29–41 (at 30), lays out the main textual variants:

P—τοῖς ἁγίοις οὖσιν καὶ πιστοῖς P46
B—τοῖς ἁγίοις τοῖς οὖσιν καὶ πιστοῖς Α* B* 424c 1739
A—τοῖς ἁγίοις τοῖς οὖσιν ἐν Ἐφέσῳ καὶ πιστοῖς most other manuscripts

96. The Greek text of P46 reads τοῖς ἁγίοις οὖσιν καὶ πιστοῖς ἐν Χριστῷ Ἰησοῦ. Thielman, 12, concludes that "although impressively early, this reading appears only in this one manuscript and so is unlikely to represent what Paul wrote."

97. Lincoln, 2, argues that this reading is the earliest, because one can see how the alternative readings came to be and because it is the most difficult reading.

98. The Greek text reads τοῖς ἁγίοις τοῖς οὖσιν καὶ πιστοῖς ἐν Χριστῷ Ἰησοῦ, with

not include "in Ephesus," and its antecedent Greek text follows the fourth-century codices. Origen postulates that Paul drew on Exod 3:14, wherein God declares, "I AM." Origen suggests that Paul intended believers should think of themselves as "saints *who are*" picking up on the "to be" verb from Exodus.[99] Basil the Great, in the fourth century, asserts that the traditional text omits "in Ephesus," although he knows texts that include the phrase.[100]

Writing in the late second or early third century, Tertullian claims that Marcion changed the title of his copy, identifying the epistle as to the Laodiceans, a church mentioned by Paul in Col 4:16.[101] Tertullian claims in his brief remark that Marcion wrongly identified our epistle's recipients as the Laodiceans. Tertullian responds with two arguments. First, he points out that the church's tradition has always held the epistle as having been addressed to the Ephesians. Second, Tertullian concludes that Marcion's title change is of no account, because the apostle's words are written to the entire church.[102] We cannot ascertain from this brief remark whether Marcion's biblical text, or Tertullian's, included "in Ephesus," but if Tertullian's copy included "in Ephesus," it would have strengthened his case to include it.[103] Aside from Marcion's claims, however, all ancient authors present this letter as to the Ephesians in the superscription or title of the epistle.[104] And most manuscripts include the phrase "in Ephesus" within the text itself; it is predominately the Alexandrian text type that omits the phrase.[105]

---

repetition of τοῖς before the participle. The Alexandrian uncials א2 (6th or 7th century) and B2 (tenth or eleventh century) include "in Ephesus."

99. Origen, in his comments on Eph 1:1, argues that the letter was sent to the Ephesians and explains the absence of the complement by declaring that Paul emphasized the believers being part of the existent one; see Heine, 80. Lincoln, 2, rejects this interpretation. See also Muddiman, 60, who rightly notes that this explanation "tells us a lot about Origen, but nothing about the origin of Ephesians."

100. Basil the Great, *Against Eunomius* 2.19 (PG 29:612–13); see Thielman, 13.

101. Tertullian, *Against Marcion* 5.17.1 (see also 5.11.12). Best, "Ephesians i.1," 30, remarks: "It is generally held that Tertullian's accusations relate to the superscription to the letter and not to the text itself: in that case Marcion cannot have had the A text [τοῖς ἁγίοις τοῖς οὖσιν ἐν Ἐφέσεῳ καὶ πιστοῖς]; this would also imply that Tertullian did not have 'in Ephesus' in his text."

102. Tertullian uses the Latin *titulum*, which refers to the superscription or title of the epistle (*Against Marcion* 5.17.1).

103. Thielman, 12, observes: "Since Tertullian charges Marcion with corrupting only the title of the letter, moreover, even he may have been working from a version without a place name in its text."

104. Thielman, 15–16. This includes both Origen (*First Principles* 3.5.4) and Basil, whose texts apparently did not include "in Ephesus." Arnold, 25, includes references from Irenaeus, *Against Heresies* 5.2.3, 8.1, 14.3, 24.4.

105. Thielman, 14, cautions that the limited geographical range of the texts that omit

B. EVALUATION OF THE EVIDENCE

The evidence from texts and the early church indicates that (1) a few of our oldest manuscripts omit "in Ephesus" and (2) all ancient authors, with the exception of Marcion, identify the epistle as to the Ephesians. The three ancient witnesses lacking "in Ephesus" are Alexandrian text types, which might suggest a local variant. Moreover, the superscription "to the Ephesians" appears in all three. The Western and Byzantine text types, and not a few manuscripts within the Alexandrian text type, include the phrase "in Ephesus." The correctors of both Sinaiticus and Vaticanus, as well as a third-century Coptic text, include the phrase "in Ephesus."[106] Origen speaks about the epistle as addressed to the Ephesians, in his discussion of 1:1: "In the case of Ephesians alone we find the phrase, 'to the saints who are.'"[107] The absence of "in Ephesus" in 1:1 did not lead him to doubt its authorship or provenance. Instead, he interpreted the awkward Greek as conveying a theological truth about believers' new life in Christ.

Modern scholars have built several theories to accommodate the information. One option postulates Ephesians as a circular letter written to the churches around Ephesus. This theory assumes that the original letter omitted "in Ephesus" but that the letter was written by Paul to be circulated in and around Ephesus. Tychicus would insert the town's name in Eph 1:1 as he read the letter to each congregation. This theory builds on the evidence taken from several of Paul's letters, that Paul's letters were shared by congregations. Paul asks Tychicus to read Colossians to the Laodiceans, and to read his letter to the Laodiceans (nonextant) to the Colossians (Col 4:15–16).[108] Paul sends greetings to the Corinthians from the churches in the province of Asia, suggesting that he knows of communities outside of Ephesus, the city from which he wrote 1 Corinthians (16:19).[109] Moreover, Paul writes to the Galatian churches, expecting the letter to pass from church to church. This theory has the additional advantage of explaining both the general nature of the epistle as a whole, and its lack of greetings. However, this theory does

---

"in Ephesus" weakens the argument for their representing the original reading. See also Hoehner, 146.

106. Hoehner, 145–46, cites copsa of the third century and copbo from the fourth century, both representing the Alexandrian text type. See also À2 and B2.

107. Heine, 80.

108. Campbell, *Framing Paul*, 323–29, argues that our Ephesians is the letter to the Laodiceans that Paul speaks of to the Colossians.

109. Trebilco, *Early Christians in Ephesus*, 71: "Paul here seems to imply . . . that the Christian community of Ephesus was the central Christian community of the province . . . This suggests that the Ephesian Christian community was a missionary centre, and maintained contact with Christians in other parts of the province."

not explain why "in" was omitted as well as "Ephesus," for one would expect the preposition to remain in the text. Nor do any of the three manuscripts that lack "in Ephesus" have a blank space into which a city's name was to be inserted. And why would Paul fail to identify the recipients as "the churches in the Lycus Valley" or "the churches in Asia Minor," as he does in his letter to the Galatians?[110] Finally, when Paul expects his letters to be read by other churches, he stipulates his intentions in the letters—but there is no statement to that effect in our letter.[111]

A second explanation argues that the original letter lacked "in Ephesus" and that Paul was not the author.[112] The epistle was written by a disciple or interpreter of Paul to an unspecified group. From this position, at least two possibilities emerge. First, the cities of Laodicea and Hierapolis have been put forward as the intended destinations for our epistle, based on the letter's close relationship with Colossians and drawing on Marcion's identification.[113] Tychicus is named in our letter as courier, as he is for Colossians, which suggests that our author capitalized on the congregation's high regard for both Paul and Tychicus.[114] Second, the possibility exists that the city of Ephesus was attached to the letter as the collection of Pauline letters developed. Since Paul spent a good portion of time in Ephesus, the collectors surmised that he must have sent a letter to this congregation. Therefore, our epistle was designated as "to the Ephesians" (cf. 1 Cor 15:32; 16:8).[115] A scribe then incorporated "to those who are in Ephesus" into the text of the letter, and later, another scribe recalled that originally the epistle did not contain a geographic location and so omitted "in Ephesus." The theory falls under the weight of its overly complex assumptions. Additionally, as I have suggested, it is most likely that Paul himself kept copies of his letters, thus a collection of letters was quite early. Moreover, if

---

110. Best, "Ephesians i.1," 36–37; Lincoln, 2–3.

111. Hoehner, 146–47.

112. Lincoln, 1–4.

113. Lincoln, 3, explains that two place names "would not only help to explain the καί but also bring this address into harmony with the syntax of other Pauline addresses where we find a dative construction simply followed by an attributive phrase." See also A. van Roon, *The Authenticity of Ephesians* (Leiden: Brill, 1974), 72–85. Best, "Ephesians i.1," 39, rightly critiques van Roon's theory.

114. Lincoln, lxxxii, suggests that "Tychicus would have been known to the recipients as one of the leading representatives of the Pauline mission." Lincoln's position suggests that the recipients knew the epistle was not written by Paul, yet it carried the authority of the apostle.

115. Ernest Best, "Recipients and Title of the Letter to the Ephesians: Why and When the Designation 'Ephesians'?," *ANRW* 2.25.4 (1987): 3278, suggests hesitantly that "Marcion or a predecessor whose copy of the letter was used by Marcion, saw the need of a geographical designation, probably read in Col 4.16 about a letter which he did not appear to possess and assumed that his unidentified letter was this letter."

our letter circulated for several decades with anonymous recipients, one would expect various locations to be supplied, but we have only a single claim by Tertullian that Marcion identified the letter's recipients as Laodiceans.

A third option promotes the view that "in Ephesus" is original to the text and that Paul wrote the epistle.[116] While no theory satisfactorily addresses all the text-critical issues, this theory seems the least problematic, as it agrees with the majority voices within the manuscripts and early Christian writers.[117] The epistle's superscription in all manuscripts identifies the epistle as to the Ephesians, and Origen understands Ephesus to be the letter's destination and Paul to be its author. The omission of "in Ephesus" in the three early Alexandrian texts could be the result of a scribe's efforts to generalize the epistle, as was done with Romans by a scribe in Codex G.[118] It is also possible that an early scribe misunderstood the "epexegetical *kai* in the first verse [1:1] as a genuine conjunction that could have led to the excision of the place name."[119] This third option explains the relationship with Colossians, allowing that both epistles come from Paul and speak to similar concerns faced by churches within the same general location. The lack of personal greetings at the end of the epistle, also absent in Galatians, Philippians, and 1 Thessalonians, could reflect the time that has passed since Paul lived in Ephesus.

III. OCCASION FOR WRITING EPHESIANS

Ephesians itself offers few specifics about the situation addressed and scarce details about the recipients' concerns. We learn from the letter that Paul does not want the Ephesians to be discouraged at the news of his imprisonment, and he asks for their prayers for his boldness in presenting the gospel as he is an ambassador in chains (3:13; 6:19). Paul did not live in a prison as we think of it today; rather, he probably rented an apartment within one of the ubiquitous and unsound tenement houses (Latin *insulae*) that filled Rome (Acts 28:20–30).[120] Brian Rapske explains that Paul was likely confined to his apartment with his guard at night, but during the day was "able to divide his time

---

116. Thielman, 11–16; Larkin, 2–3.

117. Best, "Ephesians i.1," 41, laments: "Few conclusions can be drawn other than that there is as yet no satisfactory solution."

118. Thielman, 15–16, remarks that in Codex G, Rom 1:7, 15 lack the designation "Romans."

119. Muddiman, 62.

120. Brian Rapske, *The Book of Acts and Paul in Roman Custody*, The Book of Acts in Its First Century Setting 3 (Grand Rapids: Eerdmans, 1994), 228–29, 326, 431.

between his rooms and the precincts of his tenement—perhaps wandering about the courtyard if such was a part of his dwelling."[121]

Paul capitalizes on his current situation as a prisoner of Christ, and perhaps an incipient martyr,[122] to speak with greater authority about holy living (4:1). Paul's actions fit a larger narrative of martyrdom that grew up at the time of the Maccabees in the second century BCE. Zealous Jews rebelled against their Seleucid overlords. Several Jews were martyred, and their testimony galvanized others to persevere. The Hasmoneans drove out the Seleucids, cleansed the temple, and established Jewish rule throughout Judea, Samaria, and Galilee. Paul explains his life as a Pharisee as zealous for the traditions of the fathers (Gal 1:13–14; Phil 3:6), a likely reference to the early Maccabees' zealous commitment to the law. Paul places himself in that line of Jews who died rather than be unfaithful.

Additionally, Paul wants the Ephesians to know the content of his prayers for them. He prays that they would come to understand their inheritance—their salvation, their redemption, and their membership in God's family. Such knowledge should be felt with the heart, as well as absorbed by the mind (1:18). Paul also prays that God would strengthen them, that they would know Christ's love in their hearts (3:17–18). Paul asks that God's power would dwell deeply and richly within them, as they dwell in Christ (1:23; 3:16–19). He desires that they mature in their faith, which means growing together as the body of Christ (4:15–17).

Paul explains the salvation plan of God, established before creation and brought to fulfillment in Christ's death, resurrection, and exaltation. It is not clear that the Ephesians questioned anything that Paul put forward; however, his stress on Christ's rule over all spiritual forces and his call to put on the armor of God may indicate some concern or confusion about these spiritual authorities.

Paul warns the Ephesians to have nothing to do with those who promote sexual immorality or greed, for they are deceptive and will fall under God's judgment (5:6). Paul does not name these people or offer further description. I suggest that these people reflect an immature understanding of the gospel message that plagued Corinth as well. In that city, the community accepted lawsuits between believers and men visiting prostitutes (1 Cor 5–6). Paul addresses the Corinthians with warnings that the sexually immoral and greedy will not inherit the kingdom of God. Paul offers a similar warning to the Ephesians that they avoid idolaters and immoral people (Eph 5:5).

---

121. Rapske, *Book of Acts and Paul*, 238.

122. Eusebius, *Ecclesiastical History* 2.22.2, includes the tradition that Paul was beheaded during Nero's reign.

Introduction

Paul insists on the unity of Jew and gentile within the church, which invites questions about Paul's intention in addressing the topic with such forcefulness. Some argue that gentile believers separated from the Jewish believers.[123] However, we have no evidence of factionalism in Ephesus as we find, for example, in Corinth.[124] Arranged as they are around a household unit, however, the Ephesian groups of believers would naturally gravitate toward homogeneity and clannish loyalty, reflecting wider Greco-Roman values.[125] Margaret MacDonald makes the cogent argument that unity of Jew and gentile is but one example of Paul's emphasis on unity within the letter, and as such, Paul's language and imagery is meant to "transcend its historical referents."[126]

IV. PURPOSE OF EPHESIANS

Several theories concerning the purpose of Ephesians have been put forward, often by pointing to a particular theme within the epistle. Some highlight the epistle's liturgical tone and locate its purpose within a worship context. For example, some point especially to the first chapter and conclude that the missive was used in a baptismal context.[127] MacDonald argues more broadly that "rituals were of key importance to the community life of the recipients and central to shaping the message of the letter."[128] She points to the emphasis on Spirit-led hymns and possible heavenly visions (1:15–23; 5:18–20). Developing this idea in a different direction, some argue that Ephesians is an attempt to move the church toward greater institutionalization and cath-

---

123. Ernst Käsemann, "Ephesians and Acts," in *Studies in Luke-Acts*, ed. Leander E. Keck and J. Louis Martyn (London: SPCK, 1968), 291. See also Lincoln, 136, who postulates that Paul implores the Ephesians "to see their past in terms of categories which were valid at an earlier state in the history of salvation, when God's purpose was centered in Israel."

124. MacDonald, 253, explains that viewing the epistle, and especially 2:11–22, "as offering insight into specific tensions between Jewish and Gentile Christians is probably to go beyond the evidence."

125. Trebilco, *Early Christians in Ephesus*, 98–99.

126. MacDonald, 254. She continues that the language about unity of Jew and gentile has "gained an objective quality" and is then applied to a new, later setting (255).

127. Nils A. Dahl, "Adresse und Proëmium des Epheserbriefes," *Theologische Zeitschrift* 7 (1951): 241–64.

128. MacDonald, 19. Jeal, *Integrating Theology and Ethics in Ephesians*, 177, argues that the letter is best understood as a sermon designed to encourage the Ephesians toward maturity and concludes: "The 'sermonic' language of Ephesians 1–3 impresses its ideas and themes on the audience members (θεωροί), encouraging them to remember and identify with Christian beliefs and understandings."

olicity.[129] Focusing on Jewish parallels, Pheme Perkins highlights the correspondences with Qumran texts as examples of "sectarian piety" reflected in the letter to gentile believers who are "encouraged to remember themselves as brought into a common inheritance with Jewish believers."[130] Those who locate the epistle's purpose within its historical setting offer several suggestions, including that the gentile believers grew alienated from their Jewish compatriots and drew back from the Jewish roots of the faith.[131] Still others suggest an external threat from outsiders[132] or from cosmic forces,[133] or claim the letter is an antignostic treatise.[134] The epistle's purpose is best explained as Paul's attempt to guide his congregation of primarily gentiles, to a mature faith, defined as having a deep understanding of God's redemptive plan and responding appropriately with holy living.[135]

---

129. Ernst Käsemann, "Paul and Early Catholicism," in *New Testament Questions of Today* (Philadelphia: Fortress, 1967; London: SCM, 1969), 236–37. See Conzelmann and R. P. Martin, "Early Catholicism," *DPL* 223–25, for a brief overview and critique of Käsemann's argument.

130. Perkins, 29–30.

131. Ralph P. Martin, "An Epistle in Search of a Life-Setting," *Expository Times* 79 (1968): 296–302.

132. MacDonald, 257, identifies the dual threats of external forces and "hostile cosmic powers." See also Lincoln, 440–41: "The writer is concerned to bolster his readers' confidence by reminding them again of their identity and what this means for being enabled to maintain an appropriate lifestyle in the midst of an alien society and in the face of the powerful forces that lie behind it."

133. Timothy Gombis, *The Drama of Ephesians: Participating in the Triumph of God* (Downers Grove, IL: IVP Academic, 2010); see also Arnold, 45, who argues that the purpose is to affirm the local churches in Ephesus and the surrounding area *"in their new identity in Christ as a means of strengthening them in their ongoing struggle with the powers of darkness"* (emphasis original). Arnold also holds that Paul wanted to strengthen unity between Jews and gentiles and to encourage deeper holiness in the congregations; see Clinton E. Arnold, *Ephesians: Power and Magic—the Concept of Power in Ephesians in Light of Its Historical Setting*, Society for New Testament Study Monograph 63 (Cambridge: Cambridge University Press, 1989).

134. Petr Pokorný, *Der Epheserbrief und die Gnosis: Die Bedeutung des Haupt-Glieder-Gedankens in der entstehenden Kirche* (Berlin: Evangelische Verlagsanstalt, 1965), 21. See also Rudolf Bultmann, *Theology of the New Testament*, 2 vols., trans. Kendrick Grobel (Waco, TX: Baylor University Press, 2007; originally New York: Scribner, 1951–55), 178–79. Recent scholarship has moved away from the theory that pre-Christian Gnosticism informed Ephesians.

135. Best, 74, writes that the epistle's purpose is "to ensure the corporate maturity of believers and does so by driving home the nature of the body they joined when they left the pagan world, and the type of behavior which would produce true growth in their communities." Bruce, 245, writes: "There is at least firm internal evidence that the letter was written to encourage Gentile Christians to appreciate the dignity of their calling."

INTRODUCTION

V. FIRST-CENTURY EPHESUS

First-century gentile believers faced daily decisions as they extracted themselves from pagan practices that had previously governed their lives.[136] In Ephesus, they faced this reality in two acute ways—in the worship of Artemis and in the significant presence of the imperial cult. These expressions of paganism assumed a metanarrative that reinforced Roman superiority politically, culturally, economically, and spiritually.[137] Paul explains God's alternative narrative of redemption, grounded in God's power over all things, including spiritual forces of evil and Christ's love that knows no bounds. Paul must reassure the Ephesians of Christ's supreme lordship, and he has an uphill battle.

A. CULT OF ARTEMIS

Artemis, a goddess of great renown, was honored with worship sites in many of the two thousand towns and cities across the Roman Empire. Her main temple, the Artemisium, was located about two kilometers from Ephesus's city center. At four times the size of the Athenian Parthenon, this great building was considered one of the seven wonders of the ancient world.[138] Ancient sources tell us that Artemis and her twin, Apollo, were born to Leto and Zeus in the grove of Ortygia, just outside Ephesus.[139] Hera, wife of Zeus, was jealous of Leto and sought to destroy the twins. She watched from nearby but before she could act, the wardens[140] of the Artemis cult stormed the hill, banging their swords on shields. The noise frightened Hera and she fled. The twins were saved. Each year the myth was remembered, although it is unclear exactly what rituals were followed.

What is clear is that the city of Ephesus took its responsibility to honor Artemis very seriously.[141] She was the founder of their city. Her image graced many of the city's coins, and her name was invoked in numerous official doc-

---

136. Contemporary sources for the city include Strabo, *Geography* 14.1.4–38.

137. Guy MacLean Rogers, *The Mysteries of Artemis of Ephesos: Cult, Polis, and Change in the Graeco-Roman World* (New Haven: Yale University Press, 2012), 102, remarks that Ephesus underwent remarkable architectural change at the beginning of the imperial period, such that one "could have imagined himself to have entered a Roman city superimposed upon a Greek one, complete with a Roman-style forum (with its characteristic monumental axiality), laid out on a relentlessly regular grid of blocks."

138. Antipater, *Greek Anthology* 9.58. See Trebilco, *Early Christians in Ephesus*, 20.

139. Strabo, *Geography* 14.1.20.

140. Κουρῆτες.

141. Trebilco, *Early Christians in Ephesus*, 29.

uments. Artemis saved those in need and was known as the protector of women in childbirth. The bees that decorated her skirt in her many statues emphasized her special powers.[142] She defended Ephesus, and the city's political business interwove seamlessly with her festivals. The wardens of the temple, who described themselves as devout, also functioned in the city's government.[143] These male civic leaders celebrated festivals and participated in symposia dedicated to Artemis.[144] For example, an inscription (ca. 104 CE) celebrates Gaius Vibius Salutaris for his piety in providing money and statues honoring Artemis.[145] Paul turns the gentile expectation for piety on its head, infusing the term with new meaning.

Two annual festivals determined the city's liturgical year. In one of the festivals, the Artemisia included not only athletics and arts competitions, but also a matchmaking ritual wherein young men and women found their mates. Xenophon describes this practice in his first-century CE romance novel *Ephesiaca*.[146] The text indicates the erotic appeal of braided hair and a purple chiton or dress. Xenophon describes the heroine Anthia's celebration, specifically commenting on her hair, which hung loose except for a braided portion mimicking that of the goddess.[147] Paul's concerns about sexual immorality within the Ephesian community are understandable, given the erotic

---

142. Callimachus, *Hymn* (*Suda* 3.302, 859); see Rick Strelan, *Paul, Artemis, and the Jews in Ephesus* (Berlin: de Gruyter, 1996), 48, 62, 114.

143. Philip H. Towner, *The Letters to Timothy and Titus*, NICNT (Grand Rapids: Eerdmans, 2006), 172, remarks that the "wardens of the mysteries of the Artemis cult . . . also were part of the city's governing structure." Paul's encouragement in 1 Tim 2:2 concerning reverent behavior for all believers includes the general term εὐσέβεια, which means godliness or piety (Latin *pietas*).

144. Rogers, *Mysteries of Artemis of Ephesos*, 135, observes that by declaring themselves pious in inscriptions, the wardens presented "themselves to readers as possessing a communally shared religious quality or virtue that justified and legitimated the positions of authority and power that they held within the civic hierarchy of Ephesos."

145. *Die Inscriften von Ephesos* 27. See Gary G. Hoag, *Wealth in Ancient Ephesus and the First Letter to Timothy: Fresh Insights from Ephesiaca by Zenophon of Ephesus*, Bulletin for Biblical Research Supplement 11 (Winona Lake, IN: Eisenbrauns, 2015), 32–33, who concludes: "Rich people also gave money to ensure the perpetual honor of Artemis, and in return, they were lauded for their εὐσέβεια, 'devoutness, piety, or godliness,' to the goddess with public proclamations and inscriptions that celebrated their beneficence." See also Rogers, *Mysteries of Artemis of Ephesos*, 184–85.

146. Xenophon of Ephesus, *Ephesiaca* 1.2.2–4; 24. See also Craig S. Keener, *Acts: An Exegetical Commentary* (Grand Rapids: Baker Academic, 2012), 1:212, who concludes that the centrality of Artemis worship and the Artemisium in the city's economy corresponds to inscriptional and literary evidence from Ephesus.

147. Braided hair (πεπλεγμένη) mimicked that of the goddess. Interestingly, 1 Tim 2:9 specifies braided hair using the cognate noun (πλέγμασιν), which suggests the Artemisian festivals as a backdrop to his injunctions on proper Christian prayers.

environment of the Artemis celebrations.[148] Moreover, Paul's sanction against greed could be directly related to the sumptuous clothing worn in honor of the goddess.[149] A second festival was held a month or two later, on the sixth of Thargelion (May/June). A grand parade carrying images of the goddess began at the temple, processed to the city, and then returned to the temple. About once or twice each month, devotees marched from the temple through the city; each lasted about ninety minutes as they traversed the four-kilometer round trip.

The cult of Artemis followed a pattern of devotion called "votive religion."[150] Guy Rogers describes this as the "polytheists' practice of making vows to the gods for some reason or to achieve some goal and then fulfilling those vows by making dedications to the gods."[151] The ancients sought the favor of the god or goddess, usually for an immediate need such as good health or harvest, and not for eternal salvation. The devotee made the request, offered a sacrifice, and vowed to honor the deity should it answer the prayer. It was a bit of a hit or miss approach, and supplicants kept trying until they got results. Gentile believers would naturally bring assumptions about proper devotion to their worship of Israel's God, and Paul's letter to the Ephesians distinguishes the arena of gentile darkness with the light of Christ (4:17; 5:8–16).

B. IMPERIAL CULT

The imperial cult was an innovation as the Roman Empire emerged from the period of the Republic, but also had natural roots in the pagan culture.[152] It grew organically from the pagan family practice of honoring the *genius* or life

---

148. Xenophon of Ephesus, *Ephesiaca* 1.3.1–2, describes Anthia and Habrocomes as falling in love at Artemis's temple. He could not take his eyes off her, and Anthia put "maidenly decorum out of her mind: for what she said was for Habrocomes to hear, and she uncovered what parts of her body she could for Habrocomes to see" (translation from Hoag, *Wealth in Ancient Ephesus*, 77).

149. Similar terms are used in Acts 20:33, where Paul declares to the Ephesians that he has not coveted gold (χρυσίον) or clothing (ἱματισμός).

150. Walter Burkert, *Ancient Mystery Cults* (Cambridge: Harvard University Press, 1987), 12.

151. Rogers, *Mysteries of Artemis of Ephesos*, 16.

152. Karl Galinsky, "The Cult of the Roman Emperor: Uniter or Divider?," in *Rome and Religion: A Cross-disciplinary Dialogue on the Imperial Cult*, ed. Jeffrey Brodd and Jonathan L. Reed (Atlanta: SBL, 2011), 1–22, offers an excellent overview of the issues. He rightly points to Mary Beard, John North, and Simon Price, *Religions of Rome*, vol. 1: *A History* (Cambridge: Cambridge University Press, 1998), 348, who caution readers that there is no such thing as "the" imperial cult.

force of the paterfamilias. It developed from the Greek ruler cult promoted especially in the eastern provinces of the empire.[153] The imperial cult involved negotiation, a term used by Simon Price to explain the integration of the imperial cult within daily life in the city.[154] The imperial cult could be a tool for city magistrates to demonstrate their fealty to Rome, as they incorporate and assimilate their local deities and customs with imperial Rome.

Octavian Caesar Augustus, the first emperor of Rome, postured himself as the first citizen or Princeps, and the Father of the Empire. As such, each household within the empire honored his *genius* as their supreme paterfamilias, pouring a libation in his name.[155] The Ephesians might have had this practice in mind as they heard Paul identify God as Father of every family (3:14-15) or as the one God and Father of all (4:6). Members of the imperial family, including Livia, Augustus's wife, were honored with deification if they lived exemplary lives. The honor was bestowed by the Roman Senate, who determined that the person had received an apotheosis, that is, had become a god.[156]

Augustus postured himself as Zeus/Jupiter, who defeats his enemies and brings peace in the heavens and on earth.[157] Cities viewed the emperor as their highest benefactor, and the cult brought the entire metropolis together around a common enterprise. The Priene Calendar inscription (9 BCE) declares that Caesar Augustus, "savior," brought wars to an end and established peace and order.[158] At about the same time, across the empire near modern-day Monaco, the Roman Senate established a temple to Augustus celebrating his victory over the forty-six tribes of the Alps (*tropaeum*

---

153. S. R. F. Price, *Rituals and Power: The Roman Imperial Cult in Asia Minor* (Cambridge: Cambridge University Press, 1984), 24.

154. Price, *Rituals and Power*, 99-100: "The cult became one of the major contexts in which the competitive spirit of the local élites was worked out; it formed one of a range of civic provisions by which the prestige of the city was measured; it shared in the dominance of the Greek culture as a whole." See also 62-72.

155. Lily Ross Taylor, *The Divinity of the Roman Emperor* (Middletown, CT: American Philological Association, 1931), 152. For an alternative view, see Ittai Gradel, *Emperor Worship and Roman Religion* (Oxford: Oxford University Press, 2002), 3, who holds that senators did not worship Augustus's *genius*, but rather worshiped him as a god. Gradel focuses on ancient sacrifice and ritual, not on philosophical texts. He suggests a porous boundary between human and divine, one based on social status rather than ontological categories.

156. Spencer Cole, *Cicero and the Deification of Rome* (Cambridge: Cambridge University Press, 2014), offers an excellent survey of evidence from the great orator on the changes occurring during the late first century BCE.

157. Maier, *Picturing Paul in Empire*, 72-73. He points to the Gemma Augustea (ca. 10 CE), which stylizes Augustus as Jupiter Capitolinus.

158. For a translation and discussion of the Priene Inscription, see Neil Elliott and Mark Reasoner, eds., *Documents and Images for the Study of Paul* (Minneapolis: Fortress, 2011), 35, 126-27.

Alpium). Augustus was likely represented as Jupiter set atop the rotunda. The temple included twelve statues of bound figures representing the defeated peoples and perhaps symbolizing the zodiac. The overall picture is of Augustus as Jupiter bringing order and peace to the world, even as Jupiter brings order to the heavens.[159]

Cities combined their worship of traditional gods with the veneration of Augustus and his family. An inscription from Lesbos from the early first century CE declares that honoring Augustus be added to their traditional celebration of Nedameia.[160] The first-century BCE historian Nicholas of Damascus writes, "Because mankind address him thus [as Sebastos] in accordance with their estimation of his honour, they revere him with temple and sacrifices over islands and continents, organized in cities and provinces, matching the greatness of his virtue and repaying his benefactions towards them."[161]

In 46 BCE, the city Pharsalus honored Julius Caesar as a god. Similarly, in Ephesus, Julius Caesar is declared "god made manifest" (*theos epiphanes*). In 29 BCE, Ephesus built a temple for Roma and the Divine Julius.[162] At the same time, nearby Pergamum erected the first temple dedicated to Rome and Augustus and so launched the provincial imperial cult in Asia Minor. Smyrna was granted the honor of the second provincial cult site in 23 CE, dedicated to Livia, Tiberius, and the Roman Senate.[163] Nero compared his rule to that of Jupiter and Helios, the sun god. As Jupiter's viceregent, Nero brought together tribes and peoples and established order in the cosmos. During the reigns of Tiberius through to Nero, in Aphrodisias (Asia Minor) a large temple complex was built honoring Aphrodite and the divine emperors (*theoi sebastoi*). A long processional space leading to the temple was lined on both sides with a two-story stoa, each decorated with statues and reliefs showing gods and emperors and scenes of victories in battle, as well as Greek myths and allegories.[164] The defeated peoples are represented as female, a typical presentation that emphasized the nations' pacification.[165] The visual created

---

159. Maier, *Picturing Paul in Empire*, 75, includes a photo of the model of the *tropaeum Alpium*.

160. Price, *Rituals and Power*, 3.

161. Nicolaus of Damascus, *Die Fragmente der griechischen Historiker* 90 F 125; see Price, *Rituals and Power*, 1.

162. Dio Cassius, *Roman History* 51.20.6–7.

163. Tacitus, *Annals* 4.15.37.

164. Laura Salah Nasrallah, *Christian Responses to Roman Art and Architecture: The Second Century Church amid the Spaces of Empire* (Cambridge: Cambridge University Press, 2010), 77–83.

165. The *Judea Capta* coins, minted to celebrate Vespasian's victory over the Jews and the destruction of the Jerusalem temple, typically show a female figure, bound and seated at the foot of a palm tree, with a Roman soldier towering over her.

by this large architectural space underscored Rome's power and might. It shouted that Rome's rule stretched to lands far away from the town of Aphrodisias and reached to the heavens. The *pax Romana* gathered up all peoples, pacifying and assimilating them. As Tacitus put in the mouth of Calgacus, the Caledonian leader who fought against the Roman general Agricola, "they make a desolation and call it peace."[166]

Within a generation after Paul, Ephesus further embraces the imperial cult. In 89–90 CE, the emperor Domitian granted Ephesus the honor to build the third provincial cult site. The Temple of the Sebastoi honored the Flavian line (Domitian, his wife Domitia, Titus his deceased brother, and probably Vespasian), while the earlier imperial temple was dedicated to the Julio-Claudian emperors and their family.[167] With the arrival of the imperial cult of the Flavians, Ephesus was host to two important temples. The Temple of the Sebastoi held a strategic spot along the procession route of Artemis celebrations.[168] A temple warden was assigned to the Domitian temple, and with that, the city embraced the title "twice *neokoros*" drawing on the term for temple warden to emphasize its importance.[169] The imperial cult was also embedded in pagan worship generally, as in Ephesus there were "sacrifices to Asclepius and the Sebastoi . . . , and to Demeter and the Sabastoi . . . ; the basilica on the upper agora was similarly dedicated to Ephesian Artemis, Divus Augustus, Tiberius, and the *demos* of the Ephesians."[170]

What would all this mean for the Ephesian believers in Paul's day? The peace of Rome brought economic gain for some and the end of wars for the region around Ephesus. Rome's military power brings order, but at the cost of destroying and subjugating its enemies. The price of peace is submission, paid by the blood of the nations who are subdued. Many who walked the streets of Ephesus came from conquered territories, and slaves from these areas would be regular cargo in its harbor. Such peace, Rome proclaimed, was due to the gods' favor, but Paul drew on this enforced peace to speak of Christ's generative, creative, empowering peace that grants life now and eternally. How astonishing, then, is the gospel's explanation of peace. Paul declares that Christ is our peace. It is he who dies, not his enemies. It is he

---

166. Tacitus, *Agricola*, trans. M. Hutton, rev. R. M. Ogilvie, Loeb Classical Library 35 (Harvard: Harvard University Press, 1970). Gnaeus Julius Agricola (born 40 CE) commanded the Twentieth Legion in 70 CE. In 84 CE he defeated Calgacus in what is now Scotland.

167. Trebilco, *Early Christians in Ephesus*, 31. Not every emperor was honored as a god; for example, Nero did not make the list, and Gaius Caligula was only briefly exalted.

168. Maier, *Picturing Paul in Empire*, 127–29.

169. Temple warden (νεωκόρος). Price, *Rituals and Power*, 65, explains that νεωκόρος initially meant a temple warden or the city itself as the guardian of the cult. The term grew to include a city that had an imperial cult site.

170. Galinsky, "Cult of the Roman Emperor," 5.

who brings unity as God's son, not the emperor as a son of god. This gospel peace celebrates all peoples; it does not privilege one ethnic group. This peace elevates the lowly, offers slaves an inheritance. This peace challenges those to whom society grants power and prerogative to submit and serve others. It decries the pursuit of wealth and status and the underlying individualism that promotes self over others. It pulls the rug out from under imperial political claims that domination and violence could serve good ends. Christ our peace has vanquished evil cosmic powers and has opened a way to the very throne of God. His gospel peace culminates in the unity of all things in heaven and earth, in the establishment of the kingdom of Christ and of God, wherein all believers share an inheritance.

C. MAGIC AND POWERS IN EPHESUS

Ephesians mentions "powers and authorities" in four of its six chapters. Numerous theories about the identity of these references have been put forward, including that this language refers to supernatural or spiritual beings (good and/or evil) or to human structures and organizations that dominate with their powers.[171] We do well to remember that the sacred/secular divide that shapes the modern world does not map onto the ancient world's integration of divine and natural. I suggest a *via media* approach that neither minimizes the supernatural or spiritual emphasis in Paul nor ignores the social and political power structures that play an outsized role in human

---

171. For a useful summary of the leading arguments, see Amos Yong, *In the Days of Caesar: Pentecostalism and Political Theology* (Grand Rapids: Eerdmans, 2010), 145–51. Walter Wink, *Naming the Powers: The Language of Power in the New Testament* (Philadelphia: Fortress, 1984), 39, concludes that this terminology is used in numerous contexts, "both heavenly *and* earthly, divine *and* human, good *and* evil power," and that "we must conclude, then, that the original hearers of the New Testament, whether Jewish or Gentile, understood this language to be comprehensive vocabulary for power in general and took the meaning from the context." See also Walter Wink, *The Powers That Be: Theology for a New Millennium* (New York: Doubleday, 1998). Arnold, *Ephesians: Power and Magic*, 49, critiques the methodology, stating that the comprehensive character of the terminology breaks down over the difference of essence between spiritual and human beings, adding: "Granted that both the spirit being and the human magistrate have in common a sphere of power, . . . the spheres represent two distinct dimensions." Wesley Carr, *Angels and Principalities: The Background, Meaning, and Development of the Pauline Phrase hai archai kai hai exousiai*, Society for New Testament Study Monograph 42 (Cambridge: Cambridge University Press, 1981), 21, maintains that the language of power represents the angelic hosts of heaven and adds that Luke's portrait of the early church in Acts "is never characterised in terms of principalities and powers." Carr does not accept Eph 6:12 as original to the letter, but a second-century addition, thus removing from consideration the most damaging evidence against his thesis.

culture. The immediate context will shed further light on Paul's emphasis in the particular passage.

Magic is often brought into the discussion about powers and authorities. The concept of magic is difficult to define, as what looks like magic to one person might be religious rites to another.[172] Nevertheless, the definition of magic revolves around the use of power, and the illegitimate use of power would generally be labeled as magic. Magicians might be executed or hounded out of town as dangerous to its stability.[173] Women were more vulnerable to charges of using magic.[174] It was alleged that prostitutes used magic to gain customers and that wealthy women used it in treachery.[175] A famous

---

172. Resources for information on magic in the ancient world include Karl Preisendanz, *Papyri graecae magicae: Die griechischen Zauberpapyri*, 3 vols. (Berlin: Teubner, 1928–42; 2nd ed. Stuttgart: Heinrichs, 1973–74). See also David E. Aune, "Magic in Early Christianity," *ANRW* 23.1:1507–57; Hans Dieter Betz, ed., *The Greek Magical Papyri in Translation*, vol. 1: *Text* (Chicago: University of Chicago Press, 1986); Clinton E. Arnold, "Magic," *DPL* 580–83; Clinton E. Arnold, "Principalities and Powers," *ABD* 5:467; Gideon Bohak, *Ancient Jewish Magic: A History* (Cambridge: Cambridge University Press, 2008).

173. Matthew W. Dickie, *Magic and Magicians in the Greco-Roman World* (New York: Routledge, 2001), 150–53. Documents of magical spells were destroyed as well; see Suetonius, *Augustus* 31.1, who relates that in 13 BCE Augustus ordered that two thousand scrolls be burned.

174. Lynn H. Cohick, *Women in the World of the Earliest Christians: Illuminating Ancient Ways of Life* (Grand Rapids: Baker Academic, 2009), 192, 420–26. Elizabeth Ann Pollard, "Magic Accusations against Women in the Greco-Roman World from the First through the Fifth Centuries C.E." (PhD diss., University of Pennsylvania, 2001), 27, observes: "It is precisely a woman's perceived inability to dominate the summoned powers and carry through the penetrative force of some of the spells which renders her an inadequate subject of the ritual and makes her use of *magicae artes* so problematic and reprehensible to ancient contemporary commentators." See also Elizabeth Ann Pollard, "Magic Accusations against Women in Tacitus' *Annals*," in *Daughters of Hecate*, ed. Kimberly Stratton and Dayna Kalleres (New York: Oxford University Press, 2014), 183–218.

175. Tacitus, *Annals* 2.85, lists nine women accused before the Senate of performing magical arts. Arnold, *Ephesians: Power and Magic*, 14, focuses on the pervasiveness of magic in the ancient world in relation to the discussion about powers. Strelan, *Paul, Artemis, and the Jews in Ephesus*, 83–89, 156–62, critiques Arnold's theory, arguing that (1) there is little evidence that Artemis was seen as demonic and thus was dreaded by the Ephesians; (2) Arnold generalizes material from Egypt as relevant for Ephesus; and (3) Arnold does not take full account of the Jewish worldview underpinning the epistle. For material in *Ephesia Grammata*, see Fritz Graf, "Ephesia Grammata," in *Brill's New Pauly: Encyclopaedia of the Ancient World*, ed. Hubert Cancik, Helmuth Schneider, Christine F. Salazar (Leiden: Brill, 2004), 4:1023, who defines the *Ephesia Grammata* as "a series of words devoid of meaning . . . that was used orally and in writing for apotropaic and salvation-bringing purposes. Their name comes from the fact that they were engraved on the statue of Artemis of Ephesus," according to Pausanias in Eustathius, *Ad Odysseam* 19.247; Adolf Deissmann, "Ephesia Grammata," in *Abhandlung zur Semitischen Religionskunde und Sprachwissenschaft*, ed. W. Frankenburg and F. Küchler, Beihefte zur Zeitschrift für die alttestamentliche Wissenschaft 33 (Giessen: Töpelmann, 1918), 121–24.

INTRODUCTION

first-century CE magician, Apollonius of Tyana, performed exorcisms and also proclaimed to have divination powers.[176] He offered advice to the city of Ephesus when it was overcome with a plague. Apollonius gathered the city and urged them to stone a beggar who was later determined to be a demon.[177]

Against this general backdrop, Paul reassures the church that Christ is the supreme authority in the heavens and over all spiritual beings and magical incantations and powers. The Ephesian believers lived with the tensions created by the city's identity as the protector of Artemis's honor. Pagan affinity to magic and the promise of power over spiritual forces permeated the culture. Jews and gentiles mixed in the marketplace and debated in shops and synagogue. It was in these surroundings that they interpreted Ephesians.

D. JUDAISM IN EPHESUS

The letter's emphasis on unity between Jew and gentile in Christ fits with Ephesus's social makeup, which included a sizable Jewish population.[178] In the third century BCE, two thousand Jewish families from Judea and Galilee were resettled in the general area.[179] It is difficult to determine how many Jews lived in Ephesus in the first century CE. Estimates at the high end suggest between 5 percent and 15 percent of the total population, or about ten thousand to twenty-five thousand Jews.[180] A lower estimate puts the population at

---

176. Dickie, *Magic and Magicians in the Greco-Roman World*, 224, notes that exorcism is connected with magic in the ancient world, but that when the exorcism is done by someone from the author's group, it is not disparaged as magic. Josephus, *Jewish Antiquities* 8.2.5 §§42–49, speaks of Eleazar exorcizing a demon using Solomon's name.

177. Dickie, *Magic and Magicians in the Greco-Roman World*, 204. See Philostratus, *Life of Apollonius* 4.10.

178. John M. G. Barclay, *Jews in the Mediterranean Diaspora: From Alexander to Trajan* (Berkeley: University of California Press, 1999), 82–100, speaks of Jews engaging in the Hellenistic milieu as one of "assimilation, acculturation and accommodation." The Jewish community negotiated their cultic expressions and beliefs within the rise of the imperial cult. Barclay's ideas helpfully account for the historical realities better than the term "syncretism," for the latter term carries the inaccurate assumption that a pure Judaism existed over against which diaspora expressions of the religion could be judged. For a detailed discussion, see Shaye J. D. Cohen, *The Beginnings of Jewishness: Boundaries, Varieties, Uncertainties* (Berkeley: University of California Press, 1999); Erich S. Gruen, *Heritage and Hellenism: The Reinvention of Jewish Tradition* (Berkeley: University of California Press, 1998); Martin Hengel, *Judaism and Hellenism: Studies in Their Encounter in Palestine in the Early Hellenistic Period*, trans. John Bowden, 2 vols. (Philadelphia: Fortress, 1974).

179. Josephus, *Jewish Antiquities* 12.3.4 §§148–53.

180. Mikael Tellbe, *Christ-Believers in Ephesus: A Textual Analysis of Early Christian Identity Formation in Local Perspective*, WUNT 242 (Tübingen: Mohr Siebeck, 2009), 75.

several hundred.[181] The scant evidence is notoriously difficult to interpret, but it does indicate that the Jewish community was sufficient in size to warrant special treatment by the Romans.

In the first century BCE, Ephesian officials permitted Jews to keep their traditions and Sabbath and to send money to Jerusalem for sacrifices and the temple tax.[182] Jews who were Roman citizens were exempt from military service.[183] Josephus indicates that Jews met together, although no synagogue has been discovered in the city's excavations.[184] The documents reveal tensions between gentiles and Jews, seemingly resolved in the latter's favor by the beginning of the first century CE; at least we hear no more about conflicts from Josephus. Overall, the evidence suggests that Jews were allowed to practice their traditions, such as keeping Sabbath and maintaining food laws. Jews actively sought these privileges and stayed connected to Jerusalem through sending money for the temple tax and sacrifices.[185]

E. EPHESUS AND PAUL'S VISIT (ACTS 19)

According to the book of Acts, Paul lived in Ephesus for about three years. Paul does not refer to any events mentioned in Acts in his letter to the Ephesians (nor does he refer to his time in Philippi in the Letter to the Philippians; see Acts 16:11–40). We need not expect extensive overlap as the enterprises of letter writing and historiography address different concerns. Scholars debate the historical verisimilitude of Acts, yet it remains one of our few sources for earliest Christianity.[186] Questions have been raised concerning the usefulness of Acts in reconstructing the historical church, but sometimes these are grounded in ideological assessments about Luke's theology and view of salvation history.[187] It is not my purpose to determine the historical reliability

---

181. Trebilco, *Early Christians in Ephesus*, 50–51.

182. Josephus, *Jewish Antiquities* 14.10.11 §§223–27; 14.10.25 §§262–64; 16.6.2 §§162–73; Philo, *Allegorical Interpretation* 3.315–16.

183. Josephus, *Jewish Antiquities* 14.10.13–19 §§228–30, 234, 240.

184. Josephus, *Jewish Antiquities* 14.10.12 §227. See also Acts 18:19, 26; 19:8–9. Irina Levinskaya, *The Book of Acts in Its Diaspora Setting*, The Book of Acts in Its First Century Setting 5 (Grand Rapids: Eerdmans, 1996), 146, speculates that the synagogue is in the part of the city not yet excavated.

185. Trebilco, *Early Christians in Ephesus*, 39–41.

186. Keener, *Acts*, 27, explains: "For historians interested in earliest Christianity after Jesus, Acts is the only concrete extended source we have." Colin J. Hemer, *Book of Acts in the Setting of Hellenistic History* (Winona Lake, IN: Eisenbrauns, 1990), 1–29, offers an overview of views on the historicity of Acts.

187. Wright, *Paul and the Faithfulness of God*, 1:62.

INTRODUCTION

of the events during Paul's stay in Ephesus.[188] I include a brief discussion of Paul's Ephesus visit because it presents the tensions around Jew and gentile over matters of religion, as well as Paul's Jewish abhorrence of pagan magic, which fit well with other evidence about the cultural and social climate of ancient Roman cities. The events and interactions highlighted in Acts help readers today fill out their understanding of the ancient city and the effects that Paul, his coworkers, and the gospel message had within its midst.

In Acts 18:19–21, Paul indicates to local Jews in Ephesus that he will return to discuss further his claims about Jesus the Messiah. He and his coworkers, Priscilla and Aquila, stopped briefly in Ephesus on the last leg of Paul's second missionary journey before Paul traveled to Jerusalem.[189] Later, in his third journey, he remained in Ephesus for about three years. Acts 19:1–20:1 describes several events that seem typical of Paul's ministry, including acceptance of the gospel message, rejection of the same, and violent opposition to Paul's work. Paul spoke both in the synagogue and then for about two years in a lecture hall probably located in the commercial marketplace. It may be here that Epaphras heard the gospel message and then took it to Colossae, where he founded a church in that city. Paul's teaching was accompanied by miracles, healings, and exorcisms (19:11–12). It resulted in believers rejecting their pagan past by burning their magical texts (19:19).

Paul enjoyed support from at least a few wealthy gentiles, perhaps the Asiarchs, Paul's patrons who protected him when a riot broke out (19:31). But he made powerful enemies as well, including Demetrius the silversmith. Demetrius claims that his trade in silver amulets honoring Artemis is declining because Paul's preaching pulls people away from the goddess (19:27). His comment highlights the intimate connection between religion and economy in the ancient cities. Demetrius creates a commotion; a mob forms and grabs two of Paul's coworkers, dragging them to the theater. The disruption is significant and the town clerk rushes to calm it, for Ephesus could lose its self-governing status if they failed to keep the peace. The clerk downplays Demetrius's concerns, soothes the crowd, and Paul leaves the city quietly.[190]

---

188. Keener, *Acts*, 29, concludes: "Having worked through Acts from basic and accepted criteria for historical reconstruction, I believe that I can affirm that Luke was an acceptable and responsible historian by the standards of his contemporaries." For an alternative reading that dates Acts to ca. 115 CE, written from Ephesus, see Richard I. Pervo, *Acts: A Commentary*, Hermeneia (Minneapolis: Fortress, 2009).

189. Elif Hilal Karaman, *Ephesian Women in Greco-Roman and Early Christian Perspective*, WUNT 474 (Tübingen: Mohr Siebeck, 2018), 11, reflects on the "hybrid character" of the Ephesian society and looks at inscriptions primarily to examine "ancient Ephesian women in their varied and numerous roles" (18).

190. Keener, *Acts*, 212, argues that the riot in Ephesus "likely indicates historical tradition" as Luke would have little reason to invent the crisis, and he shows evidence of having

VI. DATE AND PROVENANCE OF EPHESIANS

Having laid out the issues, and established the viability of the traditional attributions of Pauline authorship and the provenance of Ephesus, we are left to discuss the city from which Paul wrote his letter and the other "prison epistles" of Colossians, Philemon, and Philippians. These four are treated together if Pauline authorship is assumed.[191] Philemon and Colossians include Timothy as a cosender and greet several of the same people. Ephesians and Colossians include Tychicus as the courier. Traditionally, Rome is understood as the city from which Paul wrote. This conclusion is linked to Paul's final arrest in Jerusalem and detainment in Rome, described in the last chapters of Acts. Recently, however, Ephesus has been put forward in a challenge of the traditional conclusion.

A. EPHESUS

Those who argue for an Ephesian imprisonment place the event at 55 or 56 CE, perhaps after the riot mentioned in Acts 19:40–41, for Paul seems to imply an imprisonment in his remark to the Corinthians that he faced wild beasts in Ephesus (1 Cor 15:32). Alleged travel difficulties in moving between Colossae and Rome also strengthen this theory. Finally, a central element in this theory involves Onesimus, Philemon's slave. Onesimus has been identified as a runaway slave, although the Epistle to Philemon does not state as much. Onesimus, it is argued, could get to Ephesus from Colossae with relative ease and lose himself in this busy city, while getting to Rome would be difficult.[192] After reaching Ephesus, Onesimus happens to be imprisoned with Paul and is converted by the gospel message. He and Paul begin working together, and Paul sends a letter to Philemon asking that he free his slave so that he could work more closely with Paul.

The Ephesus venue theory runs aground, however, on several points. First, and least important, we have no record of Paul's being imprisoned in Ephesus. This argument from silence is weak in part because Paul speaks of having many imprisonments and beatings (2 Cor 11:23), but Acts includes only

---

a wide body of information on which to draw in recounting the event, including names of individuals.

191. Cohick, 28: "Put simply, the problem involves *four* epistles . . . *three* interconnected lists of names, *two* very similar epistles (Ephesians and Colossians) and *one* author."

192. For the argument that Onesimus was not a runaway slave but was sent by Philemon to help Paul while in prison, see Cohick, 28–30. See also Craig S. Wansink, *Chained in Christ: The Experience and Rhetoric of Paul's Imprisonments*, JSNTSup 130 (Sheffield: Sheffield Academic Press, 1996), 176, 186–98.

a few incidents. Nevertheless, we cannot read the silence of Acts or Paul as an invitation to speculate on a significant imprisonment that was not mentioned by either source. Second, and more compelling, Paul's claim to fight wild beasts in Ephesus is most likely an example of hyperbole as he describes his human opponents (1 Cor 15:32). Paul's phrase "wild beasts" is part of a series of rhetorical questions, some of which are clearly counterfactual. He also qualifies the phrase with an additional note that can be translated "pertaining to human beings."[193] Paul's point is that he faced ferocious human opponents in debates about the gospel.[194] Third, it is difficult to imagine a Roman citizen facing beasts in the arena without first being stripped of his citizenship. And if Acts is wrong that Paul possessed Roman citizenship, it is still highly unlikely that Paul, an old man, could have survived beasts. If he did, one would think this miraculous event would be worth remembering within the church. Again, if Paul had Roman citizenship, he was unlikely to be imprisoned for any length of time before being released or sent to Rome for his hearing.[195]

Concerning Onesimus, several points render his status as a runaway unlikely. First, runaway slaves were not typically imprisoned, but captured and returned to their owners, often by bounty hunters. And the odds seem astronomical that in a city the size of Ephesus a slave would be imprisoned with Paul, a Roman citizen. Second, Paul would have no authority to retain a runaway slave, and his Roman guards would have no compunction in returning Onesimus immediately to his owner. Third, the assumption that Onesimus stole from his owner cannot be substantiated by the letter, for Paul does not indicate Onesimus's repentance for such an act. The suggestion that Onesimus stole is in line with ancient assumptions about the character of slaves and thus could be an example of exegetes' prejudices slipping into the argument. Fourth, Paul's letter reveals something not usually taken into consideration today, namely, that in the ancient world, a freedman was still beholden to his or her owner. Paul's letter makes the request not only for Onesimus's freedom, but also for the freedom to serve with Paul. I think it more likely that Philemon sent Onesimus to Rome to help Paul, in much the same way as the Philippian church sent Epaphroditus (Phil 2:25).[196] This explains why Paul does not inform Philemon of his slave's whereabouts—Philemon knew where Onesimus was. It also explains why Paul states to Philemon that he

---

193. Εἰ κατὰ ἄνθρωπον. English translation from Witherington, 526.

194. Dio Chrysostom, Homily 40 on 1 Corinthians. For a general discussion, see Abraham J. Malherbe, *Paul and the Popular Philosophers* (Minneapolis: Fortress, 1989), 79–89.

195. Wansink, *Chained in Christ*, 29, cites examples of men confined for extensive time in prison as punishment for especially terrible crimes or to satisfy the emperor's cruelty (cf. Suetonius, *Tiberius* 61.5).

196. Wansink, *Chained in Christ*, 193. Less likely is the possibility that Onesimus seeks Paul to be a mediator between himself and Philemon; see Cohick, 28–30.

would rather not send back Onesimus at that time (Phlm 12–14).[197] Paul was impressed with Onesimus, and he hoped Philemon would consider releasing the latter to Paul.

And perhaps the most compelling reason against Paul writing Ephesians from Ephesus is the very oddity that one would write to people who are in the same location. In fact, often those who promote an Ephesus provenance for Colossians and Philemon suggest that Paul wrote Ephesians from Rome, or that another wrote Ephesians based on Paul's letter to the Colossians, copying the note about Tychicus delivering the letters.

B. ROME

Several factors favor Rome as the place where Paul wrote Ephesians during his imprisonment of 60–62 (Acts 28:30–31). First, it would be the only city where Paul, as a Roman citizen, could receive adjudication on his case. Second, the description in Acts of Paul imprisoned and receiving visitors matches the picture painted at the end of Colossians where Paul interacted with several coworkers (Acts 28:30–31; Col 4:7–14). Third, travel between major cities in Paul's day was faster and more common than we think. The traveler going from Colossae to Rome would pass through Ephesus, about 120 miles from Colossae. From Ephesus the traveler could take a boat across the Aegean Sea to Corinth, then on to Rome, perhaps in about three weeks, depending on weather.[198] Fourth, if Onesimus were a runaway, he could escape detection more easily in Rome. It would be more difficult to hide in the smaller city of Ephesus, which was also closer to Colossae, his hometown. Given that it would involve only a five-day journey, Onesimus's owner, Philemon, would be much more tempted to go after him and likely had connections in Ephesus that would aid in his search.

VII. STRUCTURE OF EPHESIANS

The examination of specific formal features and their purposes in the ancient epistle greatly advance our interpretation of its content. Having a clear sense of the general characteristics also alerts us to variations made by Paul that

---

197. The verb ἀναπέμπω (Phlm 12) is used to indicate the return of a messenger; see 1 Clem 65:1; Josephus, *Jewish War* 2.11.2 §207; 2.17.10 §451; *Jewish Antiquities* 6.9.4 §293.

198. Lionel Casson, *Travel in the Ancient World* (Baltimore: Johns Hopkins University Press, 1994), 150–52.

highlight his intentions and emphases. Focusing on the form as well as theological or historical themes offers a solid foundation for study.

A. ANALYSIS OF LETTER

Before turning our attention to the ancient letter's structure, we should distinguish epistolary analysis from rhetorical criticism, as both look at the literary composition of a text. Rhetorical criticism draws on Greco-Roman speech conventions, generally classified as judicial, epideictic, and deliberative.[199] The speech is structured in four basic parts: *exordium, narratio, probatio, peroratio*.[200] The orator seeks to connect with the audience through *ethos, pathos,* and *logos*. New Testament epistles have been studied as rhetorical speeches with greetings and closing attached.[201] Nevertheless, three significant cautions must be raised. First, although Paul clearly used rhetorical devices, we cannot assume that he was highly educated in the art of rhetoric. Second, the first-century Roman world used written material extensively, and even those who were unable to read functioned within a literate culture that produced books and receipts. Third, the ancient sources themselves distinguish between epistolary form and rhetoric. Epistolary theory was treated as a separate category and was not considered when dealing with rhetorical theory in the ancient handbooks.[202] It is unlikely, therefore, that the ancient readers/listeners of Paul's letters would have expected formal rhetorical compositions. Instead, they would be familiar with the typical letter-writing practices.[203]

The ancient world differentiated types of letters based on content and audience, and the distinctions should be seen as on a continuum, rather than as sharply distinguished categories. Literary letters or letter-essays were ad-

---

199. Stanley K. Stowers, *Letter Writing in Greco-Roman Antiquity* (Philadelphia: Westminster, 1986), 51–53, describes the categories and discusses the limitations of using rhetorical categories in analyzing ancient letters.

200. Lincoln, xliii–xliv, offers an outline of Ephesians using these four rhetorical speech conventions.

201. Witherington, 216–23. See also Lincoln, xlii. Witherington's general approach is critiqued by Stanley E. Porter and Bryan R. Dyer, "Oral Texts? A Reassessment of the Oral Rhetorical Nature of Paul's Letters in Light of Recent Studies," *Journal of the Evangelical Theology Study* 55.2 (2012): 336: "Oratory and epistolary theories were understood as two distinct disciplines and any formal overlap occurred much later than the time of Paul's compositions."

202. Carl Joachim Classen, *Rhetorical Criticism of the New Testament*, WUNT 128 (Tübingen: Mohr Siebeck, 2000), 23–26.

203. Michael F. Bird, "Reassessing a Rhetorical Approach to Paul's Letters," *Expository Times* 119.9 (2008): 376, provides a helpful summary of the arguments cautioning against heavy reliance on rhetorical handbooks for interpreting Paul's letters.

dressed to the public at large and conveyed general information, propaganda, or philosophical ideas.[204] These essays used the letter format as one option among others to get their message across.[205] Included in this category would be the literary letters of Epicurus, which are better described as philosophical treatises with epistolary openings and closings.[206] Paul's letters, while showing some evidence of elevated style in places, do not fit well into this category.[207] A second category included personal or official letters targeting a specific audience, who could be personally known or unknown to the author. These documentary letters addressed a particular context, offering specific information, recommendations, or advice. Personal letters presumed an intimate relationship with the recipients. Paul's letters fit well in this grouping. A third classification are those fictitious letters created often for entertainment or as school lessons, wherein the writer impersonates another, typically famous person.[208] Pseudepigraphic letters were discussed above when examining the authorship of Ephesians, and I argue that Paul's letters did not match this category.

The ancient letter is said to be composed of three, four, or five parts. All letters have an opening, body, and closing. Most include a thanksgiving after the opening. The paraenetic material could be counted as a separate section alongside the body.[209] By and large, Pauline letters share the basic structure:

204. Richards, *Paul and First-Century Letter Writing*, 122, concludes: "Public letters were essays in letter form. They were artificial and were intended to be disseminated widely."

205. M. Luther Stirewalt Jr., *Studies in Ancient Greek Epistolography*, SBL Resources for Biblical Studies 27 (Atlanta: Scholars Press, 1993), 4–12. Stowers, *Letter Writing*, 19, cautions against a sharp demarcation between literary, public letters and nonliterary, private letters.

206. Epicurus's letters are preserved in Diogenes Laertius's *Lives of the Philosophers* 10.35–83, 84–116, 122–35. Reece, *Paul's Large Letters*, 22, includes Dionysius of Halicarnassus in this category.

207. Reece, *Paul's Large Letters*, 25, concludes: "Paul's letters..., while in some cases achieving great length and rising stylistically to an ambitious literary level, remained in essence functional letters addressed and sent to historical recipients and framed by the epistolary conventions more commonly found in the situational letters of the documentary papyri." Paul M. Robertson, *Paul's Letters and Contemporary Greco-Roman Literature: Theorizing a New Taxonomy*, Supplements to Novum Testamentum 167 (Leiden: Brill, 2016), 217, suggests that Paul had a handbook-level awareness of rhetoric and that his social and literary environment was similar to that of Epictetus.

208. Reece, *Paul's Large Letters*, 20, briefly touches on the collections of Greek letters attributed to ancient philosophers and famous people, but that were written in the Hellenistic and Roman periods for entertainment, propagation of moral teachings, and as school exercises.

209. Stowers, *Letter Writing*, 95, explains the complexity of distinguishing paraenesis from advice and suggests that the former "requires some type of positive relationship, e.g., that of parent and child, or friendship."

INTRODUCTION

opening address, greeting/thanksgiving, body (including paraenesis), and closing.[210] Paul modifies the typical opening, thanksgiving, and closing to emphasize his gospel message.[211] The thanksgiving foreshadows the epistle's message, and the closing highlights the major points covered in the body. The opening in Ephesians has significant textual variants, which I have discussed above and in the commentary proper. The closing in Ephesians also deserves a word, because it is unclear exactly where it begins. Alongside final greetings and a peace benediction in 6:21–24, we find a hortatory injunction in 6:10 that begins "finally," which could signal the start of the closing. Several of Paul's letters use a hortatory closing—including Philippians, 2 Corinthians, and Galatians. At issue in Ephesians is whether the command to put on the armor of God is part of the letter's closing or part of the paraenetic section. If deemed part of the closing, then the message about standing firm in God's armor sums up the epistle's message, but evidence for this is weak.

The body holds the substance and assertions of the letter, and its structure is driven in large part by the content. Nevertheless, there are stock phrases and typical transitions that organize the argument.[212] Specific formulas guide the reader, including the appeal ("I appeal to you"), the disclosure ("I want you to know"), the "now about" transition, and liturgical elements.[213] Paul uses this stereotypical language throughout Ephesians, and it helps shape and advance his argument. For example, he appeals or "urges" the Ephesians in 4:1 as he launches into the paraenetic section. He asks that they "remember" their former life in paganism (2:11) as he develops his argument on the work of Christ for Jews and gentiles. He offers a

---

210. Richards, *Paul and First-Century Letter Writing*, 127–30, explains the basic three-part structure of opening, body, closing. Weima, *Paul the Ancient Letter Writer*, 9, postulates four sections, including paraenesis within the letter's body. William G. Doty, *Letters in Primitive Christianity* (Philadelphia: Fortress, 1973; repr. Eugene, OR: Wipf & Stock, 2014), 27–47, argues for five-part format. Interestingly, the oldest surviving handbook on letter writing does not discuss the formal components of the letter; see Pseudo-Demetrius, Τύποι Ἐπιστολικοί. Stowers, *Letter Writing*, 53, explains Pseudo-Demetrius's mission to describe epistolary types and generic formulas that correspond to the author's situation determined by the "relationship to the recipient of the letter, the current status of the relationship, and the particular occasion for writing."

211. Weima, *Paul the Ancient Letter Writer*, 82, comments on the absence of a thanksgiving in Galatians and explains that the recipients would have been surprised at the lack of a wish for good health and safety and a prayer on their behalf, as both were common in ancient letters.

212. Stowers, *Letter Writing*, 56, concludes: "The modern student of ancient letters should understand both the limitations and the logic which the various types represent and the enormous flexibility in composition which they allow."

213. Weima, *Paul the Ancient Letter Writer*, 92–123. See also Richards, *Paul and First-Century Letter Writing*, 130–34.

prayer (3:14–19) and a doxology (3:20–21) as he closes the body and moves to the paraenetic part of the letter.

The body of the letter addresses the theological argument and the paraenesis, which focuses on moral formation and ethics.[214] This pattern is clearly seen in Romans, where in chapters 1–11 Paul discusses in great detail God's salvation plan and in 12:1 begins an explanation of the ethical and moral ramifications of his theological argument.[215] We find a similar structure in Ephesians, with a compelling theological argument in chapters 1–3, and chapters 4–6 urging a holy life in community as Christ's body, the church. In both letters, Paul uses the verb "to urge" and the adverb "therefore" as he moves ahead with imperatives based on his previously argued theology (Rom 12:1; Eph 4:1). I say more about the theology of Ephesians both in my summary of the argument and as it pertains to the authorship question. Here I will pursue the question of the paraenesis as it relates to the letter's identification and structure.

Two basic arguments for understanding paraenesis are put forward by scholars. On the one hand, the term is defined as a type of content, namely, philosophical claims about morality and ethics. The format or genre is secondary and incidental to the meaning of the term.[216] The philosophical letter-essay attaches epistolary trappings to what is aimed at an extended audience, made suitable to multiple contexts as it develops general moral truths and ethical teachings. The author represents himself as a philosopher explaining the reasonable, moral life. Examples include Pseudo-Isocrates and Seneca's letters to his friend Lucilius, which demonstrate the philosopher's astute grasp of philosophical dilemmas but reveals very little personal information about the recipient or his context.[217]

On the other hand, we have ancient sources referring to paraenesis as "a style of writing rather than a form of philosophy."[218] In this case, the focus

---

214. Perkins, 94, explains that the term "paraenesis" is transliterated from the Greek term παραίνεσις, which means "moral advice or admonition."

215. Best, 353, observes that both Rom 12:1 and Eph 4:1 begin a new section and "in both the summons to behavior is followed first by a general but brief exhortation (Eph 4.2f; Rom 12.1f) and then by a reference to the church (Eph 4.4–16; Rom 12.3–8) before the detailed ethical instruction is given."

216. Andrew W. Pitts, "Philosophical and Epistolary Contexts for Pauline Paraenesis," in *Paul and the Ancient Letter Form*, ed. Stanley E. Porter and Sean A. Adams (Leiden: Brill, 2010), 272.

217. Pitts, "Philosophical and Epistolary Contexts," 279, cites Seneca, *Epistles* 89.13; 94.1; 95.1.

218. Pitts, "Philosophical and Epistolary Contexts," 286. This theory is traced to H. Lietzmann, *An die Römer*, Handbuch zum Neuen Testament 8 (Tübingen: Mohr Siebeck, 1971); and M. Dibelius, *Der Brief des Jakobus*, Kritisch-exegetischer Kommentar über das Neue Testament 15 (Göttingen: Vandenhoeck & Ruprecht, 1964).

INTRODUCTION

is on direct advice about specific situations. The epistolary paraenesis relies on the letter genre to convey specific moral teachings to specific audiences, addressing specific contexts. Examples of this sort of paraenesis are found in nonliterary letters written to directly or indirectly known audiences. The moral and ethical teachings are generated out of the crucible of everyday life and extenuating circumstances that require direct attention. As such, they have a bit of an ad hoc flavor, as these ethical injunctions are put forth with specific goals to direct or redirect behaviors and attitudes and not to promote a philosophical tradition to a wider audience.

A strong case can be made that the Pauline corpus fits into the category of epistolary paraenesis, for several reasons. First, the overall pattern of extensive, lengthy theology followed by exhortations is not found in literary letters or in the philosophical letter-essays.[219] Second, Paul addresses specific situations that reveal particular knowledge of the recipients' state of affairs. His instructions directly deal with questions and challenges faced by his churches. We learn about the circumstances and attitudes of the audience, as Paul's injunctions, warnings, and advice address their issues. Third, both philosophical letter-essays and epistolary paraenesis share common features, including the pattern of thesis/antithesis and the language of "knowing," "remembering," "friendship," and "imitation." Therefore, one cannot use these traits to argue for a philosophical letter-essay parallel in Paul. Fourth, Paul's letters are generally much longer and more complex than both the philosophical letter-essay and the epistolary paraenetic texts. Paul's innovation serves his purposes. He locates his ethics within God's redemption story. And he establishes or strengthens bonds of friendship and fellowship with his congregations, as the letter represents his presence among them. Establishing the paraenetic section as intrinsically connected to the body and as part of the nonliterary epistolary paraenetic category, with its link to Hellenistic moral instruction (rather than philosophy), helps define authorship possibilities. Specifically, this evidence allows for Pauline authorship for Ephesians.

B. OUTLINE OF LETTER

The letter can be subdivided into two halves, the first focused on praising God for his glorious provision of salvation, and the second attending to the transformation of believers to live a life consistent with their holy God.[220] The dif-

---

219. Stirewalt, *Studies in Ancient Greek Epistolography*, 156.

220. Käsemann, "Epheserbrief," 517, argues that Eph 1 is a separate opening section similar to Paul's opening thanksgiving sections in the genuine epistles. Gerhard Sellin, "Epheserbrief," in *Religion in Geschichte und Gegenwart*, ed. Hans Dieter Betz, 4th ed. (Tübingen:

ference in verb tenses also demonstrates the epistle's halves. Gustavo Martín-Asensio explains that in Eph 1–3 there is a similar number of present and aorist tenses, but from Eph 4–6 the number of present tense forms is about double the aorist forms.[221] He observes that aorist tenses are used when speaking about "the acts of God or Christ on their [believers'] behalf *without* a hortatory or paraenetic (exhortative) emphasis."[222] And I would add that aspectual theory contends that the aorist does not refer to past time, but to the totality of the event or action. This basic structure of Ephesians, nevertheless, does not prevent Paul from weaving theological and didactic threads throughout the epistle.[223] Most prominent are the references to being "in Christ" and its underpinning conviction that God's love drives his redemptive plan. Also pervasive is the apocalyptic picture of two ages and contentious spiritual forces whose efforts will be decisively defeated in God's ultimate plan of unity in Christ.

VIII. OUTLINE OF THE COMMENTARY

I. Paul's Opening Greeting (1:1–2)

II. Theological Explication of the Gospel (1:3–3:21)
   A. Eulogy and Prayer (1:3–23)
      1. Thanksgiving to God Through Christ (1:3–14)
         a. Adopted by the Father (1:3–6)
         b. Redeemed by the Son (1:7–12)
         c. Sealed by the Holy Spirit (1:13–14)
      2. God's Work through Christ's Rule over All Things (1:15–23)
         a. Prayer for the Ephesians (1:15–19)
         b. God Raised and Exalted Christ (1:20–23)
   B. The Riches of His Grace (2:1–22)
      1. God's Grace Rescues Humanity (2:1–10)

Mohr Siebeck, 1999), 2:1345, nuances Käsemann's position by describing 1:3–14 as the epistle's overture and by suggesting a chiastic structure between Eph 1 and Eph 3. John Paul Heil, *Ephesians: Empowerment to Walk in Love for the Unity of All in Christ*, SBL Studies in Biblical Literature 13 (Atlanta: SBL, 2007), 13, argues that the letter reveals an "extended chiastic structure."

221. Gustavo Martín-Asensio, *Transitivity-Based Foregrounding in the Acts of the Apostles: A Functional-Grammatical Approach to the Lukan Perspective*, JSNTSup 202 (Sheffield: Sheffield Academic Press, 2000), 44.

222. Martín-Asensio, *Transitivity-Based Foregrounding*, 45.

223. Barth, 55–56, suggests a tripartite division of the letter's body into the following three units: 1:15–2:22; 3:1–4:24; 4:25–6:20.

Introduction

        a. Human Plight in the Present Age (2:1–3)
        b. God's Actions in Christ for Believers (2:4–7)
        c. God's Gift of Grace (2:8–10)
     2. Christ Is Our Peace (2:11–22)
        a. Gentiles Far from God (2:11–13)
        b. Christ Creates One New People (2:14–18)
        c. Christ Builds His Church (2:19–22)
  C. Mystery of Salvation Revealed (3:1–21)
     1. Digression Concerning the Revealed Mystery (3:1–13)
        a. Paul's Insight into the Mystery (3:1–5)
        b. Mystery of Gentile Participation in Christ (3:6–7)
        c. Paul's Sufferings for Gentiles' Glory (3:8–13)
     2. Prayer to Be Established in Christ's Love (3:14–21)
        a. Paul Prays to the Father of All (3:14–15)
        b. Paul Prays for Christ's Love (3:16–19)
        c. Paul Glorifies the Father (3:20–21)

III.   Exhortation to Holy Living (4:1–6:20)
  A. Walk Worthy of Your Calling (4:1–32)
     1. Unity in One Spirit, One Lord, One Father (4:1–6)
     2. Christ's Gift to the Church (4:7–16)
        a. Christ Descended and Ascended (4:7–10)
        b. Christ's Body Grows to Fullness (4:11–16)
     3. Put on the New Self (4:17–24)
     4. Speak Truth with Compassion (4:25–32)
  B. Walk as Christ Walked (5:1–21)
     1. Follow God's Example (5:1–2)
     2. Inherit the Kingdom (5:3–6)
     3. Darkness and Light (5:7–14)
     4. Be Filled with the Holy Spirit (5:15–21)
  C. The Household Codes (5:21–6:9)
     1. Wife and Husband (5:21–33)
        a. Instructions to Wives (5:21–24)
        b. Instructions to Husbands (5:25–33)
     2. Children and Parents (6:1–4)
     3. Slaves and Masters (6:5–9)
  D. Armor of God (6:10–20)
     1. Be Strong in the Lord (6:10–13)
     2. Put On God's Armor (6:14–17)
     3. Pray in the Spirit (6:18–20)

IV.   Final Greetings (6:21–24)

IX. THEOLOGY OF EPHESIANS

Paul narrates a plot that began with the creation of the world and time and includes God's redemption of his people from sin and their relational distance from God. Paul explains that the gospel message was established when creation began. This story assumes that sin entered God's creation. The salvation plan centers on the cross and resurrection of the Lord Jesus Christ, who not only offers redemption but also creates unity across the cosmos and between Jew and gentile. However, full unity is not yet accomplished, and powers aligned against God are currently ruling the present age. The apocalyptic undertones echo in the call to resist the evil days of darkness and disobedience and to put on God's armor and stand fast for good.

Paul's redemption story has two final chapters. The penultimate one is being written by the church now, as believers mature and are transformed by the work of Christ. These people are sealed by the Holy Spirit so as to enjoy the final chapter of this redemption story, namely, the fully realized kingdom of God, wherein Christ brings all things to unity in himself. Having laid out the narrative, Paul also offers a guide for addressing life in this penultimate chapter. His advice reflects life in the spiritual realm, with the powers and authorities, as well as in the mundane physical world. This present time and space is contested as evil vies for power and influence. But God has prevailed over death, Christ is raised and exalted, and the Spirit's seal is effective and trustworthy. The time will come when all things are taken up in Christ, who brings unity and establishes his kingdom, the kingdom of God.

A. PAUL'S USE OF THE OLD TESTAMENT

Paul's understanding of the gospel is deeply rooted in Scripture, which frames his understanding of God's work in the world. Alongside the few quotations of the Old Testament in Ephesians, we have allusions and presuppositions about spiritual and natural reality taken from its pages.[224] As such, we would shortchange our exegesis if we viewed Paul as prooftexting from the Bible, for Scripture richly infuses Paul's ideas. To get the most from his message,

---

224. Earlier scholarship distanced Paul from the Old Testament as influential for his gentile ministry. See Adolf von Harnack, "Das Alte Testament in den Paulinischen Briefen und in den Paulinischen Gemeinden," *Sitzungsberichte der Preussischen Akademie der Wissenschaften* (1928): 124–41; Rudolf Bultmann, "The Significance of the Old Testament for Christian Faith," in *The Old Testament and Christian Faith: A Theological Discussion*, ed. and trans. Bernard W. Anderson (New York: Harper & Row, 1963), 17, who concludes that the Old Testament "speaks to *a particular people who stand in a particular ethnic history (Volksgeschichte) which is not ours*" (emphasis original).

we need to see his citations and allusions in their Old Testament context and explore how Paul elucidates the gospel based on his Old Testament reading.[225]

Paul's picture of God's salvation of his people and his victory over evil develop in conversation with Scripture from which echoes and allusions sound throughout the six chapters of Ephesians, drawing especially on the Ten Commandments, the prophet Isaiah, and the Psalms. Paul's understanding of the church takes shape as he reflects on Scripture. For example, Paul begs the Ephesians not to live as the gentiles do (Eph 4:17; see also 1 Cor 12:2); he invites them to imagine themselves as part of the people of God, adopted into God's family (Eph 2:19). When we read that God the Father places all things under Christ the Son's feet (1:22), we are drawn to Ps 8:6 (= 8:7 MT, LXX) and 110:1 (= 109:1 LXX). These passages are used by Peter in the Pentecost address (Acts 2:34–35), by the author of Hebrews in describing Christ (Heb 2:6–8), and by Paul's letter to the Corinthians when describing the culmination of this present age and the establishment of God's kingdom (1 Cor 15:25). When Paul speaks of Christ giving gifts (Eph 4:7), he likely draws on Ps 68:18. Paul highlights phrases within a hymn of praise to the God who saves, who with his tens of thousands of chariots establishes his throne and blesses his people. The picture of gentiles far from God, now drawn near through Christ (Eph 2:13, 17), evokes Isaiah's promise that God will offer peace to those far and near and heal them (Isa 57:19). Paul enjoins believers to put on God's armor as they stand fast against the evil of the present age, drawing on Isa 59. There is little question that Isaiah served as Paul's conversation partner, especially Isa 40–55. Paul's creative reflection on Gen 2:24 develops his understanding of the church's unity in Christ (Eph 5:31–32). The charge for children to honor their parents (6:1–4) is found in the Decalogue and invites reflection on the covenant story of God's people, the children of Abraham, and their call to live holy before their God (Exod 20:1–17; Deut 5:6–21). Paul's comment that believers control their anger (Eph 4:26) echoes Ps 4:4, which calls for the faithful to trust in God, who will grant them peace and safety.

Paul reads Scripture eschatologically, and he builds his ecclesiology around his findings.[226] The collections of Scripture citations and echoes have in common an eschatological thrust, emphasizing God's future plans to save his people and judge wrongdoers. Paul interprets Scripture from his vantage

---

225. Richard B. Hays, *The Conversion of the Imagination: Paul as Interpreter of Israel's Scripture* (Grand Rapids: Eerdmans, 2005), 2, explains metalepsis as the "rhetorical and poetic device in which one text alludes to an earlier text in a way that evokes resonances of the earlier text *beyond those explicitly cited*" (emphasis original). He argues that Paul uses metalepsis, citing part of a text to call to mind the whole.

226. Hays, *Conversion of the Imagination*, 6.

point as an apostle to the gentiles, seeing in Christ the fulfillment of God's promise and his warnings of judgment. The gentile members of the congregation have a new past, and the Jewish believers have a new future—together they must renew their imagination based on the cross and resurrection. Paul urges the Ephesians not to live as gentiles, a clear expression of his deep conviction that Christ has formed a new people that is also a continuation of the ancient people called by God to follow faithfully. While we do not meet Abraham or Moses by name in Ephesians, Paul's language of adoption and inheritance, as well as his references to circumcision and Israel and covenant, all invite readers to pause over the significant events found in Genesis, Exodus, Deuteronomy, and later in the Psalms and Isaiah.

The Psalms foretell that God will rule over his enemies, and Isaiah reinforces that God will vanquish his foes. Paul sees himself in the moment of fulfillment as God brings to pass the salvation, peace, and holiness promised in Scripture. If we pull together the allusions, we find that the wider contexts call to mind God's powerful victory over his foes, his mercy to the faithful, and the suggestion that time can be divided into "before" and "after": before God executes judgment and after. Paul overlays the gospel onto this grid, such that the end is now somewhat at hand, as gentiles are included in the faithful community. And Paul sees the apocalyptic victory over spiritual forces still to come.

Given Paul's strong eschatological reading of Scripture, it is difficult to see Ephesians as expressing a realized eschatology. A robust eschatology drives his view of the church. And his apocalyptic accent offers an appropriate warning of the dangers that befall those who neglect so great a salvation and continue under the rule of the prince of this present age.

B. CHRISTOLOGY OR THEOLOGY?

New Testament studies is presently embroiled in a debate about whether Paul demonstrates a high or a low Christology. The discussion centers on questions about the divine status of Jesus Christ and how positions changed and developed within the first centuries of the church. The views reflecting on Jesus's divinity can be grouped into three basic categories. First, some argue for a slow development of the claim of his divinity.[227] Those holding to a low Christology suggest that the earliest believers, Jews in Judea and Galilee, understood Jesus as God's human agent and prophet. Jewish monotheism, this view proposes, prohibited any claims of Jesus's divinity. As gentiles grew in

---

227. Bart Ehrman, *How Jesus Became God: The Exaltation of a Jewish Preacher from Galilee* (San Francisco: HarperCollins, 2014).

number within the church, opinions shifted toward Jesus having qualities of God, leading eventually to the conviction that Christ is fully divine.

Second, others suggest Paul's letters include an implicit reference to the incarnation of Jesus, labeled as "Adam Christology" by James D. G. Dunn.[228]

The third position, often identified as "early high Christology," suggests that Paul and his contemporaries within the Jesus movement held that Jesus was divine and thus worshiped him.[229] Larry Hurtado argues that Paul's claim that every knee will bow to Jesus as Lord (Phil 2:9–11), an act of worship, points to a reshaping of the understanding of God.[230] Hurtado speaks of the "triadic nature" of God within New Testament texts, including Paul's letters.[231] This "triadic" label captures several claims that Paul holds together, namely, that the God of the Old Testament cannot be rightly understood apart from Jesus the Messiah and the Spirit who is the agent and means that makes present God and Jesus to believers. Hurtado adds that the New Testament's characterization of the three in this triadic relationship is "relatively stable/fixed."[232]

A high Christology challenges the definition of monotheism used by the low Christology position, for the latter position asserts monotheism as a belief in only one god who is the single deity. The high Christology position rightly reminds us that monotheism as claimed by first-century Jews was a declaration of the one true God over against the pagan deities and thus involved decisions about worship and loyalty. High Christology posits that

---

228. James D. G. Dunn, *Christology in the Making: A New Testament Inquiry into the Origins of the Doctrine of the Incarnation*, 2nd ed. (Grand Rapids: Eerdmans, 1996); James D. G. Dunn, *The Theology of Paul the Apostle* (Grand Rapids: Eerdmans, 1998); James D. G. Dunn, *Did the First Christians Worship Jesus? The New Testament Evidence* (Louisville: Westminster John Knox, 2010).

229. Martin Hengel, "Christology and New Testament Chronology: A Problem in the History of Earliest Christianity," in *Between Jesus and Paul: Studies in the History of Earliest Christianity*, trans. John Bowden (London: SCM, 1983); Martin Hengel, *The Son of God: The Origin of Christology and the History of Jewish-Hellenistic Religion*, trans. John Bowden (London: SCM, 1975); Larry W. Hurtado, *One God, One Lord: Early Christian Devotion and Ancient Jewish Monotheism*, 2nd ed. (London: T&T Clark, 1998); Larry W. Hurtado, *Lord Jesus Christ: Devotion to Jesus in Earliest Christianity* (Grand Rapids: Eerdmans, 2003); Michael F. Bird et al., eds., *How God Became Jesus: The Real Origins of Belief in Jesus' Divine Nature* (Grand Rapids: Zondervan, 2014).

230. Larry W. Hurtado, *God in New Testament Theology* (Nashville: Abingdon, 2010), 46, writes: "One cannot adequately worship 'God' without including Jesus explicitly as a divinely authorized recipient of worship."

231. Hurtado, *God in New Testament Theology*, 45, 99; see also 129n6, which credits Arthur William Wainwright, *The Trinity in the New Testament* (London: SPCK, 1962), 248, with the term "triadic." See also Gordon Fee, *Pauline Christology: An Exegetical-Theological Study* (Peabody, MA: Hendrickson, 2007), 591, who speaks of "Paul and the Divine Triad."

232. Hurtado, *God in New Testament Theology*, 101.

the first Jewish believers understood Jesus Christ as God's divine agent and worthy of worship. Some in this camp build on divine figures such as the angel of the Lord (Gen 22:11–18) and the character of Wisdom (Prov 8:12–31), determining that these figures seem to be an extension or expression of God in some way.[233] Both low and high Christology views emphasize that Paul remained tightly tied to his Jewish monotheism, such that God's identity persisted unchanged, even as his actions in raising Jesus Christ from the dead modified Paul's understanding of God's salvific acts in history.

Several voices suggest that the high versus low Christology structure imposes a limited grid and fails to account for aspects of Paul's thought. The argument rightly claims that Paul does not typically describe Jesus Christ apart from God, except when speaking about Christ's church.[234] Said another way, Paul did not begin with a static monotheism into which he slotted Jesus.[235] Instead, Paul's views of God interacted with those he held of Jesus Christ, the Lord and the Son, defining and redefining both.[236] We see this especially in Paul's discussion of Christ's death and resurrection, which demonstrates, in creative and powerful ways, the grace and love of God.[237] Divine identity can be ascertained by seeing what God does and what God is not. God is the creator of all that is and is the God who calls a people to himself. Jesus Christ is described as having all things created in him, through him, and for him (Col 1:16) and to be exalted after his resurrection (Eph 1:20). Early Christians drew on Scripture such as Ps 110:1 and Deut 6:4 (the

---

233. David B. Capes, *The Divine Christ: Paul, the Lord Jesus, and the Scriptures of Israel* (Grand Rapids: Baker Academic, 2018), 42–43. Richard Bauckham, *God Crucified: Monotheism and Christology in the New Testament* (Grand Rapids: Eerdmans, 1998), 27–29, sharply disagrees with this position: "The key to the way in which Jewish monotheism and high Christology were compatible in the early Christian movement is . . . the recognition that its understanding of the unique identity of the one God left room for the inclusion of Jesus in that identity."

234. Neil Richardson, *Paul's Language about God*, JSNTSup 99 (Sheffield: Sheffield Academic Press, 1994), 24: "Christology, in fact, is a misleading term, in that it might imply that statements or words about Christ can somehow be studied in isolation from their surrounding language."

235. Wesley Hill, *Paul and the Trinity: Persons, Relations, and the Pauline Letters* (Grand Rapids: Eerdmans, 2015), 2–24, persuasively argues that the "high or low" vertical axis model falsely presupposes a static monotheism that Paul inherited and embraced from Judaism.

236. Francis Watson, "The Triune Divine Identity: Reflections on Pauline God-Language, in Disagreement with J. D. G. Dunn," *Journal for the Study of the New Testament* 23.80 (March 2001): 104, challenges Dunn's low Christology, arguing that "far from merely assuming or reproducing pre-Christian Jewish views of God, Paul's texts everywhere assert or assume a distinctively Christian view of God."

237. Richardson, *Paul's Language*, 307, explains that "language about Christ in turn redefines the identity of God."

Shema) to conceptualize Christ's identity as uniquely divine in the manner of Israel's God.[238] Ephesians' allusions to Ps 110:1 (Eph 1:20–22; 2:6) and to Israel's confession (4:4–6) should be seen in this light.

Rather than use categories of monotheism and Christology, Wesley Hill appeals to the relation between the Father, Son, and Holy Spirit—that is, drawing on Trinitarian concepts to elucidate Paul's thought.[239] Hill argues that readers should focus on the relationship described between the figures of God, Christ, and the Holy Spirit, rather than on the vertical axis moving from human to absolute Deity.[240] His work rightly concludes that one cannot speak about the identity of God the Father without also at the same time implicating and involving the identity of Christ Jesus the Son and the Holy Spirit.[241] God and Christ are understood in relation to each other and take their identity from that relationship. The eternal God is eternally the Father; therefore, the Son is eternal. The Son is part of God's plan established before time to adopt believers through him.[242] The focus on identity helps us avoid generating static definitions of concepts, such as transcendence or divinity, or titles such as "Lord," outside their narrative framework. The pursuit of identity asks "who" is Jesus Christ, rather than "what" the title "Lord" reflects.[243] Hill's insights help us understand the unity of God, Jesus Christ, and Holy Spirit, for "God and Jesus share the divine name; they are both together 'the Lord.'"[244] And

---

238. Bauckham, *God Crucified*, 28–38.

239. Hill, *Paul and the Trinity*, 49.

240. Hill, *Paul and the Trinity*, 74, writes: "The *person* 'God'—traditionally referred to as 'the Father' in trinitarian discourse—is who he is by virtue of this relation with Jesus ('the Son,' in traditional terms); by his act of giving up and raising Jesus . . . God defines himself as a distinct person, in such a way that the relation is internal to the self-definition." See also C. Kavin Rowe, *Early Narrative Christology: The Lord in the Gospel of Luke* (Grand Rapids: Baker Academic, 2009), 17–18, who challenges the static view of establishing identity and encourages a relationality view that stresses the interrelatedness of the Father, Son, and Holy Spirit. See also Watson, "Triune Divine Identity."

241. Hill, *Paul and the Trinity*, 43.

242. Athanasius (*Against the Arians* 1.29) and the Cappadocians (see Basil of Caesarea, *Refutation of the Apology of the Impious Eunomius* 2.4) exploited this relation against Arius's views that the Son is not coeternal with the Father. Lewis Ayres, *Nicaea and Its Legacy: An Approach to Fourth-Century Trinitarian Theology* (Oxford: Oxford University Press, 2004), 198–204.

243. Rowe, *Early Narrative Christology*, 21, takes this approach in his study of κύριος in Luke's Gospel: "This focus on narrative allows the insight that identity need not be static but can be dynamic or even relational, in the sense that certain characters may indeed be so aligned with one another that they can be said to share an identity."

244. Hill, *Paul and the Trinity*, 170.

the identity of the three persons "are constituted in and by their differing ways of relating to one another: God sends and exalts, Jesus is sent and exalted."[245]

How does this shape Paul's theology in Ephesians? By attending to the relation between God the Father, the Lord Jesus Christ, and the Holy Spirit, we track closely to Paul's language. For example, Paul proclaims that before the world was created, God purposed in Christ to redeem believers through adoption through Christ (Eph 1:4–5).[246] Such grace and peace comes from God the Father *and* the Lord Jesus Christ (1:2, see also Gal 1:1). This grace is that which saves (Eph 2:6, 8) and this peace is that which creates the church (2:14–17). The church created through Christ is a temple indwelt by God by his Spirit (2:22), and Paul prays that Christ will dwell in the hearts of believers, that they also will have God's power through his Spirit (3:16–17).

Therefore, I will not focus on Christology per se, as though an understanding of Jesus Christ can be separated from God the Father or from the Holy Spirit. Instead, I will examine how Paul speaks about Christ, God, and the Holy Spirit as they together reflect the triune God. We will first examine Paul's description of God (the Father), then look at his claims about the Holy Spirit, and finish by looking at the Lord Jesus Christ, including the titles "Lord" and "Christ." Having a better understanding of the Godhead as Paul apprehends it, we will examine two related theological emphases in Ephesians: the church and the gospel.

C. GOD THE FATHER

Paul identifies God as "our" Father, who is also the Father of "our Lord Jesus Christ" (Eph 1:2–3) and the Father of all families. These claims are developed together throughout the epistle, but we tease them apart here to better grasp their individual features. First, God the Father is the Father of the Lord Jesus Christ. God brings salvation through this one, the Beloved (1:6). God raised Christ from the dead, seated Christ at his right hand, and has subjected all authorities and powers under Christ's feet. God predestined before time began to accomplish redemption in the Son (1:4–5). God's action in raising Christ identifies him in relation to Christ the Son.[247] God kept hidden and now reveals the mystery of his redemption, that in Christ gentiles are coheirs with

---

245. Hill, *Paul and the Trinity*, 170.
246. Hill, *Paul and the Trinity*, 64, remarks: "God's Christological aim in God's foreknowledge enables Paul to discern a Christ-oriented identity of God prior to the Christ-event."
247. Hill, *Paul and the Trinity*, 70, declares: "God's *identity*—what makes God the God that he is—is revealed in that act [of raising Christ from the dead]."

INTRODUCTION

Jews as they both share in the promise of Christ (3:6). God allows believers access to him through Christ (2:18; 3:12). Paul identifies himself as an apostle of Jesus Christ, by the will of God and his grace (1:1; 3:7). Paul is called to preach the gospel to the gentiles, by the grace of God. God the Father is Father of the cosmos, every family in the heavens and on the earth (3:15).

Believers are God's people, God's family, because they are in Christ (1:1). Paul explains that believers are dearly loved as children of God (5:1). God blesses superabundantly with his adoption of believers, his promise of inheritance, and his mercy that raised up believers with Christ. God not only saves, he also prepares good works for believers to do (2:10). Believers are chosen by the Father to be holy and blameless in Christ (1:4). This "glorious" Father gives wisdom and understanding so that believers understand and know him better (1:17). The Father pours his glorious riches onto believers and works his immeasurable power, that they might know Christ's love and be filled with the fullness of God (3:16–19; see also 1:23).

D. GOD THE SPIRIT

Paul speaks of the Spirit in each chapter of Ephesians. The Holy Spirit is integral to the believers' redemption. First, the Spirit's presence in the believers' lives is assurance that they have an inheritance in God's future kingdom. Paul describes this as being marked with a seal (1:13–14; 4:30). The Holy Spirit is a deposit that guarantees the promises of redemption (1:14). The Spirit reveals the mystery of the gospel, that gentiles share with Jews in Christ's redemptive work (3:6). The Spirit fills the church, God's holy temple, as believers are joined together to make this dwelling (2:22). The Spirit is active in the church, joining Jewish and gentile believers in unity (2:18–19; 4:3). Paul links the one Spirit and the one body or church as he urges believers to act with kindness toward each other (4:2–3). The Holy Spirit is grieved when believers sin (4:30).[248] Paul commands believers to be filled with the Spirit as they worship together (5:18). The Spirit communicates God's power to a believer's inner life, strengthening him or her (3:16). The Spirit fills and strengthens now, and it offers active protection against the dark forces of evil as believers take up "the sword of the Spirit," that is, the word of God (6:17). Thus believers pray in the Spirit.

Paul's description of the Spirit suggests that we consider the Spirit's identity in relation to Jesus Christ and God the Father. I resist the language of "binitarianism," which postulates a static monotheism into which Christ's

---

248. Gordon D. Fee, *Paul, the Spirit, and the People of God* (Peabody, MA: Hendrickson, 1996), 14–15, points to Isa 63:10, which states that Israel grieved the Holy Spirit of God.

relationship to God is inserted and which explains the Spirit as the means by which Christ or God accomplishes a particular purpose or task. In this case, God and Jesus Christ can be known apart from and prior to the Spirit. Instead, I suggest that the Spirit is identified as the Spirit of God or the Spirit of Christ, and we know God and Christ as we know the character and action of the Spirit.[249] Paul declares that the Spirit fills believers (5:18), brings unity (4:3), and communicates God's strength and presence to believers (2:22; 3:16).

E. THE LORD JESUS CHRIST

Paul introduces himself as an apostle of Christ Jesus and as one sent on a mission to bring Christ's message of salvation to the gentiles. Paul speaks of Christ as the Lord, as the "head" of his "body" the church, as "our peace" and as giving gifts to his people. Believers offer reverence to Christ and model their ethical behavior after him. Paul speaks of Jesus Christ as God's Son, the beloved one, and one who with God possesses the kingdom (5:5). These qualities and titles deserve a closer look.

1. Jesus Christ as Son of the Father

In his call for the church to mature to unity and attain the full measure of Christ, Paul states specifically that Jesus is the Son of God (4:13). The previous three chapters prepared readers for this direct statement because Paul spoke of God the Father of Christ Jesus (1:3, 17). The Son and the Father existed before the creation of the world (1:4), and the mystery now revealed highlights the identity of God as Father, whose Son died and was raised so that redemption and a new people might be established. Paul explains that believers are adopted children through Jesus Christ (1:5), and he repeatedly describes believers as being "in Christ." Thus it should not surprise us that Paul can also speak about God as "our" Father (1:2; see also Gal 1:3). It is through Christ that believers have access to the Father (Eph 2:18).

2. Christ

Paul uses the title "Christ" quite often, and generally in discussions of Jesus Christ's death and resurrection.[250] This practice likely goes back to the earliest

---

249. Hill, *Paul and the Trinity*, 163–66.
250. Capes, *Divine Christ*, 55–56. David Rolph Seely, "Resurrection," *EDB* 1120–22;

disciples, as indicated by the tradition Paul cites. He reminds the Corinthians that he handed on to them what he received, including the testimony that Christ died for sins (1 Cor 15:3–5). Paul uses "Christ" or the personal pronoun to discuss his work on the cross and his exaltation to God's right hand. Paul typically uses the divine passive to speak of those acts done by God through or in Christ. Not surprisingly, then, we find the term "Christ" used extensively in the first three chapters of Ephesians, as Paul lays out the salvation plan of God. And we find the title used in the second half of the epistle as Paul speaks of "Christ" as an active agent concerning his church. It is Christ who is "our peace," who creates a new people unto himself (Eph 2:14). Christ is the head of his body (4:15; 5:23); he is the cornerstone of the living temple (2:20). It is Christ who descended and then ascended (4:9–10) and who gives a gift to his church (4:7, 11). It is Christ's life that is placed before believers as a model (4:20–21; 5:2).

3. Lord

Paul uses the title "Lord" extensively. The background for this title is Scripture's term for Israel's God, the Lord, most famously expounded in the Shema: "The LORD our God, the LORD is one" (Deut 6:4). The Septuagint often translated the Tetragrammaton (YHWH) as *kyrios*, and Paul speaks of Jesus Christ as *kyrios*. This suggests that Paul has more than a title in mind, for "Lord" is also a circumlocution for the divine, unspeakable name of God.[251] Paul draws on the Shema, modifying it to include Jesus Christ, as he instructs the Corinthians in the dangers of idolatry. Paul writes that for believers, there is one God, the Father, from whom are all things, and there is one Lord, Jesus Christ, through whom are all things (1 Cor 8:6). In rearranging the words, but not adding to them, Paul includes Jesus Christ as Lord, along with God the Father, as representing the one true God. Paul raises a similar point in Ephesians, but with an eye to church unity (Eph 4:4–6). Paul declares that there is one Spirit, and one Lord, and one God and Father. Paul typically associated the title "Lord" with Jesus's resurrection (Rom 14:9), but Ephesians does not stress the cross and resurrection as much as their effects: the exaltation

---

George W. E. Nickelsburg, "Resurrection," *ABD* 5:680-91. The term "Christ" is of Greek origin, and the term "Messiah" is of Jewish origin, and both refer to an anointed one. For discussion on these terms' meaning in Paul, see Matthew V. Novenson, *Christ among the Messiahs: Christ Language in Paul and Messiah Language in Ancient Judaism* (Oxford: Oxford University Press, 2012), 3, who concludes: "My thesis is that χριστός in Paul means 'messiah.'"

251. Hill, *Paul and the Trinity*, 94, concludes that when κύριος is used by Paul as a circumlocution for the divine name, "it is inseparable from the divine identity and being," and thus Jesus is the Lord God, not merely one who shares certain functions with God.

of Christ and the establishment of the church, his body and "a holy temple in the Lord" (2:21).

Paul uses "Lord" in the second half of Ephesians as he enjoins believers to live a life worthy of their calling (4:1). Often Paul speaks in the imperative, commanding that believers turn away from their futile thinking that characterized their lives as pagans (4:17).[252] The Lord's people (5:3) should walk in the light, for they are "light in the Lord" (5:8). We find the term throughout the household codes, and here Paul cites passages from the Old Testament (Gen 2:24; Exod 20:12; Deut 5:16).[253]

In a few places in Ephesians, Paul speaks of the "Lord Jesus Christ." He repeats this title at the beginning of the letter (1:2–3) and in his prayer to the God of the Lord Jesus Christ (1:17). He uses the phrase in his call for believers to give thanks to God the Father in the name of the Lord Jesus Christ (5:20). In these cases, Paul shapes the reader's perception of the identity of God the Father. Later in the letter, Paul describes the eternal purpose of God, his mystery revealed and his wisdom celebrated, by means of Christ Jesus our Lord (3:11). In all five cases where the title "Lord Jesus Christ" is found, Paul connects its importance or meaning to his understanding of God the Father.

Within the Pauline corpus, Paul subordinates Christ to God in several passages, including his discussion of the kingdom of God in his letter to the Corinthians. There Paul describes God the Father as placing all things under Christ's feet, and Christ handing over the kingdom to the Father (1 Cor 15:24–28). Subordination does not mean disunity, for "the Son remains the Son in his subordination to the Father."[254] In Philippians, Paul speaks of Christ's receiving the name above all names and being highly exalted (2:9–11). So too in Ephesians, Paul speaks of Christ exalted to God's right hand and giving thanks to God in the name of Christ (Eph 1:20; 2:6; 5:20). In Ephesians, God the Father and the Lord Jesus Christ offer grace and peace to believers (1:2), and this demonstrates their mutuality. God the Father raised Jesus and seated him in the heavenly places at his right hand; this suggests an asymmetrical aspect to the relation, but it need not imply that Jesus lacks equality or oneness with God the Father. Instead, Paul presents God the Father and Christ

---

252. Capes, *Divine Christ*, 58, states: "Paul utilizes *kyrios* when concrete, behavioral-ethical issues are at stake."

253. Capes, *Divine Christ*, 60–63, suggests that Paul follows the pattern found in the ethical demands of Scripture, that it is the Lord (κύριος) your God who commands the people to remember the Sabbath (Exod 20:8) or to be holy, for "I, the LORD [κύριος], your God, am holy" (Lev 19:1–2).

254. Hill, *Paul and the Trinity*, 132, concludes that the passage reflects different roles that Christ takes up before and after he gives the kingdom to God the Father, which are "non-overlapping, non-competitive, complementary" to the Father.

the Son as identified by the same name, *kyrios* ("Lord"), who are distinct in asymmetrical ways that are not competitive but reveal a mutual relationship.

4. Christ Our Peace

Paul makes the powerfully sweeping claim that Christ is "our peace" (2:14), who makes peace (2:15) and brings the gospel of peace (2:17; 6:15). Christ's peace is made concrete within the church, as Jews and gentiles are brought together in a new entity created from the peace. This peace destroys barriers, hostilities, and ethnic, social, and religious walls that prevent the flourishing of God's people. This peace should lead to unity among believers, as peace binds them together (4:3). Peace works toward unity, toward reconciliation, toward mutuality among humanity and especially within the church. Christ's peace is active, a force of creative destruction that demolishes evil and builds unity in the present age, as well as the age to come. The gospel of peace is proclaimed by those who have put on the armor of God (6:15). Christ's peace looks forward to an everlasting peace, as Paul draws on images from Isaiah to show how peace will prevail (Isa 11:1–9; 52:10; 59:14–21).[255] Christ's peace also operates at the cosmic level. It reflects the mystery now revealed of gentile inclusion into the people of God through Christ's gospel of peace (3:6).

F. TRINITARIAN LANGUAGE IN EPHESIANS

In Ephesians, Paul's discussion of God the Father, the Lord Jesus Christ, and the Holy Spirit distinguishes certain roles or actions as specific to one of the members. For example, Christ died and is raised, the Spirit is given to the church, and God predestined the redemption plan to include adoption through Jesus Christ. In distinguishing between the characteristics specific to each person and the apparent asymmetry within the Triune God, theologians use the concept of reduplication. This principle argues that when speaking of each person, we must speak of both their essence as God and of the unique properties that define their person. The relation between Father and Son and Spirit is not based on different substance or essence but describes their relation. The fourth-century CE theologian Gregory of Nazianzus explains:

---

255. Gorman, *Becoming the Gospel*, 206, concludes that the mission of the church exists as "participation in the missional life of the triune God" as the Christian is strong in the Lord Christ (6:10) and puts on the armor of God (6:11, 13) and is empowered by the Spirit (6:17, 18).

"The Three are One from the perspective of their divinity, and the One is Three from the perspective of the properties."[256]

How does this emphasis on relations (and not monotheism) among the Godhead help us understand Paul's claims in Ephesians about one Spirit, one Lord, one God and Father of all (4:4–6)? How does this aid our interpretation of Paul's statement that believers put their hope in Christ, are marked with the Holy Spirit, and are God's possession (1:12–14)? How does this illuminate Paul's prayer to God the Father that believers might be strengthened through his Spirit in their inner being and have Christ dwell in their hearts (3:14–18)? Finally, how does this help us apprehend Paul's views on Christian worship when believers are filled with the Spirit and give thanks to God the Father in the name of our Lord Jesus Christ (5:18–20)? I think we can draw at least three general statements.

First, Paul understands God to be the one who saves through Jesus Christ, fulfilling the promises made to God's people in Scripture. Paul interprets Scripture through the lens of the cross and resurrection and allows Scripture to shape his understanding of God and creation. We may identify the God of the Hebrew Scriptures without reference to Jesus Christ, but we cannot fully understand his identity apart from Christ.[257] Second, Paul understands salvation to include victory over spiritual forces of darkness, and his assertion of the one true God as Spirit, Christ, and God the Father reinforces his argument. Paul's triune God is the creator God who will bring unity to all things—the spirits and powers of darkness have no power over God and will not prevail against God's people. Third, Paul invites the church to engage in the "divine peace mission" of the triune God as believers enjoy reconciliation with God and bring the message of reconciliation to the world.[258] Reconciliation occurs as Christ makes a new people who call on Christ's Father as their Father, in the one Spirit.

G. THE CHURCH IN EPHESIANS

Ephesians emphasizes the church in its grand narrative of cosmic warfare. Paul stresses Christ as victorious over powers and authorities, describing him as having his enemies under his feet (1:22) and as having a kingdom (5:5). The

---

256. Gregory of Nazianzus, *Orations* 31.9, translation from Gilles Emery, *The Trinitarian Theology of St Thomas Aquinas*, trans. Francesca Aran Murphy (Oxford: Oxford University Press, 2007), 45. See Hill, *Paul and the Trinity*, 99–103.

257. Hill, *Paul and the Trinity*, 75, writes: "'God' ... is known by Paul always as the God of Jesus Christ."

258. Gorman, *Becoming the Gospel*, 188. He remarks that the church is "the primary means God has established for drawing a fractured, hostile, and violent world together" (194).

prince of the realm of the air who leads people into disobedience further hints at the battle that rages around the gospel truth (2:2). Christ brings peace, the end of hostilities between warring groups (Jews and gentiles); even more, he creates a new people (2:14–15). Later in Ephesians, Paul cites a scriptural passage that speaks of captives that Christ took as he ascended on high; the image is of prisoners of war (4:8). Finally, the qualities of a soldier to obey and submit to his commanders find support in Paul's exhortations that believers submit to each other out of reverence to Christ (5:21). Paul speaks of their unity, another virtue of any military unit (4:3). Of course, these virtues are reshaped in line with the gospel message of grace and their baptism into the body of Christ (4:1–6). Paul's command to put on God's armor completes his call to faithful discipleship (6:10–13).

Ephesians emphasizes the universal church in his picture of the church's past as established by God in Christ before the foundations of the world, and its future enjoyment of the kingdom of Christ and of God when Christ unifies all things. By "universal" I do not imply an abstraction or an entity disconnected from daily life. Rather the term reflects Paul's description of the church community inclusive of all geographic locations. Paul speaks this way about "the church of God," which he persecuted (Gal 1:13; 1 Cor 15:9; see also 10:32; 12:28). Paul also refers to individual churches, such as the gathering that meets in Prisca and Aquila's house (Rom 16:5) or the several gatherings in the region of Galatia (Gal 1:2) or God's churches in Judea (1 Thess 2:14). Colossians captures both senses, as Paul addresses the local church (1:2; 4:15) as well as speaks of the church universal (1:18, 24).

Paul addresses the particularities of the Greco-Roman culture as well as discusses the local church in Ephesus. Paul emphasizes the ethnic division between gentile and Jew, a particular reality within the first-century church. Christ closed the distance between the two groups, and destroyed the obstacles to fellowship by bringing peace (Eph 2:11–18). The new people constituted in and by Christ are called to abandon any gentile pagan practices that separate them from the life of God (4:17–18); instead, they are to follow God's example (5:1, likely referring to forgiveness) and walk as Christ walked (5:2).[259] Paul also takes up the particularity of the Greco-Roman social and legal division of slave/free and wife/husband. The gospel's call of mutual submission (5:21) and reciprocity (5:28–29; see also 1 Cor 7:4) is affirmed in Paul's statement that God shows no favoritism (Eph 6:9; see also Acts 10:34).

---

259. Michael J. Gorman, *Inhabiting the Cruciform God: Kenosis, Justification, and Theosis in Paul's Narrative Soteriology* (Grand Rapids: Eerdmans, 2009), 125, points to this passage as connecting the imitation of the cruciform God with emulating the crucified Christ, concluding that "Christification is deification, or theosis."

THEOLOGY OF EPHESIANS

Paul uses two significant metaphors to describe the church: Christ's body (Eph 1:23; 2:16; 3:6; 4:4, 12; 5:32) and God's temple (2:22).[260] Christ's work on the cross creates one body that brings together Jew and gentile (2:15) and is symbolically represented by the "one flesh" of husband and wife (Gen 2:24, cited in Eph 5:31).[261] The building is being constructed, and the body is maturing (4:15; 5:26-27). Here we see the "already/not yet" aspect of Paul's eschatology.[262] The church is the body of Christ, and it is growing into maturity, speaking truth in love (4:12, 14-16). The church is a building that rises up in the Lord, as a holy temple wherein God dwells in his Spirit (2:21-22). Paul uses these metaphors in other letters, speaking of the Corinthian congregation as God's temple (1 Cor 3:16; 2 Cor 6:16) and Christ's body (1 Cor 12:27; see also Rom 12:3-8). The unity among the members is based on each one being "in Christ," the crucified and risen Lord.[263]

Only in Ephesians and Colossians does Paul speak of Christ as the head of the church, his body.[264] Christ is presented as "head" in the context of the claim that God will bring together all things in the cosmos in Christ (Eph 1:10; Col 1:18). Drawing on Ps 110:1, Paul speaks of God's placing all things under Christ's feet and appointing him head over all things, all powers and spiritual authorities (Eph 1:22). Paul expands the feet/head metaphor by declaring that God gave Christ as head to the church, his body (1:22-23). With this assertion, Paul makes two claims. First, Christ as head over all things (1:22) is another way of saying that Christ will bring all things together (1:10). Second, God gave Christ to be head over all things, for the sake of the church (1:22), which parallels Paul's prayer that celebrates God's great power exerted on behalf of believers (1:19).[265] Paul explicitly links Christ as head with the church as he speaks of the latter maturing and growing in truth and love (4:15; Col 2:19). Paul identifies Christ as head and Savior of the church, caring for the church that is his body (Eph 5:23, 29-30).

The church in Ephesians was called into being by God through Christ's work.[266] The community has its roots in Israel's history (Eph 2:11-18; see also

260. For a brief discussion, see Dunn, *Theology of Paul the Apostle*, 548-52.
261. In Romans and 1 Corinthians, Paul emphasizes the community's egalitarian makeup (Rom 12:3-6; 1 Cor 12:12-28).
262. David E. Aune, "Eschatology (Early Christian)," *ABD* 2:594-609.
263. James W. Thompson, *The Church according to Paul: Rediscovering the Community Conformed to Christ* (Grand Rapids: Baker Academic, 2014), 71, citing Walter Klaiber, *Rechtfertigung und Gemeinde: Eine Untersuchung zum paulinischen Kirchenverständnis* (Göttingen: Vandenhoeck & Ruprecht, 1982), 43, writes: "The reality of the crucified and risen Christ is the basis for the unity of the congregation."
264. In 1 Cor 11:3, Paul speaks of Christ as the head of man.
265. Lincoln, 67.
266. Ἐκκλησία is used in the Septuagint to translate *qāhāl*, the "assembly" of the Lord, the covenant people of Israel (Deut 23:2).

1 Cor 10:1–4). They are coheirs with Israel and share in the fulfillment of God's promises (Eph 3:6). Believers are adopted through Christ, and the church is God's family (1:5; 2:19; 3:6). Paul emphasizes the inheritance that believers share, based on Christ's work and secured with the seal of the Holy Spirit (1:13–14, 18). As children of God, they look forward to sharing in the kingdom of Christ and of God (5:5). In light of this great inheritance, the church is called to live in holiness (4:1). The church receives gifts from Christ to aid its growth (4:11), and these gifts are given so that each member is prepared to serve the mission of the church. The corporate body is served by its individual members, even as each member takes his or her identity from the corporate unity as the body of Christ.

The church lives in the present age, but members are also seated with Christ in the heavenly places. Paul's eschatology, the "already/not yet," is woven throughout the epistle, but salvation is enjoyed now in some measure, as believers are raised with Christ, alive in him (2:5–6). Yet still to come is the fullness of God's kingdom (5:5), the inheritance of the saints (1:13–14), rewards for faithfulness (6:8), and the unity of the cosmos in Christ (1:10). Christ's exaltation is shared by believers, for they are his body (1:22–23). Nevertheless, his followers must protect themselves from evil spiritual forces that dominate the present age of darkness (2:2; 4:27; 6:12–13).

H. MYSTERY OF THE GOSPEL AND THE CHURCH

Paul speaks of the mystery that is now revealed and that he proclaims, namely, the gospel message of Christ's redemption, that gentiles are coheirs and share in the promises of God in Christ, and they are members of the church, the body of Christ (3:3–6). The mystery of God's will is that the cosmos will be unified under Christ (1:9–10), and the church manifests that unity as gentiles share in the inheritance through Christ. Paul asks the Ephesians for prayer that he might fearlessly proclaim "the mystery of the gospel" (6:19), a proclamation that resulted in his imprisonment. Paul draws on the description of marriage in Gen 2:24 and its "one flesh" language as he describes the unity of Christ with his body of Christ, and Christ's self-giving love for his body, as a profound mystery (Eph 5:29–32). Overall, Paul uses "mystery" in Ephesians to capture his claim that the gospel brings unity, now in the gentile inclusion and ultimately with all things unified under Christ.[267] Romans and Colossians

---

267. T. J. Lang, *Mystery and the Making of a Christian Historical Consciousness: From Paul to the Second Century* (Berlin: de Gruyter, 2015), 98, summarizes Paul's point well: "The mystery is synonymous with gospel, just as the gospel is synonymous [with] Christ."

speak of mystery in a context that reflects a similar concern for gentile inclusion as those who will share in the glory to come (Rom 11:25; Col 1:26–27).[268] The closing benediction in Romans asserts that the long-hidden mystery is revealed now through Scripture, that in Christ gentiles might come to believe in the one God (Rom 16:25–27).

X. THE NEW PERSPECTIVE ON PAUL AND EPHESIANS

The interpretive lens called the New Perspective on Paul takes its name from the contrast between its view and a traditional reading of Paul that presented the center of Paul's thought as justification by faith over against (Jewish) works righteousness.[269] Ephesians does not use the language of justification, nor does it include the phrase "works of the law"; nevertheless, its discussion of Jew and gentile requires us to engage with recent scholarship about Jews and Judaism in Paul's day.

The New Perspective grew out of reflection on the church's anti-Semitism (and anti-Judaism), shown most clearly during the Holocaust.[270] It also drew on recent archeological discoveries such as the Dead Sea Scrolls.

---

268. Grindheim, "A Deutero-Pauline Mystery?," 179, argues for a development in Paul's thought from 1 Corinthians, which uses "mystery" in speaking of the resurrection (15:51), and Romans, which uses the term to speak of gentile inclusion, as we also find in Colossians and Ephesians.

269. For an overview, see Hans Hübner, "Zur gegenwärtigen Diskussion über die Theologie des Paulus," *Jahrbuch für Biblische Theologie* 7 (1992): 399–413; Kent L. Yinger, *The New Perspective on Paul: An Introduction* (Eugene, OR: Cascade, 2011). Evaluations of the theory include Michael Bachmann and Johannes Woyke, eds., *Lutherische und neue Paulusperspektive: Beiträge zu einem Schlüsselproblem der gegenwärtigen exegetischen Diskussion*, WUNT 182 (Tübingen: Mohr Siebeck, 2005); Stephen Westerholm, *Perspectives Old and New on Paul: The "Lutheran" Paul and His Critics* (Grand Rapids: Eerdmans, 2003); Stephen J. Chester, *Reading Paul with the Reformers: Reconciling Old and New Perspectives* (Grand Rapids: Eerdmans, 2017).

270. E. P. Sanders, *Paul and Palestinian Judaism: A Comparison of Patterns of Religion*, 40th anniversary ed. (Minneapolis: Fortress, 2017; originally Philadelphia: Fortress, 1977), 33–59, 183–98, 222–28, addresses the overt anti-Judaism and anti-Semitism that permeates Christian scholarship, especially in Germany, in the early twentieth century; E. P. Sanders, *Judaism: Practice and Belief, 63 BCE–66 CE* (Minneapolis: Fortress, 1992). See also Anders Gerdmar, *Roots of Theological Anti-Semitism: German Biblical Interpretation and the Jews, from Herder and Semler to Kittel and Bultmann* (Leiden: Brill, 2009), 373–400. See also Amy-Jill Levine, "Bearing False Witness: Common Errors Made about Early Judaism," in *The Jewish Annotated New Testament*, ed. Amy-Jill Levine and Marc Zvi Brettler, 2nd ed. (Oxford: Oxford University Press, 2011), 760–63. See also Krister Stendahl's influential essay: "The Apostle Paul and the Introspective Conscience of the West," *Harvard Theological*

INTRODUCTION

The New Perspective is as much about a historical reconstruction of Second Temple Judaism as it is about the theology within Paul's letters. Second Temple Judaism began with the return of Jews from exile in Babylon and the rebuilding of Solomon's Temple in Jerusalem. Alexander the Great conquered Judea, Samaria, and Galilee in the late third century BCE and brought with him the Greek way of life, that is, Hellenism. Jews in the homeland and diaspora resisted, accommodated, and assimilated in various degrees to Hellenism.

Christian history has often characterized Judaism of this period as one of works righteousness, with Jews seeking to earn their salvation by their own merit. The New Perspective on Paul argues that Jews followed the law as an obedient response to God's prior election and not to earn their salvation. E. P. Sanders coined the phrase "covenantal nomism" to describe the conviction that Jews obeyed the law not to "get saved" but in response of obedience to God's commands.[271] James D. G. Dunn built on Sanders's insight and argued that when Paul spoke of works of the law, he was referring to Jewish ethnic boundary markers such as circumcision and food laws that distinguished Jews from gentiles.[272] These markers reflect Jewish social identity: "A Jew distinguished himself or herself as a member of God's people and lived into that reality by faithfully carrying out the teachings God had delivered to his people."[273] Alongside Dunn, N. T. Wright developed Sanders's insights, fo-

---

Review 56.3 (1963): 199–215; Krister Stendahl, *Paul among Jews and Gentiles, and Other Essays* (Philadelphia: Fortress, 1976).

271. Sanders, *Paul and Palestinian Judaism*. In the foreword to the 40th anniversary edition, Mark Chancey, xvi, recalls that Sanders used the phrase "new perspective" only once in this book (p. 496) and that it was James D. G. Dunn, in his Manson Memorial Lecture, who declared that Sanders's work required a "new perspective on Paul." See James D. G. Dunn, "The New Perspective on Paul," *Bulletin of the John Rylands University Library of Manchester* 65 (1983): 95–122.

272. Dunn, "New Perspective on Paul." See also James D. G. Dunn, *The New Perspective on Paul*, WUNT 185 (Tübingen: Mohr Siebeck, 2005; rev. ed. Grand Rapids: Eerdmans, 2008), 4–16, 121–40, 381–94, 413–28; James D. G. Dunn, "A New Perspective on the New Perspective on Paul," *Early Christianity* 4.2 (2013): 157–82. Countering Dunn, Francis Watson, *Paul, Judaism, and the Gentiles: Beyond the New Perspective*, rev. ed. (Grand Rapids: Eerdmans, 2007), 20–21, argues that Paul's phrase "works of the law" refers to general Jewish practices, not boundary markers such as circumcision, as Dunn concludes. For a critique of the New Perspective with a traditional view of Judaism, see D. A. Carson, Peter T. O'Brien, and Mark A. Seifrid, eds., *Justification and Variegated Judaism*, vol. 1: *The Complexities of Second Temple Judaism* (Grand Rapids: Baker Academic, 2001).

273. Lynn H. Cohick, "The New Perspective and the Christian Life in Paul's Letter to the Ephesians," in *The Apostle Paul and the Christian Life: Ethical and Missional Implications of the New Perspective*, ed. Scot McKnight and Joseph B. Modica (Grand Rapids: Baker Academic, 2016), 21.

cusing on the categories of covenant and exile.[274] The New Perspective does not represent a single or unified theological voice, although in general those who promote it critique the traditional emphasis on justification in Paul's theology, presented as faith (Christian) against works (Judaism).

The questions around grace, faith, and works of the law have taken a new turn with John Barclay's discussion of grace as gift.[275] He suggests that Sanders's evaluation of Second Temple Judaism was insufficient in its description of grace.[276] Barclay found that "grace is everywhere in the theology of Second Temple Judaism, but not everywhere the same."[277] Barclay determines six understandings (he calls them perfections) of grace that singularly or together are intended when a Christian, Jewish, or gentile author speaks of gift: superabundance, singularity, priority, efficacy, incongruity, and noncircularity.[278] The last two qualities are the most important for our study. The incongruity (unconditionality) of a gift refers to a gift giving without regard to the worthiness of the recipient. Paul presents the gospel as given without regard to the recipient's worthiness, which could suggest that God was unjust or irrational based on typical Greco-Roman assumptions. The Essenes praised God for his incongruous gift given to wretched sinners such as they were (1QHa). Paul likely held to the circularity of a gift, emphasizing the reciprocal relationship formed between the giver and recipient.[279] God gives the unconditioned gift of salvation, which is not tied to the worth of the recipient. However, the gift requires a response, for in receiving it, the recipient accepts the relationship to God in Christ that comes with it.

The New Perspective underscores the importance of the gentile in

---

274. N. T. Wright, *The New Testament and the People of God* (Minneapolis: Fortress, 1992), 299–301; Wright, *Paul and the Faithfulness of God*; Wright, *Paul and His Recent Interpreters* (Minneapolis: Fortress, 2015).

275. John M. G. Barclay, *Paul and the Gift* (Grand Rapids: Eerdmans, 2015), 151–58, offers a critique of Sanders, noting that "Sanders's analysis of the structure and content of Judaism emphasized primarily the *priority* of grace, the divine initiative that founded the people of Israel and contextualizes their observance of the Torah" (152).

276. Barclay, *Paul and the Gift*, 564, notes that Sanders generalizes from the notion of the priority of grace also to include the incongruity of grace; thereby, he "unwittingly created a spurious uniformity within Judaism." Barclay concludes: "I depart from the 'new perspective' in identifying the theological root of this Pauline mission. It is Paul's theology of the Christ-gift that shapes his appeals to the Abrahamic promises, to the experience of the Spirit, and to the oneness of God" (572).

277. Barclay, *Paul and the Gift*, 565.

278. Barclay, *Paul and the Gift*, 70–75.

279. Barclay, *Paul and the Gift*, 569: "The *incongruity* of grace does not imply, for Paul, its *singularity* (since God's act of grace in Christ is predicated on his judgment of sin) or its *non-circularity* (since the gift carries expectations of obedience)."

Paul's understanding of the gospel. This is the burden of Eph 2:11–22.[280] Two points are pertinent for our study if the New Perspective on Paul accurately sketches the dominant Jewish position in Paul's day.[281] First, Paul likely does not imagine his fellow Jews doing good works to *get saved*. Second, most Jews would nevertheless distinguish their religious behavior as monotheistic and their virtues and values as drawn from God's law.[282] In other words, the distinction between Jew and gentile was a constant social reality—not necessarily a tense one, but an obvious one. Shaye Cohen helpfully explains that Jewish identity centered on (a) religious, cultural, and political affiliation and (b) ethnicity and geography.[283] Second Temple Jews understood their ethnicity as a status of birth, and their religious identity as comprised of choices concerning following the law. They might choose the sect of the Pharisees, or the Essenes, or join John the Baptist's followers.

---

280. Cohick, "New Perspective," 28: "Just as the raised body of Christ confirms Christ's victory over death ... so too the people of God that includes gentiles as full members of the community gives clear evidence to the power of the cross to make all believers new."

281. James R. Harrison, *Paul's Language of Grace in Its Graeco-Roman Context*, WUNT 2/172 (Tubingen: Mohr Siebeck, 2003), 104, critiques the New Perspective, arguing that "two pieces of Pauline polemic (Rom 10:2–3; Phil 3:5–6) indicate that the apostle was as much critiquing the rise of a merit theology within first-century Judaism ... as the exclusivism of certain Christian Jews in the early house-churches." Harrison's thorough study of the primary material is praiseworthy, but I remain unconvinced by several of his negative assessments of the New Perspective on Paul.

282. The Hebrew Bible was translated into Greek in the third century BCE (i.e., the Septuagint), and by the first century was available in Greek throughout the Roman Diaspora.

283. Cohen, *Beginnings of Jewishness*, 70–92.

The Letter to the
EPHESIANS

Text and Commentary

I. PAUL'S OPENING GREETING (1:1–2)

¹Paul, an apostle of Christ Jesus by the will of God,
To God's holy people in Ephesus, the faithful in Christ Jesus:
²Grace and peace to you from God our Father and the Lord Jesus Christ.[1]

1 Paul begins this letter in his typical fashion, identifying himself as the sender.[2] This was the normal pattern for ancient letters and was followed by a greeting to the recipients.[3] Paul identifies himself as an apostle, the nominative noun in apposition to the name "Paul" (see also Rom 1:1; 1 Cor 1:1; Gal 1:1). The term "apostle" carries the sense of being sent by another, and in this case, Paul declares he is sent by Christ Jesus.[4] Paul adds that this sending is God's will. The Greek phrase "Paul an apostle of Christ Jesus by the will of God" is mirrored exactly in 2 Cor 1:1; Col 1:1; and 2 Tim 1:1.[5]

---

1. The printed text of Ephesians above, and elsewhere in the commentary, is from the NIV (2011 edition).

2. Paul is the Roman Latin cognomen or surname (Greek *Paulos*, Latin *Paullus*), and Saul is likely his supernomen or nickname; Saul is the Semitic name *Shaul*, transliterated into Greek as *Saulos*. See Stephen B. Chapman, "Saul/Paul: Onomastics, Typology, and Christian Scripture," in *The Word Leaps the Gap: Essays on Scripture and Theology in Honor of Richard B. Hays*, ed. J. Ross Wagner et al. (Grand Rapids: Eerdmans, 2008), 220.

3. For a description and discussion of ancient letter writing, see introduction, p. 47.

4. On ἀπόστολος see BDAG 122; P. W. Barnett, "Apostle," *DPL* 45–51; Hans Dieter Betz, "Apostle," *ABD* 1:309–11. Morris, 10, observes that typically we find the order Christ Jesus (approximately seventy-three occurrences), over against the order Jesus Christ (approximately eighteen occurrences), with about twenty-four additional passages in which the textual evidence is difficult to determine.

5. Παῦλος ἀπόστολος Χριστοῦ Ἰησοῦ διὰ θελήματος θεοῦ.

Paul locates his apostleship in the will of God, and he will reflect deeply and broadly on God's will throughout this letter.[6] Paul is aware of other apostles, including the Twelve (1 Cor 15:7; Gal 1:17, 19).[7] As he addresses the Ephesians, Paul uses the label "apostle" only here; elsewhere in the epistle he prefers terms that refer to his imprisoned status (Eph 3:1; 4:1; 6:20). When he uses "apostle" elsewhere in the letter, he speaks in general terms of those who provide foundational leadership within the churches (2:20; 3:5; 4:11).

Paul is identified as an apostle twice in Acts (14:4, 14) and calls himself an apostle who has seen Jesus our Lord (1 Cor 9:1). He distinguishes himself as the least of apostles because of his persecution of the church before his calling by God (15:8). Paul declares that he is sent to the gentiles (Gal 1:16; 2:7), and we find a similar emphasis on gentiles in Ephesians. The noun "apostle" is used primarily to identify those sent by God, but the term can also refer to those sent on a mission by a congregation (2 Cor 8:23; Phil 2:25). The author of Hebrews describes Jesus as an apostle (3:1). Paul portrays his apostleship as filled with trials and hardships (1 Cor 4:9–13; 2 Cor 1:8; 6:4–10; 11:23–28) and characterized by signs, wonders, and miracles (2 Cor 12:12).

The absence of a cosender in the salutation is unusual. We would expect to find Timothy's name (2 Cor 1:1; Phil 1:1; Col 1:1; 1 Thess 1:1; 2 Thess 1:1; Phlm 1) or Silvanus/Silas's (1 Thess 1:1; 2 Thess 1:1). In one case, Paul cosends with Sosthenes (1 Cor 1:1).[8] To the Galatians, Paul mentions a group of brothers and sisters who are with him as he dispatches the letter (1:2). Only in Romans (and the Pastoral Epistles) does Paul's name stand alone as the sender. Paul's purpose in writing Romans is to introduce himself to the city, for he has not visited them, nor did he play a role in the church's beginnings. This could explain why Paul did not include a cosender.[9] Such circumstances do not fit Ephesians, however, for Paul has

---

6. Barth, 65, observes that Ephesians has more references to God's will than any other New Testament work, except the Gospel of John. He continues that "'God's decision' describes an action and manifestation of the One who is living, personal, wise and powerful."

7. P. W. Barnett, "Apostle," *DPL* 45–51, offers a thorough overview of the term. Apart from the twelve apostles of the Gospels, others identified as apostles in the New Testament include Barnabas (Acts 14:4, 14), Andronicus and Junia (Rom 16:7), and possibly Timothy and Silvanus (1 Thess 2:6).

8. Best, 97–98, observes that the absence of Timothy's name weakens the theory that the author of Ephesians copied from Colossians.

9. Lincoln, 5, makes this argument and cites this as further evidence for non-Pauline authorship of Ephesians, a congregation that Paul knew well.

been to Ephesus and was involved in planting and growing the church there.[10] Paul's letter to the Galatians addresses an attack on his apostolic calling and authority, which may be why he does not name a specific cosender. Again, perhaps he mentions a group that joins him in the letter so as to further emphasize the reach of his ministry and authority. In the case of Ephesians, Paul's authority with the congregation seems secure; it is his imprisonment that has created consternation and confusion (3:13). In the end, an argument from silence is precarious, and I venture to say only that I would expect Timothy's name. As with Romans, so too Ephesians presents treatiselike qualities and a special focus on developing theological concepts. It may be that such emphases were factors in the decision to exclude cosenders.

Paul sends the letter to those he identifies as saints or holy ones and further describes them as faithful.[11] The two substantival adjectives share a single article, indicating they represent a single group.[12] The designation "saint" for a follower of Jesus is typical throughout Paul's letters (Rom 1:7; 1 Cor 1:2; 2 Cor 1:1, Phil 1:1; Col 1:2) and is repeated throughout Ephesians (1:15; 3:8, 18; 4:12; 6:18). Paul can inject a moral connotation to the designation, declaring that God in Christ chose believers to be holy (1:4; see also 5:26–27). Paul always uses the term in the plural and never as a title for an individual.[13] Identifying God's holy people as saints has deep roots in the history of the Israelites. The people of God are chosen by him to live in accordance with his holiness (Exod 22:31; Lev 11:45; Ps 34:9; Dan 7:18–27). The term carries the sense of being set apart for a sacred purpose, much as a temple space would be reserved for religious rituals, not profane or mundane activities (see Eph 2:21).

Paul greets the believers as "faithful" (see also Col 1:2). The emphasis is on the believers' posture of belief, not on their character as trustworthy individuals. For an example of the latter, Paul praises Tychicus as faithful at the end of Ephesians (6:21). Here in the greeting Paul emphasizes their belief in Christ Jesus. Both Paul and the Ephesians share in Christ Jesus, and this theme of being "in Christ" reverberates throughout Paul's Epistles

---

10. Campbell, *Framing Paul*, 318–19, 325, suggests that this letter was written to the Laodiceans and was composed in 50 CE, before he wrote to the Corinthians, Galatians, Philippians, and Romans.

11. On ἅγιος see BDAG 11 (2dβ); S. E. Porter, "Holiness, Sanctification," *DPL* 397–402. On πιστός see BDAG 821 (2); L. Morris, "Faith," *DPL* 285–91; Dieter Lührmann, "Faith (NT)," *ABD* 2:749–58; John Reumann, "Faith," *EDB* 453–54.

12. Larkin, 2, explains: "The article before the first but not the second of two personal plural items linked by καί indicates both groups are identical." See also Hoehner, 142.

13. Morris, 11.

and will shape his exhortations here as well. The elastic phrase sometimes carries the sense of incorporation into the community of faith and other times indicates the agency of salvation.[14] Those who are part of the people of God, Christ's body (1:22–23), are thereby equipped by being in Christ to do good works (2:10).

While the vocabulary of this clause is straightforward, the syntax and grammar are not, for we have a participle of the verb "to be," which lacks a complement, as "in Ephesus" is missing in key early sources.[15] The text in the earliest sources reads "to the saints who are and to believers in Christ Jesus." If we assume that the location was not part of the original text, then it may read as follows: the saints who are "also" (*kai*) faithful.[16] However, this makes the participle redundant and could imply that some saints are not faithful.[17] Less likely is that a deliberate space was left in the original document to be filled in by the reader of the letter, Tychicus, for no extant manuscripts demonstrate a space.[18] We will proceed with the presumption that the complement was the geographical location "in Ephesus" and was part of the original letter.[19] This position accounts for most ancient manuscripts including "in Ephesus" in their texts, and all ancient authors indicated that the epistle was sent to the Ephesians.[20]

2 Paul continues his greeting with his customary phrase extending "grace and peace" to the recipients (Rom 1:7; 1 Cor 1:3; 2 Cor 1:2; Gal 1:3; Phil 1:2; Col 1:2; 1 Thess 1:1; 2 Thess 1:2; Titus 1:4; Phlm 3).[21] The nouns "grace" and "peace" replace the typical Hellenistic greeting that employs the cognate verb of the noun "grace."[22] Paul creates a play on words, as he speaks of grace (*charis*) rather than the expected verb form of greetings (*chairein*). Paul ex-

---

14. MacDonald, 32. For a general discussion of the phrase, see the excursus "In Christ" (pp. 91–94).

15. See introduction for a detailed discussion.

16. Lincoln, 1–2.

17. Muddiman, 60.

18. Lincoln, 3. Muddiman, 61, lists several reasons why this theory is weak, including the practice of identifying communities who received a circular letter, such as Galatians, 1 Peter, James, and perhaps 1 John.

19. Thielman, 14–16.

20. Arnold, 27, observes that "the inclusion of 'in Ephesus' has the unanimous support of the Western and Byzantine text families in addition to the support of numerous Alexandrian witnesses." See also Thielman, 15–16. Moreover, the three early witnesses (B ﬡ P46) to its omission from the text include "to the Ephesians" as their superscription.

21. On χάρις see BDAG 1079 (2c); A. B. Luter Jr., "Grace," *DPL* 372–74; Gary Steven Shogren, "Grace (NT)," *ABD* 2:1086–88. On εἰρήνη see BDAG 287–88 (2a); S. E. Porter, "Peace, Reconciliation," *DPL* 695–99.

22. James 1:1 uses the typical Hellenistic verb, χαίρειν.

1:1–2 Paul's Opening Greeting

tends this grace and peace to all the Ephesians with the plural pronoun "to you," and he highlights that it is God the Father and the Lord Jesus Christ who extend such grace and peace.[23]

While "grace" and "peace" occur regularly in Paul's greetings, these terms also play a significant role in the following chapters as Paul examines the redemption story of God.[24] In Greek, the term *charis* can mean grace, favor, or gift, and Paul speaks of salvation in Christ as God's indescribable gift (2 Cor 8:9). Paul explains that God extended a specific grace to Paul as he established him as a messenger of the gospel (Eph 3:2, 7) and that Christ gives grace to each believer so that they would contribute to the overall health of the congregation (4:7, 29). Paul emphasizes that believers are saved by grace (2:5, 8) and that Christ is the believers' peace (2:14). Paul's message to gentiles, who made up a majority of the Ephesian congregation, was the good news that God in Christ has forgiven them by grace and has brought them into a new family, the body of Christ. The good news applies as well to the Jewish members of the congregation, and the new entity is now to grow together in unity and maturity in Christ.[25] Paul's wish that believers receive God's grace should not be understood as an implicit contrast with Judaism or Jewish religious practices or attitudes of alleged self-righteousness or works to merit salvation.[26] For Paul, grace is found in Christ's redemptive work, extended to all people regardless of their social worth or ethnic background.[27]

Paul develops the concept of peace to include a reference to Christ himself and his death and resurrection. In 2:14 Paul introduces Christ as "our peace" as Paul explains the creative power that makes a unity of that which was separate, namely, Jewish and gentile communities. Paul describes his message as the gospel of peace and a gospel that prepares believers for struggles of this life (6:15). The peace that is Christ is to be nurtured within the

---

23. The verb "to be" in the optative mood is implied, as Paul indicates his wish that they receive God's grace and peace.

24. Arnold, 70, counts ninety-five occurrences of the term "grace" in Paul's letters.

25. Barclay, *Paul and the Gift*, 1, explores the concept of grace as gift and rightly comments that "scholars now commonly note that Paul's theology—including his theology of justification and his famous antithesis between 'faith in Christ' and 'works of the law'—is best understood as articulated in and for this Gentile mission." Barclay traces the ways the concept of gift is used by Jews and gentiles in the Greco-Roman world, in the history of interpretation within the Church, and in modern anthropology.

26. See "The New Perspective on Paul" in the introduction, pp. 71–74. Barclay, *Paul and the Gift*, 6, accurately states: "Grace is everywhere in Second Temple Judaism but not everywhere the same."

27. The ideas of grace as gift are developed in 2:8–10.

community (4:3). The epistle echoes Old Testament passages that speak of God's Messiah bringing peace. From Isaiah we hear of the Prince of Peace (9:6 [= 9:5 LXX]), and the earliest believers drew on Zechariah's description of the king who brings peace to the nations (Zech 9:9–10; Matt 21:4–5; John 12:14–16). The Jewish term *shalom* conveys a traditional wish for peace that may underpin Paul's use, a peace that is more than absence of war, but that reflects God's blessings.[28] The peace that Paul proclaims is a reconciling peace, for "the church is to embody peace and unity so as to reflect both the reality of the cosmic reconciliation accomplished by Christ and the possibility of what the world may become."[29]

Paul identifies the givers of grace and peace as "God our Father and the Lord Jesus Christ" (see also 6:23–24).[30] Paul prays to God as the father of all peoples (3:14–15) and speaks of God as the father of glory in his prayer for the Ephesians (1:17). Paul declares God is father over all things (4:6) and is the father of the community of faith (5:20). The term "father" carried a political overtone in Paul's day, for the emperor was known as the father of the country (*pater patriae*).[31] The emperor as father is nicely filled out by a story from the Roman historian Suetonius. In 79 CE, Mount Vesuvius erupted, causing immense devastation to Pompeii and Herculaneum. Suetonius describes the Emperor Titus's generous response: "In these many great calamities he showed not merely the concern of an emperor, but even a father's surpassing love."[32] Paul's message implicitly contrasts the benefaction of the Roman emperor with that of God our Father. God is also Father of the Lord Jesus Christ (1:3), who is designated as the son of God in 4:13. Paul speaks here of the Lord Jesus Christ and in the previous verse speaks of being an apostle of Christ Jesus. The Greek term *Christos* represents the Hebrew "anointed one" or "messiah."[33]

---

28. Morris, 13, explains that *shalom* means not the absence of war or strife, but the "presence of something wonderful: the blessing of God in all its fullness."

29. Lau, *Politics of Peace*, 3.

30. Schüssler Fiorenza, 2, calls attention to the masculine terms "Father" and "Lord" having been used by some to dominate others (men over women, owners over slaves). She offers an inclusive translation of 1:3 that translates Father as "parent" and Lord as "leader" (5).

31. *Res Gestae divi Augusti* 35.

32. Suetonius, *Titus* 8.3; quotation from Lau, *Politics of Peace*, 132.

33. On Χριστός see BDAG 1091; B. Witherington III, "Christ," *DPL* 95–100; Marinus de Jonge, "Christ," *ABD* 1:914–21.

II. THEOLOGICAL EXPLICATION OF THE GOSPEL (1:3–3:21)

A. EULOGY AND PRAYER (1:3–23)

1. Thanksgiving to God through Christ (1:3–14)

³*Praise be to the God and Father of our Lord Jesus Christ, who has blessed us in the heavenly realms with every spiritual blessing in Christ. ⁴For he chose us in him before the creation of the world to be holy and blameless in his sight. In love ⁵he predestined us for adoption to sonship through Jesus Christ, in accordance with his pleasure and will—⁶to the praise of his glorious grace, which he has freely given us in the One he loves. ⁷In him we have redemption though his blood, the forgiveness of sins, in accordance with the riches of God's grace ⁸that he lavished on us. With all wisdom and understanding, ⁹he made known to us the mystery of his will according to his good pleasure, which he purposed in Christ, ¹⁰to be put into effect when the times reach their fulfillment—to bring unity to all things in heaven and on earth under Christ.*

¹¹*In him we were also chosen, having been predestined according to the plan of him who works out everything in conformity with the purpose of his will, ¹²in order that we, who were the first to put our hope in Christ, might be for the praise of his glory. ¹³And you also were included in Christ when you heard the message of truth, the gospel of your salvation. When you believed, you were marked in him with a seal, the promised Holy Spirit, ¹⁴who is a deposit guaranteeing our inheritance until the redemption of those who are God's possession—to the praise of his glory.*

Paul launches his message to the Ephesians with an emphatic call to praise God. Paul proclaims that God is the one who blesses believers with all blessings. The rest of this passage explains and extols this God who blesses believers and is worthy of all praise. Interestingly, Paul includes this lengthy eulogy or blessing before his thanksgiving, which he begins in 1:15. Typically Paul begins his letters with thanksgiving, although he begins with a eulogy in 2 Corinthians, albeit shorter (2 Cor 1:3–7; see also 1 Pet 1:3–9). The decision to write such an extended tribute invites us to explore the passage closely.[1]

While there is no debate about the qualities of God expressed here, scholars have various theories about how this text should be understood. Is

---

1. Lincoln, 19: "The eulogy fulfills the function which an introductory thanksgiving normally has in a Pauline letter, signaling or announcing in summary form much of the subject matter of the body of the letter."

it a hymn?[2] Does it function within a baptismal liturgy? Should it be read in light of Jewish blessings or *berakah* material?[3] Is Greek poetry a better backdrop for the passage? While all these options have their champions, none can claim majority support. We have little evidence that this passage was a hymn, was part of a liturgy, or reflects Greek meter. Given that Paul was a Jew, it is quite likely that his praise to God would reflect Old Testament sentiments and Jewish practices common in his day.[4] Yet the benediction is decidedly Christocentric, and that shapes Paul's vision of God and his actions in the world. The lengthy sentence, then, is best read as Paul's careful, yet unstudied, praise to the God who infuses and informs his church. These two emphases, theology (God the Father, the Lord Jesus Christ, and the Holy Spirit) and ecclesiology, will take up the remainder of Paul's message to the Ephesians. Additionally, Paul expounds throughout Ephesians on his emphasis here on the cosmos and its relation to God's redemptive plan that moves toward unity of all things. Finally, the mystery of the unity of Jew and gentile in Christ is hinted at here, to be fully developed within the epistle.[5]

This unit is a single sentence in Greek. With 202 words, it is the second longest sentence in the New Testament, behind Col 1:9–20, which includes 218 terms.[6] While this sentence is the longest in Ephesians, Paul includes several additional lengthy sentences as he addresses the Ephesians (see 1:15–23; 3:2–13; 4:1–6, 11–16).[7] Paul's extensive sentence with its numerous clauses benefits from a close analysis. By highlighting the key verbs, the important participles, and the numerous prepositional phrases that describe how God's salvation plan works "in" and "through" Christ, the reader discovers the map of redemption as portrayed in Paul's gospel.

The sentence flows from the subject, God the Father (1:3), and the verb "chose" (1:4), the only finite verb not subordinate to another element in the sentence. Relative clauses shape Paul's argument, as three times Paul uses a relative clause to develop his argument: in 1:6 he notes this grace "which he has freely given us," and in 1:8 the grace is explained as "that he lavished on us," while in 1:9 Paul notes God's good will "which he purposed in Christ."

---

2. Lincoln, 12–14, outlines several arguments and rightly points out that the passage's "language and style are too similar to the rest of the first three chapters for it to be possible to isolate an entity which is clearly different" (14).

3. Examples found in Lincoln, 10, include 1 Kgs 8:15, 56; Ps 41:13; 72:18–19; 89:52; 106:48. He points to the Dead Sea Scrolls, including 1QS 11:15; 1QH 5:20; 10:14; 11:27–33; 16:8.

4. See also Zechariah's praise (Luke 1:67–79).

5. MacDonald, 206.

6. Hoehner, 153, and Larkin, 4. MacDonald, 197, identifies it as the longest sentence.

7. This is in contrast to terse, short sentences that typically include an imperative (e.g., 4:4–6, 28, 29, 30, 31) and are generally found in Eph 4–6.

1:3-14 Thanksgiving to God through Christ

Participles are a key element in the sentence. Participles depend on finite verbs, in this case the sentence's main verb, "chose" (1:4). The participles underline God's intention and purpose guiding his actions. Paul describes God as the one who "blessed us" (1:3-4) and "predestined us for adoption" (1:5-8) and "made known to us" his will (1:9-14) and is therefore worthy of all praise and glory.[8] Paul repeats in 1:11 the participle "predestined" from 1:5, in both verses emphasizing the themes of adoption and inheritance. The passive participles in 1:11-14 focus on believers having been predestined, having heard and believed, and thus having received the seal of the Holy Spirit.

A series of four prepositional phrases "in whom," referring to Christ (1:7, 11, 13 twice), offers interior framing for the lengthy sentence and denotes Paul's supporting arguments.[9] Ephesians 1:7-10 focuses on the believers' redemption through Christ's blood, which is evidence of God's abounding grace poured out on them. Yet this redemption is but a piece of the overall plan of God, which is to sum up in unity all things in Christ. Ephesians 1:11-12 picks up the language of inheritance implicit in Paul's language of adoption (1:5), noting that God in Christ has given believers an inheritance and predetermined their end as being for the praise of God's glory.[10] The third and fourth occurrences of "in whom" (1:13-14) hold together Paul's contentions about the Ephesians' belief in the gospel message and the seal in the Holy Spirit that signifies and guarantees their inheritance.

Another approach to this passage's structure focuses on redundancy and repetition.[11] Phrases, terms, and synonyms flow rhythmically and produce a

---

8. Schlier, 39-40, argues that 1:4-10 comprises three strophes based on the key verbs ("choose" in 1:4, "bless" in 1:6, and "lavish" 1:8). Lincoln, 14, points out that Schlier's theory divides the strophes "unnaturally [at 1:6] and break[s] the relative clause's close connection with its antecedent."

9. Another important grammatical element is the prepositions. Paul uses κατά ("according to") in the following pairs of verses: 1:3-4, 5-6, 7-8, 9-10, 11-12 (including καθώς in 1:4). When κατά is considered alongside the verbs in this section, we find either a causal emphasis ("because" or "since") or a comparative sense ("in accordance with"), or perhaps both nuances. For example, in 1:5 κατά indicates that God predetermined believers' adoption as children of God "according to" his will. The last two verses (1:13-14) do not contain this preposition.

10. Arnold, 76, argues that the passage be divided into four sections and that "the first (1:4-6) and third (1:11-12) are parallel with one another and give similar reasons for Paul's praise for God related to his choosing and predestining of his people."

11. See, for example, the repetition of the participle "predestined" (προορίζω) in 1:5 and 1:11. Paul uses the noun "grace" (χάρις) and the cognate verb "graced, blessed" (χαριτόω) in 1:6 and repeats the noun in 1:7. He repeats three times the phrase "of/in accordance with his pleasure" (κατὰ τὴν εὐδοκίαν τοῦ θελήματος αὐτοῦ) in 1:5, 9, 11 and the noun "redemption" (ἀπολύτρωσις) twice in 1:7, 14. Paul uses the verb "inherit or choose" (κληρόω) in 1:11

"chantlike effect."[12] Paul presents a key phrase three times, "to the praise of his glorious grace" (1:6) and "to/for the praise of his glory" (1:12, 14). The first section focuses on God the Father's actions (1:3–6), the second section notes the work of the Son, the Lord Jesus Christ (1:7–12), and the final section highlights the seal of the Holy Spirit on believers (1:13–14). While this mapping captures Paul's stress on God receiving glory, it might suggest a separation of the Father's and the Son's activities, yet Paul stresses their interwoven harmony to effect salvation and the unity of all things. In every verse but two, Paul either names Christ or uses a pronoun to refer to him.

While one can discern three sections (1:3–6, 7–12, 13–14), it is also clear that Paul interlocks these sections by creating conceptual links between them. Can a pattern be discerned and a focal point identified? Perhaps a clue to these questions can be found in Paul's underlying narrative emphasis on time and space. The passage begins by emphasizing time, and more specifically the time before the world began. Paul moves to the present age, emphasizing believers' holiness in Christ and adoption into God's family by the redemption gained in Christ through his blood, a reference to the historical moment of Jesus's crucifixion. The mystery now revealed in the fullness of time (1:10) is yet to be fully realized, and so inheritance is secured by a seal of the Spirit upon believers.

Paul frames the structure narratively by a focus on God working in time, and even beyond or before time existed. Chronology is crucial in several ways. First, Paul establishes that God's good will/intention is not contingent, but is before, behind, under, and above what believers experience, that is, time. Second, it allows for a past, present, and future aspect to understanding salvation: the historical reality of Christ's blood shed on the cross, the inclusion of gentiles *as gentiles* into God's people, the life in the Spirit, and the future inheritance secured by Christ and confirmed by the seal of the Spirit. Third, it declares the glory that was, is, and is to come and for all time—the glory of God.

In addition to tracing time through this passage, Paul also sounds a spatial note. In 1:10 Paul declares that all things everywhere will be summed up and united in Christ—things in heaven and earth will come together in Christ. Believers' redemption, forgiveness, and inheritance provide one glimpse of this summing up of all things in Christ. Later in this chapter Paul

---

and the cognate noun (κληρονομία) in 1:14; in a similar fashion he uses the verb "purpose" (προτίθημι) in 1:9 and the cognate noun "plan" (πρόθεσις) in 1:11.

12. Lincoln, 12. He argues that the style reflects Hellenistic Judaism, based on study of the hypotaxis (subordination of one clause to another): "Its clauses are syntactically subordinated to each other rather than arranged in parataxis or *parallelismus membrorum* (couplets) as in Hebrew poetic and liturgical texts."

will emphasize Christ's victory over all things (1:20–22), and in 3:6–11 Paul emphasizes the scope of Christ's redemption to bring together Jew and gentile, a feat that awes and amazes the spiritual powers and principalities. It is this final unity of all things in Christ that leads Paul to repeat the call to praise God's glory.

EXCURSUS: EPHESIANS 1:3–14 AND ITS RELATIONSHIP TO THE EPISTLE

The unusual length of this sentence and its call to praise God invite us to consider its influence in the rest of the letter. Several topics and terms play significant parts as the drama of God's redemption unfolds in the six chapters.

First, Paul identifies the Godhead as God the Father and the Lord Jesus Christ (1:3) and speaks of the Holy Spirit (1:13), highlighting his perspective that will guide the early church in its doctrinal development as it takes shape in the later ecumenical councils and creeds. Paul shows how the Father, Son, and Holy Spirit shape redemption, build and nurture the church, and preserve believers until the consummation of all things. For example, Paul speaks of believers as having access through Christ to the Father by the Spirit (2:18) and repeats the truth that believers are sealed with the Holy Spirit (1:13; 4:30). Second, and related, Paul speaks extensively in this section about believers being "in Christ" and develops this depiction with word pictures, such as putting on the new self in Christ as one does a piece of clothing (4:24) and being made into one new humanity (2:14–15). Third, Paul describes redemption with language of family—adoption—that plays a key role in his developing picture of the church as God's household (2:19), as a body (4:16, 25; 5:23, 30), and as a uniting of disparate ethnic groups (Jew and gentile) into one covenant community (2:12–13). Moreover, God is described as the Father of all families (3:14–15; 4:6) with believers as his children (5:1, 8). Fourth, Paul uses the term "mystery" that he develops throughout the letter. Paul speaks of God's actions as a "mystery" now revealed, a mystery he is commissioned to make known, and a mystery that highlights God's wisdom to rulers of the heavenly realms (3:9–10) and to believers united with Christ (5:32).

Ephesians 1:3–14 lays the groundwork for Paul's extensive reflections on the nature of God, especially as it pertains to redemption, the life believers should live now, and each believer's secure hope for the future. Paul's attitude of praise and his extravagant expressions of gratitude model his later calls to build up others (4:29) and speak with thanksgiving (5:20).

Thematic Outline of 1:3–14

>praise be to God, the Father of our Lord Jesus Christ
>>he blessed us in Christ
>>he chose us in Christ
>>>before creation
>>>to be holy
>>
>>he predestined us for adoption in Christ
>>>in accord with his will
>>>to the praise of his glory
>>>in grace given in Christ
>
>in Christ we have redemption and forgiveness
>>God's grace lavished on believers
>>God made known the mystery
>>God purposed his will in Christ
>
>to bring unity to all things in heaven and earth under Christ
>in Christ, we are chosen
>>God purposed his plan in conformity with his will
>>God wills that we might be for the praise of his glory
>
>in Christ, you are included
>>Holy Spirit marks believers with seal of salvation
>>Holy Spirit guarantees believers' inheritance
>
>to the praise of his glory

a. Adopted by the Father (1:3–6)

For Paul, the greatness of God's enacted plan of redemption has specific ramifications for believers. Paul describes two ways in which God chose believers. First, they are chosen in Christ to be holy and blameless (1:4). Second, God chose by predestining believers to adoption as sons or children (1:5), which Paul explains as linked with God blessing believers in the Beloved, specifically Christ (1:6). The structure of this passage can be visualized as encircled with words of praise. In 1:3 Paul declares "praise be," followed by a reference to God the Father and our Lord Jesus Christ. Then in 1:6 Paul uses another noun translated "praise" in a clause that will be used twice more in the larger unit, namely, "to the praise of his glorious grace" (see also 1:12, 14).[13] The praise is rooted in the action of God choosing. Paul speaks about when that choice was made, how the choice was executed, what that choice accomplished, and how that choice reflects God's good will. Specifically, God's

---

13. The phrase in 1:6 reads εἰς ἔπαινον δόξης τῆς χάριτος αὐτοῦ.

choice was made before the world came into being. Christ is the instrument or effected the relationship that made possible the execution of the choice. As Paul puts it, the choice was done through Christ for believers to be in Christ. The choice created believers who are (to be) holy, blameless, and adopted by God the Father, through Christ. The choice reflects God's grace, with which God graced believers. This choice includes all spiritual blessings and can be summed up in the Beloved.

3 Paul indicates that believers "bless" or praise God the Father because he blessed them with blessings beyond compare.[14] Paul expands this idea using the cognate participle and noun when he adds that God is the one "blessing" believers with every spiritual "blessing." Even in English, readers experience the powerful force of the repetition "bless" and "blessings." Paul expands his claim by focusing on God's choice to make believers holy and blameless, adopting them as sons and daughters through Jesus Christ. Paul declares that such is God's extravagant grace with which he graced us.

Paul specifies that God is to be known as the Father of our Lord Jesus Christ. This implies that Jesus Christ is the Son, and Paul says as much in 4:13. Here, however, the emphasis is on Jesus as the believers' Lord and Messiah (see also Rom 15:6; 2 Cor 1:3; 1 Pet 1:3). God is described as "God *and* Father." What does Paul intend with the conjunction "and"? This syntax in which "and" connects two singular nouns, the first of which has an article, indicates that the second noun further describes the first.[15] Thus Paul identifies God as Father. Paul indicates with this phrase a complex understanding of the Godhead. He indicates that God has always been Father and, by implication, has always had a son. Said another way, there was never a time when God was not Father, nor was there a time when the Son was not. Jesus Christ is identified as "our Lord," a title used of God in the Old Testament, but here applied to Messiah Jesus. Paul elaborates on the designation "Lord" in 1 Corinthians,

---

14. Paul declares that God is praised with the verbal adjective εὐλογητός (BDAG 408). Hoehner, 163, indicates that this term in the New Testament refers only to God and never to humans. Paul continues by using the cognate verb in a participle form εὐλογήσας (BDAG 407–8) to indicate that God blesses believers. The participle can be understood as substantival, by which Paul would be emphasizing the term as the main noun/subject of the verse and would signal the key facet of God's person or character as the one who blesses. Alternatively, the participle could be attributive, in which case Paul would be highlighting God the Father's action of blessing. Is Paul qualifying God's person as predominately one who blesses? Or does Paul wish to focus on God as Father of the Lord Jesus Christ, who does things like bless (1:3), predestine (1:5), and reveal (1:9)? The scales tip in the direction of the former, in that Paul uses the article before the participle in 1:3, unlike the other two occurrences noted (1:5, 9). Moreover, Paul uses a finite verb in the next verse to describe God's action—"he chose."

15. See the Granville Sharp rule in Daniel B. Wallace, *Greek Grammar: Beyond the Basics; An Exegetical Syntax of the New Testament* (Grand Rapids: Zondervan, 1996), 270–74, 735.

when he instructs the Corinthians that there is "one God, the Father" and "one Lord, Jesus Christ" (1 Cor 8:6). Paul draws a direct ramification of this theological reality in declaring that believers are adopted sons and daughters of the Father (Eph 1:5).

The God who is himself blessed demonstrates this by pouring out all spiritual blessings onto believers, those who are in Christ. Paul uses the adjective "spiritual" in describing God's blessings, but we should not read into this a rejection by Paul of material blessings. The point Paul makes is a cosmic one—the blessings are as unlimited as the universe God created. They are given by the one who is before time and is not mastered by time. They pertain to the reconciled relationship between God and humanity through Christ. Additionally, Paul likely implies with the term "spiritual" the Holy Spirit's work in making available these blessings (see also 1:13–14; Col 1:9; 3:16).[16] Paul is more explicit in Eph 5:18–19 when he speaks of being filled with the Spirit and singing spiritual songs to each other. The spiritual life of the church is directly tied to the Holy Spirit's work in their midst. Two important pronouns emphasize how believers fit into the picture. Jesus Christ is not simply Lord, but "our" Lord. And God is not simply the one who blesses, but is the one who blesses "us." God's character in its very self blesses, and thus humans should praise God.

An unusual phrase found only in Ephesians first appears here: "in the heavenly realms" (see also 1:20; 2:6; 3:10; 6:12). In one case, the phrase stresses the believers' being raised and seated with Christ (2:6), and twice Paul emphasizes spiritual forces that dwell in the heavens and who now know God's plan of redemption in Christ (3:10) but actively seek to undermine God's faithful followers (6:12). In one sense, the phrase distinguishes between earthly and heavenly locations, but it carries a wider metaphorical sense that pertains to God's power and the permanence that underpins God's redemptive plan.[17] Though evil forces also populate the heavens, God has secured our place there with him in and through Christ.

God extends blessings "in Christ," a phrase that governs Paul's imagination about redemption, resurrection, and the world to come. The phrase "in Christ" is the third of three prepositional phrases that describe God, the one who blesses.[18] Paul uses the phrase "in Christ" and similar ones extensively

---

16. MacDonald, 197, remarks: "As is usually true in the NT, the use of the adjective 'spiritual' (*pneumatikos*) refers to the presence and working of the Holy Spirit in God's blessing."

17. MacDonald, 196, argues for a "local sense: heavenly realms or places." See also Lincoln, 20, who suggests that the phrase "designates the sphere of the spiritual blessings." Arnold, 78, explains the heavenlies as "a sphere of spiritual blessings to which believers now have access as well as the realm populated by evil spiritual powers."

18. Arnold, 78.

in his letters; moreover, this phrase does a lot of heavy lifting in this epistle.[19] The basic theological meaning can be explained as identification, incorporation, and participation—in sum, union with Christ.[20] Paul could allude to the objective nature of Christ's work of redemption, or the subjective experience that believers share in that salvation, or the ethical imperatives incumbent on Christ's followers.[21] Context is key to proper interpretation.[22]

EXCURSUS: "IN CHRIST"

Paul uses "in Christ" and similar phrases throughout his epistles, emphasizing the believers' participation in the life of Christ.[23] Exactly what Paul intends is an ongoing discussion.[24] Some argue for a mystical relationship

---

19. Hoehner, 173–74, lists all the occurrences of "in Christ" and its parallels, totaling thirty-nine. Lincoln, 21, observes that the phrase occurs eleven times in this passage alone.

20. Constantine R. Campbell, *Paul and Union with Christ: An Exegetical and Theological Study* (Grand Rapids: Zondervan, 2012), offers an excellent discussion on this phrase in Pauline material.

21. Additionally, the preposition ἐν is quite elastic, and the most widely used in the New Testament. Its meaning depends on the context, which makes determining Paul's meaning in the phrase "in Christ" difficult. Typically the preposition carries a local, instrumental, or spherical connotation. The spherical sense focuses on the realm of influence or control, the personal influence of Christ to the believer. The spatial/local sense answers the "where" question by noting location with Christ (2:6). Hoehner, 171–72, and Thielman, 47, propose that here in 1:3 Paul uses a locative sense combined with the spherical nuance to stress incorporation in Christ as the one in whose sphere is found salvation. The instrumental use answers the "how" question, pointing to the manner or means by which something is accomplished—that is, "through Christ" (1:3). Lincoln, 21, explains that this use carries a sense of incorporation into Christ. Best, 154; see also J. A. Allen, "The 'In Christ' Formula in Ephesians," *NTS* 5 (1958–59): 54–62. Lincoln, 22, critiques Allen's assessment that Ephesians lacks a local or incorporative sense of the phrase "in Christ." The focus on God's actions in providing blessings might tip the balance toward the instrumental sense, but we should not push this too far, as the blessings are available as believers participate in Christ together, his body the church. Campbell, *Paul and Union with Christ*, 73, laments: "Indeed, it may not be an overstatement to suggest that the pervading ambiguity of the theme of union with Christ is due in no small measure to the ambiguity of this little word, ἐν."

22. Dunn, *Theology of Paul the Apostle*, 396–404.

23. Best, 153–54, concludes: "For Paul the phrase may be said to have two main thrusts, the instrumental and the local, each predominating from time to time but neither ever totally absent."

24. M. A. Seifrid, "In Christ," *DPL* 433–36. Campbell, *Paul and Union with Christ*, 31–58, provides a helpful summary of recent scholarship. See also J. Todd Billings, *Union with Christ: Reframing Theology and Ministry for the Church* (Grand Rapids: Baker Academic,

with Christ,[25] which could include the believer's experience with the Holy Spirit.[26] Albert Schweitzer speaks of "being-in-Christ." He focuses on the eschatological reality of believers both living in the present age and looking for the new age to be brought about by Christ.[27] Others, such as Rudolf Bultmann, reject the mystical reading and instead explain Paul's views in connection with Hellenism, specifically the mystery religions and their dying-rising gods.[28] Karl Barth focuses on the relationship of the Father and Son, based on Paul's claims that "God was, in Christ, reconciling the world to Himself" (2 Cor 5:19)."[29] For Barth, participation in Christ spoke of an everlasting and enduring unity between Christ and the believer.

Schweitzer's emphasis on mystical union was modified decades later by E. P. Sanders, who connected Paul's language of righteousness by faith, and life in the Spirit, with the claims of being in Christ and what he called "participationist eschatology."[30] Richard Hays, in conversation with Sanders, developed the concept of participation to include four aspects: familial, ecclesial, narratival (living in the story of Christ), and political/military solidarity with Christ.[31]

2011); Michael J. Thate, Kevin J. Vanhoozer, and Constantine R. Campbell, eds., *"In Christ" in Paul: Explorations in Paul's Theology of Union and Participation* (reprinted Grand Rapids: Eerdmans, 2018); Michael J. Gorman, *Participating in Christ: Explorations in Paul's Theology and Spirituality* (Grand Rapids: Baker Academic, 2019).

25. Adolf Deissmann, *Paul: A Study in Social and Religious History*, 2nd ed., trans. William E. Wilson (London: Hodder & Stoughton, 1926), 130–36.

26. John Murray, *Redemption—Accomplished and Applied* (Grand Rapids: Eerdmans, 1955), 201–12.

27. Albert Schweitzer, *The Mysticism of Paul the Apostle*, trans. W. Montgomery (London: Black, 1930; reprinted Baltimore: Johns Hopkins University Press, 1998), 122–27. On p. 125, he writes: "The fact that the believer's whole being, down to his most ordinary everyday thoughts and actions, is thus brought within the sphere of the mystical experience has its effect of giving to this mysticism a breadth, a permanence, a practicability, and a strength almost unexampled elsewhere in mysticism." For discussion, see Peter Orr, *Christ Absent and Present: A Study in Pauline Christology*, WUNT 354 (Tübingen: Mohr Siebeck, 2014), 7–22.

28. Bultmann, *Theology of the New Testament*, 1:298, explains that "*Paul describes Christ's death in analogy with the death of a divinity of the mystery religions*" (emphasis original).

29. Karl Barth, *Church Dogmatics*, vol. 4.3.2: *The Doctrine of Reconciliation*, ed. G. W. Bromiley and T. F. Torrance, trans. G. W. Bromiley (Edinburgh: T&T Clark, 1962), 651.

30. Sanders, *Paul and Palestinian Judaism*, 514–20, 549. He writes: "The heart of Paul's thought is . . . that one dies with Christ, obtaining new life and the initial transformation which lead to the resurrection and ultimate transformation, that one is a member of the body of Christ and one Spirit with him, and that one remains so unless one breaks the participatory union by forming another" (514). He describes Paul's "participationist eschatology" as "the believer becomes one with Christ Jesus and that this effects a transfer of lordship and the beginning of a transformation which will be completed with the coming of the Lord" (549).

31. Richard Hays, "What Is 'Real Participation in Christ'? A Dialogue with E. P. Sanders on Pauline Soteriology," in *Redefining First-Century Jewish and Christian Identities: Essays*

Excursus: "In Christ"

James D. G. Dunn categorizes the "in Christ" phrases into three categories: objective, subjective, and actions or attitudes of Paul or other believers.[32] The objective focus understands "in Christ" as pertaining to Christ's redemptive act. The subjective usage attends to the reality of believers being "in Christ."

Drawing on these ideas, Michael Gorman promotes participation in Christ with his concept of "cruciformity," emphasizing believers' identification with Christ's death.[33] Gorman argues that we should understand "in Christ" in relation to baptism, which includes a union with Christ that is personal, corporate, and covenantal.[34] Participation in Christ secures salvation and entails covenant responsibilities as believers undergo transformation into Christ's likeness. For Gorman, the language "in Christ" is missional, engaging in the world, for these realities "are all indications of action in service to what God is up to in the world."[35] Gorman emphasizes that "to be in Christ is therefore to be part of God's mission as both beneficiaries of it and participants in it: in fact benefiting and participating are inseparable, even synonymous, realities."[36] Gorman suggests that the ideas encapsulated in "in Christ" and similar phrases can be traced to Israel's prophets and their emphasis on God's spirit being poured out on the people.[37] Isaiah speaks of the Spirit being poured out such that a barren field becomes fertile (32:15), and Ezekiel tells of a valley of dry bones reanimated by God (37:1–14). At Pentecost, Peter cites Joel 2:28–32, the prophecy that described God pouring out his Spirit on all people (Acts 2:16–21). In Ephesians, Paul speaks of believers sharing one baptism, also drawing on images of liquid poured out and the Spirit poured out on believers (4:5). In this passage, Paul stresses the unity shared by believers in the Spirit, drawing on the unity believers have in Christ, our peace (2:14), in whom believers are blessed with all blessings by the God and Father of Christ (1:3). Susan Eastman explores participation as it informs Paul's anthropology and Christology. She argues that Paul's "participatory worldview is grounded in his depiction of Christ's participation in and assimilation to human existence to the point of death, thereby enacting a transforming union with

---

in Honor of Ed Parish Sanders, ed. Fabian E. Udoh et al. (Notre Dame: University of Notre Dame Press, 2008), 339–47.

32. Dunn, *Theology of Paul the Apostle*, 390–412.

33. Michael J. Gorman, *Cruciformity: Paul's Narrative Spirituality of the Cross* (Grand Rapids: Eerdmans, 2001); Gorman, *Inhabiting the Cruciform God*.

34. Gorman, *Becoming the Gospel*, 28–29.

35. Gorman, *Becoming the Gospel*, 33, remarks that these realities "are all indications of action in service to what God is up to in the world."

36. Gorman, *Becoming the Gospel*, 34. See also Gorman, "Romans and the Participationist Perspective," in *Preaching Romans: Four Perspectives*, ed. Scot McKnight and Joseph Modica (Grand Rapids: Eerdmans, 2019), 59–79.

37. Gorman, "Romans and the Participationist Perspective," 63–64.

humanity operative in, but not limited to, bodily existence here and now."[38] She suggests that Paul's anthropology offers worth to each and every human because of "Christ's participation in the depths of human life."[39]

Constantine Campbell suggests that Paul speaks of union, participation, identification, and incorporation as four ways of understanding Paul's intentions.[40] Campbell focuses on the range of meanings within the prepositions used in the phrase. The preposition *en* has an extensive semantic range, including a locative or spatial ("in" or "in the sphere of"), instrumental ("with"), and causal meaning ("because of" or "on account of").[41] For example, Campbell argues that in 1:3, we find the instrumental use, wherein God accomplishes redemption through Christ. In 2:6 Campbell argues for the locative sense, the idea that believers are with Christ, in the sphere of his presence, as they are seated with him in the heavenly places.[42] Campbell argues for the causal sense in 4:32, stressing that because of Christ's work, God forgives believers.[43] The various meanings of *en* make understanding the context of each occurrence of the phrase critical. We will look at the specific cases as we address the verses in context.

Paul's use of "in Christ" and its parallel phrases focus on believers' participation in the redemption of God. Understanding "in Christ" as participation in and with Christ is not in competition with Paul's claims of salvation by grace and justification by faith in Christ.[44] Rather, they work together to encompass the full range of glorious blessings with which God has blessed believers.

4–5 God's blessings extend to believers through union with the Lord Jesus Christ, and in response, believers bless and praise God the Father. Paul fills out the picture of these magnanimous blessings by indicating God's choice,

---

38. Susan Grove Eastman, *Paul and the Person: Reframing Paul's Anthropology* (Grand Rapids: Eerdmans, 2017), 177–78.

39. Eastman, *Paul and the Person*, 179. She continues: "The incarnation affords a radical argument for the validity of every human body, irrespective of any criteria of rationality, mobility, race, gender, relationality, or any other characteristic."

40. Campbell, *Paul and Union with Christ*, 413.

41. Campbell, *Paul and Union with Christ*, 69.

42. Contra Best, 154, who assigns 2:6 as instrumental. Best argues for the local sense in 2:13, 15, 21.

43. Campbell, *Paul and Union with Christ*, 82–88.

44. Chester, *Reading Paul with the Reformers*, 175–86, 269–90, demonstrates that Calvin and Luther embraced the idea of union with Christ as central to their understanding of salvation by grace through faith.

the implementation of that choice, and the results of that choice for believers. Paul indicates when the choice was made ("before the creation of the world"), why the choice was made (to make believers holy, to create adopted sons and daughters), and how the choice was implemented (through Christ). In 1:4 we have the only finite verb of these twelve verses (1:3-14) not part of a relative clause, and thus all other verbs and participles link back to this—that is, the only finite verb, "to choose."

Paul declares that God "chose."[45] This verb is used a number of times in the New Testament and usually carries the sense that a choice is made between several options. For example, Jesus tells a parable of banquet guests who choose the seats of honor, only to have a person of higher honor come later and take their seat, thereby humiliating them (Luke 14:7). Jesus also uses this verb in a theological sense when he indicates that he chose and appointed his disciples to bear fruit (John 15:16). Paul uses the verb to speak about God choosing the foolish, the weak, and the despised of this world to shame the strong (1 Cor 1:27-28). Here in Ephesians the emphasis is the manner in which God makes possible the believers' reception of all spiritual blessings. Paul likely draws on the similar idea of God choosing a people found in the Old Testament (Deut 7:6-8; 14:2).[46] Paul does not emphasize God's *not* choosing some men and women, for here Paul stresses the composition of the church broadly as those adopted into God's family and expected to live in a worthy manner.[47] The verb "choose" is followed by the prepositional phrase "in him," meaning "in Christ." The phrase can imply Christ's preexistence with the Father, but more likely in this context, it explains the means by which God accomplished his choosing.[48]

Paul explains the timing and the purpose of God's choice. The choice was made before the "creation of the world." This need not imply that God intended humanity to sin and thought of a way out of the mess. Rather, Paul assures readers that God's choice rests in himself, not as a matter of contin-

---

45. Ἐκλέγομαι; see BDAG 305; Hoehner, 175; Best, 119; Thielman, 48; Gary Steven Shogren, "Election," *ABD* 2:441-44. The aorist middle tense "he chose" indicates an action in the past; indeed, Paul will note that the choice was made before the cosmos was established. Also, the aorist emphasizes the action as a whole, that it occurred; see Wallace, *Greek Grammar*, 554-55.

46. MacDonald, 198.

47. Best, 119, writes that our author "displays no interest in those who are not chosen." He continues: "The seemingly logical deduction that when some are chosen others are rejected is not worked out in the NT." See also Lincoln, 24.

48. Thielman, 48. Lincoln, 24, suggests that "the notion of the election of believers in Christ has been combined with that of the preexistence of Christ." He warns that this text says nothing about the preexistence of the church. Arnold, 80, contends that "in him" refers "to Christ's participation in God's act of choosing."

gent situations.[49] And God's choice has a purpose: for those in Christ to be holy and blameless.[50] These two adjectives are repeated in 5:27, describing Christ's work in preparing the church for himself (see also Col 1:22). I noted that Paul identifies the readers of this letter as "saints," or "holy ones." The same term is used here, but perhaps with the more active sense that believers should strive toward a life of blamelessness and holiness. Such language is sadly out of fashion today, for it brings to mind judgmental attitudes and holier-than-thou arrogance. Nevertheless, Paul encourages believers to reshape their understanding of what true human flourishing looks like.

Ephesians 1:4 ends with the phrase "in love," and its reference is unclear.[51] One possibility is that the phrase looks back to the believers' actions of holiness and blamelessness, indicating that their deeds should be covered in love.[52] A second possibility connects the phrase with the next term, a participle "to predestine."[53] The grammar is inconclusive, but this second option has the advantage of connecting this phrase "in love" with a similar phrase at the end of 1:6, "in the One he loves." Elsewhere in the epistle the language is connected with God's or Christ's love for believers, with the exception of noting a husband's command to love his wife. Even here, the command is rooted in Christ's love for the church. Given this emphasis overall and the rhetorical bookends created by "in love" and "in the One he loves," I connect the phrase with the participle that begins 1:5.[54] It is either God's love that led to his predetermining adoption, or love is the manner by which God acted in his preordaining adoption to reconcile himself to humanity.

In further describing God's choice, Paul announces that God predestined believers for adoption. Paul could be nuancing *when* God chose by indicating either that God selected believers after he had predestined them[55] or that God's choice and predetermination happened contemporaneously.[56] Alternatively, Paul may be stressing the *means by which* God chose, namely, that he chose by means of predetermining believers (to be adopted as sons

---

49. Best, 120.

50. On ἅγιος see BDAG 10–11 (1); on ἄμωμος see BDAG 56 (2).

51. William Klassen, "Love (NT and Early Judaism)," *ABD* 4:381–96.

52. Lincoln, 24. Thielman, 49–50, argues from the syntax of 1:3–14 that when a verbal form describing God's action is qualified with a prepositional phrase, that phrase always follows the verbal form.

53. Arnold, 82. Best, 123, argues in part that the eulogy primarily focuses on God's actions toward people, not their attitude toward God or toward each other.

54. Muddiman, 68, points out that the "same words are connected with a following participle at Eph. 3.17."

55. Hoehner, 194, describes the participle as causal: "because of having predestined us, he chose us."

56. Best, 123; Salmond, 251; Arnold, 81.

and daughters).⁵⁷ A grammatical and a theological case can be made for each of the three options; therefore, the reader must search more broadly for help in discerning Paul's emphasis. A clue may be found in the participle's repetition in 1:11, where it refers to either believers having been predetermined to receive their inheritance or believers as God's inheritance who are predestined according to his purpose. Such ambiguity does not help us determine the specific nuance in 1:5, but the participle's repetition highlights Paul's stress on the importance of God's redemptive design established beforehand and apart from human actions.⁵⁸ Such emphasis is consistent with Paul's use of the verb in Rom 8:29–30. In Romans, Paul indicates that those God foreknew he predetermined for conformity to the image of the Son, and those who are determined beforehand are called, justified, and glorified. The parallel ideas are hard to miss, for both Ephesians and Romans stress that believers are connected intimately with Christ. Predetermination or predestination for Paul, then, seems to be linked to a specific relationship with Christ.⁵⁹ The predestined activity of God is not salvation in a generic sense, but a specific preordained outcome that can be described both as adoption, which shapes the believer into the likeness of the Only Begotten Son, and as conformity to the image of the Son.

Paul expands the discussion by introducing a rare term found only four other places in Paul: "adoption" (see Rom 8:15, 23; 9:4; Gal 4:5).⁶⁰ The

---

57. Lincoln, 25.

58. MacDonald, 210, argues (unpersuasively in my opinion) that Ephesians promotes a sectarian, isolationist stance toward wider society: "The recipients of Ephesians receive no explicit encouragement to engage in dialogue with outsiders." MacDonald, 199, points to language of predestination in the Qumran material (1QH 15:15–17; 1QS 3:15–23). She observes that the concepts of predestination in Pauline literature "draw their origins from OT notions of God choosing a people" (209). Perkins, 39, rightly comments that, unlike the Qumran material, Paul does not discuss the wicked in this context, although he will speak about the children of disobedience later in the epistle (2:2; 5:6).

59. Augustine, *On the Predestination of the Saints*, speaks of unconditional election but reserves as a mystery the nonelect's damnation. For a general discussion, see Jesse Couenhoven, *Predestination: A Guide for the Perplexed* (London: T&T Clark, 2018). John Calvin, *Institutes of the Christian Religion*, trans. Ford Lewis Battles, ed. John T. McNeill, Library of Christian Classics (Philadelphia: Westminster, 1960), 926 §3.21.5. See also Herman J. Selderhuis, *John Calvin: A Pilgrim's Life*, trans. Albert Gootjes (Downers Grove, IL: InterVarsity Press, 2009), 190, who explains that the issue for Calvin was about whether a person could make a saving decision, not whether God saved some and damned some; and Jason E. Vickers, "Wesley's Theological Emphases," in *The Cambridge Companion to John Wesley*, ed. Randy L. Maddox and Jason E. Vickers (Cambridge: Cambridge University Press, 2010), 192.

60. On υἱοθεσία see BDAG 1024; J. M. Scott, "Adoption, Sonship," *DPL* 15–18. See also Erin M. Heim, *Adoption in Galatians and Romans: Contemporary Metaphor Theories and the Pauline Huiothesia Metaphors*, Biblical Interpretations 153 (Leiden: Brill, 2017).

adoption happens through Jesus Christ. The powerful metaphor of adoption deserves a closer look to understand its social context in the first century and its Old Testament context, before turning to the term's theological potency. Adoption of adult sons was quite common among gentiles in the New Testament era, while adoption of girls or adult females was rare to nonexistent. The purpose of adoption was to secure the family's heritage, including a continuation of honoring the traditional gods and goddesses and managing the family's wealth. The family might adopt a young man whose own father was still living (and gave permission for the adoption) and might adopt a son to inherit over a birth son.[61] Rarely would one adopt an infant, to avoid the great risk that the boy would not grow up to be a worthy adult son. Perhaps the most famous adopted son was Octavian, who was adopted by Julius Caesar at age eighteen and was later known as Caesar Augustus, the founder of the Roman Empire. Because Julius Caesar was declared a god posthumously by the Senate, Octavian identified himself as a "son of god" (Latin *divi filius*) on many imperial coins and inscriptions.

By contrast, adoption was rare among Jews in the Second Temple period, as well as among the ancient Israelites. The biblical text does not denounce adoption; rather, the emphasis is on God's ability to give a biological son to a patriarch and matriarch. Time and again God proved himself faithful in providing an heir to build up Israel. Yet one aspect of Roman-era adoption tallies nicely with ancient Israelite and later Jewish practice, specifically the emphasis on "son." Throughout the Old Testament, God refers to Israel as his son, and this identification signals the close relationship established by God toward his people.[62]

Paul pulls together various strands of Jewish and Roman thought and custom to explain God's redemptive plan. He relies on a common custom of adoption that shaped gentile families, such that his readers would have a ready image of God's family as inclusive of sons (and daughters) brought in by the paterfamilias's design. And Paul incorporates the common Jewish motif that Israel is God's son to encourage believers that God's plan in Christ connects with God's pattern of establishing his people. Implicit in this model of adoption is the reality that a believer is not simply "saved," but is also a member of God's family. In Paul's day, any man or woman who was persuaded of a particular philosophy or religious claim expected at the same time to follow that group's way of life; they became a member of a community. Identification with a group included behavioral commitments, and we find Paul explaining

---

61. MacDonald, 199, explains: "Paul called to mind the practice of a well-to-do, childless adult wanting to adopt a male heir, often a slave."

62. Lincoln, 25, writes that adoption in Paul "must also be seen against the OT background of Israel's relationship with God."

1:3–6 Adopted by the Father

these in the latter three chapters of the epistle.[63] Modern hyperindividualism can blind us to the corporate and community nature of the Christian life assumed by first-century readers.

6 With this verse, Paul concludes his initial comments concerning God's redemptive plan, which includes God choosing believers in Christ and adopting them as his beloved children so that they would be holy and blameless. As he reflects on this grand truth, Paul bursts forth with a refrain of praise that he will repeat twice more before the end of the long passage (1:12, 14). Paul enjoins believers to praise God's grace, a grace that reflects and contains the glory of God. The root of the noun "grace" (*charis*) is repeated in the verb "freely given" (*charitoō*); thus, the verse can be translated, "to his glorious grace with which he graced us in the Beloved."[64] This translation allows the English reader to appreciate the tight connection Paul draws between the glorious grace that belongs to God and God's amazing grace-gift given to believers in Christ.[65] In other words, believers are not honoring God for a quality unknown to them, but are praising God for a quality—grace—that they know intimately, because they know, or are known, by God in Christ. Love and praise, glory and grace—these encircle the believer because of God's great good pleasure.[66]

Paul uses the term *charis* often in his greetings and closings. Ephesians stands out for the number of times Paul uses this noun within the body of his letter. While it appears in Galatians seven times, three times in Philippians, *charis* occurs twelve times in Ephesians' six chapters. Romans' sixteen chapters include *charis* twenty-four times, thus Ephesians has a higher percentage of occurrence than Romans, the epistle most often connected with Paul's presentation of God's grace. Not only does Paul use the term repeatedly in Ephesians, but *charis* is central to the theology espoused. In 1:6–7 Paul stresses God's grace in relation to redemption and forgiveness of trespasses through Christ's blood. In 2:5 Paul reiterates grace that saves those who were dead in trespasses. Ephesians 2:5 and 2:8 each use the term in the familiar phrase "by grace you have been saved," while 2:7 includes the claim that God's grace is extended in Christ, a conviction strongly asserted in Eph 1. Moreover, grace is further explained as God's gift, which reflects the broader semantic context that intertwines "gift" and "giving."[67] In Eph 3, the term is nuanced to focus

---

63. I am indebted to my research assistant, Julie Dykes, for this observation.

64. On χαριτόω see BDAG 1081.

65. MacDonald, 199, notes that the noun "grace" is "the central Pauline term" and that the verb is used only here and in Luke 1:28.

66. Lincoln, 26, explains that grace is "the principle of God's redemptive activity which permeates it through and through."

67. Barclay, *Paul and the Gift*, 26: "The semantic field for gifts and counter-gifts embraces a broad array of terms, but prominent are nouns from the δωρ-root (δῶρον, δωρεά),

on Paul's gospel ministry to gentiles as evidence of God's gift of grace in his calling (3:2, 7, 8). In Eph 4, Paul speaks of grace in relation to gift (4:7) and of believers giving grace to each other by their encouraging words (4:29). Paul includes a traditional opening and closing that also uses *charis* (1:2; 6:24). Each occurrence of the term will be discussed in context; however, some general thoughts suggest themselves. First, Paul associates *charis* with God the Father's salvific actions in Christ the Son. Second, Paul understands this grace to operate at the individual level, for he sees *charis* penetrating his apostolic ministry. Third, Paul believes *charis* should guide believers' conversations, for it builds up and blesses.

The Greek term *charis* can be translated "gift," "grace," or "benefit" and carried a range of meanings in Paul's day among Jews and gentiles.[68] The noun did not always carry a religious overtone, but was also used frequently in contexts of social benefaction. Ancient Greeks and Romans valued the relationships gained through reciprocal gift giving. Seneca, the first-century Stoic, advocated giving generously and selectively. He maintained that gifts should not be given randomly, but benefactors should use sound judgment in distributing their gifts.[69] It was important to give generously to those who would reciprocate, so that when you were in need, that friend would be there to help. As such, the giver demonstrated his or her wisdom by giving a gift (*charis*) to someone who would use it well, someone worthy. To give recklessly is foolishness or arrogance, an example of showing off before others that the giver has so much that they could afford to waste it. The recipient, honored by the gift, would seek to return an even greater gift or, if that was impossible, give public praise to the gift giver. Seneca uses the image of the Three Graces dancing hand-in-hand in a circle to explain what happens with a gift: giving, receiving, returning the gift.[70]

In many Christian circles today, discussions about grace center on the unmerited nature of the recipients of God's grace and on grace being utterly free and unilaterally given without consideration of the recipient's qualifications. The term's meaning is polyvalent, carrying different emphases that accent aspects of either the giver, the gift itself, or the recipient. John Barclay suggests that *charis* carries at least six kinds (not degrees) of emphases:

---

with their associated verbs (δίδωμι and its counterpart, ἀποδίδωμι), interwoven with nouns and verbs from the χαρ-stem. These latter (among nouns most commonly χάρις and its plural, χάριτες) typically convey the ethos of the gift as voluntary benevolence, but are also used often for specific acts of beneficence, favor expressed in a particular object or action."

68. On χάρις see BDAG 1079; A. B. Luter Jr., "Grace," *DPL* 372–74.

69. Seneca's *On Benefits*, is a first-century Stoic discussion about benefaction. Barclay, *Paul and the Gift*, 46, explains that "Seneca shares with all his contemporaries the assumption that gifts are meant to be reciprocal, not unilateral."

70. Seneca, *On Benefits* 1.3.2.

1:3–6 ADOPTED BY THE FATHER

(1) superabundant, (2) efficacious, (3) priority, (4) singularity, (5) incongruity, (6) noncircularity.[71] A gift is superabundant as it gives an overgenerous amount of the gift. It is efficacious when the gift accomplishes its purpose. The perfect priority of the gift is one initiated by the gift giver, therefore the recipient cannot claim any rights to the gift. The singularity of a perfect gift refers to the giver's character as beyond reproach and who is singularly focused on benefaction.[72] The incongruous gift is one given to an unworthy recipient. This quality of *charis* or gift was less common. Most in the ancient world stressed congruity because giving to an unworthy recipient calls into question the character of the giver. Should God give to an unworthy person, he could be seen as giving randomly or as following an unfair or arbitrary practice.[73] Yet the Essenes at Qumran wrote hymns praising God for his incongruous gift of salvation.[74] They understood this gift as God's plan for the cosmos and their predestined place in it, while Paul found the incongruous grace in Christ. Finally, the noncircularity of the gift is one that breaks the cycle of reciprocity. This is the modern idea of pure gift, but it was rare in the ancient world (cf. Luke 6:27–36). While the ancients knew that a gift might be unilateral, as there is no guarantee the gift would strengthen a relationship or accomplish its purpose, and they knew that the gods (or God) did not require any gift in return, nevertheless, they believed that the value of creating and maintaining relationships would be lost in an unreciprocated (noncircularity) gift.[75] Thus, the altruistic, disinterested gift so highly praised today would have had few supporters in the ancient world.

All six of the perfections of grace listed above are definitions of grace, but historically not all Christians have weighted the emphases in the same

---

71. Barclay, *Paul and the Gift*, 69–75. In speaking of grace, Barclay uses the term "perfection" to indicate the kind of emphasis on grace drawn out to its purest form. He makes the point that it is not about degrees of the same emphasis, but a different emphasis altogether.

72. Philo, *On the Life of Abraham* 268, explains that God gives only good, not evil; cf. James 1:17.

73. Seneca, *On Benefits* 1.15.6.

74. Hartmut Stegemann and Eileen Schuller, eds., Carol Newsom, trans., *Qumran Cave 1*, vol. 3: *1QHodayot*a, Discoveries in the Judaean Desert 40 (Oxford: Clarendon, 2009). Barclay, *Paul and the Gift*, 239, notes that in these hymns "there is an equal emphasis on the worthlessness of the recipients of mercy, an insistent assertion that there is nothing in the material, social, or moral quality of the human object that could provide grounds for this outpouring of grace."

75. Gary A. Anderson, *Charity: The Place of the Poor in the Biblical Tradition* (New Haven: Yale University Press, 2013), discusses divine reward of human generosity. In his book *Sin: A History* (New Haven: Yale University Press, 2009), 12, he highlights the connections between forgiveness as debt repaid and merit earned: "Acts of human generosity funded a treasury that did not play by the rules of a zero-sum economy.... God has 'gamed' the system to the advantage of the faithful." See also Deut 14:29; 15:4–5; 24:13–15, and elsewhere, in which God promises to bless those who give to the poor.

way. If we talk about God's grace as unconditional, do we mean that it comes without prior conditions (incongruous), or that it requires no return (non-circular), or perhaps both?[76] If we speak of God's grace as unmerited favor, we refer to the incongruous nature of the gift.[77] What is important to keep in mind is that Paul and his readers knew of these different emphases surrounding grace and gift giving.

This fact is useful in our reading of Ephesians, as Christians have traditionally claimed that Jews do not believe in grace, but in works. Often the "free" grace of God in Christ is contrasted with the Jews' "works righteousness." However, Jews in the first century wrote about God's grace, often in ways that parallel Paul's usage.[78] This brief study highlights that Jews in the first century, including Paul who was a Jew, held different understandings on the meaning and implications of God's grace. All held the general conviction that God is a gracious God. Paul believed he had a better grasp of this grace than his Jewish compatriots who did not follow Jesus. Paul saw this grace expressed in Christ, the Beloved, with incongruity—that is, "given without regard to worth."[79]

Paul describes Christ as "the One he [God] loves." The participial phrase is found only here in the New Testament, but a similar adjectival phrase is used in Jesus's baptism (Matt 3:17; Mark 1:11; Luke 3:22; John 1:34) and transfiguration accounts (Matt 17:5; Mark 9:7).[80] To the Colossians, Paul describes God as "the Father of our Lord Jesus Christ" (1:3) who rescued believers from darkness "into the kingdom of the Son he loves" (1:13). In this beloved one, believers have redemption and forgiveness of sins.

b. Redeemed by the Son (1:7–12)

With 1:7 Paul begins a new section in his lengthy praise to God the Father in Christ the Son. In the next four verses, Paul expands on his understanding of God's plan noted in 1:4. Paul explores one aspect of God's plan for the cosmos,

---

76. Barclay, *Paul and the Gift*, 76.

77. Barclay, *Paul and the Gift*, 92–95, points to the example of Augustine and Pelagius. The latter believed in the superabundance and the priority of grace, but not its incongruity. Augustine held strongly to its incongruous nature. Both believed in God's grace, but they were poles apart on its meaning.

78. Westerholm, *Perspectives Old and New*, 341, discusses and critiques Sanders's view that Second Temple Jews believed that "'grace' and 'works' were identical."

79. Barclay, *Paul and the Gift*, 6.

80. Muddiman, 70. MacDonald, 199, adds: "Those who have stressed the liturgical and/or baptismal roots of this passage have attached special significance to the fact that Jesus is identified as the beloved [*ho agapētos*] in the baptismal scenes in the gospel."

specifically centering on Christ's work on the cross for believers' redemption and Christ's establishment of ultimate unity in the heavens and earth. Paul speaks of grace as he did in the previous verse and introduces an important term, "mystery," that reoccurs in key places later in the letter (1:9; 3:3, 4, 9; 5:32; 6:19). Finally, 1:7 is one of three verses in this section that begins "in him" (Christ), a key theological concept foundational to Paul's understanding of salvation (1:11, 13). Paul forms an *inclusio* with the phrase "in him" here and the personal pronoun "in him" (Christ) in 1:10.[81] One discerns a pattern when tracing these phrases in this passage. In 1:3 the verse ends with "in Christ," and a new section begins that concludes with "in the One he loves" in 1:6. Another section forms in 1:7, finishing with "in Christ" in 1:9. The next section ends with "in Christ" in 1:12.[82] This pattern, in stressing the expectations and privileges of believers—namely, that they are predestined to be holy, they are adopted, they are redeemed, they have an inheritance—reminds believers how this reality is accomplished.

7–8 Paul turns his attention from commenting on God's work to focusing on the results of that work in believers' lives. Paul stresses redemption and points to two additional aspects of redemption, namely, its connection to Christ's blood and its consequence, the forgiveness of trespasses. We possess redemption only "in him," that is, the Beloved of the previous verse. And we are granted redemption only by God's riches of grace—the grace so pointedly emphasized in 1:6. Colossians 1:14 offers a close parallel to Eph 1:7: "in whom we have redemption, the forgiveness of sins." Missing from the Colossians text is the phrase "through his blood"; moreover, the two letters use a different Greek term for "sins."[83] Finally, Col 1:13 speaks of the beloved Son, the one in whom believers have redemption and forgiveness of sins. From here Paul launches into an elevated portrait of the Son as the image of the invisible God (Col 1:15–20).

The noun "redemption" is not common in the New Testament, used only ten times, with three of those occurrences in our epistle.[84] The term is rare in the wider Greek world, and its meaning related to the idea of release or deliverance and often reflected payment of ransom for prisoners of war

---

81. Arnold, 85.

82. Thielman, 41.

83. Ephesians uses παράπτωμα, Colossians uses ἁμαρτία. Paul will use both nouns as synonyms in Eph 2:1.

84. On ἀπολύτρωσις see BDAG 117; L. Morris, "Redemption," *DPL* 784–86; Gary Steven Shogren, "Redemption," *ABD* 5:650–57. See also Hoehner, 205. MacDonald, 200, observes: "The only use of the term in the LXX (Dan 4:34) and many instances of cognate terms in the LXX suggest that the term could be used as a general word for deliverance from danger, and especially for deliverance from the Egyptian bondage and the Babylonian exile." See also Lincoln, 28.

or slaves.[85] It is seldom used in a cultic sense, except in Jewish writings. Old Testament texts such as Exod 30:12–13 speak of the half-shekel tax owed as a ransom,[86] a related noun used by Jesus in his pronouncement that he came to give his life as "a ransom for many" (Matt 20:28; Mark 10:45).[87] Paul speaks of redemption twice in Romans (3:24; 8:23). Interestingly, in Rom 8:23, Paul portrays believers as awaiting their adoption, described as the "redemption" of their bodies—that is, bodily resurrection. So too in our passage, Paul links adoption through Jesus Christ (1:5) with redemption through his blood (1:7). The future aspect of redemption, captured in the Romans passage, is likely expressed in Eph 1:14, and more certainly in 4:30, but here in 1:7 Paul stresses the believers' current reality of redemption by Christ's blood.

Paul continues that believers have "forgiveness of sins" in Christ. This phrase is in apposition to the term "redemption" and serves to explain or clarify it further.[88] The noun "forgiveness" is rarely used in the New Testament epistles (Col 1:14; Heb 9:22; 10:18), but is used thirteen times in the Gospels and Acts.[89] The phrase "through his blood" is a reference to Christ's sacrificial death on the cross that redeems those who believe. Paul's message to the Ephesian leaders in Acts 20:28 urges that they shepherd the flock faithfully, for the church of God has been bought with Christ's own blood. Throughout the New Testament we find an emphasis on the redemptive quality of Christ's blood, beginning with his own words. In his Last Supper, Jesus took up a cup and proclaimed that it is his blood of the (new) covenant, which is poured out for the forgiveness of sins (Matt 26:27–28; Mark 14:23–24). Peter declares that believers are redeemed by the precious blood of Christ, not with silver or gold. Peter focuses on redemption from an empty way of life, not specifically forgiveness of sins (1 Pet 1:18–19). These texts show the tight connections between redemption, ransom, forgiveness, and resurrection.

Paul praises God who makes such redemption and forgiveness possible. It is because of his riches of grace that Christ's blood redeems and forgives sins. Five times in this letter Paul refers to God's riches: the riches of his grace

---

85. Best, 130.

86. Λύτρον.

87. Hoehner, 206, argues that "future redemption is based on Christ's payment at the cross." Lincoln, 28, insists that the evidence is not conclusive, and "it appears to be overdogmatic to insist on ransom connotations for all uses of ἀπολύτρωσις in the NT."

88. Thielman, 60; Lincoln, 28.

89. On ἄφεσις see BDAG 155; L. Morris, "Forgiveness," *DPL* 311–13; Gary Steven Shogren, "Forgiveness," *ABD* 2:835–38. See also Muddiman, 71. MacDonald, 52, argues that "in the Acts of the Apostles 'the forgiveness of sins' acts as a formula for the content of salvation (Acts 5:31; 10:43; 13:38; 26:18)." She adds: "The emphasis on redemption that is experienced in the present, the adoption language, and the references to predestination work together to convey strong sentiments of being set apart from all others" (210).

(1:7), the riches of inheritance (1:18), the riches of his grace in kindness (2:7), the unsearchable riches of Christ (3:8), and the riches of his glory (3:16). The sense of overflowing abundance that spills out, refreshes, and makes new all it falls on—this is the effect of God's riches, expressed in his grace. Paul explains that this grace is not parceled out reluctantly or miserly but is poured out with lavish abundance (1:8). Paul develops a picture of God's unrestrained generosity and vast understanding that should inform and make confident the Ephesian believers. The Ephesians need not fear, for God gives abundantly and generously (cf. Rom 5:15; 2 Cor 3:9; 9:8).

Even more, God acts with intelligence and insight. The last clause of Eph 1:8, "with all wisdom and understanding," begins a new thought for Paul, as he turns to discuss God making known his will in 1:9.[90] The phrase modifies the participle in 1:9, "having made known," explaining more fully the nature of God's revelation. This reading of the syntax parallels the interpretation of the phrase "in love" found in 1:4–5, wherein the phrase "in love" that ended 1:4 is linked with the participle "having determined/predestined" that begins 1:5.[91] Less likely are the possibilities that "wisdom" and "understanding" are two of the gifts extended by God to the Ephesians, or qualities God demonstrates in establishing believers' redemption in Christ.[92] In sum, God's wisdom is shown in making his people knowledgeable as to the mystery of his purposes. The noun "wisdom" carries both the sense of having great intelligence and also prudence and enlightenment.[93] Paul uses the noun twice more in Ephesians, both to describe God's wisdom (3:10) and to ask that God's wisdom be given to believers (1:17). In his doxology in Romans, Paul praises God for his wisdom and knowledge (Rom 11:33), and to the Corinthians (1 Cor 1:30), Paul declares that Christ is wisdom from God, and our righteousness, holiness, and redemption (the same term found in 1:7 above). Paul uses the noun "understanding" only once, but the verbal form is a favorite of his as he explains proper modes or attitudes of thought.[94]

9 Paul introduces a new dimension to our understanding of God's redemption plan as he explains that God acts to make known his will, which was a mystery that has now become clear in Christ. "Mystery," a key term in this epistle, is used for the first time in this verse and forms a central aspect of

---

90. Best, 132–33.

91. Arnold, 86. Contra MacDonald, 200, who argues the phrase connects with 1:7 "because of the contents of the prayer described in 1:17 and the use of the similar phrase in Col 1:19." See also Bruce, 260.

92. Thielman, 61, argues the sense is that God lavished his grace "in his multifaceted wisdom and understanding."

93. On σοφία see BDAG 934 (1); E. J. Schnabel, "Wisdom," *DPL* 967–73.

94. On φρόνησις see BDAG 1066. For the verb φρονέω see BDAG 1065 and, e.g., Rom 12:3, 16; 14:6; Phil 1:7; 2:2; 4:10; Col 3:2.

Paul's discussion in Eph 3 and Eph 5 (3:3, 4, 9; 5:32; 6:19).[95] I will address the complexity of the term in Eph 3; for now, it is important to note that "mystery" describes an aspect of God's will.[96] The hidden "mystery" is revealed now in the Christ event that includes redemption through the cross and the unity of all things in Christ (1:10).[97]

Ephesians 1:9 begins with a participle "having made known" that links back to 1:4 and God's act of choosing "us in him [Christ]."[98] Paul argues that as God chose us before the foundation of the world (to be holy and blameless), he made known this truth, this mystery, in accordance with his will and good pleasure. Paul continues that God's good pleasure is "purposed," making clear that God accomplishes his good purposes. The verb "purposed"[99] is found only twice more in Paul's Epistles, both in Romans.[100] Paul drives home his argument that God's will is accomplished "in Christ," and from this position Paul will explore the salvific ramifications for believers who are in Christ.

Paul repeats two terms, "will" and "good pleasure," used in 1:5 (see also Phil 2:13).[101] Jesus speaks about God's good pleasure as he prays to the Father, thanking him for revealing the kingdom of God to "children" and keeping it hidden from the so-called learned (Matt 11:25–26; Luke 10:21). Both Paul and Jesus speak of God's good pleasure and its being hidden or revealed. Did Paul know this teaching of Jesus? Given that the term "good pleasure" is rare in Scripture, found primarily in the Psalms and in Ecclesiasticus (Sirach), and that both Jesus and Paul connect God's good pleasure to its being made known in their day, it is possible that Paul took his cue from Jesus's teaching, which likely circulated in the churches' liturgy and catechetical practices.

10 The sweep of history continues in 1:10, now looking ahead to the culmination of the ages. In 1:4 Paul indicates that God the Father chose believers in Christ before the foundations of the world. Now he notes that God's

---

95. On μυστήριον see BDAG 661–62.

96. Bruce, 261, remarks: "As regularly in the NT, a 'mystery' is something which has formerly been kept secret in the purpose of God but has now been disclosed."

97. MacDonald, 201, observes that "the term mystērion (mystery or secret) . . . would probably have conjured up powerful imagery. . . . In its plural form the term was used to refer to the mystery cults of Greco-Roman society." She points to Dan 2:18 LXX and 1QpHab 7:1–4, 13–14; 8:1–3.

98. On γνωρίζω see BDAG 203.

99. On προτίθημι see BDAG 889.

100. In Rom 1:13 Paul uses it in reference to his travels, but more interestingly for our purposes, in 3:25 Paul uses it to speak about God presenting Christ as a sacrifice of atonement, using the rare noun ἱλαστήριον, which refers to the golden lid of the ark of the covenant, on which was sprinkled blood on the Day of Atonement (see also Heb 9:5). Paul speaks of Christ's blood shed using the nouns "redemption" and "grace" and the verb "purposed/presented" in both Rom 3:24–25 and Eph 1:7–9.

101. On θέλημα see BDAG 447. On εὐδοκία see BDAG 404.

1:7–12 REDEEMED BY THE SON

plan will have a fulfillment, that all things in heaven and on earth be summed up in Christ.[102] The concept of fullness or fulfillment factors heavily in Paul's argument, as he speaks about fullness of time (1:10) or fullness of God (3:19) or of Christ (1:23; 4:13).[103] The term *oikonomia* (translated here "put into effect") can carry an active sense of administering a plan, or refer to the plan itself, or can signify the administrator him/herself.[104] Paul likely uses the first meaning here in 1:10 and the second meaning in 3:9,[105] where Paul describes the plan in relation to the mystery hidden in ages past, now made known to the rulers and authorities of the heavens. This plan, therefore, carries a sense of fulfillment of God's design chosen before time, revealed in Paul's time in Christ, and moving to a realization of unity of all things in Christ.

Paul writes that God planned "to sum up" all things in Christ.[106] The infinitive "to sum up" includes the prefix *ana*, which suggests repetition, and the verb *kephalaioō*, which means to sum up an argument or an arithmetic problem (see also Rom 13:9). The related noun *kephalaion* refers to an author or speaker's main point (see Heb 8:1). The gist of these terms is to sum up an argument or a set of figures. Some argue that the verb Paul uses here is related to the noun *kephalē* ("head").[107] It is certainly true that Paul uses "head" when speaking of Christ (Eph 1:22) and of husbands and Christ in relation to unity in marriage (5:23). However, we must not allow the explicit language of 1:10 to be silenced by later uses of the related noun *kephalē*.[108] Here Paul speaks about the culmination of the ages as the cosmic Christ "draws all things into himself according to God's plan (cf. Col 1:15–20)."[109]

Paul's discussion invites us to explore what he means by summing up all things. Given Paul's strong emphasis on oneness and reconciliation implied in

---

102. Lincoln, 32, points to contemporary apocalypses as reflecting similar views "of a sequence of periods of time under God's direction (cf. Dan 2:21 LXX; 4:37; Tob 14:5; 4 Ezra 4:37; 2 *Apoc. Bar.* 40.3; cf. also 1QS 4.18; 1QM 14.14; 1QpHab 7.2, 13)."

103. On πλήρωμα see BDAG 829.

104. On οἰκονομία see BDAG 697. See also Lincoln, 31. MacDonald, 202, explains that the term "referred to the management or administration of a house or city" and could be "closely associated with an administrative office."

105. Contra Lincoln, 32.

106. MacDonald, 202, comments that 1:10 "was especially influential in the development of the doctrine of recapitulation among the Latin Fathers (the Greek term *anakephalaiōsis* was translated as *recapitulation*)." See Irenaeus, *Against Heresies* (ANF 1:330, 442–43, 548).

107. Arnold, 88–89.

108. Lincoln, 33, rightly observes: "It is both legitimate and illuminating to place the thought of 1:10 in the context of the whole letter and link it with other passages in which a relation between the cosmos and Christ is posited, but this should be done after 1:10 has been exegeted on its own terms."

109. MacDonald, 202.

the language of adoption and redemption, most likely Paul intends a sense of complete cosmic unity accomplished in Christ. All that is brought together is free of any evil, full of the joy only bounteous grace can provide. All share harmoniously in the Beloved as each element and being in the heavens and on earth enjoy their created purpose. Paul does not promote a universalism of salvation outside of Christ, nor is Paul particularly interested in the individual here. Rather he is concerned to show the all-sufficiency of God's power to make all things right and God's unfailing love to accomplish this purpose (see also Rom 8:22–24).

If this is the summing up of the argument, believers today can prioritize their thoughts and actions to reflect what is to come. For example, forgiveness of sins, therefore, is not a simple washing away of evil dirt, but preparation for a unity enjoyed by the entire cosmos in Christ. Again, redemption in Christ's blood points to a future when all things are reconciled in Christ. These emphases might cause individuals to look at the conservation and care of creation with new vigor. Finally, adoption into God's family and the subsequent expectations for blameless living allow believers to participate in an eternal unity of perfect order, harmony, and joyous grace. Such truths refocus believers' attention today on the importance of connecting with and supporting sisters and brothers across the globe in partnerships of loving equality.

11 Ephesians 1:11 is the second of three sections in this long sentence that begins "in whom/Christ." The first occurrence was in 1:7, where Paul notes that "in him we have redemption." And in 1:13 Paul speaks of being included in Christ using the phrase "in him." Here in 1:11 the focus is on being chosen, having an inheritance in Christ that was predestined following the plan of God, who works all things according to the wishes of his will. The idea of inheritance picks up Paul's earlier comments about adoption (1:5). And we find Paul repeating key terms such as "predestined" from 1:5 and the phrase "his/God's will" from 1:5, 9. Paul uses the noun "purpose," related to the cognate verb "to purpose/plan" found in 1:9. What is new here is Paul's description of God as the one who works out all things.

Paul begins this verse with the phrase "in him," signaling that all that follows is tied to Christ's work. Paul uses the verb "to allot" or "to choose" as he explains how believers fit into this cosmic oneness in Christ.[110] Paul may be drawing on the Old Testament concept of individuals having a portion of the inheritance (land) in ancient Israel (Deut 10:9; 12:12). This option has the benefit of reading this verb similarly to a related noun used in Col 1:12: "to share in the inheritance of his holy people." However, the verb here probably carries the more specific sense "to inherit," related to

---

110. On κληρόω see BDAG 548. MacDonald, 203, notes that this verb appears only here in the New Testament, but a cognate noun occurs in Col 1:12.

1:7–12 REDEEMED BY THE SON

the noun "inheritance" found at the end of our passage in Eph 1:14, which states that believers have the Holy Spirit as a guarantee of inheritance (see also Rom 8:17).[111] If so, then who inherits? Paul stresses either that believers are God's inheritance or that believers receive an inheritance from God.[112] Given the parallel structure with Eph 1:7, it seems more likely Paul intends that believers receive an inheritance, even as they have received redemption and forgiveness of sins.[113]

Having established that believers have an inheritance, based on being in Christ, Paul continues that believers' inheritance is predestined or predetermined based on God's purpose. This language echoes 1:5, wherein believers' adoption was predetermined, and 1:9, which stresses God's purpose to make known the mystery of his will. Paul emphasizes that adoption and inheritance—two key aspects of membership in God's family—belong to the Ephesians in Christ. Paul describes God the Father here with a participle, "the one working," continuing Paul's focus on God's activities in establishing and implementing his plan of uniting all things in Christ.

12 With this verse, Paul both concludes the second of three sections in this passage, as well as takes a first step toward his third section that differentiates and also unites believers. Paul uses the phrase "for the praise of his [God's] glory" to bookend his remarks in 1:12 and 1:14, continuing the mood of thanksgiving that permeates this lengthy sentence (see also 1:6). Paul introduces a verb unique to the New Testament, translated "first to put our hope."[114] The verb is made up of the prefix "first" (*pro*) and stem "to hope." The verb without the prefix is used numerous times in Paul (e.g., Rom 8:24–25; 1 Cor 15:19). The participle's perfect tense signals that the action began in the past and continues to impact the present.[115]

Paul speaks of "we" who are the first to hope, and with this pronoun, he raises questions about whether he might be distinguishing himself from the Ephesian church. In Eph 1:13, he uses for the first time in the sentence

---

111. Thielman, 73, argues that the term does not refer "simply to an 'allotment' or 'portion' . . . but specifically to an 'inheritance' that has been given either to believers or to God." Contra Hoehner, 227, who argues that the "believer is viewed as God's inheritance." See also W. O. Carver, *Ephesians: The Glory of God in the Christian Calling* (reprinted Nashville: Broadman, 1979), 72, 105, who argues that Paul stresses here "God's claim of the Hebrews as his heritage was functional, provisional, and relative."

112. Both ideas are expressed in Jer 10:16.

113. Thielman, 73.

114. On προελπίζω see BDAG 868.

115. MacDonald, 203, remarks that "the verbal form suggests an action that has been completed with ongoing results." Lincoln, 37, argues that the tense "indicates some eschatological reserve despite other expressions of realized eschatology" in this blessing. See also Arnold, 91.

the pronoun "you" (plural), speaking of those who are hearing and believing and who are sealed with the promised Holy Spirit. Then in 1:14, with the phrase "*our* inheritance" (emphasis mine), Paul switches back to the inclusive "we." Some suggest that in 1:12 Paul distinguishes Jewish believers who heard the gospel in its earliest days from gentile believers in Ephesus who received the gospel message from missionaries.[116] Another possibility is that Paul does not distinguish Jew and gentile here,[117] but rather contrasts the present time with that which is to come, when God in Christ sums up all things. In this case, the verb's prefix refers to the present time, before the age to come. The advantage of this suggestion is that it defines "we" as the entire church community. The disadvantage of this view is that it does not prepare the reader for the "you" that begins 1:13. It may be that Paul intends to reassure the Ephesians that although "we" heard the gospel before "you all" did, nevertheless, we all inherit alike. The distinction in the chronology of hearing the message, and even the distinction of Jew and gentile, ultimately serve only to magnify the shared inheritance and glorious greatness of God's salvation plan.

Another way to look at the questions surrounding this verb is to see how the noun "hope" functions in the rest of this letter. In 1:18 Paul prays that the Ephesians' eyes be opened to the hope of their calling, which is further explained as the fullness of the glorious inheritance—either God's inheritance of believers or believers' inheritance of God's salvation (more on that below in the discussion of 1:18). And in 2:12 Paul indicates that "you gentiles" had no hope, because you were far from Christ, but now through Christ's blood, you are brought near to God. In 4:4 Paul reminds the Ephesians they were called in one hope. It seems that the hope itself is the same, but the experience of that hope differs between Jews and gentiles based on their relative closeness to the true God. In this, Paul expresses a Jewish truism that gentiles in their paganism are idolaters, wandering in dark disobedience. Jews, however, have God's law, including a true hope in the Messiah. Paul's gospel announces the fulfillment of this hope in Christ Jesus. Because the differentiation between Jew and gentile in matters of salvation is fundamental to a first-century Jew's mindset, most likely the participle "first to hope" in 1:12 carries a sense of Jewish chronological and religious priority. This is stated explicitly in 2:11–13. Yet because Paul stresses the shared hope of all believers several times in the epistle, including 1:18 and 4:4, the term's eschatological note rings loudly, including here in 1:12.

---

116. Bruce, 264; MacDonald, 203. Muddiman, 77, observes that it might also include "Israel's historic expectation of the coming of the Messiah."

117. Arnold, 91; Lincoln, 37.

c. Sealed by the Holy Spirit (1:13–14)

13–14 With these two verses Paul concludes his lengthy benediction begun in 1:3 and also draws attention to the Holy Spirit. In the previous ten verses, Paul stressed the salvation plan of God that includes adoption as his children in Christ, redemption by Christ's blood, and believers as inheritors of this great salvation. In this passage, Paul explains that the Holy Spirit secures those who believe the word of truth. This leads to Paul's thrice repeated shout of joy: "to the praise of his glory."

Paul begins this verse with the third prepositional phrase "in him/Christ" (see also 1:7, 11) and turns his attention to "you" Ephesian believers who, hearing and believing the gospel, are sealed with the promised Holy Spirit. The believers heard the word concerning the truth and believed. The aorist participles may reflect causal actions; that is, because of hearing and believing, a believer is sealed with the Spirit. But it is more likely, given the broken syntax of this verse, that Paul equates the "hearing" and "believing" in these two adverbial clauses as two components of the event that culminates in being sealed with the Holy Spirit.[118] The aorist tense depicts the event in its totality. This option clarifies the phrase "in him/Christ," used twice in this verse, as meaning the realm of Christ's salvation activity. Just as through Christ believers have an inheritance, so too believers first hear and believe the gospel and so in him/Christ are sealed with the Holy Spirit.

God promised this action of being sealed, as testified by the Old Testament prophets (Joel 2:28–29; Ezek 36:26–27). Believers are sealed with the Holy Spirit, so Paul assures the Ephesians (4:30; see also 2 Cor 1:22).[119] The seal in Paul's day confirmed ownership, validated a document's authenticity, and guaranteed the quality of the goods or document.[120] A sealed document was an authentic text; a sealed wine jar was an approved vessel. Paul refers to Abraham's circumcision as a seal (Rom 4:11). Pilate marked Jesus's tomb with his own seal in an effort to prevent grave robbers (Matt 27:66). Paul draws on these everyday realities to suggest that believers, now sealed with the Holy Spirit, are "owned" by God and represent God's good works to others. A limited analogy is the seal that universities use in authenticating their diplomas, assuring students of the value of their education. Alumni represent the school in the public eye. By marking believers with the Holy Spirit, God guarantees a full realization of salvation to come, and that seal

---

118. Lincoln, 39, argues the participle refers to an action "coincident in time with that of the main verb." See also Hoehner, 237.

119. On σφραγίζω see BDAG 980 (3).

120. Muddiman, 79, observes that early church fathers saw an allusion to baptism in this language (*2 Clement* 7:6; *Hermas* 8.6.3 [= 72:3]).

"brands" the believer as God's follower with all the expectations of holy living it entails (Eph 4:30).

In 1:14 Paul finishes his thoughts on the previous verse.[121] He continues to describe the work of the Holy Spirit as the believers' "down payment" or "guarantee" on salvation's inheritance (see also 2 Cor 1:22; 5:5).[122] The metaphor occurs only in Paul's writings in the New Testament. Paul paints the picture of believers' salvation as both now and not yet. Believers experience now in some measure what they will fully enjoy in the future. The Holy Spirit assures them of the certain future hope, their eternal life with God. This should lead to joyous confidence as believers go about their daily lives.[123]

Paul speaks next about redemption, which is related to being sealed with the Spirit. The noun used in 1:7 refers to receiving redemption now through Christ's blood. Thus, Paul locates the redemptive work of God in Christ with the Holy Spirit as a salvation enjoyed both now and in the age to come. The down payment points to the time when the full amount is paid. Following the term "redemption" is the rare noun translated "possession."[124] Typically, scholars chose between two possible meanings; either the term means "possession" in the sense that God's people are his possession (see 1 Pet 2:9)[125] or the noun means "acquisition," with the sense that God's people acquire their redemption, that is, their salvation, of which the Holy Spirit is the down payment.[126] A third, and commendable, alternative has it that the noun can refer to preservation in the sense of a remnant preserved in battle or difficulty.[127] This understanding works within Paul's wider cultural context and makes good sense of his specific concern, namely, the believers' redemption. Thus, the phrase would read "for the redemption of the saved remnant."

"The praise of his glory" has been used three times (with minor variation) in this long sentence.[128] Paul praises each of the three key aspects of

---

121. The relative pronoun that begins this verse is found either in the masculine ὅς, which agrees with the predicate nominative ἀρραβών (À D Ψ), or the neuter ὅ, which agrees with antecedent πνεῦμα (P46 A B F G L). Hoehner, 241n1, prefers the masculine reading. Thielman, 84, remarks that either text works well grammatically and that the passage reads the same with either variant.

122. On ἀρραβών see BDAG 134. On κληρονομία see BDAG 547–48. The cognate verb is used above in 1:11.

123. Fee, *Paul, the Spirit, and the People of God*, 60.

124. On περιποίησις see BDAG 804. Paul uses this noun in 1 Thess 5:9; 2 Thess 2:14; it is also found in Heb 10:39 and 1 Pet 2:9.

125. Lincoln, 41, notes that "elsewhere in the NT ἀπολύτρωσις is always an act of God"; cf. Muddiman, 80; Arnold, 93.

126. Schlier, 72; Schnackenburg, 67.

127. Thielman, 84–86.

128. Hoehner, 245, suggests that Paul cites the phrase "after each time the work of each person of the Trinity is extolled." See also Lincoln, 43, who more modestly observes that

1:15–23 GOD'S WORK THROUGH CHRIST'S RULE OVER ALL THINGS

God's salvation activities: adoption (1:5), inheritance (1:11), redemption (1:7, 14). In both 1:6 and 1:12, the phrase follows Paul's recognition that believers' adoption and inheritance have been predetermined or preordained by God in Christ, while in 1:14 the praise reflects the confidence of the completion of this preordained plan. By the plan and good pleasure of the will of the Father, Son, and Holy Spirit, believers are adopted into God's family, graced with great grace, redeemed, forgiven of trespasses, regarded as inheritors of salvation, and as part of the revealed mystery that all things in heaven and on earth will be united in Christ. With such awe-inspiring personal and cosmic truth, it is easy to understand Paul's song of rejoicing.

2. God's Work through Christ's Rule over All Things (1:15–23)

Having praised God for the plan to restore creation and reconcile believers, to sum up all things in Christ, Paul offers a thanksgiving for the Ephesians and then launches into an effusive prayer for the believers. These nine verses follow Paul's pattern of offering an opening thanksgiving and prayer in his letters on behalf of his congregation.[129] He encourages the saints with the Spirit's giving of wisdom and moral understanding that informs and strengthens their convictions. He reminds them that they are called, they have an inheritance, and they share through Christ the great power of God.[130] In 1:20 Paul begins a relative clause that introduces a close discussion of Christ's exalted standing over all things and powers, now and in eternity. Paul adapts a phrase ("seated him at his right hand") from Ps 110:1. In Eph 1:22 Paul alludes to a phrase from Ps 8:6, further stressing that all things submit to Christ, the head. The new focus leads some to render Eph 1:22–23 as a new sentence.[131] Paul reaches a crescendo in the final clauses, exclaiming that the church is Christ's body; it is filled with the one who fills all, namely, Christ.

The passage's structure builds from the main verb "I have not stopped giving thanks" (1:16) and follows with two requests that God would give them

---

"the flow of thought [in 1:3–14] spans past, present, and future, and its reflection on God's activity can be seen to have a trinitarian content."

129. Arnold, 98, counts 169 words in this long sentence and finds similar patterns in the introductory thanksgivings of Phil 1:3–11; Col 1:3–14; Phlm 4–6. NA27 and NA28 divide the passage into two sentences after Eph 1:19. Eph 1:20 begins a relative sentence dependent on the previous verse; 1:22–23 uses finite verbs, a shift from the participles used in the preceding verses. Best, 156, favors one continuous sentence, noting that "the thought is continuous and v. 22 provides two clauses parallel to those of v. 20."

130. Eph 1:19 includes the noun ἐνέργεια; 1:20 uses the related verb ἐνεργέω in the third-person singular aorist active indicative.

131. Thielman, 105.

wisdom and enlightened hearts.[132] Paul builds momentum as he adds three additional requests, that they may know what is the hope, what is the riches, and what is the incomparable greatness. Drawing on this last phrase, Paul elaborates on God's power that raised and seated Christ, appointing him over all things.[133]

Often in his letters, the thanksgiving introduces themes Paul will develop within the body of the epistle. Paul's prayer restates previous claims and introduces new themes. Paul connects verbally with his benediction in the previous verses and hints at what he will develop later in the epistle. He repeats his emphasis on the believers' inheritance, on God's glory and Christ's redemptive acts, and on the Holy Spirit's activity in preserving and developing believers. He repeats the noun "fullness" but now with a new object, for in 1:10 the fullness of time was stressed, but in 1:23 it is the fullness of the one who is filled with all things. Later in the epistle, Paul prays that the Ephesians be filled with all the fullness of God (3:19) and encourages them to attain the fullness of Christ (4:13) and to be filled with the Holy Spirit (5:18).[134]

New material includes a discussion about God's power, made evident in raising Christ from the dead, seating him at his right hand, putting all things in submission to him, and giving him as head over all things. This emphasis on God's power and strength will culminate in the last chapter of the epistle (6:10), as Paul enjoins believers to put on the armor of God, to be strong in the Lord against the powers and authorities (6:12), using the same language we find in 1:19 and 1:21.[135] In 3:10 the church reveals the wisdom of God, making such known to the rulers and authorities in the heavenlies.[136] Paul speaks for the first time of the church, described here as Christ's body (1:23). Paul develops this metaphor in numerous ways, including his emphasis on the unity of Jew and gentile (2:16), the unity produced through the proper use of

---

132. MacDonald, 222, comments that the brevity of the thanksgiving and the lack of details about the community support the contention that Ephesians was written to multiple communities.

133. Arnold, 101, provides a useful summary of the passage's structure, which includes four verbal clauses using two aorist participles ("to raise" and "to seat" in 1:20) and two aorist indicative verbs ("to exert or work" in 1:20; "to give, appoint" in 1:22). He concludes: "These four actions [in the four verbal clauses] are not to be understood in temporal succession occurring over time, but as four descriptions of the one event that is often summarized as 'the resurrection.'"

134. MacDonald, 223–24, contrasts the emphasis on enlightenment here and the "critique of the visionary experiences of the Colossian opponents."

135. Paul enjoins believers to be strong in the Lord (ἐν τῷ κράτει τῆς ἰσχύος αὐτοῦ) against the powers and authorities (ἀρχάς καὶ ἐξουσίας).

136. Ταῖς ἀρχαῖς καὶ ταῖς ἐξουσίαις ἐν τοῖς ἐπουρανίοις.

Christ's gift (4:4, 12, 16), and the unity of the church and Christ, analogous to the one-flesh unity of husband and wife (5:23, 28, 30).

Paul's prayer rests on an underlying narrative of God's redemption. One way of visualizing Paul's understanding is as a stage with elaborate scaffolding. Believers act their parts on the floor of the stage, while angels, rulers and authorities, and spiritual powers move about in the scaffolding. And in the unsearchable heights above the stage lighting, sits Christ the Lord, at God the Father's right hand. We might imagine the Holy Spirit speaking in a stage whisper, providing wisdom and revelation to those who, with enlightened hearts, live into their calling and take hold of the power of Christ in each of them and in the church body.[137] Paul's theology stretches back to a time before time, pertains to the present, and promises a future (1:21). It includes the granular particularity of Christ's death on a Roman cross and the cosmic magnificence of his victory over death (1:20–21). It includes the space of submission under Christ's feet as well as the exalted space of head over all (1:22). It involves not only implied emptiness, but also the fullness that is filled with all things (1:23).

As we saw in the opening eulogy, so too here in his prayer, Paul speaks of Father, Son, and Spirit. Paul designates God as the Father of glory, the God of our Lord Jesus Christ who gives believers the Spirit. He raised Christ, seated Christ at his right hand, submitted all things under his feet, and gave Christ as head over all things for the church. The Holy Spirit is the believers' seal and provides wisdom and understanding. The defeat of Christ's enemies sounds a note that is picked up in Eph 6, as Paul enjoins believers to take up God's armor and stand fast against the powers and principalities of darkness (6:10–12). God also gives to believers a threefold blessing, that they know what is the hope of their calling, the riches of their inheritance, and the great power of Christ in them. Christ's death on the cross is implied by Paul's assertion that he was raised from the dead (1:20); otherwise, Christ is described by what God accomplishes in and through him.

a. Prayer for the Ephesians (1:15–19)

15 For this reason, ever since I heard about your faith in the Lord Jesus and your love for all God's people, 16 I have not stopped giving thanks for you, remembering you in my prayers. 17 I keep asking that the God of our Lord Jesus Christ, the glorious Father, may give you the Spirit of wisdom and revelation, so that you may know him better. 18 I pray that the eyes of your heart may be enlightened in

---

137. MacDonald, 224, remarks that "taken as a whole there is a sense in which believers, and indeed the universal church, are depicted as engaged in a journey of heavenly ascent."

order that you may know the hope to which he has called you, the riches of his glorious inheritance in his holy people, ¹⁹*and his incomparably great power for us who believe. That power is the same as the mighty strength....*

15–16 Paul begins this new section by stating "for this reason," referring back to his lengthy eulogy. He explains he has heard two things about them: faith in the Lord Jesus and love for all the saints.[138] Paul declares that he does not cease to do two things: give thanks and remember them. He uses the same verb in his letter to the Colossians, noting that he has not ceased praying for them and asking that they would be filled with knowledge of God's will in all spiritual wisdom and understanding (Col 1:9).[139] These passages in Ephesians and Colossians share many of the same Greek terms, and assuming the same author wrote both, they can inform each other. Paul indicates a similar sentiment to the Romans, that he makes mention of them unceasingly ("remember you in my prayers at all times"; Rom 1:9–10).[140] To the Thessalonians, Paul thanks God always in his prayers, making mention unceasingly for all of them (1 Thess 1:2). Clearly, Paul makes it a habit to pray for his congregations. In the next few verses, he tells the Ephesians the content of his prayers. As we will see, Paul's prayer is thick with foundational realities of God's salvation plan.

The grammar is straightforward, but the content raises a few questions. First, why does Paul use the emphatic "I" ("I, myself")? Although Paul uses the first-person singular in his thanksgiving prayers (Rom 1:8; 1 Cor 1:4; Phil 1:3), he never uses the emphatic "I" as he does here. Most likely, Paul connects this "I" with the participles in Eph 1:16, where Paul gives thanks for the Ephesians and prays for them.[141] We find the same phrase in 1 Thess 3:5, in the context of Paul's expressing great concern for the Thessalonians' well-being. Less likely is the possibility that he highlights his apostolic authority. While he opens his letter with a description that he is an apostle of Christ Jesus, he elsewhere emphasizes his imprisonment and suffering on their behalf (Eph 3:1; 4:1; 6:19–20).

---

138. The phrase τὴν ἀγάπην ("the love") is not found in P46 א* B P 33 and Origen, all of which read καὶ τὴν εἰς πάντας τοὺς ἁγίους ("and toward all the saints"). This reading emphasizes the Ephesians' faith or faithfulness toward other believers. Barth, 146–47, accepts this reading, but Lincoln, 46–47, rightly recognizes the longer phrase, explaining that "nowhere else in the NT is there a failure to distinguish between faith directed to Christ and to one's fellow believers." See also MacDonald, 215, and Thielman, 102–3.

139. On παύω see BDAG 790 (2).

140. Phil 1:3 may read either that Paul gives thanks to God in every remembrance of them or that he thanks God for their remembrance of him/Paul; see Lynn H. Cohick, *Philippians*, Story of God Bible Commentary (Grand Rapids: Zondervan, 2013), 34.

141. Best, 158. Best remarks that with Paul's use of κἀγώ ("and I"), it is unlikely that Paul was including others as cosenders of the letter.

Second, why does Paul use the aorist participle, that he "heard" of their faith and love, when, according to Acts 19:8–10 and 20:31, Paul spent close to three years in this city? He hints at a similar lack of relationship in Eph 3:2; 4:21; and 6:21–24, noting only that the Ephesians hear about him. For some, this evidence points to a deutero-Pauline authorship.[142] Others note that Acts' chronology would put Paul's last visit to the city about seven years before he sent this letter; therefore, it is entirely possible that Paul did not know many in the congregation. And he might have been further hampered in maintaining up-to-date information because of his lengthy imprisonment.[143] Yet if we assume that the aorist does not indicate the time at which something happened, but the totality of the event, then Paul is likely acknowledging here his overall knowledge of the Ephesians' situation.[144] As argued in the introduction, this language in Ephesians likely reflects Paul's attempt to remain in contact and implies the difficulties he faced in doing so.[145]

Third, as Paul praises their faith in the Lord Jesus, he likely has in mind both Christ as the object of their faith, as well as the sphere in which believers exercise this faith.[146] Thus, there is an object—specifically, Christ, and also the reality of Christ in them. Not only is their life in Christ defined by faith, but also it is expressed in love to other believers. This love (*agapē*) characterizes Christ's love for the church (5:2, 25), an outward-focused, self-giving posture and attitude. The beneficiaries of this love are other believers. Paul stresses unity in this epistle, and we may hear in this call to love both the motivation and the path for unity. A sign of a believer's love is to want the best for a fellow believer who might not fit the definition of friend. Desmond Tutu notes, "You don't choose your family. They are God's gift to you, and you are to them."[147] This is especially true for the family of God, whose unity and love witness to God's love to the world (John 13:34–35).

---

142. Lincoln, 54, rightly notes that this complaint "tells only against Pauline authorship of a letter *to Ephesus* . . . but not against Pauline authorship of a circular letter."

143. Best, 158–59, rejects the possibilities that the author refers to new converts or that a lengthy time has elapsed since Paul's visit.

144. Arnold, 102, comments that the aorist could signal a causal meaning, "because I heard," but more likely conveys a temporal meaning, "ever since I heard."

145. See introduction, p. 11.

146. Lincoln, 54–55, comments that the genitive construction in this phrase typically refers to the object of the faith (Rom 3:22, 26; Gal 2:16, 20; 3:22; Phil 3:9) and observes that this interpretation provides a parallelism to the next phrase, "love for all the saints." The preposition ἐν when used with "faith" seems to focus on the realm in which the faith functions (Gal 3:26; 5:6; Col 1:4). He concludes that the balance tips toward the sphere in which the faith operates. See also Barth, 146, who concludes that the phrase should be rendered "*faithfulness [shown] among you to the Lord Jesus*" (emphasis original).

147. Desmond Tutu, address at his enthronement as Anglican archbishop of Cape Town, September 7, 1986.

17-19 The preceding two verses established Paul's practice of unceasing prayer for the Ephesians. The following three verses provide the content of these prayers. Paul identifies God as the God of our Lord Jesus Christ and as the Father of glory. Paul describes God as one who gives. Paul uses the same verb in 1:22, that God gives Christ to the church. Paul depicts God as having the power to effect and actualize the purposes of his gifts and as having the resources to give abundantly. Paul asks that God give to the Ephesians both a spirit of wisdom and enlightened hearts (1:18) and follows with a third request, which includes three subrequests (1:18-19). Paul desires that the Ephesians embrace their calling, their inheritance, and their experiential understanding of God's great power. They have access to such understanding because of Christ's work and his exaltation above all things (1:20-21). They can know this through the Spirit's working, for they are in Christ, they are his body, the church (1:23). This prayer shares language with Colossians, as we find a similar phrase, "spiritual wisdom and understanding," and the verb "to cease" in Col 1:9.

Paul describes God as the Father of glory or glorious Father.[148] Earlier, in 1:3 Paul described God as the Father of our Lord Jesus Christ. Moreover, God's glory is mentioned three times in the opening benediction as Paul writes "to the praise of his [God's] glory" (1:6, 12, 14). Paul uses the term twice in his prayer in Eph 3 as he speaks of God's glory (3:16, 21) and explains to the Ephesians that his imprisonment is their "glory" (3:12). Paul's focus on God's glory echoes traditional Jewish teaching and praise that exalt God's mighty power.[149] Glory denotes majesty and splendor of the sort beyond what humans themselves can create.[150] What is unique in 1:17 is the phrase "*Father of glory.*"[151] Paul speaks of Christ as the "Lord of glory" (1 Cor 2:8), and here "Father of glory" could be understood as "Father of the one who is himself the Glory of God."[152] Alternatively, and more likely, the genitive phrase is at-

---

148. Ὁ πατὴρ τῆς δόξης. On δόξα see BDAG 256-57 (1b); R. B. Gaffin Jr., "Glory, Glorification," *DPL* 348-50.

149. Muddiman, 84, writes: "The meaning of the Hebrew word for glory, *kabod*, as 'weight,' 'influence' or 'power,' is coloured in New Testament usage by the overtones of the Greek equivalent, *doxa*." We find God's honor magnified by the psalmist, "Who is this King of glory? The LORD strong and mighty, the LORD mighty in battle" (Ps 24:8; see also 29:3). Isaiah, offering the hope of salvation, proclaims that all people will see the glory of the Lord (40:5).

150. Best, 162, concludes that "majesty" might be a suitable English term for δόξα, as it draws on both the sense of power/might and splendor.

151. See also "God of glory" (Acts 7:2) and "Father of the heavenly lights" (Jas 1:17). Best, 161, explains that the term "father" refers to the source of glory: "Thus here he [God] is the source of glory to those who are his children."

152. Muddiman, 84. See also the discussion in Best, 161-62.

tributive, rendered as "the glorious father."[153] The glory of which Paul speaks reflects the greatness of God's person, the essence of his honor and power.[154]

Paul prays that God will give to the Ephesians a spirit of wisdom and revelation. The lack of the definite article "the" suggests to some that Paul speaks about human spirit or disposition here. He does so later in this epistle, using the phrase "spirit of your mind" (4:23; see also "spirit of slavery" in Rom 8:15 or "spirit of gentleness" in 1 Cor 4:21).[155] However, we have several examples of an anarthrous reference to the Holy Spirit (e.g., 1 Cor 4:21). Moreover, Paul describes this spirit as one of revelation, which seems to point to the Holy Spirit, as it is God who reveals his mystery (see Eph 3:4–5).[156] The Ephesians have been sealed with this Holy Spirit (1:13), so Paul emphasizes in 1:17 the Ephesians' experience of revelation, not their initial receiving of the Holy Spirit. Paul expresses a similar sentiment to the Philippians when he declares that he wants to know him (Phil 3:10); Paul certainly knows Christ already as his Messiah. Paul's point is that he desires a deeper appreciation of Christ's suffering and the power that upended death (3:10–11).

Paul prays that the Holy Spirit will impart a deeper wisdom and revelation to the Ephesians. He adds the phrase "so that you may know him better," which can be understood in at least two ways. First, this phrase could belong with the following participial phrase related to the enlightened hearts (1:18), such that Paul prays that their hearts gain enlightenment through knowledge of God. Second, and more likely, it refers to believers knowing God more deeply. Paul uses the term "knowledge" (*epignōsis*) again in 4:13, as he speaks about attaining the unity of faith and the knowledge of the Son of God, being mature and having the fullness of Christ (*gnōsis* in 3:19).[157] Paul similarly describes the Holy Spirit as searching the deep things of God and revealing such to believers (1 Cor 2:10–16).

Paul continues his prayer with an unusual phrase not found elsewhere: "eyes of your hearts."[158] The connection between eyes and illumination are alluded to in the Psalms and the Qumran material (Ps 12:4 LXX; 18:9 LXX; 1QS 2:3). Paul asks that God give not only the Spirit of wisdom, but also

---

153. Arnold, 104.

154. Arnold, 104 argues that "glory" is "an expression of [God's] omnipotence more than his splendor, holiness, or honor."

155. Muddiman, 85.

156. Perkins, 48. See also Hoehner, 256–58, and Lincoln, 57.

157. On ἐπίγνωσις see BDAG 369. See γνῶσις in 3:19 and C. M. Robeck Jr., "Knowledge, Gift of Knowledge," *DPL* 526–28. Hoehner, 258, explains that "ἐπίγνωσις is knowledge directed towards a particular object, perceiving, discerning, recognizing."

158. Eph 1:18 begins with the perfect passive participle of φωτίζω. The NIV adds the English phrase "I pray that" to show the syntactic connection with 1:17. Hoehner, 261–62, offers an extensive discussion of the syntax questions; see also Arnold, 105–7.

enlightened hearts.[159] The perfect participle "enlightened" indicates both that the Ephesians have been enlightened and that Paul wishes God would grant them further enlightenment.[160] Paul asks that they might know three things: the hope of their calling, the riches of their glorious inheritance among the saints, and in 1:19 the power of God for believers. Turning to the first clause, Paul desires that believers know what is the hope of their calling. In 4:4 Paul writes of their oneness, insisting that "there is one body and one Spirit, just as you were called to one hope when you were called" (see also 4:1). In our passage, two questions surface: the meaning of "hope" and the nuance of the genitive phrase "his calling." It is interesting that Paul speaks of knowing "hope," as typically we think of hope as something not quite settled, a bit indefinite. Yet when speaking of God's salvation plan, there is no uncertainty. Paul's point, therefore, is to remind believers that full realization and actualization of their salvation is coming.[161] They can know hope because Christ's blood brings redemption (1:7). This sure hope is related to their calling by God, put into effect through Christ (1:4), and confirmed by the Holy Spirit (1:13–14).

In addition to knowing that their calling is secure, Paul also prays that the Ephesians might know the riches of God's glorious inheritance in the people of God. Paul stresses divine riches in 1:7 and 2:7, the riches of God's grace evidenced by Christ's redemptive death. And in 3:8 Christ's riches are the focus. In the second major prayer of the epistle, Paul asks that God would strengthen believers, drawing on his glorious riches (3:16). Paul ex-

---

159. Best, 164, and Arnold, 105–6, argue that the perfect participle with the noun "eyes" in the accusative is a second direct object of the verb "to give" in 1:17. This option explains the use of the accusative case; however, there is no conjunction "and" before the participle, nor is the perfect participle given its full weight. However, Lincoln, 47 and 58, argues that this participial phrase emphasizes the result of the Ephesians' already enlightened hearts and connects this phrase to the dative "you [plural]." The participle (accusative case) does not match the dative case; this anomaly can be explained by noting that the infinitive phrase directly after the participial phrase is also in the accusative. Thielman, 97, cites G. B. Winer's explanation that when participles occur at some distance from the governing verb they often are found in an abnormal case; see G. B. Winer, *A Grammar of the Idiom of the New Testament, Prepared as a Solid Basis for the Interpretation of the New Testament*, 7th ed., rev. G. Lünemann (Andover: Draper, 1881).

160. Arnold, 106, points to a similar idea behind Paul's prayer that they be given the Holy Spirit: "Paul is not praying that God will grant them an initial reception of the Spirit; they have already received the Spirit and have been sealed by the Spirit (1:13–14)."

161. On ἐλπίς see BDAG 319–20 (1b); J. M. Everts, "Hope," *DPL* 415–17; Terrence Prendergast, "Hope (NT)," *ABD* 3:282–85. MacDonald, 218, writes: "'The hope of his calling' refers to the content of salvation, what has been hoped for: membership in the people of God." Arnold, 107–8, suggests that Paul refers to events such as the resurrection of the body and the second coming of Christ, but this might be too granular and precise for this context.

presses a similar sentiment in Rom 11:33, a short doxology that praises the depths of God's riches and wisdom and knowledge, inscrutable to the human mind, unsearchable in its vast capacity. God's riches are demonstrated in part by his glorious inheritance. The Greek text allows for the possibility that the inheritance referred to here is one gained by God, namely, that he inherits a holy people. This interpretation suggests that Paul expands the concept of believers' inheritance in Eph 1:14 to include God's inheritance of believers. However, the tenor of Paul's message is that believers inherit eternal life with God as adopted children. Moreover, the first and third clauses in the prayer focus on believers' deep understanding of God's activities and their certain results unto salvation. Thus, the evidence tips in favor of Paul speaking here of God granting a glorious inheritance, shared by all the saints.

In 1:19 we find the last of three clauses that connect back to Paul's request that believers know God better. Here the focus is on knowing God's "incomparably great power." This greatness is an aspect of God's power, which is further explained in two ways—as being exerted on behalf of believers and as being exercised in accordance with his unsurpassed strength. Believers are described as those who exhibit faith. Paul had earlier described believers as those who believed and were sealed with the Spirit (1:13).

Paul introduces the element of God's power in relation to the work of Christ in salvation and will stress this aspect in the remaining four verses of his prayer (1:20–23). Paul underscores God's power in his second lengthy prayer (3:16, 20). Paul expresses God's power with four Greek terms, thereby stressing the greatness of God's abilities. The first term, *dynamis*, carries the sense of potential power, while the second term, *energeia*, evokes active power.[162] We might think of the first term as an unlit dynamite stick, full of potential force, and the second term as the energy produced as the dynamite explodes. God has all potential power and is able to direct and control all energy for his purposes. Paul continues with two other terms, *kratos* and *ischys*, which function as synonyms. The former includes the notion of rule or victory, and we see it in the English terms "demo*cracy*" and "theo*cracy*."[163] The latter term includes the connotation of the effective exercise of power.[164] All four terms set the stage for Paul's drama that follows, which highlights Christ's victory over all perceived powers.[165]

---

162. On δύναμις see BDAG 262; on ἐνέργεια, BDAG 335.
163. On κράτος see BDAG 565.
164. On ἰσχύς see BDAG 484.
165. Lincoln, 60, observes that our author "attempts to exhaust the resources of the Greek language by piling up four synonyms for power in order to convey an impression of something of the divine might."

Jesus speaks of his power over all things in a conversation with his disciples fresh from a ministry foray into local Galilean villages (Luke 10:1–21). They returned full of joy after healing and preaching that the kingdom of God has drawn near. They exclaimed that "even the demons submit to us in your name" (10:17). Jesus's response is twofold. He addresses the issue of spiritual powers by observing that "he saw Satan fall like lightning from heaven" and acknowledging that he gave his disciples power to overcome the enemy, so that nothing can harm them. But he adds a surprising (to our ears) caveat. The disciples are focused on the wrong thing and have thereby failed to see what is most important. They exalted in their power to make spiritual forces submit; they did not rejoice that the one who enabled such power has also claimed them as his own. "Rejoice," Jesus says, "that your names are written in heaven." And Jesus himself rejoices in the Holy Spirit, thanking the Father for revealing such truth to those who are as simple, trusting children (10:20–21).

Paul may not have known this story told by Luke, but his prayer for the Ephesians matches the sentiment expressed in these dominical words. Paul desires that his congregations know God better through the power of the Holy Spirit's wisdom and revelation. The power of the gospel message is seen not only in the submission of the powers to Christ but, even more, in the riches of believers' inheritance as adopted children of God (1:4), redeemed by Christ's blood (1:7), and awaiting that day when Christ brings all things together in himself (1:10).

b. God Raised and Exalted Christ (1:20–23)

20. . . he exerted when he raised Christ from the dead and seated him at his right hand in the heavenly realms, 21far above all rule and authority, power and dominion, and every name that is invoked, not only in the present age but also in the one to come. 22And God placed all things under his feet and appointed him to be head over everything for the church, 23which is his body, the fullness of him who fills everything in every way.

Paul finishes a series of three requests in his prayer, asking God to give his people—those whose hearts are illumined—the Holy Spirit's wisdom and revelation. Paul's purpose is to have three key aspects of salvation understood with greater clarity and embraced with greater love. These three points push beyond present circumstances, inviting reflection on the world to come. Paul declares they are called by God, and so he wants the Ephesians to hope all the more in that reality. Paul reminds them that they will inherit new life from God and points to its glorious fullness. Paul introduces a third point, that believers more fully appreciate God's power, a power that defies quantification.

1:20–23 God Raised and Exalted Christ

In the next four verses, Paul develops this new topic of God's power as it relates to believers' salvation and the cosmic unity of all things in Christ. Several key terms are used here, including "church," "head," and "body," that play crucial roles in Paul's ecclesiology. Paul introduces the spiritual forces, rulers, and authorities that are exceedingly inferior to Christ.[166] These spiritual forces marvel at God's wisdom (3:10) and are to be resisted by believers, preserved by standing firm in God's armor (6:10). Paul expounds on the work of God in Christ in raising him from the dead and seating him at his right hand, exalting his name above every name.[167] Paul declares that Christ is head, and the church is his body. It is Christ in his incarnation who submitted to the Father and who in his resurrected body intercedes for his body, the church.

Commentators reflect on whether this section is a hymn, and most conclude that the hymnic traits do not add up to make this a hymn or confession such as we find in Phil 2:6–11, for example.[168] Paul alludes to Ps 110:1 in Eph 1:20, which emphasizes the Lord saying to his Lord, "Sit at my right hand until I make your enemies a footstool for your feet."[169] In 1:22 he points to Ps 8:6 (= 8:7 LXX), which includes a stanza praising God that the Son of Man (or human being) is ruler over the works of God's hands and that God put all things under his feet. Paul cites Ps 8:6 in 1 Cor 15:27 (see also Heb 2:5–8).[170]

In both 1 Cor 15:24–27 and Eph 1:20–23, Paul uses Ps 110 and Ps 8 (with a particular variant from the Septuagint) and refers to the powers; however, in Ephesians, Christ is the subject of the passage, while in 1 Corinthians, God is the subject.[171] Psalm 8 reflects on God's creation of humanity in Gen 1:26–30, emphasizing humanity's management over creation. The psalmist also notes that God's glory reaches above the heavens, and praise from children's lips silences his enemies. Contemplating the wonders of creation, the psalmist wonders why God would even take notice of humans. Nevertheless, God

---

166. For Christ's resurrection and exaltation, see also Rom 8:34; Col 3:1; Acts 2:32–33.

167. MacDonald, 219, rightly remarks that, as in most other New Testament passages, "the resurrection is depicted here as something God accomplishes, not as the accomplishment of Christ alone."

168. Barth, 153; Best, 180; MacDonald, 219. Lincoln, 50–52, notes the similarities between Eph 1:20–23; Phil 2:6–11; Col 1:15–20; and 1 Tim 3:16: "Christ's resurrection from the dead, his exaltation, his session at God's right hand, and his supremacy over the powers."

169. See also Matt 22:44; 26:64; Mark 12:35–37; Luke 20:41–44; Acts 2:34–35; 5:31; 7:55–56; Rom 8:34; Heb 1:3; 10:12; 1 Pet 3:22.

170. Best, 181, observes: "Ps 110 and Ps 8 were then probably linked early in Christian thought, even prior to Paul, and given messianic significance." Arnold, 115, points out that 1 Cor 15:24–27 speaks of the subjugation of powers at the end of time, while Ephesians speaks of the subjugation that occurred in Christ's resurrection and exaltation. He suggests that this is "an illustration of the 'now–not yet' [eschatological] perspective that pervades the letter."

171. Best, 181, concludes that the author of Ephesians is "indebted to the same tradition as Paul."

crowns them with honor, gives them to rule over God's creation, and puts everything under their feet. In 1 Cor 15:27 Paul stresses Christ's resurrection, for now as the new Adam, Christ gives life to all who belong to him; Ephesians does not include an allusion to the Adam/new Adam motif.[172] In the end, Christ puts all enemies under his feet, including the greatest enemy, death. Paul continues in 1 Cor 15:28 that the Son will then be made subject to God the Father who put everything under him, and thus God may be all in all.[173] This magnificent vision of God's plan, which Paul explains to the Ephesians in 1:10, highlights the resurrection power of God that will bring all things together in triumphal love.

Later church councils drew on Ephesians in developing Trinitarian doctrines. If we read Ephesians in light of those later confessions, we could say that our text speaks about both the ontological and the economic Trinity. The former denotes the inner life of God, God's divine self in itself. The latter addresses the work of the Father in the Son through the Holy Spirit to effect salvation and unite all things in Christ. Thus we can rightly speak of Jesus Christ, the Messiah, submitting to God the Father as the incarnate one who redeems humanity by his blood. And we can rightly speak about the one true God, who before creation and now, enjoys mutual love among the Three Persons.[174] We can know God only as we know Jesus and the Spirit, as the three are "equally primal, mutually determinative, relationally constituted."[175]

20 Paul describes God the Father and Christ the Son working to effect salvation. In the Greek text, Paul speaks of "the" Christ, which reinforces his focus on Jesus as the anointed Messiah of God. Paul declares that God "exerted" himself, using the verb form of the antecedent noun "power" in 1:19.[176] It is this working of God's mighty strength that raised Christ from the dead

---

172. Best, 181.

173. Anthony C. Thiselton, *The First Epistle to the Corinthians*, New International Greek Testament Commentary (Grand Rapids: Eerdmans, 2000), 1237, observes: "Thus *God* remains the source and goal: *Christ* remains the means through which the goal which God purposed comes to be brought about," reminding readers that the purposes of God and Christ are one and "that any differentiation occurs within the framework of a source, mediate cause, agency, means and goal which *do not compete* but belong to what Paul and other NT writers . . . express as a shared purpose."

174. The Councils of Nicaea and Constantinople formalized the orthodox understanding of the Godhead. Based on the doctrine of divine simplicity, God's attributes (such as love, justice, mercy) are fully characteristic of each of the three persons. The three persons have one, unified will and purposed and predestined the cosmos to be united in Christ, and humans in particular to be redeemed by his death.

175. Hill, *Paul and the Trinity*, 168.

176. On ἐνεργέω and ἐνέργεια see BDAG 335.

1:20–23 God Raised and Exalted Christ

and seated him at the Father's right hand (see also Rom 8:34; Acts 2:33). Paul speaks of four actions done simultaneously by God in Eph 1:20, 22: God worked, he raised and seated Christ, and he gave.[177] Paul earlier claimed that redemption comes through Christ's blood, a reference to his death on the cross (1:7). The forgiveness of trespasses is accomplished by the cross. God's unequaled power accomplishes Christ's defeat of death through his bodily resurrection (see 1 Cor 6:14; Phil 3:10). Christ's resurrection gives believers assurance that their calling and inheritance is secure. Paul speaks similarly to the Corinthians, that Christ's resurrection confirms their own future resurrection (1 Cor 15:14–23).

But it is not only that Christ is raised; he is also seated at God's right hand in the heavenlies. The phrase "the heavenly realms" is unique to Ephesians, occurring in 1:3, 20; 2:6; 3:10; 6:12. The phrase can carry a locative sense, "in the heavenly realms," or refer to heavenly things or beings.[178] Here Paul stresses the locative sense. This emphasis is consistent throughout Ephesians, as Paul emphasizes both the current blessings that believers share in Christ as well as those blessings yet to come. Therefore, we should not overread this phrase as establishing a realized eschatology in Ephesians.[179] Paul declares that Christ is seated at God's right hand. Psalm 110:1 influences Paul's understanding, as this psalm was used as a messianic text within the early church (e.g., Matt 22:43–45; Luke 20:41–44; Heb 1:13). The psalmist declares, "The Lord says to my lord: 'Sit at my right hand until I make your enemies a footstool for your feet'" (Ps 110:1). The most favored seat is next to the king; to be at his right hand indicates the king's complete confidence and favor. This custom is behind James and John's request to Jesus that the brothers sit on the left and the right of Jesus when he comes into his kingdom (Matt 20:21; Mark 10:37). The sons of Zebedee had the right idea, but the wrong motives; they desired to share Jesus's power, not his cross. Thus he challenged them whether they could drink the cup (of suffering) that he was about to drink. In their arrogant naivety, they answered affirmatively, but they abandoned him at his arrest. He faced his crucifixion, not with these overconfident men, but with his mother, a few female disciples, and the young apostle John. Paul will declare to the Ephesians in the following chapter that believers are seated with Christ now, positions of honor based on his great work.

21 This verse continues the thought begun in the previous verse by expanding on Paul's claim that Christ is now seated at God's right hand in

---

177. Best, 182, suggests these actions happen simultaneously, not in sequence.
178. MacDonald, 197.
179. Best, 117, rightly concludes: "'In the heavenlies' does not then by itself provide a realized eschatological slant." See also MacDonald, 220, who likewise explains that the epistle tilts toward realized eschatology but includes future elements yet to be realized.

the heavenlies. Paul describes further that Christ is seated far above every ruler and authority and power and dominion. Paul details the cosmic spiritual realities implied in 1:10 (see also Col 1:16). At this point, they are not deemed evil or enemies of God.[180] Paul uses this same tone in Eph 3:10 as he declares that God's wisdom is displayed to these powers through the church. Yet we will see that in the next chapter Paul speaks of the ruler of the kingdom of the air who works in those disobedient to God (2:2). Furthermore, he notes that the days are evil (5:16) and that believers struggle against the powers of this dark world (6:12). These powers can be hostile to the church; nevertheless, believers take heart that Christ reigns far above them.[181]

Paul adds that Christ's name is above every name. In Paul's day, a name indicated the sort of person one was. Additionally, if you knew a person's name, it was thought that you could have power over them.[182] In several places in the New Testament we see evidence of this. Jesus commands the demons who possess the man roaming the tombs in the region of the Gerasenes to identify their name. "Legion," they reply, revealing Jesus's power to extract their names and thus his power over them (Mark 5:1–20; Luke 8:26–39).[183] So too in Ephesus at the time of Paul, Acts tells of seven sons of Sceva who tried to cast out demons using Jesus's name. An evil spirit resisted, scoffing at such hubris, declaring that while he knew Jesus and Paul, he does not know these men—and he beat all seven, tearing their clothes. The event shook the city with fear, Luke tells us, and Jesus's name was held in high regard (Acts 19:13–17). The Christ hymn in Philippians notes that God highly exalted Christ, giving him a name above every name (2:9). Here in Ephesians, Paul indicates that these powers and names affect humans now and in the

---

180. Perkins, 51, explains: "Since the eulogy and the thanksgiving both depend upon traditional, formulaic phrases for divine blessing, the positive use of angelic powers and name formulae in Christological acclamations and hymns seems to be more appropriate in this section." Contra MacDonald, 220, who holds that the powers here are "hostile beings."

181. Muddiman, 89, observes that "the doctrine of fallen angels, supernatural beings who inadvertently obstruct or deliberately oppose the rule of God, is an ancient Jewish idea (Gen 6:1–4) which comes into major prominence in later apocalyptic (cf. Dan. 12; *1 En.* 6–9, 15)."

182. MacDonald, 220, writes: "In the ancient world the names of deities were thought to have divine power." See also Best, 173–80; Arnold, *Ephesians: Power and Magic*, 54: "The calling of the names of supernatural 'powers' was fundamental to the practice of magic." Carr, *Angels and Principalities*, 12, argues (wrongly in my estimation) that these forces were understood as positive, for the ancient world did not imagine hostile forces standing over them: "Paul moved about an Asia that was characterised by religious quiet and acceptance of the past."

183. Jesus speaks of himself as "I AM," the name God used to reveal himself to Moses (Exod 3:14), in several places in the Gospels (e.g., Matt 14:27; Mark 6:50; John 6:20, 35; 8:12, 58; 10:11; 11:25; 14:6; 15:1).

future age. He expresses similar convictions about two ages in several other letters (Rom 8:38; 12:2; 1 Cor 1:20; Gal 1:4).

Are these powers human agents or institutions? Or is Paul referencing spiritual forces in this verse?[184] Perhaps we need to examine the premise of these questions, which is that we have two spheres of reality—the natural and the supernatural world. Such a bifurcation is foreign to the ancient world's cosmology. Instead, unseen forces were believed to impact everyday life.[185] People feared being cursed and used magic to manipulate fate and spiritual forces to do one's bidding.[186] Acts describes some believers in the Ephesian church who had previously relied on magical texts and spells. They brought them into a public space and burned them, about fifty thousand drachmas worth of spells (Acts 19:19–20).[187] Paul reassures his Ephesian readers, who would remember the names of gods and goddesses that populated their magical texts and amulets and charms, that Jesus has power over all names.

The manner in which God through Christ defeated the spiritual powers deserves attention. God's victory was through the cross, a subversive way to address power structures.[188] Typically we think victory is about dominating our opponents, exploiting weakness. The way of the cross, however, is the way of self-denial, losing so as to win (Mark 8:35). Believers are to imitate this behavior and walk this path as they follow after God.[189]

22 In the previous verse, Paul notes that Christ is far above all powers and above all names. In this verse, all things are under his feet and he is head over all things, and God gives Christ to the church. Similar themes inform Peter's argument to his congregation, as he declares that the resurrected Christ "has gone into heaven and is at God's right hand—with angels, authorities and powers in submission to him" (1 Pet 3:22). Paul makes an allusion to Ps 8:6, which Paul also cites in 1 Cor 15:27 (see also Heb 2:5–8).[190] Paul places the direct object, "all things," in a position of emphasis at the beginning of the pas-

---

184. MacDonald, 225, explains: "That the powers are spiritual agencies and not human authorities is communicated especially strongly by 6:12 where conflict is said to be not against flesh and blood but against spiritual powers."

185. MacDonald, 226, rightly notes the ancient conviction that society is affected by spiritual forces, such that "what is experienced on the earthly plane has a cosmic referent."

186. Arnold, 40, summarizes: "A belief in the harmful influence of the 'powers' is attested throughout the Mediterranean world of the Greco-Roman period."

187. A drachma is a Roman coin made of silver and worth about one day's wages.

188. Gombis, *Drama of Ephesians*, 88.

189. Gombis, *Drama of Ephesians*, 88: "The manner in which God achieves his victory over the powers is crucial, since the way God triumphs determines how the church participates in his triumph."

190. Arnold, 114–15. Best, 181, observes that "Ps 110 and Ps 8 were then probably linked early in Christian thought, even prior to Paul, and given messianic significance."

sage. "All things" are "placed under" Christ's feet. Joshua, the ancient Israelite, exhorts his generals to put their feet on the necks of the five defeated Amorite kings. This act symbolized the victory aided by the Lord (Josh 10:24–25).

The verb "placed under" (*hypotassō*) can be translated "to be subject" or "to submit" (see 5:21, 22 [implied], 24).[191] The verb stem carries the sense "to arrange, appoint" (see Rom 13:1).[192] Paul adds the prefix *hypō*, which means "under," and we have the meaning "to be ordered under" and thus "to be subordinate" and "to submit." The negative tone these verbs carry in today's individualistic culture often prevents readers from appreciating the positive nuance they could hold for ancient listeners; they need not imply subjugation, but rather ordered stability. In the early Roman imperial period, the fragile veneer of civilized conduct threatened to fracture, with the resulting lawlessness overwhelming especially the poor. Law and order were maintained through a rigorous insistence on social hierarchy, to keep chaos at bay. In the New Testament, the verb is used with reference to Ps 8:6, as we find here (see also 1 Cor 15:25–27; Phil 3:21; Heb 2:7–8; 1 Pet 3:22). In this psalm, God is praised for his creation and his decision to give humanity dominion over it, such that everything is submitted under their feet. The psalmist celebrates God's ordering of the universe, including the celestial realm and the earthly domain. In Eph 1:21, the verb likely implies a victory over all things, earthly and heavenly.[193]

Paul adds that not only did God put all things under Christ's feet, but God also "gave" or "appointed" him.[194] Paul places "him/Christ" at the beginning of this clause for emphasis.[195] Some argue that with this particular syntax, the verb is better translated "appoint," so that the verse would read "God appointed Christ as head."[196] But there is little evidence for this meaning elsewhere,[197] and the dative of "the church" suggests the verb should be read with its typical sense, "to give."[198] We face two other syntactical questions.

---

191. On ὑποτάσσω see BDAG 1042.
192. On τάσσω see BDAG 991.
193. Muddiman, 91.
194. On δίδωμι see BDAG 242–43. See also Larkin, 25. Best, 180, observes that the shift to finite verbs and the "credal-type" language could reflect a preformed statement; however, he rightly disagrees with Roberts's argument that this verse is both a transition to the letter's body and a creedal statement. See J. H. Roberts, "Belydenisuitsprake as Pauliniese breifoorgange," *Hervormde Teologiese Studies* 44 (1988): 81–97.
195. Best, 181.
196. Larkin, 25.
197. Thielman, 111.
198. Best, 181, writes that the genitive of "church" (ἐκκλησία) would be used if the verb's meaning was "to appoint." MacDonald, 220, rightly argues that the verb choice strengthens Paul's point: "The importance of the church in God's plan of salvation could not be stated more strongly."

First, is the term "head" (*kephalē*) a predicate accusative, "God gave Christ as head," or is "head" in apposition to "church"?[199] Second, does the prepositional phrase "over all things" modify the verb? To the second question, if the phrase modifies the verb, that would necessitate the verb's meaning "to appoint," which we determined above to be unlikely. The better option is to see the phrase as attributive to "head." The resulting translation follows: "God gave him/Christ as head over all things, to the church."[200] Alternatively, one could argue that "head over all things" is a single phrase in apposition to "him/Christ," which would render the English "God gave him, head over all things, to be the head of the church."[201] The difference is minimal, because Paul will make clear in the second half of the verse what is implied here—namely, that Christ is the head of the church. The last piece of the puzzle focuses on the relationship of the dative "to/for the church" to the rest of the clause. While the sense could be "with respect to the church" (dative of reference), most who argue that the verb means "to give" conclude that this dative should be understood as an indirect object, "to the church."[202]

We are left to discuss the fuller meaning of two key terms, "head" (*kephalē*) and "church" (*ekklēsia*), both of which are related to a third term "body" (*sōma*). These three terms are found in Col 1:18 (see also 1:24; 2:19). As we examine the term "head" below, we must keep in mind that the term operates within the metaphor of head/body and not as an isolated term. The meaning of "head," therefore, is shaped and limited by its use in Paul's argument.[203] Paul stresses Christ as head, partly to fill out the word picture that began with the allusion to Ps 110:1 of putting all things under his feet and partly to introduce the notion of the church as his body.[204] Paul juxtaposes in a rich metaphor the human body and the spiritual impact of Christ's elevation above all names. Just as all things are in submission to Christ, under his feet, so too he is over all things as preeminent. The point Paul makes is not that Christ is the leader of "all things" but that he is above all creation.

---

199. Best, 181, sees no real difference in meaning between the two grammatical choices.

200. Barth, 157, argues for an adjectival meaning (supreme head) due to the lack of an article. Best, 182, counters that πάντα was anarthrous in the quotation in 1:22 and that its occurrence here simply matches that usage. Moreover, Christ is the only head, not the supreme head above other heads.

201. Hoehner, 288, cites Dio Chrysostom, *Ephesians* 1:15–20 (PG 62:26).

202. Contra Muddiman, 91, who concludes that it is more "fitting to say that God gave the Church to Christ (as at John 17:9) or at least that Christ gave himself for the Church (5:2, 25) or took the Church to himself (5:31)."

203. On κεφαλή see BDAG 541–42; C. C. Kroeger, "Head," *DPL* 375–78.

204. Best, 182. He adds that the headship is "certainly not simply one of overlordship as with the cosmos, for that would not entail the church being his body."

EXCURSUS: THE MEANING OF *KEPHALĒ*

The discussion surrounding the semantic range of *kephalē* grew heated in the 1980s among evangelical scholars. Some drew on the Liddell and Scott lexicon (1843), which included more than twenty-five entries, none of which defined the term as having authority. This group of scholars promoted the definition "source."[205] Gordon Fee, a leading proponent of this view, noted that the translators of the Septuagint, "who ordinarily used *kephalē* to translate *rō'š* when the physical 'head' was intended, almost never did so when 'ruler' was intended, thus indicating that this metaphorical sense is an exceptional usage and not part of the ordinary range of meanings for the Greek word."[206] A parallel is found from the Roman world, when Seneca wrote to Nero, his former pupil and emperor, that the head is the source of human well-being and, by extension, Nero should be that which brings health to his empire.[207]

Other scholars, including Wayne Grudem, suggested that the semantic range of *kephalē* included the notion of leadership or authority. He examined 2,336 examples of *kephalē* and discovered that about 87 percent of the references indicated a physical head, 5 percent exhibited a metaphorical sense, and 3 percent carried the sense of a starting point or top. Grudem concluded that only 2.1 percent of the occurrences of *kephalē* could be defined as "authority over," including several passages in Septuagint Judges, reflecting an ancient translation decision.[208] One could find both ideas in the description of the patriarch of the family as "head," for the father was both the literal, biological source for his children and the decision maker on their behalf.[209] Markus Barth examines the contemporary medical and biological understandings of "head," explaining that Paul follows the positions of Hippocrates and Galen, over against the views of the Aristotelians and Stoics.[210]

---

205. Berkeley Mickelsen and Alvera Mickelsen, "What Does *Kephalē* Mean in the New Testament?," in *Women, Authority, and the Bible*, ed. Alvera Mickelsen (Downers Grove, IL: InterVarsity Press, 1986), 98–99, 105–10.

206. Gordon D. Fee, *The First Epistle to the Corinthians*, NICNT (Grand Rapids: Eerdmans, 1987), 502–3.

207. Seneca, *On Clemency* 2.2.1. Thiselton, *First Epistle to the Corinthians*, 816–17.

208. Wayne Grudem, "Does *Kephalē* ('Head') Mean 'Source' or 'Authority Over' in Greek Literature? A Survey of 2,336 Examples," *Trinity Journal* 6 (1985): 38–59; Wayne Grudem, "The Meaning of *Kephalē* ('Head'): An Evaluation of New Evidence, Real and Alleged," *Journal of the Evangelical Theology Study* 44 (2001): 25–65.

209. George Lyons, "Church and Holiness in Ephesians," in *Holiness and Ecclesiology in the New Testament*, ed. Kent E. Brower and Andy Johnson (Grand Rapids, Eerdmans, 2007), 249.

210. Barth, 186–88. He summarizes (188): "Hippocrates' and Galen's neurological doctrine amounts to the following: the head, i.e. the brain, is the coordinator and inte-

Excursus: The Meaning of *Kephalē*

More recently, other options have been forwarded, based in part on research into metaphor.[211] Anthony Thiselton argues that *kephalē* can be used as a synecdoche; it "denotes persons or animals (for which the part denotes the whole)."[212] Additionally, *kephalē* can be understood as preeminent or foremost, that which is the public face of the entire entity.[213] Michelle Lee-Barnewall argues that the notion of preeminence without some sort of power or authority would be quite unlikely in the ancient context. The head metaphor was often used in context of political or military authority, as it is uppermost on the body. As the head of the body must be protected for the soldier's safety, so too must the general of the army, or the emperor, be protected as having the primary place within the community.[214] A common assumption is that the "body" would or should sacrifice itself for the head. She observes that the body metaphor in antiquity "was diverse and flexible and could be used to illustrate a number of different situations."[215]

Cynthia Westfall focuses on the categories of reciprocity and family, arguing that *kephalē* occurs in the context of ancestry. The progenitor of the family is the head or source of the family, and as such, he is the prominent one or the face of the family unit. The wife in the ancient world depended on her husband for food and shelter as the body depends on the head for its life. Using the lens of reciprocity, Westfall further argues that the patron/client social relationship informs the head/body metaphor, as the "head" or patron provides a benefit to her client, which the client reciprocates through honoring his patron. Westfall concludes, "Functioning as a 'head' may be the

---

grator of the body's sensations. . . . It not only receives, registers, arranges, and retains messages, but much more, it also has a causative, almost creative, function: it selects, evaluates, and steers the sensations of the body communicated to it, and decides on a proper reaction to them."

211. See commentary on Eph 5:20–32 for a detailed discussion of metaphor.

212. Thiselton, *First Epistle to the Corinthians*, 812–22.

213. Cynthia Long Westfall, *Paul and Gender: Reclaiming the Apostle's Vision for Men and Women in Christ* (Grand Rapids: Baker Academic, 2016), 38–40, examines *kephalē* in the context of reciprocity and family structures, noting that the English term "head" does not carry the same semantic range as Greek κεφαλή. In the case of 1 Cor 11:3, she argues that Paul "has drawn the metaphor of the man being woman's head from the language of kinship" (40).

214. Michelle Lee-Barnewall, "Turning ΚΕΦΑΛΗ on Its Head: The Rhetoric of Reversal in Ephesians 5:21–33," in *Christian Origins and Greco-Roman Culture: Social and Literary Contexts for the New Testament*, ed. Stanley E. Porter and Andrew W. Pitts (Leiden: Brill, 2013), 608.

215. Lee-Barnewall, "Turning ΚΕΦΑΛΗ on Its Head," 602.

grounds for holding a position of authority over a client, but it is not the same thing as the exercise of authority."[216]

A careful study of *kephalē* is found in 5:22–24.

A second critical term in Paul's theology is "church" (*ekklēsia*), found nine times in the epistle.[217] It was used in the wider culture to indicate an assembly. Paul expresses his understanding of Christian community with different metaphors, including "body" as we will see in the next verse (see also 4:15), as well as "God's household" (2:19), "God's people" (2:19), and "a holy temple in the Lord" (2:21). He paints a picture of a new humanity (2:14–15) and of a mature human, full of Christ (4:13). God's church, Christ's body, filled and led by the Spirit, is a group sustained by grace. Paul's "affirmations about the church are organized in a Trinitarian fashion—from the Spirit, through Christ, to God the Father."[218]

When Paul speaks of the church, he primarily intends the local worship gathering of Christ-followers. The ancient church drew on the practices of the synagogue, a weekly gathering of local Jews to celebrate the Sabbath with Torah reading. An ancient synonym for synagogue is "house/place of prayer" (*proseuchē*), which highlights another of its main activities (Acts 16:13, 16; see also Matt 21:13; Mark 11:17; Luke 19:46, citing Isa 56:7). So too, the church met regularly (perhaps weekly, 1 Cor 16:2) for encouragement, and to pray, read Scripture, sing psalms and hymns, and partake of the Lord's Supper together. In addition to each local congregation, Paul also speaks about the church universal, the church across time and space that is Christ's body (see 1 Cor 11:22).[219] The universal, eternal commonwealth of believers is perceived in each individual manifestation at the local level. Paul focuses on

---

216. Cynthia Long Westfall, "'This Is a Great Metaphor!' Reciprocity in the Ephesians Household Code," in *Christian Origins and Greco-Roman Culture: Social and Literary Contexts for the New Testament*, ed. Stanley E. Porter and Andrew W. Pitts (Leiden: Brill, 2013), 587. The alert reader will notice that I imagined a female patron and a male client. I did so because (1) it represents historical possibility and (2) it highlights the range of application of reciprocity.

217. On ἐκκλησία see BDAG 303–4; P. T. O'Brien, "Church," *DPL* 123–31; Allan J. McNicol, "Church," *EDB* 252–54.

218. Lyons, "Church and Holiness in Ephesians," 245.

219. Ben Witherington III, *Conflict and Community in Corinth: A Socio-Rhetorical Commentary on 1 and 2 Corinthians* (Grand Rapids: Eerdmans, 1995), 91: "Each local congregation is a full representation, whether small or large, of the whole body of Christ and of the whole Christ."

the local community in his injunctions to support and encourage each other (Eph 4:25, 32). He attends to the universal when he states that the Ephesians have a permanent address with Christ who is seated at God's right hand now (2:6), and they have an inheritance in his kingdom in the new heavens and new earth in the age to come (5:5). In a similar way, Paul declares to the Philippians that their eternal, universal citizenship is in heaven (3:20). This means that the church today includes as its "members" those from the ancient Philippian church, as the universal church is not just global, but includes each faithful generation.

These two realities of the church can be captured in the labels "church militant" and "church triumphant." In the former, the church is in a battle against evil now on earth; in the latter, the church rejoices in eternal repose in the new heavens and new earth (cf. Rev 21:1–5). Paul indicates that believers enjoy both realities now; he does not completely collapse the future into the present, but he does reimagine the temporal timeline such that believers stand in two places at the same time. The church battles now in the present age of conflict (hence the need for the armor of God; Eph 6:10) and is in a place of victorious rest, seated with Christ who is head over all things.

23 This verse completes Paul's thought from the previous verse.[220] Paul introduces a key metaphor, the church as *sōma* or "body."[221] As we consider this metaphor, it is important to note that Paul does not speak of the powers and principalities as part of Christ's body, even though he serves as head over them.[222] Not only local and universal, the church is also a living entity, as it worships the living God. In that sense, the "body" metaphor is especially useful because it calls to mind an active and growing organism. The church as a group of individuals is susceptible to sin, but the church as Christ's body is equipped for holy living, for he is head over all things. Because God is sovereign and rules and reigns through Christ, the world is his—thus his followers are to be holy and blameless (1:4).[223] Paul uses the "body" metaphor to ex-

---

220. Barth, 154, underestimates the importance of the verse: "Actually vs. 23 gives the impression of an afterthought, an added interpretation."

221. On σῶμα see BDAG 983–84; L. J. Kreitzer, "Body," *DPL* 71–76; Eduard R. Schweizer, "Body," *ABD* 2:767–72. Barth, 192–94, rightly critiques the conclusion that "body" is not used metaphorically by Paul and rejects the meaning that the church is not simply called Christ's body, but *is* his body, while Christ is himself both head and body. Here Barth reacts primarily to the argument of E. Schweizer, *Das Leben des Herrn in der Gemeinde und ihren Diensten* (Zürich: EVZ, 1946).

222. Barth, 197, comments that "without love and without the historic event of the cross there would be no body and no members of Christ." He continues: "Only the death of Christ is the means and moment of the church's formation."

223. MacDonald, 226, points out that the interest in the church throughout Ephesians

plain spiritual gifts (Rom 12:4–5; 1 Cor 12:12–27), to teach about communion (1 Cor 10:16–17; 11:27, 29), and to describe the theological impact of his own sufferings (Col 1:24).

The metaphor "body" to describe a group of people was familiar to Paul's audience, as it was used by philosophers and politicians alike to describe the body politic and to encourage each person to fulfill their role in the community, for the sake of the whole.[224] This was not a call to egalitarian social order, however, but a reinforcement of the hierarchical status quo. Paul turned this supposition on its head (pun intended), for the "head" of the church's body is the crucified Lord. Therefore, each member is of infinite worth and is graced with infinite love.

Within Ephesians, Paul stresses the church as one body, both Jew and gentile made one through Christ who is their peace (2:14; see also Col 3:15). Relatedly, he speaks of gentiles as coheirs and as comembers of Christ's body (Eph 3:6). Paul encourages believers to grow up into Christ, even as a body grows strong as each part does its work well (4:4, 12, 15–16; see also Col 2:19). Finally, Paul stresses intimacy of relationship with this metaphor in his discussion of marriage (Eph 5:21–33). He draws on the marriage pronouncement of Gen 2:24, that the husband leaves his father and mother, cleaves to his wife, and the two become one "flesh." He uses "flesh" and "body" interchangeably to emphasize the unity and oneness of marriage. Perhaps Paul's encounter with the risen Lord also shaped his understanding of the metaphor. Recall the question: "Saul, Saul, why do you persecute *me*?" (Acts 9:4–5, emphasis added; 22:7–8).[225] Technically, of course, Paul was not persecuting Jesus, but those who followed his teachings. Yet Jesus insists with this question that Paul attacks him when he goes after his followers.

---

is based on Paul's conviction that the group is exposed to hostile forces and is engaged "in a cosmic struggle that is overcome for believers by means of a new life with Christ in the heavenly places."

224. Eastman, *Paul and the Person*, 85–105, explores the concept of body in the ancient Stoics (especially Epictetus), modern scientists and philosophers, and Paul's Epistles, noting that "twentieth-century pundits may trumpet that humans beings are made of stardust, but that would have been old news to a Greco-Roman audience" (86). She concludes that "Paul's 'body language' thus discloses a close interplay between corporeal human existence as physical and social 'bodies' and larger suprahuman realities that exercise pressure on embodied human interaction" (91).

225. John A. T. Robinson, *The Body: A Study in Pauline Theology* (London: SCM, 1952), 58, uses this argument, but then concludes that Paul believes the resurrected body of Christ is revealed in the Christian community. This conclusion fails to consider Paul's insistence on Christ's literal, personal, physical resurrection in 1 Cor 15:20.

EXCURSUS: "BODY" METAPHORS IN THE ANCIENT WORLD

Aesop's fable entitled "The Belly and the Members" (#130 Perry Index) tells the story of the body's members rebelling against the stomach, refusing to give it food. Of course, this decision ends up crippling the body for lack of nourishment. The Latin historian Livy (ca. 64 or 59 BCE–17 CE) recounts a well-known story that emphasized the importance of a unified political group through the metaphor of a human body.[226] The historical scene is set in Rome, when Valerius was dictator, and he promised the plebians in his army to redress their debt (494 BCE). The situation decayed: Valerius resigned and the Senate ordered the Roman army to leave the city quietly. They relocated to a place about three miles outside the walls. Now Rome was in turmoil, as the patricians (nobility) and the plebeians (free citizens) greatly feared each other, and both feared what might happen if a foreign war erupted. The senate decided to send Menenius Agrippa to the military camp in an effort to resolve the stalemate. Agrippa told a simple fable about a human body whose various members all did what they wanted. They ignored the belly (the patricians), saying that it never worked but only enjoyed the work of others, like the hands who prepared the food and the teeth who chewed it (the plebeians). And so the body refused to eat, as a way to hurt the stomach. Yet in their attempt to influence the stomach to do as they wished, they ended up weakening themselves for lack of nutrition. This parable shows that the belly is vital to the body's survival, for it sends out nourishment in the blood that fills all the members. This convinced the army, and by extension the plebeians, on the importance of unity. While a few concessions were granted to the plebeians, by and large the hierarchical status quo was maintained. Both Agrippa and the plebeians assumed the higher social worth of the "belly," the patricians.[227]

Tacitus, a Latin historian and senator of the early second century, describes a scene during Tiberius's reign wherein the emperor skirmished with the senators about his decision to pull back a bit from leading the empire. Some senators responded that the "body of the State was one, and must be directed by a single mind."[228] The underlying assumption is that the state was a single unit and needed a single guiding figure.

Typically, Greek and Latin authors used the body metaphor to explain or rationalize the class and economic divisions within society as necessary for the proper function of the entire society. Paul modifies this general metaphor

---

226. Livy, *History* 2.32.7–11. See also Cicero, *On Duty* 3.5.22.

227. Dale B. Martin, *The Corinthian Body* (New Haven: Yale University Press, 1995), 45, calls this viewpoint "benevolent patriarchalism," a cultural structure that viewed as natural the rule of the wealthy, who should practice prudence and resist overindulgence.

228. Tacitus, *Annals* 1.12, 13.

in gospel-specific ways. He does not accept the class divisions that privilege wealth and social prestige but instead stresses the Spirit's gifts as that which creates different functions within the church (1 Cor 12:18–25).

Yet the "body" metaphor could also promote familial virtues. Plutarch, a Middle Platonic philosopher (ca. 46–120 CE), used a body metaphor to emphasize the importance of brotherly love. He explained that the body has pairs—hands, feet, eyes, ears, nostrils—for its preservation and care. So too brothers in the same family should work together and care for each other. He notes: "Just as in the same body the combination of moist and dry, cold and hot, sharing one nature and diet, by their consent and agreement engender the best and most pleasant temperament and bodily harmony . . . ; so through the concord of brothers both family and household are sound and flourish, and friends and intimates, like a harmonious choir, neither do nor say, nor think, anything discordant."[229] Paul shares the sentiment expressed by Plutarch, but with an important twist. The "brothers" are not of the same biological family, but are those united by Christ. They include male and female slaves and owners, Jewish and gentile women and men, diverse ethnicities and economic statuses. These are all adopted sons (and daughters) of God in Christ (Eph 1:5).

Paul declares that the church is *Christ's* body.[230] This evocative claim reminds us that ecclesiology and Christology in Ephesians are inseparably intertwined.[231] In our passage, the metaphor of church as Christ's body ties directly to Christ's exalted status as above all beings, because he was raised from the dead. Perhaps we could find here a hint of the mystical body of Christ, for the church as Christ's body is above all things. But we cannot push the analogy too far, for the church does not equal Christ, nor does the incarnation extend to include the church. Paul clearly teaches that Christ has his own resurrected body (1:20; see also 1 Cor 15:20). Moreover, the church is fallible, and believers die (or "fall asleep" in the Lord). The introduction of "body" language here to describe the church's relationship to Christ prepares the reader well for the next description of the church as one new humanity, Jew and gentile made one through Christ,

---

229. Plutarch, *Moralia*, translation from W. C. Helmbold, Loeb Classical Library 6 (Cambridge: Harvard University Press, 1970), 439A–523B at 479A–B.

230. Barth, 192–99, offers an extensive discussion, concluding: "The church is the self-manifestation of the crucified and risen Jesus Christ to all powers, all things, all men." See also Best, 189–96.

231. MacDonald, 226, explains: "As the thanksgiving of 1:15–23 illustrates so well, ecclesiology is the result of christology in Ephesians." Barth, 199, rightly cautions: "The body metaphor does not monopolize the discussion and perhaps [may] even have a supreme position."

1:20–23 GOD RAISED AND EXALTED CHRIST

our peace (Eph 2:14). Only resurrection power, power that is above all things, can create a new "creature." This theme of unity continues in Eph 4 with Paul's emphasis on one body, one Spirit, one hope, one Lord, one faith, one baptism, and one God and Father of all. This body grows in unity and matures into the fullness of Christ (4:13), who is the head (4:15). The terms "body" and "fullness" used in 1:23, elevate both Christ's work in the church and God's work in establishing the salvation plan executed and established in Christ.

The final clause of 1:23 is full of grammatical puzzles. The noun "fullness" (*plērōma*) and its participial clause ("him who fills") have generated a plethora of interpretations.[232] While it is theoretically possible that "the fullness" is in apposition to "him/Christ" in 1:22, the syntactical issues raised are daunting. Most likely "fullness" is in apposition to "body" mentioned directly before this noun, thus referring to the church.[233] "Fullness" carries three basic meanings: "that which is full," "that which is filled,"[234] or "that which makes something complete."[235] It is better to understand "the fullness" as passive, which means that the church is filled with Christ himself,[236] rather than argue that the church completes or fills Christ.[237] The latter interpretation finds no support elsewhere in Paul, for the possible example of Col 1:24 focuses on "Christ's sufferings as part of the messianic woes" and is not applicable to our context in Ephesians.[238] Paul insists that Christ has all fullness of deity dwelling in him, for God was pleased to do so (Col 1:19; 2:9), and here he refers to Christ's body, the church, being filled by Christ.[239]

---

232. On πλήρωμα see BDAG 829–30. The noun πλήρωμα is used in Rom 11:12, 25; 13:10; 15:29; 1 Cor 10:26.

233. Best, 183–84. See also Arnold, 116, and Lincoln, 73, who adds that "the weight of the clause in v 22b is on the end . . . , on the status of the Church in God's purposes," and thus points to the author's overall focus on the church in the passage.

234. Hoehner, 294–95; see also Barth, 158, who concludes that Paul defines the church here: "She is Christ's body, and she is his fullness."

235. MacDonald, 221.

236. Lincoln, 75. Arnold, 117, rejects the passive interpretation, that God fills Christ, because "it requires the neuter plural accusative adjective (πάντα) to be understood adverbially when it has twice been used in the immediately preceding context as a direct object." See also Barth, 205.

237. P. D. Overfield, "*Pleroma*: A Study in Content and Context," *NTS* 25 (1975): 393, concludes "that the Church is the completion of Christ." Lincoln, 75, critiques Overfield.

238. Lincoln, 75.

239. Arnold, 118, suggests that Paul draws on Old Testament images of God filling the Jerusalem temple, although Arnold notes that our noun πλήρωμα does not occur in the Septuagint—though the cognate verb and adjective occur in several places (2 Chr 7:1; Isa 6:1; Ezek 43:5; 44:4). See also Barth, 204, who concludes that, if the Old Testament has any role here, "the noun means the miracle, process, and the event of filling" as God acts to fill a place and demonstrate his power.

The participle is a cognate verb (*plēroō*) to the noun "fullness" and means "to fill or make full." It may refer spatially to filling a container, to paying a bill, or to completing or summing up something.[240] The participle is either (1) passive, (2) middle with an active sense, or (3) middle with a reflexive meaning. The ambiguity allows for either of the following translations: "of the one who fills" or "of the one who is being filled."[241] One option is to read the noun as carrying the sense "completion," with the participle as passive; this renders the verse's meaning as Christ is completed by the church.[242] The overall argument centers on a head lacking or being undeveloped without a body. However, the message of this passage is Christ's greatness over the cosmos.[243] Moreover, Christ is later described as the source of life for the church (4:16; 5:25).[244] A better option is to see the participle as middle with an active force.[245] The active sense of the participle expresses Christ filling the church, similar to Paul's claim that Christ and the Spirit fill the church (4:10; 5:18).[246]

The participial phrase includes two other phrases: "(the) all things/everything" and the phrase "in all" or "in every way." The last two phrases are found in 1 Cor 12:6, often translated as "in all of them and in everyone," and 15:28, "so that God may be all in all." I argue for an active sense of the participle[247] and a passive sense of the noun, and that leads to understanding the phrase "all things" as the direct object, indicating that Christ fills everything.[248] Paul is not establishing the church as filling Christ or filling the world. Instead, the church serves the world, as it grows to maturity in Christ.[249]

---

240. Barth, 159. On πληρόω see BDAG 827–29.

241. Barth, 159. Arnold, 117, observes that in 4:10 Paul uses the active voice of the verb, and Arnold finds an "active significance" here.

242. Barth, 159. The passive rendering of the participle would entail viewing the prepositional phrase adverbially: "totally" or "completely"; see Arnold, 119, and Thielman, 114–15.

243. Barth, 156, suggests that because the passage stresses Christ's rule over all things, Paul here stresses Christ's rule of the church as a specific example of his universal dominion. See also Arnold, 119.

244. Best, 185–89, discusses various interpretations.

245. MacDonald, 221.

246. Arnold, 117. Barth, 209, concludes: "He who does the filling is God or Christ." Larkin, 26, argues that because the clause "all things" fits most naturally as a direct object, it makes better sense to see the participle as middle with an active, reflective sense. As such, the meaning could be expressed as "Christ is filling for himself all things in every way."

247. Arnold, 119, remarks that the present tense of this participle suggests a dynamic engagement of the church in the world, as Christ fills his church.

248. Barth, 206, rightly concludes that the passage does not speak of "the implementation of Christ by the church."

249. Barth, 209: "Any notion of world dominion by the church is missing, but the church is equipped to do a 'work of service' and to 'stand against,' and 'resist,' the attacks of evil powers."

Paul has likely elevated his rhetoric by repeating the "p" sound in the four major words of the verse.[250] Ancient readers always read aloud, even if they were by themselves; they read as much with their ears as with their eyes. Moreover, most of the congregation would not have been literate enough to read this prose. Paul brings his congregation before the throne of grace, asking God to show them their great calling and inheritance, which depends on the all-surpassing power worked in Christ's redemptive act and celebrated now in Christ's exaltation to the Father's right hand. He closes by introducing a key theme within the epistle, namely, that the church is Christ's body.

B. THE RICHES OF HIS GRACE (2:1–22)

In Eph 2, Paul begins the body of the letter.[251] Paul offers a "before and after" picture of the Ephesian believers from two vantage points. In the first ten verses, he describes their past and current situation as it relates to the heavenly realm, the arena of the powers and principalities. In this, Paul continues the previous chapter's emphases on Christ's superiority over all authorities (1:21–22) and the ultimate end when Christ brings all things together in unity (1:10). In these verses the believers are assured that they now participate in Christ's victory over the evil powers that pull humans from God and his love. Believers enjoy Christ's presence as they are made alive with him, raised with him, and seated with him (2:5–6). God's love is shown in his grace-filled act of salvation accepted by faith (2:5, 8). This grace continues in the present, as God makes a way for the believers to do good in the world (2:10). The second half of Eph 2 offers the same story, now told from the cultural point of view.[252] Here it is the gentiles' past as aliens from God and his people that captures Paul's attention. Paul roots this narrative in the story of Israel and highlights the fulfillment of God's promises to unite his people. Believers participate in Christ as a new entity (2:14–15), a new household (2:19), a new temple (2:21–22). Paul lays this theoretical foundation of believers' salvation and will provide instructions in the final three chapters that detail how believers live out their new identity as followers of Jesus.[253]

---

250. Thielman, 116. Lincoln, 72, notes the use of paronomasia—the use of a noun and its cognate verb. See also 3:19.

251. Perkins, 55. Contra Muddiman, 97, who discusses the structure and concludes: "There is nothing to mark the transition to the letter's main theme." He adds that the letter's structure has been obscured by later editing (98).

252. Contra Best, 235, who suggests that 2:1–10 speaks of the redemption of the individual and 2:11–22 refers to the salvation of gentiles.

253. Lincoln, 88, remarks that in 2:1–7, "while temporal categories are to the fore in the contrast, spatial categories have been intermingled."

In this chapter, Paul draws on Old Testament and other Jewish motifs and passages, including Jewish apocalyptic overtones of the faithful reigning with God, both in the future (Dan 7:22, 27; 1 Enoch 108.12) and now (1QH 3:19–22).[254] Paul's language of dying and rising calls to mind the rite of baptism (see Col 2:11–13), and while it cannot be satisfactorily demonstrated that Ephesians is a baptism liturgy,[255] one cannot deny the heavy liturgical accent in several passages in this chapter. Paul echoes Isaiah's vision of Jews streaming up to Jerusalem, but with a twist (Isa 57:19). In Ephesians, gentiles are the ones far away who are now brought near (2:17). The community of believers becomes the temple of God (2:22).

1. *God's Grace Rescues Humanity (2:1–10)*

In 2:1–10, Paul uses a wide-angle lens as he pictures believers' redemption from their lives before conversion to their present reality and future hope. Paul emphasizes that the believers' location changes as they move from one kingdom to another, and they begin to live within two time zones, the present and the eternal. Paul explains God's salvation process and, in so doing, reveals the character of God as loving, merciful, and full of grace and kindness. In 2:1–3 Paul describes the plight of humans under the rule of the one who fosters disobedience and sin against God and neighbor, resulting in spiritual and moral death. The next four verses celebrate God's great mercy and love demonstrated in his saving grace. This grace made us alive again, with Christ, and raised us and seated us with Christ. The last three verses (2:8–10) teach that grace, a gift received by faith, renders the believers fit for good works laid out by God for them to do.

Paul begins this section after his inspiring prayer in 1:15–19 and description of God's great work in Christ by raising him from the dead and seating him at his right hand in the heavenlies. Paul desires that believers know this hope to which they are called, the power that God works on believers' behalf. Such power, decisively displayed in the resurrection, proves greater than any known power or authority or name that exists now or in the future. Believers are united as the church, Christ's body (1:23). Paul will use language from Eph 1 as he develops his picture of the church in Eph 2. For example, both Christ and the believers are raised from the dead (1:19–20; 2:5–6), both are seated in the heavenly places (1:20; 2:6),

---

254. MacDonald, 235. She also observes (237) the similar sectarian response to outsiders found in Ephesians and the Qumran literature, including descriptions of the "sons of darkness" (1QS 1:10; 3:21; 1QM 1:7, 16; 1QH 5:7).

255. MacDonald, 235.

believers receive forgiveness (1:7; 2:4–5), and they are to live holy lives (1:4, 11, 12; 2:10).[256]

As he expounds on the nature of Christ's body here in Eph 2, Paul begins with the reader's own reality. The Ephesian believers are not long out of paganism. In all likelihood, their family members and friends continue in idolatry and embrace human wisdom and values that fail to reflect God's righteousness and truth. Paul, of course, also lives in this present age. While as a Jew he does not indulge in idolatry, nor is he ignorant of God's goodness, he too is burdened by the weight of his weak flesh and the passions that turn him from God's ways. In the end, all humanity arrives at the same desperate place, alienation from God.[257]

Paul's brief sketch of the human plight sets the stage for his main emphasis, the work of God in Christ for us. In a sentence that stretches seven verses (2:1–7), Paul places God the Father at the center. God made us alive with Christ, raised us with Christ, and seated us with Christ (see also Rom 6:11–14; Col 2:10–13).[258] God is rich in mercy, full of love expressed by his actions of love, and driven by perfect kindness.[259] Believers receive all these benefits through faith in Christ, with whom they are raised and are now seated in the heavenly places. The sentence is divided in half, with each section beginning with a plural pronoun and mention of being dead in sins: "you being dead in trespasses" (2:1) and "we being dead in trespasses" (2:5). The sentence continues with the subject, God, and three verbs describing God's actions in Christ that affect believers—made alive with, raised with, seated with Christ. Paul places the subject of the lengthy sentence, God the Father, in 2:4, and the controlling verb, "made us alive," in 2:5.[260] In other words, Paul spends the first three verses explaining human reality in sin, so as to help the Ephesians better understand the magnitude of God's actions. Paul speaks of "you" (2:1) and "we" (2:3, 5) in relation to God's mercy and riches of grace. Twice Paul sounds the refrain "by grace you [plural] have been saved" (2:5, 8). Ephesians 2:8 begins with "for," and the sentence in 2:10 likewise begins with "for," expanding on Paul's discussion about "works" in the previous verse. Paul begins and ends this section with a reference to behavior, using the verb "to walk" (metaphorically: "to live"), contrasting the Ephesians' previous way of life in sin and their new life of faith, doing good works.

256. Lincoln, 85–86.
257. Perkins, 56, remarks that "the section shifts from the Gentile past of the letter's audience, 'you,' to the experience of salvation shared by all Christians, 'we.'"
258. Arnold, 125, describes this as "participationist Christology."
259. Perkins, 56, rightly notes that the "opening section stresses the graciousness of God's life-giving power, not the sinfulness of life without God."
260. The controlling verb of the passage, "made us alive" (2:5), is linked with two additional finite verbs that further explain its meaning ("raised with" and "seated with" in 2:6).

The structure of Paul's argument in 2:1–10 lacks syntactical precision; however, Paul's meaning is quite clear. Paul's decisions to present an extensive introduction before citing the subject and verb might be based on three interrelated reasons. First, he may be addressing a likely question that surfaces in his ministry, namely, how is it possible that gentiles, who by definition are also polytheists, could be incorporated into Christ's (holy) body? His discussion in 2:1–3 explains the different paths of human failure that end up at the same fatal cliff edge. Second, he may be raising the rhetorical stakes, as he creates tension by describing first the awful plight of humanity before demonstrating the magnificent redemption accomplished by God the Father in Christ. Third, he may be using these ten verses as a bridge between his declaration that the church is Christ's body, of which he is the head (1:22–23), and his description of Christ's body as two made one, with Christ as its peace (2:13–14). The metaphorical bridge, made up of theological planks, links believers to Christ. Even as walkers crossing a bridge rely on the soundness of its planks to carry them across, so too God's acts of making believers alive with, raised with, and seated with Christ serve to move believers from an earthly kingdom to life eternal in the kingdom of Christ and of God (5:5). Given their new "home," Paul can now speak about the social reality of the community of believers as a new humanity, unified by Christ our peace, and as a new temple, home to the Spirit of God (2:22).

At least three key questions arise as we study this passage (2:1–10). First, how should we understand Paul's use of "you [plural]" and "we"? This question has two parts, specifically, whether Paul stresses the pagan and Jewish backgrounds of believers and whether Paul is primarily focused on the individual, despite his use of the plural. A second issue relates to the question of authorship, for salvation is described here with aorist tense verbs; moreover, typical terms such as "justification" are absent. Finally, this passage invites a deeper discussion into the nature of grace, especially in light of new research into Jewish understandings of salvation in Second Temple Judaism, as well as into the important social institution of benefaction and patronage within the Greco-Roman world.

a. Human Plight in the Present Age (2:1–3)

¹As for you, you were dead in your transgressions and sins, ²in which you used to live when you followed the ways of this world and of the ruler of the kingdom of the air, the spirit who is now at work in those who are disobedient. ³All of us also lived among them at one time, gratifying the cravings of our flesh and following its desires and thoughts. Like the rest, we were by nature deserving of wrath.

2:1–3 Human Plight in the Present Age

Paul begins a new topic in Eph 2, though one that is tightly related to his previous declaration of Christ's complete sovereignty over all powers and authorities. Paul has finished his prayer (1:15–19), in which he asks God to show the believers their magnificent redemption gained in Christ. Paul then highlighted the authority of God in Christ over the rulers and authorities both now and in the age to come; this marvelous truth is even more so because Christ is head of his body, the church, and Christ is filled with God's infinite fullness. Paul sets before the Ephesians two sharply contrasted visions: that of victorious and risen Christ, head of his body, the church (1:22–23), and themselves as morally bankrupt and spiritually dead. Paul now places their trespasses and sins within a larger, cosmic context. While each Ephesian believer has personal experience in trespassing against God's truth, their individual sins are part of a larger reality that stretches beyond their human horizon line to the spirits of the air. Their past trespasses represent the typical behavior of those who follow the laws and customs of this realm's ruler.

These three verses are clauses related to the subject, God, introduced in 2:4, and the main verbs denoting God's actions in 2:5–6. Paul will repeat his opening line in 2:1, "*you* being dead in *your* trespasses," a few verses later, with interesting differences in pronouns noted in italic: "*we* being dead in trespasses" (2:5).[261] From here Paul gets to the center of his argument, namely, that God has made believers alive with Christ and raised them and seated them with Christ, who is now seated at God's right hand (1:20). Believers experience God's mercy expressed in his love and kindness, as his grace effects salvation in Christ.

1 Paul begins this verse "as for you," linking back to the previous verse as it develops the impact on humanity of God's exaltation of Christ and Christ's place as head over his body, the church. Rather than come straight to the point, however, Paul uses these three verses to explain the human plight and the reality of evil in the cosmos, reflecting on the entire thanksgiving of 1:17–23.[262]

Paul places the pronoun "you" at the beginning of the clause, which indicates its importance.[263] Does Paul's use of the plural "you" indicate he has his gentile audience in mind? Arguments that answer this question in the negative include the following points. First, in 2:5 Paul speaks of "we" being dead in our trespasses, which suggests that Paul implicitly includes himself

---

261. Eph 2:1 is a participial clause ("you [plural] being dead"), and the next two verses are relative clauses describing this realm of death.

262. MacDonald, 228.

263. The present tense participle is loosely connected to the main verbs in 2:5–6 and so is best translated as past, given that the human condition described in 2:1–3 is antecedent to God's actions of making them alive and raising and seating them with Christ (see also Col 2:13).

in 2:1. Second, Paul uses "we" in 2:3 when speaking about following passions, thereby incorporating himself and all people into the same group as noted in 2:1.[264] Third, Paul explicitly speaks to gentiles in 2:11, so if he wanted to make it clear he was talking about gentiles, he could have done so. Fourth, Paul's primary focus is on the individual, not the ethnic group to which one belongs.[265] In particular, Paul focuses on that individual who doubts Christ's victory over the spiritual forces.

Yet a strong case can be made that Paul is distinguishing gentiles here with his use of the plural "you."[266] First, Paul explains in 2:2 that "you" lived under the sway of the ruler of those who disobey God—a likely description of pagan religion. It is hard to imagine Paul would describe his Jewish experience with such language. Paul lived in a world divided into Jew and gentile, clean and unclean (cf. Acts 15:5–29; Gal 2:11–18). Second, Paul distinguishes himself from those who submitted to the ruler of those disobedient ones. His weak flesh drove him to follow his cravings and desires, true enough. But as a Jew, he had the advantage of identifying the true God against the deceptive spirit at work in children of disobedience. Gentiles and Jews were quite aware of their differences, as gentiles mocked Jewish Sabbath and food laws and were confounded at their resistance to idols.[267] Paul makes a similar point in Colossians. He speaks of "you [plural]" being dead in trespasses and the uncircumcision of your flesh, a clear description of gentile believers before they followed the gospel. He continues that all believers' sins are forgiven by God, using the first-person plural pronoun "our." Third, Paul retains a focus on the corporate body. The indefinite pronoun in Eph 2:9 ("one") reflects the way boasting occurs as individuals seek to elevate themselves within a group. Paul rejects such individualism. I conclude that Paul differentiates the gentile and Jewish experience outside of Christ, even as he affirms that both paths lead to the same dead end.

Anticipating their new life, Paul states directly that "you [plural]" were dead. Likely the Ephesians heard Paul's assessment of their previous way

---

264. Muddiman, 100–101, includes the possibility that Paul exercises here a literary device, "oscillating between the pointedness of direct address and rounded expressions of solidarity." He concludes, however, that the different pronouns are the result of editors using the "we" form on the existing traditions that have the "you" form (101).

265. Lincoln, 84, 88. Best, 198–200, concludes that the passage speaks of the "typical believer."

266. Perkins, 56; Barth, 212.

267. Margaret H. Williams, *The Jews among the Greeks and Romans: A Diaspora Sourcebook* (Baltimore: Johns Hopkins University Press, 1998). Erich S. Gruen, *Diaspora: Jews amidst Greeks and Romans* (Cambridge: Harvard University Press, 2002), 41–52, discusses the negative comments by gentiles about Jews in first-century Rome. See also Louis H. Feldman, *Jew and Gentile in the Ancient World: Attitudes and Interactions from Alexander to Justinian* (Princeton: Princeton University Press, 1993).

of life earlier, for we have no hint that Paul defends a contested idea. Paul reminds his readers of the "before picture" so that as he creates for them the "after photo," the contrast becomes clear. They need to know their previous life was deadness, so that as Paul encourages them to righteousness in Eph 4–6, they will have no illusions about their previous spiritual state. Later in Ephesians, Paul quotes a poem, "wake up, sleeper, rise from the dead" (5:14), which highlights the moral dimension of the term. Death entails putrefaction, decay, a retched smell, as when Martha warned Jesus that her brother Lazarus was already four days in the tomb, and the space stank (John 11:39). Yet even as Jesus called Lazarus forth to life, so too Paul argues that the Ephesians' previous state of death does not have the final word.

The death of which Paul speaks is a spiritual or moral death, tied to their trespasses and sins. Paul likely has concrete acts in mind, not an abstract idea of sinfulness. And Paul lists specific categories of sinful behaviors, such as sexual immorality and covetousness, unwholesome talk and impurity, that characterize those who are disobedient and who will experience God's wrath (Eph 5:6; more on God's wrath below in the discussion on 2:3). While the two nouns, "trespasses" and "sins," carry distinct nuances, Paul is uninterested in exploiting differences. He makes clear that their previous behaviors counted as death to them.[268] And he may be echoing Ps 19:13–14 (18:13–14 LXX), which uses both terms as synonyms expressing the psalmist's desire to be cleansed of all sins before God.

2 Paul describes the Ephesians before they confessed Christ.[269] The Ephesians lived under the influence of powerful forces antithetical to God. Paul uses two nouns to describe their reality: "the ways [*aiōn*] of the world" and the "ruler" (*archōn*) of it.[270] *Aiōn* typically refers to a period of time and within Jewish apocalyptic thought carries the idea of the present era of sin.[271]

---

268. For "trespass" (παράπτωμα) see BDAG 770 (bγ); for "sin" (ἁμαρτία) see BDAG 50 (1a). Arnold, 130, observes that the two terms "form a hendiadys (one concept through two words)." See also Barth, 212. The dative case of both "trespasses" and "sins" can be expressed by several terms: "by," which reflects the means by which they are dead; "because," which indicates the reason for their death; and "in," which indicates the sphere in which their death sentence operates. MacDonald, 228, rightly notes that both the instrumental and locative meanings apply here.

269. Eph 2:2 is a relative clause that begins with a prepositional phrase "in which" (ἐν αἷς) and continues with the second-person plural aorist verb "you walked" (περιεπατήσατε) followed by two prepositional phrases, introduced by the preposition κατά, that explain when and under whose influence they walked. Arnold, 130, rightly argues for an intensive meaning for the preposition κατά, "under the control of," rather than the typical meaning, "according to." See also Best, 202.

270. Barth, 214–15, suggests that the two phrases could be seen in apposition to each other, and if so then the noun αἰών refers to a spiritual power that he translates "World-Age."

271. On αἰών see BDAG 33 (2a). Muddiman, 103, rightly rejects the connection with

Paul usually uses the term with a temporal meaning, making it more likely he uses it with that meaning here (1:21; 2:7).[272] Paul further describes the *aiōn* as "of this world," indicating the "realm of sin" (see also 1 Cor 1:20).[273]

Paul speaks of a "ruler" (*archōn*) further defined with two phrases: "of the kingdom"[274] and "of the air." The Greek term translated here "kingdom" can be rendered "authority." In 1:21 Paul uses the same noun, but does not specify that the authorities and powers are evil. However, as he begins this new chapter, it becomes clear that at least some of these powers actively work against human flourishing and operate in opposition to God's good will. The ruler's authority can be understood as either the sphere (realm) of the ruler's influence (see also Col 1:13) or the power or collective evil that permeates the unseen world (the plural noun is used in Eph 1:21; 3:10; 6:12). Here the former meaning is intended, likely referring to the realm of the ruler, and thus translated "kingdom." The realm of the "air" is that area between the earthly and heavenly realms where stars, angels, and demons exist.[275] In the Greco-Roman world it was commonly believed that forces in this realm could be manipulated by magic.[276]

Paul speaks twice more about the spiritual world in this epistle. Using the same nouns, Paul speaks of the rulers and authorities witnessing to God's great wisdom in establishing the church in Christ (3:10). There is no direct mention of their hostility toward God or his people. Yet in 6:12 Paul speaks again of rulers and authorities and of powers that control this dark age, those spirits of evil who exist in the heavens. Paul calls on the Ephesians to put on the armor of God as they stand fast against these enemies. Ephesians 2:2 and 6:12 sound similar alarms against forces that actively incite disobedience toward God.

Paul continues with the phrase "of . . . the spirit who is now at work in those who are disobedient." The grammar allows for at least three possible

---

later Gnostic writings that use the noun as a name of a spiritual being. See also MacDonald, 229; Perkins, 59; Arnold, 131.

272. Contra BDAG 32 (4). Perkins, 58, points to similar conflict between those who follow truth and those who do evil among the Qumran literature: "There exists a violent conflict in respect of all his decrees since they do not walk together. God, in the mysteries of his knowledge and the wisdom of his glory, has determined an end to injustice and on the occasion of his visitation he will obliterate it forever" (1QS 4:17–19).

273. MacDonald, 229.

274. Ἐξουσία is translated here "kingdom" (see BDAG 352 [6]) but can also be translated "authority" (see BDAG 352 [3]).

275. MacDonald, 229.

276. Arnold, 132, cites magical texts that speak of evil forces who exist in this realm, including "protect me from every demon in the air" (Preisendanz, *Papyri graecae magicae*, 4:2699). In Acts, believers in Ephesus are described as well acquainted with such realities and testified against it when they burned their own magic books (19:19).

2:1-3 HUMAN PLIGHT IN THE PRESENT AGE

interpretations. First, "of the spirit" could be in apposition to "authority" and refer to the realm or territory of the ruler.[277] Second, as the phrase is grammatically parallel to the earlier phrase authority "of the air," it may point to a being or spiritual force over which the ruler has control.[278] Third, the genitive phrase may be in apposition to "of the ruler," thus renaming the ruler as the spirit who works in those who disobey God.[279] To make a judgment, let us review Paul's complex thought: he indicates that the Ephesians were dead in sins, and he will finish this reflection with the phrase "children of disobedience." He states that they acted in sin within a particular framework, specifically, this age, and under a particular influence, namely, a ruler aligned with the age. I suggest that the balance tilts slightly toward understanding the final phrase about the spirit who now works as in apposition to the ruler. Paul describes the ruler as part of this age and thus as actively instigating disobedience in those people who live within that domain.

Paul concludes with a description of those who live under this ruler. The Greek text reads "sons of disobedience," here translated "those who are disobedient." The Semitic phrase "sons of" reflects language of the Old Testament to refer to a group of people (Ezek 30:5 LXX; see also John 8:44). The Qumran community referred to their opponents as "sons of darkness" (1QS 1:10). The opening clause "in which" refers back to the trespasses and sins that characterized the Ephesians' previous "dead" existence. These behaviors are characteristic of the ways of this world, and Paul explains that they "walked" or conducted themselves based on values from that reference point.[280] Paul can use the verb "to walk" (translated "to live") when speaking of godly behavior, as he does in 4:1. In our verse, Paul makes it quite clear that their previous spiritual and moral gait was a death march, representative of the epoch in which they live (2:10; 4:17; 5:2, 8, 15).[281] The disobedient fall victim to the evil spirit's working. Paul uses the phrase "children of wrath" in the next verse, warning of the doom that awaits the disobedient ones. Paul explains further in 5:6 that these people indulge in sexual immorality, impu-

---

277. Lincoln, 96, who explains: "The personal power of evil is the ruler of the realm of the air, the ruler of the spirit that is now at work in the disobedient."

278. Barth, 215, offers a summary of interpretive options, concluding that the several options "reveal various dimensions of the devil's character and means of operation" and are neither mutually exclusive nor contradictory.

279. Arnold, 132. In this case the awkward genitive form results from the influence of the previous genitive phrase ("of the air").

280. On περιπατέω see BDAG 803 (2aδ). MacDonald, 228, explains Paul's use of the verb in Col 4:5, wherein Paul instructs believers' behavior relative to nonbelievers (see also 1 Thess 2:12; 4:1–12).

281. Muddiman, 103: "'Walking' is a semitic idiom for conduct or ethical behavior and is frequent in Paul (e.g. 2 Cor 4:2)." This verb in 2 Cor 4:2 can be translated "we do [not] use."

rity, and covetousness—all anathema to those who will inherit the kingdom of Christ and of God.

3 Paul centers on passions and desires of the flesh that drive "us" far from God, earning the label "children of wrath." Paul explains that all of us lived among them. The verb "to live/conduct oneself" is found extensively in the New Testament, as well as in the Septuagint.[282] We find the cognate noun in 4:22 as Paul describes the former way of life that the Ephesians discarded as an old piece of clothing, when they put on the new self, made whole and holy in the Lord. Paul emphasizes his own participation in this dark age with its disobedient actors. "We all" may refer to Jews who follow Jesus (in contrast to gentiles in 2:1–2) or to those who knew Christ before the Ephesians accepted the gospel (1:12) or to believers (1:19). Here Paul likely distinguishes himself and other Jews as those who are not complicit in the active pursuit of disobedience against the true God, but who nevertheless find themselves sinning because of weakness of the flesh.[283] Paul describes living under the influence of "our" passions and acting on the desires of the flesh and thoughts. The terms "flesh" and "mind/thoughts" do not represent what is inherently evil or wrong, but in this context reflect a person's disposition against God's ways.

Paul adds that we are children of wrath "by nature." This noun does not in itself suggest wickedness, and there is no reason to assume Paul hints at Adam's sin.[284] He uses it to speak of gentile idolatry and ignorance (Rom 1:18–32), as well as the natural order (Rom 1:26; 1 Cor 11:14) or birth (Gal 2:15). Perhaps Paul implies a comparison with the metaphor of adoption in Eph 1:5, differentiating the unregenerate who by birth are part of the human race from those adopted children of God.[285]

Paul concludes that humans are "deserving of wrath" using the Hebrew idiom "children of wrath" (Col 3:6; see also Deut 25:2; Ps 102:20; Matt 23:15). He states that he is "like the rest," for all transgress God's laws, succumbing to the pressures of this present dark age and the passions within themselves. The term "wrath" when referring to the human emotion, carries the sense of

---

282. On ἀναστρέφω see BDAG 72–73 (3b).

283. Perkins, 60, rightly notes that "though Paul can speak of all humans implicated in sin from the beginning (Rom 5:12–21), he would hardly describe the Jew as 'child of wrath' by nature."

284. On φύσις see BDAG 1069 (1). Perkins, 61, writes that Paul "does not use 'nature' to describe a principle that separates humans from God." Contra Arnold, 134, who suggests that Paul "probably intends to convey that we inherited this status and condition at birth." See also Lincoln, 99, who suggests that the notion of original sin "is not entirely alien to the thought of this verse when it speaks of the impossibility of humanity of itself, in its natural condition, escaping God's wrath."

285. Thielman, 127n30.

out-of-control anger, violence, revenge.[286] None of these traits match God's character. Instead, we find God's wrath understood within the framework of his kingship, which focuses on righteousness and salvation. Interestingly, to say that God is king is to affirm that he is a warrior (Exod 15:1–3; Ps 24:8; Isa 59:16–17); both images echo throughout Ephesians (1:19; 6:10–17).

The prophet Isaiah offers a picture of God's wrath, and the context helps us understand the term's meaning here. Isaiah declares that Israel disobeyed the Lord's laws, indulged in oppression and deceit, and sought protection from surrounding nations. Yet in the midst of their rejection, God remained gracious and compassionate, binding their wounds and restoring the people. God is described as coming from far away to rescue his people and punish the nations who oppressed them. With lips full of wrath, a tongue as a consuming fire, and breath like a rushing river, God destroys those who conquer and oppress (30:27–28). Isaiah stresses that God's apparent delay in rescuing Israel is due to their injustices and his merciful patience that seeks repentance (59:2–8). He desires that people would turn from their transgressions and follow after him (59:11–13). Isaiah is clear that the warrior king will execute judgment, using the image of crushing grapes in a winepress (63:3). Yet in the midst of judgment, there is redemption (63:4).[287]

God's wrath promises that in the end, wrongs done to the vulnerable will be punished, injustices unresolved will be paid up, and the arrogant who abuse others will be silenced. Of course, each of us has done injustice, has expressed arrogance, and has misused power; thus, each of us can rightly be called a child of wrath. Without softening this powerful warning to those who need to mend their ways (see also Eph 5:1–8), it is important to note that Paul's main argument in this sentence is that God is rich in mercy, shown in granting to believers a life in Christ and raising up and seating with Christ

---

286. On ὀργή see BDAG 720–21 (2b); C. M. Tuckett, "Atonement in the NT," *ABD* 1:518–22; Stephen H. Travis, "Wrath of God (NT)," *ABD* 5:996–98. Leon L. Morris, *Atonement: Its Meaning and Significance* (Leicester: InterVarsity Press, 1983), 147, 174–75, observes that the "wrath of God" is hard for us to accept today, in part because we have not properly understood that God loves us deeply. He states that love and wrath can coexist, for the opposite of love is hate, not wrath. God is hostile to evil, and so when he sees evil in believers, he wants to do away with it in the process of forgiveness. Humans want sin/evil accounted for; therefore, in some way God must be involved in judging sin. See also Arnold, 134.

287. Andrew Abernethy, *The Book of Isaiah and God's Kingdom: A Theological-Thematic Approach to the Book of Isaiah*, New Studies in Biblical Theology 40 (Downers Grove, IL: IVP Academic, 2016), 99, notes: "A strong taste exuding from the dregs of 63:1–6 is of bloody vengeance from YHWH, though embers of redemption and salvation intermingle, reminding us that when the warrior king comes in terrifying judgment, one of his primary goals is to redeem the repentant (cf. 63:8–64:12)."

those who embrace him by faith. No one needs to remain a child of wrath. No one is doomed to linger in spiritual death.

b. God's Actions in Christ for Believers (2:4–7)

4But because of his great love for us, God, who is rich in mercy, 5made us alive with Christ even when we were dead in transgressions—it is by grace you have been saved. 6And God raised us up with Christ and seated us with him in the heavenly realms in Christ Jesus, 7in order that in the coming ages he might show the incomparable riches of his grace, expressed in his kindness to us in Christ Jesus.

Ephesians 2:4–7 forms the backbone of this passage (2:1–10), containing both the main subject (God) and verbs (made alive with, raised with, seated with). Tension builds in 2:1–3 as Paul describes the miserable state of humanity condemned in their trespasses and greedy desires; then in 2:4 Paul introduces God, the subject of this long sentence, as rich in mercy. The mercy springs forth from God through his great love, which God activates toward us. To introduce God's mighty acts, Paul repeats his opening line of 2:1 (humans are dead in trespasses) before trumpeting God's saving acts. God makes alive what was dead, God raises up what was burdened under wrath, and God seats in the heavens those condemned to sit under the vicious rule of the prince of the air. God's tremendous exertion on humanity's behalf demonstrates his love toward them now and his plentiful grace in the ages to come.

4 Focusing on humans in 2:1–3, Paul charts in no uncertain terms the human death spiral enflamed by the ruler of the authority of the air. But in 2:4 Paul makes an abrupt, 180-degree turn and attends to his primary message. Paul introduces the sentence's subject, God, in this verse and will explain the subject's actions in the following two verses. Paul highlights God's character here and in the following two verses demonstrates his claims by outlining God's accomplishments in Christ for humanity's redemption.

Ephesians 2:4 begins with an adversive conjunction "but," indicating a contrasting idea that recalibrates the previous points. Paul sharpens the contrast between your "being" dead in trespasses and God's "being" rich in mercy. Paul expresses the reason or cause for God's demonstration of love with three main verbs in the sentence, found in the next two verses (made alive, raised up, seated). Paul finishes 2:4 with the pronoun "us," unremarkable in itself, but critical in Paul's argument as it underlines the direction of God's tender attention.

Several terms deserve closer attention. First, Paul stresses that God is "rich," an adjective found only here in Ephesians, although the noun is used

2:4–7 GOD'S ACTIONS IN CHRIST FOR BELIEVERS

five times in this epistle.[288] We observed it in Eph 1 describing God's grace (1:7) and glorious inheritance (1:18). It occurs in 2:7, highlighting God's grace; in 3:8, expressing Christ's boundless riches; and in 3:16, referencing God's glorious riches (see also Col 1:27; 2:2).[289] Second, Paul underscores God's mercy (see also Eph 1:5, 7–8), a trait contrasted with wrath stated in the previous verse. The Greek term "mercy" (*eleos*) has been used to translate the evocative and nuanced Hebrew term *ḥesed*, sometimes translated "steadfast love" or "loving deeds."[290] In Exod 34:6–7, God announces to Moses that he is a "compassionate and gracious God, slow to anger, *abounding in love* and faithfulness, maintaining *love* to thousands" (the italic conveys *ḥesed*). Another example is found in Ps 107:43 (= 106:43 LXX), as the psalmist invites the wise to consider the steadfast love (Hebrew *ḥesed*, Greek *eleos*) of the Lord. Notice the action implied in the terms: "mercy" is not a sentimental emotion, but an attitude that leads to action.[291] Third, in the Greek text, Paul uses the noun "love" and the verb "to love" in Eph 2:4 (translated "his great love for us").[292] God's love is a disposition of grace extended through his Beloved (Christ Jesus, 1:6) to humanity. Paul expresses a similar sentiment in Romans, as God in Christ demonstrates his love (Rom 5:5, 8; 8:39).

5–6 Paul emphasizes three of God's acts: he made us alive together with Christ (2:5),[293] he raised us up together (with Christ), and he seated us with Christ Jesus in the heavenly places (2:6, see also Col 2:12–13). These three verbs share the prefix "with," further emphasizing the connection of believers to Christ.[294] Earlier, Paul declared that God raised Christ from the dead and seated him at his right hand in the heavenly places (Eph 1:20). In 2:5–6 we find this assertion applied to believers, who were spiritually dead and now made alive. Paul's argument ends with a declaration that believers are God's workmanship, his masterpiece, designed for good works (2:10).

---

288. On πλούσιος see BDAG 831 (2).

289. Barth, 218, remarks that "the frequent allusion to the 'riches' of God is a peculiarity of Ephesians."

290. On ἔλεος see BDAG 316 (b). Lincoln, 100–103, offers a discussion of the Hebrew and Greek terms.

291. Lincoln, 100, states: "Διά plus the accusative of words for emotion indicates motivation."

292. Ἀγάπην αὐτοῦ ἣν ἠγάπησεν ἡμᾶς.

293. Best, 216, explains that some manuscripts include ἐν before τῷ Χριστῷ (P46 B 33), but rejects it as original, for "had the formula been already present it would surely not have been altered." See also Thielman, 140.

294. MacDonald, 231, writes: "The prefix *syn* (with), attached to this verb and those in v. 6, reinforces the solidarity of believers with Christ." Paul uses the prefix "with" in Rom 6:4, 5, 6, 8. The context in both Romans and Colossians speaks about the believers' baptism; in Ephesians the emphasis is on God's power; see Perkins, 61.

That is, God's purpose in raising up believers with Christ and seating them with Christ in the heavenly places is to serve God's kingdom work here on earth. The impossible paradox is that believers are both raised and very much on earth; they are both seated and very much active in the world. Paul reveals that Christ's own path of resurrection and exaltation is shared in a contingent and subordinate way by believers.

In 2:5 God makes alive—this is Paul's central conviction in this lengthy passage. The verb with this prefix is found only here and Col 2:13 in the New Testament. The prefix links believers to Christ, as their eternal life is gained by virtue of his everlasting intercession (Eph 3:12; Heb 10:19–23). The verb without the prefix is found in Romans, where Paul focuses on the future resurrection of the saints (4:17; 8:11).[295] The aorist tense "made us alive" may suggest a reference to the future resurrection, when God raises believers' bodies (Phil 3:20–21). Paul would thus speak proleptically; that is, the actions described are anticipated to occur in the future, and the confidence of their ultimate outworking is so great as to cause Paul to represent these events as already in effect. This accent may be at work in Colossians, which focuses on forgiveness of sins and canceling of debts before God, by means of Christ's cross. However, while it is true that believers' bodies have yet to be raised and that Christ's second coming is still on the horizon, his victory over sin and death pertains now, as his resurrection life attests.[296] And in our passage, victory over spiritual forces and trespasses stands at center stage. Therefore, the aorist tense is best understood here as constative, because it paints the action as a whole, standing from the outside, presenting God's action without concern for when the action began or ended.[297] Paul shows that believers in Christ have victory over death and the spiritual powers that promote evil and disobedience.[298] Believers were spiritually dead, now are regenerated to a holy life that honors God and blesses others, and will continue in the new heavens and new earth as they enjoy resurrected bodies, all based on God's grace exercised in Christ.

---

295. On συζῳοποιέω see BDAG 954. Lincoln, 102, reflects on the verb ζῳοποιέω ("to make alive").

296. Best, 215.

297. Hoehner, 330. Recent scholarship questions whether the apostle Paul could have expressed God's salvation with the aorist tense, assuming that Paul implies that all is accomplished. However, Paul speaks at the cosmic level about the reality of Christ's victory over cosmic powers, and the aorist reflects a panoramic view. Moreover, Paul uses the aorist tense in Rom 8:24 as he declares that believers are saved in their hope of their final bodily resurrection and the redemption of creation. A few verses later (8:30), Paul strings together four aorist verbs—predestined, called, justified, glorified—all describing believers' current reality as Christ, who is seated at God's right hand (8:34), interceding for believers, who are with Christ, as nothing separates them from his love (8:35–39).

298. Thielman, 135–37.

2:4–7 God's Actions in Christ for Believers

Comparisons with 1:20 are instructive. In Eph 1, Paul uses the same two verbs we find in 2:6, "raised" and "seated," but without the prefix "with." Paul describes the power of God that raised Christ and seated him at God's right hand in the heavenly places. Here in 2:6 Paul adds "in Christ Jesus," thus linking believers to their Lord. Again, in 1:20 Paul states that Christ was raised "from the dead," using the same term for "dead" found in 2:1 and 2:5, describing humanity as dead in their trespasses. Christ's death was a literal death, experienced by one who knew no sin; the believer's is a spiritual death that is overcome by Christ's redemption, as believers are united with Christ by God's grace. Finally, both 1:20 and 2:6 include the phrase "in the heavenly places." This prepositional phrase is key to Paul's overall argument that Christ is victorious over all spirits and powers and authorities, now and forever (1:21–22). These beings exist in the lesser domain ruled by the prince of the air, the ruler of this present age. Christ stands above them, in a higher realm. Paul employs a spatial argument based on common assumptions of his day that the high heavens were the dwelling place of the gods and the atmosphere was the dwelling of lesser (but still capricious and dangerous) deities, spiritual beings, and even human souls.

Paul begins 2:5 with a parenthetical reminder that we were dead in trespasses, before declaring that God has "made us alive with Christ." This phrase repeats key terms with which Paul began this sentence in 2:1—the participle "being" (translated "were") and two nouns, "dead" and "trespasses." Paul focuses on God's mercy and humanity's spiritual deadness as he prepares to explain the glorious riches of God's redemptive plan in Christ.[299]

Paul interrupts his description of God's actions and inserts three Greek words, translated "by grace you have been saved," that make clear the method that accomplishes such extraordinarily good news.[300] The perfect passive participle indicates an action in the past that continues to impact the present.[301] English translations try to capture both qualities of the perfect tense, but it is difficult to express the sense that salvation is as much a present reality as a past event. Thus, we often understand the phrase "have been saved" as though it were a past event only. The KJV, written five hundred years ago, perhaps expresses the perfect tense best with "for by grace are ye saved," as readers perceive themselves as currently saved, but implying a moment in the past

---

299. Merkle, 58, for a discussion of the issues. Hoehner, 328, and Thielman, 133, suggest that καί expresses an additional point, thus translate "even."

300. Χάριτί ἐστε σεσῳσμένοι. This phrase begins with the noun "grace" in the dative, which is represented in English with the preposition "by," followed by the present indicative verb "to be" and the perfect passive participle "saved" in a periphrastic construction.

301. Arnold, 136, cites three places where Paul uses this verb in the aorist: Rom 8:24; 2 Tim 1:9; Titus 3:5.

that marked their repentance unto salvation.[302] Moreover, the passive voice makes clear that the readers do not create or activate the grace; it is exclusively and entirely God's doing.

I address the topic of grace in 2:8, where Paul draws a fuller picture of the concept. Here we should note the powerful juxtaposition of death and life, of grace and Christ. The Ephesian believers were dead and now are alive through the working of God in Christ.[303] We may hear an echo of 1:7 with its connection of God's grace "to a formulaic description of the cross as sin offering" and conclude that Paul might be reminding readers here in 2:5 that being alive includes forgiveness of sin.[304] We observed this pattern in Eph 1, as Paul explained the plan of redemption. Christ is alive now, raised from the dead, seated at God the Father's right hand, having vanquished all his foes and established the church as his body. This is what "alive" means. God's great power that accomplished these feats now works in believers, who are in Christ, as they take their life from him. The stench of death gone, the spiritual grave clothes removed, senses restored and attuned to the Savior.

7 "In Christ Jesus" is Paul's closing note in both 2:6 and 2:7. This is music to believers' ears, for this chorus promises life now and eternally. God redeems believers by making them alive, raising them, and seating them with Christ. In 2:4 we learn that God's character of mercy, love, and grace energizes his actions of redemption. And now in 2:7 we learn a bit more about God's expansive purposes. Paul explains that God desires to show grace to believers for all eternity. God is rich in mercy (2:4). God is rich in grace (2:7). So rich, in fact, that he cannot contain it in this present age, but will show this great grace throughout eternity. Paul will continue in the next verse with the centerpiece of the gospel—believers are saved by grace through faith. This grace is God's gift, bursting forth from God's gracious character and his efficacious plan to kill death and make humans alive again. This grace is rooted in Christ's redeeming work on the cross, established in the resurrection, and celebrated in his ascension. This grace is available to all, through faith (more on this below).

Paul begins this verse with a conjunction, "in order that," that signals a dependent clause indicating purpose.[305] Paul indicates that God's desire is that he "might show"[306] his grace "in the coming ages," defining when God

---

302. Wallace, *Greek Grammar*, 575.

303. MacDonald, 232, observes that we might expect Paul to speak of grace and justification, not grace coupled with salvation, but admits that "salvation and justification can sometimes act as virtual synonyms in Paul's letters (e.g., Rom 10:10)."

304. Perkins, 61.

305. Lincoln, 109.

306. On ἐνδείκνυμι see BDAG 331. See also Hoehner, 337, who explains that the verb "he may show" is an aorist middle tense but should be read as active, for Paul follows the

2:4–7 God's Actions in Christ for Believers

desires to show this surpassingly rich grace. It is not clear if Paul imagines that the coming age begins with Christ's return[307] or, more likely, that the age has begun and will continue into the age to come.[308] Adding support to this last possibility is that the participle "coming" is in the present tense.[309] Paul indicates when God will show his magnificent grace, but at this point, Paul does not identify explicitly *to whom* God will show it. Believers are the beneficiaries of this grace, so it may be that Paul has them in mind. And we learn in 3:10 that God will make known his wisdom through the church to the principalities and powers.

God desires to demonstrate the surpassing wealth of his grace. Paul adds the participle "surpassing" to the noun "riches." Paul spoke of God's surpassing great power in 1:19 and will use the participle again in 3:19, describing Christ's great love. The noun "riches" is the same term that described God's rich mercy in 2:4. The entire phrase "riches of his grace" without the participle "surpassing" is found in 1:7, where Paul declared that in Christ we have redemption in his blood, the forgiveness of trespasses, because of God's great grace.[310] It is not surprising, then, that we find this phrase repeated here in 2:7, for Paul stresses death in trespasses and life anew in Christ in the previous several verses.

The verse concludes with three prepositional phrases, the first of which, "in kindness," likely refers to the proximate noun "grace."[311] This kindness is directed toward believers, and is located in Christ, as Paul stresses our union with the Lord Jesus.[312] The term "kindness" deserves a closer look.[313] We tend

---

verb with the pronoun "himself" (αὐτοῦ), which would be redundant if the verb carried the typical middle voice. The verb is rare in the New Testament, used only by Paul (nine times) and in Hebrews (twice), and never in the active voice.

307. Lincoln, 110. Best, 223, rejects this possibility because the noun is plural.

308. Arnold, 138.

309. Less likely is the interpretation of τοῖς αἰῶσιν as personal, hostile forces. See Best, 223–24, who summarizes the positions and problems with each view and concludes that the author capitalizes on the term's ambiguity ("the exaltation of reader and writers to their position in the heavenlies will indicate the grace of God to the future ages which contain personal supernatural beings") and sees the temporal emphasis primary.

310. For the verb ὑπερβάλλω in Ephesians, see 1:19; 2:7; 3:19. See also 2 Cor 3:10; 9:14.

311. Best, 225, explains that the phrase can connote either the manner by which, the means by which, or the sphere in which God demonstrates his grace. While the choices are several, the distinctions between them are negligible, for Paul's point is that God's grace works together with God's kindness.

312. Lincoln, 110, aptly writes: "If the raising of Christ from death to sit in the heavenly realms is the supreme demonstration of God's surpassing power, then the raising of believers from spiritual death to sit with Christ in the heavenly realms is the supreme demonstration of God's surpassing grace."

313. On χρηστότης see BDAG 1090 (2b).

to think of being kind as being nice, polite, with a hint of superficiality. Yet the term used in 2:7 accents moral excellence and magnanimity. This term cautions the reader today who may be tempted to intellectualize God's grace to a propositional abstraction, for in the broader Greek context, the term carries the sense of clemency. I emphasize this aspect of the term, because in the following verse Paul states that salvation is God's gift. Paul's overarching message is that salvation is God's doing, in Christ, without human engineering. "Kindness" has traces of gift giving around it, which prepares the reader for the coming announcement concerning our salvation by grace through faith.

c. God's Gift of Grace (2:8–10)

8For it is by grace you have been saved, through faith—and this is not from yourselves, it is the gift of God—9not by works, so that no one can boast. 10For we are God's handiwork, created in Christ Jesus to do good works, which God prepared in advance for us to do.

In these three verses, Paul encapsulates key qualities of the believer's salvation, including God's gift and grace, and significant concepts, such as grace, faith, works, and good works.[314] Paul summarizes his gospel message of God's work of redemption in Christ on behalf of humanity.[315] Paul makes clear in the previous seven verses that God is at work: he is making alive, raising up, and seating believers with Christ. God reveals his wealth of mercy and his inexhaustible love as he extends his kindness to us in Christ Jesus. This activity on God's part accomplishes salvation, as believers are united with Christ. Paul reiterates in 2:8 that salvation is a gift received by faith. He expands this point by distinguishing faith and works, and then works and good works. The grace is found in God's redemptive work in Christ (2:7), and in 2:8 we read the phrase "through faith," which raises the question as to whether Paul means believers' faith in Christ (objective genitive) or Christ's faithfulness, which achieves our redemption (subjective genitive).[316]

---

314. See also Rom 3:24–27; 4:2; 11:6; Gal 2:16; 3:2–5. MacDonald, 233–34, suggests that the terms in the undisputed Pauline material are narrower in scope than we find in Ephesians, as the former look at the Jewish law and the concept of justification by faith. Arnold, 140, explains that the absence of the term "justification" is not evidence of non-Pauline authorship, but can be explained as rooted in a lack of conflict with "Judaizers."

315. MacDonald, 233, writes: "Some have viewed vv. 8–10 as the most concise summary of Pauline theology in the NT."

316. Lynn H. Cohick, "The Gospel as God's Gift: Good News from Ephesians 1:1–3:12," in *Is the Gospel Good News?*, ed. Stanley E. Porter and Hughson T. Ong (Eugene, OR: Pickwick, 2018), 150–72.

2:8–10 GOD'S GIFT OF GRACE

Paul introduces a new term, "gift," and contrasts God's actions in giving the gift with human deeds or works.[317] Paul elaborates that good works are a natural outworking of humans who confess Christ. The phrase "good works" does not occur elsewhere in Paul, but a similar idea is conveyed to several congregations (2 Cor 9:8; Col 1:10; 1 Thess 1:3; 2 Thess 1:11).[318] Paul compares "of yourselves" (Eph 2:8) and "of works" (2:9) using the same preposition, *ek*, and argues his point by saying that, because it is not of yourselves, therefore no one may boast. Traditionally, Paul's language was understood to mean that "salvation has been freely given by God to the readers as undeserving sinners."[319] Typically Paul's argument is summarized as contrasting God's grace in saving humans and human pride in trying to save themselves. Augustine is perhaps the most influential theologian who promoted this view.[320] Augustine drew on Rom 5:5 in asserting that our love for God was given to us by God.[321] He pointed to Eph 2:8 as he insisted that God is the source of all virtuous deeds and thoughts.[322] Augustine held that God's grace works in a believer's life such that they are made holy and godly. Luther will pick up Augustine's views, but rejected the latter's conclusions about the efficacy of God's grace on believers.[323] Luther insisted on the alien righteousness possessed by the sinner/saint, but not infused.[324] Luther spoke of the believer as *simul justus et peccator*—that is, as simultaneously righteous and sinful.[325] At times,

---

317. On δῶρον see BDAG 267. The term "gift" (δῶρον) is found only here in the Pauline corpus, but the related term δωρεά is used in 3:7 and 4:7. See also Rom 5:15, 17; 2 Cor 9:15, for a total of eleven times in the New Testament.

318. Ἔργοις ἀγαθοῖς.

319. Lincoln, 102.

320. Barclay, *Paul and the Gift*, 87: "Augustine takes Paul as striking at the root of human pride, self-assertion, and self-congratulation; even in their virtues, believers are to acknowledge their dependence on what is not their own, but God's." Barclay explains that Augustine focuses on the priority, incongruity, and efficacy of God's gift/grace (88).

321. Barclay, *Paul and the Gift*, 87.

322. Barclay, *Paul and the Gift*, 87: "The language of gift thus serves to make clear the attribution of source: *non ex nobis sed dei donum* ('this is not from ourselves, but the gift of God,' Eph 2:8; cf. *Ad. Simpl.* 1.2.3, 6)."

323. Barclay, *Paul and the Gift*, 115, locates the modern idea of altruism in Luther's new definition of the perfect gift.

324. Barclay, *Paul and the Gift*, 89, speaks of Augustine's "dual emphasis on the incongruity of grace (given to sinners before they were worthy) and the congruity of its result (creating humans fit for God)." Barclay continues: "Luther will later find this duality in Augustine's treatment of 'merit' unhelpful, since incongruity is for Luther the abiding essence of grace."

325. Barclay, *Paul and the Gift*, 97–116, for a discussion of Luther. See also John M. G. Barclay, "Paul, the Gift, and the Battle over Gentile Circumcision: Revisiting the Logic of Galatians," *Australian Biblical Review* 58 (2010): 36–56; John M. G. Barclay, "Under Grace: The Christ-Gift and the Construction of a Christian *Habitus*," in *Apocalyptic Paul: Cosmos*

Christians have mapped these views onto Christianity and Judaism, with the latter serving as the quintessential example of human self-righteousness. Such anti-Jewish interpretation has been recently called into question. Attention has been given to problematic claims and assumptions that Jews in Paul's day, and Judaism generally, held to a "works-righteousness" religion.[326]

While human pride could be at the root of Paul's contrast of works and grace, another lens through which to analyze Paul's argument accounts for the understanding grace as gift. That is, the term *charis* can be translated "grace" or "gift."[327] John Barclay picks up this set of questions by pursuing how grace was variously understood in Paul's day (and within the history of interpretation of Paul).[328] He speaks of six different ways that grace/gift is understood in the ancient world and today, using the concept of "perfection" ("the drawing out of a concept to an end-of-the-line extreme").[329] These perfections include superabundance, singularity, priority, efficacy, incongruity (unconditionality), and noncircularity (nonreciprocity).[330] Barclay maintains that Paul, like most everyone in the ancient world, held to the reciprocity of a gift.[331] The purpose of a gift was to create a relationship between gift giver and receiver.[332]

---

and *Anthropos in Romans 5–8*, ed. Beverly Roberts Gaventa (Waco, TX: Baylor University Press, 2013), 61.

326. See introduction, pp. 71–74. Augustine viewed Judaism in this way and assessed Jews as prideful in their pursuit of merit before God (*Exposition on Romans* 60.13); see Barclay, *Paul and the Gift*, 86, 565–66, 572.

327. Lincoln, 103, suggests that the noun is used over one hundred times in the Pauline corpus. Paul uses χάρις in various ways, such as in reference to his apostleship (1 Cor 3:10; 15:10; Gal 1:15; 2:9) or in contrast to the law (Gal 2:21; 5:4).

328. Barclay, *Paul and the Gift*, 75–182.

329. Barclay, *Paul and the Gift*, 66–75, 563–65. See also 1:6 for a discussion of his theory, p. 73, above.

330. Barclay, *Paul and the Gift*, 70–75. He concludes that most people believed a gift should be congruous with the recipient's worthiness (Seneca, *On Benefits* 1.1.1–2; 1.15.6; Philo, *Allegorical Interpretation* 3.77, 79, 83, 95, 166; Wis 8:5; 9:18). Seneca, the first-century Stoic philosopher, held that the gods gave some gifts indiscriminately (such as rain, sunshine), not because the gods were morally indifferent, but because they wanted to bless the worthy and could do so only by also benefiting the unworthy (*On Benefits* 4.28). Philo, a Jewish philosopher of the early first century CE, shares Seneca's belief that God ultimately acts to benefit the worthy. Philo grants that God is benevolent to the unworthy (*On the Sacrifice of Cain and Abel* 121–25), as the gifts of creation can be enjoyed by them (*Allegorical Interpretation* 1.33–34), and that no one is entirely worthy before God (*On God* 106); nonetheless, God considers the worth of the recipients as he dispenses his gifts.

331. Barclay, *Paul and the Gift*, 74.

332. Benefaction in the ancient world was a nonlegal, complex, and pervasive system that included gift giving. Stephen Charles Mott, "The Power of Giving and Receiving: Reciprocity in Hellenistic Benevolence," in *Current Issues in Biblical and Patristic Interpre-*

2:8–10 GOD'S GIFT OF GRACE

After exploring gift giving in the Greco-Roman world, Barclay postulates that the recipient of the gift did not earn it, but rather the gift giver was wise in distributing his/her benevolence to those who would use the gift wisely and justly.[333] Most of us today think of the best gift as one with "no strings attached," but this would not be the assessment of Paul's world. Jews were not exempt from these social assumptions, as witnessed by the disciples' astonishment that it is difficult for the rich to be saved (Matt 19:16–30; Mark 10:17–31).[334] However, some Jews, including Paul and the community of the Dead Sea Scrolls, held to the incongruity or unconditionality of grace (see 1QHa).[335] Here in Ephesians, I suggest that Paul has his gentile audience in mind, and these gentiles struggled to understand the one true God apart from their culture's conviction that gifts are given to worthy recipients.[336] Paul reinforces their worth by proclaiming that God's grace chose them and by denouncing the cultural norms that evaluated a person's worth by ethnic, social, or gender criteria.[337] Paul says much the same to the Galatians, as Barclay declares: "The continuation of ethnic distinctions at meals

---

tation: Studies in Honor of Merrill C. Tenney Presented by His Former Students, ed. Gerald F. Hawthorne (Grand Rapids: Eerdmans, 1975), 60: "The act of benefitting set up a chain of obligations."

333. Barclay, *Paul and the Gift*, 64, writes: "The importance of the ties established by gifts, and the expectations of return, explain why it is important for donors to be selective in their distribution of gifts, using some criterion of 'worth' to give discriminately and well." See also Jonathan Linebaugh, *God, Grace, and Righteousness in Wisdom of Solomon and Paul's Letter to the Romans* (Leiden: Brill, 2013), 164: "For *Wisdom* . . . grace means . . . an unearned though explainable benefit given to a suitable recipient."

334. For a discussion of reward, see Gary A. Anderson, *Sin: A History* (New Haven: Yale University Press, 2009), 146–47. He focuses both on Col 2:14, that God in Christ erased the believers' "legal indebtedness" (NIV, χειρόγραφον), and on almsgiving as "loaning to God," who then repays all out of proportion to the "loan," as he explores notions of reward, work, and grace/gift (see Tob 4:11: δῶρον γὰρ ἀγαθόν ἐστιν ἐλεημοσύνη πᾶσι τοῖς ποιοῦσιν αὐτὴν ἐνώπιον τοῦ ὑψίστου: "Indeed, almsgiving, for all who practice it, is an excellent offering [gift] in the presence of the Most High" [NRSV]). Barclay, *Paul and the Gift*, 567–68, contends: "Paul opposes those who think Torah-observance is the essential expression of faith not because 'law' or 'works' are problematic principles of soteriology, but because the Torah—like every other pre-constituted norm—has been dethroned as a criterion of worth by the unconditioned gift of Christ."

335. Barclay, *Paul and the Gift*, 562, adds that "a gift can be *unconditioned* (free of prior conditions regarding the recipient) without also being *unconditional* (free of expectations that the recipient will offer some 'return')."

336. Paul does not show concern that these gentiles might drift toward taking up the Jewish law, as their Galatian and Colossian neighbors seemed tempted to do.

337. Barclay, *Paul and the Gift*, 570, explains that when the gentile mission ceased, the language of grace shifted from a focus on "undermining not their pre-Christian criteria of worth but their pride or purpose in gaining Christian worth."

in Antioch is not just a communal malfunction, but an outright denial of justification of faith."[338]

I part company with Barclay in his (brief) statements about Ephesians. He summarizes "works" in Ephesians as "moral achievement" and boasting as "pride in achievement."[339] I suggest rather that Paul's emphasis on submission among the congregation, his direct address to wives and slaves, and his focus on the new humanity that is Christ's body add up to Paul's denouncement of societal hierarchical norms even in Ephesians. The extensive social hierarchy of the Greco-Roman culture said to slaves that they had no self-worth. Freed slaves carried the cultural baggage of their former slavery with them as permanently as their physical scars. Yet Paul addressed Christ-following slaves in his epistle's audience, raising the question: What could "not by works" mean to them? I suggest that Paul was not attacking their human pride, but offering them hope that their lack of ethnic identity/social status/worth/deeds of social benefit made no difference to God.

8 Paul continues with his message begun in 2:5 that by grace one is saved. Here in 2:8 Paul offers a slightly expanded repetition, using the article before the noun "grace" so as to make clear he intends the very grace he has been speaking about in the previous verses.[340] This is the powerful grace of God that effects salvation—you have been saved. Paul writes to the predominately gentile congregation, but he is not implying here that Jews are saved by other means; Paul, himself a Jew, also is saved by God's grace, through faith.[341] Paul will add two qualifying clauses that the gift of grace is not "from yourselves"[342] and is "not by works." Paul stresses that the entire salvation

---

338. Barclay, *Paul and the Gift*, 440. Barclay continues that Paul attacks "not working as such or the subjective motivation of the worker, but the 'objective' (socially constructed) value systems that make works, or other forms of cultural or symbolic capital, accounted worthwhile or good" (444).

339. Barclay, *Paul and the Gift*, 571.

340. Lincoln, 111.

341. Best, 226: "Paul never thought, nor does AE [author of Ephesians], that Gentiles alone and not Jews needed to respond to God in faith." For an opposing view, see John G. Gager, *Reinventing Paul* (Oxford: Oxford University Press, 2000), 10, who argues that Paul "did not expect Jews to find their salvation through Jesus Christ."

342. Ἐξ ὑμῶν. MacDonald, 233, explains that the preposition ἐκ in 2:8–9 "refers to origin or cause, i.e., faith is not caused by, nor does it draw its origins from, humans." The pronoun τοῦτο might refer to "faith" in the previous clause, thus defining it as God's gift. This is unlikely for at least two reasons—first, because it is rare for a demonstrative neuter pronoun to link with a feminine noun (faith) and, second, because that would render the phrase "not of yourselves" in 2:8 parenthetical. Arnold, 139, remarks that "it is not unusual for the neuter demonstrative pronoun to have an entire clause (or even more) as its antecedent." See also Best, 226, and Lincoln, 112.

2:8–10 GOD'S GIFT OF GRACE

act is accomplished by God. For emphasis, Paul places the genitive "of God" before the noun "the gift."[343]

A key phrase in this passage is "through faith," consisting of a preposition and a noun in the genitive case.[344] Before we look at the meaning of the phrase, we must explore what Paul means by the term "faith." Typically, Greek dictionaries suggest that *pistis* means (1) assurance, confidence, trust in others, proof; (2) trustworthiness, faithfulness; (3) pledge of loyalty, promise; (4) true piety, body of belief.[345] The cognate verb *pisteuō* emphasizes the act of believing in the truth of something or someone (cf. Rom 10:9).[346] These definitions, applied to our context, suggest that Paul has in mind here faith that speaks to the events and outcomes of God's salvation achieved in Christ. Paul explains this to the Ephesians as he states that they are sealed with the Holy Spirit, having believed the gospel of their salvation (1:13).

Additionally, there are several places in Paul's letters where a similar phrase occurs: the noun *pistis* and the term "Christ" in the genitive. Turning to the phrase conveniently shortened to *pistis Christou* we find it contrasted with "works of the law" in those passages that often come under scrutiny, namely, Rom 3:22, 26; Gal 2:16, 20; 3:22; Phil 3:9.[347] This construction can be translated "faith in Christ" (objective genitive) or "faithfulness of Christ" (subjective genitive).

We will look closely at this conversation, even though in Eph 2:8 neither the pronoun nor the noun "Christ" is used. However, in 3:11–12 we find

---

343. The verb "to be" as the equative verb is implied.

344. Διὰ πίστεως. A similar phrase, ἐκ πίστεως, occurs only in Romans and Galatians twenty-one times, including often with the addition of Christ's name in the genitive.

345. BDAG 818–20. For a summary of definitions from BDAG, L&N, and LSJ, see R. Barry Matlock, "Detheologizing the ΠΙΣΤΙΣ ΧΡΙΣΤΟΥ Debate: Cautionary Remarks from a Lexical Semantic Perspective," *Novum Testamentum* 42 (2000): 1–23. Had Paul used the accusative form of "faith" with this preposition, we would translate the meaning "because of" or "on account of" or "through" in a spatial sense. Wallace, *Greek Grammar*, 432, indicates that, in the passive voice, the subject is acted upon and that agency is expressed in three ways: primary, intermediary, and impersonal means. In the διά plus genitive construction in 2:8, the agency is intermediary and is understood as "through" or "by." Lincoln, 111, explains that ἐκ πίστεως is synonymous with διὰ πίστεως. Best, 226, argues that the genitive with the preposition διά establishes that salvation is "through" a believer's faith; had the noun been in the accusative, the preposition διά would have the force of "because of," which would send the inaccurate message that salvation is because of their faith.

346. On πιστεύω see BDAG 816–18.

347. Διὰ πίστεως Ἰησοῦ Χριστοῦ (Rom 3:22; Gal 2:16), διὰ πίστεως Χριστοῦ (Phil 3:9), ἐκ πίστεως Χριστοῦ (Rom 3:26; Gal 2:16), ἐκ πίστεως Ἰησου Χριστοῦ (Gal 3:22), ἐν πίστει (Gal 2:20). In all of these verses, the context also speaks about the δικαιοσύνη θεοῦ ("righteousness of God").

a similar phrase that uses the pronoun "his," referring to Christ.[348] There Paul calls to mind the inscrutable riches of Christ (3:8), echoing 1:7 and the riches of God's grace in the Beloved whose blood brings redemption and forgiveness of sins. In these chapters, Paul asserts that these riches, found in Christ, result in our reconciliation with God, accomplished in Christ Jesus our Lord (3:11), in whom believers find bold access and confidence before God. The final phrase in 3:12 may denote Christ's work in our salvation, in the fulfillment of the mystery of the inheritance in the Messiah for gentiles alongside Jews—in which case we could translate it "through his faithfulness."[349] It may also highlight the believer's faith in Christ, and we would translate it "through faith in him."[350] In any case, the pronoun certainly refers to Christ, specifically Christ Jesus our Lord (3:11).

To argue that the phrase in 2:8 is a subjective genitive, we must assume that Paul wanted his listeners to link "riches" in 2:7 with "gift" in 2:8 through the subject of salvation by grace. Moreover, since Paul distinguishes "by faith" from "not of yourselves" it could be that he wants to create a picture in his listeners' minds that puts Christ in the forefront, and not themselves. "By faith" is their cue to imagine Christ seated in the heavenlies, full of riches unto salvation.[351] However, if one takes *dia pisteōs* in 2:8 as an objective genitive, 1:13 with its participle "believing" supports the wider context shared by these verses that stress the gentiles' faith in the gospel message.[352]

The objective/subjective genitive debate will likely continue, but perhaps a way forward is to consider it in light of the first-century benefaction system and Paul's gospel challenge to it. That is, those who argue for an objective genitive may seek to preserve the notion of "free" grace for the believer. Yet Paul's definition of "free" or "pure" grace still carries necessary obligations (not burdens) for the believer who receives this gift of salvation.[353] And if one

---

348. Eph 3:12: διὰ τῆς πίστεως αὐτοῦ.

349. Paul Foster, "Πιστις Χριστου Terminology in Philippians and Ephesians," in *The Faith of Jesus Christ*, ed. Michael F. Bird and Preston M. Sprinkle (Peabody, MA: Hendrickson, 2009), 99–109.

350. Richard H. Bell, "Faith in Christ: Some Exegetical and Theological Reflections on Philippians 3:9 and Ephesians 3:12," in Bird and Sprinkle, *The Faith of Jesus Christ*, 111–25.

351. Paul consistently promotes Christ as God's "inexpressible gift" (2 Cor 9:15; see also 8:9), as the Son who gave himself up for all (Gal 1:4; see also Rom 8:32).

352. Best, 226, argues that if Paul "had Christ in mind we should have expected a following genitive "of Christ." Moreover, he holds that 3:12 and 3:17 refer to believers' faith, further evidence that 2:8 has believers' faith in mind.

353. John M. G. Barclay, "Pure Grace? Paul's Distinctive Jewish Theology of Gift," *Studia Theologica: Nordic Journal of Theology* 68 (2014): 17, notes that J. Louis Martyn's advocacy for subjective genitive in Paul is understandable as a response to "contemporary forms of Christian moralism and the gospel-less activism." Barclay argues that Paul does not

2:8–10 GOD'S GIFT OF GRACE

is persuaded by the subjective genitive argument, with its focus on Christ's riches making possible salvation and the unity of the cosmos, then one would need to consider that a recipient of such a magnanimous gift would expect to be in a relationship with the gift giver. The subjective genitive option, therefore, would need to include recognition of the "in Christ" language so prevalent in Paul's material.

Paul speaks of "gift" using a noun (*dōron*) not found elsewhere in his letters; however, it is used nineteen times in the New Testament.[354] In 3:7 Paul speaks of the gift of grace and in 4:7 of the gift (*dōrea*) of Christ (see also Rom 5:15, 17; 2 Cor 9:15; Heb 6:4). In Eph 4:8 Paul cites a scriptural passage that uses a similar term for gift (*dōma*), a term that carries a nuance of cultic or votive gift.[355] Paul creates a picture of a gift from God; salvation as a gift presented on an altar. The gift is redemption in Christ, through Christ, with Christ. Paul contrasts God's agency in providing the gift, with the futility of humans' ability to create or establish such a gift.

9 Ephesians 2:9 is a mere seven words in Greek, yet it offers a crucial admonition and explanation concerning the salvation by grace through faith that Paul presented in the last few verses. Paul detailed that God has benefited believers by making them alive with Christ, raised and seated them with Christ, and accomplished this by the overabundantly rich grace, experienced by believers in his kindness. Paul made clear that humans cannot generate its life-giving properties or its fullness of grace or a holiness that warrants God's great gift. The verse begins with a negative conjunction "not" and then a prepositional phrase "by [*ek*] works" that matches the phrase "from [*ek*] yourselves" in 2:8. Paul provides the reason or purpose for his declaration, namely, that no one might boast.[356] There is little dispute about the straightforward grammar and syntax; it is the terms' meanings in Paul's argument that warrant close attention.[357]

---

extend his argument to include these concerns about agency, as valuable as they may be for our current Christian discussions.

354. On δῶρον see BDAG 267.

355. Jesus speaks of leaving one's gift on the altar and reconciling to one's brother or sister, and then continuing to offer the gift to God (Matt 5:23–24). Jesus contrasts the rich putting gifts of money in the temple treasure with the poor widow who gave out of her poverty (Luke 21:1–4). Hebrews discusses the gifts offered by the high priest as sacrifices for sins (5:1; 8:3–4; 9:9; 11:4).

356. Best, 227, observes that ἵνα "could be final ('and that means incidentally that no one should boast'), or consecutive ('the result of all this is that no one should boast'), or imperatival ('let therefore no one boast')." The verb is in the aorist subjunctive tense, which conveys the sense that the verb's action is possible, even probable.

357. Polycarp, *To the Philippians* 1.3, includes εἰδότες ὅτι χάριτί ἐστε σεσωσμένοι, οὐκ ἐξ ἔργων. Best, 229n64, asks whether Polycarp knew Eph 2:8–9.

What are the "works" to which Paul refers? Several options are suggested. First, one group of theories addresses the term "works" in relation to the Old Testament law: some argue that Paul refers here to meritorious efforts related to the law;[358] others suggest that Paul alludes to the Torah in a general sense, not in relation to issues like gentile circumcision;[359] still others propose that Paul speaks against good deeds done by human effort "to earn God's approval."[360] With the reevaluation of Second Temple Judaism within the New Perspective on Paul, some scholars suggest that "works" are better explained as those behaviors and rites (circumcision, Sabbath) that separate Jew from gentile and stimulate nationalism. A second alternative is that the text speaks to "human effort towards salvation in Stoicism and the contemporary religion and magic."[361] And a third option was introduced above, specifically, to view Paul's concern for "works" as reflecting typical assumptions about gift giving and receiving. That is, Paul noted that recipients of God's gift were not inherently worthy of receiving the gift, for their character, social station, wealth, ethnicity, or any other identity-defining characteristic did not make them stand out and grab God's attention.

To help us better understand "works" we will look closely at Paul's concern about boasting. First, we should define boasting.[362] We tend to think of it as an action or attitude that takes credit where none is due, or is self-promoting. Paul and his compatriots would have understood boasting as "to accord [something] value, to recognize its worth, to treat it as superior 'symbolic capital.'"[363] Second, in and of itself, boasting is not wrong, for if it represented truthfully the worth of someone or something, then it was seen

---

358. Barth, 244, argues that the phrase "works of the law" in Romans, Galatians, and Philippians pertains to Ephesians and explains those works as "'works of law' to which meritorious value was attributed." Yet Barth, 247, indicates that "in no case are Paul's polemics against 'works of law' directed against the Jews, their holy tradition, or their zeal as such."

359. Perkins, 63, claims that the text alludes to the works of the law here, but has a more general purpose. MacDonald, 239, points to the absence of tension between Jews and gentiles over the law (circumcision, for example) as evidence that Ephesians was composed at the end of the first century, when, the argument goes, issues over Jewish law were less important. She correctly observes the differences in Romans and Ephesians; however, I am less confident that the second generation of the church had "solved" the problem of gentiles and the law.

360. Lincoln, 112. Arnold, 140, points to Titus 3:5 as a parallel, with its phrase "works of righteousness" contrasted with God's mercy. He understands Paul in both cases to be informing his gentile congregations that no amount of good deeds will be enough before God on judgment day.

361. Best, 227.

362. On καυχάομαι see BDAG 536. Barth, 226, observes: "Occasionally he substitutes for *kauchaomai*, 'boasting,' the verb *physioumai*, 'to be puffed up,' or he uses both together as synonyms" (e.g., 1 Cor 4:6–7).

363. Barclay, *Paul and the Gift*, 469.

2:8-10 GOD'S GIFT OF GRACE

as offering proper honor (Rom 5:2, 11; 12:3; 1 Cor 1:31; Gal 6:14). Obviously, God should receive all glory, as Paul indicates with his quotation from Jeremiah: "Let the one who boasts boast in the Lord" (Jer 9:24; 1 Cor 1:31; 2 Cor 10:17). And Paul indicates to the Galatians that they may boast in their own works, provided they have taken proper measure of them, without comparing themselves to others in the church (Gal 6:14, which includes the terms "work" and "boast"). Third, boasting occurs in the context of a culture of honor/shame. We tend to think of shame as bad, but in the ancient world, it was also seen as that which allowed for proper honor to be given, both to other humans and to the gods. Consequently, both men and women covered their heads during religious rites, for "who is this man who dares to greet Aesculapius with an uncovered head?"[364] Being properly shamed is a way to give reverence to those deserving it. Fourth, while Paul lived in an honor/shame culture, people also could feel guilt.[365]

Paul worries in 2:9 that believers might boast wrongly, and by doing so, they would dishonor God because they would rob him of the praise and glory due him and the salvation gift. Perhaps equally concerning to Paul, boasting in the community would disarrange the body of Christ, creating factions and hierarchies and reinforcing the social status quo. Boasting would tear apart the community that is raised and seated with Christ. Boasting would deny that all are equally the recipients of the riches of God's grace in Christ (2:5; see also Rom 3:27).

Paul concludes his argument in the next verse, as he stresses God's own work, namely, making believers his handiwork and setting before them good works to do. But Paul does not imagine that this happens in isolation from other believers. So in the remainder of the chapter, Paul expands on how salvation not only makes us alive with Christ and makes us God's handiwork, but as we will see, it makes us one, new humanity with Christ as our peace and one temple for the one true God.

10 This verse summarizes the previous nine verses and outlines how the magnificent salvation plan that displays God's riches in mercy and grace, through Christ, can be lived out by the Ephesians.[366] As this creator God is at work, so too his followers are concerned to do works that bring him honor. This attention to practice would be characteristic of any philosophical or religious group in the first century. We see this with the Pharisees and Sad-

---

364. Plautus, *Curculio* 389.
365. Carlin Barton, *Roman Honor: The Fire in the Bones* (Berkeley: University of California Press, 2001), 217, notes that in the West today we draw distinctions between "the shame of inadequacy from the guilt of violation," yet in antiquity, they are "inseparable aspects of *pudor* [shame]."
366. Barth, 243, observes that God's "present work recalls what he always has been, is, and will be: the creator of heaven and earth."

ducees in the Gospels, and we learn of it from the Essenes and their writings discovered in the caves at Qumran. The Stoic, the Cynic, and the Epicurean all considered their beliefs to encompass a way of life. So too, the Ephesians would be asking how the grace extended by God should be expressed by his people in Christ. Paul addresses the implied concern by showing how believers will demonstrate their new life in Christ. Paul declares that God has made a way and will provide the resources to walk faithfully.

This verse explains the believers' reality of having been saved by grace through faith. Paul places a personal pronoun "his" at the beginning of the clause to emphasize that this is God's doing.[367] Paul explains that God prepared good works in advance, stressing God's purpose for believers.[368] Paul uses the verb "to walk," which is often translated "to do" or "to live." The image is one of activity, of discipleship as a journey (see also 4:1, 17; 5:2, 8, 15). Each individual has his or her own stride: men and women move differently, tall and short individuals have varying stride lengths, a youth's smooth, quick stride becomes rigid and halting in old age. The verb is also used to describe "walking" in transgressions and sins, as we saw in 2:2. The implicit picture is that humans are on a journey, and they choose either the way of salvation or the path of death (2:1).

Several questions arise from 2:10, including the definitions of the term "handiwork," the force of the phrase "created in Christ Jesus," and Paul's intention in describing these good works as "prepared in advance" by God.[369] The term translated "handiwork" (*poiēma*) occurs numerous times in the Septuagint in reference to works by human artisans (Sir 2:4; 3:17) or to evil deeds (Ezra 9:13; Neh 6:14).[370] The cognate verb is used to speak of God's handiwork as a potter works with clay (Isa 29:16, cited in Rom 9:20). The noun occurs only one other time in Paul's letters, when he speaks of God making creation (Rom 1:20). That the idea of creation was part of Paul's intention here is strengthened with his use of the participle "created" and the phrase "in Christ Jesus."[371] Paul emphasizes newness later in this chapter, as

---

367. Lincoln, 114.

368. Perkins, 64, states that "verse 10*b* points to the purpose of divine election, the good works that have also been preordained by God." Barth, 227, explains that the preposition ἐπί can indicate purpose, although with the dative it is typically translated "on," "above," or "at the time of."

369. Best, 229, rightly resists the translation "workmanship" because "it suggests a play on ἔργα; there is no facile connection between our works and God's work."

370. On ποίημα see BDAG 842. Lincoln, 113–14, observes that in the Septuagint ποίημα is a synonym for ἔργον ("work"). See also Barth, 226, who argues for the connotation "work of art."

371. Arnold, 141, explains that the adverbial participle functions causally, offering a reason why believers are God's handiwork or craftsmanship. Elsewhere Paul speaks of believers

he describes the new humanity that results from a unity of Jew and gentile in Christ (2:15). Again, he describes the new human (*anthrōpos*) created according to God's likeness in true righteousness and holiness (4:24). Additionally, the preposition *epi* (translated here "to do"), with the dative phrase "good works," stresses purpose or result. These details strengthen the argument that Paul explains here God's mission for his people in Christ: they are to fill their communities with acts of lovingkindness representative of their Creator (see also "works of service" in 4:12). Paul conveys a similar thought to the Philippians, that is to say, that God began a "good work" in them and will continue that working until the day of Christ Jesus (Phil 1:6).

Paul invites readers to distinguish "good works" from "works" in Eph 2:9–10. Perhaps the distinction is explained by looking at Paul's personal declaration in 1 Cor 15:10. Here Paul indicates that he worked or toiled harder than the other apostles, and then he adds that it was the grace of God that worked within him. Paul speaks of his apostolic calling, and he makes a similar charge to Archippus in Colossians, that he fulfills the "work" (*diakonia*, service) that the Lord laid on him (Col 4:17). Thus, at times believers have a specific charge given to them, and they must work in that ministry. Paul might also have in mind, when he mentions "good works," the practice of virtues and habits of holiness that he speaks about in Eph 4–6. These behaviors grow from a believer's union with Christ (4:13), being clothed with Christ (4:24) and being a member of his body (4:15).

Paul emphasizes that God "prepared" these good works.[372] Paul uses this verb only one other time, as he describes God's objects or vessels of mercy whom he "prepared" in advance for glory (Rom 9:23). God prepared the works "in advance," and it is not clear whether this refers to the foundation of the world or at the point of the believer's conversion.[373] The prior action of God, no matter how distant, affects the Ephesians in the present. They can rest assured that God has useful work for them that will accomplish the purposes he sets out. The mention of good works echoes an earlier statement in Ephesians that believers were created to be holy and blameless (1:4). Paul indicates that the present age is corrupted by evil and that humans

---

as being new creations (Gal 6:15; see also 2 Cor 5:17; Col 3:10). Best, 230, rightly rejects the idea that Ephesians speaks of a second creation.

372. On προετοιμάζω see BDAG 869.

373. Best, 232, argues for the former, based on the wider context that uses the prefix προ to speak of precreation matters (1:4, 5, 9, 11). See also Lincoln, 115, who points to, but ultimately rejects, the theory that Paul presents here of believers being created in advance, not their works. He outlines this theory: the relative pronoun "which" is a dative of reference, and Paul implied an object "us," leading to the translation: "the good deeds, for which God has designed us." Perkins, 63, may support this theory, as she explains: "The righteous have been elected to perform certain good works."

are susceptible due to their fleshly passions (2:2–3). But God has made a way for believers to experience good works of holiness and fruitful service to the people of God and the wider human community.

In sum, the believer is God's handiwork, made alive with Christ, a recipient of the gift of salvation by God's all surpassing grace. In receiving God's salvation by faith, being raised and seated with Christ, believers also live out their salvation through behaviors and attitudes that attest to God's great work in them. The deeds prepared in advance by God release the believer to serve others in the Lord. These good deeds provide the context for growing into Christ's likeness. These opportunities are realized in God's strength, thus relieving believers of the temptation of boasting in themselves. Paul encourages the Philippians in a similar way: "Work out your [own] salvation with fear and trembling, for it is God who works in you to will and to act in order to fulfill his good purpose" (Phil 2:12–13).

EXCURSUS: CHRISTIAN ANTI-JUDAISM

Paul does not draw a sharp contrast between "works of the law" and faith in Ephesians; in fact, he does not mention "works of the law" at all. Nevertheless, his emphasis on faith and not works in 2:5–9 has led to anti-Jewish exegesis, in part based on inaccuracies about ancient Jews.[374] The remedy to such an approach is to keep in mind several key points. First, Jesus and Paul remained Jews throughout their lives, and they argued with and/or agreed with other Jews in their orbits. They discussed the questions of their day, including how to understand their present and the future. Within Ephesians, we find expressions of Jewish apocalyptic thought in discussions about "this age and the age to come (1:21; 2:7; compare *Jub.* 1.29; 23.26–29; *1 En.* 10.16–22; 11; 45.3–6; *T. 12 Patr.* 18.2–14), the distinction between the children or pathways of light and those of darkness (1.18; 2.1–2; 5.8–14; compare 1QS 3.13–4.14), and the anticipation of the end-time (1.10; 3.10)."[375]

Second, Judaism at this time is characterized by a robust conversation about the proper interpretation of the law. The numerous sects (e.g., Pharisees, Sadducees, Essenes, Herodians, followers of John the Baptist) jostled in

---

[374]. For example, see Carver, *Ephesians: The Glory of God*, 12–18, who, in his otherwise excellent reflection on Ephesians, explains Judaism in Paul's day as rooted in ceremony and exclusiveness: "Paul, on his part, felt bound to defend his Gentile converts, to save Christianity from the blight of formalism, ceremonialism, and sacramentalism, and to free it for its universal, spiritual function and destiny" (12).

[375]. Maxine Grossman, "Ephesians," in *Jewish Annotated New Testament*, ed. Amy-Jill Levine and Marc Zvi Brettler (Oxford: Oxford University Press, 2011), 345.

the public square as each promoted their ideas and way of life. All embraced Scripture, its one God, and the temple in Jerusalem, even as they disagreed passionately about behaviors by which to best demonstrate such allegiance. Those who followed Jesus as Messiah entered the fray with their own interpretations. Key concerns included forgiveness of sins, purity codes, and determining clean and unclean. These were vital issues in no small part because the Jerusalem inner-temple courts were sacred space and those who entered must be clean. It was not always the case that uncleanness resulted from sin (menstrual purity is a ready example).

Third, diaspora Jews formed close communities that continued their ethnic traditions, and in this they were similar to other ethnic groups that lived in the diverse cities in the Roman Empire. Their ethnic claims included identifying themselves as *Ioudaioi* or "Judeans/Jews," the people who worship the one God and followed this God's laws, including the prohibition against images.[376] In the Greco-Roman context, Jews explained their religion as *Ioudaïsmos* or "Judaism" and identified its key practices and virtues.[377] Most people in the ancient world identified Jews by their rejection of pagan gods and observance of three laws: circumcision, Sabbath rest, and refusal to eat pork. Some gentiles might know that these practices derived from the Jews' lawgiver, Moses. These beliefs and practices separated the Jewish community from their gentile neighbors in specific ways, especially at the time of citywide pagan festivals. This led to charges that Jews were hostile to humanity (*misanthropia*),[378] but Josephus makes clear that the Jewish community welcomed proselytes, that is, gentiles who embraced the Jewish way of life, including circumcision for men.[379]

Exegetes of the New Testament must reckon with the historical reality that its material was forged in a Second Temple Jewish milieu and written primarily by Jews.[380] Nevertheless, as Denise K. Buell points out, this

---

376. Josephus, *Against Apion* 2.23 §193 (translation by Henry St. J. Thackeray in Loeb Classical Library), writes: "We have but one temple for the one God."

377. The term "Judaism" is first found in 2 Macc 2:21, written ca. 100 BCE. See also Josephus, *Against Apion* 2.15–18 §§151–78.

378. Tacitus, *Histories* 5.5.1–2.

379. Josephus, *Against Apion* 2.28 §210. Shaye J. D. Cohen, "Judaism and Jewishness," *Jewish Annotated New Testament*, ed. Amy-Jill Levine and Marc Zvi Brettler (Oxford: Oxford University Press, 2011), 515, observes: "Culture or religion can be changed even if birth cannot; achievement (changing one's beliefs and practices) trumps ascription (birth)."

380. John G. Gager, *The Origins of Anti-Semitism: Attitudes towards Judaism in Pagan and Christian Antiquity* (Oxford: Oxford University Press, 1985), 11–34, traces the modern debate regarding anti-Judaism and anti-Semitism. See also John G. Gager, *Who Made Early Christianity? The Jewish Lives of the Apostle Paul* (New York: Columbia University Press, 2015), for a distillation of his thoughts over the decades.

knowledge "leaves suspended or unarticulated how this identification and the ethnic reasoning within these writings relates to later Christian collective self-understandings."[381] She summarizes the problems thus: "The rendering invisible of how the rhetoric of a multi-ethnic universalizing potential of belonging in Christ is built precisely upon existing ancient Jewish collective self-understandings; and second, that early Christian universalizing claims themselves have an exclusionary edge insofar as making belonging in Christ potentially available to all opens the door to vilify and marginalize any who resist this invitation."[382] She rightly challenges the conclusion that early Christianity moved away from an ethnic self-identity and toward a universalist, nonethnic self-understanding, in contrast to Jewish ethnic identity.[383] We discover in Ephesians the emphasis on gentiles becoming part of a new family, which includes a new heritage and a new set of familial customs, all this based on faith in Jesus the Messiah.[384] As such, believers create their own culture as a mixture of Jewish and gentile practices shaped by worship of the true God and his Messiah Jesus. Christian readers today should not insert the foil of "Jewish" ethnocentrism against which the gospel is preached.

The intervening two thousand years since Paul penned Ephesians has witnessed horrific crimes by Christians against Jews, and these cannot be swept under the rug.[385] As Paula Fredriksen observes: "The core canon of the

---

381. Denise Kimber Buell, "Challenges and Strategies for Speaking about Ethnicity in the New Testament and New Testament Studies," *Svensk exegetisk årsbok* 79 (2014): 38.

382. Buell, "Challenges and Strategies for Speaking about Ethnicity," 50.

383. For example, Rudolf Bultmann, *Primitive Christianity in Its Contemporary Setting*, trans. R. H. Fuller (London: Thames & Hudson, 1956), 175–87.

384. Buell, "Challenges and Strategies for Speaking about Ethnicity," 42, observes that New Testament authors speak of baptism as changing the ancestry of gentiles, and of these gentiles becoming members of "a *genos*, an *ethnos*, or a *laos* with a distinctive *politeia* and customs. This is what I call ethnic reasoning." She explains ethnic reasoning as seeing both the Christian embrace of people of all ethnic groups *and* promoting its own ethnicity as the people of God. After citing Justin Martyr (*Dialogue with Trypho* 119.4) and Clement of Alexandria (*Miscellanies* 1.42.2), she adds: "Those who become Christian from different backgrounds change not into members of a non-people but a different people" (43). See also Denise Kimber Buell, *Why This New Race: Ethnic Reasoning in Early Christianity* (New York: Columbia University Press, 2005).

385. Susannah Heschel, *The Aryan Jesus: Christian Theologians and the Bible in Nazi Germany* (Princeton: Princeton University Press, 2008). See also Gavin L. Langmuir, *History, Religion, and Antisemitism* (Los Angeles: University of California Press, 1990); and Rosemary Radford Ruether, *Faith and Fratricide: The Theological Roots of Anti-Semitism* (reprinted Eugene, OR: Wipf & Stock, 1997). David Nirenberg, *Anti-Judaism: The Western Tradition* (New York: Norton, 2013), 3, notes that the "Jewish question" (German *Judenfrage*) raised in the mid-nineteenth century reflects centuries of thought and shapes our current world. According to Nirenberg, Karl Marx argued that "conversion could neither emancipate the

New Testament, in other words the Gospels and the letters of Paul, witness to that moment in the evolution of Christianity when it was still a type of Second Temple Judaism."[386] It benefits Christians to understand Jews, and Christianity to understand Judaism, so as to "achieve the *shalom* ('peace') that the children of Abraham (including Muslims) all claim to be seeking."[387] This goal is especially relevant to the study of Ephesians, where Paul explains that Christ is our peace (2:14). We dare not perpetuate a false picture of Jesus, the Jew from Nazareth who died on a Roman cross, lest we distort the biblical claims of his redemption.

2. Christ Is Our Peace (2:11–22)

Paul develops and expands his discussion concerning salvation presented in the chapter's previous ten verses. He expounds his vision of believers' new life in Jesus Christ, saved by grace, seated with Christ in the heavens, and created to do good works that God prepared. Paul shapes his argument around "you" gentiles who were in darkness and "we" Jews who were under the power of the flesh. In both cases, Paul declares, the group members are given new life in Christ through the same gift of grace unto salvation. This grace prepares believers for good works, for they are God's workmanship. In the remaining twelve verses of this chapter, Paul develops this picture of salvation from a different angle, moving his argument along in three sections.[388] First, he paints a dismal picture of gentile life as outside the blessings of God, without hope, without God (2:11–13). A key manifestation of this reality is the strife endemic to relations between Jews and gentiles, between those who enjoy the promises of God and those who are far from them. Next, Paul highlights the new humanity created by Christ's death, which brings enemies together, receives gentiles into the family of God, and draws Jews (those who are near) through Jesus the Messiah together with gentiles (who are far) to the Father

---

Jews of Germany nor free Germany of Judaism, because Judaism is not only a religion but also an attitude, an attitude of spiritual slavery and alienation from the world."

386. Paula Fredriksen, "The Birth of Christianity and the Origins of Christian Anti-Judaism," in *Jesus, Judaism, and Christian Anti-Judaism: Reading the New Testament after the Holocaust*, ed. Paula Fredriksen and Adele Reinhartz (Louisville: Westminster John Knox, 2002), 18.

387. Amy-Jill Levine, *The Misunderstood Jew: The Church and the Scandal of the Jewish Jesus* (San Francisco: HarperSanFrancisco, 2006), 5.

388. Barth, 275, declares this passage as the "key and high point of the whole epistle."

by one Spirit (2:14–18). This section includes liturgical phrases and an allusion to Isa 57:19 and reiterates the theme of peace brought by Christ (Eph 2:14, 17).[389] The third section elaborates the gentiles' new position in Christ, as members of God's family and as part of a new temple built with Christ as the cornerstone (2:19–22). The picture of gentiles as fellow citizens with God's people (2:19) is in marked contrast to the first section's description of gentiles as excluded from the commonwealth of Israel (2:11–12).

Paul fills out key themes presented in his opening thanksgiving and prayer in Eph 1 and sets the stage for further discussion in Eph 3. Earlier, Paul spoke of the magnificent inheritance that believers share in Christ, the power that God uses to effect such inheritance, and the church as Christ's body. Here he speaks of the church as one new "human" who is created by the work of Christ bringing together Jew and gentile into one family of God (2:14–15). The unity of the body of Christ offers a foretaste of the cosmic unity yet to come when all things are brought together under Christ (1:10; 3:9–10).[390] Paul further defines this reality as a mystery now revealed, namely, that gentiles are coheirs with God's people, sharing together the fulfilled promise of God in Christ (3:6). This accomplished God's purposes of making known his great wisdom to the cosmos (3:10) and bringing the surpassing love of Christ to God's people (3:17–19). From this theological foundation, Paul launches into didactic instruction in the remaining three chapters of the epistle, reinforcing the reality that believers are new in Christ and so should behave in line with their new identity.

Paul describes his present reality wherein his world is divided into two groups—the people of God and those outside this family.[391] Another way to state this division is with the terms "Jews" and "pagans." The two groups pledge allegiance to different deities and divergent worship communities. There is a second layer to this social fabric, as pagans are also gentiles.[392] For most in this group, the terms are synonyms; however, gentiles who turn to

---

389. Perkins, 66.
390. Lincoln, 132.
391. For a general discussion of this section, see Cohick, "New Perspective."
392. For a discussion on the development of the discursive category "gentile" (Hebrew *goy*, plural *goyim*; Greek ἔθνη) and how this changed the self-identity of the Jew, see Adi Ophir and Ishay Rosen-Zvi, *Goy: Israel's Multiple Others and the Birth of the Gentile* (Oxford: Oxford University Press, 2018). The authors contend that Paul's use of the term is "innovative" and that "he mentions *ethne* more than any Jewish text before him, at every critical juncture of his work: his mission, the death of Jesus, the law, ethics, and redemption" (142). They argue that Paul established the strong divide between Jew and gentile and did not inherit it from the Judaism of his day (146). They conclude that Ephesians (written in the second century) "already assumes the binary division as a given and narrates Paul's mission as breaking this division down" (147).

Christ leave their paganism, but do not become Jewish proselytes. These believing gentiles come from different social and ethnic backgrounds and continue with their cultural practices that are not overtly pagan. The group known as Christians will be predominately gentile by the second century.[393] In Paul's time, however, the communities that embrace Jesus as Messiah are more evenly intermingled between Jew and gentile (former pagan), and most of the leadership is Jewish.

Does Ephesians suggest prior hostility between these groups in Ephesus that has now been resolved? Some argue that the epistle paints a historical picture of a reconciled group and use this assessment to argue for the letter being written at the end of the first century.[394] The underlying assumption is that within Paul's lifetime, there would be strife between the two groups. Here in Ephesians, however, Paul draws a *theological* conclusion that Christ's death and resurrection accomplished a new reality that can be implemented within communities. The peace that creates one new humanity need not reflect historical rapprochement between the two groups, but rather is a goal to be actualized. Furthermore, it is difficult to determine relationships between Jews and gentiles in the first century, as the situations depended on local circumstances and could change decade to decade.

Paul addresses questions that arose within the nascent communities of Christ followers. "If Jews were God's chosen people and Gentiles were not, and if Gentile Christians were not Jews and yet the elect of God (1.4f), what were they?"[395] Paul answers this question with metaphors of body, household, and temple, describing a single community that worships God faithfully. Paul maintains that this community of believers participates in the ancient Israelites' heritage and the Old Testament promises as their own. As such, believers share an inheritance in Abraham's family.[396] Paul's expectations for the church are rooted in and grow from his understanding of the prophets, most directly in this case from Isaiah. This prophet proclaims God's promise

---

393. Buell, *Why This New Race*, 94, observes that "ideas about race and ethnicity gain persuasive power by being subject to revision (flexible) while purporting to speak about fundamental essences (fixed). Early Christians participated in this dynamic treatment of ethnicity/race, adapting it to define Christianness."

394. Lincoln, 133. He rightly rejects the historical suggestion that Paul battles gentile arrogance in Ephesians, contrasting Rom 11:13–32.

395. Best, 235.

396. Caroline Johnson Hodge, *If Sons, Then Heirs: A Study of Kinship and Ethnicity in the Letters of Paul* (Oxford: Oxford University Press, 2007), 4: "For Paul, kinship and ethnicity cannot be merely metaphorical, for lineage, paternity, and peoplehood are the salient categories for describing one's status before the God of Israel." She rightly warns against reading into Paul a critique of Judaism as narrowly ethnocentric and exclusivist, in contrast to a Christianity that is transcultural, universalistic, and culturally neutral.

that he will bring all peoples together to worship at the one holy place, the temple in Jerusalem (57:19). For Isaiah, and for Paul, God proves the power of his great love in that he can unite "natural" enemies. Such love is beyond human capacity. God's goal of unity through sacrificial love infuses and excites Paul's imagination about what Christ's shed blood has achieved.

Paul provides a spatial rendering of salvation, drawing on Isaiah's evocative description of diaspora Jews streaming into Jerusalem and up to the temple of God (Isa 57:14–19). Paul picks up that compelling visual and maps Jews and gentiles onto it. For Paul, the gentiles are distant, so far away as to be utterly aimless. Jews are near, walking toward the true God as a people blessed by God's promises. Far and near, such is the reality of these two groups. Suddenly, the predictable end to the journey shifts. Now, by Christ's work on the cross, both groups arrive at the same time, at the same destination. And they discover that they are not the same as they were—no longer two groups but a new entity. This surprising end to the prophet's vision, Paul declares, is but one piece of the unity of all heaven and earth secured in Christ and realized at the end of time (Eph 1:10). Paul imagines redemptive history to bring unity, and that unity centers on God and his people, with Jerusalem/temple as the symbolic center of worship. Paul may be reflecting on the theme of exile woven throughout the Old Testament.[397] Underpinning Paul's message is his understanding of humanity on a journey, moving closer to, or farther from, the one true God. His own pilgrimages to Jerusalem for festivals dramatized Paul's convictions (see Acts 21:20–26). Gentiles are drawn into this resurrected community by the same grace and mercy of God through Christ.

The context of Ephesus makes this image even more poignant, as the city was the keeper of Artemis's temple, and Artemis ruled over her people in the city.[398] Ephesian gentile believers would have seen parades of devotees marching to her sanctuary; indeed, they likely participated in such rituals prior to turning to Christ. Now they imagine themselves as having arrived at a different temple and as different people. Paul extends the image of temple to describe this "one new people" as it functions in the world as a holy place, representing to all around the one true God.

Nouns dominate the lexical landscape in this passage: peace, enmity, stranger, citizen. Notice the dichotomy created by these nouns. Paul sharpens the contrast with his use of adverbs: near/far, then/now. And the key figure is

---

397. David Starling, *Not My People: Gentiles as Exiles in Pauline Hermeneutics*, Beihefte zur Zeitschrift für die neutestamentliche Wissenschaft 184 (Berlin: de Gruyter, 2011), 192–93, argues that Paul understands "Israel" in his time to be in spiritual exile, awaiting God's kingdom, and that Christ's work raised "a dead Israel from the grave of their exile."

398. Introduction, pp. 34–36.

Christ, who is "our peace" and who makes peace as he establishes his church, the holy temple of God. Paul emphasizes Christ's actions through participles that stress building and making, and he describes believers using the verb "to be," thereby accenting their identity.

The passage can be divided into three sections.[399] The first and third sections focus on the gentiles' past and present in Christ, and the middle section discusses Christ's or God's actions on behalf of the church.[400] The first three verses establish the plight of gentiles and the solution wrought by God (2:11–13). Paul begins with the command to remember, and Paul's focus is on the gentile believers' miserable history of separation from God (2:11–12). Paul assures believers that the past is past, for they are now close to God. Paul uses a passive voice in 2:13, emphasizing that it is God who acts toward the believers, and not the believers' own actions that have brought them to God. The second section stretches for five verses and proclaims Christ as the one who brings peace and makes a new people in his Spirit (2:14–18).[401] Paul focuses on Christ, both his identity as peace and his actions that create and sustain that peace. The final section, comprised of four verses, expands on Paul's claim of a new humanity in Christ by shifting images to describe the church as God's temple, with Christ as the cornerstone (2:19–22). Paul shifts his attention back to the gentiles, drawing on language used in the first section and emphasizing that in Christ these gentiles are fellow citizens, members of God's family. Paul adds a new image of Christ as the cornerstone, and with this illustration, Paul speaks of the church as God's holy temple. Paul will build on the temple image in his prayer in the following chapter, as he expresses the desire that believers will be filled with God's fullness, much as the temple is filled with God's Spirit (3:19; 5:18).[402]

a. Gentiles Far from God (2:11–13)

11Therefore, remember that formerly you who are Gentiles by birth and called "uncircumcised" by those who call themselves "the circumcision" (which is done in the body by human hands)—12remember that at that time you were separate from Christ, excluded from citizenship in Israel and foreigners to the

---

399. Lincoln, 126, rightly critiques arguments that present a chiastic construction.

400. Best, 236, rightly concludes: "In this way, the connection between soteriology and ecclesiology is brought out."

401. Barth, 275, includes 2:13 with the middle section, based on the opening phrase "but now."

402. Arnold, 148.

covenants of the promise, without hope and without God in the world. ¹³*But now in Christ Jesus you who once were far away have been brought near by the blood of Christ.*

Paul begins this passage by asking the Ephesian gentile believers to cast back in their memories to the time before they heard the gospel message. This walk down memory lane is a bleak one, for Paul indicates they were far from God, alienated from God's community ("Israel"), and foreigners outside God's covenant promise. Without hope, without God—this is an awful picture. It matches the one painted at the beginning of this chapter, when Paul declared that the Ephesians were dead in their trespasses. Paul himself felt the tug of the fleshly life, but God did not leave him, or any gentile, in such a state. Paul twice proclaims "by grace you have been saved" and announces that believers are seated with Christ, having been raised with him. This joyous truth is lived out by believers in the doing of good works already prepared by God.

Ephesians 2:11–12 comprises a single sentence that begins with a strong conjunction that encourages the gentile reader to pause and take in Paul's command to remember. After the command to remember, Paul includes two lengthy clauses, each highlighting an aspect of their history. Ephesians 2:13 offers a sharp contrast of hope as Paul insists that these gentiles are drawn near to God by Christ's work.[403] Gentile believers are now close to God, alongside Jews who are also brought nearer to God, and this nearness to God takes its shape as a new people, a new temple.

11–12 Paul begins this section with the conjunction "therefore," which tightly links his forthcoming argument to that which has been asserted in the previous verses. He commands the (gentile) readers to remember.[404] Paul describes the Ephesians as *ethnē* or gentiles in the flesh.[405] Although it is grammatically possible to label "gentiles" as a predicate nominative and insert "were" ("you *were* gentiles"), such a move overstates Paul's case. Paul does not require gentiles to become Jews when turning to Christ. Rather, Paul highlights the polytheistic religious heritage of these gentiles before their conversion to Christ.

Paul further describes the gentiles as uncircumcised[406] and contrasts this label with a physical circumcision done by human hands (see also Rom

---

403. Arnold, 149, places this sentence at the center of Paul's argument, arguing that "the idea of nearness to God is the central idea of the text." This statement should be augmented to include Paul's emphasis on new community that results from Christ's redemptive work.

404. Best, 237, emphasizes the present active imperative as Paul's insistence that the gentiles "keep on remembering."

405. On ἔθνος see BDAG 276–77 (2); D. R. de Lacey, "Gentiles," *DPL* 335–39.

406. Paul uses the term "foreskin" or "uncircumcision" (ἀκροβυστία); Hodge, *If Sons, Then Heirs*, 62, writes: "I know of no other author who uses *akrobustia* to designate non-Jews."

2:25-29; Col 2:11).⁴⁰⁷ Defining and reframing the importance of circumcision is crucial for his argument on unity in Christ (see also Gal 5:6; 6:15).⁴⁰⁸ Circumcision took on special importance in the Hellenistic period as an indication of Jewish identity.⁴⁰⁹ Paul identifies believers as the (true) circumcision (Phil 3:3) and speaks of a spiritual circumcision (Rom 2:28-29), drawing on this image from the Old Testament (Deut 10:16; Jer 4:4; see also 1QS 5:5; 1QH 18:20). The phrase referencing "human hands" harkens back to the Old Testament description of idols (e.g., Lev 26:1, 30; Isa 2:18; Dan 5:4, 23) and is used in the New Testament to describe the Jerusalem temple (Mark 14:58; Acts 7:48; Heb 9:11, 24). In all cases, the phrase is used disparagingly in contrast to God's actions.⁴¹⁰

Paul uses spatial and chronological signposts to guide the readers as he develops his picture of the gentiles' past. He speaks of separation, alienation, foreignness, hopelessness, and godlessness, which carry religious and political overtones.⁴¹¹ The corporate nature of the description might sound odd to our modern ears, which are often attuned only to the individual. In the ancient world, however (and in many cultures today outside the West), the community shapes the person's identity and sense of self-worth. Paul's first readers could not imagine private, personal beliefs apart from a community group, family, or clan that shared those convictions.

Paul declares that the gentiles were in a miserable condition based on their distance from Christ. One could translate Christ "Messiah," which would reinforce for modern readers Paul's emphasis on Israel's history as God's people.⁴¹² The gentiles' plight was not simply alienation from God, but exclusion from the commonwealth with God's people, or citizenship in Israel. Paul speaks of the *politeias* of Israel.⁴¹³ The Greek term is rooted in the word for city (*polis*) and signals a civic group, a commonwealth, a constitution of

407. T. R. Schreiner, "Circumcision," *DPL* 137-39. Perkins, 67, observes: "Within first-century Judaism, references to 'spiritual circumcision' or circumcision of the heart distinguished members of sects that claim true devotion to God from other Jews (Deut 10:16; Jer 4:4; *Jub.* 1.23; Philo *Spec. Leg.* [*On the Special Laws*] 1.305; 1QpHab 11:13; 1QS 5:5)."

408. Perkins, 67, adds that it was well known that Jews required male circumcision (Josephus, *Jewish Antiquities* 1.10.5 §192; Tacitus, *Histories* 5.5.2). Best, 239, adds that circumcision was a custom of other Semitic peoples in the ancient world.

409. 2 Macc 6:10 recounts the laws prohibiting circumcision established by Antiochus IV and the Jews' rebellion against these orders. Philo, *On the Special Laws* 1.4-7, gives four reasons for circumcision's value, chief of which is more effective semen emission and thus higher fertility.

410. Best, 239.

411. Perkins, 67, notes the similarity with Rom 9:4-5; however, in Romans, Paul speaks of these characteristics positively as part of Israel's privileges.

412. On Χριστός see BDAG 1091; B. Witherington III, "Christ," *DPL* 95-100.

413. On πολιτεία see BDAG 845. The term is used only here and Acts 22:28.

Israel[414] or a way of life (2 Macc 8:17); here it likely refers to being part of the community that worships the one God.[415] Paul may include the civic rights enjoyed by Jews in Ephesus, but he also focuses here on Jewish identity as people of the true God (Deut 5:1–21; Rom 3:1–2; 9:4–5).[416] The Jews in Ephesus assembled regularly, sent money to the temple in Jerusalem, observed food laws and Sabbath, and actively preserved their community identity.[417]

Not only are the gentiles separated from the people of Israel, but they have no hope (see also 1 Thess 4:13) and are foreigners (*xenoi*) to the covenants of the promise.[418] For Paul, the promise is Christ, and the covenants are those agreements and pledges made between God and his people, found in the Old Testament (see Rom 4:13–14; Gal 3:17–19). Paul's description suggests that Jews were not actively proselytizing gentiles. Most historians agree that, while Jews welcomed gentile Godfearers and accepted those who chose to convert to Judaism,[419] the Jewish community did not actively encourage gentile conversion.[420]

Paul also describes the gentiles as "without God" (*atheoi*), using a term that does not appear elsewhere in the New Testament or the Septuagint.[421] In describing the gentiles as godless, Paul is not saying that they were atheists and did not believe that gods existed. His point is that they embraced gods that were not the one true God, and thus were impious in their ignorance.[422]

---

414. Josephus, *Jewish Antiquities* 4.3.2 §45; 13.8.3 §245.

415. Best, 241, explains the term's meaning as "membership in Israel . . . possessing the rights, privileges, and duties which go with belonging to Israel as a defined political and religious community."

416. Trebilco, *Early Christians in Ephesus*, 48, observes that Jews in Ephesus organized along a citywide structure, but we lack details about what that looked like. He adds: "It is unlikely that it formed a *politeuma* within the city" (48n226).

417. Trebilco, *Early Christians in Ephesus*, 40.

418. On ξένος see BDAG 684. Clement of Alexandria (ca. 150–215), *Exhortation to the Greeks* 2.17–21, discusses the mystery cults and cites the language of Eph 2:12 ("*xenoi* of the covenants") directly before he outlines the behavior of the priests of Cybele, a Phrygian goddess known also as Demeter. Larry J. Kreitzer, "'Crude Language' and 'Shameful Things Done in Secret' (Ephesians 5.4, 12): Allusions to the Cult of Demeter/Cybele in Hierapolis?," *Journal for the Study of the New Testament* 71 (1998): 67–68, argues that, most likely, Clement uses these priests as examples of those who are strangers and godless.

419. Cf. Josephus, *Against Apion* 2.28 §210.

420. Martin Goodman, *Mission and Conversion: Proselytizing in the Religious History of the Roman Empire* (Oxford: Clarendon, 1994); Judith Lieu, John North, Tessa Rajak, eds., *The Jews among Pagans and Christians in the Roman Empire* (New York: Routledge, 1992); Michael F. Bird, *Jesus and the Origins of the Gentile Mission* (London: T&T Clark, 2007).

421. On ἄθεος see BDAG 24 and MacDonald, 242. She continues that the term is used in the wider Greco-Roman context to refer to those who neglect religious rites.

422. Best, 243, rejects the possibility of a moral rebuke in Paul's words here.

2:11–13 Gentiles Far from God

Paul speaks of gentiles as enslaved to those that are by nature not gods (Gal 4:8). Earlier in the epistle, Paul prays for the Ephesians that they would know the hope to which they are called, which suggests an eschatological inheritance enjoyed in some measure even now (Eph 1:18). Gentiles outside of Christ have no such future, nor do they have the peace that such confidence in this sort of future would bring. Indeed, their future was godless, their world held no peace, and they were impious (2:2).

Paul holds up a merciless mirror to the gentile believers, revealing the depth of their hopelessness outside of Christ.[423] What specific concerns does he presume about their past? Paul locates these gentiles over against Jewish covenants and promises that God established. Unlike 2:1–2, which focused on the gentiles' sins and disobedience, here Paul stresses their "outsider" identity. He does this to prepare for his central argument that believers together have a new identity, for in Christ there is one new people or "man" (*anthrōpos*, 2:15). Could this thought be expressed well today in the binary contrast of believer/unbeliever? The analogy works to a degree, if one suggests that an unbeliever is an individual who is far from God and without eternal hope outside of Christ. Yet this interpretive move downplays the corporate nature of our text, for it is not individual characteristics, but an entire group of humans—gentiles, the uncircumcised—that is the object of Paul's focus. Gentiles are both far from God and also far from God's people because the laws and promises that promote godly living are at odds with the ignorance and immorality that plagued polytheistic religions. Even gentile philosophers, who shunned the excesses of pagan ritual, did not recognize the God of the Scriptures.

Notice that Paul does not assign blame to the Jews for this situation, for they do not exclude gentiles. Rather, it is the gentiles who resist God, who are far from Christ, and who are foreigners to God's promises. The enmity created is not between warring clans, or cities, or even nations. The enmity is created by the very covenants of God that are to produce holy living. In defining godly living and in calling a people to himself, God the Father made a way for all in Christ.

13 Paul sounds a joyous note in this verse, a sharp contrast to the death knell in the previous two verses that mourned the fate of the gentiles who are strangers to God's promise and who are wandering in an unholy, hopeless world.[424] Now, Paul says, God the Father has acted in Christ Jesus the Son

---

423. A separate category of gentiles, "Godfearers," embraced Jewish monotheism and certain aspects of their lifestyle, without undergoing circumcision and becoming proselytes. Cornelius the Roman centurion (Acts 10) and Lydia of Philippi (Acts 16) are two Godfearers mentioned in the New Testament.

424. Best, 244–45, observes that the verse begins with two conjunctions, νυνὶ δέ, which strengthens the contrast from the previous two verses.

by bringing into the fold those who were at a distance. The picture calls to mind Jesus's parables of the lost sheep (Luke 15:1–7), the lost coin (15:8–10), and the lost son (15:11–24); in all three cases, there is great rejoicing when the lost is found, when the sinner repents. The contrasting language in Eph 2:1–10 focuses on the gentiles' past sinful situation bound to the ruler of this age and believers' new life with Christ.[425] The general theme continues here, as Paul stresses the gentiles' past unconnected to God with the "now" in Christ. Throughout Ephesians, Paul emphasizes the believer's secure salvation rooted "in Christ."

He uses the adverb "far away" as a parallel reference to his earlier statement that the gentiles are separated from Christ. Paul's use of adverbs reflecting distance foreshadows the near/far language of Isaiah on which he draws in later verses (2:17–19; see Isa 57:19).[426] The passive verb tense indicates that God in Christ is the active force drawing in the gentiles. Paul stresses that it is the blood of Christ that effects this location change (see also Col 1:20; Rom 5:8–11). Paul alludes to Jesus's death on the cross with this reference, and he makes this explicit in Eph 2:16.

The preposition *en* with the dative noun "blood" carries the sense "by means of" and indicates that God the Father, by means of the Son's death on the cross, brings gentiles near to himself and includes them with the people of God. In 1:7 Paul connects Christ's blood and redemption, explaining it as the forgiveness of sins.[427] To the leaders of the Ephesian church, Paul declares: "Be shepherds of the church of God, which he bought with his own blood" (Acts 20:28). A key verse in the discussion is Lev 17:11, quoted in Heb 9:22: "Without the shedding of blood there is no forgiveness of sins."[428] The blood of sacrifices brought to mind for both Jew and gentile an altar in a temple and the importance of a devotee's purity.[429] Animal sacrifices, performed at the

---

425. See also Rom 5:8–11; 6:11–14; 1 Cor 6:9–11; Gal 4:3–9; Col 1:21–23.

426. Best, 245, rightly notes that the context of Isaiah refers to Jews in exile returning to Jerusalem. Lincoln, 138–39, rejects the connection with Isa 57:19; instead, he points (unconvincingly in my view) to language of proselytism found in later Jewish writings, such as the *Mekilta* on Exod 18:5 and *Numbers Rabbah* 8.4. MacDonald, 243, offers that later rabbinic interpretations understand Isa 57:19 as gentile proselytes, and this idea may have been present in Paul's day.

427. Lincoln, 28, remarks in reference to 1:7: "The author of Ephesians has tied down God's deliverance of his people to Christ's work in history by making clear that the means of redemption was Christ's sacrificial death."

428. Morris, *Atonement*, 149, observes: "The thought of the love of God seen in the cross leads immediately to the thought of justification by Christ's blood and reconciliation through the death of the Son. The love and the reconciliation go together." He further notes that in both the Old Testament and the New Testament, the term "blood" most frequently indicates a violent death (62).

429. It is unlikely that Paul draws on a belief in the sacrificial significance of Christ's

temple in Jerusalem, reminded Jews of sin's defiling power and the need for purification. Paul declares that Christ's blood serves to make clean both Jew and gentile. In the following verses, Paul explains that the reconciling capability of Christ's cross extends to reconciling people to each other.[430]

b. Christ Creates One New People (2:14-18)

14 For he himself is our peace, who has made the two groups one and has destroyed the barrier, the dividing wall of hostility, 15 by setting aside in his flesh the law with its commands and regulations. His purpose was to create in himself one new humanity out of the two, thus making peace, 16 and in one body to reconcile both of them to God through the cross, by which he put to death their hostility. 17 He came and preached peace to you who were far away and peace to those who were near. 18 For through him we both have access to the Father by one Spirit.

Paul describes redemption in Christ by declaring that Christ is our peace. This peace creates something new, a single entity reconciled to God, and this peace kills something old, the enmity that existed between humans, all made in God's image. The one, new humanity reflects the one Spirit and the Father, together with the one Lord Jesus Christ.[431] The peace that makes the two one (2:14) is not an entailment of a personal justification, a second step, if you will, in an individual's salvation journey. Instead, the new humanity created by this peace is another way of expressing "by grace you have been saved." Simultaneously the believer is forgiven and made new, reconciled to God and to enemy at one time (see also Col 1:20).[432] The scope of Christ's work on the

---

circumcision blood. See Best, 246, who accepts (without listing primary sources) that in the first century "in some circles of Judaism circumcision had been given sacrificial significance" but adds that we do not find this idea in the Mishnah (tractate *Nedarim* 3.11).

430. Scot McKnight, *Jesus and His Death: Historiography, the Historical Jesus, and Atonement Theory* (Waco, TX: Baylor University Press, 2005), 371, observes that "the design of the atonement is to create a *community*, an *ecclesia*, a *koinonia*, a *zoe*, a *new creation*. The purpose is to take humans in one condition and put them in another condition . . . put them in freedom, in Christ, and in holiness." Hans Boersma, *Violence, Hospitality, and the Cross: Reappropriating the Atonement Tradition* (Grand Rapids: Baker Academic, 2004), provides a useful summary of the major theories of atonement and argues that Irenaeus's views might provide an ecumenical way forward in bringing various atonement theories together in reflecting on the divine virtue of hospitality and on the reality of violence. See also James Beilby and Paul R. Eddy, eds., *The Nature of Atonement: Four Views* (Downers Grove, IL: IVP Academic, 2006).

431. Gorman, *Becoming the Gospel*, 181-82, 186-206, offers an extensive discussion on peace in Ephesians.

432. Best, 235, concludes: "Salvation means union with one another."

cross extends from personal forgiveness to remaking the people of God, done in a single, redemptive motion of death-resurrection-ascension. This point is especially pertinent for those who see "personal" salvation as step one and "corporate" participation in church as step two in their Christian journey.[433]

In these five verses, Paul explains the method by which God brought gentiles near and opened the way to enjoy the promises given to Israel. Paul develops one result of Christ's saving work on the cross, that is, the creation of a new entity, Christ's body, the church. In bringing together Jews and gentiles, Christ makes clear that gentiles are pure and clean by means of his blood that washes away sin. This section connects with Paul's vision of Christ's bringing unity to all things in the cosmos (1:10), and it lays the foundation for his later exhortations for unity. Paul explains in Eph 3 that the new, reconciled people demonstrates God's wisdom to the authorities of the heavenly places (3:10). He insists that the church build unity by acting with patience, humility, and lovingkindness toward their fellow believers (4:2–3). Perhaps part of the reason for Paul's insistence is his recognition that if believers grow into Christ's likeness, then such a likeness will exhibit unity, even as there is one God—Father, Son, and Holy Spirit (4:4–6).

Unity necessitates that differences remain; otherwise, one has not unity, but sameness. The unity produced in Christ celebrates difference, and the diversity is not asymmetrical in terms of power. How might this be expressed in Paul's congregations? First, all believers participate in worship (5:18–21), which centers on God, not their own honor. Second, all the saints are aware that God shows no favoritism (6:9). Their unity should undercut their social hierarchies. The rejection of favoritism helps us understand the type of unity Paul desires— it is not about creating uniformity but about renouncing cultural privilege.

Because of the passage's traditional elements and closeness to Col 1:15– 20, some see this section as indebted to an ancient hymn later modified by the letter's author.[434] Arguments for this position include the number of *hapax legomena* and the alleged conflicting concepts of reconciliation to God and reconciliation between Jew and gentile. Three observations tell against this view.[435] First, the ten *hapax legomena* are part of the more than 200 we find

---

433. Lincoln, 85, makes the case that is highly unlikely that Ephesians is drawing such distinctions; instead, the letter addresses salvation from two angles: "The former is more general and lends itself to personal application, while the latter is more specifically ecclesiological." Furthermore, "he is simply portraying his readers' experience of salvation from two different perspectives."

434. MacDonald, 251, suggests "hymnic elements." See also Lincoln, 127–31, and Barth, 260–62. Best, 250, rightly observes a major weakness in the theory, namely, that "agreement is lacking even in respect of the verses chosen to form the base for any reconstructions" of the alleged hymn.

435. Best, 248–50.

2:14-18 CHRIST CREATES ONE NEW PEOPLE

in the 2,411 terms that make up Ephesians. Thus we would expect to find at least seven *hapax legomena* in these five verses, and ten is not statistically significant. Second, those who allege a hymnic setting often assume a gnostic backdrop that promoted a barrier between heaven and earth breeched by the divine redeemer. Few today, however, accept that Ephesians relied on gnostic thought.[436] Finally, the assumed conflict between the two foci (relationship to God, relationship between Jew and gentile) was brought to the reader's attention in 2:13. The two concerns, therefore, are highlighted by Paul.[437]

14-16 In Paul's day, the virtue of peace was associated with a minor deity in Greek mythology, *eirēnē*, using the Greek term for peace. When Augustus became the sole emperor of the Roman world, he introduced the cult of *pax* (Latin "peace"). Plutarch, a near contemporary of Paul, explains the ideal *politeia* as one in which "all the inhabitants of this world of ours should not live differentiated by their respective rules of justice into separate cities and communities, but that we should consider all men [πάντας ἀνθρώπους] to be of one community and one polity."[438] However, the familiar Roman slogan *pax Romana* ("Roman peace") was often enforced with severe brutality. Paul's listeners in Ephesus would likely hear the sharp contrast implied in describing Christ as our peace, for Christ was crucified by the Romans to maintain their *pax*.[439] Both Paul and his churches would also compare Christ's peace with the *shalom* of the Old Testament.[440] In this context, God's peace reflects his salvation and his righteous reign. New Testament authors pick up these themes as they stress God's kingdom and his justice, joy, righteousness, and faithfulness. To the Colossians, Paul speaks of Christ's blood shed on the cross as both reconciling all things to himself and making peace (1:20), using

---

436. Lincoln, 128-29, argues (unpersuasively in my view) that Eph 2:14-16 originally represented a "cosmic context" and that the two entities "are the two parts of the cosmos, heaven and earth."

437. Best, 249, states that the presumed conflict "therefore has not been produced by [the author's] tampering with an underlying hymn." See also Ralph P. Martin, *Reconciliation: A Study of Paul's Theology*, rev. ed. (Eugene, OR: Wipf & Stock, 1997), 172, who argues that the author of Ephesians used a "pre-formed hymnic celebration, called maybe a 'song of reconciliation,'" to tightly connect reconciliation and Christ's cross.

438. Plutarch, *On the Fortune of Alexander* 1.6 (*Moralia* 329A-B), translation from Lau, *Politics of Peace*, 90.

439. Lau, *Politics of Peace*, 81, explores ancient philosophical reflections on civil unrest due to ethnic tensions, summarizing that "any new community that is formed from previously diverse ethnic groups has the potential to be politically unstable." See Aristotle, *Politics* 5.2.10 (1303a25); Dionysius of Halicarnassus, *Roman Antiquities* 3.10.6; Plutarch, *Numa* 2.4-5.

440. The Septuagint regularly translates Hebrew *shalom* with Greek εἰρήνη. For discussion, see S. E. Porter, "Peace, Reconciliation," *DPL* 695-99; Willard M. Swartley, "Peace," in *The Westminster Theological Wordbook of the Bible*, ed. Donald E. Gowan (Louisville: Westminster John Knox, 2003), 354-60.

similar terms (reconcile, blood, cross) as found in our passage.[441] To the Philippians, Paul notes that the peace of God will guard their hearts (4:7), even as the God of peace is with them (4:9, see also Rom 5:1).

Paul describes Christ's peace with three participles: "has made" (Eph 2:14), "has destroyed" (2:14), and "setting aside" (2:15).[442] Both Paul's vocabulary and syntax are difficult in this section. After declaring that Christ has made the two groups one, Paul speaks about Christ destroying a "dividing wall" of the "barrier."[443] The first term, "dividing wall," is found only here in the New Testament and rarely used elsewhere.[444] The second noun, "barrier," has the sense of railing or hedge used, for example, to protect farmers' fields and vineyards (Matt 21:33; Mark 12:1).[445] The second term functions appositionally to the first—that is, it restates the "middle wall" as that which is the fence.[446] To what is Paul referring? Is it the Jewish law, noted in the next clause? Or does Paul allude to the balustrade that separated the court of the gentiles from the courts of the Jews in the Jerusalem temple?[447] The second option is more attractive in this context. First, the verb "to destroy" is often used to speak of the destruction of physical objects, and "whatever the meaning of 'middle wall' it is suggestive of a real or metaphorical building."[448]

---

441. In Col 1:20 the phrase "making peace" is a unique term that combines the noun "peace" and the participle "making" (the noun "peacemaker" is found in Matt 5:9); while in Eph 2:14, Paul uses the participle "making" and the noun "peace" separately. The meanings of terms are quite similar.

442. These function as substantival participles in apposition to the personal pronoun "he himself" that introduced this sentence.

443. Καὶ τὸ μεσότοιχον τοῦ φραγμοῦ.

444. On μεσότοιχον see BDAG 635. Arnold, 160, remarks that this noun is not found in the Septuagint, Josephus, Philo, or inscriptions in Ephesus; however, in two cities fifty miles south of Ephesus, the term has been found in inscriptions. The noun τοῖχος is rather common in the Septuagint.

445. On φραγμός see BDAG 1064.

446. Arnold, 159. He notes that the noun τοῖχος and "fence" are found together in Ps 62:3 (= 61:4 LXX). Barth, 263, suggests that the two terms together indicate a barrier that keeps people from entering a building or city based on hostility, as with the "Iron Curtain, the Berlin Wall, a racial barrier, or a railroad track that separates the right from the wrong side of the city."

447. The balustrade or railing (Hebrew *soreg*) is described by Josephus (*Jewish Antiquities* 15.11.5 §§417–18; *Jewish War* 5.5.2 §§193–94). An inscription placed on the fence declared that gentiles passed through the barrier on pain of death: "No man of another race is to enter within the fence and enclosure around the Temple. Whoever is caught will have only himself to thank for the death which follows" (translation from Lincoln, 141). See Orientis Graeci Inscriptiones 5.598 = Corpus Inscriptionum Graecarum 2.1400.

448. Best, 253. He concludes, however, that the best solution is to see the wall as "purely metaphorical" (256). This solution, in my view, fails to carry the intensity of the passage and its social context.

2:14–18 CHRIST CREATES ONE NEW PEOPLE

Second, even if most of the Ephesian believers had not visited the Jerusalem temple, it is likely that they would have heard about it from those Jews who visited Jerusalem during festivals or on pilgrimages. The believers might have asked Paul himself to describe it, as the Jerusalem temple was a marvel of architecture in the ancient world. Third, Paul speaks of the church as God's temple at the end of this chapter, with Jew and gentile worshiping together as one new people. This evocative image could call to mind the Jerusalem temple. Does this mean that Paul encouraged gentile believers to ignore the barrier if they visited the Jerusalem temple? In Acts 21:27–29, Luke informs us that certain Jews from Asia (which includes Ephesus) accused Paul of bringing gentiles into the temple courtyard reserved for Jews.[449] Although Paul does not directly deny the charges, earlier in the passage, Luke tells us that Paul paid for the purification rites of four believing Jews as a way to show that he was observant of Jewish customs (Acts 21:20–26).

Paul continues in Eph 2:14 with the noun "hostility" and the phrase "in his flesh."[450] In the Greek text, these stand between the clauses "destroyed the barrier" (2:14) and "setting aside the law" (2:15). Syntactically they could both connect with the previous participle, "destroying," or point forward to the next participial clause in 2:15 that speaks of setting aside the law of commandments.[451] A third option is that the noun "hostility" links with the earlier claims about the dividing wall, and the phrase "in his flesh" joins with the phrase "setting aside the law."[452] Most likely, Paul links "the barrier" with "hostility," which has been destroyed. In this case, "hostility" is in apposition to "the dividing wall."[453] Less likely is Paul connecting "hostility" with the law in the following verse. The meaning would then be that Christ abolishes the enmity, that is, the law.[454] The weaknesses of this second position include that Paul does not speak of the law as hostile, nor is such a view found elsewhere in Scripture. Additionally, Paul makes clear in 2:16 that the enmity was put

---

449. Arnold, 159–60.

450. The Greek text of 2:14 includes the phrase τὴν ἔχθραν ἐν τῇ σαρκὶ αὐτοῦ ("the hostility in his flesh"), but the NIV includes the phrase "in his flesh" in 2:15.

451. The NRSV and ESV follow the former option, while the KJV and NASB follow the latter.

452. See TNIV and HCSB.

453. Arnold, 159. The NIV adheres to this interpretation: "destroyed the barrier, the dividing wall of hostility."

454. Lincoln, 142: "The objective situation of hostility because of the law's exclusiveness engendered personal and social antagonisms." Lincoln then pivots to blame Jews for having "contempt for Gentiles which could regard Gentiles as less than human." This argument, in my opinion, exemplifies anti-Jewish Christian interpretation, as it locates blame for gentile animosity on the Jews themselves, with sweeping charges of antisocial behavior, which is unsubstantiated by careful historical analysis.

to death, not rendered inoperative as the participle in 2:15 is generally translated.[455] Left to determine is what the phrase "in his flesh" modifies. It might describe how the middle wall, the hostility, is destroyed. But more probable is that it reflects the means by which the law is no longer operative in the lives of believers.[456] By his blood, his flesh, believers are reconciled to God and to each other; the law is not the foundation, but Christ is the cornerstone for the church, his body. Overall, the third option is better, for it focuses on the issue of separation created by the law's focus on creating and maintaining a holy and blameless (pure) people of God (1:4). Such separation is overcome in Christ, our peace.

In 2:15 Paul continues his sentence begun in the previous verse, using the third participle ("setting aside") in his series of three. This participial clause explains the first two clauses.[457] The verb can be translated "invalidate" or "make powerless."[458] Paul uses this verb with some frequency, including when discussing the law—for example, "Do we, then, nullify [*katargeō*] the law by this faith? Not at all! Rather, we uphold the law" (Rom 3:31). Paul teaches that the law's ordinances have been now taken up in Christ, such that the previous and temporary means of reconciliation have found fulfillment in the death and resurrection of Christ. Those laws that separate Jew and gentile are nullified in Christ, making a new people as a fulfillment of the covenants of promise established by God. Yet those laws are not destroyed, for Paul does not ask that Jewish believers cease to circumcise their sons or forego Sabbath rest (see Rom 14). Instead, Paul relegates these practices to following cultural customs that celebrate God's goodness but are not essential for holiness within the community.

Paul links three nouns as he speaks of the "law" of the "commandments" in the "regulations."[459] To what is Paul referring with this unusual phrasing? It could be the entire law of the Old Testament[460] or only the cultic purity laws such as circumcision and food laws. Most likely it is the latter, for Paul will cite with affirmation the commandment that children honor their parents (6:2); clearly this law is binding on the household of God. Again, he draws on Gen 2:24 in his understanding of the oneness of husband and wife (Eph 5:30–32). But it and all other laws are also summed up and accomplished

---

455. See λύσας (2:14) and καταργήσας (2:15).

456. Arnold, 161–62, suggests that the phrase "in the flesh" modifies both clauses.

457. Best, 257.

458. On καταργέω see BDAG 525.

459. Τὸν νόμον τῶν ἐντολῶν ἐν δόγμασιν. For νόμος see BDAG 677–78; F. Thielman, "Law," *DPL* 529–42. For ἐντολή see BDAG 340 (2). For δόγμα see BDAG 254 (2).

460. Andrew T. Lincoln, "The Church and Israel in Ephesians 2," *Catholic Biblical Quarterly* 49 (1987): 612, argues that the whole law (both ceremonial and moral) served to divide Jew and gentile and was abolished in Christ.

2:14–18 CHRIST CREATES ONE NEW PEOPLE

through Christ. Paul uses the term translated "regulations" (*dogma*) in Col 2:14: "Having canceled the charge of our *legal* indebtedness, which stood against us and condemned us; he has taken it away, nailing it to the cross." The context is similar to Ephesians, as Paul encourages the gentile believers in Colossae that they have been circumcised in Christ through faith. Their new life includes forgiveness and fullness and is not characterized by observances of typical boundary markers of Judaism, for example, circumcision, food laws, and Sabbath (Eph 2:16–18).

The second half of 2:15 offers the purpose of Christ's making and destroying and setting aside. Paul reasserts that Christ's work of peace creates one new *anthrōpos*, or humanity.[461] Paul's language echoes Isaiah's language of "the house of" Israel and the *anthrōpos* or people of Judah (e.g., Isa 5:7). Paul connects the creation of a new people in Christ with the vision of unity that Isaiah celebrates. Peace is something tangible, it is both Christ ("he is our peace"; Eph 2:14) and it is "one, new *anthrōpos*," a living entity of unity. Peace has the power to reconcile, for the power of the cross manifests itself in peacemaking (2:16). Peace is something preached (2:17), and its message draws together Jew and gentile to the one God (2:18).[462] Individuals are reconciled to God and to each other in the all-encompassing peace gained by Christ for the church. Yet anyone who has spent time in a local church knows that this peace is not fully realized. Nevertheless, the call to peace and the means of such peace are available in Christ. The goal of peace, which is life with God by the one Spirit (2:18), should spur believers on toward unity. Why then do believers fear a call to unity? In part the anxiety lies in the proper worry that unity comes at the cost of faithfulness to Scripture and church practices. Second, the fear can be rooted in an ignorance of the vision for the church based on what Christ has gained through his blood. Finally, the distress might be based on the inaccurate belief that unity equals sameness. Precisely the opposite is true, for unity depends upon different persons coming together. Sadly, the resistance to unity finds its safe harbor in personal, familial, and ethnic particularities that barricade itself from others. This rationalization that

---

461. On ἄνθρωπος see BDAG 81–82. See Eph 3:5, 16; 4:8, 14, 22, 24; 5:31; 6:7. Sang-Won (Aaron) Son, "The Church as 'One New Man': Ecclesiology and Anthropology in Ephesians," *Southwestern Journal of Theology* 52.1 (2009): 25, concludes: "The focus of the passage is, therefore, not on the reconciliation of individual believers with God, but on the unity of two groups of people in Christ." See also McKnight, *Colossians*, 331.

462. Gorman, *Becoming the Gospel*, 181, writes of Ephesians: "The document is liturgically wrapped in peace (1:2; 6:23), its theological substance is peace (2:14–17, where the words 'peace' and 'reconciliation' are clustered in five occurrences), it calls for the inner life of the church to be a life of peace (4:3), and it characterizes the gospel the church is to share with the world as 'the gospel of peace' (6:15)."

justifies lack of unity is an affront to God, whose call to unity is central to the redemption plan established in Christ.[463]

Paul continues to describe Christ's work as reconciling the new humanity to God.[464] Paul describes the new entity created by the cross as a "body," repeating the language of 1:23 with the additional note that the body is "one." The peace reconciles the two (Jew and gentile) into one body. Paul reinforces this metaphor in 5:30, as he proclaims that believers are members of Christ's body. This body, united in Christ, is reconciled to God the Father. Paul adds that the reconciliation is possible "through the cross." Here we find an echo of Paul's earlier statement that Christ's blood has brought near those both far and near (2:13). Paul uses the verb "to reconcile" twice more in Colossians as he proclaims Christ as the one through whom God reconciles all things (Col 1:20, 22).[465] In Eph 2:15 Paul stresses that Christ destroyed the enmity by means of his flesh, that is, his death on the cross, while in 2:16 Paul declares that Christ put to death this enmity by means of the cross. Paul contrasts life and peace with death and enmity—the new body reconciled to God through the cross, which overcomes the old divisions that spawned enmity and that was far from God. Reconciliation through the cross of Christ has a horizontal and a vertical aspect. Humans are reconciled to each other, and both are joined in one community in new, reconciled relationship to God.

In Paul's day, gentile pagans were far from God and outside the community of faith. Their need for salvation was obvious, at least to a Jew such as Paul. What might have been less obvious is God's reconciliation of Jew and gentile into a new body. Instead, the expectation was that gentiles would become Jews, proselytes to the people of Israel.[466] Paul insists that the reconciliation of Jew and gentile is also the reconciliation of gentile and Jew—neither group is privileged, for both are changed as they become a new body altogether.[467] This new entity is rooted in the existing reality of the people

---

463. Carl E. Braaten and Robert W. Jenson, eds., *In One Body through the Cross: The Princeton Proposal for Christian Unity* (Grand Rapids: Eerdmans, 2003), 14: "Because it is God who binds his people together in faith and love, work for Christian unity is always, in the end, an acknowledgement of God's present authority and activity."

464. On ἀποκαταλλάσσω see BDAG 112. The verb "to reconcile" is in the same aorist subjunctive tense as "to create" in 2:15.

465. Paul uses the verb without the prefix—that is, καταλλάσσω—five times; see Rom 5:10 (twice); 1 Cor 7:11; 2 Cor 5:18-20.

466. Barth, *People of God*, 47, writes: "The Jews formed the people of God long before Gentiles joined in." See also Markus Barth, *Israel und die Kirche im Brief des Paulus an die Epheser* (Munich: Kaiser, 1959).

467. Schüssler Fiorenza, 25, rightly explains: "Their [gentile] conversion and being brought near makes them not 'Christians,'" but her conclusion that they are "Jewish messianic converts to the commonwealth of Israel" downplays Paul's emphasis on a new entity of Jew and gentile in Christ.

of God. Paul treats this issue in Rom 9–11, using the Old Testament image of Israel as an olive tree. The tree represents God's people, and its branches those who confess Christ. Paul assumes that those Jewish "branches" that confess Christ remain connected to the tree. He laments those Jewish branches that do not confess, for they are lobbed off (although they can be regrafted if a profession of faith is made). The gentile believer is grafted onto the olive tree, which changes the tree, but does not make it an entirely new tree.[468] There is continuity, therefore, between the body of Christ and the people of God as reflected in the ancient Israelites and the Jews of Jesus's and Paul's days. The perceived discontinuity created by the inclusion of gentiles *as gentiles* in Christ's body is related to God's actions wherein the drawing near of gentiles occurs now, in the Messiah Jesus.

In our age of pluralism, it is difficult to speak of conversion, of people being far from God and needing to be reconciled, because it is deemed judgmental or intolerant. Pluralism, which seeks a unity of sorts by accepting others' religions to foster peace, is the right instinct, but does not go far enough. The vision of unity that pluralism seeks can be attained only in Christ and his work on the cross. This reconciliation brings all people together into a new group, where no single culture, language, or political entity is privileged over another. This is a unity of differences, not a union of sameness. Here in this new body, all are equally beloved by the Father, as members of the body of his Son.

EXCURSUS: SUPERSESSIONISM

The history of interpretation of Eph 2:11–22 has included a strong anti-Jewish strain, due to at least two realities. First, scholars hold an anachronistic view that in the first century one could talk about Christianity over against Judaism as if the two were distinct institutions. This position fails to account for the first leaders of the Jesus movement being Jews, and they proclaimed that the Jewish Messiah had come in the person of Jesus of Nazareth, fulfilling the promises of the prophets.[469] Second, Christianity's claims to have su-

---

468. Wright, *Paul and the Faithfulness of God*, 2:1449. Barth, *People of God*, 46, highlights that here Paul speaks of "a single people of God, of the citizenship of Israel, into which Gentiles have been accepted." He contrasts this position with Rom 9–11, which assumes a split "within Israel between the majority and the remnant, and between the hardened part of Israel and the church" (46). He holds that Ephesians provides the best lens through which to read Rom 9–11 as affirming "the one people of God," over against interpretations "of substitution or of a final split" (48).

469. Fredriksen, "Birth of Christianity," 18, writes that Paul's letters "witness to that moment in the evolution of Christianity when it was still a type of Second Temple Judaism."

perseded Judaism and replaced it as God's people is viewed as threatened by the continuing existence of Jews and Judaism.[470] When the categories of Christianity and Judaism are mapped onto this message, the content shifts to mean that Christianity supersedes Judaism. Elisabeth Schüssler Fiorenza explains: "In such a reading all honorific titles or religious values and visions are transferred from Judaism to Christianity and understood as no longer Jewish."[471] This position has justified centuries of physical violence against Jews by Christians, and today it can perpetuate erasure of Jewish identity. Adele Reinhartz comments that "as a Jew for whom [the law] remains a vital and positive element in the divine-human covenant, [I] resist the tone of exaltation" and push against the passage that "delegitimizes those Jewish groups (the majority) who did not believe Jesus to be the messiah."[472]

Too often scholars neglect Paul's emphasis that he is an apostle to the gentiles; instead, they substitute a generic "unbeliever" as his missional target. This leads to several problems. First, it sets up Jews in the texts as the typological nonbeliever. Second, it can present Judaism "as narrowly ethnocentric and gentiles/the church as abstractly universal and culturally neutral."[473] Third, it ignores that the group called "gentiles" represents a myriad of cultural and ethnic backgrounds; they are not nascent Christians. Paul's gospel message condemns gentile idolatry, and it "restricts aspects of the Jew's Torah obedience to an ethnic expression, not a set of practices to be shared by gentiles within the believers' fellowship."[474] Paul's letters indicate a lively debate among Jesus followers as to whether gentile male converts should undergo circumcision (Acts 15:5–6; Gal 2:1–10). Scholars continue to debate how the earliest Christ followers negotiated living out the gospel in their local congregations.[475]

---

470. Dunn, "New Perspective on the New Perspective on Paul," 160, writes: "That is why, even late into the twentieth century the Judaism of the time of Jesus and Paul was often referred to as 'Spätjudentum,' 'late Judaism' the logic being that with the coming of Christianity there was no longer need or place for Judaism." See also Heschel, *Aryan Jesus*, 26–27: "The presence within Christianity of Jewish teachings, albeit transformed from 'old covenant' to 'new covenant' and the Jewish identity of Jesus, Paul and the apostles, formed the heart of the problem for Christian Nazis: to be a Christian inevitably meant affirming Jewish teachings." She concludes: "Through the various methods, Jesus was transformed from a Jew prefigured by the Old Testament into an anti-Semite and proto-Nazi."

471. Schüssler Fiorenza, 29.

472. Reinhartz's comments are found in Schüssler Fiorenza, 24.

473. Cohick, "New Perspective," 24. See also Hodge, *If Sons, Then Heirs*, 47, who rightly critiques the stereotype of Jews as following unnecessary practices, contrasted with the gentiles who seem to have no cultural baggage.

474. Cohick, "New Perspective," 26, going on to say: "The gospel establishes its own religious rites, baptism and Eucharist, and insists that the entire community practice them."

475. For a general survey and helpful summary of the issues, see Michael F. Bird, *An Anomalous Jew: Paul among Jews, Greeks, and Romans* (Grand Rapids: Eerdmans, 2016).

Excursus: Supersessionism

In the early twentieth century, Dispensationalism emerged with its view that God established several eras, including the current church age and the future millennium age that would include the restoration of the nation of Israel.[476] In this scenario, Israel has a special calling by God, and the synagogue and church do not intermingle. This interpretation might avoid the label "supersessionary," but it did not promote dialogue between the two groups.

Concerned that the story of Israel has been ignored by the church, Kendall Soulen argues for a post-supersessionary theology that highlights God as the consummator of creation and the gospel as "good news about the God of Israel's coming reign, which proclaims in Jesus' life, death and resurrection the victorious guarantee of God's fidelity to the work of consummation."[477] Soulen places Jesus Christ as part of God's eschatological rule, but not as representing the fullness of that reign.

Recently, some scholars focus extensively on Paul within Judaism. Mark Nanos argues that "Christ-following Jews like Paul do not reject Torah, but develop halakhot that articulate the appropriate way to observe Torah now, in view of the revelation of Christ that the representatives of the nations are not to become Israelites, but to join with Israelites in a new community ... adumbrating the restoration of all humankind."[478] This position resonates with the *Sonderweg* ("special path") interpretation that argues that the Jews have one covenant relationship with God and gentiles in Christ have another.[479] In this case, Paul was unconcerned about the wider Jewish community and did not take a position on the future status of Israel.[480] Others promote

---

476. C. A. Blaising, "Dispensation, Dispensationalism," in *Evangelical Dictionary of Theology*, 3rd ed., ed. Daniel J. Treier (Grand Rapids: Baker Academic, 2017), 248–49.

477. R. Kendall Soulen, *God of Israel and Christian Theology* (Minneapolis: Fortress, 1996), 157. He argues that "in Jesus God demonstrates invincible fidelity to God's overarching work as the Consummator of creation" (165).

478. Mark D. Nanos, *Reading Paul within Judaism: Collected Essays of Mark D. Nanos* (Eugene, OR: Cascade, 2017), 1:37. See also Mark D. Nanos and Magnus Zetterholm, *Paul within Judaism: Restoring the First-Century Context to the Apostle* (Minneapolis: Fortress, 2015).

479. Also known as the radical new perspective on Paul, this group argues that Paul addressed non-Jews only with his gospel message. See Lloyd Gaston, *Paul and the Torah* (Vancouver: University of British Columbia Press, 1987); Stanley K. Stowers, *A Rereading of Romans: Justice, Jews, and Gentiles* (New Haven: Yale University Press, 1994), 29–33.

480. John G. Gager, "Paul, the Apostle of Judaism," in *Jesus, Judaism, and Christian Anti-Judaism: Reading the New Testament after the Holocaust*, ed. Paula Fredriksen and Adele Reinhartz (Louisville: Westminster John Knox, 2002), 70: "It becomes clear that, as the apostle to the Gentiles, Paul is focused exclusively on disputes about the law and circumcision of Gentiles *within the Jesus movement*" (emphasis original). He concludes that Paul "never speaks of Gentiles ... as replacing Israel, or of God has having rejected Israel in favor of a new chosen people" (75). See also Gager, *Reinventing Paul*.

a post-supersession approach that argues for two tracks within Paul's congregations: the Jewish believers pursued their Jewish lifestyle and practices, and the gentiles remained nonkosher.[481] N. T. Wright critiques what he calls "sweeping supersessionism," a position that argues against any continuity between the radical inbreaking of Christ into this world and anything that had gone before.[482]

Paul presents his gospel message as superseding any and all religious claims or theories, and in that sense, one could say that the Christian message is supersessionary. But this sort of exclusive claim was put forward by the Qumran sect and probably other Jewish groups in the first century. As such, it seems best to think of Paul's message with categories such as fulfillment, and not replacement.[483] In our historical moment within Jewish-Christian dialogue, Jews and Christians understand that their "appointed tasks in this world are very different and must remain so because the covenant is not the same for both of us."[484] Both groups long for the promise of final redemption to be fulfilled, captured in Paul's enigmatic phrase "all Israel will be saved" (Rom 11:26).[485] The church in Ephesians is the body of Christ, created of both Jew and gentile who now are one new humanity.

---

481. Joel Willitts, "Conclusion," in *Introduction to Messianic Judaism: Its Ecclesial Context and Biblical Foundations*, ed. David Rudolph and Joel Willitts (Grand Rapids: Zondervan, 2013), 317, lists four assumptions that characterize post-supersessionism, including that "by God's design and calling, there is a continuing distinction between Jew and Gentile in the church today."

482. Wright, *Paul and the Faithfulness of God*, 2:807–8, points to J. L. Martyn and Ernst Käsemann, who advocate for an apocalyptic reading of Paul. See also Beverly Roberts Gaventa, ed., *Apocalyptic Paul: Cosmos and Anthropos in Romans 5–8* (Waco, TX: Baylor University Press, 2013).

483. Wright, *Paul and the Faithfulness of God*, 2:810, writes that the nub of the matter is Paul's claim that Jesus is Israel's promised Messiah: "It would be extremely odd if, in a group whose whole existence depended on being the people of a promise-making God, nobody was ever allowed to claim that the promise had been fulfilled, for fear of being called 'supersessionist.'" See also N. T. Wright, *Paul: In Fresh Perspective* (Minneapolis: Fortress, 2005), 125–28.

484. David Novak, *Jewish-Christian Dialogue: A Jewish Justification* (Oxford: Oxford University Press, 1989), 155–56. See also *Nostra Aetate* ("In Our Time"), The Declaration on the Relation of the Church with Non-Christian Religions of the Second Vatican Council, October 28, 1965; and Tikva Frymer-Kensky et al., "*Dabru Emet*: A Jewish Statement on Christian and Christianity," *New York Times*, September 10, 2000. *Dabru Emet* is a Hebrew phrase meaning "to speak the truth to one another."

485. Wright, *Paul and the Faithfulness of God*, 1:368, observes: "If Paul can speak of God's call to the patriarchs as 'irrevocable,' he would certainly say the same about God's action in the Messiah, and some of his greatest (and most challenging) theological writing consists precisely of working out the relationship between those two."

2:14–18 CHRIST CREATES ONE NEW PEOPLE

17–18 Paul explains that Christ "is our peace" (2:14), that Christ is "making peace" (2:15), and here in our passage that Christ "preached peace" (2:17). Peace brings a new humanity by destroying old hatred and distance from God and from other people. Christ's peace establishes a new community unified and reconciled to the one true God. Using similar language, Paul exhorts the Colossians that in Christ God reconciled all things unto himself, through the blood of Christ's cross, which makes peace. This peace extends from the earth to the heavens; it encompasses all things (Col 1:20). In Ephesians, Paul focuses on the unity of humanity created by the cross's reconciling power.

Paul declares that Christ "came" and "preached." That Christ "came" does not refer to Christ's incarnation, as the immediate context centers on Christ's cross. Instead, Paul points to Christ's own resurrection voice that, through his Spirit, proclaims the message of peace. Paul might also suggest that he and other apostles announce Christ's message as they declare the gospel (2:20; 3:5; Col 1:23). The content of Christ's preaching is peace, and it is spoken to those both far and near. Paul includes the plural personal pronoun "you" when speaking of those who are far from God. This specificity likely reiterates Paul's comments in Eph 2:13—that now in Christ you gentiles who were strangers to the covenants of the promise have been brought near in Christ Jesus.

Continuing his sentence, Paul repeats the term "peace" and then includes those who are near, but without using a pronoun.[486] We might expect Paul to put "we" who are near, meaning the Jews who are of the commonwealth of Israel (2:12). Perhaps Paul wanted to reassure his gentile congregants that their previous distance from God has been completely rectified in the all-sufficient work of Christ. The language in 2:17 echoes with expressions from Isaiah.[487] The prophet proclaims that a child is to be born who will be the Prince of Peace (Isa 9:6–7 = 9:5–6 MT, LXX).[488] Isaiah promises that the Lord lives with those of a contrite spirit, and he will heal them. The Lord guides and restores, as the people seek him in his holy place. "Peace, peace, to those far and near," says the Lord (57:19). But the prophet continues that

---

486. Lincoln, 124, cites the textual variant that omits the second reference to "peace" (Textus Receptus, Marcion, Origen), but correctly concludes that the second occurrence is likely, as it is found in P46 ℵ A B D F G P and "it is likely that the writer has reproduced the twofold reference to peace in the underlying OT text (LXX Isa 57:19) but given it a different sequence."

487. Barth, 276–79, offers an extended discussion; his theory that already in Paul's day, Jews interpreted Isa 57:19 as speaking of gentile proselytes likely exceeds the evidence.

488. Isa 57:19 LXX (reflecting the Hebrew) reads εἰρήνην ἐπ' εἰρήνη τοῖς μακρὰν καὶ τοῖς ἐγγὺς οὖσιν. Lincoln, 147, explains that Paul drew the verb "proclaimed" (εὐηγγελίσατο) from Isa 52:7; moreover, the references to "peace" have been separated, and the text "now emphasizes that Christ's peace is proclaimed to the two distinct groups, Gentiles and Jews."

God will bring judgment to the impious, admonishing that "there is no peace ... for the wicked" (57:21). Isaiah also declares that beautiful are the feet upon the mountains that proclaim peace (52:7; see also Rom 10:15).[489]

The peace that is Christ himself, which reconciles Jew and gentile and reconciles the new community to God—this peace is available to every believer. Paul enjoins the Colossians to allow this peace to rule in their hearts (Col 3:15) as they live out their calling as one body in Christ. He encourages the Philippians to give all their worries and sorrows to God, who will grant them peace, for his is the God of peace (Phil 4:7–9). He reassures the Romans that believers have peace with God through Christ Jesus (Rom 5:1). Not only Paul; Peter also reflects on the reconciling peace brought by Christ. In Acts 10, Peter preaches to Cornelius, a Godfearing gentile who receives the message of salvation in Christ. But one could say that Peter also had a conversion of sorts, for he declares that he sees the gospel message with new eyes now. The conversion of the gentile Cornelius, and the bestowal of the Holy Spirit upon him, causes Peter to realize that God shows no favoritism or partiality toward any single group, but is drawing all nations and peoples to himself in Christ (Acts 10:34–36).

In Eph 2:18, Paul continues the sentence begun in the previous verse, explaining the purpose of Christ's preaching. Paul shifts from his focus on Christ or God the Father's actions to spotlight the believers' situation. The "we" is further defined as "both," that is, Jew and gentile (see 2:14, 16). This pair is joined through Christ "in one Spirit" and this united entity is presented to the Father. Paul will develop the idea of "one" in Eph 4, as he describes the one body, one Spirit, one hope, one Lord, one faith, one baptism, and one God and Father (4:4–6).

Paul declares that believers ("we") have access to God.[490] The noun translated here "access" sketches the picture of Christ making introductions of his body, the church, to God the Father. Courtly protocols in the ancient world included a person who would formally introduce a figure to the king or queen. At times a person approaching their sovereign would bring a gift, and in the case of drawing near to a deity, one would bring a sacrifice or petition. Paul uses the same noun in 3:12, speaking of believers' access to the Father because of the redemptive work of Christ (see also Rom 5:2). Peter draws on this image using a cognate verb as he speaks about revering Christ as Lord,

---

489. Robert H. Suh, "The Use of Ezekiel 37 in Ephesians 2," *Journal of the Evangelical Theology Study* 50.4 (2007): 717: "Although Ezekiel 37 and Ephesians 2 each has its own distinctive historical context, even at first glance it is quite recognizable that the message of both chapters run topically parallel." The evidence presented, however, fails to demonstrate more than similar broad themes.

490. On προσαγωγή see BDAG 876.

c. Christ Builds His Church (2:19–22)

> [19]*Consequently, you are no longer foreigners and strangers, but fellow citizens with God's people and also members of his household,* [20]*built on the foundation of the apostles and prophets, with Christ Jesus himself as the chief cornerstone.* [21]*In him the whole building is joined together and rises to become a holy temple in the Lord.* [22]*And in him you too are being built together to become a dwelling in which God lives by his Spirit.*

Paul begins a new section, comprised of a single sentence in Greek, that expands his message in the previous eight verses with new metaphors even as he connects to his earlier claims by stressing the role of Christ in establishing his church. In these four verses, Paul shifts the focus from one new people created from two (Jew and gentile) to believers built together as a temple fit for worship of the one God. While the shift in metaphor from "one new humanity" to "holy temple" might seem abrupt to modern readers, Paul signals his shift by introducing the term "father" in 2:18, inviting reflection on a household. Six key nouns, including "household" and "building," and the verb "to build up" share a root from the Greek term for "house" (*oikos*). These terms define gentile believers as full members of God's family and also reconfigure what the household looks like. Jews, including Paul, established identity as the holy people of God through practices such as circumcision, adherence to food laws, and Sabbath rest. Now, Paul declares, identity is rooted in Christ, and the new people of God are united around his gospel. The household of God shares one Spirit, but need not share a single language or culture. Indeed, the wise and simple, the rich and poor, the slave and free — labels assigned by the wider culture — take on different importance in Christ's body. The wisdom of this age, the wealth of this world, the political power of those who possess it — all have status similar to that of the slave or impoverished free man and woman, in Christ. Said another way, each person has equal worth in God's eyes, through Christ. The craving today underpinning much of identity politics finds its peace in Christ, who affirms cultural and ethnic differences even as he sets these realities on the solid rock of his own redemptive and reconciling work on the cross.

Alongside the new language and metaphors in these four verses, Paul continues his emphasis on Christ; three times Paul declares "in whom" and "in the Lord" after indicating that Christ Jesus himself is the building's cornerstone. And he repeats several themes and terms used in 2:12, including "strangers" (referring to gentiles) and "citizens" (referring to Jews).[491] Having despaired in 2:12 that gentiles are without God (*atheos*), he now rejoices that these gentile believers are part of the household of God.[492] Paul implies throughout the passage that it is God's work in Christ that brings forth this changed status for gentiles and this new building made up of all who confess Christ.

19 Paul begins this passage by reflecting on the gentile members of the congregation. He contrasts who they were then with who they are now in Christ. Repeating the noun "foreigners" (*xenoi*) from 2:12 and adding the noun "strangers," those who are not native of a region or city, Paul explains the gentiles' characteristic alienation from God and his people.[493] The second half of this verse stresses the gentile believers' new status in Christ. The first of the two nouns, "fellow citizens," is found only here in the New Testament, but it is similar to the term "citizenship" used in 2:12; the distinction is that the term in 2:19 has a prefix "with" attached.[494] Paul uses a related verb and noun when addressing the Philippians, encouraging them to walk in a manner that is worthy or reflective of their membership in God's family (1:27) and to hold fast to their citizenship in heaven (3:20). Here in Ephesians, Paul's new word highlights the unity of Jew and gentile in the body of Christ—or, as Paul writes here, "God's people." Paul's reference can be translated "holy ones" or "saints" and should be understood more broadly than simply Jews, or even Jews who believe in Jesus Christ. Paul includes all who follow Christ.[495]

The second noun, "household" (*oikeios*), refers to the spiritual bond that unites believers as members of a household. Paul used the same term in the first half of the sentence, but added the prefix *para*, which changed the term's meaning to "stranger." Paul speaks of the household of faith (Gal 6:10) and regularly uses kinship language such as "brothers and sisters" to describe

---

491. MacDonald, 248. She also points to similarities with 1 Peter, including references to the household of God (4:17) and to Christ as the cornerstone (2:4–6).

492. Perkins, 75, notes a parallel in 1 Pet 2:11, which uses "aliens" to describe believers as they interact with nonbelievers (i.e., gentiles).

493. On πάροικος see BDAG 779. Daniel K. Darko, "Adopted Siblings in the Household of God: Kinship Lexemes in the Social Identity Construction of Ephesians," in *The T&T Clark Handbook to Social Identity in the New Testament*, ed. J. Brian Tucker and Coleman A. Baker (London: T&T Clark, 2014), 340, explains that "ξένοι refers to *immigration status* in relation to the *polis* whereas the second πάροικοι implies temporary status in a family home."

494. On συμπολίτης see BDAG 959.

495. Perkins, 75. See also MacDonald, 248–49, who adds that "angels" might be included in this reference to "holy ones." Less likely is the option that "saints" refers to martyrs or deceased faithful; see Muddiman, 140. Best, 277–78, argues for both angels and deceased believers, "since believers raised to heaven cohabit with heavenly beings"; this seems an overly complicated interpretation.

his congregations. For his portrayal, Paul draws on generally accepted norms for familial harmony, including honor and affection between brothers (and sisters).[496] In Paul's time, households included parents, children, slaves, and perhaps relatives. The ancient family was structured on a hierarchy of social worth, a construction based in large measure on the influential work of Aristotle (384–322 BCE). Paul draws on the patriarchal familial structure of his day, as when he assumes parents deserve the highest honor from their children (6:1–4). But he also reflects his society's values when he speaks of his own work among them as a father who should care for his children (1 Cor 4:15–16; see also Eph 5:1) or as a nurse who nurtures the little ones in the family (1 Thess 2:7). We should not impose our modern Western egalitarian standards onto Paul's letters, for in doing so, we flatten and distort the apostle's variegated cultural landscape.

20 Paul widens his gaze to include both gentile and Jewish members of the church as he shifts metaphors. He enlarges the images of house and household used in 2:19 and identifies Christ as the cornerstone. Paul uses an aorist participle translated "built."[497] Paul imagines this building to be still under construction. He pursues this general line of thought later in the epistle, as he speaks of believers being built up to maturity in Christ (4:12, 16, 29; see also Col 2:7).[498]

He explains that the building's foundation rests on "the apostles and prophets." These nouns share the article, but that does not mean they are synonymous, only that they illustrate a single point or reflect a similar purpose.[499] The role of apostle is not only to present verbally the message of God's salvation in Christ, but to demonstrate the power of the cross made perfect in

---

496. For a discussion of fictive kinship in Paul, see Darko, "Adopted Siblings in the Household of God." See also Trevor J. Burke, *Family Matters: A Socio-Historical Study of Kinship Metaphors in 1 Thessalonians* (London: T&T Clark, 2003), 6, 250–53; Halvor Moxnes, ed., *Constructing Early Christian Families: Family as Social Reality and Metaphor* (London: Routledge, 1997).

497. Martín-Asensio, *Transitivity-Based Foregrounding*, 46, explains the distinctive of the aorist and present tenses in Ephesians by pointing to the aorist participle in 2:20 and the present participle in 2:22 of the same verb: "Both are predicated of the believers, but only the latter uses the present tense, for it brings to the conclusion the central idea expressed above." Arnold, 169, suggests that the aorist is best interpreted as causal, "indicating the basis for the new citizenship and membership in the household of God." Best, 279, understands the aorist to refer to time and suggests that the past act was likely the believers' conversion/baptism.

498. Perkins, 75, rightly connects the image of building with 2:18, as "access to a powerful person often implied entry into an impressive building." Paul speaks of the church as a building to the Corinthians, and he states that he laid a foundation based on his calling from God to embody the gospel (1 Cor 3:9–17).

499. Lincoln, 153, points to 4:11, which clearly speaks of two groups, as further evidence for two distinct groups.

weakness (1 Cor 1:17; 2 Cor 12:9–10). Questions swirl around Paul's specific reference here to prophets.[500] Often this term refers to Israel's prophets such as Isaiah or Jeremiah, but in this case, paired as it is with "apostles," a better suggestion is that Paul refers to prophets of his day who bring the gospel.[501] Strengthening this reading is the similar phrase in Eph 3:5 that clearly refers to people of Paul's generation (see also 4:11).[502]

Turning to the description of Christ as the chief cornerstone, Paul elaborates on his sketch of the building. The Greek term translated "cornerstone" is found in Isa 28:16 and is used in 1 Pet 2:4–6.[503] In Isa 28:16, the Lord declares that he lays a sure foundation (using the cognate noun to the participle used in Eph 2:20) and a chosen cornerstone. The one who believes on it will not be ashamed. Paul cites this verse when stressing the importance of faith (Rom 9:33). Peter draws on this verse as he develops his argument that believers are being built into a temple, are serving as priests, and are offering acceptable sacrifices to God through Jesus Christ (1 Pet 2:4–6). The noun translated "cornerstone" could refer to the capstone that finishes off the building. Such an image works well with the metaphor in Eph 4:13–16, wherein the body of Christ is growing up to its head, namely, Christ.[504] Alternatively, the term can refer to the stone that functions as the crucial piece of the foundation and provides the plumb line from which the walls were built. While both possible interpretations fit Paul's overall message, the cornerstone image is to be preferred, as it draws on Isa 28:16 and makes better sense of the claim that the building's foundation is the apostles and prophets.[505]

21–22 In both 2:21 and 2:22, Paul refers to Christ the cornerstone with the phrase "in him." The passive voice of both "joined together" and "built together" indicates that it is not the church's own actions that create the increase or build the edifice. Rather, it is God's power at work through Christ that builds a holy temple, fit for worshiping the holy God.[506] The term used

---

500. On ἀπόστολος see BDAG 122 (2c); P. W. Barnett, "Apostle," *DPL* 45–51. On προφήτης see BDAG 890–91 (1e).

501. Perkins, 76.

502. MacDonald, 249–50, supports this position with the additional argument that the Acts of the Apostles, which has several "important points of contact with Ephesians," also has an interest in prophets and apostles.

503. On ἀκρογωνιαῖος see BDAG 39–40.

504. Best, 284; see also Lincoln, 154–55. He concludes: "The exalted position ascribed to Christ elsewhere in Ephesians (cf. 1:20–23; 2:6; 4:8–10) and the special emphasis on Christ's position as over against the rest of the structure in 2:20 favor this interpretation" (154).

505. MacDonald, 249, adds that this interpretation fits with the "foundational role given to Christ in 1 Cor 3:10–11."

506. Best, 287.

for temple (*naos*) gestures to the sanctuary in Jerusalem.[507] The building efforts result in a structure that is a dwelling wherein God dwells. This noun is used to describe God's dwelling place in the Old Testament (e.g., 1 Kgs 8:39–49; 2 Chr 6:30–39; 30:27).[508] Paul adds a prepositional phrase, "by [his] spirit," that could be understood in several ways. It might indicate that this is a spiritual dwelling, in contrast to a temple made by human hands.[509] Paul makes this contrast to the Athenians, noting that God does not live in temples made by humans (Acts 17:24–26; see also 1 Pet 2:5). Another possibility is that this phrase refers to how the believers are made into the Lord's holy temple, namely, by means of the Spirit's work.[510] However, this interpretation falters because the phrase is too distant from the verb it must modify.[511] Most likely, the phrase modifies the immediately previous phrase, "of God," indicating that God's own Spirit dwells in their midst.[512] This interpretation sees a parallel in the phrase "in the Lord," found in Eph 2:21.[513] The ancient world viewed temples as the homes of the gods who lived within them (in some fashion). Paul declares that the one true God—Father, Son, and Holy Spirit—dwell in the midst of the church, the body of Christ, its savior.

Paul stresses the concept of dwelling in 2:19–22, a theme that factors in later chapters as well. In 3:17 Paul prays that the Ephesians would have the strength of the Spirit and the indwelling of Christ in their hearts by faith, using the cognate verb when describing the fullness of God dwelling in Christ (see also Col 1:19; 2:9). Just as God's fullness dwells in Christ, so too Christ dwells in believers by faith. Such indwelling creates reconciliation between Jew and gentile and establishes a new space that can be described as a building, a holy temple, in which God's Spirit inhabits.

In 2:21 Paul speaks of the "building" that is growing or rising as the Lord's holy temple (see also 4:12, 16, 29; 1 Cor 3:9).[514] While it may seem odd

---

507. Arnold, 172, adds that the entire Jerusalem temple complex would be called ἱερόν.

508. On κατοικητήριον see BDAG 534–35 and Arnold, 173.

509. Hoehner, 414, rejects this option, indicating that the grammar is not similar to 1 Pet 2:5, which is properly translated "spiritual dwelling."

510. Arnold, 173, states: "The Spirit is the manner or means by which God inhabits this corporate body of believers."

511. Hoehner, 414.

512. Lincoln, 158, seems to argue for the latter two, and indeed, these are not mutually exclusive options.

513. Hoehner, 414: "Whereas in verse 21 the temple was in the sphere of Christ, this verse may be describing 'the manner of God's dwelling in this holy temple, *viz., in the Spirit*.'"

514. On οἰκοδομή see BDAG 696. The definite article ἡ is found after the adjective πᾶσα and before the noun οἰκοδομή in À1 A C P plus Origen and Dio Chrysostom. It is missing in many early witnesses: À* B D G K plus Clement, Origen, Basil, Dio Chrysostom, and Theodoret. The shorter reading is to be preferred; see Thielman, 186. Best, 286, points to other places in the New Testament where the article is absent: Matt 28:18; Acts 1:21; 2:36;

for Paul to speak of a growing building, this language anticipates Paul's discussion of the church growing into maturity in Christ (4:11–16).[515] Paul uses the same verb, "joined together" (2:21), in 4:16, within the metaphor of a human body as the church, being joined together and growing in Christ.[516] Paul emphasizes in this later chapter the need for holy choices by each believer, as they grow up in Christ. If readers jump from 2:21 to 4:16–17, they might experience a bit of confusion, inasmuch as the first text stresses God's work in Christ, while the second insists on the believers' actions working to build up the body. Even more, the first text insists that there is a new, holy building made up of Jew and gentile, while the second text states that believers must no longer live as gentiles do. The apparent contradiction is resolved when we realize that Paul uses a similar metaphor to develop different aspects of the church's life. On the one hand, the church exists only and solely by God's power demonstrated in Christ's work on the cross. On the other hand, this holy community develops as each member makes holy decisions, always in and through the Lord Jesus Christ.[517] The continuity between these verses is Christ, in whom and from whom the church, his holy temple and his holy body, increases and grows in love.

C. MYSTERY OF SALVATION REVEALED (3:1–21)

This chapter is about prayer: the one to whom prayers are directed (the Father of all), the one praying (Paul), and the ones on whose behalf prayers are given (the Ephesians, especially the gentile believers). The prayer Paul offers in the second half of the chapter soars to lofty heights, drawing the reader up to the very heavens. This should not surprise us, for Paul has earlier stated that believers are seated with Christ in the heavens (2:6). Vocabulary from Eph 1 echoes here, terms and themes related to the fullness, power, and love that characterize God and his salvation plan in Christ. Just as Eph 1 ended with the confident declaration of Christ's sufficient and superabundant work in establishing his church, so too here the prayer ends with a celebration of that glory that belongs to the God who establishes forever the salvation of his people and the restoration of the cosmos.

7:22; 23:1; Col 1:15, 23; 4:12; 1 Pet 1:15. MacDonald, 250, suggests that the phrase indicates the universal church. Lincoln, 124, writes that the article was likely added to clarify that "every building" was not the proper interpretation. He adds: "The writer has the universal Church in mind" (156).

515. Perkins, 76.

516. On συναρμολογέω see BDAG 966. Arnold, 172, writes: "Paul uses his creativity to coin a word that appears here for the first time in the Greek language."

517. Paul uses a similar argument, but in a negative sense, in Col 2:19.

3:1–13 Digression Concerning the Revealed Mystery

Paul launches into a new thought in this chapter, a line of reasoning that builds on the theological realities of the gospel—saved by grace through faith, made one people through Christ our peace through the blood of his cross. These amazing truths deserve to be pondered, but they must also govern choices and shape the sense of purpose in this life. Paul's own life radically altered course after Christ summoned him to become an apostle to gentiles (Acts 9:1–19; Gal 1:13–24). Paul obeyed, and he might be reflecting on that moment as he writes this chapter, for he tells the Ephesians that he sits in chains for Christ because of Christ's call on him for the sake of "you gentiles." This is no burden, says Paul; rather, he is a bearer of a great mystery now revealed: the grace of God in Christ makes a new body of believers, Jew and gentile heirs together of God's great promise. Paul uses similar language in his letter to the Colossians, as he emphasizes his servant status and calling to the gentiles as he brings the mystery, which is "Christ in you" (1:23–27).

1. Digression Concerning the Revealed Mystery (3:1–13)

Yet the chapter begins not with the prayer, but with Paul's explanation of his own situation. The first half of the chapter (3:1–13) is, syntactically speaking, a digression, but in terms of content, it is a vital piece of Paul's gospel message.[518] The first thirteen verses seem to ramble as the subject, Paul, has no finite verb attached. Throughout this passage, however, the implicit subject is God the Father, who tasks Paul with presenting the mystery now revealed.[519] The revelation made known to Paul and other apostles and prophets is that gentiles are coheirs with Jews in the community of faith established in Christ. In Paul's day, Jews received gentile proselytes in the synagogue community. Paul asserts, however, that God in Christ has created a new people that grows from the covenant people of Israel. This "one new humanity" (2:15) is comprised of believing Jews and gentiles who are made one through Christ's work on the cross. Paul is not content simply to state this breathtaking proof of God's magnanimous grace. He wants this reality to animate each believer, and thus his prayer in the second half of Eph 3.

---

518. Perkins, 78, states: "This section forms a key piece of evidence for the hypothesis that Ephesians has drawn on the text of Colossians"; she provides a table that compares Eph 3:1–13 and Col 1:23–28 (79–80). See also Lincoln, 193.

519. Carver, *Ephesians: The Glory of God*, 100–101, explains Paul's grammar: "A great soul, conscious of having received a most exalted revelation with which he had struggled for years to comprehend it, at length took an opportunity to try to write down what was beyond expression."

Something in Paul's opening line triggers the need for a digression.[520] The new information is that Paul is a prisoner in chains, a shameful situation that calls into question the veracity of his gospel message. Is Paul really God's ambassador (6:20)? Does not Paul's imprisonment instead highlight the improbability of his calling? The digression is perhaps better understood as an answer to an implicit question about the trustworthiness of Paul's message and, by extension, the truthfulness of the gospel. It is not surprising, then, that Paul anticipates questions about his theological claims of gentile inclusion in the people of God.[521] These latter concerns necessitate Paul's explanation as administrator of God's redemptive plan, to reassure his readers that his interpretation of Scripture is accurate in light of the Christ event. Explaining his hermeneutical conclusions, Paul invokes a "mystery" that is now revealed, the lens through which to view Israel's history and God's redemptive plan.[522] Paul expresses an eschatological perspective highlighting the new heavens and new earth and a new people reconciled in Christ through his blood shed on the cross.

In his digression, Paul clarifies his role in God's redemption plan and, by extension, the gentiles' role as well. In the first sentence (3:1–7), Paul states his task as steward of God's grace. He focuses on the content of this grace, explaining the mystery as gentiles blessed with an inheritance in Christ, coheirs with Jews who follow Christ. The second sentence (3:8–12) draws on the language of the first sentence as Paul spotlights his role as administrator of God's plan and explains the result: that God shows his wisdom to the "rulers and authorities" by having gentiles enfolded into the church.[523]

In the previous chapter Paul emphasizes that Scripture lines up with his assertions, but here he indicates that the final pieces of the puzzle were not available until God revealed them. Hidden in ages past, now the apostles and prophets see with Christ-tinted lenses the awe-inspiring truth of the gospel. Paul holds together these seemingly opposite positions—that Scripture held

---

520. Arnold, 179, states that "the nature and content of his [Paul's] digression does not appear to follow any contemporaneous rhetorical forms of *digression* as known through the rhetorical handbooks of antiquity."

521. Starling, *Not My People*, 185, unpacks Paul's hermeneutics by helpfully suggesting that Paul spends the early part of Eph 3 defending his earlier claim that "the (eschatologically revealed) mystery is the story of how the Gentiles have become heirs in Christ of the (scriptural) promise embedded in (scriptural) covenants to which they were once strangers, through the (scriptural) gospel that has now been preached to them." Starling's insight is that Paul sees Christ's death as having soteriological, ecclesial, *and* hermeneutical ramifications.

522. Starling, *Not My People*, 193, argues that the mystery is grounded in the "retelling of the ancient scriptural story of Israel's exile and promised restoration."

523. Thielman, 187, argues for two sentences. Hoehner, 417, states the passage is a single sentence comprised of 3:2–13.

the gospel truth and that God hid the truth—through his sophisticated hermeneutics of the Old Testament and his careful explication of the specific aspect of the gospel truth he attends to in this portion of Ephesians.

First, Paul interprets the impact of the Scriptures in light of Christ. He does what Christ did with the disciples on the road to Emmaus: "Beginning with Moses and all the Prophets, he explained to them what was said in all the Scriptures concerning himself" (Luke 24:27). Christ's death and resurrection transform believers' ability to understand Scripture.[524] Second, Paul understands the gospel to be both simple and complex. It is simple in its demonstration of the creator God's love and grace on his creatures. It is complex in that it involves the history of Israel, the person of Jesus Christ and his redemptive work, the church, and the world—all affecting each other. Paul teases out a thread of this tapestry in the opening three chapters of Ephesians and examines it from several angles. That thread is the inclusion of gentiles *as gentiles* by faith through grace.

An additional point should be made about Eph 3. After two thousand years of Christian reflection, we take for granted Paul's imprisonment. But in his own lifetime, the physical violence he endured, as well as the social shame that attended his missional activities, led some within the ecclesial community to distance themselves from him. His imprisonment put at risk any credibility he might have with the Ephesians (Gal 2:4; Phil 1:15–17). This digression anticipates concerns about social shame regarding his current imprisonment and its potential to impede the gospel. Paul's response is instructive: he does not promote his own record, but highlights God's salvation plan and his part in its unfolding. Paul explains God's triumph in Christ through the reality of human weakness.[525] And gentiles experience God's grace as church members, which is also a demonstration of God's wisdom to the powers of the cosmos.

Moreover, Paul takes advantage of his predicament by highlighting his similarity to the gentiles. His shame as a prisoner makes him a social outsider, much as were the gentiles in relation to the people of God (2:12). His past

---

524. Starling, *Not My People*, 185. See also Richard B. Hays, *Echoes of Scripture in the Letters of Paul* (New Haven: Yale University Press, 1989), 67, who writes: "It is as though the light of the gospel shining through the text has illuminated a latent sense so brilliant that the opaque original sense has vanished altogether." Hays highlights Paul's use of Hosea and Isaiah in Rom 9–11. He argues that Paul does more than simply draw an analogy from God's mercy shown to Israel to God's mercy shown to gentiles. Instead, Paul argues that Hosea's words indicate God's intent to call gentiles to himself. Hays suggests that Paul's Spirit-led study, done from an eschatological vantage point in Christ, finds hidden in the Deuteronomy passage the gospel that was in fact always close to Israel.

525. Gombis, *Drama of Ephesians*, 109–10; see also Timothy G. Gombis, "Ephesians 3:2–13: Pointless Digression, or Epitome of the Triumph of God in Christ?," *Westminster Theological Journal* 66 (2004): 316.

as one who hounded the church located him far from God, just as were the gentile believers (2:13; see also 1 Cor 15:9). Paul then speaks of himself as a servant of the gospel (Eph 3:7). The similarities found in Col 1:23–29 reiterate Paul's views on his apostleship. Paul the servant of God suffers affliction as part of the full message of the gospel (Col 1:24). God revealed the mystery to Paul and to all the Lord's people, that Christ dwells in Jew and gentile and is their hope of glory (1:27). Paul experiences his administering of the apostolic call that God bestowed upon him, this grace, as a gift.

Finally Paul's imprisonment is rightly also the gentiles' glory, for both the gentiles and Paul are living proof of God's revelation of grace that defeats the powers and reconciles humans to God, as Christ's cross creates a new community of faith.[526] This new community reveals God's wisdom to the powers, the same powers that are now under Christ's feet (Eph 1:22) and against which the Ephesians now stand dressed in God's armor (6:12–14).

a. Paul's Insight into the Mystery (3:1–5)

¹For this reason I, Paul, the prisoner of Christ Jesus for the sake of you Gentiles—
²Surely you have heard about the administration of God's grace that was given to me for you, ³that is, the mystery made known to me by revelation, as I have already written briefly. ⁴In reading this, then, you will be able to understand my insight into the mystery of Christ, ⁵which was not made known to people in other generations as it has now been revealed by the Spirit to God's holy apostles and prophets.

This section is a single thought if not technically and grammatically a sentence. Paul distinguishes 3:1–7 with an *inclusio* by repeating "God's grace given to me" (3:2, 7). This passage focuses on Paul's current situation as one imprisoned by authorities (likely imperial authorities, not Jewish authorities). The chains serve as a visual, visceral contrast to the remarkable revelation that had been bound up in God, but now is revealed to humanity. The imprisonment could be misunderstood as Paul's failure of ministry, as God's yanking Paul from ministry circulation. Therefore, Paul explains his

---

526. Aaron Sherwood, "Paul's Imprisonment as the Glory of the *Ethnē*: A Discourse Analysis of Ephesians 3:1–13," *Bulletin for Biblical Research* 22.1 (2012): 106, concludes that the second half of the digression clarifies the first half, and its meaning can be summarized as "the above *charis* was given to me—and it is indeed a *charis* for me to do the following—in order to evangelize the Gentile, with the result that now the church might make God's wisdom known."

3:1–5 Paul's Insight into the Mystery

assignment given to him by God: a ministry or stewardship of grace, the grace reflected in the cross. Key terms in this section include "mystery," "administration," and "grace," all concepts introduced earlier in the epistle. The echoing theme is grace as gift. Paul uses this same interplay in 2:8–9 as he speaks about God's gift of salvation. Paul creates new words as he captures the enormous scope of God's redemptive work. He speaks of gentiles as "heirs together," as "members together of one body," and "sharers together" in the promise (3:6).

1 The verse begins with a transition phrase "for this reason," which Paul repeats in 3:14. This connector points back to 2:11–22 and the message of Christ's reconciling work that makes a new people before God the Father, in one Spirit, bringing together Jew and gentile. This transition phrase is unusual in the New Testament, but not unprecedented.[527] Paul emphasizes his current situation as a prisoner by stating "I" emphatically, followed by the noun "prisoner" with the article.[528] Paul qualifies his situation as a prisoner in two ways; he states that he is a prisoner "of" Christ Jesus and "for" the gentiles in his congregation.[529] The first prepositional phrase is interpreted in at least two ways. The genitive "of Christ Jesus" could mean that Christ and his gospel message preached by Paul is the cause of his current chains.[530] It may also carry the sense of possession, namely, that Paul is "owned" by Christ, his Lord.[531] The two possible meanings are not at odds, and both might be at work in the passage.

The second prepositional phrase, "for the sake of you Gentiles," highlights Paul's solidarity with gentiles as they both serve Christ. Because he later says that his imprisonment is the gentile believers' "glory" (3:13), he might also introduce here the idea that suffering in Christ's name is honorable, not shameful. Paul says as much to the Colossians, that he suffers his imprisonment as part of his calling in the church, so that the mystery of redemption in Christ might be made known (Col 1:23–25).

There is no finite verb in this sentence, and so some translations insert the verb "to be," rendering the translation "I, Paul, *am* the prisoner." This complete sentence, however, raises more issues than it solves. By inserting

---

527. Hoehner, 418. Paul uses the phrase in Titus 1:5, and χάριν by itself as "because" in Gal 3:19; see also 1 Tim 5:14; Titus 1:11.

528. On δέσμιος see BDAG 219; D. G. Reid, "Prison, Prisoner," *DPL* 752–54.

529. The phrase τοῦ Χριστοῦ Ἰησοῦ (P46 B A, also geographically diverse) and τοῦ Χριστοῦ (Ἀ D F G). Thielman, 208, explains that "at an early date the name Ἰησοῦ was added to the text under the influence of the two references in Philemon" (Phlm 1, 9). See also Best, 294.

530. Hoehner, 226.

531. Arnold, 185, concludes the phrase is a "simple genitive of possession and thus indicates that Paul is a prisoner ultimately belonging to Christ and not to Caesar."

"am" before "prisoner of Christ Jesus," the spotlight shines on Paul himself, not on the gentiles under his care, which he emphasizes in the prepositional phrase "on behalf of you gentiles." Moreover, if Paul had implied the verb "I am," then the use of the article before "prisoner" would mean that Paul believes he is *the* (preeminent) prisoner, a sentiment unsupported by the rest of the passage. Therefore, it seems best to see this opening phrase as teeing up his prayer, which begins in 3:14. The intervening verses are a grammatical digression filled with pertinent information about the nature of God's gift of grace in Paul's own calling and in bringing grace to the gentiles, now members of God's people by faith.

EXCURSUS: PAUL'S ARREST IN JERUSALEM

Paul's imprisonment discussed in 3:1 grew from charges that he brought gentiles beyond the Jerusalem temple barrier, restricting access to the inner courts to Jews and circumcised proselytes (Acts 21:33). Jews guarded the sanctity and purity of their temple in Jerusalem, even as gentile polytheists protected the specific purity codes (such as they were) of individual deities and their "houses" or temples. The Jewish leaders were given extraordinary authority by the Romans to put to death any gentile who went beyond the balustrade that separated the court of the gentiles from the inner courts reserved for Jews (see commentary on Eph 2:14). Romans tolerated (more or less) indigenous religious groups within their imperial borders, but tensions in Jerusalem were high in the 60s CE and boiled over in 66 with the First Revolt.

A similar situation of strong nationalism and resistance to Roman occupation existed at this time in Britain, led by Boudicca, queen of the Iceni. Stephen Dyson notes that Boudicca's forces devastated three cities and destroyed the imperial cult temple in Camulodunum.[532] This occurred after her husband's death and the refusal by Rome to honor his will. The king left half his estate to his two daughters and the other half to the emperor. Rome rejected the terms of the will and the possibility of female rule and made clear their position by publicly raping the daughters in front of their mother.

Martin Goodman perceptively observes the distinctive aspect of Jewish leadership compared with typical Roman authorities, namely, that the former were not necessarily the wealthiest of their group. He remarks: "In essence, when faced by societies in Judaea, Gaul and Britain where high status was accorded to many who were not rich, the Romans could explain such societies

---

532. Tacitus, *Annals* 14.31.6–7. Stephen L. Dyson, "Native Revolts in the Roman Empire," *Historia* 20 (1971): 239–74.

to themselves only by assuming that their 'unnatural' attitudes were the result of religious fanaticism."[533] Rome explained the nationalistic zeal by these groups in Britain and Judea as the result of "stubborn and vicious religious instincts of the inhabitants."[534]

---

2 Paul begins with a conjunction, "if" or "surely," emphasizing that the Ephesians have heard about Paul's calling as an apostle to the gentiles.[535] Paul will not offer the apodosis or "therefore" part of his thought until 3:13.[536] He reminds the Ephesians that they have heard about Paul's ministry, and he is refreshing their memory.[537] Paul describes his ministry with the noun *oikonomia*, which can refer to the plan that is administered, the position of administrator, or the tasks and responsibilities of the administrator.[538] The latter two options should not be sharply distinguished, for an administrator administers plans and tasks. Paul repeats the noun in 3:9, there referring to God's plan, which included the revealing of a mystery that was hidden (see also 1:10). If Paul intends a similar meaning in 3:2, then the verse focuses on God's plan as it relates to Paul's specific responsibilities to preach the gospel to gentiles. Alternatively, Paul may be pointing to his position as administrator.[539] Finally, we might have the spotlight trained on the responsibility itself. To decide on the better option, we turn to the phrase "of the grace of God." On the one hand, Paul could be speaking about the administration concern-

---

533. Martin Goodman, *The Ruling Class in Judaea: The Origins of the Jewish Revolt against Rome A.D. 66–70* (Cambridge: Cambridge University Press, 1987), 240.

534. Goodman, *Ruling Class in Judaea*, 244.

535. Εἴ γε. Paul uses a conditional conjunction with an enclitic participle adding emphasis or nuance.

536. Arnold, 185–86, translates the thought this way: "If you have heard about my stewardship of God's grace . . . then don't lose heart in my suffering."

537. Paul uses the aorist tense of the verb ἀκούω. Constantine R. Campbell, *Basics of Verbal Aspect in Biblical Greek* (Grand Rapids: Zondervan, 2008), 34, explains the semantic property of the aorist tense as providing "an external view of the action." Campbell cautions against assuming that the aorist "*always* depicts a punctiliar, once-occurring, instantaneous action" (35). He adds that "only about eighty-five percent of aorist indicatives refer to the past in New Testament usage" (36).

538. On οἰκονομία see BDAG 697–98. Carver, *Ephesians: The Glory of God*, 103, rightly points out that the KJV's "dispensation" has been assigned a false meaning used to support dispensational theology: "The term is never once used in the Scriptures . . . in the sense of one of a succession of 'ages' in which God's principle of working with men changes from age to age."

539. Hoehner, 422–23.

ing the gospel of grace that he preaches.[540] On the other hand, because the attention is on explaining his apostolic mission, Paul is likely here describing his responsibility to preach the gospel as a special grace from God.

Further support for the latter option comes in the next verse, as Paul discusses how his commissioning happened; it was by revelation (3:3; see also Gal 1:12). God's grace is given to Paul, reflected in his calling as apostle and the responsibilities thereof. By extension, it is a grace given to the Ephesians who heard and accepted the gospel message.

Paul remarks that the Ephesians "heard" about Paul's administration of God's grace. Yet Paul lived in Ephesus for over two years in the early 50s, so one would expect him to say that they "knew" about his administration (Acts 19:1–10). For some scholars, Paul's use of the verb "to hear" reflects a "device of pseudonymity."[541] However, it may be that with this verb Paul includes the new members of the church who joined after his departure approximately seven years earlier.[542]

3–5 These verses set the stage for the central message of the digression. They confirm with the congregation what they know already about Paul, namely, his authority given by God for preaching the gospel.[543] Paul indicates this revelation was made known to him. The divine passive voice signals that it is God who revealed. Paul describes what was made known as a mystery revealed to him (see also Rom 16:25–26). The revelation Paul has in mind is most likely his encounter with the risen Lord on the road to Damascus (Acts 9:1–6; 22:1–21; 26:1–23; Gal 1:12), but it seems reasonable to assume that his understanding of this epiphany developed as he pondered its content and ramifications. His claim could include his subsequent visions from God (2 Cor 12:2, 7).[544]

Paul uses the term "mystery" twice in Eph 3:3–4 to express that which was made known to him by revelation.[545] In 3:3 Paul speaks only of the mys-

---

540. Larkin, 87, offers several options succinctly.
541. Lincoln, 173.
542. Arnold, 186; Thielman, 192.
543. Best, 299, considers ὅτι in 3:3 original, although a few important early manuscripts lack it. He argues that internal evidence pushes in favor of including it, for if ὅτι was not present, then 3:2 would become an uncharacteristically short sentence for this epistle, and a new sentence would begin in 3:3.
544. Arnold, 187; Lincoln, 175.
545. On μυστήριον see BDAG 661–62; P. T. O'Brien, "Mystery," *DPL* 621–23. Lang, *Mystery and the Making of a Christian Historical Consciousness*, 90, writes that "Ephesians 3:2–13 represents the lengthiest and most detailed development of μυστήριον and the accompanying hidden/revealed schema in the Pauline corpus." He continues: "Exactly why this mystery so frequently lands him in bondage and distress is never stated, but the correlation is a consistent and prominent theme in Ephesians and Colossians" (107).

3:1–5 Paul's Insight into the Mystery

tery, but in 3:4 he further describes the mystery as "of Christ" (see also Col 2:2). Christ's death and resurrection have redeemed humanity and set in motion the reconciliation of all things under God. Christ's redemptive work is described in greater detail in Eph 3:6, namely, that gentiles are members of one body with Jews in Christ (see also Col 1:27).[546] Again, in Eph 3:9, Paul uses the term in the phrase "the administration of this mystery," as he contends that what was long hidden is now made known to the powers and authorities in the heavens (see also 1 Cor 2:7; Col 1:26), that the gentiles may receive the unsearchable riches of Christ (Eph 3:8). In 3:10 Paul draws on the message of 1:9–10 as he declares that the mystery of Jew and gentile is in Christ, his body.[547] By this point the reader knows that this mystery includes (1) the unity of Jew and gentile in the body of Christ, leading to the unity of all things in the cosmos under Christ, (2) the revelation of God's plan, and (3) the demonstration of God's superabundant grace in Christ and unsearchable wisdom that redeems his people. We will find that Paul uses "mystery" with a similar emphasis on unity, but this time expressing the union of husband and wife (5:31–32). Paul cites Gen 2:24, that the "two become one flesh," and continues that this union is a great mystery.[548] Finally, at the end of the letter, Paul asks for prayer that he might boldly preach "the mystery of the gospel" (Eph 6:19; see also Col 4:3–4). The request to be fearless in preaching mirrors a similar statement Paul makes to the Corinthians when he declares that he and Apollos are servants of Christ and ones "entrusted [*oikonomos*] with the mysteries [of] God" (1 Cor 4:1).

Paul continues in Eph 3:3 with the assertion that he had already written about this mystery briefly. The verb is used four times by Paul, including in Rom 15:4 when speaking of Scripture written long before his time (see also Gal 3:1; Jude 4). In our case, Paul is likely referring to what he wrote just before this passage, especially Eph 2:11–22, where he lays out the message of

---

Arnold, 188, reminds readers that in Paul's time the term was quite common among the gentile religious cults, including those that stressed initiation rites; he cites *Die Inscriften von Ephesos* 3059.3-6, which includes the line "all the mysteries of the goddess" (πάντα τὰ μυστήρια τοῦ θεοῦ).

546. Lang, *Mystery and the Making of a Christian Historical Consciousness*, 97: "The identity of Israel must, of course, be inferred here but, given the preceding context of 2:11–22, such an inference is uncomplicated."

547. Lang, *Mystery and the Making of a Christian Historical Consciousness*, 102, explains that the church exhibits "this wisdom to the heavenly powers [that] in some sense prefigures the comprehensive ends of God's mystery as described in 1:9–10."

548. Lang, *Mystery and the Making of a Christian Historical Consciousness*, 105, makes clear that prior to Christ's revelation, such a reading of Gen 2:24 would not be evident within the text. Lang concludes that such a hermeneutical move shares similarities with Rom 11:25–27 and 1 Cor 15:51–57 in its creative reapplication of Jewish Scripture.

reconciliation through Christ, our peace.[549] Paul begins 3:4 with the phrase "in reading this." Paul likely refers to the previous mention of mystery, and this mystery is that about which he wrote at the close of Eph 2. This letter is read aloud to the congregation, and Paul provides an auditory reminder that he will develop his previous argument, now with attention to his own part in the drama of salvation. Paul desires that they should understand his message. The verb is used at the end of this chapter, as Paul exalts the one able to do more than we can "imagine" (3:20; see also Matt 16:9, 11; Rom 1:20; 1 Tim 1:7).[550] The Ephesians should have a solid grasp of God's revealed mystery by listening to Paul's explanation.

Paul offers new information about this mystery in Eph 3:5, specifically that it was unknown to previous generations. Paul repeats from 3:3 the verb "was made known" but now in the negative, indicating that past generations did not know of this mystery because God had not yet revealed it. Paul further describes these generations as "the sons of men" (*tois huiois tōn anthrōpōn*), a Semitic expression that means humans. Paul might be referring to ancient holy men and prophets, a parallel to the apostles and prophets in Paul's day that he speaks of later in the verse. The idea here might be similar to Jesus's claim that many prophets and righteous ones desired to see what his followers saw (Matt 13:17). The exact phrase is found only once in the New Testament, in Mark 3:28 (the parallel in Matt 12:31 has only "men"). Given the slender amount of data, it seems best to regard "the sons of men" as a poetic reference to human history that lacked knowledge of the mystery because it had not yet been revealed.

Paul contrasts the previous situation with the current one, as now a revelation has occurred, this by the Spirit to holy apostles and prophets.[551] These New Testament figures, among whom Paul counts himself, have been shown the mystery of Christ, the gospel of redemption and reconciliation. Paul describes the apostles and prophets as "holy," a term used fifteen times in the epistle, reflecting his emphasis on the proper disposition of God's people. While this adjective is found only before "apostles," its force is projected to the second noun "prophets."[552] Paul writes the possessive pronoun "his" (translated "God's") only once, but because the two nouns are joined by a common article, the pronoun refers to both apostles and prophets.[553] The

---

549. See Schlier, 149; see also Arnold, 187. Less likely is the theory that Paul draws on Col 1:25–27, which contains in brief form what Paul spells out here in Eph 3; Bruce, 312. See also Perkins, 82.

550. On νοέω see BDAG 674–75.

551. On ἀπόστολος see BDAG 122–23; P. W. Barnett, "Apostle," *DPL* 45–51. On προφήτης see BDAG 890–91; C. A. Evans, "Prophet, Paul as," *DPL* 762–65.

552. Hoehner, 442–43, and Best, 307. Contra Lincoln, 179, and Thielman, 199.

553. Contra Thielman, 199.

3:1–5 Paul's Insight into the Mystery

unusual phrase "apostles and prophets" could reflect two traditions that circulated on the mission to the gentiles, one that emphasized Paul as the apostle to the gentiles and another that stressed Jesus's commissioning of the Twelve to go to the gentiles (Matt 28:19–20; Luke 24:47; Acts 1:8).[554] Paul uses the pronoun "his" (God's) to describe the apostles and prophets, but typically he speaks of "*us* apostles" (1 Cor 4:9), a fact that some point to as evidence that Paul is not the epistle's author.[555]

A question arises around the conjunction "as" that separates the two halves of Eph 3:5. Does this conjunction suggest that the era of the Israelites partially understood the revelation, but now with Christ's coming, the revealing is complete?[556] Or is Paul drawing a sharp line between the past, which had no understanding, and the present, which enjoys the revealing of the mystery?[557] The latter conclusion fits with Paul's comments in 3:9, that the mystery was hidden in ages past (see Rom 16:25–26; Col 1:26). Moreover, while the theme of gentile inclusion is found throughout Second Temple literature, Paul's emphasis on the equal status of gentiles with Jews in the community is not obvious in these works, nor in the Old Testament itself.[558]

Paul speaks of the Holy Spirit's work in the revealing of mystery. Throughout Ephesians, the Spirit is active with the Father and the Son in effecting the salvation plan. Earlier Paul indicated the Spirit seals believers (1:13), and below he prays that the Spirit will give believers' strength for their lives now (3:16). This same Spirit is the basis of their unity and evidence of the sure promise of inheritance in God (4:3–4). The Spirit works *now* in providing access to the Father of both Jew and gentile in Christ (2:18).[559] Paul fills out this marvelous unveiling of God's mystery in Christ in the following verse, that gentiles are coheirs with Jews in Christ, as together they share in God's promised redemption.[560]

---

554. Lincoln, 180, concludes: "Ephesians is unconcerned about this actual historical process and is content to attribute original revelation on this to those other apostles and prophets as well as Paul."

555. Perkins, 83.

556. Eadie, 217.

557. Lincoln, 177–78; Barth, 334.

558. Thielman, 198. Perkins, 82, describes the apocalyptic genre that flourished in Second Temple Judaism, noting that the seer typically has a vision and is given an interpretation (Dan 10:1), or the vision is sealed until a later revelation reveals its meaning (Dan 12:9).

559. Fee, *Paul, the Spirit, and the People of God*, 61, writes: "Thus the Spirit for Paul is the key to the *present fulfillment* of the *eschatological* inclusion of the Gentiles in the people of God."

560. On ἀποκαλύπτω see BDAG 112.

b. Mystery of Gentile Participation in Christ (3:6-7)

⁶*This mystery is that through the gospel the Gentiles are heirs together with Israel, members together of one body, and sharers together in the promise in Christ Jesus.*

⁷*I became a servant of this gospel by the gift of God's grace given me through the working of his power.*

6 Paul continues his discussion of the mystery by focusing on the gentiles' place in Christ's redemption. It is "through the gospel" that gentiles share together with Jews the inheritance of and fellowship with God. Paul refers to the gentiles' non-Jewish heritage; however, in 4:17 he addresses their pagan background, enjoining the Ephesians not to live as do "the gentiles." Paul can distinguish the redeemed gentile from the unredeemed, who still live in the bleak space of hopelessness (2:12). Later in the letter, Paul uses the adjective "sharers together" as he exhorts the Ephesians not to return to this desolate place, nor to have any fellowship or partnership with those who reside there (5:7).

The three adjectives that describe gentile believers deserve a closer look. The first refers to the gentiles as "heirs together" with Jews who believe in Christ, identified here by Paul as "Israel."[561] Throughout the letter, Paul stresses the believers' inheritance in Christ (1:11), as believers are sealed by the Holy Spirit who guarantees believers' inheritance (1:14). Paul prays that the Ephesians would grasp the riches of such a glorious inheritance (1:18). Later he will warn that those who are immoral or greedy (which amounts to idolatry) will fail to inherit the kingdom of Christ and of God (5:5). The image of inheritance fits naturally with the wider metaphor of family and household that Paul developed in Eph 2. Christ's reconciling work on the cross creates new, forgiven members of God's family. Paul uses the same term in Rom 8:17 as he argues that believers are "coheirs" with Christ (see also Heb 11:9; 1 Pet 3:7). A further parallel with Ephesians is the adoption language found in Romans and earlier in Eph 1:5 (Rom 8:15; 9:4; see also Gal 4:5). Paul proclaims to the Romans that those who are in the Spirit of God are adopted as children of God. From this position of adoption, Paul speaks about being an heir of God and a coheir of Christ, God's Son.

The second term, "members together of one body," is unique to the New Testament and is not found in outside literature.[562] However, the root "body" without the prefix is used extensively by Paul. Paul declares that the church is Christ's body (1:23) and that this body has the distinctive characteristic of

---

561. On συγκληρονόμος see BDAG 952.
562. On σύσσωμος see BDAG 978.

3:6–7 MYSTERY OF GENTILE PARTICIPATION IN CHRIST

incorporating Jew and gentile together (3:6). Implied is the sense that neither group assimilates the other, but both are drawn up into Christ.

After asserting that gentiles are coheirs and members of the same body, Paul includes his third predicate adjective, "sharers together."[563] He follows with the phrase "the promise." In this, Paul insists that gentiles share equally in the need for reconciliation and redemption with their Jewish compatriots. The term is found only here and in 5:7; and in 5:7 Paul speaks of joining with those who are disobedient and will not inherit the kingdom of God. The same noun, but without the prefix, carries the sense of a business partner (Luke 5:7) or fellow believers (Heb 3:1, 14; 12:8; see also 6:4).

Paul emphasizes the church as Christ's body, with gentiles as members together with believing Jews. The metaphor of the church as Christ's body has become commonplace, such that its radical implications might be missed. Paul stresses the intimacy between Christ and his followers, and among his followers. The mysterious union of all believers, and believers in Christ, is likened to the marriage union of husband and wife that results in "one flesh" (Eph 5:30). The Ephesians would also have heard in this metaphor the overturning of a traditional argument about social unity and political cohesion. Paul promotes Jew and gentile as having the same social value within the body, thereby upending the social assumption that the body is hierarchically composed. Paul's congregation would not be surprised at his emphasis on unity of the group. However, they would have been amazed that unity could be achieved in the Spirit and not by imposing a social hierarchy.

7 Paul concludes his thought, if not the sentence, that he began in 3:2. Paul declares that he has become a servant of the gospel of Christ. The divine passive voice highlights that Paul did not choose such a lofty position, but rather God has called and equipped him. Paul is a *diakonos* of this gospel, a minister or deacon.[564] The image of "servant" suggests both a call of God upon the believer and a royal mission undertaken on behalf of God. Paul will use the feminine noun *diakonia* as he encourages the Ephesians to do works of "service" that build up the body of Christ (4:12). Paul speaks of Christ as becoming a servant to the Jews so that God's promises to the patriarchs might be confirmed (Rom 15:8). To the Colossians, Paul speaks of himself as a servant of the hope of the gospel that they heard (1:23). He continues that he is a servant according to the *oikonomia* of God given to him (1:25), with language that echoes our passage (see also 1 Cor 3:5; 2 Cor 3:6).

---

563. On συμμέτοχος see BDAG 958.
564. On διάκονος see BDAG 230 (1); C. G. Kruse, "Servant, Service," *DPL* 869–71. Thielman, 206, explains: "Paul frequently uses this and the closely related words διακονέω and διακονία to refer to his special work of urging people to be reconciled to God through faith in Christ."

Paul continues that he is a minister according to "the gift of God's grace." The feminine noun "gift" (*dōrea*) is used in 4:7, and the neuter noun "gift" (*dōron*) is found in 2:8. The root *dōr-* shares a similar meaning with the root *char-*, from which we get *charis* or "grace."[565] In Paul's day, "gift" and "grace" were linked semantically and in social conventions. The recipient of a gift was expected to be worthy of it. One's worth was determined by one's wealth, social standing, or ethnic background. A suitable recipient would use the gift wisely, thus demonstrating the wisdom and generosity of the gift giver. Paul's readers would expect that God gave this gift to Paul because he was in some way worthy or would become worthy. Paul turns such expectations upside down and inside out, as he highlights his own unworthiness of this gift (3:8) and emphasizes God's power to make his gift effective in Paul's ministry.[566] What is true of Paul is true of all believers. Their worth is not based on the standards of this world (wealth, social position, cultural influence), but according to the membership in God's family that they now enjoy through Christ.[567] There is no obvious reason why God should include the gentiles in his family, why they should be coheirs and sharers in the promise. Christ's redemption of gentiles *as gentiles* created a new family, together with Jewish believers sharing God's inheritance.

Paul qualifies the gift as "of grace," and this phrase likely defines the gift. This grace was given to Paul by God in his call to be an apostle to the gentiles. Paul further explains this giving as a manifestation of God's power.[568] Paul elsewhere speaks of God's strength and power working in his weakness (Rom 15:19; 2 Cor 4:7; 6:7; 12:9; Col 1:29). God tasked Paul with preaching the gospel of reconciliation. God's plan itself and Paul's stewardship of his part express God's grace. And the grace continues, for it is God who equips Paul. The circle is complete—God establishes the salvation plan and Paul's specific role of service in it, then gives this administration to Paul, and finally empowers Paul to accomplish that which God desires.

c. Paul's Suffering for Gentiles' Glory (3:8–13)

⁸*Although I am less than the least of all the Lord's people, this grace was given me: to preach to the Gentiles the boundless riches of Christ, ⁹and to make plain to everyone the administration of this mystery, which for ages past was*

---

565. Using language of "gift" found in our passage, Paul argues in Rom 5:15–17 that Christ's work as the "new Adam" is far more powerful than the sin of the "old Adam," which infected humanity.
566. Best, 315, writes: "When God gives he is not simply conferring a benefit; the gift entails also a particular duty."
567. For a detailed discussion of these ideas, see Barclay, *Paul and the Gift*, 494–96.
568. On δύναμις see BDAG 262–63.

kept hidden in God, who created all things. ¹⁰*His intent was that now, through the church, the manifold wisdom of God should be made known to the rulers and authorities in the heavenly realms,* ¹¹*according to his eternal purpose that he accomplished in Christ Jesus our Lord.* ¹²*In him and through faith in him we may approach God with freedom and confidence.* ¹³*I ask you, therefore, not to be discouraged because of my sufferings for you, which are your glory.*

Ephesians 3:8–9 in the digression raises the question of purpose: why did Paul exclaim here that he is the least of the saints? Is this a parenthetical thought?[569] Or does 3:8 begin a new sentence that continues through 3:12, a sentence that expresses an additional thought about Paul's role in God's plan?[570] The answer likely lies with an understanding of the rhetorical structure of Paul's argument. Throughout this digression, Paul insists on his role as preacher of the gospel to the gentiles and describes this from several angles. Paul declares (1) that God gave this task to him, (2) that he has insight from God about the message, and (3) that he stands with other holy apostles and prophets in declaring this message of salvation.

The two halves of the digression look at two different aspects of the message, as throughout the entire passage Paul is the humble servant of God, who is imprisoned for the sake of Christ and whose imprisonment is the gentiles' glory. In 3:2–7 Paul describes the content of the gospel message, focusing on the impact of the gospel for gentiles, namely, that they are coheirs with Jews who have faith in Christ. Paul is a servant of Christ, and his fellow Jews have been under the care of the one true God; however, the same cannot be said of the gentiles, who were without God and without hope (2:11–13). They were under the ruler of the kingdom of the air (2:1–2). Yet now, Paul indicates that these same gentiles are in Christ, part of a new people, and no longer bound to the spiritual forces of this age.

In 3:8–13 Paul summarizes the result of such a message on the powers and authorities who have governed gentiles and who continue to rule the pagan gentiles. Paul begins a new sentence with this verse, having concluded in 3:7 his claim that he is a servant of God, who has been given a gift of grace. The language "of God's grace given to me" is a verbatim repetition of his statement in 3:2, tying together that sentence. Here in 3:8 Paul uses "gift" as a synonym for *oikonomia* or administration/plan of God's redemptive work in Christ. Through the use of three infinitives—"to preach," "to make plain," and "to not be discouraged"—Paul begins to develop the tasks he has undertaken with God's strength, which result in the gentiles' receiving of the gospel.

569. Hoehner, 452.
570. Arnold, 181.

8 Paul begins this verse with a personal pronoun in the emphatic position; "I myself" is the force of the grammar. He further describes himself with an adjective, "less than the least," and identifies the comparison group as "the Lord's people." The comparative form of "least" is used here as a superlative.[571] Paul identifies himself to the Corinthians using the same adjective. Speaking of those to whom Christ appeared in his resurrected state, Paul announces that Christ also appeared to him, "the least of the apostles" (1 Cor 15:9).[572] Paul presents himself as a servant, as a prisoner, and now as least among the congregation. The admission here is unlikely to have been composed by a pseudepigraphic admirer of Paul, but instead supports the claim that Paul is the epistle's author.[573] This is no effort at false humility, but rather is descriptive of his calling and his actual situation. Furthermore, he might be drawing on "the rhetorical requirements of self-praise."[574] He really is chained, under house arrest, and restricted in his movements. He really did seek to destroy the church and now experiences God's grace. He really is a servant of the Lord—this is a common label that church leaders used, acknowledging that their master is the Lord (Rom 1:1; Gal 1:10; Phil 1:1; Jas 1:1; 2 Pet 1:1; Jude 1). And finally, "least of all" is a reference to his actions before Jesus called him on the road to Damascus, the time when Paul was determined to stamp out the "the Way," as Jesus's followers were known (Acts 9:2; Gal 1:13). We should not read Paul's specific identity claims in the abstract, as though Paul speaks for all believers "imprisoned" in their sin or as though Paul merely sets a good example of humility that all should follow. To make this interpretive move eviscerates Paul's testimony.[575]

"This grace" serves as the subject of this sentence, and the main verb is "to give" with God as the implied agent who gives this grace to Paul. Paul declares that this grace is shown in God's call to Paul to preach to the gentiles. Paul uses the infinitive "to preach" here, and in 3:9 he will use another infinitive, "to make plain." Both highlight the purpose of God's gift. Paul describes the content of his preaching as "the boundless riches of Christ." Paul speaks about the riches of grace that are ours through Christ's blood (1:7) and the

---

571. On ἐλάχιστος see BDAG 314.

572. Best, 317, rejects Pauline authorship, but adds: "In the light of 1 Cor 15.9 there can be no possible psychological objection to his penning Eph 3.8."

573. Muddiman, 157, observes that if one assumes the letter to be pseudepigraphic and written by an admirer of Paul, then one cannot logically explain this comment as false modesty. He concludes: "For only a genuine speaker can strictly be guilty of false modesty." See also Bruce, 53.

574. Perkins, 84.

575. Thielman, 194, observes: "With Paul specifically, God's grace is evident in his use of a former persecutor of the church . . . to preach the good news that the Gentiles are now included among God's people."

3:8–13 Paul's Suffering for Gentiles' Glory

riches of our glorious inheritance (1:18). God shows the surpassing riches of his grace in the coming ages (2:7) and makes available these glorious riches to strengthen believers (3:16). The rare adjective, "boundless," describing riches, is not found outside biblical texts. The adjective expresses the idea of something beyond searchable.[576] The book of Job describes God's ways as unsearchable (5:9; 9:10), a refrain also found in one of Paul's doxologies (Rom 11:33).

9 Paul declares that God's grace given to him has made him a servant. As a servant, he is to preach Christ's surpassing riches (3:8). Paul continues this thought in 3:9 with a conjunction "and" plus the infinitive "to make plain" (see also 1:18), indicating his role in illuminating God's now revealed plan.[577] Following this infinitive in many manuscripts is the masculine adjective "all" or "everyone."[578] Paul is likely not referring to the gentiles of the previous verse as the term "gentiles" is a neuter noun. More likely, Paul speaks of the saints mentioned in the previous clause.[579] The content that Paul illuminates is the plan (*oikonomia*) of the mystery, repeating the term used in 3:2. In the earlier verse, Paul emphasized his own part as a steward of the mystery. In 3:9 he focuses on God's strategy that centers on the unveiling of the mystery that gentiles with Jews are coheirs in Christ (3:6).

Following his statement that the mystery is made known, Paul explains where the mystery was hidden. Paul does not say that God hid the mystery, but that the mystery was "hidden in God" from the beginning of the ages. The phrase "for ages past" is found in one other place in the New Testament, Col 1:26. This passage (Col 1:25–27) has numerous connections with our current set of verses, including references to Paul becoming God's servant according to God's plan and to the mystery hidden in ages past, now revealed to his people. The term "ages past" likely caries a temporal emphasis.[580] There is little to link this with the rulers and authorities in the next verse. Readers may

---

576. On ἀνεξιχνίαστος see BDAG 77. See also Arnold, 194, and Muddiman, 158.

577. Lincoln, 184.

578. Thielman, 223, and Larkin, 54, support its inclusion. The adjective πάντας is found in most manuscripts but is absent in codices Sinaiticus (א) and Alexandrinus (A) and a few early witnesses. Larkin explains that the inclusion is most likely original, as it "is well attested and is also difficult" (54). The inclusion of "all" aligns with its use in Col 1:28.

579. Πᾶς follows the infinitive in an unemphatic position, unlike the previous clause where the phrase "to the gentiles" was in the emphatic position, preceding the verb. Perkins, 84, points to parallels with the Dead Sea Scrolls: "Comparison with Essene language indicates that 'all' stands in place of its designation of those illuminated through the Teacher, 'the many.'"

580. On αἰών see BDAG 32 (1). Arnold, 196, states that "nowhere else in his writings does Paul use this term as part of his vocabulary for demonic powers." He adds that Col 1:26–27 supports a temporal reading. See also Perkins, 86.

recall Eph 1:4–10, where Paul underscores God's magnificent salvation plan established in Christ before the foundations of the world. The completion of this plan is the unity of all things under Christ. The echo of these verses reverberates here, as Paul points to God, who created all things. Paul brings into view the cosmic aspect of God's plan and, in the next verse, highlights the powers and rulers in the heavens. His attention turns from his own place in the redemption plan to the plan itself. In the following three verses, Paul expounds on God's eternal purpose accomplished in Christ, to reconcile by faith both Jew and gentile, that all might have access to God by his grace.

10 Paul explains that the rulers and authorities in the heavenly realms will see God's wisdom demonstrated through the church. Paul adds the adverb "now," making a contrast with the previous verse's emphasis on the past ages. The passive voice of the verb "to make known" emphasizes God's action in establishing the church. The church's existence, through the work of God the Father in Christ and sealed with the Holy Spirit, demonstrates God's wisdom (1:3–14). The recipients of this wisdom are the rulers and authorities in the heavens. Paul does not suggest that God created the church and then that the church should make known God's wisdom to the principalities.[581] In this case, the church plays a passive role. Later, however, Paul insists that the church put on the armor of God to stand firm against the rulers of this dark age (6:12–13).

Paul describes God's wisdom with an adjective not found elsewhere in the New Testament, which emphasizes great variety and diversity.[582] Paul emphasizes God's sagacity and knowledge here, which is distinct from the personified figure of Wisdom that we meet in Prov 8:27–30. God's wisdom is infinitely greater than human wisdom or the figure of Wisdom from the Proverbs, and God establishes the church as evidence of this wisdom. Paul writes an extensive discussion about God's wisdom to the Corinthians. Contrasting the foolishness that passes for wisdom in this world, God's wisdom is evidenced in the cross of Christ, and Christ has become for believers the wisdom of God (1 Cor 1:30). The rulers of this age know nothing of this wisdom, nor do they understand it. Paul declares that this wisdom is a mystery, hidden until now, and prepared by God for believers' glory (2:6–8). The language of our Ephesians passage echoes these notes to the Corinthians. Using

---

581. Contra Wink, *Naming the Powers*, 89, who concludes that the church preaches to the powers. Arnold, 197, notes that God "is thus revealing his plan, and the outworking of this plan is a witness to the powers." Contra Schüssler Fiorenza, 43, who argues that the church's task is to proclaim Divine Wisdom to the powers.

582. On πολυποίκιλος see BDAG 847. Arnold, 197, explains that the term carries the meaning of rich variety, as in a beautiful, multicolored garment; the *hapax legomenon* connects two common adjectives: πολύς ("much") and ποικίλος ("manifold").

3:8–13 PAUL'S SUFFERING FOR GENTILES' GLORY

language found in our passage, Paul raises his voice in a song of praise: "Oh, the depth of the riches of the wisdom and knowledge of God!" (Rom 11:33).

Unfortunately, at times, the church has assumed a triumphal posture based on a misapprehension that it possesses such power and wisdom in itself. When Paul penned this epistle, however, the followers of Jesus were a small group with no political prestige or social clout. Indeed, Paul himself writes this while in chains.[583] Acknowledging the wisdom of God in and through the church should lead the church not to a posture of arrogance, but to one of humility.

Why does Paul emphasize God's wisdom here?[584] It may be to address a social assumption about gift giving and grace. In Paul's time, when resources were scarce, a wise leader or benefactor gave resources to those who would use them wisely and productively. Foolish patrons tossed their wealth about indiscriminately, thereby appearing shameless and frivolous.[585] Paul might be anticipating a question about God's great gift of Christ given to such unworthy subjects such as himself, a man who once tried to destroy Christ's church, and to gentiles, who denied the true God. Or Paul might be countering an unspoken worry that the gift of grace was not so special at all, for it was flung about with no forethought as to the worthiness of the recipients. Paul's answer to both misperceptions points to God's wisdom, a mystery to those operating with the world's calculus.

Who are the "rulers and authorities" in the heavens to whom God's wisdom is made known? Earlier in the letter Paul spoke in a neutral or mildly pessimistic way concerning rulers and authorities in the heavens (1:21), but he turns negative as he describes the ruler of the kingdom of the air, who works in those who reject God (2:2; see also 1 Cor 2:6–8). The existence of this false prince underpins Paul's urgent command that the Ephesians put on God's armor to defend against these rulers and authorities (Eph 6:12). In Eph 3, these rulers likely represent the entire spiritual realm, both good and bad.[586] Walter Wink argues that these rulers are best understood as superhuman forces that

---

583. Perkins, 87: "Depiction of the church as heavenly reality, not as a human institution, should not be taken as triumphalism since its truth is a mystery of God's plan known to the elect, not an expansionist socio-political program."

584. Schüssler Fiorenza, 38, discusses the "Wisdom of G*d, which manifests Herself in a great variety of forms and colors" by exploring "the figure of Divine Wisdom ... [and] its roots in Jewish-Hellenistic Wisdom the*logy, which was articulated in interaction with widespread Isis worship."

585. For a discussion of this issue, see Barclay, *Paul and the Gift*, 475, 555.

586. Bruce, 321, writes: "All created intelligences are in view here." Perkins, 85, concludes that "there is no reason to treat the 'aeons' and 'powers' in verse 10 ... as mythological, hostile powers actively seeking to prevent souls from reaching heavenly regions as in Gnostic accounts of salvation (*pace* Schlier 1957)."

grow from human institutions and power structures.[587] Elisabeth Schüssler Fiorenza refines her argument by identifying the domination as kyriarchy, drawing on the Greek term *kyrios*, which means lord, Lord, or master and can refer to husband and father. Kyriarchy describes exploitation of "gender . . . , race, class, ethnicity, imperialism and age."[588] Both Wink and Schüssler Fiorenza rightly point to the necessity of speaking and acting against racism, sexism, jingoism, and the like. And they recognize that large corporations and governments can take on a life of their own, developing a destructive culture that seems more than the sum of its individual members. However, simply to conflate institutions with the powers that Paul speaks about here fails to take full account of Paul's description of the powers as part of the spiritual realm.[589]

11–12 Paul elaborates that God demonstrates his purpose in making known his wisdom. Paul describes this purpose as "eternal." This echoes from earlier in the epistle when Paul explained that believers are chosen in Christ, according to God's design, and are established in accordance with his purposes (1:11). Paul continues that God accomplished his plan in "Christ Jesus our Lord." Paul uses both his earthly name "Jesus" and his title "Messiah/Christ," which suggests that Paul envisions Christ's accomplished work on the cross. Moreover, in the next verse, Paul applies a ramification of the accomplished purpose, namely, that Christ's work provides free and full access to the God of grace.

Paul begins 3:12 with the prepositional phrase "in whom," referring to Christ Jesus our Lord mentioned in the previous verse. Paul explains that this access to God occurs "in him," that is, Jesus Christ our Lord.[590] Such exclusivism might sound triumphant, but Paul and his tiny congregations had no social or political power from which to impose their belief on others. Paul lists two things that "we" believers have in Christ Jesus. First, Paul indicates that believers have boldness or freedom. He uses the same noun in his request for prayer at the end of this letter, that he might have boldness of speech in making known the mystery of the gospel (6:19).[591] Second, Paul declares that believers may approach God. While the noun "God" is not found in the Greek text, it is implied. The phrase "we may approach" translates the noun "access," which is used in the previous chapter as Paul states that believers are now one

---

587. Wink, *Naming the Powers*, 109–10.

588. Schüssler Fiorenza, xlviiin9.

589. Gombis, *Drama of Ephesians*, 117, stresses: "The powers have ordered the present evil age in such a way as to exacerbate the divisions within humanity (Eph 2:11–12). God confounds them by creating in Christ one unified, multiracial body consisting of formerly divided groups of people."

590. Perkins, 87, explains: "Therefore, anyone who does not respond to the gospel and become one with Christ has no hope of salvation."

591. On παρρησία see BDAG 781 (3).

new humanity in Christ and in the one Spirit have access to God (2:18; see also Rom 5:2).[592] The two nouns, "boldness" and "access," used together here, form a single thought, a figure of speech known as a hendiadys. Paul declares that believers may access God freely, frankly, openly, candidly.[593] Paul adds that such bold access to God is done with "confidence."[594] The self-assured access is one dimension of the riches of Christ (3:8).

Paul declares that "through faith in him" believers may approach God. This phrase in Greek can also be translated "through his [Christ's] faithfulness." This prepositional phrase begins with "through," and Paul uses this preposition in 2:16 to speak of the cross as that through which God reconciles humanity to each other and to himself. Following the preposition is the definite article "the," which plays an important role in the wider debate about how to translate the remaining noun and pronoun "faith of/in Christ [him]." Both translations reflect aspects of the gospel, for believers trust God's salvation plan in Christ, and Christ the Son faithfully accomplished the work of his Father. The question is not likely to be solved through grammar, but rather through exegetical decisions.[595]

EXCURSUS: "FAITH IN CHRIST" OR "THE FAITHFULNESS OF CHRIST"

We have this access to God, Paul declares, *dia tēs pisteōs autou* (3:12).[596] The primary interpretative issue centers on the genitive pronoun "his" or "in him," specifically whether to translate the phrase "through [our] faith in Christ" (objective genitive)[597] or "through the faithfulness of Christ" (subjective genitive).[598] The article is used in 3:12,[599] and this construction is found both in Rom 3:3, which speaks of God's faithfulness, and in 4:12, which refers to Abra-

---

592. On προσαγωγή see BDAG 876.

593. Arnold, 198, makes the point that such candidness was a quality of ancient Greek democracy, as the citizens could speak freely in the assembly. I mention that only elite males were citizens.

594. On πεποίθησις see BDAG 796.

595. J. H. Moulton, *A Grammar of New Testament Greek*, vol. 1: *Prolegomena* (Edinburgh: T&T Clark, 1908), 72, writes: "It is well to remember that in Greek [the] question is entirely one of exegesis, not of grammar."

596. Διὰ τῆς πίστεως αὐτοῦ.

597. The objective genitive is advocated by Arnold, 199; Best, 226, 330; Hoehner, 466–67; Larkin, 57; Lincoln, 190–91; MacDonald, 267.

598. The subjective genitive is advocated by Wallace, *Greek Grammar*, 115–17.

599. In six passages (Rom 3:22, 26; Gal 2:16, 20; 3:22; Phil 3:9), Paul uses this phrase

ham's faithfulness.[600] The grammar of these two verses suggest that in Eph 3:12 Paul emphasizes the faithfulness of Christ that achieved salvation. Paul Foster concludes: "In this context a subjective rendering of διὰ τῆς πίστεως αὐτοῦ most satisfactorily coheres with the overarching train of thought that the new administration . . . is inaugurated and revealed through Christ."[601] Foster's argument need not devalue a believer's faith or trust in God's salvation plan. The apostle addresses the believer's faith or trust in God's salvation plan at the beginning of 3:12 with the prepositional phrase "in whom," namely, in Christ. The believers participate in Christ's life, accepting God's call to live worthy of this calling (4:1, 4).

Elsewhere in Paul, the phrase *pistis Christou*[602] is contrasted with "works of the law"[603] in the context of discussions about the righteousness of God (Rom 3:22, 26; Gal 2:16, 20; 3:22; Phil 3:9).[604] The noun is anarthrous in all these verses (but carries the definite article in Eph 3:12). Barry Matlock argues for the objective genitive in these six verses and critiques the subjective genitive reading by arguing that proponents of the objective genitive wish to convey that Christ was "faithful unto death."[605] They are not interpreting the phrase with reference to "Christ's faith or believing."[606] John Barclay picks up this thread, explaining that "the concern with questions of agency which motivates the work of J. Louis Martyn, and lies behind many

---

without the article, and the majority view is that these occurrences are best translated as an objective genitive: "faith in Christ."

600. Rom 3:3: τὴν πίστιν τοῦ θεοῦ; and Rom 4:12: πίστεως τοῦ Ἀβραάμ.

601. Paul Foster, "The First Contribution to the Πίστις Χριστοῦ Debate: A Study of Ephesians 3:12," *Journal for the Study of the New Testament* 85 (2002): 75–96.

602. Διὰ πίστεως Ἰησοῦ Χριστοῦ (Rom 3:22; Gal 2:16); ἐκ πίστεως Ἰησοῦ (Rom 3:26); ἐκ πίστεως Χριστοῦ (Gal 2:16); ἐκ πίστεως Ἰησοῦ Χριστοῦ (Gal 3:22); ἐν πίστει (Gal 2:20); διὰ πίστεως Χριστοῦ (Phil 3:9).

603. Matlock, "Detheologizing the ΠΙΣΤΙΣ ΧΡΙΣΤΟΥ Debate," 21, asks "why the πίστις Χριστοῦ formulations only occur in contexts where 'works of law' and 'faith in Christ' are set in antithesis."

604. For an excellent discussion of the issues, see Michael F. Bird and Preston M. Sprinkle, eds., *The Faith of Jesus Christ: Exegetical, Biblical, and Theological Studies* (Peabody, MA: Hendrickson, 2009). See also Richard B. Hays, *The Faith of Jesus Christ: An Investigation of the Narrative Substructure of Galatians 3:1–4:11*, Society of Biblical Literature Dissertation Series 56 (Chico, CA: Scholars Press, 1983); 2nd ed. *The Faith of Christ: The Narrative Substructure of Galatians 3:1–4:11*, Biblical Resource 56 (Grand Rapids: Eerdmans, 2002).

605. Matlock, "Detheologizing the ΠΙΣΤΙΣ ΧΡΙΣΤΟΥ Debate," 11. He concludes that the objective genitive is the stronger reading, but its sense is not to separate Christ from justification, for such issues evolve later in church tradition (22–23).

606. Kenneth Schenck, "2 Corinthians and the Πίστις Χριστοῦ Debate," *Catholic Biblical Quarterly* 70 (2008): 524–37, examines 2 Cor 4:13 and the quotation of Ps 115:1, suggesting that Paul believes Jesus is the one who believes, and thus Paul uses the Scripture to argue that just as Christ believes, so too we imitate him in our belief.

of the arguments for the 'subjective genitive' interpretation of *pistis Christou* (as 'the faithfulness of Christ'), seems fully comprehensible as a reaction against contemporary forms of Christian moralism and gospel-less activism. But it is liable to overload Paul's discourse and his theology of grace with additional dimensions and perfections beyond the horizon or the interests of Paul himself."[607] Barclay translates *pistis Christou* as "Christ-faith" in Gal 5:6, suggesting that believers experience the reality of the faith, the gospel, through their orientation toward this singular moment of God's redemptive history, namely, the death and resurrection of Jesus Christ.

The definition of "faith" (*pistis*) in the ancient world includes such characteristics as (1) proof, assurance, trust in others; (2) trustworthiness; (3) loyalty, promise kept; and (4) piety or a body of belief.[608] The cognate verb conveys the sense of a person's trustworthiness and the action of believing that something is true or trustworthy. First-century Jewish writers Josephus and Philo express that "one gives signs *of* faithfulness, but entrusts valuable things *to* the faithful."[609] The term "truth" (*alētheia*) refers to evidence that is trustworthy or reliable. It seems to me that those who argue for objective genitive translations desire to defend the notion of "free" grace for the believer. Barclay's work on gift and grace in Paul argues that "free" or "pure" grace still obligates the believer who receives this gift of salvation to live rightly. Those persuaded by the subjective genitive argument often emphasize that Christ's riches make possible our salvation and his redemption brings about the unity of the cosmos. In this case, the recipient of such a magnanimous gift would expect to be in a relationship with the gift giver. The subjective genitive option, therefore, needs to include recognition of the "in Christ" language so prevalent in Paul's material.

---

13 With this verse, we come to the close of Paul's digression begun in 3:1. Throughout these thirteen verses, Paul emphasizes his role in God's salvation plan and spotlights the mystery now revealed, the gospel that makes gentiles coheirs with Jews through Christ. Paul began this digression by remarking

---

607. Barclay, "Pure Grace?," 15. See also Barclay, "Paul, the Gift and the Battle," 55. Analyzing Galatians, Barclay continues that "Christ-faith" (πίστις Χριστοῦ), which is described here as "faith working through love" (5:6), is also a regulative schema for life in the world" (42).

608. Matlock, "Detheologizing the ΠΙΣΤΙΣ ΧΡΙΣΤΟΥ Debate," 6–10, offers a helpful summary of the definitions found in the major lexicons, such as BDAG, L&N, and LSJ.

609. Douglas Campbell, *The Quest for Paul's Gospel: A Suggested Strategy* (London: T&T Clark, 2005), 179.

that he is in chains for Christ, and he will close by mentioning his afflictions.[610] Paul explains his apostleship without using that specific term; instead, he speaks of his *oikonomia*, that responsibility to preach the gospel as a special grace from God (3:2). Paul describes himself as a servant because of God's grace and power, not by his own initiative (3:7). And Paul declares that he has insight into the mystery, he and the prophets and apostles who received revelation by the Spirit (3:5). The mystery demonstrates God's wisdom to the rulers in the heavens, and this wisdom is expressed by creation of the church, made up of gentiles and Jews as coheirs in Christ (3:6).

Paul begins 3:13 with a conjunction, "therefore," that draws an inference from the preceding verses. He stressed in 3:1 that he sits imprisoned on behalf of his gentile congregation, and he uses the same phrase, "for you," in 3:13, indicating that his focus directly relates to the situation of these gentile believers. The verb "to ask" follows here in the middle voice, commonly used in Paul's day between people making requests to each other. The active voice is often used as humans make requests to God. While the grammar allows for this alternative reading, namely, that Paul asks God that he, Paul, would not be discouraged about his imprisonment,[611] such an interpretation works against the points Paul makes in the previous verses. The gospel message of the gentile inclusion into God's family through Christ draws the Ephesians into the center of the story. Therefore, it is important that they not forget their part in God's cosmic drama nor feel defeated when their champion is in chains. Paul requests that they not become discouraged or lose heart because of his afflictions.

The final clause of this passage begins with a pronoun, "which," denoting Paul's afflictions and imprisonment.[612] These afflictions are for the Ephesians, but do not carry the salvific qualities that pertain to Christ's afflictions on the cross. Rather, Paul speaks of the trials that accompany life in this present age. He makes a similar comment to the Colossians, that he is filling up what was lacking in Christ's afflictions for the sake of the church, his body (Col 1:24; see also 2 Tim 2:10). Paul recognizes that participating in Christ's suffering deepens his knowledge of Christ (Phil 3:10–12).[613]

---

610. On θλῖψις see BDAG 457 (1).

611. Larkin, 57, explains that this option "is unlikely (contra Barth, 348), since it creates complicated syntax with a different subject for the infinitive than the supplied object for the verb," and rightly notes that Paul's prayer to God begins in the following verse.

612. Larkin, 58, explains that the singular feminine pronoun has as its antecedent the plural feminine "afflictions" but the pronoun is in the singular due to attraction to the predicate nominative "glory."

613. MacDonald, 267, offers a historical perspective based on Paul's honor culture: "Afflictions can act as external manifestations of honor, because in Pauline Christianity they have come to symbolize the promise of salvation. Suffering will be followed by

3:8–13 Paul's Suffering for Gentiles' Glory

Paul has one more thing to say about his tribulations. They are the Ephesians' "glory." These four words are explosive in their power. Paul does not say *for* your glory, but that his sufferings *are* your (gentiles') glory.[614] In this context, "glory" means honor or reputation.[615] Their reputation is based on Christ, who suffered and is raised, and they are raised with Christ (Eph 2:6). Their honor is based on being members of God's family (2:19), being a part of God's temple (2:22), and having an inheritance secured in the Holy Spirit (1:13–14; see also Rom 8:17). Paul's chains bring honor to the gentiles, as his afflictions reveal the gospel truth that gentiles are sharers in the promise through Christ. The Romans would hardly imprison Paul for preaching about a Jewish Messiah to Jews, but his claims about Messiah Jesus, that his death and resurrection are on behalf of all people, strike at the heart of the pagan empire. Before the rulers and authorities in the heavens, these gentiles in Christ stand as testimony to God's wisdom.

Paul describes his sufferings, his imprisonment, as part of the grace-filled plan of God. This jarring claim highlights the paradox of the gospel in at least two ways. First, the suffering and death of Christ proves the worth of the prize—life eternal with God. This is no "cheap" grace.[616] Second, Paul's chains reveal the paradox of God's justice. To the casual observer, God could be charged with being unfair in giving grace to those who are unworthy, such as the gentiles who are far from him. God's wisdom, however, is deeper than human understanding. Where is justice? It is taken up in love, but it will also cost each person their life as well. Each believer is made something new, and they become part of a new community in Christ. No believer can claim that their heritage, culture, language, social status, or wealth (or lack of it) gives them special advantage within the church. This new community is entered through death, both Christ's literal death and the death of one's own social and cultural privilege. God's justice is seen in the one, new humanity created by Christ's redemption.

---

glory." Schüssler Fiorenza, 44, offers an important pastoral warning against using this verse to justify domestic violence: "This text ... is potentially life-threatening when, for example, battered wo/men are told that their sufferings, like Paul's, will also lead to glory."

614. The pronoun "your" (ὑμῶν) has stronger manuscript support, but the variant "our" (ἡμῶν), is found in some early sources, especially from the Alexandrian tradition; see Thielman, 223.

615. Perkins, 86, comments that "'glory' is always associated with praising God or God's gift of salvation in Ephesians (1:6, 12, 14, 17, 18; 3:16, 21)."

616. Dietrich Bonhoeffer, *The Cost of Discipleship* (New York: Touchstone, 1995; originally *Nachfolge* [Munich: Kaiser, 1937]), 43, writes: "Cheap grace means the justification of sin without the justification of the sinner."

2. Prayer to Be Established in Christ's Love (3:14–21)

Paul offers his prayer now, after digressing in the previous verses of this chapter. This is Paul's second prayer in the epistle (see 1:15–19), and he ends here with a doxology celebrating God's power to accomplish his purposes in Christ and in the church. As in his earlier appeal, Paul prays that the Ephesians will have a deeper appreciation for the character and power of God and a better understanding of God's work of redemption in Christ and by the Spirit. The prayer in Eph 1 centered on the future inheritance of the saints, based on the current reality that Christ has been raised and has defeated all heavenly powers in this age and the next. The prayer before us in Eph 3 builds on the earlier picture of redemption, and now Paul focuses on the experience of Christ's love. Paul requests that God's power be directed to the grounding and growing of the Ephesians' inner self, that God's fullness would fill them to overflowing.

The prayer consists of eighty-six words in Greek, another long sentence in Ephesians, and the doxology adds an extra thirty-seven words. The structure of the passage includes Paul's opening description of God the Father of all families, to whom he bows and prays (3:14–15). The prayer itself has three main sections all introduced by the term "that" (3:16, 18, 19). It is possible that this conjunction has two meanings within the passage. In the first clause, the term introduces the content of Paul's prayer, and the remaining two clauses express the outcome of that prayer. In this case, Paul prays for strength by the Spirit in the inner self and for Christ to dwell by faith in their hearts (3:16–17). The second and third clauses would enumerate the goals of such prayer, namely, that the Ephesians would know Christ's expansive love and be filled with God's fullness. On the other hand, one could analyze the prayer as having three main requests introduced by the term "that": that God grant them strength for Christ to dwell and be established (3:16–17), that they would have the power to understand the magnitude of Christ's love (3:18), and that they would be filled with God's fullness (3:19).[617] The second request focuses on Christ's love, with two infinitival clauses expressing Paul's desire that they grasp and know this love. The final request summarizes the prayer by using the verb "to fill" and its cognate noun, repeating the refrain of his earlier prayer (1:23). The practical difference between the two structures is minimal, for in both cases Paul's hope is the same. He desires that God strengthen believers with his fullness and the love of Christ.[618]

---

617. Arnold, 206–7; Barth, 368–77.

618. Barth, 368, discusses the two structural options. He rightly concludes that we should not expect a logical progression, for "at this point Paul's thinking follows the form of devotion and meditation rather than that of deduction, induction, careful subordination or coordination."

Paul offers his prayer to God the Father of all families; the cosmic and global reach provides an eternal perspective for the congregation. Here is the one true God, who lays claim to all peoples and who loves all peoples. To this God Paul bends his knees and asks that believers be given the strength they need to grasp the enormity of their reality in Christ. Paul offers a prayer for the Ephesians that pulls together his convictions about the power of God to bring salvation to Jew and gentile alike through Christ's work on the cross. Redemption and reconciliation are found by those far and those near, for Christ is our peace (2:14). The community of God is being built into a holy sanctuary for God in his Spirit, and each believer is seated with Christ in the heavens. This marvelous mystery has been revealed now to Paul and other apostles and prophets, about which the heavenly rulers and authorities stand in awe. This superabundant gift of grace reflects God's love demonstrated in Christ. Paul's prayer celebrates this love and asks that God would fill believers to the fullest with the surpassing love of Christ.

a. Paul Prays to the Father of All (3:14-15)

14For this reason I kneel before the Father, 15from whom every family in heaven and on earth derives its name.

14 Paul begins this verse with the same opening phrase found in 3:1, "for this reason." His repetition invites the reader to return to 3:1, wherein Paul declares that he is a prisoner for Christ. His congregations likely knew he was imprisoned, but may not have understood the connection between his apostleship, gospel message, and this imprisonment. Paul digresses for twelve verses to explain that connection. Now as he repeats "for this reason," he invites listeners and readers to recall his words at the end of Eph 2. In those verses, Paul declares that gentiles in Christ are no longer strangers or foreigners, but are full members of God's household. They make up, with believing Jews, the community of the saints or holy ones. Christ Jesus is the cornerstone of the new temple built by his work on the cross, wherein God dwells by his Spirit. Christ Jesus is our peace, the one who made this new people, reconciling Jew and gentile through his blood and destroying the enmity between them. This new people is reconciled to God together.

From this theological vantage point, Paul begins his prayer. Paul describes his posture as "kneeling."[619] He could have used the verb "to pray" or he could have indicated that he lifted hands in prayer (1 Tim 2:8) or stood in

---

619. On κάμπτω see BDAG 507. Barth, 378, observes that this is the only place in the Pauline corpus where Paul indicates that he knelt in prayer.

prayer (Luke 18:11, 13); all are typical ways of describing the act of praying in his day (Acts 7:60; 9:40; 20:36; 21:5). The posture of kneeling indicates intensity of emotion or magnification of honor. In Gethsemane, Jesus is described as falling to his knees in prayer (Luke 22:41).[620] Paul points to those ancient Israelites who did not bow their knees to Baal (Rom 11:4) as model disciples. In the Old Testament, we read of Daniel kneeling in prayer (Dan 6:10) and find Solomon kneeing as he dedicated the Temple (1 Kgs 8:54). Why might Paul use the metonymy of bending the knee? Perhaps he is echoing Isa 45:23, which declares that every knee will bow to the Lord (see Phil 2:10; Rom 14:11). The Israelite prophet declares in this chapter that there is no God but the Lord, a righteous God and Savior who calls to the ends of the earth that people turn to him and be saved.

Paul declares that he bends his knee "to the Father."[621] By using the preposition "to, toward," Paul stresses the person to whom he prays. This is God the Father, the Father of the Lord Jesus Christ (Eph 1:3), the Father of glory (1:17) who gives his people the Spirit of wisdom, who grants them an inheritance, who exerts his great power on behalf of his people (1:18–19). Elsewhere, he speaks of Abba Father (Rom 8:15; Gal 4:6) as a form of address available to Christ's followers. This usage is similar to Christ's prayer, which begins "our Father" (Matt 6:9). Here, however, Paul has a broader scope in mind when addressing God as Father, declaring that he prays to the Father of all the families in heaven and earth. Paul includes under the title "Father" all of God's creative power as the one who generated the universe and every living thing (see also Jas 1:17). He expresses a similar thought in Eph 4:6, describing God the Father with three prepositional phrases depicting God as over and through and in all things.

15 Paul uses a play on words in Greek, speaking of "families" or "peoples" with the term *patria*, which is related to *patēr* ("father").[622] Paul remarks that families derive their name from God the Father. Here Paul reflects the customs of his day wherein the family name continues through the father to

---

620. Luke 22:41 speaks of Jesus falling (τίθημι) to his knees, and the same verb and noun are used to describe Stephen's posture as he prays his final prayer (Acts 7:60). Perkins, 88, explains: "Kneeling is often the gesture of suppliants begging for a favor from a powerful or important person."

621. Larkin, 60; Barth, 380. A variant reading adds "of our Lord Jesus Christ," a common formula in other Pauline letters (2 Cor 1:3) and found in Eph 1:3. The variant is likely a gloss, as (1) the manuscript evidence is late, (2) the phrase harmonizes with 1:3, (3) it limits what is likely the scope of God's fatherhood, and (4) it disrupts the wordplay between "father" and "families" (3:15) developed in the Greek text.

622. Barth, 368, observes that in the Septuagint the noun πατριά "is never used to denote the abstract concept 'fatherhood,' but always means a specific, concrete group of people, i.e. a family, a clan, a tribe, or a nation."

3:14–15 Paul Prays to the Father of All

his child. The connotation behind the act of naming in the Old Testament is one of power, as the one who names is over that which is named (cf. Isa 40:26). Paul uses the same verb and its cognate noun in Eph 1:21 as he describes Christ raised and seated above all the powers and rulers and "every name that is invoked." Peter uses the term to refer to the blessing of Abraham and his seed (or progeny) extending to all peoples (*patria*) (Acts 3:25, citing Gen 22:18; 26:4).

The adjective "every" modifies "family," and Paul further describes this group with two prepositional phrases: "in heaven" and "upon the earth." Paul emphasizes that God is the God of all nations, all peoples, all tribes and languages, both in the past, now, and until Christ returns.[623] Paul draws this conclusion not only from Israel's prophets such as Isaiah, but also from the reality that in Christ, Jew and gentile are made one new people, reconciled to God by Christ's cross. Paul's claim that God the Father is the God of all ethnic and language groups was not a dominant view at the time, for most people believed that gods ruled over territories and those born in those territories were under the care of and were responsible to that deity.

The reference to "heaven" could mean that Paul speaks of heavenly beings, for as creator of all that is, God would be their father.[624] Yet the context is prayer for believers, and Paul's argument is that both Jews and gentiles are now included in God's household through the reconciling work of Christ (see also Col 1:20). Moreover, he will address slave owners in Eph 6:9, cautioning them that the Lord is in the heavens and shows no favoritism toward them, but rules impartially, even protectively over the poor and disadvantaged. Paul speaks of all believers as citizens of heaven (Phil 3:20), contrasting the Christian's allegiance to Christ with the world's focus on earthly power structures. Paul's mention of "heaven," then, emphasizes God's power and fatherly care over humanity, and it is to this God that Paul prays.[625]

The reference to the heavens might carry a secondary note for Paul's gentile readers, inasmuch as gentiles revered ancestors, offering libations to the deceased fathers of the clan. This form of honoring comes close to worship, at least to our modern ears. Yet it might be better to understand this practice as supporting the belief that the ancestors remained a part of the

---

623. MacDonald, 275, remarks: "The church transcends the historical realm." Contra Edgar J. Goodspeed, *The Meaning of Ephesians* (Chicago: University of Chicago Press, 1933; reprinted Eugene, OR: Wipf & Stock, 2012), 48–49, who suggests that the reference is to the local church; he adds: "We cannot prove this to have been a Mysteries term for a local group, but such groups were sometimes headed by a Father, πατήρ, and I cannot doubt that this is the meaning of the much-discussed πατριά."

624. MacDonald, 275, suggests that the reference to heavenly family is to "the company of angels."

625. Best, 339.

family even beyond the grave, and honoring their memory was the proper civic thing to do. Paul may be nuancing that view, reshaping the sense of family as that which is rooted in God the father of all.

b. Paul Prays for Christ's Love (3:16–19)

> [16] *I pray that out of his glorious riches he may strengthen you with power through his Spirit in your inner being,* [17] *so that Christ may dwell in your hearts through faith. And I pray that you, being rooted and established in love,* [18] *may have power, together with all the Lord's holy people, to grasp how wide and long and high and deep is the love of Christ,* [19] *and to know this love that surpasses knowledge—that you may be filled to the measure of all the fullness of God.*

16 Paul begins 3:16 with a conjunction that links back to the main verb in 3:14, "to bend or bow."[626] Paul signals with this conjunction that he is now providing the content of his prayer to God. He asks God the father of all families that he might give strength to the Ephesians. The grammar includes the finite verb "to give" with the infinitive direct object "to strengthen or prevail." In 3:17 we find a second infinitive "to dwell." The two infinitives could be parallel and "interdependent."[627] Yet because the infinitives are not linked by "and" and because the finite verb "to give" is far from the second infinitive, it seems better to suggest that the second phrase states the result of the believers receiving strength.[628] The third clause in 3:18–19 includes two perfect participles, "rooted" and "established." It is possible that Paul offers a third request, but more likely he describes parenthetically the believers' state as God grants them strength and Christ indwells them.

Paul uses the same verb in 3:16 ("to give") as he does in Eph 1 in his prayer that God will grant the Ephesians the Spirit of wisdom, that they might better grasp the hope of their calling (1:17). Paul stacks the noun "power" with the infinitive "to strengthen or prevail" (see also 1 Cor 16:13) to reinforce the impact of his point. God's power brings life, it makes new, it unites. Paul asks that this strength be given "out of his glorious riches." Paul stresses God's riches or wealth throughout Ephesians, including in the opening prayer that

---

626. The conjunction ἵνα is not translated in the NIV.
627. Lincoln, 206; Best, 341; Arnold, 211; and Bruce, 327, suggest that the two infinitive clauses, "to strengthen" and "to dwell," refer back to the main verb, "to grant." Thielman, 229, continues: "The second infinitive and its modifiers restate in other terms the first infinitive with its modifiers." He concludes, however, that the second infinitive phrase supplies "the result of the first infinitive phrase."
628. Hoehner, 480–81, argues that the second infinitive further describes and details the first infinitive and renders the first infinitive "to strengthen."

3:16–19 PAUL PRAYS FOR CHRIST'S LOVE

stressed the glorious wealth of his inheritance.[629] God's glory reflects who God is, rich in grace and mercy, full of love for all peoples.[630] In the opening chapter of the epistle, glory carries the sense of radiance (1:6, 12, 14), while in 3:13, 16 the emphasis is on power.[631] Earlier in 3:8 Paul speaks of Christ's abundant riches that bring redemption and reconciliation to the gentiles. In 3:13 Paul declares that his imprisonment for Christ is the Ephesians' glory. In this case, "glory" carries the sense of honor and worth and is connected to the gospel that brings the promises of reconciliation to gentiles in and through Christ. In our passage, God's glory in all its wealth comes to the fore.

Paul asks that the Ephesians receive strength at the center of their being. This strength flows from God's Spirit into the believer's inner being. From this position of power, the sort of power that comes from the cross, believers may drink from the vast reservoir of love that is theirs in Christ. Paul uses the adverb "inner" with the noun "human" to speak of the person's mind or perspective on circumstances. The parallel phrase "in your hearts" in 3:17 further explains this phrase as referring "to the basic intelligence and will of human persons."[632] He uses the phrase in Romans when he contrasts his mind's joy in God's law and the rebellion of his flesh against this same law (Rom 7:22–23). The only other place Paul uses this phrase is in describing his trials and tribulations to the Corinthians; he indicates that while his physical body is battered by afflictions, nevertheless his "inner man" is renewed (2 Cor 4:16). Given the similarities in circumstances described in 2 Corinthians and Paul's current situation as he writes this letter, it is no surprise that he draws on the phrase "inner being."[633] We should distinguish this phrase, however, from the phrase "new self" used in Eph 4:24. The new self relates to the redeemed position of believers in Christ and contrasts with the old self that did not confess Christ.

17 Paul expresses the hoped-for result of God through his Spirit granting believers strength with power, specifically, that Christ would dwell in believers' hearts. Paul includes the three persons of the Godhead in his prayer, an emphasis that permeates the epistle. Parallels with 3:16 include the two phrases "inner being" and "heart," plus the two clauses "through

---

629. On πλοῦτος see BDAG 832. Bruce, 326, observes that God's glory is "inexhaustible, and provides the measure of his generosity when he bestows his gifts."

630. On δόξα see BDAG 256–57 (1); R. B. Gaffin Jr., "Glory, Glorification," *DPL* 348–50.

631. Best, 339.

632. Perkins, 90. Best, 340, suggests that the phrase expresses "the moral and spiritual side in people."

633. Bruce, 326, rightly rejects connections with gnostic thought—"Gnostic speculation about the 'inner man' does not help us to understand Paul's use of the phrase"—arguing against Heinrich Schlier, *Christus und die Kirche im Epheserbrief*, Beiträge zur historischen Theologie 6 (Tübingen: Mohr Siebeck, 1930), 32.

the Spirit" and "through faith."⁶³⁴ Paul describes a believer's life moving to ever-increasing faithfulness.⁶³⁵ The verb "to dwell" carries the sense of settling down in an area⁶³⁶—which we might translate "take up residence,"⁶³⁷ calling to mind Paul's discussion earlier where, using the cognate noun, he describes believers being built up into God's dwelling (2:22; see also Col 1:19; 2:9). With two additional phrases, Paul indicates that Christ dwells "through [the] faith" and "in their hearts."⁶³⁸ The Ephesians' trust in the redemptive plan of God in Christ allows Christ to dwell in their hearts. While to the modern ear the heart implies the seat of emotions, the ancients held the heart to be the seat of physical and spiritual life, the place of soul, mind, and conscience. Therefore, Paul stresses with the metaphor of "heart" more than emotional affections. He includes a commitment of the will and intellect as believers follow Christ.

The passage continues with the prepositional clause "in love," which qualifies the terms "rooted" and "established."⁶³⁹ Paul does not clearly state whether believers are rooted and grounded in God's love, or Christ's love, or God's love in Christ, as he does in the following verse when he speaks of the "love of Christ" (3:18; see also 2:4). While we may not be able to state Paul's emphasis definitively, the context does not suggest human love, unless it refers to the love within the believer, stemming from the indwelling of Christ in their hearts.⁶⁴⁰ In speaking about being rooted and established, Paul does not offer additional requests to God, but points forward to the next verse and his desire that believers will attain some perspective on the enormity and grandeur of Christ's love.⁶⁴¹

---

634. Best, 341.

635. The aorist infinitive of κατοικέω does not imply a specific moment, but the progression of transformation in its entirety, viewed as a single entity.

636. On κατοικέω see BDAG 534.

637. Bruce, 327.

638. Paul uses the phrase "through [the] faith" in 3:12, where the phrase can refer to either Christ's faithfulness or the believers' faith in him. A similar phrase without the article is found in 2:8. See excursus "'Faith in Christ' or 'the Faithfulness of Christ,'" pp. 221–23.

639. These two nominative participles are in the perfect passive tense; the passive voice indicates that God and not the believer is the source of the action, and the perfect tense presents a current condition based on a past action. Barth, 371–72, remarks that it is unlikely that these participles carry an imperatival force, for this would be odd syntax in the middle of a prayer. Hoehner, 483, advocates a causal sense, but Arnold, 212, counters that there is no place in the NT where we find a "nominative participle (in an adverbial relationship to the following verb) followed by a ἵνα with a subjunctive verb."

640. Best, 343, discusses the options and concludes that the evidence tips in favor of divine love. See also Arnold, 214. Perkins, 90, suggests that "'love' means both God's love in the faithful and their love for others (1:15)."

641. Best, 342.

3:16–19 Paul Prays for Christ's Love

The first participle, "being rooted" speaks of something firmly fixed in the ground.[642] The second participle, "being established," carries the sense of having a secure and solid foundation.[643] Both serve to present a picture of immobility and solidness, a constancy cemented in place and anchored by love. Paul uses both of these participles in Colossians, although the context is not Christ's love as it is here in Ephesians (Col 1:23; 2:7). This love that God grants to the believer's heart is a love whose depth and height, whose width and length, is beyond human comprehension, yet can be experienced and grasped by believers.

18 This verse continues Paul's prayer that Christ might dwell in the believers' hearts, reflecting their solid grounding in love. Paul stresses the power of God that flows from the riches of his glory, the strength provided by the Spirit, and the indwelling of Christ that roots believers deeply in love. In the Greek text, the verse begins with a conjunction (*hina*) that may signal that Paul's thought builds on and offers the purpose for Paul's request above. More likely, Paul makes a second request to God, after asking that the Ephesians have strength (3:16). This option is captured in the translation in 3:17 with the phrase "and I pray that you." Paul prays that every believer, and together the church, mentally grab hold of the magnitude of Christ's indwelling power through faith. In his prayers in Eph 1 and Eph 6, Paul mentions the Lord's holy people (1:15; 6:18), so it is no surprise to find a reference here to believers in all the local churches.

The connecting thread in Paul's prayer is the love of Christ. In 3:17 Paul stresses that Christ dwells in the believer's heart through faith, described as being rooted and grounded in love. Then in 3:18 Paul focuses on the scope of Christ's love, which in 3:19 he admits is beyond human comprehension. Christ's love, while emphasized, is not sharply distinguished from the love of the Father, expressed through the Spirit who resides in the inner being of believers.

Paul uses the verb "to be able, have power" with a prefix. This compound form occurs only here in the New Testament and rarely in the broader Greek literature of Paul's day.[644] The verb without the prefix is more common in the Gospels and Acts and is found twice in Paul's letters (Gal 5:6; Phil 4:13). Why might Paul use this rare form? The next verb, "to grasp or comprehend," might give a clue.[645] Paul asks God to give supernatural strength of mind and imagination to the Ephesians because

---

642. On ῥιζόω see BDAG 906.
643. On θεμελιόω see BDAG 449.
644. On ἐξισχύω see BDAG 350. For the verb without the prefix, ἰσχύω, see BDAG 484.
645. On καταλαμβάνω see BDAG 519–20 (4).

the mystery of the gospel and the afflictions of their apostle are so wildly beyond natural comprehension and worldly wisdom. In a similar vein, Paul enjoins the Romans to renew their minds, and thus their lifestyles and goals, to be conformed to God's perfect will (Rom 12:2). Paul emphasizes that this comprehension is not a mystical experience available to a chosen few, or a private revelation, but is something to which all saints have access.

What are they to comprehend? Paul provides four nouns with a single article ("the") before the first noun, and all four terms are joined by the repeated conjunctive "and." This indicates that the reader should consider all nouns together, but not as synonyms. There is no stated referent to these terms of measurement, so the reader is invited to think expansively. Perhaps Paul points to God's presence throughout the cosmos (Ps 139:7-12; Eph 1:20-23) or God's wisdom (Job 11:7-9; Eph 3:10) or Christ's love (Eph 3:19).[646] His lack of specificity suggests that Paul hopes readers will meditate on the spatial references and contemplate the magnitude of God's salvation plan, the one established before the foundations of the world and accomplished in Christ. A possible parallel is the Essene apocalyptic emphasis on understanding the dimensions of the heavens and "participation in divine wisdom."[647] It is unlikely, however, that this passage reflects gnostic reflection on the *plērōma* or that the text implies a response to magical incantations, as Paul will emphasize Christ's love that goes beyond human knowledge.[648]

19 Paul recognizes that God is infinitely more than any human can fully know, yet believers can know much more in their whole selves—their hearts and minds and experiences. This verse contains the second half of Paul's request that believers have power, namely, that they would know Christ's love. Paul uses the conjunction "and," but the Greek term used here (*te*) is softer and emphasizes the close relationship with the previous verse. This conjunction is often used in poetry, so Paul choosing this term may suggest that *te* is not found only in poetic literature. Most people in Paul's day viewed poetry as a proper vehicle to express profound truth, goodness, and beauty that lifts the human soul to higher contemplation of the nature and purpose of our existence. Paul draws on this tradition to express the truth, goodness, and beauty of the one true God and his redemption plan.

---

646. Best, 344-46, lists and dismisses several interpretive options—philosophical thought, magical texts, gnostic thought, or a heavenly Jerusalem. See also Barth, 395-97.

647. Perkins, 91: "Exaltation to the heavens where Christ is seated on the divine throne would certainly endow the saints with such knowledge."

648. Perkins, 92.

The object of knowing is the love of Christ, that is, Christ's limitless love bestowed to believers.[649] Paul qualifies such knowing with the phrase "that surpasses knowledge," using the cognate noun. How can we know that which is beyond knowing? Paul's contrast is not between true and false knowledge, or even between theoretical and practical knowledge. Paul highlights the knowledge that believers, immortal in Christ but not infinite, are able to grasp in relation to the eternal God who is Life itself.

Paul finishes this verse with the third and final clause signaled by "that." The lack of a coordinating conjunction indicates that this clause presents either the purpose or a summary of his prayer and not a third request. Paul desires that believers are continually filled, and he uses the cognate noun to describe the content poured out, "the fullness of God."[650] This fullness likely refers to that fullness that God possesses.[651] The picture Paul paints is of believers receiving love poured out by God. The preposition used, "to the measure of," denotes the filling up toward a goal.[652] Paul will speak of the Holy Spirit filling believers (5:18) to promote a healthy, holy community. The prayer for fullness in the church reminds the Ephesians that they are also seated with Christ in the heavenly places now (2:6) and as Christ's body are filled with God's fullness.[653] Colossians focuses on the indwelling fullness in Christ that is accomplished and that believers share (Col 1:19; 2:9-10).[654]

c. Paul Glorifies the Father (3:20-21)

20Now to him who is able to do immeasurably more than all we ask or imagine, according to his power that is at work within us, 21to him be glory in the church and in Christ Jesus throughout all generations, for ever and ever! Amen.

---

649. Barth, 373, remarks that while "God's revelation is complete and clear," nevertheless, "the saints' knowledge and understanding of the secret is still 'imperfect' (1 Cor 13:12)."

650. On γινώσκω see BDAG 199-200 (3); on γνῶσις see BDAG 203 (1); C. M. Robeck Jr., "Knowledge, Gift of Knowledge," *DPL* 526-28. Barth, 374, translates the verb "to make perfect" and the noun "perfection" so as to capture the eschatological and dynamic dimensions of the argument. Perkins, 94, explains that Paul "asks God to bring to perfection the work of salvation that has already begun among the elect."

651. On πληρόω see BDAG 827-28 (1); on πλήρωμα see BDAG 829-30 (3); D. S. Lim, "Fullness," *DPL* 319-20.

652. Barth, 373, argues: "The teleological and eschatological meaning of the Greek preposition 'into,' or 'toward' [*eis*], ought not to be allowed to disappear in the translation."

653. Perkins, 92, writes: "The community must become what the church in its heavenly reality already is, 'filled with all the fullness of God.'"

654. Arnold, 218; Barth, 374.

These two verses form the benediction or doxology of Paul's prayer that began in 3:16. A doxology typically encompasses an expression of praise that includes the term "glory" (*doxa*) and a reference to eternity, closing with an "amen."[655] The doxology usually occurs at the end of the letter (Phil 4:20), but might also conclude a section, as it does here and in Rom 11:36 (see also Gal 1:5).[656]

20 The language of the opening phrase, "to him who is able," is also used in Rom 16:25 and Jude 24. The reference is God the Father, the subject of this paragraph. God is able to do greater things than we can quantify. To express this, Paul uses the adverb *hyper* and a second adverb "immeasurably more" that includes the prefix *hyper* (see also 1 Thess 3:10; 5:13).[657] Such repetition emphasizes the magnitude of God's power. Paul further qualifies God's surpassing abilities as those that are, to use a modern idiom, off the radar. Humans are unable to form adequate questions to probe God's work. Paul suggests that even as believers grasp at understanding the scope of Christ's love and God's power, they will never be able to wrap their minds around God's fullness.

Nevertheless, a power animates believers; this power raised Christ from the dead (Eph 1:19–20). The final clause includes the noun "power" and the participle "working." The participle could be middle or passive. If middle, it stresses the power as a "relatively free agent." If passive, the participle points to the Holy Spirit's work in believers.[658] Most likely Paul refers here to the Holy Spirit in believers. Paul indicates that this power is at work "in us," which could suggest a limitation on God's abilities to work superabundantly and without measure. But Paul likely speaks here of the power that sustains believers' asking and imagining as they think of God's great love. The Ephesians' experiences of God's actions demonstrate God's limitless power expressed in unsurpassed and immeasurable love.

21 Paul closes the prayer with a second and final line of doxology. He refers to God the Father by using a personal pronoun, "to him." The equative verb ("to be") is implied, and the mood could be either optative ("may"), indicative ("is"), or imperative ("let"). Because all three are fitting postures before God, Paul might not have had a single mood in mind, but allowed all three to inform the Ephesians' reflection on this praise. He follows with the article and noun "the glory," an emphasis throughout Ephesians. Paul declares

---

655. Perkins, 93.
656. Bruce, 330, points to Rev 1:6; 5:13; 7:12; 19:1; Ps 29.
657. On ὑπερεκπερισσοῦ see BDAG 1033. Arnold, 219, points out that this adverb has a double prefix (ὑπέρ and ἐκ), thereby intensifying its meaning.
658. Barth, 375, chooses the passive voice.

praise to God's glory in the opening chapter (1:6, 12, 14) and describes God as the Father of glory (1:17) who gives to his people a glorious inheritance (1:18) out of his glorious riches (3:16). Paul speaks of his afflictions as the Ephesians' glory; their confidence in Paul's apostleship and apostolic message is well placed, for Christ has indeed established reconciliation with God and with each other (3:13).

Paul follows the reference to God's glory with two phrases: "in the church" and "in Christ Jesus." Perhaps Paul speaks of the church here because the church is with Christ in the heavenly places (1:22–23; 2:6). Paul does not place the church on equal footing with Christ, but rather reaffirms his earlier claims that the church is God's masterpiece in Christ (2:10).[659] God receives glory and displays his glory in the church, the sacred temple in which his Spirit dwells (2:22). The church, made up of Jew and gentile brought together into one new people, stands as testimony to God's wisdom (3:8–10) and reconciling power (2:15). The church is Christ's body, of which he is the head (1:22–23), so it is fitting that Paul adds "in Christ Jesus" as the expression of God's glory. Paul declares that Jesus Christ brings glory to God the Father in his closing doxology to the Romans (Rom 16:27; see also 1 Pet 4:11; Heb 13:21).

The conclusion of this doxology combines two rather common expressions related to time and eternity. Paul declares that God's glory extends "throughout all generations" and "for ever and ever." Such effusive language is typical of Paul's rhetorical flourish throughout this letter. As timebound creatures who do not have life in themselves but share immortality through the Son, this praise to God the Father is appropriate, even celebratory and joy filled. Horizons vanish into infinity, and God's glory is there.

---

659. Bruce, 331.

III. EXHORTATION TO HOLY LIVING (4:1–6:20)

Ephesians 4 begins the second half of the epistle, and Paul addresses proper Christian conduct consistent with the soaring theology presented in the first three chapters. In the paraenesis of Eph 4–6, the theological indicative drives the ethical imperative.[1] The focus shifts from the redemptive act of God the Father in Christ the Son, expounded in Eph 1–3, to an ethical focus on the church and its health and growth in the epistle's second half. Paul concentrates on how believers might live into their salvation and their calling to be holy and blameless (1:4; 4:1). A similar pattern of laying out doctrine and following with ethical injunctions is most clearly seen in Romans, wherein the first eleven chapters focus on theological questions, and the latter four on how these doctrines can be lived out in the church.[2] Yet I must also point out that in Ephesians and Romans, the theologically rich chapters also contain hortatory injunctions.[3] And Paul does not leave theology behind in the second half of Ephesians, for the didactic is infused with the kerygmatic, as seen by the continued reminder of Christ's efficacious work that makes a way for ethical behavior suitably reflective of God's kingdom (5:1–6).[4]

Paul encircles the second half of the epistle with references to his chains (4:1; 6:20). He writes this epistle while under house arrest that allows some visitors but restricts his movement and prevents him from preaching in the marketplace (Acts 28:16).[5] Paul awaits an audience with the emperor, who might condemn him to death. For that reason, Paul asks the Ephesians to pray that he would be bold and fearless in preaching the gospel (Eph 6:20). Paul

---

1. See introduction, pp. 51–52, for a discussion of paraenesis. Stowers, *Letter Writing*, 23, explains: "Paraenesis includes not only precepts but also such things as advice, supporting argumentations, various modes of encouragement and dissuasion, the use of examples, models of conduct, and so on."

2. Best, 353, observes that Romans' exhortation is briefer from a percentage basis of the total length of the epistle in comparison to Ephesians.

3. Stowers, *Letter Writing*, 23, rightly cautions that within Romans, and all of Paul's letters, the "earlier part of the letter also contains hortatory materials." Best, 353, notes that both Eph 4:1–2 and Rom 12:1–2 talk about the church after a brief exhortation. He points out the sharp divide between paraenesis and doctrine, which is most evident in Romans, while in Galatians the imperatives are more general. Best cites K. Berger, "Hellenistiche Gattungen im Neuen Testament," *ANRW* 2.25.2: 1331, that secular letters did not have paraenesis.

4. Barth, 54–55, rightly cautions against imposing a limiting grid onto the epistle, for it "may be as inappropriate as the attempt to measure the beauty of a symphony with a yardstick or a barometer."

5. For a general discussion of imprisonment, see Daniel G. Reid, "Prison, Prisoner," *DPL* 752–54; B. M. Rapske, "Prison, Prisoner," in *Dictionary of New Testament Background*, ed. Craig A. Evans and Stanley E. Porter (Downers Grove, IL: InterVarsity Press, 2000), 827–30; Wansink, *Chained in Christ*; Cassidy, *Paul in Chains*.

reminds the readers of his imprisonment to establish rapport between him and the Ephesians, as "was also considered fundamental to hortatory discourse."[6]

Unity is a key theme throughout the epistle. We saw earlier that God's ultimate goal is to bring all things together under Christ (1:10) and that Christ has brought together Jew and gentile into one community/body (2:14–16). The newly constituted body of Christ represents the wisdom of God to the heavenly powers and authorities (3:10). In this section of the letter, Paul focuses on the oneness of the people of God in Christ, urging behavior that matches the lofty truths expressed in the first three chapters. The social framework for this call is the liturgical life of the church, its confession of faith tied to life in the Holy Spirit (4:3, 30; 5:18) and to mature knowledge of the Son of God (4:13). Paul focuses on unity achieved by Christ's gift extended to every member (4:7), reinforced by putting on the new self (4:24). Paul highlights how unity is demonstrated by submitting to each other as to Christ (5:21) and standing firm in the armor of God against evil forces (6:11–13). Paul urges members to grow together, with Christ as their head (4:15–16), and to understand their oneness with Christ through the analogy of the "one flesh" of husband and wife (5:32). Paul emphasizes Christ's role as the source of unity.[7]

Within this unity, there is differentiation, based both on responsibilities within the church (4:11) and in recognition of the wider social and legal codes (5:22–6:9). The diversity is not presented as one member ruling over another, for Paul insists on humility and love as the guiding virtues for the community. Christlike humbleness and self-effacement overturn the social assumptions of social worth and hierarchy. Christlike love offers forgiveness in the manner of God's forgiveness to each believer through Christ's sacrificial death on the cross (5:1–2).[8]

What is behind Paul's urgency with regard to his theme of unity?[9] Some postulate external threats from the wider pagan community and from the

---

6. Perkins, 94. Best, 360, adds that the author was not "attempting to win their sympathy," but stresses Paul's "authority within the church."

7. Julien Smith, *Christ the Ideal King: Cultural Context, Rhetorical Strategy, and the Power of Divine Monarchy in Ephesians*, WUNT 313 (Tübingen: Mohr Siebeck, 2011), 220, observes that the "unity that Christ establishes in the church through his benefaction is but a part of the larger vision of the reconciliation of the cosmos."

8. MacDonald, 297, observes both that "there is even the suggestion of a reversal of cultural expectations governing relationships" and that an argument develops "in which some will be given authority over others." To this latter point, I add that having authority based on gifts from Christ is a different thing from having authority based on Greco-Roman values of the worth of a given individual.

9. Lincoln, 233, who holds the letter is deutero-Pauline, argues that the issues the writer "is addressing are how, without the apostle, the Pauline churches can remain unified and how, without the apostle, they can remain apostolic."

spiritual forces of the present dark age.[10] Internal forces likewise can tear apart a community, and Paul experienced such pressures in the Corinthian community.[11] Likely both external and internal concerns animate Paul's injunctions, but we have no evidence of a specific crisis. Paul's emphasis on unity could reflect his conviction that unity testifies to God's activity within the community. Josephus argues similarly as he stresses the unity of Jewish belief and practice around the law of Moses.[12] His slogan, "the one Temple for the One God," might have been a rallying cry for Jews in his day.[13] For Paul, the cry is "one Spirit, . . . one Lord, one faith, one baptism; one God and Father of all" (4:4–6). Paul uses language that later factors into discussions of the Trinity—Father, Son, Holy Spirit. In Eph 4, Paul speaks of Spirit, Son, and Father.[14]

Paul proclaims the unity of the faith as he encourages the Ephesians to walk in a manner worthy of their salvation gift (4:1, 17). As members of Christ's body, believers should speak truthfully and gently, without gossiping, without anger and rage. Paul continues a focus on ethics in Eph 5, reinforcing believers' proper attitudes and behaviors as heirs of God's kingdom, as those who live in the light of the Lord (5:5–8) and as those who are filled with the Holy Spirit (5:18). Living within the household takes up the rest of Eph 5 and the beginning of Eph 6, and Paul closes with a call to put on God's armor and stand fast against the powers that seek to undermine a faithful life (6:12–13).

Paul's call for a moral lifestyle would likely have been received in the context of friendship, for paraenesis was generally given by "the recipient's friend or moral superior (e.g., older, wiser, more accomplished)."[15] Ethical instruction, moreover, reinforced what was generally held to be useful and proper. We need not assume, therefore, that Paul's injunctions imply a church

---

10. MacDonald, 298.

11. Best, 366, observes that the author would have been aware of divisions within early Christian communities and adds "as a wise pastor AE [author of Ephesians] knew that unity was always at risk unless zealous care was taken to preserve it."

12. Josephus, *Jewish Antiquities* 18.1.6 §§23–25, argues that it is only when a sect of radical Jews (the "fourth philosophy") broke unity that the disastrous First Revolt occurred.

13. Josephus, *Jewish Antiquities* 4.8.5 §§200–201; *Against Apion* 2.23 §193. Jonathan Klawans, *Josephus and the Theologies of Ancient Judaism* (Oxford: Oxford University Press, 2012), 174, explains: "Indeed, the overall unity of the Jewish people is a motif of both *Jewish Antiquities* and *Against Apion*, with *Jewish Antiquities* emphasizing historical continuity under divine providence (esp. *Jewish Antiquities* 1.1–26) and *Against Apion* emphasizing general unity of practice and belief (esp. *Against Apion* 2.179–87)."

14. MacDonald, 296, remarks that Paul's language serves "to articulate the identity of the church as a unified whole that ultimately draws its origins from divine oneness."

15. Stowers, *Letter Writing*, 96.

that disregarded a moral life.[16] Dio Chrysostom, a first-century CE orator and philosopher, argues: "Since I observe that it is not our ignorance of the difference between good and evil that hurts us, so much as it is our failure to heed the dictates of reason on these matters and to be true to our personal opinions, I consider it most salutary to remind men of this without ceasing, and to appeal to their reason to give heed and in their acts to observe what is right and proper."[17]

The tempo of these chapters is brisk and quick, which contrasts to the earlier chapters, with their expansive, extravagant sentences.[18] Here Paul uses shorter sentences and more imperatives.[19] The present tense found extensively in these chapters underlines Paul's message and highlights the central purpose of the epistle.[20] The participles used in this section are "a common feature of paraenetic style."[21] The structure of Eph 4–6 can be organized around five sections that contain "therefore" and the verb "to walk" or "to be" (4:1–16; 4:17–32; 5:1–5; 5:6–14; 5:15–6:9).[22]

A. WALK WORTHY OF YOUR CALLING (4:1–32)

In the opening section of the paraenesis, Paul develops links with the first half of the epistle, as well as expands key metaphors and themes. For example, Paul addresses the believer's calling in 1:3–14 as he outlines the redemption established by God's great love, gained through Christ, and sealed by the Holy Spirit. Paul indicates that believers are to be holy and blameless (1:4); now in this section, he begins to explain what that looks like. As a second example, Paul describes the Ephesians as having formerly walked in the ways

---

16. Perkins, 94, remarks: "Therefore the Epistle's parenesis need not reflect actual vices among the addressees."

17. Dio Chrysostom, *On Covetousness* 17.2 in his *Discourses 12–30*, translated by J. W. Cohoon, Loeb Classical Library 339 (Cambridge: Harvard University Press, 1939), 189.

18. Bruce, 241, speaks of the "plerophoric style (notably the piling up of genitival phrases)." See also Best, 353.

19. Larkin, xx, observes that "thirty-nine of the forty imperatives in Ephesians are found in the ethical section."

20. David L. Mathewson, "The Abused Present," *Bulletin for Biblical Research* 23.3 (2013): 362, observes: "In Ephesians the present tense dominates chs. 4–6 (120 present-tense forms over against 59 aorists). . . . The present tense is used to emphasize what is most central to the author's purpose—exhortation and hortatory change in the readers."

21. Lincoln, 224.

22. Larkin, 67. However, this configuration separates 4:32 and 5:1, which are held together by a repetition of the verb "to be" (γίνομαι). Moreover, 5:6 does not include "therefore," which is found in 5:7. Yet the structure has the advantage of highlighting similar sections of thought.

of the world (2:2) and as having good works prepared by God in which they can walk (2:10); now he describes how they can walk worthy of their calling (4:1). Paul warns believers against walking as they did before they knew Christ (4:17). Paul repeats his stress on walking worthy (5:2, 8, 15). Third, Paul develops his metaphor of Christ as head and his body the church (1:22–23; 4:12–16), including an expansion of the place of apostles and prophets (2:20; 3:5; 4:11).[23]

In 4:17 Paul repeats his exhortation that he began in 4:1, that believers walk worthy of their calling. He states that they should avoid acts of gentiles, who have a darkened understanding. The latter are filled with disobedience and greed, and the former with the character of Christ. Believers in their new self, and as members of Christ's body, speak truthfully and gently, without gossiping, without anger and rage.

Paul proclaims the unity of the faith as he encourages the Ephesians to walk in a manner worthy of their salvation gift. This chapter can be divided in half, with the chapter's first sixteen verses focused on believers' discipleship and growing in Christ. The second half draws a sharp contrast between the behavior of the Christ follower and an unbeliever's mindset. The opening section takes a step toward ethical injunctions, but pauses for a theological declaration on the nature of believers' unity (4:1–6). Then Paul resumes the discussion of a worthy life, now with a focus on Christ's gift of grace to each believer, enabling them to grow to maturity (4:7–16). The second half of the chapter can be broken down into three smaller sections: 4:17–19, 20–24, 25–32. The first two sections contrast the gentile polytheistic life with one rooted in Christ. Paul presents the pagan as a piteous figure lost due to ignorance, even while stressing that pagans are culpable for their actions.[24] The Ephesians' previous ignorance has been remediated, not by learning specific doctrines or creeds, but by learning a person, namely, Christ (4:20–21). And their behavior changes, not because they were carefully trained in a Christian catechesis, but because they changed their "clothing." Paul thus provides a vivid image of taking off the old self and putting on the self that is righteous before God.[25] This new self must act in ways consistent with its new identity. The godly behavior is first and foremost to be directed to other members of the church, but it also will have ramifications for the wider society as believers' gracious speech and generous actions support its members and by extension those who come in contact with them.

---

23. Lincoln, 231.
24. Thielman, 294.
25. Thielman, 295, suggests that Paul reflects on the story of the first humans created by God (Gen 1:26).

4:1-6 Unity in One Spirit, One Lord, One Father

1. Unity in One Spirit, One Lord, One Father (4:1-6)

¹*As a prisoner for the Lord, then, I urge you to live a life worthy of the calling you have received.* ²*Be completely humble and gentle; be patient, bearing with one another in love.* ³*Make every effort to keep the unity of the Spirit through the bond of peace.* ⁴*There is one body and one Spirit, just as you were called to one hope when you were called;* ⁵*one Lord, one faith, one baptism;* ⁶*one God and Father of all, who is over all and through all and in all.*

To know Christ's love in all its expansiveness is to respond with behavior that honors the magnificent gift of grace. In a sentence that extends for six verses, Paul lays the foundation for his call to living in light of God's salvation gift. The foundation is unity, a central theme of this epistle. Unity is the goal of the cosmos, when all things will be summed up in Christ (1:10). Unity is the accomplishment of Christ's reconciling work through his blood, which brought Jew and gentile together in one new people and brought that people to God, fully redeemed by the cross. Unity is the daily practice of believers, for each is saved by the one faith, shares the one baptism, and lives by the power of the one Holy Spirit, giving honor to the one God and Father of all.

1 Paul builds on his previous prayer, taking its message forward into the daily lives of believers. The finite verb "to urge" is one Paul often chooses as he exhorts his congregations (see Rom 12:1; 2 Cor 10:1; 1 Thess 4:1).[26] Paul urges "you" (believers) to walk or live in a certain way.[27] Paul uses the verb "to walk," often translated "to live," several times in the remaining chapters (Eph 4:17; 5:2, 8, 15).[28] He draws on the metaphor's extensive use in the Old Testament as he conjures up the image of moving through daily life.[29] Paul might be further drawn toward this metaphor because of his own peripatetic lifestyle.[30] By speaking of the Christian life as a walk, Paul

---

26. On παρακαλέω see BDAG 764-75 (2); C. G. Kruse, "Call, Calling," *DPL* 84-85.
27. We might expect Paul to reference "brothers" here, as he does in Rom 12:1 and 1 Thess 4:10. Best, 360, suggests that "its absence enhances the authority and diminishes the friendliness of the phrase." This theory, however, fails to fully account for Paul's concern that they not get discouraged (Eph 3:13) and the cultural expectation that teachers would instruct their disciples.
28. On περιπατέω see BDAG 803 (2).
29. Joel B. Green, *Conversion in Luke-Acts: Divine Action, Human Cognition, and the People of God* (Grand Rapids: Baker Academic, 2015), 65, explains: "Several hundred of the more than fifteen hundred occurrences of the verb [in the Hebrew Scriptures] carry this metaphorical sense—famously of David, who walks 'through the valley of the shadow of death' (Ps. 23:4)."
30. Robert Banks, "'Walking' as a Metaphor of the Christian Life: The Origins of a Significant Pauline Usage," in *Perspectives on Language and Text: Essays and Poems in Honor*

envisions a journey in which each step, each day, is an opportunity to live well and faithfully.

Paul asks that believers walk "worthily," an adverb whose meaning will be unpacked in the next several verses. Their worthy walk reflects the calling they received. In the Greek text, Paul uses both the noun "calling" and the verb "to call, invite."[31] The repetition emphasizes Paul's concern that believers recognize that they are Christ's, grounded in love, enfolded into his life. The verb is in the passive voice, which highlights God's actions in calling believers. This calling, secure in the Holy Spirit, provides the courage necessary to live worthily (see also Col 1:10; 2 Tim 1:9).

Paul's emphasis on calling reflects his claims that God has predestined the plan of salvation before the foundations of the world, such that believers would be adopted as children of God through Christ's work of redemption (Eph 1:4–7). Paul writes to the Romans in a similar vein, that those whom God predestined, he also called, and justified, and glorified (Rom 8:30). Paul does not engage in the philosophical questions about free will and election; his point is focused on believers' conduct.[32]

A worthy life is a bold life, one that embraces the fetters of imprisonment. Paul writes, "I, a prisoner for the Lord" (Eph 4:1). Several points are worth noting. First, Paul identifies himself as one imprisoned (3:1) and as an ambassador in chains (6:20).[33] Second, the phrase "for the Lord" could modify "I urge you," yet because in 3:1 he explains his chains as "for Christ," it seems best to see this idea reiterated here. Third, Paul uses the emphatic "I" in apposition to "a prisoner." He points to his previous digression (3:2–13), wherein he underscores that his current imprisonment testifies to his apostolic appointment. Few in Paul's world are as vulnerable as a prisoner, and we might be tempted to read Paul's advice about being humble and gentle as a practical strategy to avoid offending guards who could abuse him. Paul, however, sees these virtues as conforming to Christ's own character and, thus, as summing up the perfection and full flourishing of a human, made in the image of the Creator God. To look like Christ is to radiate patience, gentleness, and humility. In a similar vein, Paul assures the Romans that they are predestined to be conformed to the image of the Son (Rom 8:29). He

---

of Francis I. Andersen's Sixtieth Birthday July 29, 1985, ed. Edgar W. Conrad and Edward G. Newing (Winona Lake, IN: Eisenbrauns, 1987), 303, states: "Paul's most characteristic way of talking about the Christian life is as a 'walk.'" He refers to Paul as a "walkabout theologian."

31. On κλῆσις see BDAG 549. On καλέω see BDAG 502–3 (4). The Greek reads τῆς κλήσεως ἧς ἐκλήθητε ("the calling to which you have been called").

32. Best, 361, concludes: "His later stress on conduct shows that he does not regard the call as affecting freedom of action."

33. On δέσμιος see BDAG 219. On ἅλυσις see BDAG 48; D. G. Reid, "Prison, Prisoner," *DPL* 752–54. See also discussion in introduction, pp. 10–11.

4:1-6 UNITY IN ONE SPIRIT, ONE LORD, ONE FATHER

urges the Corinthians to embrace the freedom of the Lord, as believers are transformed into his image with ever increasing glory (2 Cor 3:18).

Paul states that he is a prisoner for/of Christ in four other letters, including 2 Timothy and three that, with Ephesians, are known as the Prison Epistles (Colossians, Philippians, Philemon). Few doubt that Paul experienced imprisonment in his life, but those who argue that Paul is not the author of the epistle must account for the autobiographical note that the writer is in chains. Some suggest that the author used the well-known fact of Paul's imprisonment to add verisimilitude to the epistle. This suggestion, however, does not take full account of the importance of martyrs and confessors in the Jewish and Christian traditions. Jews honored the Maccabean martyrs, including elderly Eliezer and the faithful mother and her seven sons, who remained steadfast under horrific torture because they trusted in God's resurrection power (2 Macc 6–7). Stephen, the first Christian martyr (Acts 7), held an early place of honor in Christian memory. Given the high regard that martyrs held in the church's eyes, it seems unlikely that an anonymous author, especially a disciple of Paul, could write with a clear conscience as though he or she were facing martyrdom.[34]

2-3 Paul exhorts his congregation to live out their calling in a manner that matches their "called" status before God. They are to show humility and patience, bearing with each other in love and making every effort to maintain unity. Paul's words "make every effort" carry a sense of urgency and priority.[35] While some commentators find imperatival force behind the participles "bearing with" and "make every effort,"[36] I suggest that they are dependent on the finite verb in 4:1, Paul's appeal to walk worthy.[37] The first participle in 4:2 encourages the Ephesians to bear with or be patient with each other. The second participle in 4:3 insists that the community prioritize its unity. The two participles express parallel ideas, as the first encourages individuals to practice virtues and the second looks to the unity of the community. Paul reminds believers to stay the course and protect their community values, for while they do not create unity on their own strength, they can by their own willfulness destroy it.[38] Paul encourages the Colossians and the Galatians in a similar

---

34. See introduction, pp. 10–11, for discussion.

35. On σπουδάζω see BDAG 939 (3). Barth, 428, remarks: "It is hardly possible to render exactly the urgency contained in the underlying Greek verb."

36. Hoehner, 505; Lincoln, 235.

37. Arnold, 230–31. Drawing on Wallace, *Greek Grammar*, 652, Arnold explains: "This expression has a similar semantic force to an imperative (e.g., περιπατήσατε), after which it is common to have present participles in the nominative case clarifying how the action is to be carried out." I note that the two present tense participles parallel Paul's two prepositional phrases.

38. Best, 364.

manner, that through love they serve each other (Gal 5:13) and that they bear one another and forgive (Col 3:13). Such behavior rubs against the embedded social hierarchy of the wider Greco-Roman culture. In this latter case, aid was given to those who could repay, for helping a neighbor was a way to insure one's own future help in time of need. In the context of the church, however, believers are to give to each other regardless of the possibility of return.

Paul fills out the meaning of the adverb "worthy" mentioned in the previous verse. Such a life includes the virtues of humility, gentleness, and patience. The same phrase, "be completely humble," is found in Paul's farewell message to the Ephesians, as he portrays his ministry in their midst (Acts 20:19). Paul describes Christ as humble in his obedience to God, even though it meant death on a cross (Phil 2:8), and urges believers to follow his example (Phil 2:3, 5; see also 1 Pet 5:5). Paul uses the adjective "all" before the noun "humility," and the adjective modifies both "humility" and "gentleness."

The term "humility," however, was not used by philosophers in discussions of the virtues.[39] Epictetus uses it only once, in a negative way.[40] Seneca speaks of the related virtue of *clementia* or mercy.[41] He advocates that those who hold power, such as Emperor Nero, should show forbearance in dealing with reprobate behavior, thereby demonstrating mercy and self-control. Seneca argues that in certain cases it is more honorable to forego an insistence on one's right to impose a response of honor due to one's person or office.[42] Paul's understanding of humility challenges the very social hierarchy that Seneca embraces. Paul insists on a humility wherein every believer shows deferential honor to all other believers, regardless of their social class or rank. As we will see in Eph 6:9, Paul insists that masters demonstrate to their slaves the same honor due a slave owner, for God does not esteem certain humans over others as does Roman culture. In this Paul follows the Old Testament references to God's exaltation of the humble (Ps 34:18 [= 33:19 LXX]; Isa 11:4; 49:13; 66:2; Jer 22:16; Prov 3:34, quoted in 1 Pet 5:5; see also Jas 1:9–10). This virtue was extolled within the Qumran documents (1QS 4:2).[43]

---

39. On ταπεινοφροσύνη see BDAG 989. Perkins, 95, observes that "humility" is found only in Jewish and Christian virtue lists: "To the non-Jew, 'humility' suggests demeaning lowliness."

40. Epictetus, *Discourses* 3.24.56.

41. For an English translation of Seneca's *De clementia*, see Susanna Braund, *Seneca: De Clementia, Edited with Text, Translation, and Commentary* (Oxford: Oxford University Press, 2009).

42. Lincoln, 235, adds: "Humility was an attitude that was . . . associated with contemptible servility (e.g., Josephus, *Jewish War* 4.9.2 §494; Epictetus, *Discourses* 1.9.10; 3.24.56)."

43. Lincoln, 236; see also Perkins, 95, who observes: "'Humility' does not appear outside Jewish and Christian lists."

4:1–6 Unity in One Spirit, One Lord, One Father

The second noun in the series, "gentleness," carries the sense of self-control and kindness.[44] Paul uses "gentleness" when describing Christ's character (2 Cor 10:1), in line with Jesus's words to his followers that he is gentle and humble in heart, that his yoke is easy and light, and in him the weary find rest (Matt 11:29–30).[45] Paul includes this virtue in his list of the fruit of the Spirit (Gal 5:23). The philosopher Aristotle, centuries before Paul, valued the virtue of gentleness, describing it not as timidity or weakness, but rather as a position between excessive anger and lack of anger.[46] It suggests a person with self-control and the wisdom to discern injustice and then act to rectify it. James uses the term in the context of resisting anger because such outbursts do not lead to righteousness (Jas 1:19–21; 3:13).

The third virtue is patience (see also Col 3:12 for these three virtues). The one who walks worthily is the one who acts with patience. The term carries the sense of being calm under fire and slow to anger.[47] The term is a combination of the root "anger" and the adjective "a long time," which we might describe as having a long fuse.[48] Later Paul will speak against anger and rage (Eph 4:26, 31; 6:4). God is patient (Exod 34:6; Rom 2:4; 9:22; 1 Pet 3:20), and Christ is patient (1 Tim 1:16; 2 Pet 3:15). Believers are called to bear suffering patiently and to endure patiently (Jas 5:10), awaiting the coming kingdom of the Son (Col 1:11–13). This fruit of the Spirit (Gal 5:22) equips believers to remain steadfast on the journey of faith.

For Paul, the believer is never an island unto himself, or a solitary figure making her own way. The believer demonstrates patience and humility by caring for others and, by implication, receiving care by others. Reciprocity is assumed here; however, believers are to give to each other regardless of the possibility of return. Paul knows what it is to be free to move about and show patience to others, and what it is like to be chained and thus humbly accept care from others. That is why humility is a key virtue and gift of the Spirit in the context of the church.

Paul urges the Ephesians to protect or "keep" what they have, namely, unity. Paul does not say that they must *create* unity; rather, they should main-

---

44. On πραΰτης see BDAG 861.

45. Perkins, 95, observes that "patience" is a quality found in God (Jer 15:15; Rom 2:4; 9:22; 1 Tim 1:16; 1 Pet 3:20) or in humans (Prov 25:15; 2 Cor 6:6; Gal 5:22), in both the Jewish and Christian traditions.

46. Aristotle, *Magna moralia* 1.22.2–3; see also *Nicomachean Ethics* 1.13.20.

47. On μακροθυμία see BDAG 612–13; C. G. Kruse, "Virtues and Vices," *DPL* 962–63; John T. Fitzgerald, "Virtue/Vice Lists," *ABD* 6:857–59.

48. Arnold, 230, explains the etymology of the term: it is a compound based on a noun for anger (θυμός) and an adjective meaning "a long time" (μακρός) with the resulting meaning "slow to anger." He rightly cautions against using a term's etymology to discern meaning, but acknowledges that in this case "this particular word bears a close association to its etymology."

tain what they already have. The noun translated "unity" is used only here and in 4:13 and is rarely used in Greek, which makes it difficult to know why Paul chose this term.[49] Perhaps its rarity attracted Paul as a way to catch his listeners' attention, for Paul emphasizes oneness in 4:4–6.[50] Additionally, the term includes as its first syllable the term for the number "one" in the neuter, which is picked up as the first word in the next verse (4:4). Such verbal repetition is a feature of Ephesians. The Ephesians possess this unity, for they are guarding it. While the noun "unity" is rare, the general concept is not, including in the political realm.[51]

The unity is "of the spirit," most likely a reference to the Holy Spirit, the originator of this unity (see also 2:22), rather than a reference to human spirit. Reasons for this position include that Paul assumes this spirit is stable and secure, something that cannot be said about an individual or community. Second, if Paul wanted to indicate a human spirit, he would have written "spirit of unity," rather than "unity of the Spirit." Finally, Paul continues in the next verses to speak of one Spirit in parallel with one Lord and one Father, clearly implying the Holy Spirit.[52]

The unity they share through the Holy Spirit binds the believers together. Paul includes two prepositional phrases to end this verse: "through the bond" and "of peace." The phrases together parallel the phrase "in love" in the previous verse.[53] The term translated "bond" (*desmos*) is similar to the term Paul uses to describe himself as a "prisoner" (*desmios*), which suggests that even as Paul is bound in the Lord (4:1) so too all believers are bound together in peace in the unity of the Spirit (4:3). This bond is not the restrictive chain of a prisoner, but the blessing of peace, even as Paul's chains are not ultimately Rome's restrictions but are evidence of his sharing in the afflictions

---

49. On ἑνότης see BDAG 338. Lincoln, 237, adds that the term is more common in the second century, citing Ignatius, *To the Ephesians* 4.2; 5.1; 14.1; *To the Philadelphians* 2.2; 3.2; 5.2; 8.1; 9.1.

50. Thielman, 254, explains that "the term 'one' will appear six times within the space of thirty-four words and itself serves as a transition to the next major section (vv. 7–16)."

51. Lau, *Politics of Peace*, 100, observes that this call for unity "can be understood within the ancient political frame of concord and discord." One might expect the noun ὁμόνοια rather than Paul's choice of the synonym εἰρήνη, and Lau speculates that Paul's choice (1) follows the Isaianic allusions in 2:14, 17; 6:15 and (2) reflects the term's use when speaking about humanity's relationship to God/gods (102).

52. See Barth, 428, for a discussion of these arguments. See also Best, 365, who observes that Paul does not answer the question as to what happens to the church if it loses its unity. Does it cease to exist? He speculates that perhaps Aquinas and Calvin pondered these questions and concluded that Paul meant the human spirit in this verse, because the community can both create and destroy it.

53. Best, 365, who adds: "Love (v. 2) may be the assumption for unity; peace is the cement of its working out in the church."

4:1-6 UNITY IN ONE SPIRIT, ONE LORD, ONE FATHER

of Christ.[54] In Eph 6, Paul speaks of the "gospel of peace" that prepares the Ephesians to stand firm (6:15). The latter context centers on the armor of God that the believer puts on as protection against threatening spiritual forces. Peace takes on a special significance within this letter, as Paul identifies Christ as "our peace" (2:14). With this image, Paul reinforces his overarching claim that believers are "in Christ." As individuals participate in Christ's life, as their lives are made new in Christ, they are also made new to each other and become a new entity, Christ's body. The "bond of peace," therefore, speaks to the interconnections of believers within the church who are all "in Christ."

4-6 Earlier in Ephesians, Paul declares that Christ is our peace (2:14), and from this peace, he has created one new people of God. Here in this section, we find additional connections to Paul's discussion of Christ's peace. Paul underscores the oneness of the body, the one hope and calling that reflect the one faith professed by believers in the one true God. The one body is Christ's body, the church, brought into being through the blood of the cross and sustained by the Holy Spirit. The declaration in these verses prepares the way for Paul's discussion in 4:7-16 as he speaks of the different members all growing together into maturity in Christ.

The confessional nature of these verses suggests that Paul draws on creedal statements (see also Rom 10:9-10; 11:36; 1 Cor 8:6).[55] Paul incorporates his own emphases, for example, his focus on "one body," a theme that permeates Ephesians. We find similar language in 1 Cor 12:12-13, including a focus on Christ, the one Spirit, and believers baptized into one body.[56] Perhaps Paul uses language from a traditional baptismal confession, as the phrases "one baptism" and "one faith" suggest.[57] Evidence for this position includes its traditional understanding of water baptism. Moreover, it is unlikely that Paul knew the tradition of describing Jesus's death as a "baptism" (Mark 10:38-39; Luke 12:50). Instead, Paul speaks of baptism as being buried *with* Christ (Rom 6:3-6; Gal 3:27; Col 2:11-12).[58]

---

54. Perkins, 96, concludes that Paul's message is "the fruit of the Spirit is peace" and includes both "communal concord" and "fullness of salvation" (Rom 14:17; 15:13).

55. Barth, 429 and 462-63, argues that the entire passage reflects traditional acclamations compiled by the author. However, Lincoln, 228-29, rightly cautions that this conclusion outruns our evidence.

56. Perkins, 96, concludes: "First Corinthians 12:12-13 . . . provides the initial framework for verses 4-5, while 1 Cor 8:6 provides a formula for God's creative activity." See also Muddiman, 183.

57. Arnold, 235; see also Lincoln, 229, and Barth, 468-70.

58. Barth, 469-70, suggests that Paul references baptism after speaking of one Lord and one faith because it "is a comprehensive, practical, public, binding, joyful confession." Contra Best, 368, who concludes that the material is pre-Pauline and not confessional in this context; rather "it is a statement for internal church use."

The passage repeats the number "one" seven times, which invites comment. First, from a rhetorical standpoint, Paul uses the masculine, feminine, and neuter nouns in 4:5 that produce three ways of saying "one" (*heis, mia, hen*), and this would catch a listener's ear. Second, Paul tends to use numbers in a literal way, not symbolically; therefore the sevenfold use of "one" need not imply perfection.[59] Third, the confession of the one God carries heightened theological significance as gentile believers reject their polytheism and embrace Jewish monotheism (cf. Deut 6:4–6; 1 Cor 8:6). Later creedal statements draw on this language, but reverse the order of nouns, starting with God the Father and moving to Christ and then the Holy Spirit. Here in Ephesians, Paul's focus is the church. Paul includes units of three in 4:4–6, including "body, Spirit, calling"; "Lord, faith, baptism"; and his description of God the Father as "over all, through all, and in all."

Paul begins 4:4 rather abruptly without any conjunction connecting this verse to the previous three verses. This lack of conjunction is best represented by including a semicolon at the end of 4:3. It also suggests an implied equative verb ("to be"), such that the English would read "there is one body."[60] Paul declares that there is "one body," which refers to the body of Christ, the church. At the end of Eph 1, Paul indicates that Christ is the head of his body, the church (1:23), and in Eph 2 he underlines the single body made up of Jew and gentile believers (2:14–15). Paul will emphasize the body metaphor again in 5:29–30. Its emphasis here in a liturgical setting reminds believers that "one body" is not simply a theological doctrine but is a reality that the church is encouraged to live by.

Paul continues that there is "one Spirit," here referring to the Holy Spirit who binds believers together and inhabits the church, who is God's holy temple (2:18, 22; see also 1 Cor 12:13). The Holy Spirit seals believers (Eph 1:13–14; 4:30), and thus each believer shares a common bond with others. Believers are empowered by the Spirit, as they experience ever more deeply the love of Christ (3:17). Paul's emphasis on "one" here reinforces the superiority of the Spirit over all other spiritual forces and authorities. Paul may draw a contrast between the Spirit of God and spirits, known as *paradroi*, that were subordinate to the gods upon whom pagans called for help. Paul urges Ephesian believers to renounce reliance on such "helper spirits" and demonstrate allegiance to the Holy Spirit of God, who seals them in their redemption.[61]

---

59. Arnold, 232.

60. Arnold, 232, notes that it is less likely that Paul continues his exhortation from 4:1, for the imperative would make little sense in 4:5 where Paul speaks of "one Lord." Best, 366, observes that while a causal connection would make sense for 4:4, we would expect a "for" to begin the section, and then 4:5 would make little sense.

61. Arnold, 233, offers a quotation from a magical text: "An assistant who will reveal everything to you clearly and will be your companion and will eat and sleep with you" (*Papyri*

4:1–6 Unity in One Spirit, One Lord, One Father

Paul adds a second clause with the conjunction "just as" to draw a comparison of "one hope" to his statement about one body and one Spirit. He repeats the verb "to call" and the noun "calling" from 4:1. Paul emphasizes that God has called believers and has called them to a special inheritance in the Son, who is lauded in the following verse as "one Lord." This calling happens in the realm of hope, a confident trust in the future because God is faithful to his promises (see 1:18).[62] In Paul's day, the reigning philosophy of Stoicism focused hope on the near future, the human future. Epictetus expressed that even as a ship should not rely on a single anchor, so too a man should not have only one hope.[63] Paul did not pay attention to this somber warning, but drew on the Old Testament's confident portrait of God fulfilling his promises. Jesus explained his ministry as the Servant in Isaiah, in whom all nations would put their trust (Matt 12:15–21; see Isa 42:1–4). Paul points to that eschatological promise as he reassures believers that their hope is secure in Christ. Although the gentile believers once stumbled in darkness and sin, without God, without hope (Eph 2:2, 12), now they are members of God's people, a dwelling place for God's Spirit (2:19–22). The single hope they share is rooted in the one Lord (4:5) who redeemed and reconciled them to God, who is over all (4:6). Paul adds an eschatological thrust in the next chapter, when he speaks about the kingdom of Christ and of God as the believers' calling (5:5; see also 1:10).[64]

Paul continues in a staccato pace with three nouns and three adjectives, but no verbs. The number "one" is repeated three times (4:5), with the nouns "Lord," "faith," and "baptism." The three nouns in this verse are part of a list of seven; the final noun in the next verse is God the Father.

The noun "Lord" (*kyrios*) is used in the Old Testament to address the God of Israel, and Paul uses it regularly to identify Jesus Christ.[65] His opening salutation to the Ephesians speaks of the Lord Jesus Christ (1:2–3). The Lord Jesus Christ is the head of the church and rules over all powers and authorities (1:17, 21–23; Col 1:18). Twice in Eph 6, however, Paul uses the noun to refer to slave masters (6:5, 9), reflecting another meaning of the widely used term. Paul's use of the title "Lord" for Jesus Christ is ubiquitous throughout his epistles. Paul declares to the Corinthians that there is one God and Father and one Lord, Jesus Christ—both of whom together created and sustain the universe (1 Cor 8:6). "Jesus is Lord" is the confession of the believer who

---

Graecae Magicae: Die griechischen Zauberpapyri, ed. Karl Preisendanz, 2nd ed. [Stuttgart: Teubner, 1973–74], 1:1–2).

62. On ἐλπίς see BDAG 319–20 (1); J. M. Everts, "Hope," *DPL* 415–17.

63. Epictetus, *Fragment* 30 (89).

64. Lincoln, 239, sums it up well: the author of Ephesians "recognizes that what his readers hope for in the end will determine what they practice in the present."

65. On κύριος see BDAG 576–77 (2); L. W. Hurtado, "Lord," *DPL* 560–69. Paul uses the title for Jesus Christ twenty-four times in Ephesians.

speaks by the Holy Spirit (Rom 10:9; 14:8–9), and every knee will bow and tongue confess that Jesus Christ is Lord (Phil 2:9–11). In these latter verses, Paul takes the title for God, "Lord" (*kyrios* in the Septuagint), and applies it to Jesus Christ.[66] While Paul does not identify Christ here as "Son" the implication hangs in the air, for Paul distinguishes God as Father of all in the next verse. We hear an echo of Eph 1:2–3 wherein God is identified as "our Father" and as the Father of "our Lord" Jesus Christ (see also 1:17). And in the middle of Eph 4, Paul speaks of Christ as the "Son of God" (4:13). Thus the "Lord" is also the "Son" of the Father, even as God's people are his children who inherit his kingdom (5:5–8).

There is one "faith," and this noun carries either the sense of trust in Christ or a summary of the beliefs of the church.[67] Paul uses it in the former sense earlier in this epistle (see also Col 2:7), but here in Eph 4 draws on its latter meaning (see also 4:13; Col 1:23; 2:7; Jude 3). For Paul, "faith" in this verse is similar to the phrases "word of truth" and "gospel of salvation" in which the Ephesians believed (Eph 1:13).

There is one "baptism," Paul declares.[68] This term has three general meanings. It can refer to (1) the rite of being dipped into water or carry the metaphorical sense of (2) being martyred (Mark 10:38; Luke 12:50) or (3) being buried with Christ (Rom 6:4; Col 2:12). In this passage, Paul probably underscores the liturgical sense and yet also retains the metaphorical meaning of the term. Ephesians were likely baptized with water in some way, as that was Paul's practice (Acts 9:18; 16:15, 33; 18:8; 19:5; 1 Cor 1:14–17). Paul encourages them to think about their identity as those who died with Christ, are raised with Christ, seated with Christ, and being built into God's temple (Eph 2:5–8, 22). Later in the letter, Paul speaks of Christ washing the church with water to make it holy (5:25–27). Those who are baptized are cleansed from sin and made new in Christ. The ritual could involve removing old clothes and putting on new clothes after being baptized with the water. The language of putting on Christ, or the new self, reflects this practice (4:22–24; Gal 3:27; Col 3:9, 12). Paul addresses the Corinthians in a similar vein, stressing that they as one body have been baptized in one Spirit (1 Cor 12:13). He encourages the Romans that they have been baptized into Christ, buried with him in his death and raised to new life, with the sure promise of resurrection (Rom 6:4–5).

With Eph 4:6, Paul finishes the sentence he began in 4:1. He encourages believers to live in accordance with their profession of faith, their unity in

---

66. Wright, *Paul: In Fresh Perspective*, 92–94, offers a discussion of these passages. For a detailed discussion, see introduction, pp. 64–66, above.

67. On πίστις see BDAG 818–19 (2); L. Morris, "Faith," *DPL* 285–91.

68. On βάπτισμα see BDAG 165 (1); G. R. Beasley-Murray, "Baptism," *DPL* 60–66; Lars Hartman, "Baptism," *ABD* 1:583–95.

4:1–6 UNITY IN ONE SPIRIT, ONE LORD, ONE FATHER

the Spirit, and their conviction that God the Father through Jesus Christ the Son has brought them into a reconciled relationship with God and with other believers. This verse begins with the term "one," repeating a theme that Paul began two verses earlier in listing seven points of unity shared by believers. This final item is also the crescendo and fulfillment of all other "ones." This "one God" is the God of Israel, the God who blessed Abraham and Sarah, the God who led his people out of slavery in Egypt, the one testified to by Moses, David, and the prophets. God is the creator of the universe, the giver of the law, the one to whom worship is due.[69] In 4:6 Paul sums up the Jewish conviction: "Hear, O Israel: The Lord our God, the Lord is one" (Deut 6:4). Interestingly, Paul rarely speaks of God as one, likely because the belief was so well known in his day among gentiles (Acts 15:21).[70] The depiction of "God" throughout the New Testament presupposes the God described in the Old Testament, but now including redemption through Jesus Christ, both Jew and gentile, as seen in Eph 3:1–10.[71] In those passages where Paul stresses God's oneness, we often find reference to Christ or to Christ and the Holy Spirit. Our passage "puts into creedal form the affirmation that God is *experienced* as a triune reality."[72]

Paul continues that God is "Father." This description has an important history in the Old Testament, as it highlights three aspects of God. First, God is the source of Israel who gives an inheritance to his "child." Second, God is the protector of his child. Third, God as father is to be honored and obeyed.[73] At significant moments in Israel's history, God reminds them that he is their father. As he calls the people out of Egypt, he declares, "Israel is my firstborn son," stressing their inheritance (Exod 4:22–23). The same idea is echoed in the prophet Hosea: "Out of Egypt I called my son" (Hos 11:1–3). Not only has God established and rescued his people, but he also holds an inheritance for them. Both Jeremiah and Isaiah speak of God the father as redeemer who will in the last days forgive and establish the people (Isa 63:16; 64:8; Jer 31:9). Paul uses the phrase "God and Father" several times in Ephesians, usually in the context of praying or praising God (Eph 1:2–3, 17; 3:14–15; 5:20; 6:23).

---

69. Wright, *Paul: In Fresh Perspective*, 86, speaks of Jewish monotheism as "creational and covenantal monotheism."

70. Gordon D. Fee, *Jesus the Lord according to Paul the Apostle: A Concise Introduction* (Grand Rapids: Baker Academic, 2018), 183.

71. So Hurtado, *God in New Testament Theology*, 70.

72. Fee, *Jesus the Lord*, 183, surmises that the belief about the one God "is so presuppositional for Paul and assumed to be true for his readers, the need seldom arises for him to make a point of it."

73. Marianne Meye Thompson, *The Promise of the Father: Jesus and God in the New Testament* (Louisville: Westminster John Knox, 2000), 39.

Paul describes God as father "of all." The question arises whether Paul has in mind believers, all humans, or all things. The immediate context suggests believers, because Paul is speaking of the church.[74] Yet in Eph 3, Paul suggests that God is the father of all peoples. Moreover, throughout the epistle, Paul emphasizes God's ruling care over all creation (1:22; 3:9, 15).[75] It may be that we should keep the ambiguity, as we think about believers, who are drawn from all humanity and who are part of God's plan for the unity of all the cosmos under Christ (1:10). Something of this picture can be seen in Paul's first missionary journey. In preaching in Lystra, a small city in Asia Minor, Paul and Barnabas declare that the living God has blessed the gentiles with rainfall and crops, food and joy (Acts 14:15–17). Jesus spoke of the Father in heaven giving sunshine and rain to both the good and the evil, the righteous and unrighteous, and he enjoined his followers to do likewise (Matt 5:43–48).

Paul continues with a series of three prepositional phrases that include the term "all": God is "over all and through all and in all." This way of describing God was common in Stoic thought and in Jewish writings of Paul's day. Stoics held that God/Reason was present everywhere, and Josephus and Philo promote the view that the God of the Jews is the creator of all.[76] As Paul discusses God's rule over all the cosmos and the eventual unity of the cosmos, he underlines the role of Christ (Eph 1:9–10), suggesting that we should hear a similar note in this passage.[77] Paul stresses both God's sovereignty, which may carry a sense of distance, and his presence, which brings to mind his intimacy with the church. Paul speaks in a similar way to the Corinthians, when he declares that there are a variety of gifts but the *same* Spirit, and a variety of services but the *same* Lord, and a variety of workings but the *same* God who works all things in all (1 Cor 12:4–6).

2. Christ's Gift to the Church (4:7–16)

From the beginning of this chapter, Paul stresses the importance of "one"— one body, one Spirit, one hope, one Lord, one faith, one baptism, one God and Father over all. Such is the unity of believers, based on the unity of the

---

74. A pair of textual variants makes this explicit in two different ways. The Textus Receptus includes "all of you"; other witnesses have "all of us" (D F G K L). The earliest manuscripts do not qualify "all"; see P46 À A B C P. See MacDonald, 289, and Lincoln, 223.

75. Lincoln, 240, remarks that "Ephesians does not completely collapse cosmological categories into ecclesiological ones."

76. Lincoln, 240, cites the second-century Roman emperor and philosopher Marcus Aurelius: "All things are from you, all things are in you, all things are to you" (*Meditations* 4.23); see also Thielman, 260, who provides a list of ancient sources.

77. Lincoln, 240.

4:7–10 Christ Ascended and Descended

Godhead, and the single salvation that all believers enjoy. This unity, however, must be exercised by the church, or disunity and dissention throw the church into tumult. Christ provides for believers, equipping them in their work of service, and so the body, the church, is strengthened.

This section includes an opening sentence (4:7), a quotation from the Old Testament (4:8; Ps 68:18 [= 67:19 LXX = 68:19 MT]), a brief interpretation (Eph 4:9–10), and a second, lengthy sentence (4:11–16). The final six verses interpret each other, although their meaning is highly contested in the history of interpretation. The following sketch of the passage orients the reader to the path taken in this commentary, while various alternative readings are presented within the discussion of individual verses. Paul speaks in 4:7 of the grace given to each member of the community. This grace is explained as that which accords with or is in line with Christ's gift. The one who gives this gift is Christ, the one who descended and ascended and is now over all things (4:8–10). The recipients of the gift are the church, the saints who are equipped by the gift (4:12). The gift is made up of teaching and evangelizing functions that foster believers' growth as they serve in ministry (4:11). The terms "grace" and "gift" are linked with the topic of salvation, for salvation is God's gift, and the salvation plan reflects God's grace extended in the work of Christ. There is no mention of the Holy Spirit in these verses, even though elsewhere in the epistle the Spirit figures prominently. Paul is not speaking about spiritual gifts in 4:11, but about the gift of grace evidenced in the new composition of God's family as Jew and gentile are made one in Christ and now together grow into maturity in this new body.

a. Christ Ascended and Descended (4:7–10)

7But to each one of us grace has been given as Christ apportioned it. 8This is why it says:

"When he ascended on high,
he took many captives
and gave gifts to his people."

9(What does "he ascended" mean except that he also descended to the lower, earthly regions? 10He who descended is the very one who ascended higher than all the heavens, in order to fill the whole universe.)

7 The sentence opens a new train of thought, based on Paul's discussion of unity in the opening verses of Eph 4. In this section, Paul focuses on individual believers working out the unity they share in Christ and thus becoming mature followers. This verse contains no obtuse grammar or unusual vocabulary; nevertheless, it gives rise to several different interpretations. The key

nouns include "the grace" (notice the definite article), "gift" (*dōreas*), and "measure," while the main verb, "to give," is in the aorist passive tense, describing the giving in its entirety. Paul begins with the prepositional phrase "to each one of us." The repetition of the term "one" links 4:7 with the previous verses' emphasis on the number "one." Yet here, the focus is not on community but on individuals in the community. It is unlikely that Paul limits the individuals in this group to leaders such as apostles, for Paul has not stressed his apostleship to the Ephesians. Thus, he is not saying "to those of us leaders Christ gave the grace," but includes all Ephesian believers in the scope of this verse.[78] Paul speaks of "us," thereby including himself in the group he is describing.

The verb "to give" is in the aorist passive, and the implied giver is either God the Father or Christ. In favor of the former theory is God the Father being the closest antecedent, and in 3:8 Paul, using the same noun and verb found here, speaks of "the [same] grace" given him by God, referring to his apostolic ministry to the gentiles (see also 3:2). Moreover, declaring Christ as the intended agent of the action renders the final phrase, "of Christ" (*tou Christou*), awkward; we would expect "his." Yet Christ is clearly the actor in the next several verses as the one who distributes the gift, which is an expression of God's grace, an expression of Christ's riches. If Paul intends Christ to be the giver, then the genitive phrase at the end of the verse should be translated "from Christ."[79] It may be that Paul intends an ambiguity to stress the interwoven actions of God the Father and Christ the Son in granting grace. As I suggest below, the evidence tips in favor of seeing God the Father as the one who gives the grace, but it is Christ as the head of the church, his body, who also gives the functions of apostle, prophet, teacher, and others to aid the body's growth in wisdom and works of service.

The subject of the sentence, "the grace," can be translated "grace" or "gift." While the term can be used of salvation, as in 2:8's "by grace you have been saved," Paul does not state here that God gives more salvation grace to certain people or that he limits his salvation grace such that others do not have enough for eternal life.[80] God's grace in Christ is infinite, as the church father Jerome illustrates by picturing God's grace as the ocean and Christ standing in the water ready to fill all those who come to him with their empty jars. Jerome thinks of the sea as containing an infinite amount of water, while the

---

78. Lincoln, 241. Arnold, 246, explains: "Every individual member receives grace from God to use in the building up of others in the body (4:16)."

79. Arnold, 246; Lincoln, 241.

80. Fowl, 136, explains that "grace" is given to each so as to maintain the unity of the church.

jars hold only a finite amount. Yet all are filled, even as God's grace is sufficient for each person and the tasks they are assigned.[81]

The article with the noun ("the grace") suggests that Paul wants the reader to focus on a particular aspect of this abstract noun. Paul explicates the meaning with several prepositional phrases: "according to the measure of the gift of Christ."[82] The term "gift" (*dōrea*) is found in 3:7, where Paul identifies himself as one who preaches the gospel "according to the gift [*dōrea*] of God's grace."[83] In 2:8 grace is described as God's gift, using a related term (*dōron*).

The term "measure" carries a range of meanings, including standard, quantity, and number.[84] On the one hand, interpreters suggest that Paul distinguishes different levels or amounts of grace parceled out to individual believers based on Christ's particular gift to them.[85] In this case, the list of leaders in 4:11 represents those who have been given special amounts of grace for their tasks.[86] The problem with this view is that in 4:11 the focus is on the duties that aid the church, not on the persons who perform those responsibilities. Here in 4:7 the term "gift" is singular, while in 4:11 Christ's gift includes several items. Additionally, Paul includes himself as one who receives the gift. This means either that Paul is speaking only about leaders here in 4:7, which seems unlikely, or he includes everyone as having received God's grace.

On the other hand, one can argue that the comparison is not between believers' levels of grace but between the infinite capacity of Christ's riches of grace and the believers' finite abilities to receive and use such grace-filled gifts. A decision on this point is in part related to whether God the Father or Christ is determined to be the actor in giving the grace. If God the Father gives the grace, then the "measure" describes the grace as rooted in the riches of Christ's work on the cross. If Christ is the agent of the verb, then he is measuring out or apportioning amounts of grace to individuals based on his gift to them for the upbuilding of the congregation. In this case, Paul is noting that the measurement or standard of the grace is Christ's gift, not believers' abilities.

Two passages in Paul offer a possible comparison. In Rom 12:6 and 1 Cor 12:4, Paul speaks of "different gifts," *charismata*.[87] Paul does not use *charis-*

---

81. Jerome, *Commentary on Ephesians* (in Heine, 171).

82. The NIV translates the phrase "as Christ apportioned it." This translation assumes that "grace" and "gift" speak of the same thing.

83. On δωρεά see BDAG 266.

84. On μέτρον see BDAG 644 (2).

85. Arnold, 246, adds that Paul implicitly speaks against good works and merit to "earn a better gift or a greater portion of a gift," which overreads the theological context.

86. Thielman, 264, explains the phrase: "Christ gives 'grace' to each believer, and he does so in proportions appropriate to each gift." This meaning parallels 3:2, 7, 8.

87. Arnold, 246, explains that χάρισμα means "'a manifestation of grace' (the μα suffix

mata in Eph 4:7 or 4:11. And in Rom 12:3–6, Paul speaks of the "measure of faith" and of different gifts given according to the grace. He cautions believers not to think more highly of themselves, but to have a sober opinion, for God apportioned a measure of faith to each person. This sober opinion is measured over against the gospel, the work of Christ, and not in comparison to other believers.[88] The passage in Romans warns against saying, in effect, "At least I'm not like so-and-so." Paul continues that believers receive different gifts (*charismata*) that spring from the same grace (12:6). However, Ephesians emphasizes unity, not difference, and on equipping believers for ministry based on what Christ gives the church (apostles, prophets, teachers). The gift given includes the resources of apostles and pastors, evangelists and teachers. Therefore, the passages in Romans and 1 Corinthians provide no parallel to our verses.

8 Paul begins this verse with a citation formula found only here and in 5:14 in Paul's Epistles.[89] The phrase "this is why it says" introduces a passage from Ps 68:18 (= 68:19 MT = 67:19 LXX).[90] In our passage we read: "When he ascended on high, he took many captives and gave gifts to his people." In the Hebrew and the Septuagint the verse reads: "You ascended to the height; you captured captivity; you received gifts among humanity."[91] Paul's quotation changes the verb "to ascend" to the third-person singular participle from the second-person singular finite verb. Paul also changes the verb in the last clause, such that our passage reads "to give," while the Hebrew and Septuagint have "to receive." He also changes the singular "human" to plural "humans." The prepositional phrase "on high" indicates where Christ ascended. The aorist indicative active "to lead captive" or "to take" and the cognate plural noun "captives" or "captivity" indicate an action done in its totality by Christ. The final clause includes the verb "to give" and the cognate plural noun "gifts," highlighting another action by Christ. The gifts are given to people. To summarize the changes, Paul speaks about Christ giving gifts to people, while the biblical texts speak of God receiving gifts from people. The passage focuses on the ascent/descent theme and speaks of captives taken prisoner by Christ.

---

indicates a result of the action," citing A. T. Robertson, *A Grammar of the Greek New Testament in the Light of Historical Research* (Nashville: Broadman, 1934), 153.

88. Cohick, 106–8; C. E. B. Cranfield, *A Critical and Exegetical Commentary on the Epistle to the Romans*, International Critical Commentary (Edinburgh: T&T Clark, 1975), 613–16; Joseph A. Fitzmyer, *Romans: A New Translation with Introduction and Commentary*, Anchor Yale Bible 33 (New York: Doubleday, 1993), 645–46. An opposing view is offered by James D. G. Dunn, *Romans 9–16*, Word Biblical Commentary 38B (Grand Rapids: Zondervan, 1988), 721–28.

89. The phrase is used in Jas 4:6, citing Prov 3:34.

90. Hoehner, 524, observes that the Septuagint follows the Hebrew verbatim.

91. Translation from Thielman, 265, who captures the similar sounding Greek terms.

4:7–10 CHRIST ASCENDED AND DESCENDED

What should we make of these changes? It is possible that Paul rewrote the psalm to demonstrate its argument more clearly. Another possibility is that Paul is familiar with quotations from a Jewish tradition later codified in the Targum, the Aramaic version of the Hebrew.[92] The verse reads: "You, Moses the prophet, ascended to the firmament; you took captivity captive, you learned the words of the Torah, you gave them as gifts to the sons of men."[93] The Targum is from the fourth or fifth century, however, and so likely reflects a later rabbinic response to Paul's quotation and the tradition that grew up around it in the early church.[94] Again, we do not find the figure of Moses in our epistle, nor a discussion about Torah and Christ.[95]

Most likely, Paul himself altered the text. Jerome indicates that Paul understood the work of Christ to have fulfilled the victory to which the psalmist pointed.[96] It may also be that Paul chose this verse as a way to connect Christ's work with the Father's grace, for the Father gives grace and the Son gives the gift necessary to grow his body, the church.[97] Why did Paul choose Ps 68, especially given the changes made? At least three possibilities suggest themselves, and these are not mutually exclusive. First, as we read the psalm in its entirety, the psalmist exalts in God's victory over his enemies and describes the procession of the victorious Lord to the Jerusalem temple, receiving gifts from the defeated kings and praise from those he saved. In Paul's day, victorious Roman generals, after gathering plunder, would give some of it as gifts to their steadfast soldiers. The psalm reflects an important theme in Ephesians, namely, the exaltation of Christ over all rulers and authorities (1:20–21; 3:10; 6:12, 16).[98] So too in Colossians, Paul declares that Christ disarmed the powers and makes them a public spectacle with his death on the cross (Col 2:15).

---

92. Lincoln, 243; Yoder Neufeld, 176.

93. Translation from Hoehner, 526. For a general discussion, see David M. Stec, *The Targum of Psalms*, Aramaic Bible 16 (Collegeville, MN: Liturgical Press, 2004).

94. Lincoln, 243, argues for an "ancient rabbinic tradition" underpinning the Targum, from which the author drew and modified the focus from Moses to Christ. Lincoln suggests that "Moses mysticism" was widespread and our author reacts against it by positing Christ as greater than Moses. Arnold, 251, suggests that the Peshitta (Syriac translation of the Psalms), which has the variant "he gave," predates Ephesians and thus could have influenced Paul's interpretation.

95. Arnold, 250, rightly observes that 2:15 is not a polemic against the Torah per se, but is an argument explaining the gentiles' new status as those near to God through Christ. Contra MacDonald, 290, who observes that "the author of Ephesians takes the psalm as referring to Christ and seems to understand him as the new Moses."

96. Jerome, *Commentary on Ephesians* (in Heine, 172).

97. Salmond, 325, concludes that this was a messianic psalm and that, "in any case, it is an *application* rather than an *interpretation* in the strict sense of the word that we have here."

98. Arnold, 247, explains that Paul "wants his readers to grasp the incomparably great power of God, who strengthens his people to stand against their enemies."

Second, the psalm uses the term "ascend," which plays an important role in Paul's Christology.[99] For example, in Rom 10:6-8, Paul uses Deut 30:12-14 as a message to the church that Christ is close at hand and offers redemption to all who have faith (see also Ps 107:23-30). And the Christ hymn in Phil 2:6-11 presents Christ as one who descended to earth in the incarnation and ascended back to God in exaltation following the resurrection and victory over sin and death. Third, and related to the second view, Paul may reflect the exegetical approach known as pesher.[100] This reading method is used in the Qumran scrolls and involves citing a biblical text and then explaining how the text applies to events past, present, and future associated with the group.[101] Interestingly, among the scrolls is a fragment of a pesher on Ps 68, but it is too fragmented to discern the interpretation (1QpPs = 1Q16).[102] In our case, the interpretation focuses on the phrase "he ascended." Note that while the phrase "he gave" is found in both Eph 4:7 and 4:11, "the connection is not in the exegetical style of a pesher."[103] This insight emphasizes the importance of the descent/ascent motif found within early Christian reflection on Jesus (John 3:14; Acts 2:32-35).

Paul begins this quotation with the phrase "when he ascended" and indicates that he rose "on high."[104] Paul's focus on the verb "to ascend" becomes clear in 4:9-10, where he makes the case that to ascend implies that one has descended. As such, the one now ascended is over all the heavens and fills all the cosmos. Paul continues with the verb "to take captive" and follows with

---

99. Lincoln, 242, who points to 1:20-22 as evidence of the epistle's emphasis on "Christ's exaltation."

100. The Aramaic term means "solution" or "interpretation." For a discussion of the term and the related method of midrash, see Richard N. Longenecker, *Biblical Exegesis in the Apostolic Period*, 2nd ed. (Grand Rapids: Eerdmans, 1999), 24-30. See also Shani Berrin, "Qumran *Pesharim*," in *Biblical Interpretation at Qumran*, ed. Matthias Henze (Grand Rapids: Eerdmans, 2005), 110, who defines pesher as "a form of biblical interpretation peculiar to Qumran, in which biblical poetic/prophetic texts are applied to postbiblical historical/eschatological settings through various literary techniques in order to substantiate a theological conviction pertaining to divine reward and punishment." For the corpus of Qumran pesharim, see Maurya P. Horgan, *Pesharim: Qumran Interpretations of Biblical Books*, Catholic Biblical Quarterly Monograph 8 (Washington, DC: Catholic Biblical Association of America, 1979).

101. Perkins, 97, cites Isa 40:3 in 1QS 8:13-16 and Isa 24:17 in CD 4:13-15.

102. Perkins, 97, adds: "Ephesians may have taken its citation from a comparable text."

103. Perkins, 98. She concludes that the author drew on a "fragment of early Christian exegesis," but it is also possible that Paul himself combined a pesher approach with one that focused on the key terms "to give" and "gift." Lincoln, 226, widens the lens by suggesting a midrashic approach that "fulfills a typical function of Haggadah, filling out possible gaps in the meaning of a text."

104. On ἀναβαίνω see BDAG 58.

the cognate noun "captivity" or "captives." Paul does not develop this image here, but most likely Paul refers to Christ taking the principalities and powers captive or leading their captives to freedom.[105] These powers would include the ruler of the kingdom of the air (2:2), who has authority over those who stand in disobedience to God, and the evil authorities in the heavens (6:12).

The final line of the quotation includes the verb "to give" and the direct object "gifts," a noun used here and in Phil 4:17 (see also Matt 7:11; Luke 11:13).[106] These gifts are given to "the people." The verb "to give" repeats from the previous verse, and the term "gifts" is a synonym to the singular "gift" found in Eph 4:7. Paul picks up the verb "to give" again in 4:11 as he declares that Christ gives apostles, prophets, evangelists, pastors, and teachers to the saints for their equipping in ministry. In the intervening two verses, Paul expands on the idea of ascending and descending to show Christ's superior power and authority over all things. Thus, he is able to give gifts that build the church, his body. Paul exegetes the question in 4:9–10.

9 After citing from Ps 68, Paul analyzes the psalm in this and the following verse. The verse opens with Paul asking a rhetorical question: What does the phrase "he ascended" imply? and the answer that it must mean that "he descended." Paul elaborates that Christ descended to the lower regions of the earth. This verse includes two interesting textual variants in our ancient manuscripts. First, we find the addition of the term "first" after the phrase "he descended"; second, we have the term "regions" after the adjective "lower." The inclusion of "first" was likely the effort of an early copyist to make clear the order of descent and ascent, lacking in the original quotation.[107] Second, the addition of "regions" is unattested in some of the oldest texts.[108] One can imagine a scribe adding this term to make the sentence read more smoothly. Paul describes the area as "lower," using a term found only here in the New Testament.[109] Paul could be referring to a place under the earth's surface, what was known as Hades.[110] The wider Greco-Roman world had an intense, terrifying

---

105. Arnold, 251; Lincoln, 242. Best, 382, observes that the decision about the identity of the captives is linked with the interpretation of 4:9.

106. On δόμα see BDAG 256.

107. Lincoln, 224. The adjective "first" is omitted in P46 א* A C* D G and in Irenaeus (Lat.), Clement, Tertullian, Origen. The variant appears in Àc B and others, plus most Latin manuscripts and the KJV.

108. The noun is omitted in P46 D* E F G and Irenaeus, Theodotus, Clement, Origen. On μέρος see BDAG 633 (1). Lincoln, 224, observes that the variant might be original and that, in the end, the meaning of the verse remains the same whether the noun is included or not.

109. On κατώτερος see BDAG 535.

110. William Bales, "The Descent of Christ in Ephesians 4:9," *Catholic Biblical Quarterly* 72 (2010): 99, suggests that Ephesians reflects a "three-tiered cosmology that includes an underworld," citing 1:20 and 5:14.

mythology surrounding the place of the dead to which the gods and humans descended and ascended.[111] The Ephesians would have been familiar with stories of the god Hades kidnapping Persephone, daughter of Zeus and Demeter, and taking her to the underworld. They would have heard about Aeneas and Pythagoras making the journey to the underworld and back to the land of the living.[112] Yet if Paul wanted to speak of this region, he had at least two terms ready at hand, "Hades" or "the abyss" (Rom 10:7).[113] Alternatively, Paul could intend to speak of a lower place relative to heaven, namely, the earth. If Paul includes the regions of the air in his cosmology, as was common in his day, then the comment here must refer to the earth and not to Hades.[114]

Three basic views are put forward explaining Paul's intention with the phrase "he descended." First, some argue that the verse indicates that Christ descended into hell and ascended to heaven (Rom 10:6–7).[115] This view can be linked to the doctrine of the "harrowing of Hell" (Latin *descensus Christi ad inferos*) as found in the Apostles' Creed and the Athanasian Creed.[116] Yet the context in Ephesians contrasts an ascent to heaven with a descent from heaven, not a descent from earth to the underworld.[117]

---

111. Bales, "Descent of Christ," 90, concludes: "So prevalent was the idea of an 'underworld' in the Greco-Roman culture of the day that it can be reasonably assumed that the average person would have understood the phrase 'he descended to the lower regions of the earth' as indicating . . . a descent (of some sort) to the underworld, the realm of the dead." Arnold, *Ephesians: Power and Magic*, 57, concludes that the reference to the lower regions of the earth "makes most sense in its first-century Hellenistic and religious context if it is understood as an expression for the underworld or Hades."

112. Arnold, *Ephesians: Power and Magic*, 57–58, discusses the possibility that Paul stresses Christ's superiority over the deities of the underworld in his insistence that Christ descended to that realm.

113. Hoehner, 535.

114. Perkins, 98, contrasts this passage with Rom 10:7; 1 Pet 3:18–21; Rev 1:18, which refer to "some region below the earth."

115. Bales, "Descent of Christ," 84, cites several church fathers' support of this view: Irenaeus, *Against Heresies* 4.22.1; Tertullian, *The Soul* 55.2; Ambrosiaster, *Ephesians* 4; Dio Chrysostom, *Homilies on Ephesians* 11; Jerome, *Commentary on Ephesians* 2.4. Bales concludes (100) that the descent phrase is used metaphorically "to indicate Christ's sacrificial death."

116. Gen 6:1–8 speaks about the sons of God coming down from the heavens to be with the daughters of men. These spiritual beings wreaked havoc, bringing all sorts of evil on the earth and great misery to humans. During Paul's day, an influential elaboration of this text circulated under the name 1 Enoch. In this work, God punishes the spiritual beings, called the "watchers," by condemning them to the earth, no longer able to ascend to the heavens from which they came (1 Enoch 1–36). First Pet 3:19–22 likely draws on this text when declaring that Christ preached to those in prison.

117. Lincoln, 245, who adds that if the contrast was between the underworld and heaven, the author would have used superlative, rather than comparative language.

4:7–10 CHRIST ASCENDED AND DESCENDED

Second, some argue that it is Christ who ascends and then, after this, the Holy Spirit descends to the church at Pentecost.[118] In this case, Paul draws his understanding of Ps 68 from the Moses tradition wherein Moses ascended Mount Sinai to receive the law, then descended to the people with the gift of the law. Paul substitutes Christ for Moses, and Christ descends as the Pentecost experience. It is suggested that the experiences of the Spirit among the Ephesians might be underneath this reference, as Paul encourages them to know the love of Christ that surpasses knowledge (3:19) and to recall that they are seated with Christ in the heavenlies (2:6).[119] This interpretation has a necessary corollary that Christ descends in some way in the Pentecost event to give gifts, a view that would be "unusual."[120] Additionally, 4:10, which stresses that Christ fills the universe, focuses on the ascent as the climactic moment, while this theory seems to privilege the descent moment when the gifts are given.

Third, some suggest (and I put myself in this camp) that Paul supposes the descent in the incarnation and the ascent in Christ's exaltation, pointing to Phil 2:6–11 as a parallel example of this christological view (see also John 3:13; 6:62).[121] In Phil 2:10, Paul identifies the heavens above the earth, the lower regions (specifically the earth itself), and the regions below the earth. Paul declares that every knee will bow in heaven and on earth and under the earth—perhaps a reference to the all-encompassing victory of Christ. So too in Ephesians, the triumph of Christ is in view, for the final two clauses of 4:10 speak of Christ's ascent extending far above the heavens and thus filling the cosmos. Paul stresses that no part of the cosmos is beyond Christ's grace and judgment.

10 Paul uses the intensive pronoun "himself" or "the very one" as he further emphasizes his argument that there is but one figure who has descended and ascended, namely, Christ. Paul describes the ascension as reaching far above all things in the heavens. Earlier, Paul underscored that Christ is above all things, all rulers and authorities and powers and dominions (1:21). Christ is seated at God's right hand in the heavenly realms (2:6). Christ's love extends beyond any human horizon, further than anyone's imagination can carry them, beyond the scope of human comprehension (3:18). Paul closes this verse with a purpose clause "in order to fill the whole universe." Paul

---

118. W. Hall Harris III, *The Descent of Christ: Ephesians 4:7–11 and Traditional Hebrew Imagery*, Arbeiten zur Geschichte des antiken Judentums und des Urchristentums 32 (Leiden: Brill, 1996); Lincoln, 244–48.

119. MacDonald, 296–97.

120. Lincoln, 247. His claim that "a close association, and indeed virtual interchange, between Christ and the Spirit is evidenced elsewhere in Ephesians" seems to stretch the evidence beyond what it can bear.

121. Bruce, 343–45; Barth, 432–34; Perkins, 97–99; Best, 383–88.

uses the verb "to fill" several times in Ephesians, including his description of Christ's body (the church) being filled with Christ (1:23) and his prayer that believers will know the love of Christ in order to be filled with the fullness of God (3:19).[122] In both cases, the language is part of Paul's prayers. We likely have a liturgical echo here as well, as Paul cites a psalm of praise and contemplates Christ's work on behalf of his church. Paul expounds to the Colossians that God was pleased to have his fullness dwell in Christ, using the noun cognate of the verb "to fill" (Col 1:19). This filling is for the sake of God's world that he might reconcile humanity to himself and bring unity to all things (Eph 1:10).

b. Christ's Body Grows to Fullness (4:11–16)

11So Christ himself gave the apostles, the prophets, the evangelists, the pastors and teachers, 12to equip his people for works of service, so that the body of Christ may be built up 13until we all reach unity in the faith and in the knowledge of the Son of God and become mature, attaining to the whole measure of the fullness of Christ.

14Then we will no longer be infants, tossed back and forth by the waves, and blown here and there by every wind of teaching and by the cunning and craftiness of people in their deceitful scheming. 15Instead, speaking the truth in love, we will grow to become in every respect the mature body of him who is the head, that is, Christ. 16From him the whole body, joined and held together by every supporting ligament, grows and builds itself up in love, as each part does its work.

These verses form a lengthy sentence (4:11–16), as Paul discusses the local church growing and maturing into Christ's likeness. Paul assures believers that Christ, the one who ascended to the heights of heaven, has given his church all they need to walk faithfully and in one accord. This section is often read as parallel to Rom 12 and 1 Cor 12, which speak about spiritual gifts (*charismata*) given to individual believers. These are manifested as the gifts of healing, teaching, giving, prophesying, or speaking in tongues (for the lists, see Rom 12:6–8; 1 Cor 12:7–11). In these two epistles, Paul addresses the *diverse* gifts and the *same* Spirit who gives the gifts to believers. Here in Ephesians, however, the singular gift is given to the church by Christ himself who fills all things. Moreover, we do well to reflect on the key terms "gift" and "grace" found in 4:7 and earlier in the epistle. In 2:8 Paul declares that believers are saved by grace, using the term we find also in 4:7 (*charis*). This grace is described as God's gift, using the noun *dōron*, related to *dōrea* found

---

122. On πληρόω see BDAG 827–29.

in 4:7. In 2:10 Paul declares that believers are God's handiwork, for his gift of salvation makes it possible to do the good works that he established for them to do. Then in 3:7 Paul speaks about his servant status as one who preaches the gospel "by the gift [*dōrea*] of God's grace." In 3:8 Paul declares that "this grace," which made gentiles coheirs with Jews in God's family, is given him to preach the gospel to the gentiles. These terms, "grace" and "gift," are linked with the topic of salvation, for salvation is God's gift, and the salvation plan reflects God's grace extended in the work of Christ. There is no mention of the Holy Spirit in these verses, even though elsewhere in the epistle, the Spirit figures prominently. These points add up to the conclusion that Paul is not speaking about spiritual gifts in 4:11. Instead, his focus is on the gift of grace evidenced in the new composition of God's family as Jew and gentile are made one in Christ and now together grow into maturity in this new body.

In our epistle, Paul focuses on a single gift given to the entire church, and that gift is the equipping of the saints for ministry. Paul declares that each believer has been given (the) grace by God, grace that is defined as or is measured as the gift of Christ (4:7). This grace is exceedingly abundant and entirely suitable for preparing believers to walk worthy of their calling (4:1). The gift is given by the one who descended and now is ascended (4:10), who sits at God's right hand in the heavens (2:6). The gift Christ gives serves to instruct his body, the church. These formational functions make up the singular gift given by Christ.

To accomplish the task of equipping the church, Christ gives apostles, prophets, evangelists, pastors, and teachers—the emphasis is on a team who by God's grace strengthens the church. Christ's gift centers on teaching about the truth of God and his plan of salvation. We do not hear about church order here, nothing about overseers or deacons as we find in Phil 1:1 or in 1 Tim 3:1–13. Said another way, Paul is not interested here in a particular church structure,[123] but in the dissemination of correct knowledge and wisdom about the gospel. Paul takes advantage of the vivid image of the church as Christ's body to explore maturation and growth metaphors. In Eph 4:14 Paul notes that believers are not infants, and in 4:15 he exhorts believers, including himself, to grow unto Christ the head of his body, the church. Just as in a healthy human body, the parts grow together and proportionally to each other, so too in the church community, each member grows in relation to the other members, as well as maturing in its own function.

11–12 Paul continues his discussion about the gift that Christ gives the church. Paul repeats the verb "to give" that he used in 4:7. I argued that in 4:7 God is the gift giver and that Paul uses the psalmic quotation to focus on

---

123. Contra Barth, 435, who observes: "By his gift the exalted Christ establishes an order and gives the church a constitution."

the gift that Christ brings the church. This allows Paul to talk here about the ascended one, Christ, giving the gift to the church. The verse continues with five components of the gift that Christ gives the church: apostles, prophets, evangelists, pastors, and teachers. Another way to read this verse is to insert the verb "to be" before each of these nouns, with the resulting translation: he gave some *to be* apostles and so on. This addition makes sense if the reader believes that Paul focuses on an individual believer's spiritual gift.[124] However, if the focus is on equipping the church, as I argue here, then the gift itself is made up of several functions or offices, including apostles, prophets, evangelists, pastors, and teachers.

Paul draws out the conclusion he set up with his statement in 4:7. In the earlier verse, Paul declares that each believer receives "the grace" from God, and this grace is reflected in the gift of salvation, established based on the measure, the riches, of Christ's gift (3:8). Each believer has the same grace, as they are established by the same God and Father of all, sharing the same Spirit and enjoying the same hope of their calling (4:4–6). Not only is Christ the gift, he also gives the gift, as Paul explains by citing Ps 68 and explaining that Christ is the ascended one who fills all things. This very one gives to his followers the resources to walk in a worthy manner (Eph 4:1; see also 2:10). The means to this glorious end includes the strengthening of knowledge about who God is and who they are in Christ, as Paul prayed in 3:18–19. Such understanding comes in part through teaching and modeling by individuals equipped for these tasks.

Paul begins 4:11 with "so," which links this verse to the previous one as the conclusion to the exegetical claims made about the scriptural quotation.[125] Paul stresses Christ as the actor with the personal pronoun "he" and Christ's action with the verb "to give," repeated from 4:7 and from his quotation of Ps 68, which substitutes "he gave" for the Hebrew and Greek textual reading "he received." Paul proceeds with a list of five functions, including apostles, prophets, evangelists, pastors, and teachers. Four of these nouns have the article attached, and all are in the accusative case. To group the items, the list uses the construction of two Greek particles, *men* and *de . . . de*. The question for interpreters comes in deciding the syntax of the sentence. It is possible that the article functions as a pronoun, in which case the reader inserts the implied verb "to be" and the phrase reads "he gave *some to be* apostles." The noun is understood as the predicate.[126] Supporters of this position point to the practice of using the article as a personal pronoun with *men . . . de* (see

---

124. Arnold, 256, sees the list as describing "gifted people" who have leadership roles.
125. Hoehner, 540.
126. Lincoln, 226, states: "The gifts turn out to be a variety of particular people, all of whom have ministries involving some form of proclamation of the word."

1 Cor 7:7; Heb 7:5–6); however, in these instances, the article is in the nominative, not in the accusative, as is the case in our verse.[127] It is more likely that Paul intends the list to be understood as discrete functions performed in the church for the strengthening of believers so that they can do what is expected of them, namely, works of service. The phrase would then read, "he gave apostles, and so on," with the article serving as an attributive modifier.[128] The potential problem with this option is that we then have no indirect object, no statement about who receives this gift. We might expect Paul to say, Christ gave *to the church* apostles, prophets, and so on. However, because the context clearly focuses on the body, with the explicit mention of "his people" and "the body of Christ" in 4:12, the problem recedes.[129]

Looking closely at the specific aspects of the gift to the church, Paul lists apostles, prophets, evangelists, pastors, and teachers. The focus is not on how the Spirit gifts individuals for ministry, but on the duties of such roles in helping the church mature.[130] Paul speaks in a similar way to the Corinthians when he notes that he is God's servant and it is God who gives the growth to the church (1 Cor 3:6–9). The group of five services performed for the church concentrate on properly presenting the gospel message. Central to their duties is speaking, although their words must match their deeds.[131] Paul focuses on speaking well and truthfully throughout this chapter, stressing the unity of the faith and the knowledge of the Son of God that matures the church (Eph 4:13–14), cautioning against falsehoods and unwholesome talk (4:25, 29) and promoting uplifting speech that builds up others (4:15).

Paul has mentioned apostles and prophets twice in Ephesians, in 2:20 and 3:5. In Eph 2 he notes their role as the foundation of the church, and in Eph 3 he stresses that they received a revelation hidden in ages past and now made known in Christ. Paul introduces himself as apostle to the Ephesians (1:1), a pattern we find in other epistles (Rom 1:1; 1 Cor 1:1; 2 Cor 1:1; Gal 1:1; Col 1:1; 1 Tim 1:1; 2 Tim 1:1; Titus 1:1). The noun "apostle" generally refers to a key leadership position in the church, whose duties include presenting true

---

127. Wallace, *Greek Grammar*, 212–13.
128. Lincoln, 249. Yet Lincoln argues that in Rom 12 and 1 Cor 12 the gifts are ministries or functions, but in Eph 4 "the focus is narrowed to particular ministers of the word."
129. MacDonald, 291, states: "What is implied is that the gifts the ascended Christ gives to believers for service to the church have led to the creation of apostles, prophets, evangelists, pastors, and teachers."
130. Barth, 435, observes that the gift from Christ is a "unit: the one 'grace' given corresponds to the one gift of the Messiah." He adds: "This gift is the same and has the same measure for 'each one of us' (4:7)."
131. Paul speaks of doing the signs and wonders that are expected of an apostle (2 Cor 12:12).

doctrine and moral guidance in accordance with the gospel.[132] The person is sent with authority and represents that authority. Paul declares that the authority of his apostleship is Christ (Gal 1:1). The cognate verb "to send" emphasizes the sender's purpose, not the messenger's activities (Isa 6:8; see also 61:1, quoted in Luke 4:18–19).[133] The noun is rarely used in the Septuagint or in Greek-speaking Judaism, which suggests that this word takes on a special significance for the early church as apostles act as representatives of Jesus Christ.

"Apostle" can refer to "the Twelve," those Jewish men whom Jesus chose as special disciples. They represented the twelve tribes of Israel restored in the messianic kingdom, which is why when Judas, the apostle who betrayed Jesus, killed himself, the other eleven apostles replaced his number (Acts 1:26). Paul mentions the Twelve when he speaks to the Corinthians about Jesus's postresurrection appearances (1 Cor 15:5) and distinguishes his own apostolic calling from this group (15:9).

Paul represents a second use of the term "apostle," one who was called after Jesus's earthly ministry. In Paul's case, the risen Jesus called him as Paul journeyed to Damascus in pursuit of Jesus's followers (Acts 9:1–6; 14:4, 14). Other men and women in this category include James, the Lord's brother (1 Cor 15:7; Gal 1:19), Barnabas (Acts 14:4, 14; 1 Cor 9:5–7), Apollos (1 Cor 4:6, 9), and Andronicus and Junia (Rom 16:7). A third use of the term centers on denoting a person who is commissioned by the congregation for a specific duty (2 Cor 8:23; Phil 2:25).

Paul speaks next about "prophets," a term that is widely used in religious contexts by both gentiles and Jews.[134] This person makes known the will of the gods/God. In the Old Testament, the prophet speaks on behalf of God, receives visions, offers signs, and brings warnings to the people. In the New Testament, the noun occurs extensively, most often in the Gospels, and refers to an individual who proclaims God's will. Several women are identified as prophetesses, including Miriam (Exod 15:20–21), Huldah (2 Kgs 22:8–20; 2 Chr 34:14–28), and Anna (Luke 2:36; see also Acts 2:17; 21:9; 1 Cor 11:5). Paul encourages the Corinthians to desire the gift of prophecy, because a prophet encourages, comforts, edifies, and strengthens the church (1 Cor 14:1–4). Paul indicates that men and women prayed and prophesied in the church (1 Cor 11:4–5).

"Evangelist" is the third noun in the list. The term appears only three times in the New Testament (see also Acts 21:8; 2 Tim 4:5).[135] The evangelist's

---

132. On ἀπόστολος see BDAG 122 (2); P. W. Barnett, "Apostle," *DPL* 45–51.
133. Arnold, 256.
134. On προφήτης see BDAG 890–91 (1).
135. On εὐαγγελιστής see BDAG 403.

task is to proclaim the gospel message, so in that sense, they function as do the apostles; nevertheless, they lack the specific apostolic call from Christ. Evangelists serve as missionaries, but also can lead a specific community with their preaching.[136]

The fourth term, translated rightly "pastor," is the noun usually translated "shepherd."[137] This term has strong Old Testament antecedents, as God is described as Israel's true shepherd (Isa 40:11; 63:11; Jer 23:3; 31:10; Ezek 34:2–10), and the latter prophets look for the day when Israel will be led by shepherds after God's heart (Jer 3:15; Zech 11:15).[138] The New Testament carries forward these positive connotations, including identifying Christ as Shepherd (John 10:1–30; Heb 13:20; 1 Pet 2:25; 5:4). Shepherds visit the Christ child in the nativity story (Luke 2:8–20) and appear in the poignant parables of the shepherd seeking his lost sheep (Luke 15:4–6), caring for his sheep (John 10:2–14), and meting out judgment in the last day (Matt 25:31–32). The cognate verb, "shepherding," is used to describe the actions of leaders in Ephesus (Acts 20:28; see also John 21:16; 1 Pet 5:2).[139]

The fifth and final term in this list, "teachers,"[140] does not have an article, which may indicate that it should be linked with the fourth noun to create a single group "pastors and teachers."[141] In this case, Paul would be stating that pastors should be teaching their congregations, perhaps with a specific focus on discerning true from false doctrine. Yet in 2:20 we have a similar construction with the single article serving both nouns, so it is more likely that Paul simply dropped the final article to avoid repetition.[142] Teachers include those who present the message of the gospel to the congregation. Paul speaks of his apostolic calling and his role as a true and faithful teacher in his letter to Timothy (1 Tim 2:7; 2 Tim 1:11).

In sum, these five functions or tasks serve to equip the church for its ministry. These responsibilities are not limited to men, for the plural mascu-

---

136. Barth, 438.

137. On ποιμήν see BDAG 843 (2). MacDonald, 292, observes that the terms "evangelist" and "pastor/shepherd" are not found in the undisputed Pauline letters. Perkins, 99, points to the Cairo Genizah copy of the Damascus Document (CD 13:7–11) as an example of the Essenes identifying a community leader as shepherd.

138. My thanks to Julie Dykes, my research assistant, for her observations on the shepherd in the Old Testament.

139. MacDonald, 292.

140. On διδάσκαλος see BDAG 241.

141. Barth, 438–39. He adds that καί can be translated as "that is" or "in particular."

142. Wallace, *Greek Grammar*, 272, 284, shows that the Granville Sharp rule does not apply with plural substantives. Arnold, 260, suggests that the two groups, teachers and pastors, are not a single group, but have related functions, such that "pastors are to be gifted to teach." See also Best, 393.

line pronouns are not exclusive, and we have examples of women as apostles (Rom 16:7), prophets (Acts 21:9), and teachers (Acts 18:26).[143] Moreover, this passage is not promoting a hierarchical structure as would later characterize the church, for "each of the ministers takes a part in the integrated whole of the church."[144]

After listing the five functions that comprise the gift Christ gives to the church, Paul offers a series of three prepositional phrases that connect with the previous verse's verb "to give." The first prepositional phrase includes the article and noun (translated "to equip" in NIV) and is found only here in the New Testament, though the cognate verb is used often. The verb has a range of meanings, such as "to restore" or "to outfit."[145] Outside the biblical text, the noun is used in medical writings to speak of setting bones, and this connotation could be operating in the background, given that Paul speaks of Christ's body in this verse.[146] The second prepositional phrase "for works" expresses the aim of equipping believers. This work is further described by the noun *diakonia*, which carries the meaning of "service" or "ministry."[147] This activity is broad ranging, including help in daily life and promoting the common good, as well as serving at tables and providing gospel-centered teaching.[148] The third prepositional phrase "for the building up" expresses the outcome of the work of service. Paul uses the same noun in 2:20–22 when he speaks about the community of faith, Jew and gentile together in Christ, being built up into God's temple. Paul speaks of apostles and prophets as forming the foundation for this building, with Christ as the cornerstone by which all is aligned. Paul repeats this emphasis in 4:16, that every member of the church matures together, as Christ the head of the body supports his body's growth.

Two primary theories seek to explain the precise relationship between the phrases themselves, as well as their relationship to the verb in the previous verse and their relationship to the list of apostles, prophets, and so on. The three prepositional phrases include "to [*pros*] equip the saints," "for [*eis*] works of service," and "so that [*eis*] the body of Christ may be built up." Notice that the first preposition (*pros*) is different from the remaining two (*eis*). Paul tends to be careful in choosing his prepositions and gives them their distinct emphasis.[149] Notice also that Paul does not use any conjunctions such as "and"

---

143. Best, 394.
144. MacDonald, 298. She continues, less persuasively in my view, that the author wants to reinforce leadership because of the loss of Paul, a charismatic leader of the movement.
145. On καταρτίζω see BDAG 526.
146. MacDonald, 292.
147. On διακονία see BDAG 230 (2); C. G. Kruse, "Servant, Service," *DPL* 869–71.
148. Barth, 439–40; contra Lincoln, 253.
149. Contra Lincoln, 253.

between the phrases, leaving it to the reader to determine their relationship. If one sees the three preposition phrases explicating the responsibilities of the five leadership roles, the resulting church structure emphasizes a high degree of distinction between laity and clergy. In this case, the leaders do three things: equip the church, do works of service, and build up the church.[150] A second possibility follows the distinctive prepositions, separating the first clause from the second and third prepositional phrases. Thus, the actions of the apostles, prophets, and so on equip the saints (1) for their work of service so that the latter might (2) build up the body of Christ. This theory presents the church structure as less hierarchical, and the emphasis falls on the priesthood of all believers.[151] This second option is the most likely for several reasons. First, within the first prepositional phrase the object carries the article, while within the other two phrases, the two objects are anarthrous. Second, this position does not overload the term "equipping" but follows the verb's meaning as "to prepare, outfit."[152] Third, this option makes the best sense of the change in prepositions between the first and second clauses.[153] Finally, while elsewhere the New Testament discusses ministerial roles, in Ephesians ministerial functions are filled by the members of the congregation; here the context is the same, namely, the building up of the church (see also Rom 15:14; 1 Cor 14:26; Eph 5:19; Phil 1:15; Col 3:16; 1 Thess 5:11).[154]

13 These works of service, which build up the church, have as their goals the unity and maturity of the church. Ephesians 4:13 begins with a conjunction, "until," which implies that the goal will be attained.[155] The verb "to reach" is used by Paul when he speaks of attaining to the resurrection of the dead (Phil 3:11).[156] It is less likely that this opening clause refers back to the phrase "Christ gave" (Eph 4:11), because the focus is not on Christ continually giving apostles, prophets, and so on, but on the continuing upbuilding of the church.

The verse continues with three phrases that express the same goal from different perspectives.[157] The three key nouns are "unity," "mature man" (translated "become mature" in NIV), and "measure." In the first clause, Paul

---

150. Lincoln, 253; MacDonald, 292.
151. Arnold, 262; Hoehner, 548-49; Best, 398.
152. Arnold, 263.
153. Best, 398, concludes: "The change in preposition between 12a and 12bc confirms that the movement from the discussion of the work of the ministers (v. 11) to that of the whole church takes place between 12a and 12bc."
154. Best, 398.
155. Arnold, 264, adds that the common conjunction ἵνα does not express such certainty.
156. On καταντάω see BDAG 523 (2).
157. Arnold, 264; Best, 399-403.

repeats the term "unity," found only in 4:3, followed by "in the faith." Given that Paul will distinguish proper and false doctrine in the next verse, it is best to see this mention of "faith" as right teaching given to the church and not as a reference to a believer's personal trust in Christ's redemptive work.[158] The focus is the whole church, not on individuals who make up the body. Paul will speak to individuals later in the chapter when he asks that each person put off the old self and put on the new, which is created to be like God (4:22–24). Paul continues with a second phrase "in the knowledge of the Son of God." While "the faith" refers to Christian teaching, "the knowledge" is likely a subjectively discovered conviction about Christ. The syntax links Son of God only with "the knowledge" as its object.[159] Paul stresses a similar thought in his prayer in 3:14–19, where he prays that they would know the love of Christ that surpasses knowledge. And in 1:17–18, he prayed that they would know the glorious Father of the Lord Jesus. This sort of knowing is more than an intellectual ascent to a truth claim, but involves a personal understanding and love of God.

Paul uses the phrase "Son of God" only here in Ephesians, but it is found throughout Paul's letters (Rom 1:3–4; 2 Cor 1:19; Gal 2:20).[160] What might be invested in this language? As noted in the introduction, the conversation often ranges along a continuum of "high" to "low" Christology.[161] I suggest a relationality perspective that insists one can understand God only in relation to Jesus, and Jesus only in relation to God. What is that relationality? Descriptions of this must include the salvation plan, which speaks of Christ as sent and raised, as well as the reality that God's eternal nature as Father includes, even requires, the eternal nature of the Son. The language describing Jesus as sent from God and as raised by God from the dead implies an ordered relationship that includes "grammatical subordination" of Christ to God.[162] Kathryn Tanner speaks of "full mutuality of co-implication" that maintains in creative tension the asymmetrical descriptions of Christ and God the Father, with those indications of mutuality in unity.[163] Wesley Hill posits that in

---

158. Lincoln, 254. Salmond, 332, explains: "The *unity* in view, therefore, is oneness in faith in Christ and oneness also in the full experiential knowledge of him."

159. Lincoln, 256.

160. Jarl Fossum, "Son of God," *ABD* 6:128–36.

161. See introduction, pp. 57–61. Arnold, 265, speaks of "exaltation Christology" as a "major theme in the letter (1:20–23; 2:4–6)." He also points to 1:3–4 as perhaps reflecting Jesus's "eternal sonship."

162. Richardson, *Paul's Language about God*, 255, adds: "Yet if Paul's Christ-language is grammatically subordinate to his God-language . . . , nevertheless, Paul's Θεός-language is dependent on Χριστός-language for its full explication."

163. Kathryn Tanner, *Christ the Key* (Cambridge: Cambridge University Press, 2010), 152. Tanner rightly warns against using "trinitarian relations when making judgments about

4:11–16 CHRIST'S BODY GROWS TO FULLNESS

Paul's letters we find "bi-directionality,"[164] wherein the asymmetrical sending of the Father with Jesus's obedience does not "compromise the fundamental 'oneness' or 'unity' that obtains between God and Jesus."[165]

The second major clause in this verse speaks of attaining to the complete or mature man. Paul uses the term for an adult male instead of the general term for humanity (see 2:15). The adjective reflects the sense of mature, perfect, complete (see also Matt 5:48). The picture is of a fully formed adult, which will be contrasted with an infant in Eph 4:14 (see also 1 Cor 13:11). The mature man is representative of the body of Christ, not of individual believers (see also Eph 2:15).[166] In Paul's day, Roman culture followed Aristotle's views that only a male could be representative of full adult maturity and that only a male could represent the entire community made up of men, women, and children. If Paul wanted to stress individuals, he would have used the plural here, in contrast with the plural "infants" in 4:14. Thus, for Paul's rhetorical purposes, only "male" will serve his purposes and convey his meaning to the first-century audience.

The final clause speaks of the "measure" using the same term found in 4:7 (translated "apportioned" in NIV). The noun "measure" is modified by "whole." Believers together as the church attain the measure of the maturity or height/stature of the fullness of Christ (see also Col 1:28). Paul describes a fully grown or complete man in the previous clause, which could suggest that the term implies the full stature or height of an adult male. However, because in the next verse Paul distinguishes the mature believer from the one who is immature, an infant, and susceptible to false teachings, it is more likely that here Paul emphasizes maturity. The noun "fullness" has been used earlier when describing Christ who fills the church (Eph 1:23).[167] In 1:23 the filling is accomplished, while here the filling is ongoing and to be complete in the future. The tension between "now" and "not yet" is found throughout the epistle (see also 3:19).[168]

---

the proper character of human ones in Christian terms" (207). Additionally, she makes the point, commenting on John 20:17, that "this is no general relationship of sonship which includes both Christ and us, but a unique relationship between the two of them which we come to share in virtue of our connection with this one Son (1 Cor 1:9; Rom 8:29)" (151). Kathryn Tanner, *Jesus, Humanity, and the Trinity: A Brief Systematic Theology* (Minneapolis: Fortress, 2001), 2–9, argues that a proper understanding of Christ comes when readers consider divine transcendence and noncompetitiveness between God and his creatures.

164. Hill, *Paul and the Trinity*, 78.
165. Hill, *Paul and the Trinity*, 81.
166. Best, 401, who continues that "man" is "the corporate Christ ... who is the church" (402).
167. Barth, 491, rightly observes: "A translation of vs. 13c which suggests quantitative or qualitative increase of Christ by the addition of men is therefore not acceptable."
168. Contra Arnold, 266, who argues for the possessive genitive and concludes that here Christ is the "perfect standard" to which the church aspires.

14 Paul provides a result of the church growing and maturing, specifically, that believers avoid being taken in by false teachings and deceitful people. Ephesians 4:14 links back to Paul's statement in 4:11 that Christ gave apostles, prophets, evangelists, pastors, and teachers to the church. Here in 4:14 the emphasis is on what these functions help prevent, while in 4:13 and 4:15 we see what they support. The plural "infants" could suggest a focus on individual believers in the church, in contrast to the "mature man" who represents the church. Additionally, Paul could be implying that childish behavior fragments the community.[169] Paul includes himself in this warning, demonstrating his humility before them, for few teachers in Paul's day would have presented themselves in such a way.[170] The overall flow of the passage suggests that the corporate nature of the body is never far from Paul's mind.

Paul continues to discuss aberrant teachings, now with a nautical metaphor conjuring a boat adrift in heavy seas.[171] Paul knew about the dangers of rough seas and indicates that he has been shipwrecked (2 Cor 11:25). Acts speaks of a violent storm that nearly sunk Paul's vessel as he traveled to Rome (Acts 27:14–44). In our verse, the first participle, "tossed back and forth," is found only here and once in the Old Testament (Isa 57:20).[172] Paul alluded to this same section of Isaiah earlier in Ephesians when speaking about peace to those near and those far away (Eph 2:17), making it likely that Paul had this Isaiah passage in mind in his warning to the Ephesians. The second participle, "blown here and there," is used three times in the New Testament (see also Mark 6:55; 2 Cor 4:10), but only here in a figurative sense.[173] Using cognate terms, the image of being tossed by winds of doubt is found in Jas 1:6, while Jude 12 warns against self-serving leaders who are as wild waves in their ruinous force within the community.

Three prepositional phrases further describe this destructive teaching. First, the teaching is by means of human trickery or guile. The noun "cunning" reflects dice playing, and we might compare it to the phrase "loaded dice," which reflects dishonesty and chicanery.[174] Second, the teaching is characterized by craftiness.[175] The same term is used in 2 Cor 11:3 to describe Satan's

---

169. Best, 404, rightly observes that the "infants" are not the believers' preconversion state, for that is described as being in sin (2:2; 4:17–19).

170. Sarah Ruden, *Paul among the People: The Apostle Reinterpreted and Reimagined in His Own Time* (New York: Pantheon, 2010), 185–86.

171. Thielman, 283, comments that "it was perhaps the changeable, seemingly random, and potentially dangerous aspects of the weather that made it a metaphor of choice for doubt and false teachings in early Christianity."

172. On κλυδωνίζομαι see BDAG 550.

173. On περιφέρω see BDAG 808.

174. On κυβεία see BDAG 573. See also Thielman, 283.

175. On πανουργία see BDAG 754.

cunning deception of Eve. Paul distinguishes his teaching from such deviousness (2 Cor 4:2).[176] The third prepositional phrase indicates the direction or goal of the second phrase.[177] This phrase includes the noun "scheming," which occurs only twice in the New Testament, both in Ephesians.[178] In 6:11 Paul refers to the devil's schemes that seek to destroy the faithful. Here the term also has a negative connotation, further reinforced by the term "deceitful." The deceitful scheme, the craftiness, the trickery—all these together create a sobering picture of the havoc within the church generated by false teaching.

The warning is real, the danger ever present, and the consequences catastrophic. Yet Paul is not specific about the content of the false teaching, as he is in Col 2:8–23. Paul worries about false teachings because they lead to false practices, which in turn draw people from the true fellowship of Christ and his church.[179] Paul underlines the reality of the spiritual world, including those forces antagonistic to God and his followers. Paul knows that the gentile Ephesians are familiar with this reality, for they used to live according to the ruler of this dark age, the one who works in those who disobey God (Eph 2:2). It is against these powers, and not against humans, that believers must stand firm, wrapped in God's armor (6:11–12). For Paul, there is one faith, one baptism, one Lord (4:4–6).

15 Paul contrasts "speaking the truth," specifically speaking the gospel truth, with the deceitful lies propagated by cunning charlatans noted in the previous verse.[180] Earlier Paul describes the gospel of salvation as the word of truth (1:13) that "you all" heard; now he presumes that these believers are speaking the gospel truth. This assumption is based on his conviction that Christ has equipped believers for their ministry that further builds up the church (4:12). Paul continues with the prepositional phrase "in love," which modifies truth telling. In the next verse, Paul declares that the body grows in love, but in this verse "in love" repeats Paul's usage in 4:2, where he urges believers to walk in a worthy manner before the Lord, including bearing each other in love (see also 5:2).[181] The repeated phrase "in love" serves as bookends for this section of the epistle. The believers' conduct, teaching, and declaration of unity must be grounded in the all-surpassing love of God in Christ.

---

176. MacDonald, 297, remarks: "The competition and deception that characterize the marketplace of philosophies and new religions in the ancient world have no place in the lives of believers."

177. Thielman, 284.

178. On μεθοδεία see BDAG 625.

179. Best, 405, suggests that because Eph 4–6 focuses on ethical behavior "this suggests that that the false teaching may be about behaviour."

180. Best, 407.

181. Contra Salmond, 335, who suggests that the phrase "in love" is best attached to "to grow" because growth is the key argument of the passage.

The promise is that as believers speak the truth in love, they will "grow" into more faithful disciples and, together, into a more faithful church. The verb was used in 2:21 to describe the church made up of Jews and gentiles growing into God's holy temple.[182] The emphasis on unity here in Eph 4 echoes the insistence on the oneness of Christ's body, one new humanity created by Christ's reconciling work on the cross. Believers grow up into him, that is Christ. The goal of growth is maturity in Christ (4:13), the scope of which covers "all things." The phrase "in every respect" can refer to the cosmos (1:10; 3:9; 4:10); however, here the focus is on the church, and so the phrase is better understood as an adverbial accusative.[183] The church's growth in Christ includes every thought and action as the body matures.

Paul closes this verse with the clause "who is the head, that is, Christ." In 1:22–23 Paul declares that Christ is the head of his body the church, for God the Father put all things under his feet and gave him to be head of his body (see also Col 1:18). Paul adds later in the epistle that Christ is head of his church, the savior of the body (Eph 5:23) who cares for his body (5:29) of which each believer is a member (5:30). Paul continues in 4:16 to describe how the body, fitted properly to each other member and to the head, Christ, grows to its full stature. A body disconnected from the head cannot function, as Paul warns the Colossians in his exhortation to avoid false humility and unspiritual teachings (Col 2:16–19). But a body that builds up each part with lovingkindness develops into the fullness of Christ. Paul does not use "head" here to emphasize Christ's rulership over the church or cosmos. The physiology assumed by Paul in this metaphor, that the body grows into the head, is foreign to our modern way of talking about human development, but his point that the church grows through Christ's work and care seems clear nonetheless.

16 With 4:16, Paul concludes his discussion about the gift given by Christ to the church, equipping believers for ministry. He continues with ancient medical terms as he describes the human body to explain, via metaphor, the church. Christ enables and facilitates the joining together of his body. Having established Christ as the source of the growth, Paul introducing the subject of this clause, "the whole body." Paul explains the body as composed of united members with interconnecting joints that supply the body with its life. From Christ the head, the body is able to work together as each does its job for the whole.

---

182. On αὐξάνω see BDAG 151 (2). The verb is best understood as a hortatory subjunctive, an exhortation in which Paul includes himself. Less likely is a possible link with the conjunction "so that" (ἵνα) that begins 4:14 and that requires a subjunctive verb.

183. Best, 408. Greek τὰ πάντα.

Paul uses two participles, "joined" and "held together," to describe the bonding together of the body.[184] Paul used the first verb only one other time, in 2:21, describing the church as a building joined together. The second verb, found seven times in the New Testament, carries the sense of imparting knowledge as well as the idea of holding things together. For example, Paul uses this verb in his argument to the Corinthians, citing Isa 40:13: "Who has known the mind of the Lord so as to instruct him?" (1 Cor 2:16).[185] Paul uses the verb in a similar passage in Col 2:19, which speaks about the parts of the body being held together. In this latter passage, Paul warns against false teachings as they disconnect believers from Christ, the head of the body. The two passages also share the rare noun, "ligament," found only here in the New Testament. In Colossians, it is clear the noun refers to ligaments of a human body, with "body" here used metaphorically for the church. Given the close parallels with the Colossians passage, it seems best to interpret the noun in Ephesians also as "ligament."[186]

Paul indicates that each believer should do his or her part in building up the body, with the expression "as each part does its work."[187] The noun translated "does work" is used in 3:7 as Paul explains the working of God's power in his ministry. In 4:16 Paul reinforces that believers are empowered by God as they do their part individually to cause the entire body to grow and mature. The goal of this growth is for the body's building up in love. This love is above human knowledge and fills believers with the fullness of God (3:18–19), yet it is also a love expressed between believers as they humbly care for each other (4:2).

3. Put on the New Self (4:17–24)

17 So I tell you this, and insist on it in the Lord, that you must no longer live as the Gentiles do, in the futility of their thinking. 18 They are darkened in their understanding and separated from the life of God because of the ignorance that is in them due to the hardening of their hearts. 19 Having lost all sensitivity, they have given themselves over to sensuality so as to indulge in every kind of impurity, and they are full of greed.

20 That, however, is not the way of life you learned 21 when you heard about Christ and were taught in him in accordance with the truth that is in Jesus. 22 You

---

184. On συναρμολογέω see BDAG 966; on συμβιβάζω see BDAG 956 (1).
185. Arnold, 270.
186. Arnold, 270. Best, 411, offers "ligaments, arteries and nerves" as the bodily systems that could be contained in the term. Contra Lincoln, 263, who argues that the noun refers to the leaders of the church.
187. On ἐνέργεια see BDAG 335.

were taught, with regard to your former way of life, to put off your old self, which is being corrupted by its deceitful desires; 23to be made new in the attitude of your minds; 24and to put on the new self, created to be like God in true righteousness and holiness.

Paul began the chapter with a call to walk worthy of the identity the believer has in Christ. He then offered a brief summary of the believers' one hope, one baptism, and one faith, established in the one Lord, one Spirit, and one God and Father of all. The gift of Christ to his body, the church, equips believers for works of service and enables believers to grow together in unity even as they each grow in their calling. Christ provides the ongoing power to build up the church. In 4:17 Paul picks up again his call to walk in a worthy manner (4:2), but now it is paired with the exhortation not to walk in immoral ways (4:17–19). Paul cautions in the following verses that believers must discard immorality, which exemplified their lives as polytheists. He worries that believers might slide back into such ways.[188] Paul discusses the futility of a pagan's perspective, for it is based on blindness and ignorance. He contrasts such impious and impure behavior with that of those in Christ, who are renewed in their minds and spirits and are able to live holy and righteous lives. Paul contrasted the gentile Ephesians' past and present life in Eph 2, when he highlighted their distance from the people of God and God's promises. In Eph 3 Paul distinguishes the past and present of these gentiles, who are now fellow citizens with God's people (2:19) and heirs together with Israel (3:6), based on the mystery of the gospel.[189]

The gentile believers must give up their immoral and idolatrous behaviors, but they are not asked to become Jewish proselytes. Said another way, they remain "gentile" in their heritage and culture, even as they reject the aspects of their culture that denied the gospel message of redemption in Christ.[190] Indeed, among the gentiles that made up the Ephesian church community, we might expect different ethnic backgrounds and cultures, given that Ephesus was a large, cosmopolitan city. Paul assumes the possibility that the gentile believers might slide back into their former, pagan way of thinking and acting, and so he cautions them to think rightly and worship faithfully.

What might these Ephesian gentiles have encountered that could have drawn them back into their former way of life? We know that Ephesus was

---

188. Best, 415, explains that the Ephesian community does not face external threats from their pagan neighbors or a promotion of "heretical intellectual ideas," but the possibility of a "relapse into their former pre-Christian ways."

189. Fowl, 145, remarks that Eph 2 focused on the alienation experienced by gentiles, while in Eph 4 "Paul focuses on the behaviors that flow from such an alienated position."

190. Fowl, 145.

quite proud of its goddess, Artemis, and promoted her worship. In Acts 19 Demetrius incites a crowd to riot with his allegations that Paul and his followers dishonored Artemis. The town clerk, attempting to quiet the crowd, assures them that Artemis's reputation is secure, for her statue fell from heaven and her temple is protected by the city of Ephesus (Acts 19:35).[191] We can add to this the emphasis on venerating the imperial family and Rome through the imperial cult. Paul paints a stark picture of life within this worldview and yet also suggests an active, redemptive engagement with this world. For example, he explains that the church's existence is a witness to the powers and authorities of God's wisdom (Eph 3:10). Paul prays to the Father of all families (3:15). Paul urges believers to do good works (2:10), and there is no indication that these efforts should focus solely on the church.[192]

The larger passage can be broken down into three smaller sections: 4:17-19, 20-24, 25-32. Both 4:17 and 4:25 begin with a strong conjunction, and 4:20 offers the contrastive conjunction "however." The first two sections contrast the gentile pagan life with one rooted in Christ, and the third section builds on that latter vision to encourage proper behavior within the church, Christ's body. Paul presents a piteous figure lost due to ignorance, even while stressing that such a one is culpable for his or her actions.[193] The Ephesians' previous ignorance has been remediated, not simply by learning specific doctrines or creeds, but by learning a person, namely, Christ (4:20-21). And their behavior changes, not only because they were carefully trained in a Christian catechesis, but because they changed their "clothing." Paul provides a vivid image of taking off the old self and putting on the self that is righteous before God.[194] This new self must act in ways consistent with this new identity. The behavior is first and foremost to be directed to other members of the church, but it also will have ramifications for the wider society as believers' gracious speech and generous actions support its members and by extension those who come in contact with them.

---

191. On the historicity of this account in Acts, see Trebilco, *Early Christians in Ephesus*, 155-63.

192. Paul R. Trebilco, "Engaging—or Not Engaging—the City: Reading 1 and 2 Timothy and the Johannine Letters in the City of Ephesus," in *The Urban World and the First Christians*, ed. Steve Walton, Paul R. Trebilco, and David W. J. Gill (Grand Rapids: Eerdmans, 2017), 162, asks how the Ephesian communities addressed in 1-2 Timothy and 1-3 John would have responded to the endowments of religious ritual concerning Artemis and the bimonthly processions through the city. He concludes "that 1-2 Timothy demonstrate a strong degree of engagement in city life, while 1-3 John demonstrate a high degree of disengagement."

193. Thielman, 294.

194. Thielman, 295, suggests that Paul reflects on the story of the first humans created by God (Gen 1:26).

17–19 In contrast to the previous verses' complicated sentence structure and elaborate metaphors, Paul's language in 4:17–19 is straightforward, and his directness alerts us to the importance of his message. In this single sentence in Greek, it is as though he turned up the volume a bit with his strong warning against immoral behavior rooted in a corrupt mindset.[195] Paul indicated in the previous verses that Christ is the head of his body the church, and he will cause it to grow. He worries that this bright future could be shattered if believers fall back into their old habits and convictions. He launches into a warning in these next few verses against greed and impurity. Such actions, Paul warns, are "futile."[196] Interestingly, he does not lead with the claim that such actions are bad or wrong, although they certainly are that too. There is much sadness, pain, and regret packed into the word "futile"—endlessly striving and never arriving, forever searching and never finding.[197] Paul uses the same noun in Rom 8:20 when speaking of creation's sense of frustration (see also 2 Pet 2:18). The adjective is used to describe the futility of a faith that denies the resurrection of the dead (1 Cor 15:17). Paul warns against such a fruitless and empty mindset; however, tucked into this word is a call for compassion concerning the one who is acting in a futile way. Paul's stern warning is tempered by a recognition that gentiles are caught in a maze of ignorance and blindness that turns hearts to stone and minds to covetousness.

Paul begins Eph 4:17 with two emphatic verbs: "I tell you" and "I insist." Further, Paul testifies "in the Lord," which adds weight to his admonition and perhaps implicitly sketches his own current situation as in chains for Christ (4:1). Paul frontloads the adverb "no longer" for emphasis, acknowledging that at one time in the past, the gentile believers did live in disobedience to God and thus wandered futilely. The term translated "live" is the Greek verb "to walk." Paul uses this expression repeatedly in his letters to speak about a lifestyle. In 4:1 Paul instructed the Ephesians to walk in a worthy manner, and now in 4:17 he contrasts the worthy walk with a walk of futility (see also 2:2, 10; 5:2, 8, 15).

These gentile believers should avoid acting like gentiles! Paul uses "gentiles" with religious force, not ethnic connotations. Paul distinguishes ungodly habits of gentiles as now foreign to the non-Jews who are believers in Christ. The non-Jewish believers are still "gentile" in their uncircumcision,

---

195. Lincoln, 276.
196. On ματαιότης see BDAG 621.
197. Schüssler Fiorenza, 61, argues that "the characterization of the Gentiles as unclean, lascivious, and ignorant, or characterized by vanity of mind, is a dangerous case of 'othering.'" While her caution against othering is important, she does not give adequate weight to Paul's concern for moral codes (5:3–5) or to his condemnation of such behavior in himself or other Jews (2:3); moreover, it is clear that it is as a gentile that one comes to Christ and is in Christ (2:11–15).

4:17–24 PUT ON THE NEW SELF

but Paul declared they are part of a new people created by Christ, together with Jewish believers, redeemed and reconciled to God (2:14–18; see also, "a new circumcision" in Col 2:11).

Paul refers to futile "thinking" (Eph 4:17) and "understanding" (4:18; see also 2:3). The first noun refers to the mind and its mental and moral state, while the second carries the idea of reasoning and comprehending.[198] Because of their ignorance and due to their hardened hearts, gentiles live with misguided reason and futility. Paul describes futile thinking further with two participial phrases that focus on being in the dark and separated.[199] Paul previously stated that gentiles are separated from God (2:12; see also Col 1:21). Interestingly, here Paul indicates that they are separated from "the life of God"; we would expect something like separated from God or from salvation. The phrase "life of God" does not mean a godly lifestyle, although it is clear that gentiles do not practice godly piety. Rather, Paul means life in the fullest sense of that word, an immortality gained in Christ.[200]

A third participle begins Eph 4:19, as Paul describes another characteristic of gentile polytheistic lifestyle, specifically, an inability to feel appropriate piety before God and respect for fellow humans. These gentile pagans have "lost all sensitivity" or become callous. This verb can also point to a feeling of despair, and since Paul has just indicated that these gentiles are alienated from God, one could imagine that such people felt despair.[201] Earlier in this letter, Paul declares that these gentile believers were once dead in their sins, but now they are alive by God's mercy (2:1, 4–5). They were once far from Christ, separated from the commonwealth of Israel (2:12).

Paul indicates that it is "because of the ignorance" that the gentiles are in their predicament (4:18). He adds that they experience a hardening of their heart.[202] Does that mean the gentiles cannot be held responsible for their

---

198. On νοῦς see BDAG 680 (2); on διάνοια see BDAG 234 (1). Fowl, 146, translates the second noun and participle as "they reason in the dark."

199. These participles are in the perfect tense. On the perfect tense, see Campbell, *Basics of Verbal Aspect in Biblical Greek*, 51, who argues that the perfect tense form is imperfective in aspect: "The perfect semantically encodes imperfective aspect and the spatial value of *heightened proximity*." For an alternative, traditional view, see Hoehner, 586, who holds that perfect participles indicate an action completed in the past but continuing to have results or effects in the present.

200. Best, 420, is likely correct when he locates Paul's emphasis as "not God's own life but the life he gives ... eternal life." Fowl, 148, might be stretching Paul's theological implications too far when he writes: "Gentiles outside of Christ are disconnected from the ends for which God made them, that is participation in God's own life."

201. On ἀπαλγέω see BDAG 96. The verb occurs only here in the New Testament. Thielman, 299, argues that the best meaning in the context is severe despondency leading to loss of hope.

202. Phrases in the Old Testament that speak of hardness of heart reference both non-

actions or thoughts?[203] This question occurs because the participles "darkened" and "separated" are both in the middle/passive voice, which could suggest that another being (God or evil forces) was responsible. Paul, however, maintains that the gentiles are accountable for their disobedience. First, their ignorance implies lacking knowledge of self or of God, things that a wise person knows and the ignorant person chooses not to explore. The one who is ignorant of God and himself or herself perpetuates such ignorance with a steadily hardening heart. Second, Paul declares they "gave themselves over," using a reflexive pronoun ("themselves") to further stress personal responsibility and choice (4:19). The verb "to give over" indicates that the gentiles have succumbed to their impulses and inclinations. The same verb is used by Paul in Rom 1:24-28 to describe God's actions of giving over to sin the gentiles who have failed to give God glory or thanksgiving, so their minds became futile and their hearts hard. Here in Ephesians, their hard hearts lead to ungodly behavior. Earlier, Paul describes this posture as being children of disobedience (2:2).

Those whose understanding is darkened can act in wicked ways; those whose hearts are hardened might behave in callous ways toward others. Paul describes their behavior in broad terms, stressing "sensuality" and "greed."[204] Paul indicates that they purpose to commit such deeds; Paul uses the noun "practice" or "indulge," which has the idea of habitual behavior. In the vice lists found in the New Testament, "sensuality" carries the idea of sexual immorality, which would certainly be part of Paul's concern here (cf. Rom 13:13; 2 Cor 12:21; Gal 5:19). More broadly, the noun reflects behavior deemed socially offensive and lacking in self-restraint. Additionally, the gentiles indulge in acts of "impurity."[205] While this term can be used in a cultic sense, here Paul emphasizes immoral behavior. These deeds are done in an attitude of greed. Paul uses these same terms, impurity and greed, alongside sexual immorality in Eph 5:3. Idolatry's great crime is that the self becomes god. All is done to serve the self—no care for neighbor, no love of community, no thought for tomorrow. Instead, the unbelieving gentile takes from those who have little and does shameful acts that reflect their callous heart and darkened mind.

Paul presents a vicious circle that entraps the futile thinker in a death spiral of immorality that further hardens and darkens their understanding. Paul realizes that alienation from God in one's heart can mean unrestrained

---

Jews (Exod 4:21) and Jews (Isa 6:10; Jer 7:26); it also occurs in the New Testament (Mark 3:5; 6:52; John 12:40). See also Best, 421.

203. In Acts 3:17 and 17:30, the gentiles' ignorance is not counted against them. Thielman, 298, rightly argues that Paul speaks of their ignorance in relation to their disobedience.

204. On ἀσέλγεια see BDAG 141; on πλεονεξία see BDAG 824.

205. On ἀκαθαρσία see BDAG 34 (2).

sinful behavior in one's community. These sinners have lost hope, but should we paint them as unfortunate souls whose unhappiness leads them to unfortunate decisions? The sins committed include sexual sins and greed, which in Paul's day would have involved others—male and female slaves, lower status males and females, and what we would call domestic violence. The actions taken in despair are not, therefore, less abhorrent because the oppressor is feeling alienated from God. Nor is the sexual crime done against the slave or lower-class neighbor less culpable because the perpetrator felt sad and distant from God. Paul makes clear with his use of reflexive pronouns that these gentiles sought to fill up their greedy appetites; such behavior was not a necessary consequence of their ignorance, but in these cases, it was a series of decisions that fed their lust.

I add a caveat here that is likely implied by Paul but should be made explicit. Paul is not saying that all nonbelievers are bad people, or that all nonbelievers are greedy and immoral. He encountered gentiles who were kind, caring, and friendly, and some who saved his life (Acts 19:31). Nor, as we will see below, does Paul imagine that believers are by definition loving and generous. He knew some professed believers who were envious and jealous and sought to ruin his ministry (cf. Phil 1:17). His point here is that as a whole, paganism leads nowhere, and those on such a miserable, dark path often give into unholy and unloving attitudes and actions.

20–24 In this sentence that extends over five verses, Paul stresses the intimate, relational reality of a believer's walk with God in Christ, presenting a vision of a new person with a new comprehension of truth and a new way of living that reflects God's holiness. The Greek order of words in 4:20 reads, "you did not in this way learn [the] Christ." Paul places the plural pronoun "you" in the emphatic position at the beginning of the sentence to bring home to the Ephesians their part in God's work. The first two words in 4:21 refer back to the plural "you" and can be translated "when" or "assuming that."[206] This phrase does not express Paul's doubt; rather, it conveys his confident hope in them, even though he has been absent several years from their congregation (see also 3:2).

The verb "to learn" is in the aorist, which describes the totality of their catechesis in the faith (see 1:13).[207] To the Philippians, Paul declares that he wants to "know" Christ, and this sounds more natural to our ears, for we desire to know better a person whom we love (Phil 3:10; see also Col 2:6). We

---

206. Εἴ γε. See also 3:2. Hoehner, 595, translates "if as I assume it to be the case."
207. On μανθάνω see BDAG 615 (1). Best, 427, however, argues that the aorist likely points to the moment when they began to follow Christ. Fowl, 150, rightly adds that the "logic" of the passage includes that "although one may have 'learned Christ,' there is still room for growth."

tend to think about *knowing* a person and *learning* an object. But if we think of "the Christ" as "the Messiah," a title that speaks to God's redemptive work promised in ages past and now fulfilled in Jesus, we get a sense of how Paul intends us to understand this passage.[208] Paul sees the Messiah as the one who brings peace between Jew and gentile (Eph 2:14). This Messiah creates an organic body, the church, of which he is the head (1:22–23). This body is loved beyond measure (5:2) and is gifted by the Messiah to be strengthened and to grow to maturity (4:12). This Messiah builds a holy temple with his faithful followers, a temple indwelt by the holy God (2:22). Indeed, this Messiah dwells in each believer, renewing and establishing each member (3:16–17). This Messiah triumphs over all spiritual forces, including dark forces (1:20–21). All these fulfilled promises point to God's final goal in the Messiah, which is uniting all things in him (1:10). And the Messiah has a name: Jesus of Nazareth.[209] This Jesus died on a Roman cross and was raised to life eternal and is now seated at God the Father's right hand in the heavens (2:6). By God's grace, believers are seated with him (2:6). Paul declares that in Jesus one finds the truth (4:21), that "word of truth" (1:13) that leads to salvation.

To learn Christ implies experience with Christ. Paul continues in 4:21 that they "heard him [Christ]," using the same unusual syntax and aorist tense as in the previous verse. We expect Paul to say "you heard *about* Christ" not "you heard Christ."[210] Paul's unusual expression captures the reality that Christ Jesus is alive and in relationship with his church and individual believers.[211] Paul continues that believers were taught in him, again with an aorist verb and followed by the unlikely dative phrase "in him." Typically, the verb "to teach" is followed by the accusative that identifies the content of the teaching. Most likely, Paul emphasizes with this unusual syntax the reality that the learning and hearing and teaching are all done "in Christ."[212] The believer

---

208. Barth, 504–5. Best, 143, argues that the "use of the article with Christ seems quite haphazard and no significance should be attached to it."

209. Schüssler Fiorenza, 62, argues the unlikely case that the definite articles reflect Paul's need to distinguish Jesus Messiah from the "many Messiahs/Christs and also many persons named Jesus." While Jesus was a common name in Roman Palestine, it is not clear it would be so in the diaspora; moreover, Josephus (*Jewish War* 2.13.4–5 §§258–63; *Jewish Antiquities* 20.5.1 §§97–99; 20.8.6 §§167–72) speaks of several messiahs, not many messiahs, and especially not in diaspora settings.

210. The NIV inserts "about." Fowl, 150. Best, 427, explains that the accusative points to hearing a sound, not a person, but that perhaps the point is that believers hear Christ in the preaching of the gospel.

211. Thielman, 300. Hoehner, 594–95, does not quite capture the personal emphasis when he remarks that Paul is reminding the Ephesians of earlier catechetical teachings.

212. Best, 428, refers back to the phrase "in the Lord" (4:17) and suggests that the message here is that Christ was introduced to believers in such a way as to establish a relationship.

grows and develops through actively engaging head, hearts, hands, and feet because the content of study is not a body of literature, but a person, namely, Jesus. In a similar vein, Paul encourages the Philippians: "Whatever you have learned or received or heard from me, or seen in me—put it into practice" (Phil 4:9).[213] In this Paul follows Jesus's own example, as Hebrews indicates that as the Son, Jesus "learned obedience from what he suffered" (Heb 5:8).

Paul adds that the teaching they received was truth. The noun "truth" is anarthrous (that is, it lacks the article in the Greek), which might mean it is the predicate and translated "there is truth in Jesus." However, with abstract nouns such as "truth," this rule does not always hold. Better is to see the noun as the subject, which would identify truth as in Jesus.[214] Paul does not suggest that *some* truth is found in Jesus and that truth might also exist elsewhere; instead, his point is that the gospel contains and sums up truth.[215] Paul infrequently uses the name "Jesus" on its own, and here he probably has in mind the historical Jesus and his incarnation, death, and resurrection (Rom 8:11; Gal 6:17; Phil 2:10).[216] Paul makes a similar point to the Romans, as he argues that those who believe in Jesus are justified, using the Greek term found also in Eph 4:24, translated "just" or "righteous" (Rom 3:26).

Central to the gospel message is the new life believers have in Christ (Eph 4:22-24). The rich metaphor of putting on and taking off clothes illustrates the catechism. Believers take off their old self, which is corrupt and deceitful, and put on their new self, which has a renewed "attitude."[217] The elite Romans had a coming-of-age ceremony surrounding the donning of the toga. This ritual, *toga virilis*, transformed the male youth to a man, now having dignity and authority.[218] The new clothing symbolized the maturity of the young man, who was to practice virtue and act wisely.[219] Paul's picks up this ubiquitous image and expands it. His teaching culminates in the recognition

---

Hoehner, 595, explains that the prepositional phrase points to the sphere of the teaching and can be translated "in communion with him."

213. Fowl, 151, makes the important point that "early Christian formation was primarily conveyed orally.... The teacher was someone known to the student, someone whose daily life, pattern of prayer, and habits of worship could be as instructive as anything conveyed in a classroom."

214. Lincoln, 281.

215. Best, 429.

216. Best, 429; contra Lincoln, 282.

217. Πνεύματι or "spirit." On πνεῦμα see BDAG 832-33 (3).

218. Quintilian, *Institutio oratoria* 2.3.137-42; Seneca, *Epistles* 4.2; *Epistulae ad Atticum* 5.20.9. See the discussion in Rosemary Canavan, *Clothing the Body of Christ at Colossae: A Visual Construction of Identity*, WUNT 334 (Tübingen: Mohr Siebeck, 2012), 155-56, who observes "a rich culture of clothing as a means of identity and used in ritual for changes in identity" (156).

219. Plutarch, *Moralia* 37.1.

and reality that the new self is created to be like God in true righteousness and holiness. There are several important layers in these three verses (4:22–24), including the act of taking off and putting on, the "old self" contrasted with the "new self" (*anthrōpos*/human), and the reality of the new self that is created to be like God.

First, believers are instructed to remove the old self and put on the new self. Paul uses three infinitives ("to put off," "to be made new," "to put on") that likely link back as objects to the verb "to learn" (4:21).[220] The first and third infinitives are in the aorist middle, the second is present middle. Have the Ephesians been taught that they *have* put off the old self, or that they *must* put off the old self? The aorist tense used of putting off and putting on suggests to some that Paul makes a statement about their past conversion, while the present tense of being renewed suggests a daily practice. However, the aorist is better understood as conveying, not the time of an action, but its totality or comprehensiveness. In this case, Paul stresses that believers fully remove their old self and fully put on their new self. Infinitives can be used as imperatives, and some commentators argue that the context of Paul's ethical instructions warrants this position.[221] Further support for this position is Paul's heavy use of imperatives within the chapter, including the following verse (4:25). Yet both positions rightly interpret Paul to be urging the Ephesians to right behavior, for the context stresses proper behavior befitting one who has learned Christ; all three infinitives speak to believers living worthy lifestyles now.

Is Paul pointing to baptism with the metaphor of taking off and putting on clothing? Those who argue for a baptism imagery point to the early church's practice of removing clothes before stepping into the baptismal waters and putting on garments after coming out of the water. In Col 2:11–12, Paul notes that the Colossians' old self was put off in the "circumcision" done by Christ, as they were buried with Christ in their baptism. They are raised to new life, and thus they are commanded to put to death the behaviors that reflect their former life in paganism (3:5–7). Paul draws a similar picture of baptism for the Romans, explaining that they have died in their baptism and are raised to new life (Rom 6:4). Specifically, Paul indicates that the old self was crucified (6:6) and believers can thus count themselves "dead to sin but alive to God in Christ Jesus" (6:11). To the Galatians, Paul declares that all those "who were baptized into Christ have clothed [them]selves with Christ" (Gal 3:27). In the end, however, the claims that Paul alludes to bap-

---

220. Hoehner, 599; Best, 430.

221. Best, 431; Lincoln, 283–84. However, Hoehner, 599, points to the rarity of such an interpretation, claiming only two undisputed examples in the New Testament (Rom 12:15; Phil 3:16).

tism in Ephesians are weak, primarily because the focus in Ephesians is on believers' behaviors, not on the single event of baptism. Additionally, there is no talk of the "new self" in these other passages. Paul uses the language of putting off/on clothing to describe rejecting vices and pursuing virtues in other letters (Rom 13:12–14), and he speaks of putting on God's armor in Eph 6:11. In Col 3:8–12, Paul moves back and forth between statements and commands, where he commands them to get rid of evil talk and lying and to put on virtues such as compassion and kindness and states that they have taken off the old self and put on the new self (see also Rom 6:6, a statement, and 13:12, a command).[222]

Paul insists that the Ephesians put off their "old self" and put on their "new self."[223] The term translated "self" is *anthrōpos* or "human." The old self is part of their pre-Christ life, when all was darkness and despair (Eph 2:1–5). The old self lives in ignorance and behaves without regard to others or to God. This former lifestyle followed deceitful passions, acted in greed, and objectified others. This path leads to corruption or destruction; the present tense participle indicates that the activity is unfolding before the audience's eyes.[224] This is far from the picture of the truth in Christ that leads to holiness and purity.

Paul holds that a continuity exists between the old self and the new self, as pertains to the skills, qualities, and mannerisms that make the believer a unique person.[225] The artist remains artistic, the athlete, athletic, and the optimist, optimistic. A similar sort of continuity exists between the current body and the raised, glorified body (1 Cor 15:53–58). Based on his conviction that humans are made in God's image, Paul focuses on understanding the self not only from the individual's perspective, but as located within community.[226] Based on Christ's work of redemption, a human's identity cannot be understood merely from the natural order of things, but must factor in the transcendent God who is attentive to humans.

---

222. Thielman, 303.

223. On παλαιός see BDAG 751 (2). On καινός see BDAG 496–97 (3). In Col 3:10 Paul describes the new (ἄνθρωπος) with the adjective νέος, and the participle ἀνακαινούμενος includes the root καινός. Best, 435, makes the point that by the New Testament period, the two terms for "new" were used as synonyms.

224. Campbell, *Basics of Verbal Aspect*, 41–42.

225. Best, 439.

226. Eastman, *Paul and the Person*, 177, astutely observes that Paul's anthropology insists that the person is made in God's image, is "grounded in a second person perspective," and is not based on a "purely individualistic notion of the self." She argues that Paul does not see humans as autonomous, free individuals, but as "relationally constituted beings from the very beginning of life"; therefore, "self-knowledge is always mediated through interpersonal interaction, both for good and for ill."

Before speaking of the new self, Paul adds that believers are being made new "in the attitude" of their minds.²²⁷ The passive voice of the infinitive "to be made new" indicates that God in Christ works in the believers' minds to help shape their holy lives. Paul's use of the present tense here draws attention to this element of his argument.²²⁸ The term "attitude" translates the Greek term for "spirit," here referring to the human spirit. It stands as a synonym to the term "mind" in the following phrase. Less likely is Paul referring here to the Holy Spirit, as the divine passive stresses God's actions on behalf of the believer. The term "mind" reflects the thinking of the individual. Paul draws a contrast between what fills and governs the human mind—ignorance or truth (see also 4:17).²²⁹

The new self is "created to be like God" (4:24). Paul may have in mind the creation narrative that declares humans made in God's image (*eikōn*), although he does not use this term here in Ephesians (Gen 1:26).²³⁰ In Col 3:10 Paul indicates the new self is being renewed in knowledge in the *image* of its Creator. Paul proclaims that believers are predestined to be conformed to the *image* of God's Son (Rom 8:29). Even now, believers "are being transformed into his [the Lord's] *image* with ever-increasing glory" (2 Cor 3:18). Instead of focusing on image, however, Paul highlights God's actions as creator. It is God who has shaped the outline of the new self and imbued it with God's holiness and righteousness. The aorist tense does not point to a past event, such as that moment when a believer received the gospel truth, but rather highlights the totality and completeness of God's creative act. Earlier Paul indicated that God made a new people in Christ (Eph 2:19) and that believers were created to do good works (2:10).

Paul continues that believers were created to be like God "in true righteousness and holiness" (4:24). The term "righteousness" carries the sense of both moral uprightness and acting justly, while the term "holiness" speaks of a person's goodness.²³¹ The terms are paired in a few places in the New

---

227. Τῷ πνεύματι τοῦ νοὸς ὑμῶν ("by the spirit of your mind"). Usually Paul speaks of the Holy Spirit when using the noun "spirit," but the qualifying phrase "of your mind" suggests that Paul is thinking of the person's inner self (cf. 3:16). See Best, 435, and Hoehner, 608.

228. Mathewson, "Abused Present," 362, explains: "Outside of narrative, the present tense is often used to highlight important thematic elements in the discourse."

229. Best, 436, perceptively observes: "In a sense the spirit and the mind represent what continues from the old person to the new, though they are changed in their continuation."

230. Lincoln, 287. Thielman, 306, probably extends the implication too far in his remarks that Paul points to Adam here. Fowl, 153, rightly cautions that all humans are made in God's image. Paul's focus here is on the proper goal of human life, to image the Creator.

231. On δικαιοσύνη see BDAG 247–48 (3); on ὁσιότης see BDAG 728. Paul uses the more common term "holy" several places in Ephesians to identify the Holy Spirit (1:13; 4:30),

Testament,[232] likely influenced by Old Testament passages (such as Deut 9:5) that link the two nouns.[233] Paul concludes this passage with the phrase "of truth."[234] The phrase describes righteousness and holiness and contrasts with the term "deceitful" that defined the old self's corruption (4:22).[235] Paul bookends this passage with the notion of truth, first identifying Jesus as the source of truth (4:21) and now indicating that believers' righteousness and holiness are rooted in that truth.

4. Speak Truth with Compassion (4:25–32)

25*Therefore each of you must put off falsehood and speak truthfully to your neighbor, for we are all members of one body.* 26*"In your anger do not sin": Do not let the sun go down while you are still angry,* 27*and do not give the devil a foothold.* 28*Anyone who has been stealing must steal no longer, but must work, doing something useful with their own hands, that they may have something to share with those in need.*

29*Do not let any unwholesome talk come out of your mouths, but only what is helpful for building others up according to their needs, that it may benefit those who listen.* 30*And do not grieve the Holy Spirit of God, with whom you were sealed for the day of redemption.* 31*Get rid of all bitterness, rage and anger, brawling and slander, along with every form of malice.* 32*Be kind and compassionate to one another, forgiving each other, just as in Christ God forgave you.*

In these eight verses, Paul builds on his previous argument concerning the believers' restored connection to God through the picture of being clothed with Christ. The deliverance from sin and membership in God's family can be described as having "put off" the old self so as to "put on Christ." This new self reflects the goal or telos of the human, to live in holiness and righteousness, reflecting their maker's character. Having established the contrast between the old self and the new self, in the remaining verses of Eph 4, Paul explores "truth" as rooted in the person of Jesus and thus a crucial aspect of believers' participation in Christ's life. He does so with short, direct sentences that

---

the church as the "holy" temple (2:21), believers (1:1), the "holy" apostles and prophets (3:5), and Christ's actions in making the church "holy" (5:26–27).

232. Luke 1:75 and 1 Thess 2:10 use the adverbial forms; Titus 1:8 uses the adjectival forms.

233. See also Deut 32:4, which uses the adjectival forms: "A faithful God who does no wrong, *upright* and *just* [righteous] is he."

234. On ἀλήθεια see BDAG 42 (2).

235. Best, 438.

command good behaviors and warn against bad ones. He adds reasons for his injunctions, which focus on edifying the church and, by extension, all people.

The Ephesians were familiar with the general scope of Paul's injunctions; Jewish moralists and Stoic philosophers warned against the dangers of an unchecked tongue and unbridled anger.[236] Their surprise would come in Paul's rationale for such behavior and attitudes. Paul roots his call for truth in his picture of Christ and in the nature of Christ's body, the church.[237] Together, believers are members of Christ's body; they are members of the one who is truth. This passage is deeply theological, as it draws on God's redemption plan to create a people whose character reflects their Lord. Truth-telling and truthful living communicate the overflowing of God's life within the believer. Paul explores with deep nuance the practices of speaking truth and living truthfully in community. Speaking truth heals and builds up. Speaking truth humbles the speakers, keeping them from manipulating power. Speaking truth empowers and builds up others. Seeing truthfully recognizes the needs of others and one's own responsibility in meeting those needs. Acting in truth involves using one's possessions to help others.

Living truthfully is living in the light of Jesus Christ, who is Truth. We shortchange Paul's exhortations if we label them "practical advice," for they sew together word and deed in a way that expresses the reality of believers being "in Christ." Moreover, isolating each verse as useful moral injunctions minimizes the unifying theme of truth in its many dimensions: personal, communal, spiritual. As believers put on their new self and speak truthfully, they reflect their true end, which is not good deeds, but life together and forever with Christ.[238] Doing good has as its end not an abstract perfection but new life by God's power.

The argument Paul makes is not linear, nor does it build on a series of claims. Instead, Paul provides a 360-degree view of what truth-speaking looks like in the community of believers. Paul established that Jesus is the truth (4:21) and that the believer's new self is rooted in a life of participation in Christ and thus a life of righteousness and holiness (4:24). Paul now turns to living truthfully, which begins with the mouth and extends to the hands and to the heart. Believers speak truth to each other (4:25), which means their anger is resolved quickly and without selfish indignation (4:26–27). Believers live the truth when they deal truthfully with their employees or

---

236. Perkins, 108–10, cites Plutarch, *Moralia* 452E–464D, and the Essene material (1QS 7:2–11; CD 7:2–3). Best, 443, states that these injunctions originated in "Judaism, if not in the secular world" and we see them here "christianised ... usually through the motivation he offers."

237. Fowl, 154.

238. Perkins, 108, observes that the corporate life of believers lies at the heart of Paul's injunctions.

4:25–32 Speak Truth with Compassion

employers, their merchants, and those who depend on their care—no thumb on the scale, no fabricating the numbers, no withholding wages (4:28). Paul next focuses on truth-telling as it honors others rather than demeans them (4:29), for shaming another believer is, by extension, shaming the Holy Spirit who establishes their inheritance and indwells them (4:30; see 1:13–14; 2:22). Finally, Paul insists that violence, such as verbal threats and screaming, has no place among believers. The believer speaks words of forgiveness and extends compassion, drawing on the infinite source of all compassion and forgiveness, Christ Jesus (5:1–2).

Paul proceeds with a pattern of giving a negative command, followed by a positive command and a rationale to motivate the Ephesians.[239] For example, in 4:25 we have the negative command not to speak falsely, the positive command to speak truthfully, and the rationale, that believers are all members of Christ's body. By setting up his argument in this way, Paul crafts a dynamic image of the believer as one who (1) is a member of Christ's body, (2) works to create surplus so as to share it with others in the body, (3) speaks truthfully to bless the body, and (4) forgives with compassion others in the body. By implication, each believer will also receive from others forgiveness for his or her own anger, help in their need, and encouragement as the body grows and is strengthened in the Lord.

The danger for believers today is to see these verses as a list of dos and don'ts, or to hear them as commands geared to an individual self-enhancement regime or a method to persuade God to love us or forgive us. Paul does not present life with Christ as a series of lists, for that would create a false vision of God and of believers. Paul will continue in 5:1–2 that as we imitate God's character, we too give good things, speak true things, and believe true things. God's superabundance of goodness flows into creation and into believers. Moreover, God is not static, but dynamic and active. Thus believers draw on the bottomless love of Christ in every action and thought and are thus transformed as they grow in him.[240]

25 As members of the body of Christ, believers enjoy the blessings of forgiveness of sins and an inheritance secured in the Holy Spirit. Paul appeals to this reality as he addresses what it looks like for believers to put on their new self. He begins this section with the conjunction "therefore" and links to the previous passage with the participle "put off." He used this same verb

---

239. Hoehner, 461.

240. Tanner, *Jesus, Humanity, and the Trinity*, 75, explains: "Jesus' sinlessness is not a static property for our imitation, but something that takes shape in a process of overcoming temptation as that process is empowered by the fact of Jesus' being the Word incarnate." She continues: "God's attributes become in some sense our own; they are to shine through our lives in acts that exceed human powers and in that way become established as part of a reborn sense of self" (111).

in 4:22, as he urged believers to put off the "old self," which is characterized by all that is false or opposed to the truth of God in Christ.[241] Paul wants believers to refrain from falsehoods, a foundational position enshrined in the Decalogue (Exod 20:16; Deut 5:20; see also John 8:44).[242] Later in this passage, he speaks against stealing, another of the Ten Commandments (Exod 20:15; Deut 5:19).

Paul insists that the Ephesians "speak truthfully to your neighbor." The Greek text repeats almost word for word the text in Zech 8:16 LXX.[243] Although Paul does not use an introductory formula for this quotation, its similarity to the biblical text suggests Paul's knowledge of the passage. The context of the prophet's words helps us understand Paul's concern. To the ancient Israelites, God declares that he will do good among them, and the seed will grow, the rain will fall, the remnant will receive their inheritance, and the nation will be a blessing to all peoples. God will draw people from all languages to Jerusalem, and they will say to an Israelite: "Let us go with you, because we have heard that God is with you" (Zech 8:23). Zechariah called Israel to speak truthfully to each other, judge rightly in their courts, and resist evil. Paul echoes the prophet's themes of godly community life and mission to the nations throughout Ephesians. Here in Eph 4 Paul focuses on truth-telling as an essential behavior of a community called by the Lord.

Paul offers a reason for his charge to speak truthfully, namely, because believers are members of one another.[244] Paul uses the noun "member" here and in 5:30, as he speaks of the unity of the church, Christ's body.[245] Paul offers a detailed presentation of this idea to the Corinthians, as he speaks of body made up of many "parts" or "members" (1 Cor 12:12–27). The body of Christ is a resounding theme within Ephesians. Paul introduces it in Eph 1:23, declaring that Christ is the head and believers his body. This body is composed of Jew and gentile, one new humanity brought into being by Christ, who is our peace (2:14–15). Such is the amazing mystery that gentiles are members of one body (3:6), and Paul insists that there is one body (4:4), which is to grow up into Christ the head (4:15). The unity of the church with Christ is demonstrated in the union of marriage when husband and wife become one

---

241. In 4:25 Paul uses the aorist middle participle form, translated as a command in the English translation: "put off." In 4:22 Paul uses the aorist middle infinitive: "to take off" the old self.

242. Eph 4:17 uses ματαιότης; 4:25 uses ψεῦδος; both terms are found in Ps 4:3 LXX [= 4:2 MT].

243. Zech 8:16 LXX has πρὸς τόν while Paul writes μετὰ τοῦ.

244. Best, 448, notes that Stoics promoted the idea that humanity is "a body with members" (Seneca, *Epistles* 95; Marcus Aurelius, *Meditations* 7.13).

245. On μέλος see BDAG 628. Hoehner, 618, observes that the term is always used in relation to "members of an organism" and never for those of an organization.

flesh (5:30–32). Even as each believer is in Christ, nourished by the head, so too each member depends on the others to speak truthfully. The question arises whether Paul limits truth-telling only between fellow believers. The text implies that Paul's focus is on the community of believers. Yet it seems hard to fathom that Paul would accept blatant falsehoods spoken by believers to those outside the church, for that would not reflect God's holiness or love of neighbor (cf. Rom 13:8–10; Gal 5:14).[246]

26–27 Paul drew on Zech 8:16 in the previous verse as he emphasized speaking truthfully to each other in the body of Christ. In Eph 4:26 he follows exactly the wording of Ps 4:4 (= 4:5 LXX), again without an introductory formula, and then continues with admonitions against allowing anger to simmer, for this opens the door to further damage relationships.

Paul cites the psalm using the passive voice of the imperative, "to be angry."[247] Paul later states that believers should remove all anger from their midst, using the cognate noun (Eph 4:31). In its current form, the verb seems to command believers to "be angry," but Paul follows with the second imperative verb in the negative, "to [not] sin." Most interpreters conclude that the first verb is concessive or conditional, cautioning against sinning when angry.[248] Such anger can control a person, rather than the person demonstrating self-control. Paul warns against such attitudes (Phil 1:17–18; see also Matt 5:21–24). However, others offer the stronger suggestion that the imperatives should be read at face value, such that Paul commands the Ephesians to be angry but not to sin.[249] In this case, Paul likely points to two types of anger. First, Paul warns against self-righteous indignation. We must distinguish this from anger against sin and injustice, which should lead to righting the wrong or stopping the transgression.[250] It is an easy thing for humans to conceal their own smugness in a cloak of public anger or justify their own pride under the cover of righteous anger. Cain expresses such anger at God and his brother Abel, and God warns Cain that this anger causes him to contemplate sin, which is "crouching at your door; it desires to have you, but you must rule over it" (Gen 4:5–7). Cain's anger destroyed his relationship with his brother and alienated him from God.[251] Second, Paul underscores the importance of being angry at sin within the church. That is, Paul warns against a complacent

---

246. Best, 447, remarks that "if the point has been put directly to AE [author of Ephesians] he would almost certainly have denied any such restriction."

247. On ὀργίζω see BDAG 721. The verb is used in the passive in each of the eight occurrences in the New Testament and in reference to human anger. Hoehner, 619, notes two exceptions: the anger of the dragon (Rev 12:17) and the nations (Rev 11:18).

248. Best, 449.

249. Wallace, *Greek Grammar*, 491–92.

250. Best, 450; Hoehner, 621.

251. Fowl, 156.

attitude toward sin within the body of Christ. Paul says as much in the next verse, as he alerts the church to the devil's schemes.

Paul continues his admonition that believers should not let the sun set on their anger. If Paul is thinking of the Jewish day, which begins at sundown, then he asks that believers start each day with forgiveness and reconciliation. It may also have been a proverb among gentiles, that anger should be resolved between the two parties before the day ends.[252] Paul uses the uncommon noun that means to provoke to anger ("still angry"), found only here in the New Testament. The verbal cognate is used twice, including Eph 6:4 where it is translated "exasperate" (see also Rom 10:19).[253] Paul's emphasis is to keep short accounts and address sins within the community quickly. This could be an example of what Paul means when he urged believers to bear with each other in love (Eph 4:2).

Paul introduces a new element in the topic of anger, namely, the devil (see also 6:11). Jesus identified Satan as the father of lies, contrasting that with his own message of truth (John 8:31–45).[254] Paul's emphasis here on truth telling fits well with Jesus's charge. Paul indicates that the devil looks for opportunities to defeat believers in their attempts to build unity in love.[255] Paul warns against giving the devil a "foothold," a metaphor for opportunity. Paul points to the spiritual forces of darkness that dominate the present age, rule over the children of disobedience, and afflict the church. Christ has triumphed over all powers and authorities (Eph 1:21–22), yet the church must put on God's armor to ward off the fiery arrows of the evil one (6:16). While the church as the body of Christ is reconciled both to God and to each other (2:16), it is still vulnerable to dissension in its ranks as enemies, including the devil, seek its destruction.[256] Paul speaks a similar word of advice to the Corinthians in a moment when they had admonished a sinful member, who then repented. Yet rather than rejoice at his repentance, the community was reluctant to welcome the repentant one back in their midst. Paul warns them

---

252. Hoehner, 621, cites Plutarch, *Moralia* 488C. Lincoln, 302, argues that "a similar practice is enjoined on the Essenes in the Damascus Rule . . . (CD 7.2, 3)."

253. On παροργισμός see BDAG 780.

254. This passage in John's Gospel has been interpreted in violently anti-Jewish and anti-Semitic ways by the church in its history; however, in John's day, this story highlighted the disagreement between Jesus and Jewish religious authorities.

255. Lincoln, 302, points to a parallel in Testament of Dan 5.2, which states: "Avoid wrath, and hate lying, in order that the Lord may dwell among you, and Beliar may flee from you."

256. Paul uses διάβολος here and in the Pastorals and uses σατανᾶς in his other letters, leading some to conclude that the former epistles are non-Pauline. Yet Paul uses both terms in the Pastorals (1 Tim 1:20; 5:15), and διάβολος is used throughout the Septuagint, including Zech 3:1–2, from which Paul quotes a latter verse (Zech 8:16) in Eph 4:25.

that such hardheartedness on their part could play right into Satan's schemes to promote disunity and discord (2 Cor 2:5–11).

28 After speaking for three verses about truth telling, Paul's warning against stealing catches the reader off guard. Paul uses the participle "the one stealing" and the imperative "to steal" as he commands those who steal to cease from such behavior.[257] The participle is in the masculine singular, which might suggest that Paul had in mind only men in this injunction because women had few opportunities to earn money.[258] This assumption is not supported by our evidence, however, including the role of women within Paul's circle (e.g., Lydia, Phoebe, Priscilla).[259] Moreover, Greek grammar rules dictate that the masculine is used when speaking of only men or of men and women. Only if the subject were female would the feminine be used.

Paul is not likely referring to a thief stealing bread or a robber lying in wait for his victim. Rather, he imagines members of the church who might trick customers to pay a bit more, or put a bit less food in the jar than what the customer rightly paid for.[260] Paul may be concerned about the slave who does not return all the change from the purchase, rationalizing that her owner surely has more than she needs.[261] Paul could have in mind the Christian lender who does not want "to leave any money on the table" and extorts the highest possible interest from her debtors.[262]

A poignant example of lying about money is found in the story of Ananias and Sapphira, a husband and wife who falsified the amount of their gift to the church. Peter declared that they lied to God (Acts 5:1–11). Scripture does not state specifically why these two believers misrepresented their gift as

---

257. On κλέπτω see BDAG 547. Best, 453, notes that the participle serves as a substantive here.

258. Best, 452.

259. For a general discussion about women's work in the ancient world, see Cohick, *Women in the World of the Earliest Christians*, 225–84.

260. See also John Calvin, "The Thirty First Sermon, which Is the Eleventh on the Fourth Chapter," in *Sermons on The Epistle to the Ephesians*, trans. Arthur Golding (1562; 1577; reprinted Edinburgh: Banner of Truth, 1973), 452.

261. Slaves accused of thievery was a common trope in the ancient world; Paul's words are not targeting slaves, but he speaks to the entire church. Contra Best, 453, who argues that slaves cannot earn money and that, because slaves are addressed in Eph 6, our author does not have them in view here. Yet slaves could earn money, and while technically it was their owner's property, nevertheless it was typically treated as their own (*peculium*). It could be used to buy their manumission or that of other slaves. For a general discussion, see Bruce W. Frier and Thomas A. J. McGinn, *A Casebook on Roman Family Law*, American Philological Association: Classical Resources Series (Oxford: Oxford University Press, 2004), 263–90.

262. Hoehner, 624, suggests that Paul points to Christian shopkeepers who steal from their customers. See also Ernest Best, "Ephesians 4:28: Thieves in the Church," *Irish Biblical Studies* 14 (1992): 2–9.

being all the money from their land sale, instead of honestly stating that they retained part of money. But a likely possibility is that they feared they would be in need in the future. We lie to others so as to keep for ourselves what we think we might need in the future, forgetting that God supplies all our needs. Stephen Fowl speaks about the anxiety that sinks deep into our being, causing us to hoard or covet: "Anxiety over scarcity not only drives stealing, it eliminates the conditions under which speech might be truthful."[263] Fowl gets to the heart of the matter as he connects truth with wealth within the church.[264] He surmises that the Ephesians knew about each other's possessions, perhaps even "borrowed" without asking first. Such stealing could be dealt with if believers told the truth to each other, asking for forgiveness and challenging those who keep extra while others lack basics. Interestingly, Paul does not ask the thief to repent, perhaps because the context implies as much.[265]

In the second half of the verse Paul points to work as the antidote to stealing. The verb "work" carries the connotation of toiling labor, strenuous enough to create weariness.[266] Paul assumes that many of the Ephesian believers are healthy enough to work and that there are jobs to be had. This suggests that few among them are destitute, and perhaps even that some might have resources to hire members of the church. We should not assume that Paul imagines that only those closest to poverty are tempted to steal. White-collar crime in the modern industrial economies reveals that it is not always actual need that drives stealing. Nor are the poor less capable of moral actions. Wealthy and poor alike can succumb to the temptation to steal.

Debates continue about the size of the first-century economy in the Roman world, yet information from this period suggests a rather robust system of distribution and consumption largely fueled by Rome's military victories and subsequent need to support its wide-flung army.[267] Perhaps 50 percent of the imperial budget went to maintaining its military, which enhanced trade routes and provided a purchaser for local goods. Moreover,

---

263. Stephen E. Fowl, *Engaging Scripture: A Model for Theological Interpretation* (Malden, MA: Blackwell, 1998; repr. Eugene, OR: Wipf & Stock, 2008), 169.

264. Best, 455, argues that the passage does not deal with "financial theft."

265. Best, 454, notes the absence of repentance language, yet Paul uses the verb only in 2 Cor 12:21 and the noun only in Rom 2:7; 2 Cor 7:9-10; 2 Tim 2:25. Yet Paul will ask the Ephesians to forgive each other in 4:32.

266. On κοπιάω see BDAG 558 (2).

267. For a review of major theories, see Helen Rhee, *Loving the Poor, Saving the Rich: Wealth, Poverty, and Early Christian Formation* (Grand Rapids: Baker Academic, 2012); Bruce W. Longenecker, *Remember the Poor: Paul, Poverty, and the Greco-Roman World* (Grand Rapids: Eerdmans, 2010). See also Walter Scheidel, Ian Morris, and Richard Saller, eds., *The Cambridge Economic History of the Greco-Roman World* (Cambridge: Cambridge University Press, 2007).

consumption of nonlocal goods was high, as locals participated in trading and consuming goods. Ephesus benefited from its position as a government and trade hub.[268] Additionally, the great Temple of Artemis/Diana brought visitors from around the Mediterranean and helped support the local economy. In sum, the picture created by economic historians fits well with the assumptions underlying Paul's orders that believers earn income.

Paul encourages believers to roll up their sleeves, as it were, and get busy with manual labor (1 Thess 4:11–12; 2 Thess 3:6–13). He qualifies the work as "useful," using the same Greek term that describes those "good" works that God prepared in advance for believers to walk in (Eph 2:10).[269] The term "useful" could be adverbial, contrasted with the bad work of stealing, or it could be the direct object of "working/doing" and describe the quality of the labor. Given the emphasis on contrast, most likely Paul stresses here that the former thief must now labor honestly.[270] Paul gives dignity to manual work over against his culture, which looked down on such physical exertion. It is true that the Roman sages waxed eloquent on the glories of farming, but they were imagining what we would call a gentleman farmer, one who has a large income and does not actually work the fields. In reality, most adults, and most children above the age of seven, would be working in shops or at tasks such as weaving or baking or, as Paul did, leather working.[271] Thus we should populate the large marketplace in Ephesus with women and men making, selling, and purchasing goods. One could imagine Priscilla working with customers while Aquila, her husband, finished sewing a patch on the torn leather tent (Acts 18:1–4, 18–19). On a given day, they might pause in their efforts and spend an hour or so teaching Apollos more deeply in the Scriptures (18:26).

Paul offers a reason for his command to toil, namely, so as to have resources to share with those in need. Paul began this section by stressing the need to speak truthfully (Eph 4:25). Truth-telling is also truth "seeing," or being aware of the true needs of those within the body of Christ. Being truthful about working is also being truthful about one's own resources. Serving Jesus who is truth means serving Christ in each member of his body. How might

---

268. Lynn H. Cohick, "Poverty and Its Causes in the Early Church," in *Poverty in the Early Church and Today: A Conversation*, ed. Steve Walton and Hannah Swithinbank (London: T&T Clark, 2019), 16–27.

269. Best, 452, highlights two minor textual variants, including the position or omission of τὸ ἀγαθόν and the omission of the phrase ταῖς ἰδίαις χερσίν or only the term ἰδίαις, but he rightly concludes: "Whatever the reading the meaning is clear."

270. Best, 454–55.

271. For child labor practices, see Lynn H. Cohick, "Women, Children, and Families in the Roman World," in *The World of the New Testament: Cultural, Social, and Historical Contexts*, ed. Joel B. Green and Lee Martin McDonald (Grand Rapids: Baker Academic, 2013), 179–88.

the early church have lived this call? Luke writes that the earliest believers in Jerusalem had a single heart and mind and they shared all things, such that there were no needy persons in their midst (Acts 4:32–35). This occurred through the unleashed power of the Holy Spirit, who worked signs and wonders through the apostles, and many came to faith (5:12–16). And when problems arose with the distribution of resources, believers spoke the truth and acted truthfully by changing how food was distributed so that no divisions, based on ethnocentrism or racism, could fester (6:1–4). As the church spoke the truth, and as individuals were truthful about their possessions, the word of God spread and the number of believers grew (6:7). Jesus addresses the issue of possessions and giving of one's resources as he answered the rich young man's questions about inheriting eternal life (Matt 19:16–23; Mark 10:17–23). Jesus looked lovingly at this earnest young man and advised him to sell all his possessions and give to the poor—a message followed by Barnabas, but ignored by Ananias and Sapphira (Acts 4:36–5:11).[272]

Paul experienced the outpouring of generosity through the impact of the Spirit on his fellow believers. For example, Paul praises the Philippians for remembering his need and making the ministry of the gospel their priority (Phil 4:10–19; see also 2 Cor 8:13–15). Even more, Paul lived out this call to labor so as to help others. Luke writes of Paul's address to the Ephesians, wherein he invites them to recall his own actions in their midst (Acts 20:18–35). Paul reminds them that he worked with his hands so as not to burden anyone with paying for his keep. Nor did he covet the wealth of other believers, their silver or fine clothing. Instead, he worked so as to help those who faced hardship. He supports his actions by citing Jesus's saying: "It is more blessed to give than to receive" (Acts 20:35). This phrase has become a cliché, but when we pause to reflect on it, we find this outrageous claim works in God's economy because God is the giver of all good things and gives all good things with superabundant generosity.[273]

29–30 Paul circles back to discussing believers' speech, now focusing on the importance of building up others. Paul stresses the believers' responsibility to reflect the reality of their reconciliation to God in Christ made secure by the deposit of the Holy Spirit within each of them. Paul warns against unwholesome talk, then describes appropriate conversation. There is an overlap

---

272. Best, 454, comments that our author's injunction to help the needy "contrasts" with Jesus's words to give to the poor in Mark 10:21. Yet Jesus's words to the rich young ruler suggest he should help the needy Jews among whom he lives. Anderson, *Charity*, 153, remarks about Mark 10:17–31: "Just as the inner core of disciples found the crucifixion to be shocking, so the young man finds the giving up of all his wealth to be a sacrifice beyond calculation."

273. Anderson, *Charity*, 159, explains: "The economy of the Kingdom of Heaven, Jesus teaches, reflects the type of world God has created. Showing mercy to the poor taps into the larger font of mercy that governs God's providential hand."

of key terms with the previous verse as Paul repeats "useful," here translated "helpful."[274] Just as believers use their hands for good purposes, so too their mouths should be trained to speak helpful words. Paul also repeats the call to care for those in "need," now stressing the power of words as helping to meet believers' emotional well-being or treating them with the honor they deserve in Christ. Moreover, Paul draws from language and concepts used in earlier chapters as he reflects on upbuilding the body (2:20, 22; 4:16), on the role of the Holy Spirit (1:13–14), and on redemption gained in Christ (1:7).

Paul commands that they refrain from speaking in nasty or mean-spirited ways. Elsewhere the term "unwholesome" is used of putrid or rotten fruit or fish (Matt 7:17–18; 12:33; 13:48).[275] Paul draws on the physical images to make his point here about words that do the same as eating bad fish or smelling rotten fruit. The saying "sticks and stones may break my bones, but words will never hurt me" does not apply here, any more than one can say eating bad food causes no discomfort or injury. Instead, Paul asks that believers speak "only what is helpful for building others up." Earlier Paul commanded that believers speak truthfully to each other, but Paul does not mean laying out "the cold, hard truth." True speech should have the effect of "building up" others where they have a need.[276] Paul uses the noun "building up" earlier in this epistle as he speaks about the church as a building constructed as the temple of the Lord, a dwelling for the Spirit of God (2:21–22). Earlier in our chapter he spoke of the body of Christ being built up through works of service done in love (4:12, 16). To the Corinthians, Paul stresses the importance of prophetic speech as it builds up the church (1 Cor 14:3, 5, 12, 26).

The command to build up the church does not imply the absence of criticism, for Paul himself points out wrong behavior and actions. The purpose behind the words is that a believer will understand more fully or trust more deeply in their redemption. Implied in these instructions is that believers know each other's needs so as to address them. This involves openness and vulnerability between believers and a trust that none will take advantage of another's needs. In other words, such conversation must be infused with grace.

And it is to grace that Paul turns, when he says "that it may benefit those who listen." The term "benefit" is the same noun translated "grace" in the phrase "by grace you have been saved" (2:5, 8). The term carries several connotations, including (1) God's favor toward a sinner, (2) a patron's care of her client (Rom 4:4), (3) a commission by God to a human (Eph 3:8), or (4) gifts given between humans (2 Cor 8:4). The expansive semantic range of the

---

274. On ἀγαθός see BDAG 3–4.
275. On σαπρός see BDAG 913 (2).
276. On οἰκοδομή see BDAG 696–97.

term is narrowed by our immediate context, which emphasizes the benefits of building up of the church.[277]

Paul connects his comments about grace-filled talk with a warning against grieving the Holy Spirit: "And do not grieve the Holy Spirit of God" (Eph 4:30). This phrase is found in Isa 63:10 (the Greek text of Isaiah uses the verb "provoke"). Does Paul allude to Isaiah here? An affirmative answer suggests that Paul was aware of the Hebrew text and chose to render it in Greek. We might not be able to confirm the hypothesis, but several details point to the possibility. First, both the Jerusalem elite and the community at Qumran used Hebrew. Paul might be considered a Jerusalem elite, if one draws on the claim in Acts that he was a student of the great scholar Gamaliel (Acts 5:34; 22:3). Second, Isa 63–64 is used elsewhere in the New Testament. Stephen's speech in Acts includes a condemnation that ancient Israelites "resist[ed] the Holy Spirit" (7:51), likely reflecting Isa 63:10.[278] Finally, the content of Isaiah fits well with Paul's emphasis on the church as God's people redeemed in the promises now fulfilled in the Messiah Jesus, including the inclusion of gentiles in the family of Abraham.[279] The benefit of discerning whether Paul drew on Isa 63:10 here is that we can then imagine the larger context for Paul's understanding of the phrase. In Isa 63–64 the prophet praises the Lord for his care and compassion for his people, even when they rebel and grieve the Holy Spirit. For God is their Father, their redeemer, who comes to the aid of his people.[280]

What then could Paul mean when he speaks of grieving the Holy Spirit?[281] The picture Paul paints is of believers, each sealed with the Spirit, choos-

---

277. Col 4:6 uses χάρις but the context is speaking the message of the gospel to outsiders.

278. Hays, *Echoes of Scripture in the Letters of Paul*, 211.

279. Hays, *Conversion of the Imagination*, 27, writes: "I believe that Paul had read and pondered the scroll of Isaiah as a whole, over the years of his apostolic ministry, and developed a sustained reading of it as God's revelation."

280. Isa 64:4 includes a reference to "no ear has perceived, no eye has seen" (see 1 Cor 2:9), and Isa 64:8 includes: "We are the clay, you are the potter" (see Rom 9:21).

281. The question of God experiencing emotions such as grieving is complex. The doctrine of God's aseity or divine impassibility argues that God's person or character is not contingent on circumstances, nor does his being change as do creatures through time. To some readers this might sound like God is removed and distant from humans, but that is not the intent of this position. Rather, the doctrine of God's aseity reminds believers of God's constancy, his unchanging and unfailing love that remains forever, without diminishing. The point is not that God has no "feelings," but that God is above all contingent circumstances and the effects of time. See J. Todd Billings, "Undying Love," *First Things* 248 (December 2014): 46, who, in the midst of his cancer treatment, realized that "if the suffering of Christ is not, finally, a revelation of the triune God's faithful, impassible love, then the cross could no longer be my solace in the midst of my physical agony and existential despair." For a broad

ing whether to walk in their new self or fall back into old pagan ways. Do they speak from the redemptive power within them, a Holy Spirit–shaped deposit guaranteeing their inheritance? Or do they spew rotten words at another believer, who is sealed with the same Holy Spirit (1:13)? Do they tear down the temple wherein God dwells by his Spirit (2:22)? Putrid talk weakens the Christian community, and what diminishes God's temple grieves God's Spirit. Truth-telling in its many dimensions expresses life as the new self, which, by God's grace and resurrection power, will continue into eternity.

31 Paul swings from the joyous promise of redemption for God's people, who are sealed by the Holy Spirit, to the fearful present possibility that evil thoughts and words might infect the faithful community. Paul advocates not a private, abstract, personal piety, but the hard work of community building amidst the rough and tumble reality of living with other people. He has no illusions about the difficulties of community life and the strife that bubbles to the surface from the envy and jealousy within individuals' hearts. Paul continues his focus on speaking that began in 4:25. Words create meaning and define circumstances. With a word, God created the world (Gen 1:3). With a word, Jesus declared his work of redemption finished (John 19:30). With a sound deeper than words, the Spirit prays for believers (Rom 8:26–27). And with words believers can build up—or, as Paul warns here, tear apart.

Ephesians 4:31 offers a list of five attitudes and actions that the believer is to put away, and the next verse finishes with a general appeal to live virtuously (see also Col 3:8). Paul further emphasizes the seriousness of these vices by declaring that "all" bitterness, rage, anger, brawling, and slander must be removed, as must "all" malice. We need not make too much of the order of these vices, yet it seems that the first term, "bitterness," identifies the root cause of the resulting anger and shouting.[282] Paul uses the term "bitterness" in a string of Old Testament quotations to warn the Romans that no one can claim righteousness before God (Rom 3:14). The mouth full of bitterness leads to feet that walk into ruin and create mayhem. James argues much the same, as he cautions that the wisdom of his day promotes "bitter envy" and "selfish ambition," condemning it as "unspiritual" and "demonic" (Jas 3:14–15). Bitterness emerges from a sense of being treated unfairly by comparing one's situation to another person's lot.[283] Bitterness is that attitude that looks only to the immediate and not to the past great gift of God in Christ, nor to the future resurrection and glory shared with Christ. Paul declares that the center

---

discussion, see James F. Keating and Thomas Joseph White, eds., *Divine Impassibility and the Mystery of Human Suffering* (Grand Rapids: Eerdmans, 2009).

282. On πικρία see BDAG 813 (2).

283. Lincoln, 308, observes that bitterness indicates "hard-heartedness that harbors resentment about the past."

of attention is not the believer himself or herself, but others in the community of God, who have also been sealed with the Holy Spirit unto the day of redemption.

From this attitude of bitterness, "rage and anger" spring up. These two nouns serve as synonyms and are used together to describe God's judgment against those who follow evil (cf. Rom 2:8; Rev 14:10).[284] Paul uses the nouns, along with "malice" and "abusive speech," in his warning to the Colossians, for they have put on their new self in Christ (Col 3:8–10). In Paul's description here in Eph 4:31, the escalating intensity grows from smoldering frustrations in one's heart (bitterness) to open flames of anger, to a wildfire of the tongue that shouts and slanders, culminating in "malice," the utter lack of virtue.[285] The term "malice" can refer broadly to wickedness or more specifically, as here, ill-will.[286]

Paul commands the Ephesians to "get rid" of evil thoughts and speech. This verb is one of thirteen imperatives in 4:25–5:2, and while the only one in the aorist tense (and not in the present tense), nevertheless, the verb depicts the need for constant vigilance against bitterness taking root and producing all manner of evil speech. Paul believes that words have power, either to build up the community or tear it down. For Paul, the very unity of the body of Christ is at stake. In this, Paul's purpose in creating a list of vices may differ from similar Greco-Roman vice lists, for his goal is not the moral perfection of the individual, but conformity to Christ and love of fellow believers. So too today, countries have laws against hate speech, for governments recognize that hateful speech against a minority group can lead to hateful actions. And we recognize the tremendous damage that harsh words have in the home, crushing children's or spouses' spirits and fracturing relationships. Paul's warnings are applicable not only in churches, but also in the home and at work. Believers must watch against bitterness and anger and should cultivate kindness and compassion, which Paul encourages in the following verse.

32 Paul concludes the list of virtues and vices by contrasting the vile speech flowing from the springs of bitterness (4:31) with the compassion that characterizes the gracious actions of God in Christ.[287] The same concern for community is front and center here, as Paul puts the phrase "to one another" directly after the opening imperative "to be." Three actions are required of believers: kindness, compassion, and forgiveness. We rightly locate the com-

---

284. On θυμός see BDAG 461 (2); on ὀργή see BDAG 720 (1).
285. Best, 462.
286. On κακία see BDAG 500 (2). See also Salmond, 349; Hoehner, 637.
287. The conjunction δέ is lacking from early manuscripts (P46 and B), yet the majority of manuscripts support it.

munal aspect of Paul's injunctions within his Jewish heritage, contrasting it with the individualistic focus of gentile moralists.[288]

The idea of "kindness" has suffered a bit today as a bland vanilla virtue, a small gesture that lightens another person's day. The biblical virtue is much more robust and often linked to God's salvation love for his people (Luke 6:35; Rom 2:4; 11:22; Titus 3:4; 1 Pet 2:3).[289] Earlier in the epistle, Paul declares that God demonstrated his kindness in extending his saving grace to us (Eph 2:7). Jesus explains that God the Father's kindness extends to the ungrateful and wicked, and he bids his followers to love their enemies and do good to them (Luke 6:35). Following Jesus's injunction, Paul too recognizes that kindness will not be a simple, small gesture, but at times will include a heroic act of the will.

Along with kindness, Paul asks the Ephesians to extend "compassion" to each other. The only other place the term is found is in 1 Peter, encouraging believers to love each other (1 Pet 3:8); however, Paul uses similar nouns in his list of virtues to the Colossians (3:12). A similar verb describes Jesus's actions in reaching out to the widow of Nain (Luke 7:13) and to the leper (Mark 1:41) or gazing at the crowds who were as sheep without a shepherd (Matt 9:36).[290] Overall, the terms reflect the proper response to a situation of need. The expectation is that the one who feels compassion will seek to right the wrong.

The third term, a present participle, can be translated "forgiving" or "be gracious," and carries the sense "unlimited succession of acts of forgiveness."[291] The root of this verb connects to the noun "grace" used by Paul to describe God's salvation gift in Christ (2:5, 7, 8). Paul spoke of the grace or "benefit" given in the good words that build up those who listen (4:29), and the same idea is in play here, for Paul insists that believers do this "to each other." Beyond the sense of graciousness, Paul wants to emphasize even more the idea of forgiveness. Paul finishes the sentence here with the same emphasis, that God in Christ "forgave you all."[292] The final phrase holds the key to understanding Paul's call for kindness, compassion, and forgiveness—these traits demonstrate the work of God in each believer's life. Additionally, these traits confirm the great work of renewal of believers in Christ. The renewal and maturity flow from the wellspring of forgiveness that fills to overflowing the

---

288. So Perkins, 112, who explains: "Virtues are not the result of individual reason and its ability to order human life. Rather, God calls together a community of persons to life in holiness and justice."

289. On χρηστός see BDAG 1090 (3). See also Best, 463.

290. On σπλαγχνίζομαι see BDAG 938.

291. On χαρίζομαι see BDAG 1078 (3); see also Best, 463. Contra Hoehner, 639, who argues for the translation "gracious."

292. Best, 463, notes that the textual evidence for ἡμῖν is strong, but that the evidence for the second plural ὑμῖν is stronger.

hearts of believers. Paul begins the clause with the causal conjunction "just as" and continues with the article and noun "God" and the prepositional phrase "in Christ," before concluding with the aorist tense verb "to forgive" and the plural pronoun "you." The aorist tense speaks of the totality of the forgiveness gained by Christ's redemptive work, rather than pointing to the moment of the believer's salvation.

We come to the end of Eph 4's list of virtues and vices. Why does Paul begin his list by reminding the Ephesians that they put on the new self, created to be like God (4:24)? Salvation is not only about receiving forgiveness of sins; it is also about being a new creation in Christ, being a member of his body, the church.[293] The list of virtues is not simply an outline of goals to pursue, but reflects the very nature of God and who we are becoming in Christ. Paul knows the power of God that melts stone hearts and heals broken spirits. However, he is also aware of the power to abuse God's call to forgive. This can happen in at least two ways, by either refusing to forgive or by demanding that another forgive. In the first case, the Corinthians faced a situation in which a church member grieved Paul, perhaps challenged Paul's gospel, and threatened to turn the church away from the truth (2 Cor 2:1–5). Paul asked that the community confront this person's sin, which they did, and the person repented. At this point, they held great power over this individual. They needed to follow Paul's injunction to forgive the repentant member of their community, or they risk overwhelming that believer in hopeless sorrow. Even more, they need to forgive so as to "outwit" Satan (2 Cor 2:11), who is eager to divide and destroy Christ's body. Withholding forgiveness destroys both the repentant person *and* the person (or church) who fails to forgive.

In the second case, the church today has used Paul's call to forgive to cover abuse within the home and church. Wives are bullied by pastors to forgive abusive husbands, and the evidence of such forgiveness is that the wife must remain in the abusive home. Historically in the church, a similar charge was made to slaves, that they forgive their abusive owners and submit to further mistreatment as a testimony to their own faith. Paul does not condone the covering up of violence. Indeed, he has earlier instructed the church to care for those in need (Eph 4:28), which would certainly include an abused spouse or child. Paul's injunction to forgive does not entail that the sinner is allowed to continue to sin against the fellow believer. Each believer is called to forgive but is not called to submit to abuse by family or church members. The church must step in to protect the vulnerable and needy in their midst and prevent further violence.

---

293. Fowl, 160, stresses that rather than moral perfection, Paul desires that the church follow "practices designed to repair and enhance relationships between believers."

B. WALK AS CHRIST WALKED (5:1-21)

Paul paints a vivid picture of the Christian's new life as safeguarded by Christ's sacrifice, established in God's loving forgiveness, and empowered by the Holy Spirit. Juxtaposing the concepts of light and dark, fidelity and idolatry, Paul draws sharp contrasts between the life of godly obedience and sinful disobedience. Underneath his admonitions to act honorably and joyfully is the secure hope of inheriting the kingdom of Christ and of God. Paul presents a future-facing orientation not only to encourage the Ephesians to obey God daily, but also to expose the evil of the present age. As believers await their inheritance, they serve each other, for they are all members of Christ's body, his church. Paul invites readers to pause over the richness of salvation, who they are in Christ, and to link that identity with actions and thoughts that reflect that identity. Paul asserts that the Ephesians are "beloved" children, loved before the world's foundations. They are "in Christ," coheirs with him through belief in his death and resurrection for the forgiveness of sins. As such, they are to mimic or imitate God, as embodied in the life, ministry, death, resurrection, and ascension of Jesus Christ.

1. Follow God's Example (5:1-2)

¹Follow God's example, therefore, as dearly loved children ²and walk in the way of love, just as Christ loved us and gave himself up for us as a fragrant offering and sacrifice to God.

Debate centers on whether 5:1-2 should be connected with the previous several verses in Eph 4 or, as presented here, start a new section. Favoring the former position is the repetition of the verb "to be/become" in 4:32 and 5:1.[294] Further, this view has the content of the two verses concluding and drawing implications from the previous section. Finally, this position argues that a new section begins in 5:3 with the conjunction "but" and a change in topic to issues of sexual morality. The position taken here, however, holds that 5:1 begins a new section and relies on several points. First, Paul uses a conjunction "therefore" in 5:1, which often signals he is moving ahead, based on his previous statements. Second, if we hold that 5:1-2 is with the previous verses, then it means Paul begins the next section with a series of vices, but this is quite atypical for the period.[295] Third, the pattern in 5:1-2 is different from the previous verses, as the latter would begin with a negative injunction and

---

294. The Greek verb is γίνομαι. Best, 443; Lincoln, 295; MacDonald, 310.
295. Perkins, 112.

follow with a positive, while here we have Paul promoting pious acts before contrasting them with sinful behaviors in 5:3–7.[296]

1–2 In these two verses, we find the reverse side of the same coin of salvation that Paul described in the opening chapter of Ephesians. Recall that in 1:3–7 Paul outlines the breathtaking love of God the Father. Before time began, God purposed that through the incarnation of the Son, the Father provided humanity with adoption into God's family and, through the Son's death and resurrection, redemption of sin. Paul explains that believers are God's dearly loved children, teases out the implications of such salvation, and connects several points that bear on the meaning of human life and human purpose. First, Paul asserts that believers' demonstration of kindness to their fellow believers correlates to God's own gesture of kindness in salvation, including forgiveness of sins (4:32). Second, Paul proclaims that the people of God should imitate God—even as children imitate their parent. Paul treats this as natural, given that believers are adopted children of God, their Father. Paul points to the Holy Spirit's work in sealing believers unto the day of redemption (4:30) and now explains that the forgiveness extended by God the Father through the Son must be visible in the body of Christ. Third, Paul draws on the deep reality that believers' very self, the *imago Dei*, is made whole "in Christ," whose body was broken that they might be made complete.

In 5:1 Paul begins with the conjunction "therefore," linking this verse with the previous argument and moving it forward. Paul continues to develop his charge for believers to forgive as God in Christ forgave them their sins. He connects the preceding call to show godly compassion and forgiveness with the charge to imitate God. Such a command would be unthinkable outside the firm knowledge that we are members of Christ's body, we are forgiven in him, and we are sealed with the Holy Spirit.

Paul repeats the imperative used in 4:32, "to be made, be performed."[297] This verb conveys a dynamic sense of producing or performing, of a new condition based on a change in circumstances. Jesus uses this verb when he bids his disciples to follow him: "I will make you become fishers of men" (Mark 1:17 ESV). Not only does Paul repeat the verb of Eph 4:32, he also follows the same pattern in using a noun, in this case "imitator," as he calls on believers to "follow God's example" or "be imitators of God."[298] In a grammatical sense, 5:1 parallels 4:32, yet 5:1–2 also heighten Paul's injunctions by connecting them to God's character and actions.

---

296. Barth, 555.
297. On γίνομαι see BDAG 196–97.
298. On μιμητής see BDAG 652 (a); S. E. Fowl, "Imitation of Paul/of Christ," *DPL* 428–31 (which, however, does not address this passage).

5:1–2 Follow God's Example

The exhortation to follow God's example is found only here in the entire Bible, although we have Paul calling on the Corinthians to imitate himself as he imitates Christ (1 Cor 4:16; 11:1; Phil 3:17; 1 Thess 1:6) and to imitate other believers (1 Thess 2:14).[299] The notion of an object imitating another object, or a person imitating another person or a god, was common within the wider Greco-Roman world, but the notion of imitating God rarely appeared in Second Temple Judaism.[300] The emphasis, instead, was on obeying God and on living a holy life as a result of such obedience (Lev 19:2; see also Matt 5:44–48; 1 Pet 1:15).[301] Yet if we press beyond a narrow understanding of imitation, we find that the creation narrative in Genesis invites humans to imitate God in their acts of working, resting, creating, and ruling.[302] Paul indicates to the Ephesians that God has created good works for them to do (2:10) and has seated them with Christ above who rules in the heavenly places (2:6).

As adopted children, beloved of God, they are to model their father's character. Paul's injunction draws on the ancient family setting wherein children mimic their parents.[303] Others might think that the call to imitate God borders on recklessness, for did not Adam and Eve seek to be like God and fall into sin (Gen 3:5–6)? Paul, however, is not asking that believers be like God in the sense that Adam and Eve attempted to be. Rather, Paul has stated that they are already new creatures in Christ; they have put on the new self, which is created to be like God in true righteousness and holiness (Eph 4:24). Paul has earlier indicated that believers are God's handiwork (2:10), a new humanity or people created in Christ (2:15). It is precisely because they are like God, by being in Christ and members of his body, that they can think

---

299. Perkins, 114, cites Philo, *On the Special Laws* 4.34, 186–87, who enjoins those with authority to use it for others' benefit: "The best is to use all their energies to assist people and not to injure them; for this is to act in imitation of God, since he also has the power to do either good or evil, but his inclination causes him only to do good." Best, 467, however, points out in a related Philonic passage: "Though Philo's statement in *Spec. Leg.* [*On the Special Laws*] 4.73 may appear similar, his reason is God's creation of people and not his love for them." Lincoln, 311, suggests that the author of Ephesians was familiar with "similar traditions to those used by Philo."

300. Best, 466, who adds: "The thought of the imitation of the invisible God is paradoxical." However, Willis Peter De Boer, *The Imitation of Paul: An Exegetical Study* (reprinted Eugene: Wipf & Stock, 2016), 8–13, explains that the Pseudepigrapha uses the language more frequently.

301. Best, 467.

302. Christopher J. H. Wright, *The Mission of God's People: A Biblical Theology for the Church's Mission* (Grand Rapids: Zondervan, 2010), 105–9. See also Jason B. Hood, *Imitating God in Christ: Recapturing a Biblical Pattern* (Downers Grove, IL: IVP Academic, 2013), 130.

303. De Boer, *Imitation of Paul*, 12, who explains that Philo speaks about "the imitation of God in the figure of a teacher and father. Philo does not hesitate to speak directly about the imitation of God."

and act as God the Father, their father. Paul insists that believers are greatly loved by God as his children; from this position of forgiveness and blessing, they step out to show such graciousness to other believers.

Implied in Paul's identification of believers as God's beloved children is the concept that God is their parent. Earlier Paul prays to this "glorious Father" that believers might know him better (1:17), for this Father adopted them through Christ Jesus by his eternal love that existed before he created the world (1:4–5). Paul makes clear that it is love that empowers and sustains Christ's redemptive work. The Ephesians have heard this through Paul's earlier prayer, which extolled the all-encompassing love that fills the universe and will continue beyond anything created (3:17–19). Paul prayed that they would know the strength that comes from the glorious riches of the Father of all families (3:14). This strength roots believers in love, specifically the love of Christ, a love that surpasses human comprehension (3:16–20). God's love is greater than anything known or experienced, and it sustains life.

Paul continues to explain what he means by the audacious call to imitate God. He uses one of his favorite images, "to walk," as he asks the Ephesians to live their calling "in love" (5:2). Paul continues with the conjunction "just as" and cites Christ and his love. Paul uses two aorist tense verbs—"to love" and "to give over, to deliver"—followed by a reflexive pronoun, "himself." At the end of the chapter, Paul again stresses Christ's love and giving, using the same two verbs in the aorist tense, in the context of Christ's care for his church. Paul indicates with the aorist tense that he sees Christ's loving and giving as the foundation for his call to holy living by believers.[304]

Paul speaks of the Christian life as a walk that must be done in a worthy manner (4:1) and not as gentiles comport themselves (4:17). This dynamic interchange is captured by Kathryn Tanner's comment: "Christ forms us but what is so formed is our action."[305] Paul enjoins believers to walk "in love," repeating the term from the previous verse. Such love is demonstrated not only in our adoption as God's beloved children, but also in the sacrificial death of Jesus Christ, the Son. This love is outwardly focused; it gives instead of takes. This love is self-giving; it gives itself, not for itself, but for others.[306]

---

304. David L. Mathewson and Elodie Ballantine Emig, *Intermediate Greek Grammar: Syntax for Students of the New Testament* (Grand Rapids: Baker Academic, 2016), 115–25, discuss the aorist tense.

305. Tanner, *Jesus, Humanity, and the Trinity*, 72.

306. Schüssler Fiorenza, 76–77, warns that violence against women and children and stereotyping women can be couched in love language: "Feminist the*logical work on violence against wo/men and child abuse has pointed to four key traditional the*logical discourses of 'love' that are major roadblocks in the way of abused wo/men and children who seek to change their violent situations," including (1) patterns of submission/domination, (2) linking women with sin, (3) exalting suffering as Christ suffered, and (4) preaching for-

5:1–2 FOLLOW GOD'S EXAMPLE

The giving is generous and sincere, or, in the language of the Old Testament, it is "fragrant" (see Gen 8:20–22; Exod 29:18; Lev 17:6).

Paul summarizes the redemptive act of Christ, that he gave himself as an "offering and sacrifice for us." Paul explains the purpose of Christ's death, which was to redeem humanity and reconcile all to God and to each other. He highlights for the Ephesians their forgiveness of sins (1:7) and future inheritance (1:14), their status as a new people (2:15), and their having a new citizenship (2:19). Paul lays out this redemption path to the Corinthians, as he explains the gospel as Christ dying for our sins, being buried and raised from the dead, and appearing to many of his followers, including Paul (1 Cor 15:3–8). Jesus explained that his death was "a ransom for many" for "the Son of Man did not come to be served, but to serve" (Mark 10:45).

Christ's death has effectively resulted in the forgiveness of sins, as his offering of himself has been received by the Father. Paul continues that this offering is made "to God" and that the offering is a sweet fragrance. Both Jews and gentiles in Paul's day were quite familiar with sacrifices of animals, grains, and wine. Both groups would imagine the liturgically rich setting when presenting an animal to be ritually slaughtered on their behalf to appease the gods or atone for sins or celebrate God's blessings. Into this colorful and dramatic setting, Paul inserts Jesus Christ, who as our Passover lamb was sacrificed (1 Cor 5:7).

Paul highlights God's approval of this sacrifice with his detail that it has a pleasing aroma. Here he draws on the Old Testament's picture of an acceptable sacrifice, as when God received Noah's offering after the floodwaters receded (Gen 8:21) and as God instructs the priests (Num 15:3–24; 29:2–36). The prophet Ezekiel writes that God will accept his people as a fragrant incense as he gathers them from the nations (Ezek 20:41). Paul uses the same adjective, "fragrant" (*euōdia*), to describe the believers in the midst of the world: "We are to God the pleasing aroma of Christ among those who are being saved and those who are perishing" (2 Cor 2:15). And he draws on the same phrase as found in Ezekiel to describe the Philippians' financial gift.

Paul draws on this rich imagery to portray Christ's death, resurrection, and ascension. Christ's death on the cross was a sacrifice, and the aroma arising to God reflects his ascension. Paul emphasizes both the death and the ascension of Christ, and while much is made (rightly so!) of Christ's work of redemption and new creation based on the cross, readers should also be alert to ascension themes in this epistle. Paul speaks of Christ being raised by God

---

giveness without repentance and restitution. For a review, see Regula Strobel, "Der Beihilfe beschuldigt: Christliche Theologie auf der Anklagebank," *Feministisch theologische Zeitschrift* 9 (1993): 3–6.

from the dead (Eph 1:20–21), seated at God's right hand (2:6), and ascended (4:8–10, citing Ps 68). The ascension demonstrates Christ's rule over all creation.[307] Paul declares that even now we are seated with Christ in the heavenly places, for we are "in Christ" through his redemptive work (Eph 2:6).

EXCURSUS: IMITATE GOD AS BELOVED CHILDREN

Later Christian writers explored Paul's teaching in 5:1–2. The fifth-century church father Augustine develops the rich theological interplay between the doctrines of the Trinity and the *imago Dei* ("image of God") in his *De Trinitate* by locating the *imago Dei* in the mind.[308] As Janet Soskice summarizes his views, it is with "the *activities* of remembering, understanding, and willing or loving (these last here interchangeable), . . . that the inner self is most Godlike."[309] Augustine draws primarily on Gen 1:27 for his ideas on the *imago Dei*. Augustine presents the Christian progress toward God as knowing oneself through remembering, understanding, and loving God, by which God shapes the believer to become what he intends. Augustine's position has the advantage of concluding that all men and women are made in God's image, for this image resides in the mind or reason.[310] However, locating the seat of God's image in the mind has the disadvantage of downplaying the body. In downplaying the transient realm of cooking, cleaning, and caring for the sick as "a mere staging post in the soul's ascent to a higher wisdom," believers might miss the power of Paul's call to imitate God, who is known through and in the incarnate Christ.[311] Believers might miss the full embodiment of the *imago Dei* in themselves and in those with whom they share their resources (Eph 4:28) and build up with their words (4:29).

---

307. Gerrit Scott Dawson, *Jesus Ascended: The Meaning of Christ's Continuing Incarnation* (London: T&T Clark, 2004), 53, writes: "Of all the meanings of the ascension, this one is pre-eminent: Jesus has gone up to the right hand of God the Father, exalted above every name and power."

308. Augustine, *The Trinity* (NPNF¹ 3). See also, Augustine, *The Trinity*, translation from Edmund Hill, *The Works of Augustine: A Translation for the 21st Century* (New York: New City Press, 1991); for discussion, see Lewis Ayres, *Augustine and the Trinity* (Cambridge: Cambridge University Press, 2010).

309. Janet Martin Soskice, *The Kindness of God: Metaphor, Gender, and Religious Language* (Oxford: Oxford University Press, 2007), 132.

310. Because Augustine (following the pattern of his time) labels wisdom as male and knowledge of temporal matters as female, his conclusions tend to elevate the male and masculinity.

311. Soskice, *Kindness of God*, 136.

Excursus: Imitate God as Beloved Children

Julian of Norwich, a thirteenth-century mystic, develops her views on the Trinity and the *imago Dei* through reflection on the incarnation.[312] Julian explores the theology of the Trinity and incarnation based on a vision she received in the midst of a serious illness. *The Revelation of Divine Love* can be read as "a deeply considered essay on the doctrine of the Trinity (of which she displays a profound and surefooted knowledge), and on the human predicament."[313] Her starting point is the wounds of Christ, the blood that flows down his face from the crown of thorns. As she gazes on a crucifix near her sickbed, she sees not only Christ's body, but the Trinity. The incarnate Jesus is "the image of the invisible God" (Col 1:15), which Julian sees in a Trinitarian sense. Julian embraces the human body in light of the incarnate Lord.[314] God is now at work in both mind and body; indeed, they are so intertwined as to be almost inseparable.

Julian asserts that God loved us before the foundations of the world, which means he loved us and then gave us embodied existence. Julian writes: "I saw very certainly that . . . before God made us he loved us, which love was never abated and never will be. . . . In our creation we had beginning, but the love in which he created us was in him from without beginning" (passage 86). Augustine will suggest something similar in *De Trinitate*: "Indeed I observe that the Father loved us not merely before the Son died for us, but before he founded the world, as the apostle bears witness" (13.5, citing Eph 1:4). It was always in God's plan to conform us to the image of the Son, to be coheirs with Christ, the incarnate one. Therefore, the incarnation was not God's ad hoc rescue mission that required the use of a fleshly body because, as it happened, humans are made of flesh. Rather humans are made of flesh because Christ is the incarnate one and believers are his coheirs, as Paul declares to the Ephesians.

---

312. Julian of Norwich, *Showings*, trans. Edmund Colledge and James Walsh, Classics of Western Spirituality (Mahwah, NJ: Paulist Press, 1978); see also Julian of Norwich, *Showings: Authoritative Text, Contexts, Criticism*, ed. Denise Nowakowski Baker, Norton Critical Edition (New York: Norton, 2005).

313. Soskice, *Kindness of God*, 125. She explains: "Where Augustine sees the cup half empty, she sees it half full; where he looks backward to the Fall, she looks forward to union with God. *De Trinitate* speaks of our thirst for God, Julian of God's thirst for us" (152).

314. Marc Cortez, *Christological Anthropology in Historical Perspective: Ancient and Contemporary Approaches to Theological Anthropology* (Grand Rapids: Zondervan, 2016), 61, states: "Julian views the cross primarily as the supreme demonstration of divine love." He continues: "Julian's crucicentric theology, then, is inescapably a theology of love, the love displayed on the cross."

2. Inherit the Kingdom (5:3–6)

> ³*But among you there must not be even a hint of sexual immorality, or of any kind of impurity, or of greed, because these are improper for God's holy people.* ⁴*Nor should there be obscenity, foolish talk or coarse joking, which are out of place, but rather thanksgiving.* ⁵*For of this you can be sure: No immoral, impure or greedy person—such a person is an idolater—has any inheritance in the kingdom of Christ and of God.* ⁶*Let no one deceive you with empty words, for because of such things God's wrath comes on those who are disobedient.*

Paul's previous three verses (4:32–5:2) summarized the believers' lifestyle as one that imitates God and walks in Christ's love. Paul describes believers as beloved children, as forgiven by God in Christ. His exhortations to be kind and forgiving to members of Christ's body imply that God has empowered believers through the sacrifice of Christ to walk in love. I remind readers of this, because in the following verses, Paul pulls no punches against the ways of darkness and makes clear that those who habitually practice evil will not enjoy God's inheritance. We must remember that Paul's judgment against sexual immorality, debauched speech, and greed stems from his firm conviction that the Ephesians are beloved children of God who can now live in the beautiful light of God's redemption. Additionally, Paul's language is characteristic of Jewish moral exhortations of his day, which warns against immoral living.[315] It is most likely that Paul speaks about a group outside his congregation, a group that seeks to influence their behavior. They press the Ephesians toward a return to their old lifestyle characterized by a moral code inimical to the gospel. Less likely is the possibility that members of the congregation promote these behaviors, because in that case we would expect Paul to be more forthright against them.

Our post-Freudian era holds that almost all sexual expression is good, and any curtailing of sexual desire leads to repressive mental ailments. We confuse love with sexual satisfaction. We also live with pervasive consumerism, enabled by crony capitalism, that dulls our senses to the damaging power of excessive consumption. Paul counters that the well-lived life is that which offers thanksgiving to God and extends openhanded generosity to others. Paul sees no reason to apologize for a holy life, a life that decries sin and embraces goodness. Perhaps we have an allergy to the term "holiness" because today it is understood as a "holier than thou" attitude and judgmental hypocrisy. The church is partly to blame for this perception, because it has defined holiness at times as only avoiding gross sexual sins or as following a

---

315. See 1QS 4:9–10; 7:16; 10:21–24; Wis 14:12; Philo, *On the Life of Joseph* 43–44; *On the Special Laws* 1.23, 25; and the discussion in Perkins, 115–16.

5:3-6 Inherit the Kingdom

list of "don'ts." Christian communities can neglect the importance of Christlike generosity and Godlike forgiveness, leading to thanksgiving to God. Paul stresses the importance of becoming like Christ, which involves both the pursuit of virtue and avoidance of vice. To this end, Paul spotlights the believer's redemption and new life in Christ.

Paul addresses three key practices in 5:3-6, specifically, "sexual immorality" (*porneia*), "uncleanness/impurity," and "greed." With nouns sharing the same root and used in the same order in 5:3 and Col 3:5, Paul warns believers against such actions. This section repeats vices discussed in Eph 4, including idolatry and immorality (4:18), greed (4:19), and depraved speech (4:29). The list in Ephesians has several verbal echoes in Col 3:5-8, but in the latter, these vices have been put to death in the believers, while in Ephesians, Paul states that these vices characterize gentile pagans (4:17).[316] Paul includes similar injunctions in other letters (2 Cor 12:21; Gal 5:19).

Paul further defines the greedy person as an idolater (Col 3:5) and insists that believers act with holiness, consistent with their new status as beloved, redeemed children of God. Not only these actions, but also speech that minimizes and mocks debauchery and selfishness—this too has no place in the church. Why? Because the kingdom of Jesus the Messiah and God the Father includes a community of equally worthy members. No one should make another believer the butt of a crude joke, nor take advantage of another as an object of their desire. As we will see below in Eph 6 with a discussion of parents and children, slaves and owners, Paul's world was filled with those who satisfied their lusts for sex and power by using others as objects. God executes his loving justice as he condemns such abuse; Paul speaks of this as God's wrath (5:6).

3 Paul contrasts walking in love (5:2) with avoiding three deadly sins that cut to the heart of personhood (5:3, 5). In decrying sexual sins and greed, Paul addresses the root cause of alienation from God, namely, the disordering of love such that the self is privileged over God. Jewish writings of this period also decry these vices.[317] The verse begins by listing the three sins, and then Paul commands that such actions not even be named in their midst. It is not necessarily the case that such sins are occurring; rather, Paul explains that as members of God's people, they should behave with holiness.[318]

The first noun, "sexual immorality" (*porneia*), expresses disdain for another as an object of desire and confuses sexual freedom with power over an-

---

316. Perkins, 112–15.

317. E.g., Wis 14:12; Testament of Judah 19.1; 23.1; Philo, *On the Special Laws* 1.23, 25. Perkins, 116–17, for this list of ancient works.

318. Wallace, *Greek Grammar*, 724–25, indicates that the "force of a particular present prohibition will not always be focused on the cessation of an activity in progress."

other.[319] It refers to sexual sins such as adultery, sexual immorality, and prostitution.[320] Jesus uses the term when speaking about marital infidelity (Matt 5:32; 19:9), and Paul uses it to describe the sort of sexual sin at which even pagans balk (1 Cor 5:1; see also 1 Cor 6:12–20; 2 Cor 12:21; Gal 5:9; 1 Thess 4:3). The second term speaks to moral uncleanness, which includes sexual "impurity."[321] Paul uses this noun in 4:19 when describing the futile thoughts of gentiles who separate themselves from life with God. Paul uses the same pair of terms, "sexual immorality and impurity," in his description of deeds done in the flesh or expressions of the sinful nature that resides in all humans (Gal 5:19; Col 3:5; see also 2 Cor 12:21).

The third term, "greed," might have a sexual connotation, as one lusts to consume another's body.[322] Yet Paul separates this noun from the other two with the particle "or," not the conjunction "and," which may suggest a separate vice.[323] In the end, the grammar does not encourage readers to establish a hard and fast line between these sins; rather, the conceptual link is idolatry.[324] Paul uses impurity and greed together in the previous chapter as he describes the pagan whose ignorance and hard heart leads to impurity and greed (4:19; see also 1 Thess 4:6). The ancient Israelites described idolatry with the metaphor of sexual infidelity (Num 14:33 LXX; Jer 3:9; Ezek 16:36; Hos 1:2; Mic 1:7). They also warned of trusting wealth rather than God, a form of idolatry (Deut 8:17–18). We might note that greed shares with idolatry a love of gold or silver; the greedy and the idolater both frequented pagan temples, for the temples also served as banks.[325] Demetrius the silversmith makes this connection plain in his attack against Paul's preaching in Ephesus (Acts 19:24–27). Paul clarifies to the Colossians with similar language that greed is idolatry and must be put to death as part of a believer's earthly nature, for believers have died a spiritual death and are alive now with Christ (Col 3:3). We in the

---

319. On πορνεία see BDAG 854.

320. Ruden, *Paul among the People*, 14–15, speaking of adultery, explains: "Altogether, nearly everybody in the Roman Empire would be prone to feel that Paul, rather than making a harsh new rule, was only seconding a humane and sensible one they had always had."

321. On ἀκαθαρσία see BDAG 34 (2).

322. MacDonald, 311, makes the interesting suggestion that "the greed in view here is sexual greed." Her astute observation reminds us today that slaves often provided sexual pleasure and as "property" could be "consumed." See also Lincoln, 322.

323. Best, 476, wonders whether the author of Ephesians "regarded avarice as a sin which can be the source of other sins" and continues: "This sentiment was widely accepted in the ancient world."

324. P. W. Comfort, "Idolatry," *DPL* 424–26; Edward M. Curtis, "Idol, Idolatry," *ABD* 3:376–81; Susan Ackerman, "Idol, Idolatry," *EDB* 625–27.

325. So Brian S. Rosner, *Greed as Idolatry: The Origin and Meaning of a Pauline Metaphor* (Grand Rapids: Eerdmans, 2007), 150–51.

5:3–6 Inherit the Kingdom

West are not tempted with actual temples such as the Artemisium, yet with internet pornography, for example, we greedily consume others' bodies and create a virtual world of power and instant gratification. We desire objects made of silver and gold and of pixels.

Paul declares that such behavior has no place within the community of believers.[326] He uses the verb "to name" or "to note," translated "no hint" above, in an effort to express his concern about sinful actions related to believers' identity.[327] In a similar passage in Colossians, Paul enjoins believers to put to death these vices, which reflect earthly life,[328] for the Colossians have died and are now alive in Christ (3:3–5). The church must be known as a holy people by the wider society, not as holier-than-thou and arrogant, but pious, moral, and generous. Even though Paul makes a sharp contrast with his reference to the immorality of the pagans, he nevertheless wishes that these pagans would be drawn into the communion of the saints. Thus, Paul does not ask the church to separate out of the society, but to walk in love such that the wider society would be attracted to the group of beloved children of God.

4 Paul knows that words do things, as when God spoke and creation came into being. Jesus declared that words matter, for they reflect the heart (Luke 6:45). Therefore, Paul not only addresses sexual immorality and greed, he also challenges improper, vulgar speech as antithetical to Christian witness. This verse draws on the previous verse's finite verb "to be mentioned or named."[329] Paul continues his concern over behavior, by offering a second triad of vices to be avoided. Paul warns the Ephesians that vile speech is unfitting for those in God's family.

Paul uses three nouns found nowhere else in the New Testament: "obscenity," "foolish talk," and "coarse joking" (5:4); and he contrasts them with a common command to offer thanksgiving to God. These terms can also carry a more general sense of vulgar behavior. The term "obscenity" includes speech that scorns social decency codes and brings shame to the speaker.[330] Paul repeats the noun "obscenity" in its adjectival form when he

---

326. For a discussion of vice lists, see John T. Fitzgerald, "Virtue/Vice Lists," *ABD* 6:858.

327. On ὀνομάζω see BDAG 714 (2). Best, 477, rightly comments that the statement cannot be taken literally because these words would be read aloud to the congregation and thus "named"; instead, the point is likely that "unnecessary discussion of these sins concentrates attention on them." Twice before in this epistle, Paul uses this verb as he highlights the spiritual powers and the earthly families that can be identified (1:21; 3:15).

328. Τὰ μέλη τὰ ἐπὶ τῆς γῆς in Col 3:5.

329. Best, 477. Lincoln, 322, however, may exceed the evidence in his comment that "the new triad of vices should be seen as simply continuing the thought of the previous verse by making explicit the sort of naming of sexual sins that is being forbidden."

330. On αἰσχρότης see BDAG 29.

declares that it is shameful even to speak of deeds of darkness (5:12). And he uses a similar noun when cautioning the Colossians against behaving according to the practices of the old self, pandering to the earthly nature (Col 3:5–8). The second noun, "foolish talk," is used by the first-century moral philosopher Plutarch in his descriptions of drunkenness at a Roman banquet.[331] Paul might have a similar thought in mind here, for later in Eph 5 Paul warns against drunkenness and paints a picture of a Christian "banquet" that includes hymns, joyous music, and thanksgiving. All this comes from being filled with the Holy Spirit (5:18–20). "Coarse jokes," the third noun used in this verse, also have no place, for they twist the beautiful intimacy that God created between lovers into a transactional event as common and ordinary as shopping at the market.[332]

In Paul's day, there were no pornography laws, and sexual adventures were pursued with abandon, especially among free men.[333] There was, however, a recognition that lust was a result of lack of self-control, a key virtue among Stoics. Self-control extended to governing the tongue, speaking with seriousness and restraint. Seneca warns against glib talk,[334] and the Essenes against vulgarity.[335] Yet other ancient authors, to justify their crude poems and epigrams, hide behind elegant poetic forms and claim that they were virtuous even as their words sketched a coarse subject. For example, Catullus writes: "For it is right for a pious poet to be chaste / himself, but there's no need for his little verses to be so."[336] Both Pliny and Martial follow similar paths, as their elegant verse contains sexually explicit and indecent content. "The effect is to remove the erotic poetry itself as far from reality as possible" by proclaiming that one's personal piety stands apart from one's words. Martial could thus declare that "his verses are lascivious but not harmful."[337]

Paul, however, will have none of that hairsplitting nonsense. He asserts that vulgar, tasteless, and coarse comments must be banished from the believers' community. None of these actions and conversation represent God and his gospel; in fact, they make a mockery of it. Paul declares they are not fitting; they misrepresent the holy God and his self-giving love. The antidote to such tempting power grabs is a thankful heart toward God (5:4). Paul asks

---

331. Plutarch, *Moralia* 504A–C. On μωρολογία see BDAG 663. See Thielman, 330.

332. On εὐτραπελία see BDAG 414. Lincoln, 323, notes that Aristotle viewed this term as positive (*Eudemian Ethics* 3.7.1234a.4–23) and negative (*Nicomachean Ethics* 4.8.1128a.14–15).

333. Ruden, *Paul among the People*, 45–118.

334. Epictetus, *Epistles* 52.8.

335. Perkins, 116, also points to 1QS 7:16; 10:21–24.

336. Catullus 16, translation from Amy Richlin, *The Garden of Priapus: Sexuality and Aggression in Roman Humor*, rev. ed. (Oxford: Oxford University Press, 1992), 2.

337. Richlin, *Garden of Priapus*, 7.

5:3-6 Inherit the Kingdom

believers to offer thanksgiving, which puts actions and attitudes in proper order (5:4).[338] When believers thank God, they recognize their dependence on him and not idols. When they praise the Lord, they remember his holiness and their own call to reflect that holiness.

5 The concern for right living in Christ is a resounding refrain throughout Ephesians. Here, the concept "kingdom of Christ and of God" pulls together forgiveness of sins and right living for life now and life in the new creation (for a similar phrase, see Col 1:13).[339] Paul begins the verse with a conjunction, "for," that signals a connection with the previous two verses. Paul follows with an unusual periphrastic phrase using the perfect imperative (or indicative) of "to know" (*oida*)[340] and the infinitive of "to know" (*ginōskō*), translated "of this you can be sure."[341] Paul repeats his concern in 5:3, citing three similar nouns; here, however, the nouns refer to persons rather than behaviors.[342] In this verse, he focuses on individuals who chose these sins, while in 5:3 he focused on the actions. Paul casts a wide net in describing sexual sins, knowing that such sins often include violence and abuse of power.[343] The actions are insupportable, and those who do such actions will not share God's inheritance.

Paul announces that those who engage in sexual immorality or act greedily have no inheritance. The semantic range of the term "inheritance" includes both a present actuality (one is an heir) and a future experience (one

---

338. Fowl, 167.

339. For a discussion of the theme in 1 Corinthians, see Samuel D. Burnette, "The Kingdom in First Corinthians: Reevaluating an Underestimated Pauline Theme" (PhD diss., Southern Baptist Theological Seminary, 2016).

340. The textual variant ἔστε is found in Dc E K L; the most likely reading, ἴστε, is found in A B D F G. Stanley E. Porter "'Ἴστε Γινώσκοντες in Ephesians 5,5: Does Chiasm Solve a Problem?," *Zeitschrift für die neutestamentliche Wissenschaft* 81 (1990): 270, explains that the variant "make[s] the construction into a simple periphrastic" and that the more difficult reading of ἴστε is the most likely.

341. Porter, "'Ἴστε Γινώσκοντες in Ephesians 5,5," 273, finds a chiastic structure in 5:3-5 and also in our verse. He continues: "There is also a chiastic arrangement: τοῦτο ἴστε γινώσκοντες ὅτι, with the pivot point around the two words for knowledge" (275). He suggests that the two verbs be treated separately, with the first verb and the demonstrative pronoun ("this") pointing back to the previous verses, and the participle with the conjunction pointing forward. This reading suggests that the finite verb should be rendered as an indicative.

342. Best, 480, wonders if the shift indicates a focus on those who habitually indulge in such vices.

343. Best, 476. Fowl, 165, perceptively notes: "Then as now, sex was always tied up with issues such as purity, identity, power, and desire, which touch on most aspects of life." He argues that "misconduct in one's sexual practices reflects a wider and deeper level of disorder."

realizes their inheritance).³⁴⁴ The heir shares the family's honor as their own honor. The heir acts consistently with his or her family's values. Paul introduced the noun "inheritance" in 1:14, explaining that the Holy Spirit is the believers' seal confirming that they are redeemed and that their redemption will be accomplished in the time of fulfillment. He repeats the noun in 1:18 as he speaks of believers' hope, the riches of this glorious inheritance, and now uses it in 5:5 to distinguish those who will not inherit the kingdom.

Paul uses a similar line of reasoning with the Corinthians, as he cautions them against bringing lawsuits against each other. The issue precipitating the lawsuits involves money, and Paul challenges them: "Why not rather be wronged?" (1 Cor 6:7). I pause here because in Ephesians, Paul equates greed with idolatry, and in his first letter to the Corinthians Paul isolates cheating as that which rendered people ineligible to inherit the kingdom. In both epistles, Paul warns against the sexually immoral and the idolaters. Those who cheat, due presumably to their greed, are in fact idolaters. Paul calls attention to the greedy explicitly in 1 Cor 6:10. The context in both epistles warns against habitual, serious sin that places people outside the inheritance (see also 1 Cor 15:50).³⁴⁵ In Galatians, Paul speaks of the inheritance of Abraham as coming from God's promise, not from the law (Gal 3:18).³⁴⁶ It is the children of the promise who inherit (4:30), but those who live according to the flesh will not inherit the kingdom (5:21).³⁴⁷

Thus, in three different epistles, looking at three different situations, Paul speaks about those who will not inherit the kingdom based on their habitual patterns of idolatry and sexual immorality.³⁴⁸ And importantly from

---

344. On κληρονομία see BDAG 547–48. Perkins, 116, highlights parallels to Paul's inheritance language in 1QS 5:18–19; 10:7–8.

345. Hans Conzelmann, *1 Corinthians: A Commentary on the First Epistle to the Corinthians*, Hermeneia (Philadelphia: Fortress, 1990), 106, explains that "the original apocalyptic sense of the concept 'kingdom of God' is maintained. . . . Paul did not spiritualize the concept."

346. For a discussion of inheritance in Galatians, see Chee-Chiew Lee, *The Blessing of Abraham, the Spirit, and Justification in Galatians: Their Relationship and Significance in Understanding Paul's Theology* (Eugene, OR: Pickwick, 2013), 56–57. See also Esau D. McCaulley, *Sharing in the Son's Inheritance: Davidic Messianism and Paul's Worldwide Interpretation of the Abrahamic Land Promise in Galatians*, Library of New Testament Studies 608 (London: T&T Clark, 2019).

347. In Gal 3:18 we read the noun κληρονομία; in Gal 4:30 and 5:21 it is the verb κληρονομέω. Paul draws on both the typical or literal meaning of inheritance, that of a father giving the family property to the son (or children in the Roman tradition), as well as the spiritual inheritance provided to all who are in the Spirit. The spiritual inheritance involves avoiding a life of the flesh with its sinful ways.

348. Gary Steven Shogren, "'The Wicked Will Not Inherit the Kingdom of God': A Pauline Warning and the Hermeneutics of Liberation Theology and of Brian McLaren,"

a pastoral standpoint, in these epistles, Paul declares that believers are not like that, for believers are light (Eph 5:8); they are washed, sanctified, justified (1 Cor 6:11). They live in the Spirit. Paul does not threaten believers with the vision of an angry Father ready to disinherit, although I think today some Christians (and many nonbelievers) see God that way.

Scholars speculate as to whether Paul speaks of two kingdoms, or a sequential rule of a single kingdom, or has a millennial kingdom in view.[349] A full answer to this question pulls us into the study of the relationship between Paul and Jesus's teachings, which is beyond our scope. The scholarly landscape has been shaped by the views of the early-twentieth-century scholar Albert Schweitzer (1875–1965). He argued that both Jesus and Paul believed the end of the world was to come within a few years or decades. When this event did not happen, the church had to explain the delay in Christ's return (parousia). Schweitzer held that both Jesus and Paul created an ethic for the church to follow in the interim before the immanent return of Christ. Schweitzer concluded that Paul held to a messianic kingdom before the final judgment and the establishment of the kingdom of God. The idea of an interim kingdom continues in premillennial thought.[350]

Trinity Journal 31 (2010): 97. See also Gary Steven Shogren, "The Pauline Proclamation of the Kingdom of God and the Kingdom of Christ within Its New Testament Setting" (PhD diss., University of Aberdeen, 1986). See also Günter Haufe, "Reich Gottes bei Paulus und in der Jesustradition," *NTS* 31 (1985): 467–72.

349. For an extensive discussion of kingdom language, see Scot McKnight, *Kingdom Conspiracy: Returning to the Radical Mission of the Local Church* (Grand Rapids: Brazos, 2014). He suggests there are three basic positions on the concept of kingdom of God today. First, "kingdom" refers to the spiritual rule of God in a believer's life, begun and sustained by Christ's salvific work. Second, "kingdom" reflects social action, bringing the love of Christ to serve those experiencing hardship. Third, "kingdom" includes all activities of everyday life done for God's glory. Each option captures an aspect of the kingdom, and, drawn together, these descriptions remind us of the communal nature of the kingdom. Each kingdom citizen is in Christ, and together citizens serve each other and the needy world. Kingdom language underscores unity within the church and service to those not (yet) citizens (Phil 3:20–21). "Kingdom" language connects the present with the future, the earthly body and the resurrected body, the pursuit of holy living, and the confidence in salvation by God's grace alone.

350. Schweitzer, *Mysticism of Paul the Apostle*, 90, concludes: "The eschatology of Paul is therefore quite different from that of Jesus. . . . Instead of thinking as Jesus did along the lines of the simple eschatology of the books of Daniel and Enoch, he represents the two-fold eschatology of the Scribes." Ben Witherington III, *Jesus, Paul, and the End of the World: A Comparative Study in New Testament Eschatology* (Downers Grove, IL: InterVarsity Press, 1992), 15, discusses Schweitzer's influence and offers critique. He suggests that (1) Rudolf Bultmann saw little connection between Jesus and Paul's teachings, (2) Ernst Käsemann was persuaded that they had only minimal continuity, and (3) later scholars such as F. F. Bruce and J. D. G. Dunn argue for greater continuity stretching from Jesus to Paul.

The Letter to the Ephesians

In Ephesians, the unique phrase "the kingdom of Christ and of God" probably emphasizes Paul's earlier claims that Christ is now seated at God's right hand and that his enemies are under his feet (2:6; 1:20–22).[351] With death's final "death," when all things are under Christ's feet, Christ hands the kingdom to the Father (1 Cor 15:24–28). The phrase "kingdom of Christ and of God" reflects the injunctions in Eph 5:1–2, which closely align the love of God and of Christ toward believers.[352] And the image of Christ's enemies being under his feet presented in 1:20–21, echoes Ps 8:6 and 110:1. These enthronement psalms celebrate the establishment of God's (Messiah) king over his kingdom (1 Cor 15:25–26; Eph 1:21–22).

Both Colossians and 1 Corinthians highlight Christ's rule over this present age of darkness and death. Additionally, Paul speaks of "the law of Christ" (Gal 6:2; 1 Cor 9:21), which reinforces the image of Christ as King, for a king's wish is the law of the land.[353] When we link the notion of kingdom with the obvious need for the kingdom to have a king, we then become aware of how much Paul speaks of Christ's kingdom. Paul asserts that Christ rules over death, life, his people, and ultimately all things. Paul says as much in Rom 14:9, that Christ died and was raised so as to be "the Lord of both the living and the dead."

These examples highlight that Paul believes the kingdom of God is yet to come. But that is not the sum total of his opinion on the matter, and two other examples demonstrate that the kingdom of God is also present now. The redemption story does not end with Christ's resurrection, but continues with his ascension and exaltation to God's right hand. When we speak about Jesus reigning, we necessarily imply the existence of a kingdom over which he rules. This reality helps us make sense of Rom 14:17, our first example, wherein Paul speaks of the kingdom of God as a matter of "righteousness, peace and joy in the Holy Spirit," and not of kosher food habits. The context is a church of Jews and gentiles seeking to establish a holy life together as the people of God.

Would that the Corinthians were so concerned about holy life! In our second example, Paul cautions the arrogant among them that "the kingdom of God is not a matter of talk, but of power" (1 Cor 4:20). Paul speaks against the cliques that grew up around key leaders. These verses in Romans and 1 Corinthians make plain that believers exist in the midst of the kingdom of God, they are established by the work of Christ, and their lives are empowered by the Holy Spirit. "Thus the kingdom of God/Christ might even be

---

351. Thielman, 334, argues that Paul emphasizes "the present reign of the Messiah together with God himself."
352. Perkins, 117.
353. My thanks to Courtney Zboncak, my research assistant, for this excellent point.

described as 'life in the Spirit' or 'life within the Body of Christ,' both much more prominent themes within the Pauline letters."[354]

Paul's emphasis on the believers' behavior shapes his discussion of God's kingdom. Paul tends to use "kingdom of God" language when speaking about the future, eternal aspect of God's rule and to speak of Christ's kingship in reference to present realities; nevertheless, "those whose lives are marred by the vices mentioned cannot be in any sense joint heirs with the Christ who is at present reigning until all his enemies are subjugated, just as they cannot hope for admission to the eternal kingdom: they are self-excluded from the kingdom in all its phases—the kingdom which is both Christ's and God's."[355] In other letters, Paul warns believers not to be deceived into believing that the sexually immoral and idolaters (in Ephesians they are also called greedy) will inherit the kingdom (1 Cor 6:9; 15:50; Gal 5:21). Paul also speaks to the church in Rome that the kingdom of God is about righteousness, peace, and joy in the Holy Spirit, not about eating and drinking, that is, about kosher foods (Rom 14:17). His answer addresses the church's internal argument about whether and how food laws should be implemented. Again, Paul comforts the Colossians with the sure hope that they inherit the kingdom of light, which is the kingdom of the Son, the beloved of the Father (Col 1:12–13).

Paul indicates that ungodly behavior characterizes those who do not inherit God's kingdom. Today it is difficult to avoid the label "judgmental" when speaking about sexual immorality.[356] This is due in no small part to the church's own failings in this area, as well as its tendency to ignore the greed in its midst. Kingdom language provides a way to talk about the duties and responsibilities of those who claim its citizenship. Sexual sins and greed harm others and grieve the Holy Spirit.[357] Personal piety develops in the crucible of personal interactions. Paul faced the disunity between Jewish and gentile believers, and he identified the root cause as judgmental posturing (Rom 14:10). Similarly, today believers face racial and ethnic tensions, and a contemptuous attitude casts an ominous shadow over the church's witness. Recognizing

---

354. Larry J. Kreitzer, "Kingdom of God/Christ," *DPL* 524–26; Dennis C. Duling, "Kingdom of God, Kingdom of Heaven: New Testament and Early Christian Literature," *ABD* 4:56–69. The phrase "kingdom of God" occurs eight times in Paul, and "kingdom of Christ/Son" twice.

355. Bruce, 372.

356. Richard B. Hays, *The Moral Vision of the New Testament: Community, Cross, New Creation; A Contemporary Introduction to New Testament Ethics* (San Francisco: HarperSanFrancisco, 1996), 385, writes: "God's judgment allows the irony of sin to play itself out: the creature's original impulse towards self-glorification ends in self-destruction."

357. Best, 483, takes the author of Ephesians to task for not showing "any concern for those who suffered through the sexual indulgence and greed of church members." This overstates the case, as 4:25–32 stresses the importance of caring for others and avoiding hurtful behaviors and language.

God's kingdom as a place of right living and a space of forgiveness draws together the poles of Christian truth.

6 Paul worries that the Ephesians would be deceived into tolerating sinful behavior as acceptable for kingdom subjects. The Ephesians must reject deceptive arguments that minimize the dangers of immoral actions. Paul begins the verse with a strong negative adjective, "no one," that serves as the subject, and follows with a plural personal pronoun "you," followed by the imperative verb "to deceive." Paul uses the cognate noun "deceitful" in describing the "old self" with its deceptive desires, which the Ephesians are to take off (4:22) and replace with the new self in Christ. The deception takes advantage of "empty" words. The term "empty" has the sense of vain, fruitless, hollow, and foolish.[358] Paul alerts the Colossians to the deceptive philosophy based on human traditions and the ways of this present age (Col 2:8; see also 2 Thess 2:10).[359] If the Ephesians allow such deception, they would be partners with the sons of disobedience (Eph 2:2), who do not inherit the kingdom, but rather experience God's wrath.

Who is Paul referring to as he warns the Ephesians? It could be that he is pointing obliquely to a group within the Ephesian church that justifies their disobedience.[360] However, Paul would be uncharacteristically vague here if he had a specific group in mind. Others suggest the influence of gentile outsiders who lure the believers back into their old ways.[361] This view picks up on Paul's stress on the insider/outsider motif throughout this section of the epistle. A third possibility is that Paul offers a general warning against those who twist the gospel message in order to turn believers to their way of thinking and acting (4:14; see also Acts 20:28–30).[362] This third possibility rightly recognizes the general character of Paul's injunction.

In the second half of Eph 5:6, Paul declares that God's wrath falls on those whose lives are characterized by sexual immorality, impurity, lewd jokes, and greed, which is idolatry. Paul writes "because of such things," pointing back to the vices noted above.[363] Paul continues with the present

---

358. On κενός see BDAG 539 (2).

359. James warns his congregation in a similar manner, that those who consider themselves religious but do not keep a tight rein on their tongues, have deceived themselves about their religiosity—indeed, "their religion is worthless" (Jas 1:26). In the parable of the sower, Jesus admonishes against the deceit of riches that warp the heart and choke off godly living (Matt 13:22; Mark 4:19).

360. Best, 484; Barth, 566.

361. Perkins, 117–18; MacDonald, 312–13; Lincoln, 325.

362. Arnold, 326, summarizes Paul's move here as "more of an immunization than a prescription."

363. Arnold, 326, argues that "these" does not refer to the "empty words" earlier in the verse.

tense indicative verb "to come" but the verb also carries a future sense here.[364] Earlier, Paul states that the wrath of God comes on the disobedient (2:2–3). Several points should be noted about Paul's teaching on God's wrath.[365]

First, we must dismiss our modern misrepresentations of the wrathful God. The biblical picture of God does not match the modern caricature of an angry Father who allows the murder of his innocent Son to appease some vendetta or grudge against humans. Nor is God the violent domestic partner who with one hand slaps his child's or partner's face and with the other seeks to embrace them. Instead, God reveals himself as fully love, giving of himself in love for love's sake.

Second, the reference to "wrath" draws on Old Testament teachings on God's judgment against the wicked who exploit the poor and mock God, who set up idols and worship false gods. While the image of a wrathful God sounds harsh to our ears today, the first listeners to this epistle might have initially shrugged their shoulders at such characterization, for the Greek gods were notorious for their angry outbursts and temper. Sicknesses and sufferings represented the gods' wrath, leading pagans to offer vows and prayers in blind hope that they might receive relief. For the Jews, however, God's wrath reflects his concern against idolatry and his desire for relationship with a holy people called into fellowship with him. The wrath of God was the counterpoint to his love, his response to that which is unlovely and unloving.

Third, and here we get to the meat of Paul's argument, God directs his wrath on sin, and those who sin stand under judgment. And sin should make us angry, as it harms and destroys the innocent. When we see harm done, exploitation, degradation, should we not be angry? Yet God's wrath is not an angry emotion; it is action that sets the wrong to right.[366] The sober fact is that to make all things new, the old ways of sin and violence must be destroyed.

---

364. Lincoln, 325; Arnold, 327. Mathewson and Emig, *Intermediate Greek Grammar*, 125, point out that "the present tense-form is the one chosen by the author to portray an action as in progress, as developing or unfolding, irrespective of the time or the nature of the action itself."

365. On ὀργή see BDAG 720–21 (2); Stephen H. Travis, "Wrath of God (NT)," *ABD* 5:996–98.

366. Fleming Rutledge, *The Crucifixion: Understanding the Death of Jesus Christ* (Grand Rapids: Eerdmans, 2015), 130, wisely writes: "The wrath of God is not an emotion that flares up from time to time, as though God had temper tantrums; it is a way of describing his absolute enmity against all wrong and his coming to set matters right." See also Miroslav Volf, *Exclusion and Embrace: A Theological Exploration of Identity, Otherness, and Reconciliation* (Nashville: Abingdon, 1996), 233, who writes: "One could further argue that in a world of violence it would not be worthy of God *not to wield* the sword; if God were *not angry* at injustice and deception and *did not* make the final end to violence God would not be worthy of our worship" (emphasis original).

This is necessary for the equation of God's new creation plan to work. In the forthcoming unity of all things under Christ (1:10), there is no place for those who reject or resist the mercy of the loving Father. Those who perpetuate violence, abuse of power, and unchecked desires are invited, through the rich mercy of God, to be made alive in Christ (2:4–5).

Paul does not describe believers here as falling under God's wrath, but rather those who do not embrace the gospel.[367] Paul reassured believers that Christ rules from God's right hand (1:20; 2:6), that they are sealed with the Holy Spirit (1:13) and made alive with Christ (2:5); they are not disobedient children, but beloved children of God (5:1).[368] They have the equipment to stand firm against the battles and skirmishes brought on by the powers of this dark age (6:10–17). And they have the promise that God will act justly against those who stand against God's peace-filled love.[369]

Wrath is a consequence of God's deep love and perfect holiness. On account of these qualities God acts in Christ to redeem humanity and through the Holy Spirit enables the redeemed to walk in new life.[370] The broad biblical witness holds in proper tension the dual reality that God's wrath is revealed against wickedness (Rom 1:18) and that God is not a wrathful, vengeful deity. God is love (1 John 4:16), and Jesus declared himself the good shepherd who gives his life for the sheep (John 10:11). Through Christ's shed blood God reconciled the world to himself, that all who are in Christ enjoy an inheritance as children of God (2 Cor 5:19; Col 1:19–20). God invites us to see sin as he does, as those thoughts and practices that prevent our flourishing and tarnish the *imago Dei*.

3. Darkness and Light (5:7–14)

> [7]Therefore do not be partners with them.
> [8]For you were once darkness, but now you are light in the Lord. Live as children of light [9](for the fruit of the light consists in all goodness, righteousness and truth) [10]and find out what pleases the Lord. [11]Have nothing to do with the fruitless deeds of darkness, but rather expose them. [12]It is shameful even to

---

367. Arnold, 327.

368. Thielman, 335, argues that the disobedient "are not believers who struggle against such sins and sometimes fail, but . . . are people dead in their transgressions and sin."

369. Volf, *Exclusion and Embrace*, 230, draws a compelling picture: "For the sake of the peace of God's good creation, we can and must affirm *this* divine anger and *this* divine violence, while at the same time holding on to the hope that in the end, even the flag bearer will desert the army that desires to make war against the Lamb" (emphasis original).

370. My thanks to Julie Dykes, my research assistant, for her comment that God's patience must be considered when speaking of his wrath (1 Cor 13:4; see also 2 Pet 3:9).

mention what the disobedient do in secret. ¹³*But everything exposed by the light becomes visible—and everything that is illuminated becomes a light.* ¹⁴*This is why it is said:*
"*Wake up, sleeper,*
    rise from the dead,
    and Christ will shine on you."

Paul continues his admonishment to the Ephesians as he gives further reason for his warning that they not partner or fellowship with the children of disobedience. He reminds them of their own past as disobedient ones, and calls out as evil those deeds of darkness that blighted their lives. But Paul does not stop here, as if to say that we in the church should circle the wagons to guard against any outsiders.[371] Instead, Paul encourages believers to take their role as light to be light to others so that they too might come into the light, which is Christ. In other words, Paul asks believers to remember their own plight and redemption and to draw others into the light.

Paul structures his argument by first stating that the Ephesian believers are children of light in Christ. He reminds them that they produce fruit or deeds suitable to the light. As children of light, they have nothing to do with darkness and the hideous deeds associated with secret, hidden, and shameful spaces. Paul recognizes that a clear stand against such secret deeds clarifies the picture of the holy life. There is no possible middle ground when it comes to idolatry (greed) and sexual immorality, and certain forms of these sins have to be called out as heinous. But they are identified as such, not to bolster a feeling of superiority among the saints, but to rescue those trapped and sinking in the sinful cesspool. The believer reproves the deeds of darkness in hope that the light of truth, goodness, and righteousness will pull others into the light. In a final metaphor, Paul likens believers to those who were once asleep and have risen from the dead now that the light of Christ shines on them.

7 This short verse of five words in Greek serves to conclude Paul's previous argument and to introduce a new argument using metaphors of light and darkness to describe believers' moral comportment. Paul uses the noun "partners" followed by the pronoun "them."[372] The noun occurs only one other

---

371. Contra Perkins, 117–18, who sees a parallel with the Essenes who self-identify as children of light and who battle darkness. Unlike the Essenes, the letter to the Ephesians does not present social structures to support withdrawal from the wider society. MacDonald, 321, argues that "Ephesians demonstrates a much stronger sense of introversion" and that "the community is adopting an increasingly defensive strategy in relation to nonbelievers."

372. Lincoln, 326. Contra Best, 486, who suggests that the pronoun refers to the vices.

time in Paul, in 3:6 of this epistle.[373] In that earlier chapter, Paul uses this noun in a set of three terms to describe the shared redemption in Christ enjoyed by Jew and gentile believers. Paul asserts that Jew and gentile believers are now one in Christ. Conversely, Paul emphasizes here in 5:7 that believers must not join together with nonbelievers whose habitual behavior mocks the living God by indulging in greed/idolatry and sexual immorality, which tarnishes those made in God's image.[374] Paul does not tear down gentile culture here or elevate Jewish ethnicity; his point is narrowly focused on destructive habits and attitudes that distance a person from God.[375]

8-9 Paul builds on his admonition in 5:7 that the Ephesians are not to partner with the children of disobedience, for that path leads to disaster. Instead, Paul reminds them that they have come out of darkness into light and are indeed light because of Christ.[376] Paul's description calls up a "before" and "after" picture that each believer should carry with them in their imagination. Paul begins 5:8 with the conjunction "for" as he develops his argument stated in 5:7. Paul uses the particle "once/formerly," contrasted in the next clause with "but now."[377] Paul states that these believers were once "darkness." Paul does not use the preposition "in," likely in order to further emphasize that if one walks in the realm of darkness, then one is characterized by darkness.[378] Paul continues that they now "are light" in the Lord. Again, the phrase lacks the preposition "in" so as to reinforce the believers' identity as fully committed to Christ. Paul specifies that this light is "in the Lord," thereby emphasizing their "union with Christ."[379]

Metaphors have the power to shape our actions and allow us to see new things, and Paul realizes that simply stating rules of behavior can lead to sterile obedience without joy or discernment. Paul uses the metaphor of light and darkness to make clear the contrast between the current dark age

---

373. On συμμέτοχος see BDAG 958.

374. Contra Best, 486, who argues that "those who offer the specious arguments and sin are within the community."

375. Lincoln, 326.

376. Best, 487-88. Arnold, 328, remarks that the image of darkness and light was common across all religions in the ancient world and suggests that the book of Isaiah might have had special influence on Paul's thought here (Isa 9:2; 60:1-2, 19).

377. Thielman, 338, observes that ποτέ and νῦν δέ "set up a contrast between preconversion and postconversion existence [that] was common in early Christian literature (e.g., Rom. 11:30; 1 Pet. 2:10; cf. Gal. 1:23)." Lincoln, 326, picks up the conversion theme and adds the unlikely observation that "the imagery of darkness and light suggest that baptismal paraenesis is being employed."

378. Fowl, 169; Thielman, 338.

379. Arnold, 329, who adds: "Paul calls believers to reflect their true nature in their daily behaviors."

5:7–14 DARKNESS AND LIGHT

of sin, ruled by the prince of the kingdom of the air (2:2), and the kingdom of Christ and of God (5:5).[380] Paul describes the dark world ruled by powers and authorities (6:12) and characterized by evil.[381] Paul conjures up a dark desolation in which evil lurks and victims succumb to its power. When light enters, when the sun rises, people can see the evil as it is. Acts presents Paul as testifying that the Messiah would bring the message of light to both Jew and gentile (Acts 26:23). Paul presents a similar claim to the Colossians, declaring that God the Father has made an inheritance for those in Christ and rescued them from the dominion of darkness into the kingdom of light, the kingdom of the Son, the Lord Jesus (Col 1:12–14).

Paul commands that believers "live as children of light" (Eph 5:8). The verb can be translated "to walk," which Paul uses throughout his letters when speaking about conduct. Earlier, he warned the Ephesians not to walk in darkness under the power of this age, as children of disobedience (2:2), and to avoid walking as those gentiles with futile minds (4:17). Instead, Paul invites believers to walk in those good works that God prepared for them (2:10) and to walk in a worthy manner (4:1), walking in Christ's love such that it spills over onto others (5:2). He will use the verb a final time in this epistle in 5:15, commanding the Ephesians to walk wisely now, because the days are evil—this a reflection on earlier observations that this age is ruled by forces hostile to God.

Paul identifies believers as "children" of light.[382] Paul earlier described the Ephesians as beloved children of God (5:1). Paul insists that God the Father blesses his children with every spiritual blessing (1:3), works his great power for their redemption (1:18–19), and welcomes them into his glorious presence through Christ (3:12). This loving father provides a lighted space for his children to grow and bear fruit. Paul does not present God the Father as threatening his children, nor does Paul urge believers to act rightly to avoid God's wrath.[383]

Paul digresses briefly as he describes the faithful child's deeds as "fruit" (see also Phil 1:11).[384] The one walking in the light produces effective results of such obedience, the virtues of goodness, righteousness, and truth (see also Col 1:10). Broadly speaking, these virtues were embraced by everyone in the first century, but Paul infuses them with particular meaning reflecting the redemption values in Christ. "Goodness" is listed as a fruit of the Spirit (Gal

---

380. See G. L. Borchert, "Light and Darkness," *DPL* 555–57.
381. Arnold, 328. Best, 489, puts it well: "There is no twilight; it is either light or darkness."
382. On τέκνον see BDAG 994–95 (6).
383. Fowl, 169.
384. On καρπός see BDAG 509–10; D. S. Dockery, "Fruit of the Spirit," *DPL* 316–19.

5:22);[385] it calls believers to a vibrant, active concern for others so as to benefit them (Rom 15:14; 2 Thess 1:11). Such behavior is the opposite of the greed Paul cautioned against in Eph 5:3–5. The term "goodness" is not found in the wider Greek literature of Paul's day, but is used in the Septuagint (Judg 9:16 Vaticanus; 2 Chr 24:16; Ps 51:5 [= 52:5 MT = 52:3 English].[386] "Righteousness" includes both the idea of personal integrity and of community justice and fairness (Rom 6:13; 2 Cor 9:9–10).[387] Paul used this term earlier in describing the Ephesian believers' new self as created to be like God in true righteousness (Eph 4:24). To the Corinthians, Paul contrasts the righteousness that characterizes believers with the wickedness of the world and then juxtaposes light and darkness. Paul also uses this term to speak of God's justification of sinners (Rom 3:21–26). "Truth" is the third noun describing the believers' fruit. Paul points to Jesus as our truth (Eph 4:21), the gospel message that is "the word of truth" (1:13) and the belt of truth, part of the armor of God that enables believers to stand fast against evil (6:14).[388] Paul enjoins believers to speak the truth in love (4:15), for the goal of truth-telling is to increase love.

10–11 Paul resumes his discussion using a present active participle "find out," which refers back to the verb "to live" in 5:8.[389] Paul uses this verb frequently as he discusses believers' evaluation of their actions and God's appraisal of human behavior.[390] Paul asks the Ephesians to do what pleases the Lord. When Paul asks that believers "find out what pleases the Lord," he is not imagining that the answers are hidden. Quite the opposite, for the Lord teaches his followers (4:20–24), the Spirit brings unity (4:3), and the church is equipped for ministry (4:11–13) so that believers grow up into Christ, the head (4:15). Paul recognizes that believers face daily choices that either move them more in the direction of evil or mold them closer to the image of Christ. Believers who affiliate with those practicing vile habits risk missing what is theirs in Christ, namely, a life guided by the light and filled with goodness and truth.

Paul speaks similarly to the Romans, that they offer their bodies as living sacrifices that are holy and pleasing to God. Paul continues that as they do so, they will be able to test and approve ("find out") what is pleasing to God (Rom 12:1–2; see also 2 Cor 5:9). Later in Romans, Paul gives examples of what pleases God, which includes treating fellow believers with utmost respect, even when your views differ. Paul also highlights what displeases

---

385. On ἀγαθωσύνη see BDAG 4.
386. Thielman, 340.
387. On δικαιοσύνη see BDAG 247–48 (3); K. L. Onesti and M. T. Brauch, "Righteousness, Righteousness of God," *DPL* 827–37.
388. On ἀλήθεια see BDAG 42 (1); L. Morris, "Truth," *DPL* 954–55.
389. Larkin, 115; Best, 491.
390. On δοκιμάζω see BDAG 255 (1).

God, namely passing judgment on other believers (Rom 14:13-18). God is also pleased when believers support each other with prayer and financial help (Phil 4:14-18). Pleasing God, then, involves not only abstaining from sinful behaviors, but also active care and concern for others in the body of Christ.

Having described a light-filled life characterized by goodness, righteousness, and truth, Paul commands believers "to have nothing to do with" dark deeds.[391] The verb carries the prefix "with" and harkens back to Eph 5:7 where Paul warned the believers not to have anything to do "with" the immoral and greedy disobedient ones. In both cases, the prefix "with" reinforces the sense of habitually participating in a certain group or action. The cognate noun to this verb is *koinōnia*, a term used frequently by Paul to describe believers' fellowship.[392] The focus here, however, is on fruitless "works" of darkness, not fruitless people. Paul does not ask that believers withdraw from relationships with unbelievers, only that they refuse to engage with them in fruitless works.[393]

Paul continues with the adverb "rather" and the imperative "to expose."[394] Paul commands the Ephesians that they expose dark deeds. The verb includes the sense of reproving and convicting persons; however, in this verse Paul addresses deeds, not people.[395] Some argue that Paul asks believers to confront nonbelievers, based on 5:12-13 and its mention of the disobedient, in an effort toward their conversion.[396] However, Paul does not ask that believers censure either other believers or nonbelievers; instead, the focus is on denouncing unfruitful deeds.[397] Irrespective of who does such deeds, believers or unbelievers, Paul's point is that such deeds must be exposed.[398]

---

391. Lincoln, 329, speaks of such deeds as "sterile, lacking direction and futile."

392. On συγκοινωνέω see BDAG 952. For the verb with the prefix, see Phil 4:14 and Rev 18:4. The noun is used by Paul in Rom 15:26; 1 Cor 1:9; 10:16; 2 Cor 6:14; 8:4; 9:13; 13:13; Gal 2:9; Phil 1:5; 2:1; 3:10; Phlm 6. The noun with the prefix is found in Rom 11:17; 1 Cor 9:23; Phil 1:7.

393. Arnold, 331.

394. Best, 492, remarks on the emphatic introduction μᾶλλον δὲ καί.

395. Lincoln, 329, observes that the Greek verb does not have an object and that the reader must assume it is the "deeds" mentioned in the previous clause. Best, 492, remarks that if 5:12 is used to define the object, it would refer to people who are disobedient.

396. Perkins, 119, explains: "The Epistle presumes that its readers are familiar with the process of conversion in their own experience of moving from darkness to light, from death to life." Lincoln, 330, suggests that the exposure takes "place through the readers' behavior" and not through "verbal correction."

397. Lincoln, 329. He points out that in other contexts the verb is used "for admonishing members of the Christian community (cf. Matt 18:15-17; 1 Tim 5:20; 2 Tim 4:2; Titus 1:9, 13; Rev 3:19)." Best, 492, rightly rejects the possible meaning of "disciplining or punishing ... those whose works belong to darkness."

398. Thielman, 344: "It is the deeds, however, that are exposed as evil, not the people

Exposing sin certainly includes avoiding such behavior. Does it also include stating that such behavior is evil? It is popular to cite a phrase (falsely) attributed to Francis of Assisi: "Preach the gospel at all times and when necessary use words." Not only did the great saint *not* speak those words, but his life reveals that he strongly urged the preaching of the gospel. Paul stresses that the gospel is a *message* about the life and reality of Jesus Christ, the incarnate Lord who died and was raised for humanity's redemption (1 Cor 15:1–8). Paul explains that the statement that "Jesus is Lord," and the conviction that God raised him from the dead, is evidence of the believer's life in God (Rom 10:9–10). This reality cannot be expressed fully without words. When we look at the Ephesian church, then, the purpose of exposing such deeds might be missional as Paul desires the Ephesians to demonstrate, by word and deed, a better way to live to a watching pagan community.[399]

12–14 These verses draw to a close Paul's injunctions for believers to walk in Christ's love and embrace the light, bearing fruit of goodness, righteousness, and truth. Paul concludes his warnings to believers of the dangers faced by those who habitually engage in sexual immorality and idolatry expressed by greed. Paul enjoins believers to expose the dark deeds, that they might be known as such and that those doing them might be drawn into the light. The exposure to light has healing properties. The light destroys the darkness that cultivates evil deeds; the light also provides brightness that causes goodness to flourish.

In this passage, Paul continues his contrast of light and darkness, now by adding that darkness hides secrets and light exposes all things. With the verbs "to illuminate" and "to shine," he develops his argument that believers' new life in the Lord is one of light and brightness. Paul offers what was likely an early Christian poem or hymn celebrating a believer's rising up from the dead, with Christ shining as a light on them. Perhaps it was recalling this poem or hymn that nudged Paul to draw out further the power of publicly confessing Christ, for in the next several verses Paul encourages believers to worship together in songs and thanksgiving, in a supportive community (5:15–20).

Paul frontloads the adverb "secret" for emphasis, as he describes how the disobedient people act (5:12). Deeds done in secret are too shameful to mention. Paul speaks in hyperbole to underline his insistence on the evil nature of the deeds of darkness. Paul here shifts from discussing deeds to a

---

who practice them." Contra Arnold, 331, who suggests it is believers whose evil deeds should be exposed by fellow believers.

399. Fowl, 171, argues that "it is most likely that Paul is speaking about exposing the deeds of the world relative to what he hopes will be the deeds of the church."

focus on people.[400] Paul likely has in mind unbelievers, for he has identified them as disobedient (2:2; 5:6) and he has admonished believers to avoid their behaviors.[401] The question remains whether unbelievers would do their behavior in secret. Some suggest that Paul focuses here on believers' attempts to hide their disobedient, shameful deeds, for they would feel shame at such behavior.[402] Yet pagan gentiles could feel shame (1 Cor 5:1) and had ethical mores that if abandoned could result in a loss of reputation.[403]

In Eph 5:13-14, Paul uses repetition to reinforce his message. He repeats the verb "to expose" used in 5:11 and explains that believers should expose fruitless deeds of darkness.[404] The result of such exposure is that deeds become "visible" and are "illuminated," as Paul draws on the same verb.[405] Paul has in mind believers who are the light that illuminates the evil deeds.[406] Paul expects that believers are lights because they are in Christ, and thus they make visible God's truth, goodness, and righteousness. As Paul stated in 5:8, believers were themselves at one time in darkness, and now they stand in the light of Christ. This light revealed their sin, but also showed them the way to fellowship with God in Christ. Their path of redemption now lit, they must bring such light to those around them.[407]

Paul adds that the light shines by Christ's resurrection power (5:14). In some English versions, this poem begins 5:14, while in other versions, the final clause of 5:13 is pulled into 5:14. The structure does not impact the meaning of the passage or the text itself.[408]

---

400. Γινόμενα ὑπ' αὐτῶν.

401. Thielman, 345. Lincoln, 330, probably is too specific in limiting the deeds to "the same sexual vices that have been discussed earlier."

402. Arnold, 332; Best, 495.

403. Thielman, 345.

404. Paul uses the preposition "by" and the genitive "light" to qualify the participle. Thielman, 346, points out that the preposition ὑπό occurs three times in Ephesians; with the other two cases, the phrase "qualifies the preceding verb." Contra Arnold, 333.

405. On φανερόω see BDAG 1048 (1). The second occurrence of the verb, τὸ φανερούμενον, is either a middle participle with active force or a passive participle. The middle voice emphasizes the noun "light" as that which reveals all things. However, the verb never occurs in the New Testament in the middle voice; moreover, Paul uses the passive voice with the same verb earlier in the sentence, making it likely that this second occurrence is in the passive voice. See Thielman, 347.

406. Thielman, 347.

407. Lincoln, 331. Thielman, 347-51, draws on 1 Cor 14:24-25 and 2 Cor 4:6 as he explains this passage as one of conversion and transformation. See also Fowl, 171, who points to John 16:8 and Phil 2:15. Contra Arnold, 333-34, who suggests that this verse speaks to mature believers correcting other believers who exhibit sinful patterns.

408. The NIV begins 5:14 with the phrase "this is why it is said." The Greek text begins 5:14 with the phrase "and everything."

This is why it is said:
"Wake up, sleeper,
   rise from the dead,
   and Christ will shine on you."

Paul introduces a saying or confession with a formula ("it is said") that usually signals a scriptural passage (see also 4:8).[409] However, the phrase "Wake up, sleeper, rise from the dead, and Christ will shine on you" is not found in any biblical passage and shares only some commonalities with Isa 26:19 and 60:1.[410] Though not a direct quotation from the Old Testament, the content of the passage shares with the Judaism of Paul's day the connection between waking from sleep and resurrection of the dead.[411] Because the passage refers to Christ, we likely have here a confession or line from a church poem or hymn that was familiar to the early churches.[412] The liturgical context might be baptism or a hymn celebrating the resurrection.

The passage flows as might a Hebrew poem, as each line begins with a verb, and the first two lines exhibit the characteristic parallelism of Hebrew poetry.[413] The poem includes two clauses using the imperative mood, followed by the third line that includes a promise "to shine" with the verb in the future tense. The verb "to shine" shares the root with the verb "to be visible, to illuminate" (5:13). The listener is commanded to "wake up" from sleep and "rise" from the dead.

Is the passage describing the believers' current situation, or is it a call to unbelievers who accept the promise of new life in Christ? Some argue that Paul warns believers. This position must logically conclude that the metaphor of sleep and death refers to a lack of understanding about sin and their own backsliding.[414] However, in the context, Paul is not discussing believers' shortcomings, but is intent on distinguishing believers' and unbelievers'

---

409. Paul often uses the verb "to speak" when he introduces a scriptural quotation; see Rom 3:19; 4:3, 6; 9:15, 17, 25; 10:11, 16, 19, 20, 21; 11:2, 9; 12:19; 15:12; 2 Cor 6:2; Gal 3:16; 4:30. Thielman, 349–50, observes that "the present tense verb λέγει occurs thirty-five times in the Pauline corpus, and in all but three of these instances (1 Cor 1:12; 12:3; 1 Tim 4:1) it is connected with the speech of Scripture."

410. Bruce, 376, rightly remarks that the "the echo, especially in Greek, is a distant one." See also Best, 497, and Thielman, 348.

411. Thielman, 349, points to 1QHa 11:19–22; 12:5–6, 23.

412. Contra Bultmann, *Theology of the New Testament*, 1:175, who views this as an example of Gnostic influence. His generation of scholarship often pointed to Gnosticism as a backdrop or explanation, but this set of assumptions and arguments is no longer persuasive within scholarship.

413. Thielman, 348; Best, 498.

414. Best, 498–99; Arnold, 334–35.

behaviors. Most likely, then, the first two lines are parallel in thought and, as such, refer to unbelievers who have yet to confess Christ. The statement highlights the conviction that Christ shines his redemptive light on those who have been "asleep" or dead in sin and now have turned to the light.[415] Elsewhere Paul encourages believers to stay awake, not to sleep, for they are children of the light, not unbelievers who work in the darkness of night (1 Thess 5:4–8).[416] The contrast between believers and unbelievers is similar to our passage in Ephesians. Paul wishes that all people would declare this confession.[417]

4. Be Filled with the Holy Spirit (5:15–21)

15Be very careful, then, how you live—not as unwise but as wise, 16making the most of every opportunity, because the days are evil. 17Therefore do not be foolish, but understand what the Lord's will is. 18Do not get drunk on wine, which leads to debauchery. Instead, be filled with the Spirit, 19speaking to one another with psalms, hymns, and songs from the Spirit. Sing and make music from your heart to the Lord, 20always giving thanks to God the Father for everything, in the name of our Lord Jesus Christ.

21Submit to one another out of reverence for Christ.

Paul concludes his discussion of light and darkness and begins a new avenue of thought focused on life in the Spirit. He continues his overarching theme of a proper moral lifestyle, but now emphasizes that believers walk as prudent people, guided by the Holy Spirit. Paul sketches the worship of the congregation as a key space for developing habits that build up the body of Christ (see also Col 4:2–6). Underneath his injunctions is the conviction that the current age is evil and must be negotiated with care. Paul urges the development of wise habits of heart and mind, demonstrated in daily decisions that please the Lord and benefit others.[418]

---

415. Contra Best, 498, who understands the poem as challenging believers who "seem to be in darkness and Christ needs to shine on them through the words of those believes who have not fallen back into darkness."

416. Arnold, 334–35, points to the commonality between 1 Thess 5:4–8 and Ephesians as that of encouraging believers to live moral lives; however, I suggest that the common ground is the distinction between believers and unbelievers that both passages depend on.

417. Fowl, 173. Lincoln, 335, is right to observe that the passage teaches that the church is to be "nothing less than a community whose conduct shines as a beacon to others, illuminating how life should be lived." However, his insistence that Paul does not refer to the "proclamation by word" but only by actions lived in the light goes beyond the evidence.

418. Fowl, 176, speaking of 5:17–20, states that the passage "can be read as offering a set

The passage begins with a series of three antithetical statements: "not this, but that." The contrasts include being wise not foolish, and being filled with the Spirit not drunk with wine. Paul finishes with a lengthy description of the Spirit's filling within the community as believers sing, make music, and offer thanksgiving to the Lord. The passage includes five present imperatives and six present participles.[419] Paul uses the present indicative "to walk/live" (5:15), a note he sounded five other times in the latter half of the epistle (4:1, 17 twice; 5:2, 8). One final grammatical observation is necessary, and that is my decision to discuss 5:21 in this passage and also in the next section. I chose to include it in both places, for several reasons.[420] First, the participle ("to submit") in 5:21 depends on the finite verb in 5:18 and the participle is implied in 5:22, which lacks any verb. Second, the worship activities reflected in these verses likely took place in homes, which were organized using the three categories of husband/wife, master/slave, and parent/child. The space for worship and families therefore overlapped. Third, the reference to "fear" in 5:21 is also found in 5:33, forming an *inclusio*.

15–16 Paul instructs the Ephesians to be careful as they live ("walk"), using the imperative "to see, watch," which can be translated "be careful." Paul includes the adverb "carefully."[421] We might say something like "watch out," to a person walking on an uneven footpath. Here Paul asks that believers walk carefully as wise people, not foolish ones. Paul first mentions wisdom when speaking of God's wisdom demonstrated in revealing to believers the mystery of his will (1:8) and the Spirit's wisdom and revelation that leads to better understanding of God (1:17). God's wisdom is made manifest in the church (3:10), and Paul prays that the Ephesians might grasp the enormity of Christ's love that surpasses human knowledge (3:19).

---

of habits or practices that will aid the cultivation of such practical wisdom, and a contrasting set of habits and practices that will frustrate the cultivation of such wisdom."

419. Best, 502, explains that "as is normal in paraenesis, participles are extensively used in dependence on imperatives."

420. Best, 515–17, offers a lengthy discussion of the options and concludes that 5:21 should be linked with the previous section. His main argument revolves around the pronoun "one another," which includes a sense of equality and mutuality that Best holds is absent from 5:22–6:9, with its theme of subordination. In his argument, he makes the dismissive statement that not until the feminist movement had the term "one another" been seen otherwise, "and it is therefore not an obvious solution" (516).

421. The manuscripts are divided in their placement of the adverb. Early sources and manuscripts mainly of the Alexandrian text type place the adverb before the particle, ἀκριβῶς πῶς; Larkin, 122; Lincoln, 337, 341. Hoehner, 690, argues for a reading that reverses that order, but the manuscripts attesting it are later.

The wise understand the time, while the foolish fail to appreciate their surroundings; they cannot discern events or evaluate ideas well. Paul explains that the wise apprehend that the "days" or current age is evil (see also 6:13).[422] As such, Paul encourages believers to "make the most" of their opportunities." The verb carries both the sense of buying up or gaining advantage as well as the notion of redeeming.[423] Paul uses the verb to speak of Christ's redeeming work (Gal 3:13; 4:5), and here Paul speaks metaphorically about using time with utmost effectiveness toward particular opportunities (see also Gal 6:10; Col 4:5).[424] Paul urges the Ephesians to view their context from an eschatological standpoint, realizing that evil is abroad, but God's power that raised Christ from the dead will overcome (Eph 1:10). Indeed, it has prevailed in their lives, which are now in the light and resurrection life of Christ. As such they are to buy up the present moments and use them for good.[425]

17 Paul begins a new sentence here with "therefore," drawing a conclusion from his claim about the evil days in the previous verse.[426] He continues with two imperatives. Paul makes the general statement that foolish behavior must stop, and he continues with the strong adversative "but" and the imperative "to understand."[427] The wise believer understands that the world and its wisdom often lead not to holy living but to the opposite. Paul bids believers not to settle into foolish patterns of thought and deed. Today, we tend to think of foolishness as goofy or silly, but Paul has in mind the fool who discredits himself through ruinous decisions (see also Luke 12:20; 1 Cor 15:36).[428] He calls himself a fool in his boasting when he contrasts his ministry in terms of worldly achievements with pseudo-preachers who confuse the Corinthians (2 Cor 11:1–21; 12:6–11). It is a fool who looks to fancy rhetoric or pedigree; what counts is obedience under the grace of God (2 Cor 12:6–9).

Because the days are evil, believers must understand the Lord's will. The imperative "understand" urges believers to use their minds and rational

---

422. Best, 504, observes that when speaking of the end times, the term "days" would be modified by "last" or made clear by the context.

423. On ἐξαγοράζω see BDAG 343.

424. Fowl, 175, rightly observes the awkwardness of the phrase "redeeming the time," as it presents time as a captive, and it suggests a soteriological function for humans. See also Best, 505.

425. Thielman, 357.

426. Best, 505–6; Thielman, 357. Contra Arnold, 347, who contends that Paul refers to the message of walking wisely in 5:15–16.

427. Best, 506, observes that the verb appears as a participle in a few, later texts, but the imperative is the stronger reading, and in any case, the force of the imperative would be found if the participle was read.

428. On ἄφρων see BDAG 159.

thought to choose wisely and act accordingly.[429] Such understanding is not simply knowing the "right" answer, but living rightly. Paul calls the Ephesians to comprehend, to gain insight, into the Lord's will. Most likely, Paul intends Christ when he speaks of "Lord" here, as he has throughout the epistle.[430] Earlier, Paul explains that God's will includes that believers be adopted as children through Christ Jesus, through grace and the redemption gained in the cross and resurrection (1:5, 11). Paul indicates that Christ desires that his people be equipped for ministry and that they would mature into the fullness of Christ (4:11–13). Believers were taught Christ (4:21) and have put on the new self that is created in God in true righteousness and holiness (4:24; see also 1 Thess 4:3). As such, they can discover what pleases the Lord (Eph 5:10).

18–21 Parallel to the command to not be foolish is the injunction not to be drunk with wine, for this leads to immorality. Why mention drunkenness here? Paul draws on the well-known gentile cultural practice of the banquet, a meal that involved much alcohol and sexual immorality. In the fifth century BCE, during the classical Greek period, wealthy men attended a banquet followed by a symposium, which might be an intellectual conversation or a rowdy party with drink flowing and prostitutes present. By the Roman period, husbands and wives attended banquets together, and the event was not limited to the wealthy elite.[431] Many of the Ephesians would have previously attended banquets hosted by their guild or funerary *collegia*, as well as attended birthday parties and weddings. Such meals could involve excessive drinking, which led to immorality. The term translated "debauchery" is used here and twice more in the New Testament (Titus 1:6; 1 Pet 4:4).[432] The noun is related to the cognate verb "to save" with a negation, and thus the noun denotes wastefulness on an immoral scale, indulgence and dissipation. Given the cultural context, most likely Paul views debauchery as including sexual immorality, but we need not limit it to that. In an environment where food was at a premium, wasteful dining meant others might go without. And the extravagant display of wealth that often attended such meals was an affront to poor believers.

This dining practice was of great concern for the second-century BCE Jewish writer Ben Sira. He cautioned his young scribes to be careful at these meals, to stay away from other men's wives, and to avoid too much wine when talking with women (Sir 9:9; 31:12–32:13). The first-century CE Jew Philo described a group of male and female Jewish contemplatives who gathered

---

429. On συνίημι see BDAG 972. See also Best, 506.

430. Lincoln, 343.

431. For a general discussion, see Cohick, *Women in the World of the Earliest Christians*, 86–91.

432. On ἀσωτία see BDAG 148.

weekly for a common meal. He was at pains to stress their proper decorum during the meal and at the symposium, where they worshiped, not drunk with wine, but "intoxicated" with the pleasures of chaste worship.[433] Paul follows this line of reasoning, developing his picture of church worship as filled with the presence of the Holy Spirit, with the congregation offering praises to God and thanksgiving.[434]

Rather than being drunk with wine, Paul urges believers to be filled with the Spirit (5:18).[435] The imperative is in the present tense, which might indicate that Paul desires believers be filled continually.[436] Insisting on this nuance, however, is likely more than the tense can bear in the context.[437] The present tense does not indicate, in itself, the duration of time or continuation of an action. Thus Paul's imperative "to be filled" signals that the action is "in progress, without saying anything about its duration or continuance."[438]

Paul commands that the believers be filled, not with wine, but "with the Spirit." Because Paul speaks of the Holy Spirit in this way throughout the letter, it is unlikely that here Paul points to the human spirit (2:22; 3:5; 6:18).[439] The preposition can be translated "with" or "by" or "in." The question is whether Paul is interested in what fills believers (they are filled "with" the Spirit), or whether he emphasizes the action of the Holy Spirit (believers are filled "by" the Spirit),[440] or whether Paul speaks about the realm of the Spirit "in" which the believers live.[441] As we look at earlier references to the Holy Spirit, we see that the Spirit offers access to the Father (2:18) and is placed as a seal on believers (1:13; 4:30). Paul speaks of praying "in the Spirit" in 6:18. Throughout the epistle, when Paul uses this preposition alongside the

---

433. Philo, *On the Contemplative Life* 40.

434. Lincoln, 342, rightly rejects the argument that the Ephesians had problems of drunkenness in their congregational meetings: "There is no evidence at all that the earlier problems in Corinth were being duplicated in the churches which this letter is addressing."

435. Paul is probably not drawing on the Pentecost event, wherein believers filled with the Spirit spoke in other human languages, leading the crowd nearby to jeer that the group was drunk. Peter explains that they were not drunk, but had experienced the outpouring of the Holy Spirit prophesized by Joel (Acts 2:13–16).

436. Lincoln, 344; Hoehner, 704.

437. Best, 508; Thielman, 358. For an excellent discussion of the present tense, see Mathewson, "Abused Present," 345; he explains the present tense from the verbal aspect perspective: "Aspectually, the present tense form's viewpoint is internal: it looks at the action from the perspective of its development and unfolding, *irrespective of the actual duration or time of the action being portrayed*" (emphasis original).

438. Mathewson, "Abused Present," 356.

439. Ἐν πνεύματι. See also Thielman, 359.

440. Hoehner, 703–4.

441. John Paul Heil, "Ephesians 5:18b: 'But Be Filled in the Spirit,'" *Catholic Biblical Quarterly* 69 (2007): 506, makes the point that "verbs of filling take a genitive of content."

mention of Spirit, he communicates the Holy Spirit's presence in the believer and the church as the one "who fills and the filling itself."[442] In the end, "with" is probably the better translation.[443] The overriding concern for Paul is that believers are fully influenced by the Spirit so that their actions are worthy of their Lord.

In the next three verses, Paul offers a series of five present tense participles to further explain what this filling of the Spirit looks like. The adverbial participles modify the main verb "be filled" in 5:18. Typically, a present tense adverbial participle following its verb will "explain or define that verb further."[444] In our case, this string of participles cannot stand on their own, but point back to the command to be filled with the Spirit.[445] We might say that Paul answers the implicit question: What does it look like to be filled with the Spirit?[446] These expressions of being filled with the Spirit occur in the community, during their weekly gatherings and fellowship meals. The believers speak, sing, make music, offer thanks, and submit to each other.[447]

Paul asks that believers speak to each other with "psalms, hymns, and spiritual songs" (5:19). Paul does not draw sharp distinctions between these three nouns, but offers them as examples of Old Testament psalms and hymns. Paul draws on Jewish practice of including psalms, hymns, and songs in their celebration to God.[448] Paul includes the adjective "spiritual," which could modify all three nouns or only the last noun "songs."[449] Most

---

442. Fowl, 175; contra Thielman, 360, who points to Heil, "Ephesians 5:18b," 507, who argues that a better translation would be "be filled *in* the Spirit," which indicates a realm "characterized by having been given the Spirit."

443. Arnold, 350. Best, 508, allows for either "by" or "with."

444. David L. Mathewson, "Being Filled with the Spirit," in *Devotions on the Greek New Testament: 52 Reflections to Inspire and Instruct*, ed. J. Scott Duvall and Verlyn D. Verbrugge (Grand Rapids: Zondervan, 2012), 86.

445. Steven E. Runge, *Discourse Grammar of the Greek New Testament: A Practical Introduction for Teaching and Exegesis* (Peabody, MA: Hendrickson, 2010), 248, rightly concludes: "The net result of choosing a participle over a finite verb is to have the main verbal action of the clause receive primary attention."

446. Runge, *Discourse Grammar*, 262, explains that those participles that follow the main verb "elaborate the action of the main verb, often providing more specific explanation of what is meant by the main action."

447. David E. Aune, "Worship, Early Christian," *ABD* 6:973–89.

448. Thielman, 361, points to Josephus's remark about the celebration of the rededication of the Jerusalem temple by Judas Maccabeus, which included psalms and hymns (*Jewish Antiquities* 12.8.7 §323).

449. Best, 511, argues that the adjective modifies all three nouns; Thielman, 361, argues that the adjective modifies only the noun "songs." Lincoln, 337, discusses the variant omission of the term "spiritual" (πνευματικαῖς), which has strong early support in P46; nevertheless,

likely the adjective qualifies only "songs" as those created with the inspiration of the Spirit.[450]

The second participle ("to sing") and the third participle ("make music") are the verbal forms of the nouns "song" and "psalms" Paul used in the first half of this verse. Their songs and music are directed to the Lord and spring from their heart. Paul is not encouraging emotionalism or private worship with his mention of "from your heart," but rather points to the place where Christ dwells (3:17). Their heart's contemplation should match their words and songs expressed in the congregation.

With the fourth participle, Paul enjoins believers to "give thanks" (5:20), repeating his call to give thanks in 5:4. Paul explains that the Spirit-filled life is one that offers thanks "always." Paul has in mind here a thankful heart and mind constantly fixed on gratitude. Paul demonstrates this behavior in his opening blessing of praise to God (1:3–14). He expresses thanksgiving "always" to his congregations (1 Cor 1:4; Col 1:3; 1 Thess 1:2; Phlm 4) and encourages them to be thankful in everything (Col 3:17; 1 Thess 5:18).[451]

He continues that believers offer thanks "for everything." What might Paul include in "everything"? Based on the letter, we could assume he intends believers to thank God for the redemption brought through Christ, for the inheritance secured in the Spirit, and for the oneness of the body, of which each is a member. Paul emphasizes that believers are children of light (Eph 5:8), forgiven by God, beloved by Christ (5:1–2). Paul might also include in "everything" the sufferings that attend to a disciple's walk (3:8, 13). Paul writes this line while imprisoned for his testimony to Christ. He can embrace "everything" because he is confident that God has the final word, and that word is love. Paul declares to the Romans that *nothing* can separate believers from God's love (Rom 8:37–39). Another way to say this is that *everything* is given believers in Christ. For God did not spare his Son, but gave him for humanity's redemption and new life (Rom 8:31–32).

Paul asks that the Ephesians offer thanksgiving "in the name of our Lord Jesus Christ" "to God the Father."[452] The language in 5:20 that links

---

he considers the term original and its omission explained as an example of homoeoteleuton. See also Best, 510.

450. Thielman, 361, suggests that the adjective "probably does have special reference to the kind of spontaneous, Spirit-inspired singing to which 1 Cor 14:15, 26 refer." See also Lincoln, 346, who does not insist on the quality of spontaneity as necessary for Spirit-inspired songs.

451. Thielman, 362.

452. The Greek text reads τῷ θεῷ καὶ πατρί, although some manuscripts reverse the order. Best, 514, offers that the phrase means "to him who is God and also Father." Arnold, 355, points to the Granville Sharp rule, that when two nouns joined by "and" have only a single article preceding the first noun, "then the two nouns indicate unity, equality, or identity."

the name of Christ and God the Father is in keeping with the wider liturgical language found in Pauline letters. Paul bows his knees before God the Father of all families in heaven and earth as he prays for the Ephesians (3:14). To the Philippians, Paul indicates that at the name of Jesus, every knee in heaven and on earth and under the earth will bow, and every tongue confess him as Lord (Phil 2:9–11).

The final participle enjoins believers to "submit" to each other "out of reverence for Christ." Speaking together in psalms, singing and making music in one's heart, giving thanks to God in Christ's name—all lead to believers placing others above themselves. The verb "to submit" generally indicates subordination and subjection, including in social relationships.[453] Paul uses the verb when speaking of a failure to submit to God's law (Rom 8:7; 10:3) or when encouraging law-abiding practices (Rom 13:1, 5; Titus 3:1). He urges the Corinthian believers to submit to those who lead them (1 Cor 16:16) and slaves to submit to their masters (Titus 2:9). Here Paul emphasizes the mutual submission of all believers to each other, whereas in other occurrences, only a specific group (wives, slaves, children) are called to submit.[454]

Paul speaks of submitting to "one another," and this reciprocal pronoun has been used to speak of the congregation earlier (Eph 4:2; 25, 32). Paul offers reason here for the congregation's mutual submission, namely, reverence for Christ. The noun "reverence" can also be translated "fear" with the sense of awe.[455] The motivating factor for mutual submission is their fear or reverence for Christ, a phrase found only here in the New Testament. Paul intends with this unique phrase to highlight a theme he will then develop in the household codes, for he will repeat the injunction that wives should fear/respect their husbands (5:33) and that slaves should respect their masters (6:5). Moreover, Paul will stress the title "Christ" throughout the household codes.

Both these points suggest that Paul signals here the interpretive key to understanding the following teachings. It is Christ who is the measure of submission and obedience and love, and it is our reverence for him that motivates and empowers our own imitation of his character. Earlier in the epistle, Paul offered a parallel to this passage as he urged believers to be humble, gentle, patient, and supportive in love (4:2). He enjoined believers to build up each other and avoid anger and bitterness (4:29–32). These actions are examples of submitting one to another. Believers revere or fear the Lord and, by extension, the members of his body. Paul's thoughts here echo his Damascus

---

453. On ὑποτάσσω see BDAG 1042 (1). Best, 517, states that "subordination implies a sense of order in society."

454. Lincoln, 365. I suggest that 1 Cor 16:16 would be a second example of a congregation asked to submit, but in this case they are not submitting mutually (as in Ephesians).

455. On φόβος see BDAG 1062 (2). See also Thielman, 374, and Lincoln, 366.

5:15–21 Be Filled with the Holy Spirit

Road dialogue with Christ, who asked: "Saul, Saul, why do you persecute *me*?" (Acts 9:4). In that encounter, Christ revealed the intimate connection between his followers and himself. Paul declares that Christ is the head and that the church is his body, which is growing up in unity and knowledge of him (Eph 4:15–16).

Colossians might help us in exploring Paul's intentions here in Ephesians. In his instructions to slaves, Paul emphasizes that their motivation in serving their earthly masters should be the "fear of the Lord" (Col 3:22), using the same term "fear" that we find in Ephesians. The overriding theological emphasis in Colossians is Christ as Lord and, by extension, the believer as the Lord's servant or slave (1:7, 23, 25; 4:7, 12). This theme is brought into sharp focus in Paul's lengthy admonition to slaves, whom Paul treats as morally capable and responsible individuals. Owners and slaves have a reciprocal relationship to each other based on their mutual standing before Christ as Lord.[456] So too, in Ephesians, the unique phrase "reverence for Christ" represents or summarizes the Christology advanced in the letter and is given concrete shape in the call for mutual submission among believers.

In many English translations, 5:22 begins a new paragraph, and the participle "submitting" is rendered "submit," leading the reader to assume Paul begins a new thought. Yet 5:22 does not have its own verb, but relies on 5:21 and its participle. This grammar points to the logical connection between the two verses and points to both verses' reliance on the main verb in 5:18. While we might debate what submitting entailed in Paul's churches, it is clear from a grammatical standpoint that he is not *commanding* wives to submit. Had Paul wanted to command this, he could have used a finite verb in the imperative, much as he does in 5:25 in his command that husbands love their wives.[457]

Because of the complicated syntax, I treat 5:21 both here and as part of the household codes. It is important to see the grammatical connections between the household codes and the church's worship life and to shape our hermeneutical approach accordingly.[458] The household was the place where believers gathered to sing, fellowship, share a meal, and partake of communion. Paul encourages believers to live as children of light and as filled with the Spirit among their families. Ephesians uses language and motifs of the

---

456. Hering, *Colossian and Ephesian Haustafeln*, 135, concludes: "The admonitions and Christological motivation enjoined to the slaves are particularly significant for the general reader, if not paradigmatic for the Christian life."

457. Runge, *Discourse Grammar*, 267, rightly states: "To infer an imperative in v. 22 is an interpretation, unsubstantiated by the grammar." He continues: "The statements to wives regarding submission are illustrating mutual submission, not signaling women out."

458. Gorman, *Becoming the Gospel*, 199, wisely observes that our reading of the household codes must be shaped by the previous verses in Eph 4–5, which describe believers living in unity and peacemaking, offering sacrificial love and submission to each other.

household throughout Ephesians, comparatively more than all but one of Paul's writings.[459] Paul explains the inclusion of gentiles into God's family or household as fellow citizens with God's people (2:19), uses familial language of adoption (1:5), describes believers as God's children (5:1) and as brothers and sisters (6:21). It should not surprise, then, that Paul continues this topic with a lengthy discussion of the household.

EXCURSUS: THE HOUSEHOLD CODES IN THE ANCIENT WORLD

Some historical background on household codes in the ancient world is in order. The household codes are those sections in Ephesians, Colossians, and 1 Peter that look closely at relationships typically found in the ancient household, including husband/wife, parent/child, and owner/slave.[460] The first two pairs are quite familiar to us, while the last pair has a dark history for Americans, and its heavy legacy continues to infect our culture and the church. The ancient world, by including the institution of slavery under the umbrella of the family, understood the domicile as an economic unit as well as one that fostered care and affection. While the economic piece is still a consideration today, we tend to speak about the ideal family as a unit joined by love between two adults who then raise children together.

Today some countries allow the marriage of two men or two women, and other countries allow polygamy. Neither of these options were available in Greco-Roman law. Certain types of sexual relations between males were relatively common in the Greco-Roman culture (although not within the Jewish subculture), but this was not considered marriage in a legal sense. And Romans did not practice polygamy; if one wanted another spouse, he or she divorced their current spouse before marrying the other.[461] Today,

---

459. So Lau, *Politics of Peace*, 127, who states that this epistle has the "second highest percentage of οικ* words within the Pauline corpus."

460. First Peter does not include parent/child, nor does it include mention of slave owners.

461. There is some evidence that Jews allowed polygamy, or at least bigamy. The documents of Babatha, a second-century Jewish woman, indicate she had a bigamous relationship. Kimberley Czajkowski, *Localized Law: The Babatha and Salome Komaise Archive*, Oxford Studies in Roman Society and Law (Oxford: Oxford University Press, 2017), 56, writes: "Since Babatha lived in Maoza and Miriam in Engedi, I do wonder whether it is possible that the wives did not know about each other until after Judah died." For a translation of some of the texts, see Ross S. Kraemer, ed., *Women's Religions in the Greco-Roman World: A Sourcebook* (Oxford: Oxford University Press, 2004), 143–52.

the institution of slavery is illegal in Western nations, but the scourges of sex trafficking and pimping remind us to be vigilant against the human impulse to control another's body for personal gain.

The modern reader is tempted, when approaching the household codes, to isolate a pair for discussion, or even one member of the pair. For example, one might look just at wives, or simply at husbands, or only at parents. The danger to this approach is twofold. First, it misses the ancient context, which is concern for community cohesion, often at the expense of the subordinate. This is most clearly seen in the master/slave pair. Second, it ignores the foundational premise for arranging the pairs, which is a form of reciprocity, or the hierarchical social structuring of society.[462] The structure might be deemed ontological, with each of the pair following their "nature" (as in Plato and Aristotle). The configuration might be seen as necessary for the effective running of the state (Aristotle) or to keep social chaos at bay (Musonius Rufus and Plutarch). Western democracies, however, assume an individualism, an equality of human nature, and a freedom of choice that underpin its laws and social configuration. As a result, the institution of slavery is outlawed and women are enfranchised. The wide gulf separating our society from the ancient one requires readers to be careful exegetes, discerning what the biblical text describes or takes for granted within their social world and what the apostle prescribes as fitting for all human cultures within their local churches. Isolating the ancient culture, then ascertaining Paul's affirmation of or challenge to it, will help us discover applications for these texts in our contexts.

The household played a crucial role in shaping and influencing the theological message of Paul's letters. N. T. Wright observes that, even as Jewish households were structured around Torah faithfulness, so too Paul "sees the home life of the new people to be a vital context within which the practice of following and imitating the Messiah is to be inculcated and sustained."[463] We find that the biblical household codes reflect the range of views held by ancient philosophers, but every popular position comes under the scrutiny of Christ's incarnation, ministry, death, resurrection, ascension, and return. As James Hering succinctly states about the household codes: "The common

---

462. Westfall, "This Is a Great Metaphor!," 561, explains that the common theme of reciprocity permeates Ephesians, but Paul "interprets it in such a way that it is consistent with Pauline teaching and theology on servanthood and so effectively undermines the assumed privileges of the patron in the patronage system without denying social realities of power and dependency."

463. Wright, *Paul and the Faithfulness of God*, 2:1108. David L. Balch, *Let Wives Be Submissive: The Domestic Code in 1 Peter*, Society of Biblical Literature Monograph Series 26 (Chico, CA: Scholars Press, 1981), 81, 97–105, argues that missional and apologetic themes run throughout 1 Peter, including in the charge to wives to win over their husbands through their moral behavior.

matters of obedience, love, submission and honour might, perhaps, find their Christian meaning and *Verwertbarkeit* [applicability] to the degree in which they are Christ's."[464] We will pay attention to how the household codes illuminate teachings in Ephesians, at times comparing this epistle to Colossians and to 1 Peter as a way to more deeply appreciate Paul's injunctions to believers in Ephesus.

The household codes go back to the time of Plato and Aristotle, the golden age of Athenian democracy, and are deeply connected to their political reflections on the state.[465] Additionally, their works reflect their philosophical views and reveal their positions on the ontology of male, female, child, and slave. In the next few centuries, several philosophers embraced and modified these views on family and state. The apostles drew on existing themes concerning household codes, yet as the survey below will show, no evolutionary pattern is discernable in the extant sources. Each ancient author had his own interests, and yet our sources share certain common themes.

Plato (428–348 BCE) founded the Academy in Athens and taught Aristotle. He argued that the state and the household should be governed by the same sort of rule, and he developed a basic dichotomy of "ruler/ruled" as a necessity and ontological reality.[466] In Plato's schema, parents ruled children, older people ruled younger; in general, the stronger ruled the weaker, with women included in the latter category.[467] Slaves were defined as impersonal property, yet it was possible, though unlikely, for a slave to have a noble soul. Slaves should be treated justly, and a just master demonstrates his good character in so doing.[468] As such, Plato relies on reciprocity, as each member of the pair fulfills their obligations and responsibilities. The apostle Paul would agree with Plato as far as he goes, but Paul also addresses the slave directly and warns the slave owner that the master of both owner and slave is in heaven and shows no favoritism (Eph 6:9). There is no ontological difference between the slave and the master, because both are in Christ and heirs of God's blessing. While Plato defends his theory from the laws of nature as he observes and reasons them, Paul relies on Christ's authority.

---

464. Hering, *Colossian and Ephesian Haustafeln*, 262.

465. Lau, *Politics of Peace*, 133–34, explains that "the primary sources of influence [for the household codes] are discussion regarding household management . . . in the Hellenistic world under the influence of Aristotle." Lau notes alternative theories, including (1) the growth of household codes from Stoic thought and (2) Hellenistic Jewish codes.

466. Hering, *Colossian and Ephesian Haustafeln*, 206, observes: "Though the dichotomy expresses the pragmatic, organisational reality of the political and domestic order, it also reflects a corollary and *essential* aspect of the natural order, which Plato terms as κατὰ φύσιν," which can be translated "according to nature" or "according to an individual's aptitude."

467. Plato, *Republic* 5.455c–e.

468. Plato, *Laws* 3.776d–777e.

Excursus: The Household Codes in the Ancient World

Aristotle builds on Plato's teachings of an ontologically stratified household by including virtue as the grounding principle on which rests the social hierarchy. He argued for a different sort of virtue for the ruler and for the ruled, and this had the result of weakening Plato's call for justice applied universally, including among slaves. Also, he modified Plato's view that by nature women are inferior to men by adding that men and women had different virtues. Moreover, rather than a single form of government that oversaw each of the three traditional pairs, Aristotle concluded that each pair required a different type of governing structure. In a marriage, the husband rules in a republican manner, but is nevertheless always in the position of ruler. The wife shows the female version of courage by subordinating herself to her husband.[469] The father rules as a monarch over his children, and owners rule over their slaves as tyrants. Slaves are thought to be deficient in virtue and could not use reason (although they could understand reason when used by others), so the owner rules absolutely. There is no call for justice because there is no relationship or friendship between the two persons.[470]

Paul in Ephesians does not follow Aristotle's interest in maintaining class distinctions or isolating virtues to specific groups on a sliding scale of social worth. Instead of Aristotle's discussion about whether someone is morally fit to practice a particular virtue, Paul insists that in Christ, all are called to love and are empowered to live out all the excellent virtues through the Holy Spirit. This is a good reminder to those who read the ethical demands as oppressive or overbearing. To a slave or woman in Paul's churches, his charge to act with virtue would have been empowering and affirming of their inherent worth in Christ.

In the first century CE, philosophers who looked at the three household categories did so with much less systemization and might consider only one pair in a given work. Yet they operated in a world that understood the household to include husband/wife, parents/children, and masters/slaves. They accepted reciprocity as the grease that kept the wheels of the social hierarchy turning smoothly. Yet they tended to be less interested in politics and focused on social and philosophical questions concerning the household.

In the generation prior to Paul, the Jewish philosopher Philo wrote extensively about God's law. He did not write systematically on household codes as did Plato and Aristotle, but he spent much time reflecting both on the parent/child relationship and on slavery. He based much of his deliberation on the fourth commandment (to rest on the Sabbath) and the fifth commandment (to honor parents). He also called on wives to obey and to

---

469. Aristotle, *Politics* 1260a.
470. Aristotle, *Nicomachean Ethics* 8.11.6–7.

serve their husbands, using the verb related to the noun "slave."[471] In this he is unique, but he might also be speaking with rhetorical flourish or defending Judaism's conservative home life against gentile slander. Paul uses the same verb in 6:7, describing the work of slaves.[472] Philo's extensive discussion on slavery emphasizes reciprocity and warns owners against unjust actions toward their slaves. Although he does not speak in his writings directly to slaves, he insists that the slave is equal in nature to the master. Philo draws his conclusions based on God's law, to which Paul also turns. Yet for Paul, it is Christ who is the final judge and arbiter.

The diatribes and discourses of the first-century CE Stoic philosopher Gaius Musonius Rufus focused on social ethics and philosophy as he explored the household.[473] He spent little time on masters/slaves, except to chide those owners who, unable to control their sexual appetite, went after their female slaves.[474] In urging husbands to self-control, he argues that just as a husband would not tolerate his wife having sex with their male slave, so too the husband should demonstrate greater self-control, for he is stronger in judgment and superior in character.[475] Musonius Rufus speaks in glowing terms about marriage as a union of perfect companionship and mutual love, looking to each other's interests. Each should demonstrate virtue, leading to a harmonious home and self-control.[476] He uses ontological categories when describing husbands and wives, as he pushes for philosophical training for wives. Philosophy helps the person lead a good life, and in the case of a wife, philosophical training enables her to keep house well; to be chaste, courageous, and just; and to resist extravagance and excessive desires. Musonius Rufus's rationale for such education is that she would be a better wife to her husband and mother to her children.[477]

Martha Nussbaum argues that Musonius Rufus fails to consider the importance of *sphere of life* in which such virtue is demonstrated. The male sphere of citizenship and statecraft was considered superior to the domestic sphere of women. She concludes: "Here we encounter a limitation that

---

471. Philo uses the verb δουλεύω in the phrase: "Other rules again there are of various kinds: wives must be in servitude to their husbands, a servitude not imposed by violent ill-treatment but promoting obedience in all things" (*Hypothetica* 7.3, translation from Hering, *Colossian and Ephesian Haustafeln*, 234–35).

472. On δουλεύω see BDAG 259.

473. For a translation of his works, see *Musonius Rufus: "The Roman Socrates,"* ed. Cora E. Lutz, Yale Classical Studies 10 (New Haven: Yale University Press, 1947).

474. Musonius Rufus, "Lecture 12: On Sexual Indulgence." See also Hering, *Colossian and Ephesian Haustafeln*, 246–52.

475. Musonius Rufus, "Lecture 12: On Sexual Indulgence."

476. Musonius Rufus, "Lecture 13A–B: What Is the Chief End of Marriage."

477. Musonius Rufus, "Lecture 3: That Women Too Should Study Philosophy."

Excursus: The Household Codes in the Ancient World

Musonius Rufus shares with many other Stoics: the failure to understand the extent to which human dignity and self-respect require support from the social world."[478] We will see this limitation in Seneca's discussion of slavery, discussed below in Eph 6:5-9. Nussbaum recognizes that the Stoic ideal of disinterest toward external conditions, coupled with Seneca's "unwillingness to challenge entrenched structures of power,"[479] creates what today would be a gaping blind spot. The same holds for Musonius Rufus, whom Nussbaum critiques as having failed "to acknowledge the extent to which female virtue may be undermined by the very fact of social hierarchy."[480] The apostle Paul shares some superficial similarities with Musonius Rufus, including his call for mutuality in marriage. Yet Paul's injunctions to husbands is much more sweeping, going beyond a call for a husband's sexual self-control to active sacrificial love of his wife as his own body (5:28).

Our last example is Plutarch's "Advice to the Bride and Groom," addressed to the newlyweds Eurydice and Pollianus. As did Musonius Rufus, so too Plutarch encourages wives to learn philosophy so that they will be more chaste and less irrational, making themselves a more pleasant companion for their husbands. He speaks of mutual fondness and kindness between the couple, but this affection is expressed in a hierarchical way, indicating that there is agreement between husband and wife, but the husband's preferences are paramount.[481] The wife worships her husband's gods, shares his emotions rather than having her own private ones, and refrains from speaking in public.[482] There is complete union, Plutarch argues, but as the reader discovers, it is united insofar as the wife accepts her husband's wishes, friends, gods, and relations.

Unlike Plutarch, Paul seems unconcerned about the wife working to make her husband happy. Instead, Paul emphasizes a husband's sacrificial, self-giving love that is more in keeping with Plutarch's description of a wife. Paul spends no time describing possible character flaws a wife is to avoid, but implies that husbands might be tempted to disregard their wife's needs, so he insists that the wife is to be treated as the husband does his own body. Paul does

---

478. Martha C. Nussbaum, "The Incomplete Feminism of Musonius Rufus, Platonist, Stoic, and Roman," in *The Sleep of Reason: Erotic Experience and Sexual Ethics in Ancient Greece*, ed. Martha C. Nussbaum and Juha Sihvola (Chicago: University of Chicago Press, 2002), 302.

479. Nussbaum, "Incomplete Feminism," 303.

480. Nussbaum, "Incomplete Feminism," 303.

481. Plutarch, *Advice to Bride and Groom* 11.

482. Plutarch, *Advice to Bride and Groom* 19, speaks of the wife not making her own friends, but enjoying her husband's friends, foremost among them being her husband's gods; only these gods is she to know and worship, avoiding all superstition. Plutarch would certainly have included Christianity in the category of superstition.

not separate husband and wife into the hierarchical union of "soul" (male) and "body" (female); rather, he highlights their bodily oneness based on Gen 2:24: "They will become one flesh." Paul connects this with the ecclesiological claim that all believers are members of Christ's body. Hering sums up well the unique emphasis in the biblical household codes: "The person of Christ represents both the central and unique element of the HT [household codes] ethic."[483]

A few concluding remarks are in order. First, many believers in the first-century churches lived as widows, widowers, orphans, and freedmen and freedwomen; in other words, they did not fit into the categories discussed here. Most people were poor, although not destitute.[484] By the time they reached adulthood, many had lost one or both parents. It was not uncommon for a spouse to die, whether in childbirth, or due to disease, infection, or accident. As such, many listening to Ephesians would not immediately place themselves in any particular category: they might be a divorced husband who previously lost a child, or a freed widow without children, or an adult child unmarried and without surviving parents, or a slave child who did not obey a father but an owner. This does not take away the importance of Paul's instructions, but rather recognizes that these three pairs in the household are stylized categories that constitute the family structure but are not descriptive of everyone's own life. A similar situation exists today, with families blended by divorce and remarriage and with widowed, single mothers or fathers raising children. Additionally, given that Paul promotes singleness as a laudable option in service for Christ (1 Cor 7), we should be careful not to assume that in Ephesians Paul mandates or assumes that all men and women should marry.

C. THE HOUSEHOLD CODES (5:21–6:9)

1. *Wife and Husband (5:21–33)*

Paul transitions from his discussion about worship in the church to living in harmony within the home.[485] Most English translations make a sharp distinc-

---

483. Hering, *Colossian and Ephesian Haustafeln*, 265.
484. Cohick, "Poverty and Its Causes in the Early Church," 17, 23–24.
485. Craig S. Keener, *Paul, Women, and Wives: Marriage and Women's Ministry in the Letters of Paul* (Peabody, MA: Hendrickson, 1992), 258–66, makes a strong case that Paul contrasts the moral behavior of Christian worship gatherings with the debauchery and revelry that characterized pagan mystery cult gatherings. See also G. F. Hawthorne, "Marriage and Divorce, Adultery and Incest," *DPL* 594–600.

5:21–33 Wife and Husband

tion between 5:21 and 5:22; however, this mutes the Greek grammatical structure, which connects the two through the participle "submit." The participle links with the imperative in 5:18, "be filled with the Spirit," and is assumed (not repeated) in 5:22. The participle is either passive or middle, and most likely Paul stresses the middle with its emphasis on the believers' choice to submit to others in the community's worship life as believers soberly and joyfully celebrate their new life in Christ. Submission is a Christian virtue because it demonstrates proper respect for Christ and those who are "in Christ."

The verb "to submit" and the noun "submission" were commonly used in the highly stratified Greco-Roman world, where subordinates honored their social superiors by deferring to them. This included children submitting to their parents, as Jesus did to Mary and Joseph (Luke 2:51; see also Heb 12:9; the noun is used in 1 Tim 3:4) and as younger believers to older members of the church (1 Pet 5:5). All believers are enjoined to submit to governing authorities (Rom 13:1, 5; see also Titus 3:1; 1 Pet 2:13). Communities should submit to those who work hard as Paul's coworkers in their midst (1 Cor 16:15–16). The spirits of prophets are in submission to the male and female prophets (1 Cor 14:32), and women are charged with learning in full submission (1 Tim 2:11). The Epistle to Titus implores slaves to submit to their masters in everything (2:9), as does 1 Peter, adding that this submission should be done both to kind and harsh masters (2:18). Of course, "A command to submit does not constitute a reversed mandate for the other to subjugate."[486]

The spiritual realm is not excluded from this hierarchy.[487] Demons submit to disciples in Jesus's name (Luke 10:17), while the flesh does not submit to God's law (Rom 8:7). James charges believers to submit to God and resist the devil (4:7). Paul implores the gentile Galatian believers not to submit to the false teaching that gentiles need to follow the law's ethnic requirements, such as circumcision, food laws, and Sabbath (Gal 3:1–6). As we saw earlier in Eph 1:22, Paul quotes from Psalm 8:6 describing Jesus Christ: "God placed [submitted] all things under his feet" (see also 1 Cor 15:27; Heb 2:6–9; 1 Pet 3:22). Paul reflects a similar idea using the same verb when he speaks to the Philippians about Christ's return when he brings everything under his control (3:21).

As the brief survey of passages shows, the concept of submission organized the social world of the New Testament. Yet is it really possible for

---

486. Westfall, *Paul and Gender*, 76.

487. Balch, *Let Wives Be Submissive*, 98, observes that the root of "to submit" is used thirty-one times in the Septuagint, most often describing human submission to God. It is never used to describe the relationship between parent and child, owner and slave, or husband and wife.

a paterfamilias to submit to his child or an owner to her slave? On the one hand, within the structure of the ancient culture, the answer would be "no," inasmuch as the term implies an asymmetrical relationship that depends on submission of the subordinate to reinforce and maintain the honor and status of the superordinate. In line with this observation, some argue that the pronoun "one another" in Eph 5:21 includes such implied limitations. On the other hand, the answer is "yes," if their submission to one another is done with an eye to the submission they exhibit toward Christ. This would mean foregoing non-Christlike actions that society allows, such as threatening slaves (6:9). And it would entail relinquishing honor, which was the most valuable commodity in the ancient world, and accepting social humiliation and shame. Further support for this conclusion comes from the strong antithesis Paul draws between the life within the community and those outside the community.[488] He bookends the household codes with a warning against living as gentiles do (5:8) and a charge to put on the armor of God to defend against the "devil's schemes" (6:11). These warnings frame the household codes as part of the church's overall stance against the present age of darkness, ruled by the prince of the kingdom of the air (2:1–3).

a. Instructions to Wives (5:21–24)

21Submit to one another out of reverence for Christ.
22Wives, submit yourselves to your own husbands as you do to the Lord. 23For the husband is the head of the wife as Christ is the head of the church, his body, of which he is the Savior. 24Now as the church submits to Christ, so also wives should submit to their husbands in everything.

Having spoken to all believers in 5:21, Paul now turns to the wives in the congregation. In many English Bibles, this verse is introduced with a new subheading as though it begins a new section. In the Greek text, however, there is no conjunction indicating a new topic. The absence of a conjunction is quite unusual for Paul, as he almost always uses a conjunction if he was introducing a new thought. The reader has to go back to 1:3 to find a case where Paul does not use a conjunction when beginning a new subject. Thus, Paul does not begin a new topic so much as continue to reflect on the makeup of the church. A quick comparison with Col 3:17–18, which lacks any transitional terms, shows that Paul can begin his discussion about the household rather abruptly. That he does not do so here, plus the repetition of the participle,

---

488. Carolyn Osiek and Margaret Y. MacDonald with Janet H. Tulloch, *A Woman's Place: House Churches in Earliest Christianity* (Minneapolis: Fortress, 2006), 122–23.

signals Paul's intention to connect these two passages.[489] As such, 5:21 offers the reader an introduction to the key themes of the household codes to follow, namely, the importance of mutual submission and its foundation on the fear or reverence of Christ.

22 Paul stresses a wife's submission to her husband, but that still does not tell us the nature of that relationship vis-à-vis the mutual submission enjoined in the previous verse. Readers today ask about underlying reasons or presumptions for this call for the wife to submit. Does this passage encourage submission to husbands because women are in some way inferior to men? We will trace similar questions concerning slaves, who likewise were considered inferior to one degree or another to free individuals.[490] Relatedly, is the husband's place as "head" an indication of male authority over females? The wider Greco-Roman culture would answer "yes" to these questions, but did Paul? Is Paul qualifying his charge in 5:21 that believers submit to each other by exempting husbands here in 5:22 from submitting to their wives?

Before we answer these questions, a quick look at similar passages in contemporary material is in order. Paul's near contemporary, Josephus, provides an alternative Jewish position. He declared that Scripture teaches a woman is inferior to her husband in all things.[491] He follows this directly with a call for the wife to be obedient to her husband and for the husband not to abuse his wife. Josephus's conclusions about the nature of women reflect the views of his first-century world. It is crucial to note that Paul does not ask the wife to *obey* her husband. Conversely, we have only two other examples of wives told to submit. Plutarch, the first example, uses the verb "to submit" once.[492] When speaking about a wife's conduct toward her husband, he ex-

---

489. Best, 531, cites the textual variants in a number of manuscripts, which insert either ὑποτασσέσθωσαν or ὑποτάσσεσθε after either γυναῖκες or ἀνδράσιν. He rightly concludes that "the absence of any form of the verb is the correct reading."

490. It might seem to readers today that the ontological reality of sex difference in male/female is not analogous to the social category of slave. However, while it is true that slaves could become free, they were never "free" men or women but always "freed." They carried their previous legal status of slave as a terrible legacy and were required to stay with their previous owners, now more as clients who owed honor and usually a percentage of wages to their previous owners.

491. Josephus, *Against Apion* 2.25 §204. Unfortunately, he does not identify his source, and scholars today cannot find any place in the biblical text that matches Josephus's claim. Philo states much the same: "Organized communities are of two sorts, the greater which we call cities and the smaller which we call households.... The government of the greater is assigned to men, under the name of statesmanship, that of the lesser, known as household management, to women" (*On the Special Laws* 3.169–71).

492. The only other occurrence is ca. 100 BCE author Pseudo-Callisthenes, *A Narrative, Remarkable and Really Marvelous, of the Lord of the World, Alexander the King* (*Historiae*

plains that a wife receives praise for submitting herself to her husband, over against a desire to rule her husband. Plutarch prefers the more typical "obey" and describes the husband as one who makes decisions and rules his wife.[493] In the same passage, Plutarch urges the husband to rule and to control his wife, while warning the wife against controlling her husband. Plutarch distinguishes this sort of control from that exercised by an owner over his property, and he urges the husband to seek to delight his wife, much as the soul cares for the body. Plutarch explains that the husband is the soul, and the wife the body; together they make one human.

Having reviewed contemporary voices, we return to our question of whether Paul qualifies his charge in Eph 5:21 that believers submit to each other by exempting husbands in 5:22 from submitting to their wives. The answer is a complicated "no" that starts with a qualified "yes." It would be almost impossible from a cultural standpoint for Paul's audience to make sense of a direct statement for husbands to submit to their wives, for the social expectations would not have envisioned it. Moreover, the legal codes treated adult women as "minors," which would have made nonsense of Paul's request. Yet in terms of actual practices, Paul does in fact ask husbands to submit—in his command that they love their wives as Christ loved the church and gave himself up to death on the cross that the church might live. Such actions undermine the gender hierarchy by ceding honor to the wife as worthy of the husband's self-sacrifice.

Paul does not command wives to *obey* their husbands, nor does he use the imperative when asking the wife to submit. Indeed, Paul never addresses the wife with any imperatives, in contrast with the husband, who is commanded twice to love his wife and is also told that he "ought to love," which carries the force of an imperative (5:25, 28, 33). Likely Paul's use of the imperative with husbands is related to cultural authority vested in the husband, for he had the social clout to change the marriage relationship.

Paul asks that wives submit to their own husbands, "as to the Lord." This final phrase matches that found in Col 3:23, that slaves work with all their heart, as to the Lord (see also Titus 2:9).[494] Paul encourages believ-

---

Alexandri Magni 1.22.4) 1.22.19–20. Pseudo-Callisthenes writes about Alexander the Great, who speaks to his mother after she has been wronged by his father, Philip: "It is proper for the wife to be submissive to her own husband" (translation from Balch, *Let Wives Be Submissive*, 98).

493. Plutarch, *Advice to Bride and Groom* 11, uses terms such as ἡγεμονία and προαίρεσις and κρατεῖν (passage 33). The verb "to submit" is used in *Advice to Bride and Groom* 33. Hering, *Colossian and Ephesian Haustafeln*, 253, explains: "The man is characterised as the ruler, the woman as the obedient member."

494. Hering, *Colossian and Ephesian Haustafeln*, 142, observes: "The motivation which implied direct service for the slaves is now implemented in Eph. to generalize the intense and unmitigated nature of Christ's lordship in *all* HT [household codes] relations."

ers to think about aspects of the marriage relationship as analogous to the church's relationship to Christ. But Paul does not draw a one-to-one correspondence—he does not say that the husband is the lord *of the wife*, but that the wife's submission to the husband is as valuable as if it is done to Christ himself. Nor is Paul saying that the wife shows her submission to Christ by submitting to her husband, as if her husband were a substitute for Christ or her intermediary with Christ. The wife is the active agent who is mindful that her posture of submission to her husband is in keeping with her active submission to Christ. "As to the Lord" circumscribes the submission to that which a holy God would ask of his follower.

Submission and authority can be viewed often as mutually exclusive postures. But that is not how we learned Christ, to borrow Paul's language from Eph 4:24. Jesus the Messiah came not to be served, but to serve. In serving he retained his authority as Lord, even as he washed his disciples' feet (John 13). Today some link male authority with "head" as they construct a definition of masculinity. The man is the initiator, the essence of proper leadership; the female is passive, a receiver or responder. This is certainly the case with the ancient Jewish and Roman authors, but Paul's view of believers does not map masculine and feminine on the spectrum of active/passive or leader/subordinate. (I demonstrate this below, when we look at Paul's call to the husbands to love their wives as their own bodies.)

23 Paul continues his discussion of the wife with the conjunction "for," offering an explanation for his statement that wives submit to their husbands as to the Lord. Paul's reason takes the form of a metaphor using "head" and "body." A word about metaphors: they are not equivalent to prescriptive statements. A metaphor is a figure of speech, a type of analogy, that brings together two ideas or subjects in a new way that creates a new idea, new meaning. A metaphor is not shorthand for a literal statement, but is designed to bring a new perspective to the reader. Metaphors pervade our thinking and actions. Indeed, "our ordinary conceptual system, in terms of which we both think and act, is fundamentally metaphorical in nature."[495]

To appreciate the impact of the head/body metaphor in antiquity, we need to recognize that it draws its rhetorical significance by comparing two similar things (both are part of the human being) that also are distinct in honor and thus social importance. This social grid is overlaid with an ontolog-

---

495. George Lakoff and Mark Johnson, *Metaphors We Live By* (Chicago: University of Chicago Press, 1980), 3. They use the example of "argument is war" to expose the metaphor's hold on our thinking, as we speak of winning and losing arguments, attacking them, defending them. They explain that we do not think of arguments in terms of dance, for example: "Our conventional ways of talking about arguments presuppose a metaphor we are hardly ever conscious of. The metaphor is not merely in the words we use—it is in our very concept of an argument" (5).

ical grid that puts mind/spirit above body/material, according to the classical dualism found in Plato and Aristotle and pervasive in the first century CE. In his discussion of slave and master, Aristotle described the master as ruling the slave as the soul rules the body through the head. The comparison depicts the master as soul and the slave as body. The metaphor demonstrates a symbiotic relationship, and Aristotle maintains that both benefit from it because "the slave is a part of the master—he is, as it were, a part of the body, alive yet separated from it."[496] Aristotle's understanding of the slave as a human tool, and as unable to be in a relationship with the master, would undoubtedly color his picture of what a slave might consider a "benefit." Finally, these two grids were perceived through a gendered lens that viewed mind/head/spirit as male and body/material as female. As such, male was esteemed superior in rationality, more noble in character, and more spiritual. Female was viewed inferior to the male in an ontological, social, and rhetorical sense. The body/head metaphor, then, carries with it the hierarchically stratified and gendered social world.

In our verse, the head/body metaphor is compared with the descriptive statement that Christ is the head, the savior of the church. Because the meaning of "head" is contentious, we might do better to start at the end of this verse and explore Paul's description of Christ as savior of his body.[497] Earlier in Ephesians, Paul described Christ as the head of the body, which he sustains and causes to grow (1:22–23; 4:15–16; see also Col 2:19). Of course, husbands are also "brides" in this passage, for they are members of the church, and they too call Christ their savior. Even as the husband submits as a bride to Christ, so too he receives his wife's submission as she models for him the submission all believers offer to each other in fear of Christ. Conversely, the wife metaphorically becomes "male" as she shares her husband's body as her own (Eph 5:28).[498]

The title "savior" is rarely used of Christ in the New Testament. The Samaritans confess Jesus as the savior of the world after the Samaritan woman testifies about him and the townspeople speak to Jesus (John 4:42). Paul encourages the Philippians that their citizenship is in heaven, from which will come their savior, Jesus Christ (Phil 3:20–21). In both cases, Christ is implicitly contrasted with Caesar's claim to be savior of the world (see also

---

496. Aristotle, *Politics* 1255b, translation from Hering, *Colossian and Ephesian Haustafeln*, 224.

497. On σωτήρ see BDAG 985; A. B. Luter Jr., "Savior," *DPL* 867–69.

498. Westfall, *Paul and Gender*, 93–94. Paul asks husbands to treat wives as their own bodies. Westfall calls this the Golden Rule in gender relationships. Westfall writes: "A husband should treat his wife as he treats himself as a man" (95). She continues that the wife is not a significant other, which would make her an object, but is part of the flesh and bone of her husband, one body.

5:21–24 INSTRUCTIONS TO WIVES

Luke 2:11; Acts 5:31; 13:23).[499] Those in Philippi remembered the great victory won by the "saviors," Marc Antony and Octavian (Augustus), over Brutus and Cassius in the plains outside the city. Exuberant celebrations and extravagant parades marked the military saviors' triumph.[500] In another example, the Priene Calendar inscription (Asia Minor, 9 BCE) configures the calendar of festivals for the province around Augustus's birthday. This inscription exalts Augustus as the savior who ends all wars, surpasses all benefactors, and is filled with virtue. Writing about forty years later, Philo of Alexandria writes of Gaius Caligula as "savior and benefactor."[501] Interestingly, a coin from 55 CE shows the "divine" Claudius seated at the right hand of Augustus, now declared "son of god."[502] Christ's victory is greater still. Paul indicates to the Ephesians that Christ now sits at God the Father's right hand, with believers also seated with him (2:6). The reversal motif echoes here as the one who died on a Roman cross is the true savior who brings true peace (2:14), the true "son of God" (4:13). Paul juxtaposes "head" and "savior," which suggests that Christ's self-surrender unto death is part of his actions as head of the church. Clearly, the role of savior does not emphasize "leadership" but redemption and deliverance.[503]

How does Paul understand the term "head" in this metaphor? In English, we can say that this woman is the head of her company, and because the term "head" can mean "leader" the sentence is not perceived as holding a metaphor. The same is true in Hebrew (*rō'š*)[504] and Latin (*to caput*), but in the Septuagint, the Hebrew term "head" would be typically translated with the term "leader" (*archōn*), not "head" (*kephalē*). As we discuss below, discovering the meaning of "head" in Greek is not so simple, as Paul invites readers to think about four concrete concepts—Christ, church, wife, husband—through

---

499. Additional examples include 2 Tim 1:10; Titus 1:4; 2:13; 3:6; 2 Pet 1:1, 11; 2:20; 3:2, 18; 1 John 4:14.

500. Perhaps the most infamous triumph was celebrated when Vespasian was emperor and his son, Titus, brought the spoils of the Jerusalem temple to Rome; the Arch of Titus remains as a monument to the destruction of the temple in 70 CE. See Josephus, *Jewish War* 7.5.4–6 §§123–57.

501. Philo of Alexandria, *Against Flaccus* 74; *On the Embassy to Gaius* 148.

502. Harold Mattingly, *Coins from the Roman Empire in the British Museum*, vol. 1: *Augustus to Vitellus* (London: British Museum, 1965 [originally 1923]), 201 and pl. 38.

503. Westfall, "This Is a Great Metaphor!," 581, explains that the title "savior" is "used as an honorific expression of gratitude to the Roman emperor as the patron or benefactor of the people and belongs to the register of patronage." Westfall, *Paul and Gender*, 83, continues: "Κεφαλή occurs in contexts of leadership, because the metaphoric importance of the head is consistent with the function of authority; but they are not synonymous."

504. Kenneth E. Bailey, *Paul through Mediterranean Eyes: Cultural Studies in 1 Corinthians* (Downers Grove, IL: InterVarsity Press, 2011), 302, offers an example of a metaphorical meaning in Hebrew: *Rosh Hashanah* or, literally, the "*head* of the year."

the vivid images of body and head. After examining the various meanings of the term "head" we will focus on its use in head/body metaphors, as we draw conclusions about Paul's intentions in this verse.

The vast majority of times, the Greek noun "head" refers to the physical head that sits between a person's shoulders.[505] When used metaphorically, it may mean (a) "preeminence," (b) "source," or (c) "leader."[506] Jesus Christ is identified in Colossians as being head over all rulers and authorities (2:10), which suggests to some that *kephalē* means "leader" in the New Testament. Yet the argument Paul makes in Colossians is Christ as the believers' source of life, even as he is the source of all things, both visible and invisible, including powers and rulers and authorities. The evidence is weak and limited, then, for *kephalē* as "leader" in the usual English sense.

Several church fathers discussed "head" as "source" when discussing Christ as head. Athanasius, fourth-century bishop of Alexandria, wrote that "the Son is the Head, namely the beginning of all: and God is the Head, namely the beginning of Christ; for thus to one unbegun beginning of the universe do we religiously refer all things through the Son."[507] Also from the fourth century, Archbishop Cyril of Alexandria spoke of Adam as the first head of the human race and of the earth. Christ, the second Adam, is the head, the source, of those whom he has made new and immortal. Cyril continues:

> Yet he though God by nature, has himself a generating head, the heavenly Father and he himself, though God according to his nature, yet being the Word, was begotten of him. Because head means source, he establishes the truth for those who are wavering in their mind that man is the head of woman, for she was taken out of him. Therefore, as God according to

---

505. On κεφαλή see BDAG 541–42. The 1843 edition of the Liddell and Scott lexicon included over twenty-five entries under κεφαλή, including the metaphorical meaning "source," but no entry referring to "leader" or "authority over." The ninth edition, published in 1996, likewise does not include "leader" or "authority over" as possible meanings for κεφαλή. Additionally, ancient lexicons do not define κεφαλή as "authority" or "leader"; see Richard Cervin, "Does κεφαλή Mean 'Source' or 'Authority Over' in Greek Literature? A Rebuttal," *Trinity Journal* 10 (1989): 85–112.

506. Plutarch, *Cicero* 14.6–7, uses the term "head" to speak of a political leader, but the term is embedded in an analogy of the body, not as a direct synonym for leader, as we find in English. Plutarch describes the failed revolt of Cicero's enemy Catiline: "Catiline, thinking that there were many in the senate who were desirous of a revolution, and at the same time making a display of himself to the conspirators, gave Cicero the answer of a madman: 'What dreadful thing, pray,' he said, 'am I doing, if, when there are two bodies, one lean and wasted, but with a head, and the other headless, but strong and large, I myself become a head for this?' Since this riddle of Catiline's referred to the senate and the people, Cicero was all the more alarmed" (translation from Lau, *Politics of Peace*, 135).

507. Athanasius, *De synodis* 2.27, Anathema 26 (*NPNF*[2] 4:465).

his nature, the one Christ and Son and Lord has as his head the heavenly Father, having himself become our head because he is of the same stock according to the flesh.[508]

Cyril emphasizes the similar nature between Father and Son, between man and woman, and between Christ in his incarnation and humanity. Both he and John Chrysostom write against the position that Christ is a subordinate being to God the Father. Chrysostom declares that Paul teaches in 1 Cor 11:3 that Christ is the same substance as the Father, and he adds that if Paul wanted to emphasize the Father as ruler, he would have chosen the master/slave pair, not the male/female pair.[509]

The position that *kephalē* means "source" is vigorously argued by some,[510] while others promote the figurative meaning "honored part" or "prominent."[511] Cynthia Westfall draws these ideas together under the category of reciprocity and family, arguing that *kephalē* occurs in the context of ancestry. The progenitor of the family is the head or source of the family, and as such, he is the prominent one or the face of the family unit. Using the lens of reciprocity, Westfall further maintains that the patron/client social relationship informs the head/body metaphor, as the "head" or patron provides a benefit to her client, which the client reciprocates through honoring his patron.[512]

Michelle Lee-Barnewall comes to similar conclusions, but by a different route. She argues that the notion of preeminence without some sort of power or authority would be quite unlikely in the ancient context. The head metaphor was often used in the context of political or military authority, as it is uppermost on the body. As the head of the body must be protected for the soldier's safety, so too must the general of the army, or the emperor, be protected as having the primary place within the community.[513] The first-century philosopher Seneca speaks of Emperor Nero as the head of his people, who show their love to him by sacrificing their lives for the preservation of his

---

508. Cyril of Alexandria, *De recta fide ad Arcadiam et Marinam* 5.6 (translation from Westfall, *Paul and Gender*, 86n69).
509. John Chrysostom, *Homilies on First Corinthians*, Homily 26.3.
510. E.g., Fee, *First Epistle to the Corinthians*, 502–3.
511. Thiselton, *First Epistle to the Corinthians*, 821.
512. Westfall, "This Is a Great Metaphor!," 587, writes: "Functioning as a 'head' may be the grounds for holding a position of authority over a client, but it is not the same thing as the exercise of authority." The alert reader would have noticed that I imagined a female patron and a male client. I did so because it represents historical possibility and to highlight the range of application of reciprocity. Wealth trumps gender, to put it bluntly, and the ancient writers noted when the wife was of higher social rank or wealthier than her husband. See Plutarch, *Advice to Bride and Groom* 8.
513. Lee-Barnewall, "Turning ΚΕΦΑΛΗ on Its Head," 608.

life. Nero shows them mercy in response.[514] Notice the roles played here: the people give their lives for the ruler who does not love them, but who extends mercy. Aristotle argued similarly that the ruler is not expected to love those he rules, while those whom he rules are to love him.[515] Lee-Barnewall concludes that a common way the body/head analogy worked was to stress the head as "primary leader and source of provision for the body."[516] The expectation would be that the body sacrifices itself for the head—a conclusion directly at odds with the gospel message, as we have seen already in Ephesians. Christ the head of the church in love laid down his life for his beloved (5:2). This reversal is a consistent motif within the gospel story, as it reflects the actions of the Lord who humbled himself to die on a cross and who bids his followers do likewise (Matt 16:24–26).

24 Paul concludes with the claim that the church submits to Christ. The tight connection Paul makes between Christ the church's savior and the church's submission to Christ reveals the important social reality of reciprocity underpinning the household codes discussion. The verse begins with a conjunction translated "now" that also can be translated "but" or "on the contrary." This signals that the characteristic of "savior" is limited to Christ alone. Paul indicated as much in the previous verse, when he used the personal pronoun "he" in identifying Christ as the savior of *his* body, the church. In this way Paul limits the analogy, for he does not allow that husbands are saviors of their wives.

Paul repeats the verb "to submit" here in the indicative, not as a command. Paul frames the scope of his call to submit by speaking of the church's submission to Christ first and then asking the same of wives. As in 5:22 so too here the verb "submit" is assumed when speaking of wives, for the verb appears only once in the Greek text of 5:24. Paul asks that wives submit to their husbands "in everything," which at first seems to put no limits on wifely submission. However, the governing principle is Christ's love for the church, a self-sacrificial, saving act of marvelous humility. It is to that love, goodness, and beauty that the church submits.

A similar phrase is found in Col 3:20 and 3:22 directing children and slaves to obey "in everything." No Colossian believer would think Paul encourages slaves to willfully follow the sinful practices of their owners. Instead, Paul makes clear that the slave obeys "in everything" inasmuch as they are working for the Lord and so gives their whole heart to the task, however menial. In working for the Lord, the slave's efforts take on an honored status. Likely a similar idea operates here in Eph 5:24, as "in everything" has

---

514. Seneca, *On Clemency* 2.2.1.
515. Aristotle, *Eudemian Ethics* 7.3.4.
516. Lee-Barnewall, "Turning ΚΕΦΑΛΗ on Its Head," 605.

the built-in qualification that "everything" includes only what Christ himself would ask of any believer, including the husband.

b. Instructions to Husbands (5:25–33)

25Husbands, love your wives, just as Christ loved the church and gave himself up for her 26to make her holy, cleansing her by the washing with water through the word, 27and to present her to himself as a radiant church, without stain or wrinkle or any other blemish, but holy and blameless. 28In this same way, husbands ought to love their wives as their own bodies. He who loves his wife loves himself. 29After all, no one ever hated their own body, but they feed and care for their body, just as Christ does the church—30for we are members of his body. 31"For this reason a man will leave his father and mother and be united to his wife, and the two will become one flesh." 32This is a profound mystery—but I am talking about Christ and the church. 33However, each one of you also must love his wife as he loves himself, and the wife must respect her husband.

Paul sees the husband/wife pair as reciprocal, including that the husband will provide marital relations, food, and clothing and, in turn, his wife will honor his care by submitting to him. Yet the submission, as we saw above, is of the sort that every believer is obligated to extend to the other, out of reverence for Christ, as part of being filled with the Holy Spirit.

25 Paul commands husbands to love their wives, which in itself is not a bold claim. Husbands spoke of their love for their wives in letters, treatises, eulogies, and inscriptions in the ancient world. "In Praise of Turia" (*Laudatio Turiae*), a lengthy, first-century BCE funerary inscription, provides an example of love between spouses. In this recorded speech, the wife's deeds are recounted with much praise. She avenged her parents' murders, deterred the attempts by pseudo-relatives to steal her inheritance, and procured her husband's release from exile.[517] Her husband describes her loyalty, obedience, reasonableness, modesty, and devotion to her parents and his mother, and he concludes: "Marriages as long as ours are rare, marriages that are ended by death and not broken by divorce. For we are fortunate enough to see our marriage last without disharmony for fully forty years."[518]

---

517. Inheritance laws in the XII Tablets indicated that sons and daughters inherit equally if the father dies intestate. The wife in a *sine manu* marriage would inherit from her father; in a *cum manu* arrangement, she is treated as though she was her husband's daughter.

518. *Laudatio Turiae* 27 (= *Inscriptiones Latinae Selectae* 8393); E. Wistrand, *The So-called Laudatio Turiae: Introduction, Text, Translation, Commentary*, Studia Graeca et Latina Gothoburgensia 34 (Göteborg: Acta Universitatis Gothoburgensis, 1976). For an in-depth

From the early second century CE, Pliny the Younger applauds his young wife, Calpurnia Hispulla, as "highly intelligent, and extremely frugal; she loves me, which is a sign of chastity. Her love for me has made her take up books. She reads and rereads my writings and even memorises them."[519] She likes to hear him read his works aloud to an audience, and she "sits discreetly behind a curtain and soaks up the praise."[520] He concludes that this behavior adds up to "evidence that the harmony between us will continue to grow stronger for the rest of our lives. For it's not my youth or body she loves—they are gradually declining—but my glory."[521] In another letter he declares: "It is incredible how much I miss you—first of all because I love you, but then because we are not used to being apart."[522] Love for these two husbands meant shared life together, but with the focus on the husband's success.

Unfortunately, because our literary artifacts were written by men, we do not have the wife's perspective on her marriage. Given the expectations expressed in the ancient household codes, however, most likely they would consider themselves to be adequately loved. Concord between the spouses was of paramount importance, and the first empress, Livia, promoted her marriage's harmony by dedicating a temple to Concord in her late husband's honor.[523] The late-first-century CE philosopher and orator Dio Chrysostom (ca. 40–110) spoke on the topic, claiming that bickering between husband and wife is as sailors who mutiny against their captain and bring danger to the ship. Harmony in the household included the wife's worshiping her husband's gods.[524] Concord was perhaps bought at the price of the wife's silence. A story in Valerius Maximus suggests that some couples sought the temple Viriplaca in Rome to restore domestic tranquility. The goddess would hear both the husband and the wife's perspective, and by some means the disagreement was settled. Valerius praises the goddess Viriplaca (her name means "man-placater") for her work in honoring the "majesty of the husband by the wife

---

study, see Josiah Osgood, *Turia: A Roman Woman's Civil War* (Oxford: Oxford University Press, 2014).

519. Pliny the Younger, *Letters* 4.19; translation from Mary R. Lefkowitz and Maureen B. Fant, eds., *Women's Life in Greece and Rome: A Source Book in Translation*, 4th ed. (Baltimore: Johns Hopkins University Press, 2016), 233.

520. Lefkowitz and Fant, *Women's Life in Greece and Rome*, 233.

521. Lefkowitz and Fant, *Women's Life in Greece and Rome*, 233.

522. Pliny the Younger, *Letters* 7.5, in Lefkowitz and Fant, *Women's Life in Greece and Rome*, 234.

523. Ovid, *Calendar* 6.637–40, in Osiek and MacDonald, *Woman's Place*, 280.

524. Dio Chrysostom, *To the Nicomedians* 38.14–16 (*Oration* 38). See Balch, *Let Wives Be Submissive*, 88–89, for translation and discussion.

in the equal yoke of love."[525] The home was not the place to show disharmony, and the temple precinct was a space for the wife's voice, so long as it ultimately privileged her husband's words.

The love that Paul speaks of here in Ephesians, however, is not that of his wider social world.[526] In fact, this verb, *agapaō*, is never used in any household codes outside the New Testament, though it is used in other contexts in the wider Greco-Roman world.[527] Why would Paul use it to describe a husband's love for his wife? The noteworthy aspect of this command to love is the subsequent definition of love as modeled in the self-sacrificial love of Christ, which led him to die by crucifixion (see also 5:2). If Paul were consistent with his times, he would have asked for the wife to sacrifice herself (body) for her husband, her head. But Paul turns social convention upside down, in line with the gospel message that those who are given honor and privilege are to lay it aside in service of others.[528]

In calling for a reversal of privilege, Paul also challenges conventional definitions of masculinity. Death by crucifixion, hanging naked before others, was one of the most shameful phenomena in Paul's day, and Hebrews remarks that Jesus "endured the cross, scorning its shame" (Heb 12:2).[529] Crucifixion took away a man's control of his situation, emasculating him. In the Roman world, masculinity and authority are closely linked, and a free man would expect to exercise power over women and slaves or suffer shame in the eyes of the community.[530] Jesus invites each follower, however, to pick up his or

---

525. Valerius Maximus, *Memorable Deeds and Sayings* 2.1.6, in *Daily Life in Ancient Rome: A Sourcebook*, ed. and trans. Brian K. Harvey (Indianapolis: Hackett, 2016), 57.

526. For a general overview of Paul on man and woman, see Craig Keener, "Man and Woman," *DPL* 583–92.

527. On ἀγαπάω see BDAG 5 (1); Witherington, 329. See also Fowl, 188, who adds that some of these Greco-Roman household codes use other terms for love, some with a sense of romantic love.

528. So Lee-Barnewall, "Turning ΚΕΦΑΛΗ on Its Head," 609, who states: "When Paul asks husbands as heads to sacrifice themselves for their wives, he asks them to do that which goes against this fundamental order of society." She continues that the order to love and sacrifice would be natural for the woman, but "shocking in light of traditional status conventions because he tells the most honored part, the head, to perform the duties of the less honored member" (610). She points to 1 Cor 12:22–23, wherein Paul declares that the church as the body of Christ protects those who seem to be the "weaker" or "less honorable." She finds this reversal motif throughout Scripture, summed up well in Jesus's teachings that the first shall be last and the last shall be first (Matt 19:30; 20:16; Mark 9:35).

529. Very few women were crucified. In one instance, a freedwoman planned and helped execute a wicked scheme against a highborn woman and was crucified (Josephus, *Jewish Antiquities* 18.3.4 §79).

530. Lee-Barnewall, "Turning ΚΕΦΑΛΗ on Its Head," 613, perceptively observes:

her cross, embracing the eschatological reality that enduring public shame now by serving others will reap eternal reward.

As we will see in the following verses, the husband is called on to do those things normally reserved for the "lesser" member of the pair. Paul describes Jesus doing "women's work" in feeding, nurturing, making clothes, washing clothes, all in service to his bride, the church. The implicit analogy is that the husband is to do the same for his wife, who is his body.[531] Said another way, Paul reconfigures the cultural expectations of masculinity expressed within a marriage between the submissive partner (wife) and the superordinate spouse (husband).

This verse parallels 5:2, which commands all believers to walk in love, as Christ loved us and gave himself for us. The difference here is that Paul uses the noun "church," because he is drawing an analogy between the church and bride of Christ. Three points are worth noting. First, husbands are asked to do no more and no less than believers in general (5:2). Second, as believers, husbands are Christ's bride and so receive themselves the surpassingly gracious love of Christ, their bridegroom. Third, the command to love is followed by an emphasis on unity, one-flesh-ness of husband and wife and of Christ and the church.[532] In the previous three verses, the distinction between body and head allowed Paul to frame the wife's submission in such a way as to call into question the ancient social hierarchy between men and women. In 5:25 Paul completes this effort by defining love as self-sacrificial, a position that Paul's culture would deem unfitting and dishonoring to the superordinate member of the pair.

26–27 Paul focuses on how Christ loves the church in these two verses. This might be judged a digression if we assume that the only point Paul wants to make is establishing the roles of husbands and wives. But we have seen that Paul develops the household codes from his call to the church to be filled with the Spirit (5:18). And Paul has reshaped the social hierarchy by calling all believers to submit to one another as they reverence Christ. The discussion about the church, therefore, is not an afterthought, but is central to the understanding of the metaphorical use of "head" and "body."

The activities in these verses include the common actions of washing, spot cleaning, and ironing, as well as the spiritual actions related to believers' salvation, including making holy and blameless. On the one hand, Christ's actions are specific to his role as redeemer. This role is reserved to Christ

---

"The greater question may not be whether or not the passage sees a patriarchal headship, but how headship is redefined in the eschatological age of a crucified Christ."

531. Westfall, *Paul and Gender*, 23.

532. MacDonald, 328, suggests: "This verse offers perhaps the strongest indication of the transformation of the marriage relationship that occurs in Christ."

alone, in whom both husbands and wives place their faith. Paul reiterates this by using personal and reflective pronouns that reinforce Christ's agency. On the other hand, the descriptions of his actions call to mind "women's work" within the household, including caring for children. These tasks appear demeaning to the superordinate in the pair, but are reordered by Christ's own example to be the mark of a virtuous person.

Paul structures the verses as two purpose clauses, with an additional purpose clause connected to the second. The reasons Christ gave himself up for the church are, first, to make her holy and, second, to present her to himself as radiant and blameless. At the beginning and the end of these two verses, Paul stresses Christ's effort in making the church holy. Notice that believers do not make themselves holy, but it is Christ's work that makes them so. Holiness can be misunderstood as a "holier-than-thou" arrogance, but when we realize that the holiness is rooted in Christ's work, all boasting is rendered worthless.

Paul uses the verb "to sanctify" or "to make holy" as he describes Christ's work (5:26). This verb offers a purpose for Christ's giving of himself, stated in 5:25 (see also 5:2 which uses both verbs, "to love" and "to give"). "To make holy" denotes being set apart, consecrated, or made ethically pure and purified from sin.[533] The verb is used only here in Ephesians and probably carries the sense of ethical purity, as in the following verse Paul stresses the church's blamelessness (1:4; see also 1 Thess 5:23; Jude 24). The concept of holiness is related to ritual purity and sacred space, two concepts that are emphasized less today than in the ancient world. Paul encourages the Corinthians that they were washed, sanctified, and justified in Christ's name and by the Holy Spirit (1 Cor 6:11; see also Col 1:22). Hebrews describes the ritual purity aspects of holiness as it explains that the blood of sacrificial animals can make impure people outwardly clean (Heb 9:13), but that believers are made holy through Christ's sacrifice once for all (10:10; 13:12).

Making believers holy involves "cleansing . . . by the washing with water through the word." The participle "cleansing" usually means making someone ethically pure or free from the guilt of sins.[534] The cleansing happens with water, and immediately the question arises whether Paul alludes to baptism or is developing the imagery of a bride's wedding preparations. Evidence

---

533. On ἁγιάζω see BDAG 9–10 (2); S. E. Porter, "Holiness, Sanctification," *DPL* 397–402. See also Arnold, 387.

534. On καθαρίζω see BDAG 488–89 (3). The aorist participle signals that Paul describes the situation in its completeness and, because it follows the main verb, offers further description of what is entailed in Christ's love and giving of himself. Lincoln, 375, concludes that while the aorist participle can indicate that the cleansing happened prior to the making holy, it is probably best to see these two actions happening in a single motion, as "cleansing" describes how the church is made holy.

for the latter comes from two quarters. First, the verse lacks the verb "to baptize," which Paul uses in 1 Cor 12:13. Second, the image seems to call to mind the common practice of bridal baths.[535] Following this analogy closely in the context of this verse, however, would require the bridegroom giving his bride a prewedding bath, which would contravene custom and modesty codes. Responding to this challenge, some argue that Paul draws on Ezekiel's vision of adulterous Jerusalem, in which the Lord washes and clothes her, but then she commits idolatry (Ezek 16:1–43). In this vision, the Lord enters into a covenant with Jerusalem and declares: "You became mine" (16:8), after which the Lord bathed his wife and clothed her (16:9–13). In any case, the Lord serves Jerusalem, his "wife," with love and compassion by washing and putting ointment on the wounded flesh, adorning her with beautiful clothes. The prophet's picture of Israel's infidelity and God's faithfulness help illuminate Paul's emphasis that Christ does not overlook the church's sin, but has "pledged himself to the church [and] will establish the church's holiness."[536]

If the bridal bath is in view here in Eph 5:26, then 5:27 fills out the picture in possible ways. Christ's actions as menial household chores of laundering and ironing implicitly contrast the typical masculine tasks of the public square.[537] The spotless, wrinkle-free garment might be compared to the vision of the bride adorned for her husband—the new Jerusalem, descending from heaven (Rev 21:2). The bride, the wife of the Lamb, is also the holy city Jerusalem, which shines with God's glory as a precious jewel (21:9–11). This verse has been understood as highlighting the brilliant beauty of the young bride, the church.[538] From here, some commentators stress the physical beauty of a young bride, even after acknowledging that the verse itself speaks to moral uprightness. This subtle switch, praising female physical beauty and connecting ugliness and sinfulness, runs counter to several strands within the biblical text and reinforces a troubling cultural message that women's worth is tied to physical appearance. Both Peter and Paul enjoin women to develop an inner beauty and eschew pearls, gold, fancy hairstyles (1 Tim 2:9–10; 1 Pet 3:3–6). And are wrinkles to be erased as ugly, even immoral? Is maintaining a youthful appearance a godly activity? I wish the church answered with a resounding "no," but too often women's self-worth is measured by society's definition of beauty. Viewing others as beloved members of God's family, being made new from the inside out, could mitigate against our culture's obsession on external appearance.

---

535. Thielman, 384.
536. Fowl, 190. Arnold, 387–88, points to Ezek 36:25–27 and its emphasis on cleansing with water as evidence that this passage speaks of renewal by the Holy Spirit.
537. Westfall, *Paul and Gender*, 57–58.
538. Thielman, 385–86.

Those who favor an allusion to baptism in Eph 5:26 offer several arguments. First, they observe that Paul uses an article before the noun "washing," thereby specifying "the washing."[539] A parallel with 1 Cor 6:11, which is more directly tied to baptism, strengthens this, but the claim cannot rest solely on the tenuous argument of the article's presence. Second, Titus 3:5 is the only other time the noun "washing" is found, there most likely referring to baptism. Paul mentions baptism in Eph 4:5 in his proclamation of the oneness of believers in the Lord, and will reemphasize unity in 5:30 as believers are members of Christ's body. Finally, the enigmatic phrase "through the word" is best understood as part of a liturgical setting. The "word" might refer to a liturgical phrase, perhaps drawing on the testimony in 4:2–5 and covering the actions of sanctifying and cleansing with water performed by Christ.[540] Or it may refer more broadly to the gospel message that is testified to in the rite of baptism. Paul uses the noun again in 6:17 in describing the sword of the Spirit as the word of God.[541] Paul describes the message of faith with the same noun as he explains to the Romans that the word is near you (Rom 10:8, citing Deut 30:14). Even though the phrase's grammatical place in the sentence is not clear, the message rings out that Christ's actions in making his people holy occurs in and through the power of God's word. Taken together, these arguments tilt the scales in favor of seeing Paul allude to baptism as part of Christ's work in creating a radiant church.

Ephesians 5:27 begins with the second of two purpose clauses that further explain Christ's loving self-giving for the church in 5:25. With the cleansing by washing in the waters of baptism, Christ presents to himself a church radiant.[542] The adjective could mean "beautiful"[543] or "reflect a moral perfection."[544] Paul uses the reflexive pronoun to emphasize that the church's holiness is accomplished by Christ's work. Paul contrasts "radiance" with "stain" and "wrinkle"; the first term is found elsewhere only in 2 Pet 2:13, and

---

539. On λουτρόν see BDAG 603; G. R. Beasley-Murray, "Baptism," *DPL* 60–66. See also Lincoln, 375. Mathewson and Emig, *Intermediate Greek Grammar*, 74, rightly conclude that the presence or absence of the article is "notoriously elusive of concrete explanation."

540. Best, 544. Lincoln, 376, explains that the phrase ἐν ῥήματι does not refer to a testimony of faith given by the baptized person, but the "baptismal formula pronounced over the candidate."

541. On ῥῆμα see BDAG 905.

542. On ἔνδοξος see BDAG 332–33.

543. Best, 545–46.

544. Lincoln, 377. MacDonald, 329, sees in this picture a reflection of the ancient Mediterranean culture wherein the "chastity of women is understood as a resource that must be carefully protected." MacDonald's comments are accurate, but I suggest Paul is not confirming his culture's picture here, but merely using it to further his larger point about the church's purity.

the second noun is used only here in the New Testament.[545] There is no discernable distinction between the two terms, and Paul follows with a general catchall "or any such thing," which can be translated "any other blemish." Paul concludes that Christ's love for the church, expressed in his death, resurrection, and ascension, is effective in making the church holy and blameless. This very goal was established before the foundation of the world and purposed by God, who predestined believers' adoption by grace through Christ (1:4). Each believer now puts on their new self in Christ, by which they might live in "true righteousness and holiness" (4:24). As God's holy people (5:3), believers shun immorality as they walk in a manner fitting those who will inherit the kingdom of Christ and of God (5:5).

28 Paul asks husbands to love their wives "in this same way"—that is, as Christ loves the church. This rendering of the adverb looks backward to what Paul stated in the previous three verses. However, the adverb can point forward to the qualification that Paul makes at the end of the sentence, explaining how husbands are to love their wives: "as their own bodies." Paul might intend both, to remind readers that Christ's love is what defines Christian love.

Paul shifts the head/body metaphor to focus only on the body, as he addresses two bodies united in marriage and the members of the church united in Christ. Paul repeats his earlier command that husbands love their wives as their own bodies, reinforcing his countercultural charge against the social structure that promoted self-serving behavior by the superordinate person (husband, father, male or female slave owner). Paul does not ask the husband to remind his wife to submit to him or to obey him, as would the ancient philosophers. Paul does not insist on a "natural" or created hierarchy between husband and wife, as did Aristotle and Plutarch. Rather, Paul insists on the new creation brought by Christ, which challenges the social construction of levels of worth and worthiness.[546]

Three times in this verse Paul uses the verb "to love," the same verb used in 5:25. Christ's love included the redemption of his beloved church, his salvific death that brings life to all—this aspect of Christ's love is singular and unrepeatable, for only in Christ are believers saved. Nevertheless, husbands can imitate aspects of Christ's love in giving themselves for their wives. Paul uses the reflexive pronoun four times: "his own wife" (twice), "his own body," and "himself." Paul enjoins the husband to look at himself very differently. Moreover, because this letter is read aloud to the church, the wife is asked to think about her body differently too. Paul earlier invited the husband to think of himself as a bride wed to Christ. And here he asks a wife to think of herself as metaphorically male, as one body with her husband.

---

545. On σπίλος see BDAG 938. On ῥυτίς see BDAG 908.
546. Witherington, 320.

5:25–33 INSTRUCTIONS TO HUSBANDS

Paul concludes his teaching that a husband should treat his wife as he treats himself, for the wife is not an object, but his own body. Reciprocity has been extended in new ways as the husband serves his wife through tasks usually assigned to slaves and women—washing and nurturing, much as Jesus did in washing his disciples' feet (John 13:1–17).[547] Paul speaks similarly to the Corinthians, that the wife does not have authority over her own body, but her husband does (this was normal in Paul's culture), and the husband does not have authority over his own body, but his wife does (1 Cor 7:2–4). This latter statement would be met with incredulity, for it was assumed that the husband had sexual prerogatives. Paul confronts one of the most entrenched social customs of his day: the honor of the free male. Paul's boldness comes from Christ's own example of true love and honor, which humbly serves (Phil 2:5–8). Honor and shame take on new dimensions in God's kingdom, and those with social privilege must demonstrate humble service. Christ's love is a self-sacrificial love that overturns the ancient world's expectations about the subordinate serving the superordinate.

One more point about the love required of the husband: it is a love that frees the wife to be her own person. The ancient examples of marital harmony indicate that a wife becomes more like her husband as love grows. The self-sacrificial love of Christ extended by the Christian husband, however, creates a unity that celebrates the wife and the husband as individuals made one flesh—not one person subsumed into another. The wife's freedom is also seen in Paul's encouragement of the celibate life, inasmuch as Paul holds that women can be fully human apart from marriage (men can as well, but this was assumed). Sarah Ruden points to Paul's encouragement for men and women not to marry, and not to remarry, as offering unheard of opportunities for women. Her comments stem from 1 Cor 7:40: "In my judgment, she is happier if she stays as she is." Focusing on the term "happier," she invites readers to imagine a young Christian woman hearing Paul's letter read in the church.[548] Ruden suggests a scenario where a young suitor sends her little gifts and introduces himself to her parents, who like him. Yet our young Christian woman also is drawn to a life of prayer. For Paul, the decision is hers.[549] Paul's picture of a husband loving his wife as his own body includes the caveat that a

---

547. Westfall, *Paul and Gender*, 165.

548. Ruden, *Paul among the People*, 117. On μακάριος see BDAG 610–11.

549. Ruden, *Paul among the People*, 118, observes: "She has life more abundantly than women before her have ever had it, the shock of it, the glaring light of it." This contrasts sharply with the culture portrayed in Asne Seierstad, *The Bookseller of Kabul*, trans. Ingrid Christophersen (Boston: Little, Brown, 2003), which chronicles the life of an Afghanistan family from this Norwegian journalist's six-month stay with them. The oppression of women is palpable on the pages.

single Christian woman can choose not to be married, for her identity comes not from her husband, but from Christ.

29–30 A subtle shift occurs in 5:29 that is not always reflected in the English translation. Paul states that no one hates his own "flesh" (*sarx*), rather than use the term "body" (*sōma*).[550] With this change, Paul prepares the reader for the scriptural passage he quotes, which speaks of the married couple becoming one "flesh." Paul can use "flesh" to imply the "sinful nature" (Gal 5:17; 6:8), but he also uses it as a synonym for a human being. Earlier, he refers to Christ's crucified body as "flesh" (2:14; see also Col 1:22). He qualifies the gentiles' past by describing them as "gentiles in the flesh" (Eph 2:11), and he will distinguish "lords/masters according to the flesh" from the Lord, who shows no favoritism between slaves and their masters (6:5; see also Col 3:22).

Paul's argument depends on the obvious point that, typically, people do not hate their own bodies. The verb "to hate" signifies the opposite of love.[551] Jesus uses the same verbs "to love" and "to hate" in his call to "love your enemies, do good to those who hate you" (Luke 6:27; see also Matt 5:43). Paul explains that loving one's body includes nourishing and cherishing it. Paul uses the verb "to nourish" in his injunction to fathers "to bring up" their children (Eph 6:4).[552] Paul uses the latter verb, "to care for," only one other time, as he describes himself as a nurse who gently cares for her own children (1 Thess 2:7).[553] The picture is of a personal, intimate relationship.

The context indicates that Paul speaks about husbands loving their own bodies. He does not have in mind training the body for athletic games or shaping the body's physique, but rather the man treating his body tenderly and gently. This is the way Christ behaves toward the church, for believers are members of his body. Ephesians 5:30 begins with the conjunction "for" and follows with the plural noun "members" and concludes with a genitive phrase "of his body."[554] The church is his body and experiences the fullness of Christ (1:22–23). Each believer is a member of Christ's body, and together the church is Christ's body. Christ cares for his church because the church

---

550. On σάρξ see BDAG 914–16. On σῶμα see BDAG 983–84 (1).
551. On μισέω see BDAG 652–53 (1).
552. On ἐκτρέφω see BDAG 311.
553. On θάλπω see BDAG 442. For a deeper discussion on maternal imagery, see Beverly R. Gaventa, *Our Mother Saint Paul* (Louisville: Westminster John Knox, 2007). See also Jennifer Houston McNeel, *Paul as Infant and Nursing Mother: Metaphor, Rhetoric, and Identity in 1 Thessalonians 2:5–8* (Atlanta: SBL, 2014), 147, who explains that the metaphor is "deeply emotional," for "even as the image is a hierarchical one, it is also filled with intimacy, nurture, and love, implying that Paul would do anything for the Thessalonian church."
554. Some manuscripts include "out of his flesh and out of his bones" drawing on Gen 2:23, however, Best, 550–51, rightly argues that "the textual evidence for inclusion is weaker than for exclusion." See also Hoehner, 769–70n3, and Lincoln, 380.

is his body. The same creative power that brings husband and wife together to make one new flesh from two is able to bring all believers together as his body. In this short verse, Paul pulls together two key images of the church in this passage: his bride and his body.[555]

EXCURSUS: PRINCIPLE OF RECIPROCITY

Reciprocity is the social convention that insists on each member of the pair acting their part in the relationship.[556] Reciprocity relies on the circularity of gift giving and the obligation of a return.[557] Several characteristics of the principle of reciprocity should be noted. First, on the nature of gift giving, the ancient culture viewed reciprocity as social glue that held together a community.[558] While we today in the West value the "free" gift and decry obligation, the ancients would have had no disagreement with the phrase "there is no free lunch." Second, reciprocity often assumed an unequal or asymmetrical social relationship between members of a group. The highly stratified, hierarchical social configuration operated as the subordinate received social honor for submitting, and the superordinate retained the privileged position and assumed responsibility for the subordinate. Third, reciprocity functioned within the community, as neighbor helped neighbor with the expectation that the other would return the favor. Give aid to one who pays it back, and refuse to give to a stingy person.[559] The adage, "I'll scratch your back if you scratch mine," adequately sums up the ancient sentiments. This was the basis for the patronage system, which connected nonfamily members in tight webs of social and economic concerns. Life was hard, existence tenuous, families

---

555. Lincoln, 379.

556. Reciprocity existed within the larger cultural pattern of patronage. Alan B. Wheatley, *Patronage in Early Christianity: Its Use and Transformation from Jesus to Paul of Samosata*, Princeton Theological Monograph Series 160 (Eugene, OR: Pickwick, 2011), 1, writes: "In its various forms, patronage consisted of long term relationships, bonded by a reciprocal exchange of resources between partners of unequal position."

557. Peter Garnsey and Richard Saller, *The Roman Empire: Economy, Society, and Culture* (Berkeley: University of California Press, 1987), 149, explain that the Roman emperor gave benefactions to the Roman people, and the "reciprocity ethic dictated that they [subjects] make a return in the form of deference, respect and loyalty."

558. Barclay, *Paul and the Gift*, 23.

559. David A. deSilva, *Honor, Patronage, Kinship, and Purity: Unlocking New Testament Culture* (Downers Grove, IL: InterVarsity Press, 2000), 100, points to Seneca (*On Benefits* 4.18.1), who states: "How else do we live in security if it is not that we help each other by an exchange of good offices? It is only through the interchange of benefits that life becomes in some measure equipped and fortified against sudden disasters."

were vulnerable to illness, famine, and fate; reciprocal relationships offered a safety net and peace of mind in this precarious environment.[560]

Reciprocity functioned to join two halves of a socially unequal pair, including husband/wife, master/slave, and parent/child. Additionally, the patron/client system fits in here, often as freed slaves remained part of the household, but now with different legal status.[561] A patron provides a financial benefit to a client, who reciprocates by offering honor to his patron. The patron accepts his praise, and in turn, she likely continues to watch over the social and material needs of her client. For example, Paul honors Phoebe as his "benefactor" who met his needs and others within the church (Rom 16:2–3).

If we apply the concept of reciprocity to the church, we can point to Paul's encouragement to the Corinthians to contribute money to aid the Judean churches, who in turn will praise God for the Corinthians' generosity (2 Cor 9:11–13). Yet Paul did not embrace the hierarchical framework of reciprocity, but subverted and nuanced it according to gospel principles.[562] God is the father of all families (Eph 3:14–15), while leaders are slaves to the community as well as patrons responsible for the well-being of their clients, especially the needy in their midst.

---

31 Paul develops his argument that believers together are members of Christ's body, the church, by citing the opening passage on marriage in the Bible (Gen 2:24). The Genesis quotation explains the husband's responsibilities to his birth family so that his wife is not relegated to second-class status.[563] The customs both in ancient Israel and in Paul's day assumed that the bride left her

---

560. Barclay, *Paul and the Gift*, 25–31.

561. Zeba A. Crook, *Reconceptualising Conversion*, Beihefte zur Zeitschrift für die neutestamentliche Wissenschaft 130 (Berlin: de Gruyter, 2004), 68, explains: "Embedded within kinship is the institution of patronage and benefaction, taking on a form of fictive-kinship. . . . What we are left with is a constellation of social systems and social values, all of which are inter-related—kinship, as over-arching social structure, with the values of honour and shame informing the interaction of families and individuals, and the institution of patronage and benefaction embedded within kinship and informed by honour and shame."

562. Stanley E. Porter, "Paul, Virtues, Vices, and Household Codes," in *Paul in the Greco-Roman World: A Handbook*, ed. J. Paul Sampley, rev. ed. (London: Bloomsbury T&T Clark, 2016), 2:387, explains that Paul's "reciprocity is not based upon self-interest but is based upon the work of Christ, and in fact somewhat mitigates the reciprocity by appeal of all parties to a higher level of responsibility."

563. Best, 552, explains that the quotation follows the Septuagint and observes the use of ἄνθρωπος instead of ἀνήρ and the addition of οἱ δύο.

family, sometimes in a physical sense by moving to another town. She might have minimal contact with her birth family after her wedding. The husband continued in his father's trade or worked the family farm, but now he and his wife (and their children) made a new unit within the family.

Paul's citation of Gen 2:24 is quite close to the Septuagint, as well as to the quotation Jesus offers in answer to the question about whether it is lawful for a husband to divorce his wife (Matt 19:3–6).[564] Paul uses the preposition "for this reason" instead of the Septuagint's "because of" or "for the sake of," thereby keeping the focus on Christ and his church found in the previous verse.[565] Paul's argument about the unity of Christ and the church relies on Jesus's conviction about the indivisible bond between husband and wife in this life. Jesus also addresses the Sadducees' question about marriage and the resurrection of the body (Matt 22:23–33). He explains that marriage does not continue into the new creation. When we line up this teaching with Paul's discussion in Ephesians, we notice a constraint on the analogy of marriage and union of Christ and the church. The former is limited to this age, while the latter continues from this age into eternity.

Paul cites the Old Testament twice in the household codes, referring to marriage and to children obeying parents. The only other direct Old Testament quotation in Ephesians also occurs in a paraenetic section, where Paul draws on Ps 68:18 (Eph 4:8). Paul alludes to or echoes the Old Testament in his reference to all things being placed under Christ's feet (Eph 1:22; see Ps 8:6), the gentiles being far and now coming near to God (2:13; see Isa 57:19), Christ being the cornerstone of the church (Eph 2:20; see Isa 28:16), and Christ's death being a pleasing sacrifice (Eph 5:2; see Gen 8:21; Ezek 20:41). We might have an echo of the command to "love your neighbor as yourself" (Lev 19:18) in Paul's call for husbands to love their wives (Eph 5:25, 33). Paul shapes his theology and understanding of discipleship around these Old Testament quotations and allusions. The Old Testament guides Paul's expectations for unity—oneness between Jew and gentile and one-flesh-ness between husband and wife.

32 Paul refers back to the Genesis question as he speaks of "mystery," specifically the point that the two become one flesh.[566] Paul indicates that

---

564. In Matt 19:4 Jesus cites from Gen 1:27 that the creator "made them male and female" and this uncommon language for man (ἄρσην) and woman (θῆλυς) is used by Paul in Gal 3:28. This suggests that Paul, and other first-century Jews such as Matthew, were familiar with the Greek text of the creation narrative in the opening chapters of Genesis.

565. Thielman, 389, argues that Paul uses ἀντί to stress the unity of Christ and the church, his body, rather than the Septuagint's ἕνεκα. He observes that ἀντὶ τούτου "refers most naturally to the preceding statements about Christ's care for his church." Contra Best, 552, who sees no significance in the change.

566. Lincoln, 380.

the unity of Christ and his church is a "profound" mystery.[567] The adjective emphasizes the significance of this mystery.[568] Marriage, the two becoming one flesh, heralds the unity of Christ and his body.[569] It is not simply about marriage, nor is it only describing the church. Hermeneutically, Paul's rhetoric centers on its "christo-ecclesial" meaning.[570] Paul discovers beyond the natural sense of the Genesis passage a prefigured and now-realized truth, namely, that the redemptive work of God includes the union of Christ and the church. Less likely is that Paul uses "mystery" in a distinct sense here to refer to marriage.[571] Paul anticipates the Ephesians' bewilderment at his interpretation and so adds that he is "talking about" a mystery.[572] Paul uses "mystery" earlier in the epistle to describe what was previously hidden and now revealed, specifically the gospel (1:9; 3:9; 6:19), which proclaims gentiles as coheirs with Jews in the body of Christ (3:3–4).[573]

33 Having established that Christ is united to the church in such a way that believers are members of Christ's body, Paul returns to the social reality of actual marriages. Paul repeats his command that each husband is to "love his wife" (see also 5:25). The love is self-sacrificial and self-giving, as is Christ's love for the church. Paul speaks to individual husbands and uses the reflexive pronoun twice to reinforce reciprocity between husband and wife. The husband's wife is as his own self, which implies that the wife's husband is as her own body (see also 1 Cor 7:2–4). Paul repeats the term "respect" used in Eph 5:21, that believers submit to one another out of "reverence" for Christ. Interestingly, Paul does not repeat the call to submit, nor does Paul speak of the husband as "head." Instead, he points to the wife respecting her husband.[574]

As discussed above, the ontological hierarchy between husband and wife (male and female) in Paul's wider context was expressed in the social

---

567. Best, 557.

568. On μέγας see BDAG 623–24. See also Best, 554.

569. Lang, *Mystery and the Making of a Christian Historical Consciousness*, 104, explains that Paul speaks of mystery to describe the superimposition of the one-flesh reality of marriage and the oneness of Christ and his church, concluding: "The mystery is what emerges when the two are superimposed."

570. Lang, *Mystery and the Making of a Christian Historical Consciousness*, 104.

571. Lincoln, 380–81, rightly critiques this view.

572. Thielman, 390.

573. Lincoln, 381, explains that "in the other five occurrences of the term in Ephesians . . . , 'mystery' has reference to the once-hidden purpose of God which has now been revealed in Christ."

574. Snodgrass, 313, remarks on the misuse of Eph 5:21–33: "Christians must take a much more forceful stand against wife abuse and against all denigration of women," including demeaning attitudes and ridicule.

2. Children and Parents (6:1–4)

¹*Children, obey your parents in the Lord, for this is right.* ²*"Honor your father and mother"—which is the first commandment with a promise—*³*"so that it may go well with you and that you may enjoy long life on the earth."*
⁴*Fathers, do not exasperate your children; instead, bring them up in the training and instruction of the Lord.*

Paul continues with the second of three pairs in his household codes, as he focuses on the parent/child relationship. Consistent with his practice, Paul addresses the subordinate member of the pair first. In the previous pairing, Paul drew on Old Testament teachings, and he will do the same as he addresses children. Paul engaged with his culture's categories and spoke counterculturally as he undermined the strict hierarchical patterns of husbands to wives. So too, here, his words to children seem to reinforce the status quo; however, when we realize that he addresses slave children alongside free and freed children, we grasp the revolutionary potential of his message. Paul's actions in speaking publicly to children creates an inclusive environment that welcomes children as church participants.[575] Church is their "home" and "family." All children are promised life in Christ as members of Christ's body, the church, and coheirs in Christ as God's people (2:14–19; 3:6). On average, younger children made up about 40 percent of a congregation and were active participants in the worship liturgy.[576]

---

575. Margaret Y. MacDonald, *The Power of Children: The Construction of Families in the Greco-Roman World* (Waco, TX: Baylor University Press, 2014), 153, writes that "in Col 3:20 and Eph 6:1, the 'performative' quality of children being called out by name in the midst of the assembly *constructs* a world of belonging: children are drawn into the community and a sense of membership and allegiance is reinforced."

576. Blake Leyerle, "Children and 'the Child' in Early Christianity," in *The Oxford Handbook of Childhood and Education in the Classical World*, ed. Judith Evans Grubbs and Tim Parkin (Oxford: Oxford University Press, 2013), 566–57. Leyerle concludes: "The first significant difference that Christianity made to the lives of children was an enhanced attention to their lives and pursuits. This surge of interest was prompted in part by their visible presence and active participation in religious rites and rituals" (566).

1–3 Paul commands children to obey their parents.[577] In this he follows his culture, and most cultures then and now. He makes a similar charge to the Colossians (3:20–21).[578] In both letters, moreover, Paul warns fathers against exasperating or provoking their children, and in Ephesians, Paul commands that they nurture and educate them in the Lord. Expressing the same concern but from a different angle, Paul lists as a sign of wickedness those who disobey their parents (Rom 1:30). Paul does not define children by their age, for in his culture, adult children should respect their parents, who have much legal and social authority over them.[579]

In Ephesians, Paul makes the qualification that children obey "in the Lord."[580] The phrase modifies the verb "to obey," not the direct object "parents."[581] This phrase may limit obedience to those parents who are believers, but more likely it explains how the child obeys, namely, he or she fulfills Christian duty in obeying his or her parents.[582] When we compare this command to the previous one given to husbands, to love their wives as Christ loved the church, we see the importance of modeling behavior on Christ's own humble service. Interestingly, when some commentators look at the phrase "in the Lord," they speak of the similarity between wives obeying their husbands and children obeying their parents.[583] Yet Paul is clear that wives "submit" to their husbands, and this is not given as an imperative, but rather as a participle linked with the previous verse that believers submit to each other out of reverence for Christ (5:21–22). Had Paul wished to use the verb "obey" when speaking of wives, he could have done so and would have been well in line with his wider culture that viewed adult women as having much in common with children from a legal standpoint and with regards to rational thought.

Paul continues that obedience to parents is "right" or fitting. Colossians expresses a similar idea, "in all things" (Col 3:20). The injunction carried an

---

577. On ὑπακούω see BDAG 1028–29.

578. The similarities include using the same first five terms, "the children, obey the parents" after which Ephesians includes the plural possessive pronoun "your" and "in the Lord" and Colossians instead reads "in everything" (3:20). The final clauses in the sentences are also similar, as both begin "for this is," and then Ephesians adds "right" while Colossians finishes "pleasing in the Lord."

579. On τέκνον see BDAG 994–95.

580. The phrase ἐν κυρίῳ is missing from B D* F G. However, it is likely original, based on its inclusion in P46 ℵ A, with much external support. Paul uses this phrase elsewhere in Ephesians—2:21; 4:1, 17; 5:8; 6:10, 21. See Lincoln, 402; Arnold, 416.

581. Lincoln, 402; Fowl, 193.

582. Arnold, 415–16. Contra Best, 564.

583. Lincoln, 402. Thielman, 376, writes: "Christ is the submissive party's authority, and when wives, children, and slaves render obedience, they do so out of obedience to Christ, not because of any innate authority in the male head of the household." See also Salmond, 366, who stresses the wife's obedience.

6:1-4 CHILDREN AND PARENTS

implicit limitation, for no one assumed it was fitting for a child to obey her father when asked to commit a crime, or his mother if asked to behave immorally. To the question of whether a son should obey his father if the latter forbids him to study philosophy, Musonius Rufus answers that philosophy is obeying the gods, and this is the son's higher calling. He announces that the son has the duty to obey the father of all, Zeus, over his individual father.[584]

Paul cites Scripture in support of his point. The quotation is close to the Greek text of Exod 20:12 and Deut 5:16, with the omission of the final clause "that the LORD your God is giving you." This exclusion allows Paul to generalize the "land" as the place where believers live, in this case Ephesus.[585] This is the second time Paul cites Scripture in the household codes, and here the verse fills out the definition of "obey" as it commands children to "honor" father and mother. By honoring parents, children show respect. Obeying parents displays the child's respect for the parent's wisdom.[586]

The fifth commandment promises that an obedient child will have a good and long life. How might Paul understand this promise in light of the gospel message? First, he would not imagine that it means a life without suffering, for he declares that believers face suffering for their testimony to Christ (6:10-13) and should live a life of self-giving service (2:10; 4:2, 12). He is imprisoned as he writes, because of his apostolic witness (3:1; 4:1). Nor can it mean a life of many years, for he encourages the Thessalonians not to grieve their dead as those who have no hope, for all will see the return of Christ (1 Thess 4:13).[587] Paul likely speaks about the quality of life when he speaks of life "going well," for when one acts in accordance with God's plan, one enjoys in the deepest sense God's favor. Jesus promises that his yoke is easy and his burden is light (Matt 11:30), *and* he asks his disciples to take up their cross and follow after him (Matt 16:24). The good life is one walked with Jesus, for the journey's blessed end is sure.

Paul describes this commandment, the fifth of ten, as the "first" commandment with a promise. The problem with this claim is that the second commandment against worshiping idols seems to give a promise. Paul's description has puzzled commentators since the third century when Origen questioned Paul's meaning of "first."[588] Typically, the term means first in a list

---

584. Musonius Rufus, 16.30-31, 104-6. See his collected and translated work in Lutz, *Musonius Rufus: "The Roman Socrates."*

585. Thielman, 400n5, demonstrates that Paul follows Exod 20:12 LXX. See also Best, 565-66.

586. On τιμάω see BDAG 1004-5 (2). Salmond, 375, speaks of obeying as doing one's duty and of showing honor as displaying one's disposition.

587. Fowl, 194, concludes: "Long life in itself is not an ultimate goal for Christians."

588. On πρῶτος see BDAG 892-94. Best, 566, states that Origen (and Jerome) suggested that Paul may be treating the Decalogue as a single unit.

of things. Some commentators, however, nuance the term to mean the first in importance or significance.[589] Others suggest that the apparent promise of the second commandment is rather a description of the God who warns against idol worship (Exod 20:3–6).[590] Most likely, Paul means "first" in the list of the Ten Commandments that offers a direct and specific promise for obeying a direct charge. The second commandment to avoid idolatry describes God's character as one who blesses those who follow his commandments.

EXCURSUS: CHILDREN IN THE GRECO-ROMAN WORLD

To grasp the nuances of Paul's expectations, we must appreciate his context.[591] In three important ways, the category of "child" differs widely from the common Western understanding.[592] First, the ancient world did not hold to a developmental model of childhood, as does the West today. Instead of seeing stages of growth in cognitive and emotional abilities, the ancient world saw the child as a miniature adult in need of strict discipline so as to grow straight. Plato spoke of tutors training children much as herdsmen watch their animals, for children are "treacherous, sly and insolent" until they develop reason.[593] Seneca spoke of children as irrational, and Marcus Aurelius laments his current mindset by asking: "Whose soul inhabits me at the moment? A child's, a [youth's], a woman's, a tyrant's, a dumb ox's, or a wild beast's?"[594] Ancient Roman society believed character was set at birth and that circumstances merely revealed what was already true about the person. Romans did not romanticize childhood, and indeed, it was a period of great peril. Only about half the children born lived beyond age ten,[595] and most were working in fields or shops by the time their adult teeth came in (about age seven).

---

589. Best, 567, concludes: "In the end may it not be simplest to take first as indicating a pre-eminent commandment, one of great importance because it is included in the Decalogue and has a promise?"

590. Lincoln, 404; Arnold, 416–17.

591. Thielman, 396, offers an extensive list of Greco-Roman sources that discuss the duties of children.

592. For a general overview, see Cohick, "Women, Children, and Families in the Roman World."

593. Plato, *Laws* 7.808d; translation from Hering, *Colossian and Ephesian Haustafeln*, 208.

594. Marcus Aurelius, *Meditations* 4.23. See Sharon Betsworth, *Children in Early Christian Narratives* (London: Bloomsbury T&T Clark, 2015), 9.

595. Osiek and MacDonald, *Woman's Place*, 78, citing Keith Bradley, "Images of Childhood," in *Plutarch's Advice to the Bride and Groom and a Consolation to His Wife*, ed. Sarah B. Pomeroy (Oxford: Oxford University Press, 1999), 184.

Excursus: Children in the Greco-Roman World

If the ancient world did not romanticize childhood, nevertheless they did love their children. In the funerary art preserved from this period as recorded in panels of a sarcophagus, a son might be shown playing rough games outside or practicing public speaking, while a daughter might be shown playing a lyre or involved in a game inside. Both might be shown at their mother's breast, and both parents are portrayed as grieving their child's death.[596] Plutarch's letter to his wife on the death of their two-year-old daughter, Timoxena, represents a philosophical approach espoused by the elite and presumably followed by the people.[597] Plutarch remembers fondly his daughter's joyful, gentle, and kind spirit, how she shared her toys. She was their fifth child, after four boys; his wife grieved deeply at her loss. Plutarch's overriding concern, however, is not to eulogize his daughter, but to instruct his wife to contain and restrain any show of grief and thus bring honor to the family. A century earlier, Cicero bragged about his daughter as being "the image of my face and speech and mind."[598] Tullia died through childbirth complications, and he mourned her death.[599]

Second, the ancient world emphasized the responsibilities of adult children toward their parents as the highest form of piety apart from worship of the deity.[600] Adult children were expected to care for their aged parents. Children were not to be independent or on their own. On the one hand, the church follows this principle in urging families to care for their aged relatives (1 Tim 5:8). On the other hand, the church family supplanted the biological family as the locus of loyalty. The early-third-century martyrdom account of Perpetua highlights the tension. She rejects her father's pleas to renounce Christianity

---

596. For a general description of sarcophagi art, see Janet Huskinson, "Representing Women on Roman Sarcophagi," in *The Material Culture of Sex, Procreation, and Marriage in Premodern Europe*, ed. Anne L. McClanan and Karen Rosoff Encarnación (New York: Palgrave, 2002), 17–19.

597. Plutarch, *Consolation to His Wife*.

598. Cicero, *Letters to Quintus* 3.1.3 (translation from D. R. Shackleton Bailey, Loeb Classical Library). See discussion in Cohick, *Women in the World of the Earliest Christians*, 34.

599. Cole, *Cicero and the Rise of Deification at Rome*, 1, explains that Cicero made two innovations in mourning his daughter's death: (1) he wrote his own consolation and (2) he "proposes to turn his deceased daughter into a god."

600. Hanne Sigismund-Nielsen, "Vibia Perpetua—an Indecent Woman," in *Perpetua's Passions: Multidisciplinary Approaches to the Passio Perpetuae et Felicitatis*, ed. Jan N. Bremmer and Marco Formisano (Oxford: Oxford University Press, 2012), 112, remarks: "It is no exaggeration to say that pagan Roman society was built on the notion of *pietas*." See also Judith Evans Grubbs, "Promoting Pietas through Roman Law," in *A Companion to Families in the Greek and Roman Worlds*, ed. Beryl Rawson (London: Wiley-Blackwell, 2010), 377, who explains the difficulties in translating the Latin noun: "'Family feeling' is too nebulous, and 'sense of duty and responsibility to family members (and to the gods and the state)' conveys the idea only very imperfectly and leaves out the more affective aspect of *pietas*."

and thereby humiliates him.[601] Augustine, writing about two hundred years later, explains that Perpetua was a loyal daughter, and so the devil used her father in an attempt to have her renounce her faith. Augustine argues that she did in fact follow her familial duty, because she grieved her father's lack of faith. It was the devil, not her father, to whom she showed disloyalty.[602]

Third, within the church gathering, both slave and free children hear Paul's message. An ancient household raised slave children together with free children; they ate the same food and had the same access to health care (that is, to what would have passed as health care in Roman antiquity).[603] Slave children had no official father, and many did not know their father or their mother. Instead, their owner served as the authority over them. Yet in the church they would have surrogate fathers and mothers who cared for them in the Lord. It likely happened that a believing slave woman or man who minded their household's children would bring both free and slave children to the house church.[604] The slave child could expect no inheritance; the slave boy was a *filius neminis*, a son of no one. Thus, Paul's language of adoption must have excited them and perhaps perplexed some free people in the congregation. The classicist Sarah Ruden points to the strong desire for inheritance as a badge of honor in the ancient world and paraphrases Paul's message: "We offer you an equal share of the community, such as most of you could only dream of before."[605]

Couples expected children to result from marriage, for birth control was essentially nonexistent.[606] Infant mortality (and maternal death) was

---

601. *Martyrdom of Perpetua and Felicitas* 5.4; translation in Thomas J. Heffernan, *The Passion of Perpetua and Felicity* (Oxford: Oxford University Press, 2012). Keith R. Bradley, "Sacrificing the Family: Christian Martyrs and Their Kin," in *Apuleius and Antonine Rome: Historical Essays* (Toronto: University of Toronto Press, 2012), 107, observes: "Through the vehicle of martyrdom Christianity promoted familial discord in a way that was new, and not at all part of the Roman family experience in the pre-Christian epoch." See also Keith R. Bradley, *Discovering the Roman Family: Studies in Roman Social History* (Oxford: Oxford University Press, 1991).

602. Augustine, Sermon 281.2, in *The Works of Saint Augustine: A Translation for the 21st Century, Sermons III/18 (273–305A) on the Saints*, translation and notes by Edmund Hill (New York: New City Press, 1994), 78–79.

603. MacDonald, *Power of Children*, 36–48. Christian Laes, *Children in the Roman Empire: Outsiders Within* (Cambridge: Cambridge University Press, 2011), 22–49. He explains that the "skeletal remains of the male and female adults aged over 20 bear traces of prolonged exertion, pointing at labour activity from childhood" (154). Peter Garnsey, *Food and Society in Classical Antiquity* (Cambridge: Cambridge University Press, 1999), 52–53, explains that skeleton evidence shows diets deficient in protein, plus vitamins A and D.

604. MacDonald, *Power of Children*, 70–75, 92.

605. Ruden, *Paul among the People*, 37, 164–65.

606. The second-century CE physician Soranus in *Gynecology* 1.60, 65, outlines techniques for abortion.

Excursus: Children in the Greco-Roman World

quite high, about one in five births. And the percentage grows over the next few years, to about 35 percent of all toddlers dying in their first few years.[607] In addition, infanticide and exposure of newborns were accepted practices within gentile communities.[608] Circumstantial evidence suggests that more female than male babies were exposed, as we have double the number of wet-nurse contracts to care for female foundlings. Both Jews and Christians spoke strongly against infanticide, and later church writers encouraged believers to raise exposed children.[609] By the age of seven, most children were doing work in the home or shop, and some boys began their studies in school. We have little evidence about girls specifically, but the hints we have suggest that they attended school when they were young. Most girls, and slave boys, however, would be educated at home as they grew older.[610] By age ten, only 75 percent of children had a living father, and once they reached adulthood, many had lost both parents.

Two historical realities, the sexual exploitation of slave children and the use of children in Roman imperial propaganda art, must be emphasized for us to understand the impact of Paul's message to children. The Greco-Roman culture accepted the sexual use of slave boys and girls (usually above the age of seven) by male slave owners, who might prostitute them. An important caveat: we have no evidence that Jewish families treated slaves this way, and the sexual mores of the Old Testament would condemn sex with slaves. The condemnation included sex with both boys and girls and was heard from Jewish authors such as Philo and Josephus, as well as Christian writers in the early second century.[611]

Within gentile culture, however, sexual activities with child slaves were celebrated in art and literature. The Warren Cup from the first century CE includes sex scenes with a slave boy and of a child viewing a sex act. A lengthy poem eulogizes the death of a twelve-year-old slave boy named Glaucias, a

---

607. Laes, *Children in the Roman Empire*, 27.

608. Judith Evans Grubbs, "Infant Exposure and Infanticide," in *The Oxford Handbook of Childhood and Education in the Classical World*, ed. Judith Evans Grubbs and Tim Parkin with Roslynne Bell (Oxford: Oxford University Press, 2013), 83–84.

609. Josephus, *Against Apion* 2.24 §§202–3; Philo, *On the Special Laws* 3.110–19. See also Didache 2:2; Barnabas 19:5.

610. Osiek and MacDonald, *Woman's Place*, 86. Inscriptions provide evidence of girls' education, but intellectual acuity was not among the celebrated female virtues; therefore, the paucity of monuments dedicated to women of learning might not reflect the actual lives of most women as having some education.

611. Philo, *On the Life of Abraham* 133; *On the Special Laws* 3.37–42; *On the Contemplative Life* 60–62; Josephus, *Jewish Antiquities* 1.11.3 §§200–201; *Against Apion* 2.37 §§273–75. See the discussion in Laes, *Children in the Roman Empire*, 269–70. Christian texts include Didache 2:2; Barnabas 10:8.

delicium or sexual favorite of his owner.[612] The most famous *delicium* was Antinous, the handsome adolescent consort of Emperor Hadrian.[613] He died tragically, and Hadrian ordered that temples and cities across the Roman Empire erect statues in his honor. With the exception of Augustus and Hadrian, more statues of Antinous survive than of any other ancient figure.[614]

The sexual use of slave children affected the church, inasmuch as sexually used children attended, and likely the adult slave members had been used for sexual pleasure by their owners. Paul's insistence throughout Ephesians that believers have put on Christ, are "in Christ," and are accepted as members in God's household must have sounded almost too good to be true to those who suffered sexual violation.[615] And believers who owned slaves now were challenged to view their slaves as in Christ; to violate a believing slave was to violate Christ.

The Romans depicted children in different ways to demonstrate their imperial power. In the wider artistic depiction of children, we see sons linked with imperial Rome and daughters connected with defeated armies.[616] Roman children are shown in scenes that reveal their high status, such as being part of a public event with the emperor. While the art distinguishes Roman and non-Roman children, the historical situation included much mingling and integration of the two. Non-Roman children tend to be associated with their mothers, not fathers. An exception would be when non-Roman fathers give their children to the emperor. For example, the Boscoreale Cup portrays children given by defeated fathers to the emperor.[617] This child-transfer motif signals the victory of Rome. Non-Roman children are most commonly presented in submissive poses.[618] What would this mean for children in Ephesus?

---

612. Laes, *Children in the Roman Empire*, 223–30.

613. Caroline Vout, *Power and Eroticism in Imperial Rome* (Cambridge: Cambridge University Press, 2007), 67, explains: "Romans routinely found sexual pleasure in their slaves: no doubt they wished that theirs were as attractive as Antinous."

614. Vout, *Power and Eroticism in Imperial Rome*, 53.

615. MacDonald, *Power of Children*, 152.

616. Maureen Carroll, *Infancy and Earliest Childhood in the Roman World: "A Fragment of Time"* (Oxford: Oxford University Press, 2018), 118–46. Jeannine Diddle Uzzi, "The Power of Parenthood in Official Roman Art," in *Constructions of Childhood in Ancient Greece and Italy*, ed. Ada Cohen and Jeremy B. Rutter, Hesperia Supplement 41 (Princeton: American School of Classical Studies in Athens, 2007), 64, concludes that the images show "that the visual language of parenthood is consistently employed by the Roman ruling elite to mark the power and political potential of children."

617. Uzzi, "Power of Parenthood in Official Roman Art," 76, includes a photo of the cup.

618. Uzzi, "Power of Parenthood in Official Roman Art," 72, adds that "scenes of violent military activity are those in which the non-Roman mother-child pair is most prominent in Roman art."

6:1–4 Children and Parents

Rome's political propaganda and the military dominance reinforced some children's lack of social worth and normalized physical violence against non-Romans. By contrast, Paul respects children by addressing them publicly as his letter is read aloud for everyone to hear.

---

4 Paul contrasts two behaviors of fathers, namely, frustrating their children and raising them well. He reflects the longstanding expectation that parents will oversee their child's proper development. Plato taught that it is natural and just for a father and mother to rule their children.[619] Aristotle discussed the household using the same three pairs we find in Paul. The classical philosopher argued that a father rules his son as a king his subject, but sees the rule as primarily offering guidance.[620] Aristotle held that fathers are obligated to instruct and care for their children.[621] Paul expresses a similar sentiment, commanding that fathers not provoke, or that they stop exasperating, their children.[622] The cognate noun is used earlier as Paul warns believers against allowing anger to rule them (Eph 4:26).[623] Why might Paul single out fathers here, for surely mothers can also exasperate their children?[624] The hierarchical social structure bestowed on fathers the power to make ultimate decisions over a child's future as well as oversee daily chores and schooling.[625]

Fathers are commanded to bring up their children well, to nurture and "bring them up." Paul repeats the verb used earlier to describe the husband's care of his wife as he "feeds" his own body (5:29). If a man is both a husband and father, he would hear twice within a few sentences that his behavior toward those society has entrusted to his care must be treated as he would like to be treated. Paul encourages training and offering instruction of the Lord.[626]

---

619. Plato, *Laws* 3.690a–b.
620. Aristotle, *Politics* 1259b.
621. Aristotle, *Nicomachean Ethics* 8.11.3.
622. On παροργίζω see BDAG 780.
623. The only other time the verb παροργίζω is used in the New Testament is in a quotation from Deut 32:21, cited by Paul in Rom 10:19.
624. Lincoln, 406, points to οἱ πατέρες as an example of the plural "fathers" rightly translated "parents."
625. Arnold, 417; Lincoln, 406. Yet a husband might work with his wife in managing family affairs. For example, Cicero's wife, Terentia, oversaw the third marriage of her daughter during the period of Cicero's proconsul duties in Cilicia in 51 BCE. Therefore, Arnold, 418, goes beyond the evidence when he states: "Fathers are ultimately responsible for their children's spiritual and religious education."
626. On παιδεία see BDAG 748–49 (1). On νουθεσία see BDAG 679.

The genitive "of the Lord" can be understood as Christ instructing children through their fathers (subjective genitive),[627] but more likely the sense is that instruction centered on the Lord (objective genitive).[628]

Education was treated with great seriousness in the ancient world, and many philosophers wrote about proper content and pedagogy or manners of teaching. As told by Hermogenes (second century CE), the ancient philosopher Isocrates (436–338 BCE) was known for his saying, "The root of education is bitter but its fruit is sweet."[629] A father's authority was commonly expressed through a beating with a whip.[630] Dionysius of Halicarnassus (30–7 BCE) spoke favorably about Roman tradition that promoted children obeying parents in every way and fathers using as much physical force as necessary to ensure obedience. He explains that a father had more control over his son than a master did over his or her slave.[631] By the first century CE, philosophers such as Seneca softened the punitive nature of education in favor of arguing that hardship was formative to developing endurance and courage. The author of Hebrews picks up on this sentiment, declaring that God as the Father of believers disciplines his adult children to increase their endurance and build their character (Heb 12:5–11). He speaks of Jesus's learning through suffering, using a catchy phrase in Greek that is similar to the English "no pain/no gain" (Heb 5:8).[632] And Hebrews makes the common observation that while discipline or education seems difficult in the moment, it brings great reward. The Jewish sect of the Essenes promoted kindness and humility in teaching their children, drawing on Mic 6:8.[633] Both girls and boys were taught the beliefs and practices of the group, as well as Scripture.[634]

Both mother and father taught their children, with mothers especially important in the education of young children. A few famous women of the late Roman Republic, such as Cornelia the mother of the Gracchi, were praised for educating her sons; while Hortensia, one of few women who addressed the

---

627. Arnold, 418.

628. Lincoln, 408.

629. Hermogenes, *Preliminary Exercises* 3.7. See George A. Kennedy, *Progymnasmata: Greek Textbooks of Prose Composition and Rhetoric* (Leiden: Brill, 2003), 77.

630. Laes, *Children in the Roman Empire*, 141–43.

631. Dionysius of Halicarnassus, *Roman Antiquities* 2.27.1.

632. Ἔμαθεν . . . ἔπαθεν (Heb 5:8). See discussion in David A. deSilva, "How Greek Was the Author of 'Hebrews'?," in *Christian Origins and Greco-Roman Culture: Social and Literary Contexts for the New Testament*, ed. Stanley E. Porter and Andrew W. Pitts, Early Christianity in Its Hellenistic Context 1 (Leiden: Brill, 2013), 630.

633. CD 13:7–19; see Cecilia Wassen, *Women in the Damascus Document* (Atlanta: Scholars Press, 2005), 164–65.

634. Wassen, *Women in the Damascus Document*, 165–67, cites several Qumran texts. She also points to Josephus, *Jewish War* 2.8.12 §159.

6:1-4 CHILDREN AND PARENTS

Roman Senate, is honored as well educated by her father.[635] From a second-century CE letter we learn that Eudaimonis, a grandmother, oversees the education of her granddaughter on behalf of her daughter-in-law, Aline, who lives in another town. Aline visited her mother, leaving behind some money and slaves to aid her mother with her weaving.[636] In this we see an example of the common practice of adult children caring for their parents, and the grandparents deeply involved with their children's and grandchildren's lives. A similar picture emerges from the brief remarks about Timothy's upbringing, overseen by his grandmother Lois and mother Eunice (2 Tim 1:5 with 3:15).

Parents educating children, therefore, was a central feature in the Roman world and also in the earliest house churches. MacDonald concludes that children's education was "a determining factor in the shape and growth of early Christianity."[637] As the church sang hymns and spiritual songs, children learned about God's character and their redemption. Perhaps Lois and Eunice sang psalms to Timothy as they raised him in the worship of the one God (2 Tim 1:5; 3:15). We must not assume that children had their birth parents with them, for by age ten as many as 25 percent of children lost their father. Again, about 20 to 25 percent of a congregation would be made up of slaves, including slave children who did not know who their fathers were and slave parents who had no official rights over their flesh and blood. The church, therefore, included believers who took the role of surrogate parents and helped educate children.

Interestingly, in a countercultural move, Paul does not link human fathers with God the Father. Several centuries before Paul, Aristotle established his position on human fathers and children by pointing to Zeus, drawing on Homer who explains that Zeus is "father" because he cares for humans.[638] Philo, a Jewish author writing in the first century CE, argues along similar lines, but based on his understanding of the fifth commandment. Philo believes parents should receive honor because it accords with nature, and, pragmatically, parents nourish and educate their children. He argues that parents are midway between the divine and human nature. Like the former, they beget life; like the latter, they have been born, and they will die. Philo insists that parents are the supreme benefactors after God, for they both feed their children and educate them in body, mind, and social decorum. Children honor their parents in part by living a virtuous life, as they have been trained to do.[639]

---

635. Osiek and MacDonald, *Woman's Place*, 84-85; see also Cohick, *Women in the World of the Earliest Christians*, 34, 45-46.
636. Cohick, *Women in the World of the Earliest Christians*, 45.
637. MacDonald, *Power of Children*, 151.
638. Aristotle, *Nicomachean Ethics* 8.10.4.
639. Philo, *On the Special Laws* 2.224-36.

Paul does not link the human father with the heavenly Father, nor does he explain the father's role as similar to God's role in caring for his people.[640] Fathers are not asked specifically to model their behavior after God, most likely because all believers are to exemplify Christ and walk in his love (5:2). Interestingly, Paul speaks of God as the father of all families on earth and heaven (3:14–15). It is to this God that he prays for believers to know the magnitude of Christ's love (3:16–18). And Paul confesses it is this Father of all who is over all and through all and in all (4:6). The human father's role offers no comparison; instead, Paul insists that the father act toward his children with the same responsible care that a husband does to his wife and believers do toward each other. Once again, the privilege of the superordinate is reversed.

There might be another reason that Paul does not link fathers with the heavenly Father. The commandment cited speaks of honoring father *and mother*. It is not only the father, but also the mother who is to be obeyed and honored. Paul singles out the father in 6:4 because Roman society gives him more legal control over children, not because the father is the more important parent in God's sight. The ideology of the Roman family centered on the paterfamilias, the eldest male of the family. In philosophical writings, some Roman authors speak about the absolute authority of the father over his family, for he gives life (literally in his sperm) and thus has the power to put his child to death.[641] In point of fact, the paterfamilias did not have such power, although he did have authority to choose the husband for his adult daughter or send his adult son to work on the family's rural estate or withdraw from school.[642] Richard Saller explains that the term "paterfamilias" is typically found in legal texts and relates to running the family estate. Therefore, the term denotes estate ownership and not tyrannical parenting.[643]

---

640. Judith M. Gundry-Volf, "The Least and the Greatest: Children in the New Testament," in *The Child in Christian Thought*, ed. Marcia J. Bunge (Grand Rapids: Eerdmans, 2001), 56.

641. Dionysius of Halicarnassus, *Roman Antiquities* 2.27.1–2.

642. Betsworth, *Children in Early Christian Narratives*, 8.

643. Richard P. Saller, "*Pater Familias, Mater Familias*, and the Gendered Semantics of the Roman Household," *Classical Philology* 94 (1999): 188, concludes: "As the figure who exercised *potestas* over his children the paterfamilias was emphatically male. But in its barest sense, *pater familias* was used by jurists to denote no more than a property owner *sui iuris* (of his own right) and by extension subsumed female owners." He notes that daughters inherited with their brothers under Roman law, if she were *sui iuris* or had her own rights. See also Beth Severy, *Augustus and the Family at the Birth of the Roman Empire* (New York: Routledge, 2004).

3. Slaves and Masters (6:5–9)

⁵*Slaves, obey your earthly masters with respect and fear, and with sincerity of heart, just as you would obey Christ.* ⁶*Obey them not only to win their favor when their eye is on you, but as slaves of Christ, doing the will of God from your heart.* ⁷*Serve wholeheartedly, as if you were serving the Lord, not people,* ⁸*because you know that the Lord will reward each one for whatever good they do, whether they are slave or free.*

⁹*And masters, treat your slaves in the same way. Do not threaten them, since you know that he who is both their Master and yours is in heaven, and there is no favoritism with him.*

EXCURSUS: SLAVERY AND INTERPRETATION OF THE HOUSEHOLD CODES TODAY

Ephesians 6:5–9 of the household codes is difficult to interpret today, particularly because we are dismayed that Paul does not critique the institution of slavery directly.[644] Yet to conclude that Paul ignores or tacitly accepts slavery fails to judge his words within their historical and theological context. As we look closely at context in 6:5–9, the astute reader will discern my assessment of the biblical text as more than a set of propositional truths understood merely by common sense. Such a flat reading often leads to prooftexting rather than to grasping the full account of God's redemptive work in Christ.[645] Moreover, it can hide preconceived notions about reality, as in the case of the racism that infected the American discussion of slavery. In assuming the Bible has no context but rather floats above all cultures, the reader might ignore or discount their own historical situation.

---

644. MacDonald, 341, rightly notes that "it is important to acknowledge that the text presents a vision of household relationships, rooted in an ancient setting, that is considered unjust today (and, in the case of slavery, completely immoral)." See also Jennifer A. Glancy, *Slavery in Early Christianity* (Oxford: Oxford University Press, 2002).

645. For an excellent discussion of hermeneutics and interpretations of key biblical passages that shaped the slavery debate in the United States, see Mark A. Noll, *The Civil War as a Theological Crisis* (Chapel Hill: University of North Carolina Press, 2006). Noll cites Philip Schaff, a German theologian who perceptively pointed to the underlying issue with American slavery: "*The negro question lies far deeper than the slavery question*" (51, emphasis original).

WHAT PAUL SAYS

Paul's language of salvation—redemption, justification, and reconciliation—draws on terms also used to describe a slave's freedom. Redemption in its most straightforward sense meant being redeemed from slavery.[646] The term connects with the concept of ransom and the idea of giving money to ensure release. We observed that Paul sees believers' redemption through Christ's blood, which provides forgiveness of sins (Eph 1:7; see also Acts 20:28). Justification for Paul entails a "not guilty" verdict for the believer "in much the same manner as the slave who has received the most perfect of manumissions, the restoration of his natality with the legal fiction that he had been wrongfully enslaved."[647] The third term, reconciliation, includes for Paul adoption into God's family.[648] Paul stresses this in his declaration that Christ is our peace (Eph 2:14) who made one new humanity from Jew and gentile. The scope of Christ's work on the cross extends from personal forgiveness to remaking the people of God, done in a single, redemptive motion of death-resurrection-ascension. The insistence on this new humanity jars modern Western sensibilities, so comfortable with individualism.

Reconciliation between brothers and sisters in the faith, regardless of social status or ethnic background, presents a powerful image of a new reality in Christ. This new status comes not because the slave died and so is released from his plight (e.g., through the noble suicide promoted by Seneca).[649] Instead, all believers are now "slaves" to God and to righteousness, because Christ Jesus died on their behalf (cf. Rom 6:17–18). As Orlando Patterson explains, Christ "annulled the condition of slavery in which man existed by returning to the original point of enslavement and . . . gave his own life so that the sinner might live and be free."[650] The church abandons this truth to

---

646. On ἀπολύτρωσις see BDAG 117.

647. On δικαιόω see BDAG 249 and Orlando Patterson, *Slavery and Social Death: A Comparative Study* (Cambridge: Harvard University Press, 1982), 70.

648. On καταλλάσσω see BDAG 521. Paul uses this verb in Rom 5:10 (twice); 1 Cor 7:11; 2 Cor 5:18–20. The cognate noun occurs in Rom 5:11; 11:15; 2 Cor 5:18, 19.

649. Seneca, *Epistles* 70.20–23, recalls the bravery exhibited by a German gladiator. This clever man asked that he might use the bathroom before going into the arena. It was the only room men were allowed to go without a guard. Once there the man grabbed a dirty sponge on a stick and shoved it down his throat, choking himself. Another man pretended to be falling asleep while riding in the cart heading to the arena. He let his head slowly sink down to his chest, then further through the bars of the cart, and at last between the spokes of the revolving wagon wheel, thus snapping his neck. But what a man should not choose is endurance without honor. Thus Seneca scoffs at Maecenas who desires above all to live through illness or torture, though it incapacitates him. He labels such extreme love of life "effeminate" (*effeminatus*) (*Epistles* 101.13).

650. Patterson, *Slavery and Social Death*, 71. Patterson fails to fully appreciate the es-

Excursus: Slavery and Interpretation of the Household Codes

its peril. An overemphasis on the justified sinner and the hope of eternal life in the hereafter relegates the present moment to secondary importance. The stress on spiritual change and the disinterest in social realities allows social injustices to be ignored as not relevant to the eternal destiny of the soul. But reconciliation in Christ between all believers reminds us that not only is the individual redeemed by the cross, but the cross creates a new humanity.

In Paul's time, Christians numbered as a fraction of society and often lived at the margins; therefore, social change would seem beyond reach. Yet the broad testimony of the New Testament indicates that the wider society noticed a difference in the Christian community. When the Thessalonian townspeople cry out against Paul as a dangerous man, the charge is that he envisions a different empire, with a different emperor (Acts 17:5–9). The gospel proclaims that God's kingdom admits no social hierarchy and that its king is a crucified and risen lord. The early Christians did not tackle the Roman legal system, but they acted counterculturally by treating slaves as full members of their communities.[651] In the letter to the Ephesians, Paul addresses slaves directly as full members of Christ's body, God's children who await an inheritance. With this public recognition in front of slave owners, Paul honored slaves as worthy children of God.

Theologically speaking, Paul uses slavery as a metaphor for understanding his own calling and for explaining the importance of the bodily resurrection. First, Paul insists on describing himself as a slave of Christ.[652] This continues the biblical tradition of faithful Israelites declaring themselves servants of the one God.

Second, Paul understands humans to be trapped or enslaved by sin, which preys on the weakness of their mind and body (cf. Rom 6:17–20). Stoics taught that the body was to be discarded at the end of life, and thus saw little need to challenge slavery other than to argue for the master's moderation in controlling slaves. Unlike Stoics, Paul does not wish his mind to be freed from the body, but rather he desires Christ to free him, body and soul, from the clutches of this present evil age. The resurrection of the body cuts to the heart of slavery's power, for in Christ, the slave's body is not a commodity but a redeemed treasure of God. Slave masters do not "own" the slave, for his or

---

chatological aspect of Paul's theology that focused on the continuing struggle with the flesh during this age, but Patterson rightly laments that the symbolism of the believer as a slave of God supported the institution of slavery (72).

651. Ulrike Roth, "Paul and Slavery: Economic Perspectives," in *Paul and Economics*, ed. Raymond Pickett and Thomas R. Blanton IV (Minneapolis: Fortress, 2017), 160, argues that Paul was a co-owner with Philemon of the slave, Onesimus. Her questions are useful, but her conclusions rest on several weak assumptions and are unpersuasive.

652. See Rom 1:1; 2 Cor 4:5; Phil 1:1; Titus 1:1. See also the disciples James, Peter, and Jude; Jas 1:1; 2 Pet 1:1; Jude 1.

her body is eternal, sealed by the Holy Spirit, and beyond the master's reach. The doctrine of the resurrection impacts the view of the body now, bestowing dignity on it as God's possession.

Third, Paul speaks not only of himself as Christ's slave, but he remarks that the body of Christ, the church, is composed of slave and free members, even as they are also made up of Jew and gentile believers. He recounts to the Galatians the tense Jerusalem conference held early in the church's life (Gal 2:1-10; see also Acts 15). Paul fought against the proposal that gentile men needed to be circumcised to be full members of Christ's body. He spoke against the movement that encouraged Jewish believers to distance themselves from their fellow gentile believers vis-à-vis kosher laws.[653] Paul insists that the "separate but equal" approach inappropriately elevates the clean/unclean distinction that food laws perpetuate, thereby making gentiles second-class citizens in the kingdom of God. It is against this separateness that Paul reacts, and he concludes that "there is neither Jew nor Greek, neither slave nor free, nor is there male and female" (Gal 3:28).[654] Paul insists that all believers are in Christ, having been baptized and clothed with Christ (3:26-27).

Paul declared that gentiles remained gentiles, but left paganism. Jews remained Jews, but now followed the promised Messiah, Jesus of Nazareth. The unity came, not at the social, cultural, ethnic, or linguistic level, but at the foot of the cross. The unity experienced by the church is not an "either/or" but a "both/and."[655] But this does not mean that difference has been eliminated.[656] Brad Braxton comments that Paul "is not asserting the obliteration of difference, but rather the obliteration of *dominance*."[657] Paul spends most of his energy in Galatians on the first pair, Jew and gentile, but his interpretive principle holds for the second and third pairs. Those groupings are key in the Ephesians household codes. Paul eliminates the power of the superordinate—husband and (male or female) slave master—and elevates the importance and worth of the subordinate. By so doing, he effectively cuts the bottom out of the institutions of patriarchy and slavery.

---

653. Brad Ronnell Braxton, *No Longer Slaves: Galatians and African American Experience* (Collegeville, MN: Liturgical Press, 2002), 75, observes: "The food laws gave tangible, ritual, and regular expression to the principle that Jews were to maintain their separateness from Gentiles."

654. In the third pair "male and female," the language echoes Gen 1:27 LXX.

655. Braxton, *No Longer Slaves*, 69, writes: "Many African Americans would share Paul's understanding of unity, namely that unity is not an antithesis (either/or) but rather a dialectic (both/and)."

656. Bock, *Ephesians*, 80-81, explains, "There is no segregation in Christ, even in the midst of recognizing a distinction in where each group came from before being united, for reconciliation is only clear when the former estrangement is appreciated."

657. Braxton, *No Longer Slaves*, 94 (emphasis original).

Excursus: Slavery and Interpretation of the Household Codes

WHAT PAUL DOES NOT SAY

Some interpreters state that Paul never addresses the problem of evil social structures, for it is the transformation of individuals that will make a new society.[658] But Paul knew Israel's history and the call of God toward social action and responsibility. Even as God rescued the Israelites from slavery in Egypt, so too they were to show justice to strangers and aliens in their midst (Deut 15:15; 24:17–22). To argue that Christianity is about individuals is to ignore the social capital that so many Christians have today. Micah's words about justice should ring loudly in wealthy churches in the West (Mic 6:6–8).

In analyzing this section of the household codes, it might be tempting to talk about the *roles* that slaves played in society and to conclude that Paul affirms the duties performed by both slaves and owners. Some suggest that Paul spoke of slaves and masters as equal before Christ, but as having different roles and responsibilities and specific lines of authority.[659] Speaking of slaves as performing certain roles, however, masks the social reality that slaves were the property of another human.[660] The distinction was not at the level of roles—most jobs that slaves did were also done by free men and women. And it was not at the level of responsibilities, as though owners earned their place by greater intellect or other merit. The owner *dominated* the slave. The distinction was about social worth, even ontological worth. Slaves were human tools, Aristotle declared. The Roman legal system gave them almost no rights; generally speaking, the owner could kill his or her slave with impunity, and slaves were routinely beaten. This treatment was consistent with the belief that slaves were of lesser value. The institution of slavery included at its core the humiliation of the slave, denying the dignity of any past, present, or future.

Some argue that because he never asks the owner to submit to her slave, or the slave to command his master, that Paul is addressing lines of authority.[661] By zeroing in on the issue of authority, commentators implicitly connect the ancient system of slavery, including the slaves' roles and the owners' responsibilities, with a hierarchical position about the social structure of marriage today and its discussion about the roles of husbands and wives. This herme-

---

658. Hoehner, 804: "Christianity's emphasis has always been on the transformation of individuals who will in turn influence society, not the transformation of society which will then transform individuals (1 Cor 1:18–2:16)."

659. Hoehner, 804.

660. Bock, *Ephesians*, 192, rightly cautions that the analogy between a slave and today's employee is limited to the attitude with which believers should work. "The employee chooses by contract to give his or her labour and has options to continue that service or not under that contract. That difference is significant."

661. Hoehner, 804.

neutical move conceals the foundational beliefs that supported slavery and patriarchy, namely, the convictions that slaves were ontologically less human and women were less rational (human) than men. Without these fundamental beliefs, the systems of patriarchy and slavery would not have survived.[662]

Paul uses the social reality of slavery to make a theological point about believers being God's sons (children) who inherit. He states what was common knowledge, specifically, that a slave does not inherit, and contrasts this with sons and daughters who receive an inheritance at the proper time (Gal 4:1–7). As Sarah Ruden explains: "One of the greatest cruelties of slavery was that, having no legal family, a slave was boxed off in time, without a real tomb or recognized descendants or anything else to ensure he was remembered."[663] The social construct favored those in power and allowed those with money and influence to solidify their power.

The biblical case against slavery is strong, even in Ephesians. Paul undermined the basis of slavery, as well as sought immediate protection for slaves within the church.[664] He did so primarily by giving the slave their personhood and a family and an inheritance, as due them through the gospel of Jesus Christ. The reader requires an agile interpretative method that does not simply rely on common sense, but allows the exposure of the reader's blind spots, such as ethnic superiority and racism. It is true that the New Testament world did not know the white/black racism of the United States' experience. However, they share a deeper commonality with many cultures today, namely, the belief that one sort of person is superior to another. The ancient slave was inferior to the free person; in the United States, the black slave was inferior to the white owner.[665] The damage done to the slaves by this way

---

662. Schüssler Fiorenza, 106, rightly argues that simply observing the admonition to slave masters does not fully address the exegetical concerns. However, she goes further than I am willing to go in her call to reject the passage altogether: "Caution! Dangerous to your health and survival!"

663. Ruden, *Paul among the People*, 161.

664. John M. G. Barclay, "Paul, Philemon, and the Dilemma of Christian Slave-Ownership," *NTS* 37 (1991): 161–86, highlights the tension present in Paul, with an insistence on kinship language that promoted brotherhood and the reality of the institution of slavery. Barclay argues that a wealthy church member such as Philemon or Gaius (Rom 16:23) could not have hosted the church or maintained their social status without slave labor.

665. In 1854, the slave owner George Fitzhugh remarked: "Some men are born with saddles on their backs, and others booted and spurred to ride them, and the riding does them good"; cited in Braxton, *No Longer Slaves*, 16, from G. E. M. De Ste. Croix, *The Class Strug-*

of thinking is obvious; what is less apparent is the damage such superiority-minded ideology inflicts on the owners.[666] If pride is the greatest sin, then racist or ethnic prejudice could be the most dangerous human invention.

EXCURSUS: SLAVERY IN THE ANCIENT WORLD

The institution of slavery was widespread in the ancient world, with slaves making up about 10 percent of the population of the first-century Roman Empire. The number rises to about 30 percent, one in three persons, in the city of Rome.[667] The institution of slavery was woven into the fabric of ancient society, crucial for the political, economic, familial, and social hierarchy that framed the cultural landscape. Slavery was a legal category supported by codes and courts. It was a key component of the economic system as free men and women, freed persons, and slaves worked alongside each other in most jobs. Yet Paul includes slavery within the context of the household, because the basis of economic life was the home, not the factory or office. Much of the production of goods used by humans prior to the industrial revolution were made at home, thus slave labor was integral to household management. Perhaps most importantly, slaves formed the foundation, the basement, of the social hierarchy on which was built the imperial skyscraper. The Greco-Roman world esteemed honor above all else, and the slave was without social capital, even if he or she had material wealth. Orlando Patterson coined the apt phrase "social death" to describe the slave's life.[668] The graphic event of the slave on the block, stripped and examined as one would a horse for defects, bought and sold, threatened and mistreated, was as common as air.[669]

---

gle in the Ancient Greek World: From the Archaic Age to the Arab Conquest (Ithaca: Cornell University Press, 1981), 417.

666. Braxton, *No Longer Slaves*, 16, writes: "The slaves' humanity was real. Yet a ruling class discourse had prevented many white Americans from seeing this reality. The inability to perceive reality accurately ... is a form of oppression."

667. Sandra R. Joshel, *Slavery in the Roman World*, Cambridge Introduction to Roman Civilization (Cambridge: Cambridge University Press, 2010), 8.

668. Patterson, *Slavery and Social Death*, 38. Patterson explains that laws governing Roman slavery addressed the critical issue, namely, "that all human beings can be the object of property and that, strictly speaking, property refers to a set of relationships between persons" (31). Sandra R. Joshel, "Slavery and Roman Literary Culture," in *The Cambridge World History of Slavery*, vol. 1: *The Ancient Mediterranean World*, ed. Keith Bradley and Paul Cartledge (Cambridge: Cambridge University Press, 2011), 234, adds that slaves experienced "the loss of ethnicity, family, membership in the community, honour and integrity."

669. Seneca, *Epistles* 80.9.

ARISTOTLE'S VIEW OF SLAVERY

Aristotle lived in a slave-based economy in fifth-century BCE Athens. Out of the total population of 250,000 in the city and the surrounding lands (Attica), approximately 80,000–100,000 were slaves, many who were non-Greeks.[670] This high percentage of slaves makes the ancient Greek society one of the few societies based economically on slavery; others include Rome and central Italy in antiquity, and Brazil, the Caribbean, and the American South in modern times.

Aristotle develops his theory about the political nature of the city-state in part by drawing parallels with the household. Three subordinate/superordinate pairs formed the household unit, including wife/husband, child/parent (father), and slave/owner. Aristotle advocates the despotic rule by the master over the slave; this is in contrast to the royal rule of the father over the son as noted above in the discussion of parents and children (Eph 6:1–4). The despot advanced his own interests, while the king or father ruled benevolently, caring for the subject or son.[671] One can say that the master ruled by means of the whip, while a father controlled without resorting to the whip.[672] The slave bore scars, the child received instruction, a dichotomy noted above. In discussing his view of male and female, Aristotle posited an inferiority of the female body, which prevented the full realization of her rational capacity.[673] Aristotle holds that the free male has the capacity to appreciate supreme good, while the female and the slave enjoy lesser goods, based on their lesser physical capacities.[674] Therefore, as the mind/soul rules the body, so too the master rightly rules the slave.

---

670. The approximations are from Paul Anthony Cartledge, "Slavery," *The Oxford Classical Dictionary*, 3rd ed., ed. Simon Hornblower and Antony Spawforth (Oxford: Oxford University Press, 1996), 1415.

671. Aristotle, *Politics* 1278b32–37; *Nicomachean Ethics* 8.10.1160b29–31.

672. Henrik Mouritsen, *The Freedman in the Roman World* (Cambridge: Cambridge University Press, 2011), 26–28.

673. Aristotle declared that women have fewer teeth than men (*History of Animals* 2.3.501b19–21) and smaller brains (*Parts of Animals* 2.7.653a28–29); however, he saw the brain as regulating body temperature and the heart as the seat of the intellect. And women generally ate diets deficient in vitamins C and D, which we know today often lead to dental hygiene problems, especially in pregnant and lactating women. He might have innocently concluded female bodily inferiority based on neutral observation, yet its use in concluding overall female inferiority remains.

674. Aristotle talks of female as the deformation or deviation of the perfect, that is, male. Sarah Borden Sharkey, *An Aristotelian Feminism* (Switzerland: Springer, 2016), 13n42, reminds us that Aristotle "does not argue ... that women and 'natural slaves' are equally able as free males to flourish as human beings, but nonetheless, still ought to be subordinated."

Excursus: Slavery in the Ancient World

Aristotle presents a moral foundation for the institution of slavery as he sees it in his Athenian context.[675] Aristotle argues against claims that slavery was unjust and created by humankind. Instead, he theorizes that nature created some peoples to be slaves and others to be masters.[676] Because nature is just and beneficent, both the slave and the owner benefit from the institution of slavery. The theory of the "natural slave" grew from his thoughts on the contrast between soul and body, and so between reason and emotion.[677]

Aristotle's theory also grew from his observations that barbarians (non-Greek speakers) had no natural rulers and thus were all slaves in that sense.[678] Aristotle begins with the idea that the free male in his natural state is good, with the elite free male as the highest good. The elite free male depends on ample leisure time to pursue the good and thus on slave labor so that the city runs well. Aristotle views the non-Greek, with their perceived lack of reason and hierarchical social structure, as the "natural" slave.[679] Said another way, Aristotle believes the ethnic Greek was a natural master, and it seems painfully obvious today that his conclusions were built on some measure of cultural bias. Aristotle defends his position through describing the Greek language as providing the vehicle for exploring reason and other languages as mere babble.[680] Nicholas Smith writes: "Hence, when the barbarian/natural slave is captured and enslaved, he finally has the opportunity to come into contact with the proper use of *logos*—reasoned arguments designed to identify right from wrong."[681]

---

675. In his day, the Greek city-states were being brought under the single rule of Philip of Macedon, whose son, Alexander the Great, would go on to conquer much of the East. Aristotle was Alexander's teacher.

676. Aristotle, *Politics* 1252a30-34.

677. Peter Garnsey, *Ideas of Slavery from Aristotle to Augustine* (Cambridge: Cambridge University Press, 1996), 108-27, discusses the complexity of Aristotle's thought on "natural slave" in his *Ethics* and *Politics*. Nicholas D. Smith, "Aristotle's Theory of Natural Slavery," in *Phoenix* 37 (1983): 109-13, recounts the numerous contradictions and discrepancies within Aristotle's thought on the natural slave who lacks reason. This theory of the natural slave shaped discussion through the ages, including debates in the eighteenth and nineteenth centuries regarding American slavery.

678. Aristotle, *Politics* 1252b5-9.

679. Aristotle, *Politics* 1255a28. Garnsey, *Ideas of Slavery from Aristotle to Augustine*, 126, observes that "this was a crucial decision, for otherwise the category of natural slaves might be thought of as entirely academic." See also Benjamin Isaac, *The Invention of Racism in Classical Antiquity* (Princeton: Princeton University Press, 2004), 178, who observes: "For Aristotle, however, it is clear that slaves by nature are non-Greeks and the masters by nature Greeks, which means that the division between superior and inferior men is essentially one based on ethnic identity."

680. Herodotus, *Histories* 2.158.2 explains that *barbaros* likely reflects etymologically the ba-ba-ba sound of a foreign tongue.

681. Smith, "Aristotle's Theory of Natural Slavery," 119-20. Cohick, *Women in the*

PHILO OF ALEXANDRIA'S VIEW OF SLAVERY

The first-century Jewish philosopher and exegete Philo of Alexandria focuses on slavery and the Torah.[682] Philo lived at the turn of the ages, when the Roman Republic became imperial Rome and when Stoicism held pride of place in the Roman worldview. While these political and philosophical sea changes certainly affected him, Philo's approach to slavery was rooted in his reading of the Decalogue. Philo maintains that slaves and owners were of the same nature, even as they have different social status, thus no person is by nature a slave.[683] Philo picks up the idea of freedom in his discussion of freeing Israelite slaves in the seventh year (Deut 15:12–18). As we saw with Aristotle, so too Philo is against enslaving a fellow countryman or countrywoman. Philo declares the slave is also a human; the master has the opportunity to do a great deed by freeing the slave in the seventh year, as freedom is a great blessing. Philo asks the owner to go further by giving gifts to freed slaves, so that they do not fall back into slavery based on poverty.[684] Therefore, slaves must be treated justly based on divine law.[685] The master who violently oppresses his slaves will not stop at this foul deed, but pursue even greater tyrannical exploits as he attacks other cities and nations to satisfy his insatiable lust for power. Moreover, the owner who beats his slave to death will not escape justice, for the judge will not accept the rationale that the master only sought to correct, not kill, with his physical blows. Philo concludes that a slave accused of wrongdoing that warrants death should be judged by a court, not the master. Philo's conclusion greatly mitigates the owner's authority.

Philo draws on the teachings about the Sabbath for his understanding of slaves and slavery. This holy day of rest is for contemplation of God's law, and both masters and slaves abstain from work. For slaves, it is a day of freedom, and for the masters, a day to reacquaint themselves cheerfully with doing some things themselves.[686] Philo speaks of the master "submitting" on Sabbath to doing the tasks typically done by his household slaves. It is not that the master submits to the slave, but rather to the tasks; nevertheless, the theme of reciprocity that we see in Ephesians is represented here. Philo locates such principle in the law, whereas Paul locates it in Christ and his body, the church.

World of the Earliest Christians, 229–30, adds that wet nurses are chosen based in part on whether they speak Greek well (Soranus, *Gynecology* 2.19).

682. For a general discussion of Jews and slavery, see Catherine Hezser, *Jewish Slavery in Antiquity* (Oxford: Oxford University Press, 2005).

683. Philo, *On the Special Laws* 2.69; 3.137.

684. Philo, *On the Special Laws* 2.85.

685. Philo, *On the Special Laws* 3.137–43.

686. Philo, *On the Special Laws* 2.66–67.

Excursus: Slavery in the Ancient World

SENECA'S VIEW OF SLAVERY

Seneca, the Stoic philosopher and teacher of Emperor Nero, discusses slavery on several occasions. He follows the Stoic concern for the slave owner's morality, endangered through the misuse of the master's absolute power over his or her slave. Seneca cares most about the owner's self-control or self-mastery. Slavery served as a metaphor for the human mind or rational self that was trapped by the body and its fleshly passions. He declares that "it is a mistake to think that slavery penetrates the entire man," since "the better part of him is exempt . . . bodies can be assigned to masters . . . but the mind . . . is its own master [*sui iuris*] . . . that inner part can never come into anyone's possession."[687]

Yet slavery was not merely a metaphor for Seneca, as he owned many slaves. He rejects the idea of "natural slave" and argues that all humans come from the same stock. But he never sought to reform the system, only to encourage owners to act mercifully toward slaves.[688] In a personal example, he recalls that a failure of his household slaves to prepare for his visit provided him the opportunity to practice patience and temper his hunger. He writes to his friend, Lucilius, that slaves are our humble friends, who could have a free soul.[689] He rejects the maxim "you have as many enemies as you have slaves," stating: "We do not acquire them as enemies; we make them so."[690] Instead, he asks that owners treat their inferiors as they would wish their superiors to treat them.[691] He also suggests that his friend train his slaves, for "good material [a slave] often remains unused without a craftsman [the owner]; try and you will learn from your experience."[692] Seneca's letter exposes the reality of slavery, which, coupled with the metaphor of the enslaved mind, created a vortex of anxiety within Seneca. He recognizes that the very domination required for maintaining slaves' obedience could at any moment be used against a freeborn man.[693] In an ironic twist of fate,

---

687. Seneca, *On Benefits* 3.20.1–2. See Peter Stacey, "Senecan Political Thought from the Middle Ages to Early Modernity," in *The Cambridge Companion to Seneca*, ed. Shadi Bartsch and Alessandro Schiesaro (Cambridge: Cambridge University Press, 2015), 291.

688. Seneca, *Epistles* 123.1–4. Mouritsen, *Freedman in the Roman World*, 13, summarizes: "The slave enjoyed no legal protection of his or her person, no right to own property, no formal marriage, and no authority over his own children."

689. Seneca, *Epistles* 47.17.

690. Seneca, *Epistles* 47.5.

691. Seneca, *Epistles* 47.11.

692. Seneca, *Epistles* 47.16.

693. Thomas Habinek, "*Imago suae vitae*: Seneca's Life and Career," in *Brill's Companion to Seneca: Philosopher and Dramatist*, ed. Andreas Heil and Gregor Damschen with Mario

his own slaves likely helped him commit suicide to prevent Nero from imposing a humiliating death.

ROMAN IMPERIAL VIEWS ON SLAVERY

As in Greek thought, so too Romans did not question the existence and utility of slavery. Romans tended not to enslave another Roman, even as Greeks tried not to enslave a fellow Greek. Owning slaves was a status symbol; thus we see freedmen and freedwomen owning slaves. Similar to Aristotle's contention that conquered slaves might benefit from their Greek master, the Roman orator Cicero suggests that Rome's conquest of the provinces is beneficial because Rome protects them even as it also subjugates them.[694]

Romans rejected the idea that some groups were by nature slaves. They admitted that it was Fortune or plain bad luck that caused most to be enslaved.[695] Nevertheless, Cicero smeared the Jews and Syrians as "peoples born to be slaves."[696] Typically, slaves were captives in war, or taken by pirates or brigands, and not a few were homeborn (Latin *vernae*). Yet slaves were seen as inferior, made so by the very institution to which Fate consigned them. The slave was characterized as cowardly, weak, lazy, conniving, cruel, and lacking in judgment and wisdom. Therefore, the slave must be beaten in order to work hard and speak truthfully. Such circular logic reached a hideous pinnacle in the courts as slaves were uniformly tortured before they gave testimony.[697]

A further word about the reality of slavery must not be swept under the rug. An ancient saying proclaimed the social reality: "Losing one's virtue is a crime in the freeborn, a necessity in a slave, and duty for the freedman."[698] The male and female slave's body was owned, including the sexual use of that body by the male family members and by anyone to whom the owner made the slave available. It is likely that female owners also used

---

Waida (Leiden: Brill, 2014), 22, perceptively notes that "for Seneca, as for many Roman writers, the experience of dominating intensifies the fear of being dominated."

694. Isaac, *Invention of Racism*, 184. See Cicero, *On Duty* 2.26.

695. Cicero, *Stoic Paradoxes* 5.33–34. See also Seneca, *On Benefits* 3.28.1, which concludes that all humans come from the same source. See also *Epistles* 31.11.

696. Cicero, *On the Consular Provinces* 5.10; see Hezser, *Jewish Slavery in Antiquity*, 61; Mouritsen, *Freedman in the Roman World*, 24–25.

697. Mouritsen, *Freedman in the Roman World*, 28, explains: "The use of torture was therefore rooted in the social construction of the slave as a natural stranger to the truth—which therefore had to be extracted through the application of physical force."

698. Mouritsen, *Freedman in the Roman World*, 27, citing Seneca the Elder's quotation by Haterius.

Excursus: Slavery in the Ancient World

their slaves for sex, but social conventions would frown on a free woman's having sexual relations with anyone but her husband. Christian slaves, including boys and girls from the age of seven, would be sexually used by their nonbelieving owners (and by their Christian owners, against church teaching). These same Christian slaves attended church gatherings. Paul says nothing here in Ephesians about this treatment,[699] which likely means that he does not hold the slave guilty of sexual misconduct. The slave is in the same position as the rape victim, noted in Deuteronomy, who cries out in the field for help, but no one is there to aid her (Deut 22:25–29).[700] Earlier in Ephesians, he speaks against sexual immorality and stresses in the strongest possible terms that such a person will not inherit the kingdom of Christ and of God (Eph 5:5).

MANUMISSION

To better understand the complicated, seemingly contradictory view that slaves were both tools of the owner and also human beings, we turn to the practice of manumission. Romans took the process seriously, for it was both practically necessary and theoretically paradoxical. On the practical side, the promise of freedom motivated slaves to work all the harder. Yet theoretically, the slave was inferior to the free person, and this hierarchical relationship was staunchly maintained. How then could a slave become free? The answer is twofold. First, the legal process was well defined and involved three possible options. Second, the social reality was that slaves were never "free" but rather joined the ranks of the "freed." We will examine both more closely.

Underpinning the legal process of manumission was the legal fiction that the slave had been wrongfully enslaved and that the legal change was merely doing justice. One process involved a mock trial wherein an owner and their slave stood before a Roman magistrate and a Roman citizen. The citizen touched the slave with a rod, spoke words of emancipation, and the magistrate validated the legal change.[701] A second possible process of manumission was less involved, as the owner merely included the slave's name on

---

699. Glancy, *Slavery in Early Christianity*, 60, draws the opposite conclusion in her analysis of 1 Thessalonians, suggesting that Paul allows sexual access to slaves.

700. Ruden, *Paul among the People*, 41, notes that Jewish families would not accept sexual relations with slaves, seeing such actions as abuse.

701. Mouritsen, *Freedman in the Roman World*, 11, describes this process known in Latin as *manumissio vendicta*. The citizen would pronounce the free status of the slave and touch them with a rod and state: "Hunc ego hominem liberum esse aio ex iure Quiritium." This phrase can be translated: "I declare this man to be free by right of the Quirites," with "Quirite" indicating "Roman citizen."

the census record. A third option had the owner testify that their slave shall be free. After any of these processes, the slave was one no longer in the eyes of the law.

The reality is, however, that the slave was not entirely free, if by "free" we refer to a person with self-determination. Instead, the slave joined the ranks of the "freed." This category likened the former slave to a client of the former owner, now viewed as a patron. The former slave became a part of the owner's family circle, but still an outsider. This new social configuration gave the former slave a home, relations of a sort, protection, and community. Freedmen or freedwomen served their patron and were legally obligated to share income from a business. Furthermore, the previous owner would not be charged with committing adultery with his former slave, now a freedwoman.

Moreover, the stain of slavery remained, and the former slave was forever deemed inferior. Why did the stain of slavery remain? It was not because the slave's skin color marked him or her as inferior. Rather the Romans believed that the bodily humiliation, endemic to a slave's existence, forever rendered them servile in mind and character. The scars from whippings, beatings, and shackles marked the body and the mind as subservient. Free people were at risk of being contaminated by a freed person's low morality and lack of virtue. For example, Emperor Augustus formed a military unit of freedmen to increase the size of his army without infecting the regular army.[702] Again, a senator divorced his wife upon discovering that she spoke to a freedwoman in public.[703]

Interestingly, Paul refers to this group only once, in 1 Cor 7:22.[704] The context has been interpreted to refer to slave's using their own money to buy their freedom. This "savings" was known as *peculium*, which was technically under the control of the owner. The same term described a son's money controlled by his paterfamilias. A few remarks from ancient authors lead many to believe that slaves regularly earned their freedom, but recently that assessment has been challenged. Mouritsen suggests that the slave's savings were a symbol of status, which the slave carried as they became freedmen and freedwomen. This explanation fits well with Paul's charge to the Corinthian believers not to change their social status as pertains to marriage, or Jew/gentile, or slavery. For in all cases, it is not society that pronounces a person's worth, but God in Christ, and God has declared each believer a member of Christ's body and a coheir with Christ. Yet Paul is mindful of the slave's lot and

---

702. Suetonius, *Augustus* 74. Also noted is Augustus's decision not to meet with freedmen.

703. Valerius Maximus, *Memorable Deeds and Sayings* 6.3.11; see Mouritsen, *Freedman in the Roman World*, 21.

704. Paul uses the term ἀπελεύθερος.

so encourages them to embrace manumission if given. These words were read in the church that included owners; it is entirely possible that Paul implicitly and rhetorically throws down the gauntlet to owners that they manumit their believing slaves.[705]

SLAVERY IN ANCIENT AND MODERN TIMES

The paradox of slavery is that it flourishes where one might least expect it. In classical Greece, the cradle of democracy, we find Aristotle defending the institution as natural and therefore just (in certain circumstances). In the United States, we find a rapid growth of capitalism and modern democratic institutions and proclamation of individual rights alongside the enslavement of Africans as means of production and as the political and social identification of white and black races. In both imperial Rome and colonial America, the owner's rights to the slave's labor and obedience was of primary importance. As noted above, Seneca worried that the owner's pursuit of virtue might be derailed by giving into passionate rage and violence against his or her slave, because the owner had absolute power. Yet such qualms did not induce Seneca to suggest eliminating slavery, for ultimately the elite life he and other philosophers desired could be achieved only (so it seemed to him) by slave labor. So too in the American South, the slave obeyed based on the owner's absolute authority.

Those who compare the slavery of the American South with that of ancient Rome are quick to point out that slaves in the ancient world could gain their freedom, while the American slave had no such opportunity. This observation, while true in some sense, is misleading in several ways. First, few agricultural or mining slaves in the ancient world were released; most died on the job, a job similar to the hard labor of American slaves. Second, few female slaves received freedom, unless it was to marry their owner or their owner's son. Third, manumitted slaves joined the ranks of freedmen and freedwomen, not of "free" persons. This middle category included obligations toward the owner's family, including a percentage of any wages or income, as noted above. Most importantly, the stain and shame of slavery remained. In sum, slavery in the ancient world was not a more civilized, beneficent, or necessary societal institution than that which existed in the American South.

---

705. Scot McKnight, *Philemon*, NICNT (Grand Rapids: Eerdmans, 2017), 11, concludes differently, namely, that "Paul did not so much turn a blind eye to the morality of slavery as he did not realize slavery was an issue of morality. He was blind to the immorality of slavery as an institution."

Perhaps the most salient difference between the two slavery institutions is the lack of racism in the ancient system.[706] In the ancient world, the dark-skinned person, identified as an Ethiopian, was not considered inferior based on physical appearance. Instead, the Greco-Roman slave was constructed socially as an inferior based on ethnic background (barbarian) or on the social degradation done by the enslavement itself. So too within early European history, the person's skin color was immaterial to their place as servant, and white and black alike held this position. Yet as "Christianity" came to mean "civilized" in some circles, the "heathen savage" in Africa seemed barbarous, and so racism developed within the church supported by "natural" reasoning.[707]

Paul develops his argument in the third pair of the household codes by stressing Christ as Lord. This involves a play on words in the Greek, for *kyrios* ("lord") can signify both a superordinate (a slave owner [e.g., Col 3:22] or a husband [e.g., 1 Pet 3:6]) and a deity. Paul continues his emphasis on Christ, using this title at the beginning of the household codes (Eph 5:21) and drawing out the implications here as he stresses that both slaves and owners serve Christ. Paul links the two positions by using the term "slave/servant," which has a cognate verb "to serve." In Greek, the passage identifies slaves (6:5) who, as "slaves of Christ" (6:6), serve (6:7) with good will as to the Lord, for the Lord will reward both slave (6:8) and free.[708]

While the first two pairs of the household codes, wife/husband and child/parent, are ideally grounded in love, this final pair is supported by violence. The master dominates the slave; otherwise, the slave would not remain in slavery. The master has complete power, to which the slave obeyed or was punished. It is true that in the ancient world philosophers encouraged masters to be gentle with slaves and that some poor, free people starved while slaves had bread from their owners. But these observations do not change the underlying reality that slavery fostered, as a necessary part of its continuation, the domination of one human over another human. The control included not only the use of brute force, but also the loss of natal and paternal heritage in perpetuity. Having no ancestors or descendants made the slave the "ultimate human tool, as imprintable [sic] and as disposable as the master

---

706. Frank M. Snowden Jr., *Blacks in Antiquity: Ethiopians in the Greco-Roman Experience* (Cambridge: Harvard University Press, 1970), 176.

707. Patterson, *Slavery and Social Death*, 7.

708. On δοῦλος see BDAG 259–60; on δουλεύω see BDAG 259; A. A. Rupprecht, "Slave, Slavery," *DPL* 881–83; S. Scott Bartchy, "Slavery," *ABD* 6:58–73.

wished."[709] A slave had no honor, due to his or her lack of power or agency. The seventeenth-century philosopher Thomas Hobbes comments on the relationship between power and honor: "To obey, is to Honour; because no man obeys them, whom they think have no power to help, or hurt them. And consequently, to disobey, is to Dishonour."[710] Patterson concludes that slavery is best defined as *"the permanent, violent domination of natally alienated and generally dishonored persons."*[711]

5-7 Paul begins his charges to slaves and owners by commanding that slaves obey their earthly masters or lords, using the same verb found in 6:1 enjoining children to obey their parents. The English rendering "earthly" attempts to understand the unusual Greek phrase "according to the flesh" that modifies "masters."[712] Paul includes this qualification to distinguish "lord" as owner from the Lord Jesus Christ in 6:7-8. The term "flesh" likely carries a negative evaluation of the master's position.[713] Paul speaks of the "flesh" earlier in the epistle, its passions and desires that drive humans to sin (2:3). He speaks about temporal things, such as being a gentile "in the flesh" (2:11) or having a body ("his own flesh," 5:29; see also 6:12). At best the term is neutral; at worst it signals this present age of darkness.

He adds that slaves should obey with fear and trembling, a phrase that Paul uses several times, including to the Philippians as he enjoins them to obey his call to work out their salvation with fear and trembling (Phil 2:12; see also 1 Cor 2:3; 2 Cor 7:15). We saw the importance of the term "fear" or "reverence" at the beginning of the household codes, as Paul insists that all believers submit to one another out of fear (reverence) for Christ (Eph 5:21). And wives are to respect or fear their husbands (5:33). The posture is one of the subordinate honoring the social position of the superordinate. There is another sort of fear that was all too common in a slave's life—fear of brutality. First Peter suggests that this sort of fear might be common among believing wives married to unbelieving husbands (3:6) and to the wider unbelieving community (3:13-17). Neither Peter nor Paul countenance such treatment by one believer toward another. That domestic violence exists within believing families today reveals that churches must do a better job at explaining Paul's meaning "fear and trembling" as indicating honor or deference. In no way

---

709. Patterson, *Slavery and Social Death*, 27.

710. Thomas Hobbes, *Leviathan* (London: Dent, 1914 [originally 1651]), 44. Patterson, *Slavery and Social Death*, 12, remarks on what "slavery really meant: the direct and insidious violence, the namelessness and invisibility, the endless personal violation, and the chronic inalienable dishonor."

711. Patterson, *Slavery and Social Death*, 13 (emphasis original).

712. Κατὰ σάρκα.

713. Thielman, 405; Lincoln, 420.

does this phrase allow for the husband or parent to intimidate their wife or child.[714]

Paul asks not only that the slave obey with honor, but also with "sincerity of heart" (6:5). At this time, slaves were characterized as lazy and greedy. But Paul is not reinforcing that view—indeed, he praises Philemon's slave, Onesimus, for his great help in Paul's ministry (Phlm 11, 13). Rather, Paul holds up the slave's behavior as worthy of emulation, as they demonstrate godly obedience to Christ. They have a heart fitted for serving God. Paul prays that the Ephesians will have the eyes of their hearts enlightened so as to see their glorious future hope and inheritance (1:18; 3:17). It is a hard heart that lives in ignorance and darkness (4:18), but a faithful heart that sings psalms to the Lord (5:19). Paul declares to the Romans that, though once they were slaves to sin, now they obey from the heart (Rom 6:17). The confession of faith includes believing in one's heart that God raised Christ from the dead (10:9–10).

The final clause "as to Christ" describes the sort of sincere obedience that slaves offer, because they are also followers of Jesus Christ. The NIV adds the verb "obey," which could lead readers to the false conclusion that Paul sees masters as a proxy or representative of Christ. Instead, Paul indicates that the slaves' work, although mandated by their owner, is nevertheless an opportunity for them to model the character of Christ.[715] Paul makes a sharp contrast between this sincerity and the sort of work that is done only when one believes they are being evaluated (6:6). Paul uses two unusual nouns as he speaks about insincere work. The noun "eye-service" is translated "when their eye is on you," and "people-pleaser" is translated "win their favor" (6:6; see also Col 3:22).[716]

In 6:6–7 Paul uses two present participles that elucidate the obedience Paul has in mind. He speaks of "doing" (6:6) and "serving" (6:7). The first participle emphasizes doing the will of God, and the second echoes the same sentiment with its encouragement to serve wholeheartedly. The will of God is qualified with the phrase "from the heart."[717] In 6:5 Paul speaks of *kardia*, from which we get the term "cardio," but here the term is *psychē*, from which we get "psychology." The latter Greek noun has a wide range of meaning, from "life," to "spirit" or "soul," and also "mind" or "person." Debate in Paul's day centered on dichotomies of soul/body and master/slave,

---

714. Fowl, 197, writes that domestic violence "should always be unacceptable to Christians, even though sometimes churches invoke passages such as Eph 5:21–6:9 to underwrite such violence through advocating the comprehensive submission of wives to husbands."
715. Thielman, 406; Lincoln, 421.
716. On ὀφθαλμοδουλία see BDAG 743–74; on ἀνθρωπάρεσκος see BDAG 80.
717. On ψυχή see BDAG 1098–99 (2). See also Best, 578.

and about how the slave was in some ways a human and in others, an inferior shell of a human. Paul puts such a dichotomy to rest with his remark that the slave's whole person—their body, mind, and soul—can apprehend the will of God and his marvelous power demonstrated in the redemptive plan through Christ (1:5, 9, 11).[718]

The verb "to serve" is a cognate of the noun "slave," so we discover a wordplay in Greek between slaves as a social category and serving the Lord as godly action and attitude. Notice the contrast between Lord and humans; Paul emphasizes the temporary, earthly status of the owner by locating it within humanity's sphere. The slave of Christ, however, serves with zealous dedication of their entire person. Paul identifies those who do God's will as "slaves of Christ" and choses this label "slave of Christ" (Rom 1:1; Gal 1:10; Phil 1:1) as one way to speak of his apostleship, thereby imbuing it with honor. Paul does not minimize the reality of physical slavery, but signifies its temporary claims on those who share Christ's eternal life. The service rendered is with a good heart or mind, with one's whole person focused toward the Lord and not humans (Eph 6:7). To the Galatians, Paul insists that he does not please humans, but only Christ, for he is a slave/servant of Christ (Gal 1:10). Paul explains that doing God's will requires a person to relegate human praise to a secondary status. It requires constancy and steadfastness with one's whole being, and not just to receive some sort of favor. The slave exhibits godly character for the entire church, including their masters in the flesh.

8 Paul asserts the impartial justice of God and the lack of favoritism that defines his kingdom rule. Still speaking to slaves, but with owners listening in, Paul acknowledges what is common information, specifically, that whoever does good will be rewarded by God. What is good? Paul noted that God has prepared good works for believers to walk in (2:10). Paul challenged the Ephesians to do good works with their hands so as to share with others and to speak "what is good" or helpful to build up others (4:28–29). Both slave and free, then, are under obligation to do good deeds and speak good thoughts so as to bless the church and live out the gospel before all peoples. Paul describes slaves as having the capacity to know the will of God and to do it (6:6), an astonishing statement given the prejudices of the day that viewed slaves as untrustworthy and lazy. Paul elevates the slaves' deeds as those done unto Christ, effectively undercutting the evaluation of the slave owner.

---

718. Contra J. Albert Harrill, *Slaves in the New Testament: Literary, Social, and Moral Dimensions* (Minneapolis: Fortress, 2006), 90, who assumes this connection and concludes: "The author of Ephesians identifies the will [*thelēma*] of the human master with that of the Lord more clearly than Colossians does and targets paraenesis more squarely on the slave's inner self [*psychē*] as an object to bind and so to control."

God "rewards" those who do good, a special promise to slaves who have no earthly rewards coming to them.[719] But in Christ, they inherit with all believers a place in God's kingdom (5:5). Paul does not mention judgment alongside reward here, but he does so to both the Corinthians and the Colossians. To the former, Paul indicates that believers' goal should be to please the Lord, for they will face him on the judgment seat and receive just recompense for good and bad deeds (2 Cor 5:10). To the Colossian slaves, Paul assures them that they will receive an inheritance as a reward, but that those who do wrong will also receive just punishment, for God does not show favoritism (Col 3:24–25).

9 After several verses devoted to slaves, Paul's message to owners is succinct and severe (see also Col 4:1). He gives no space to special privilege—the very bedrock of the institution of slavery. Slavery is maintained by domination, by brute force and the threat of it. It is "social death" as it dehumanizes the individual, taking from them their ethnicity, community, family, and future.[720] Paul equalizes the owner with the slave by declaring that the legal and social title "master" is of no account in God's eyes, for he is the true Lord and Master of all humans.[721]

Paul commands masters to "treat slaves in the same way." The Greek phrase reads "the same things" and could refer to the wholehearted service (6:7) or the good deeds that slave and free are to do in their service to Christ (6:8).[722] But it probably carries more specificity.[723] Philo believed that the law obligated owners to care for themselves on the Sabbath so that their slaves could rest. The owners submitted to doing the slaves' tasks in obedience to Sabbath laws. The fourth-century church father Chrysostom argues that Paul urges owners to serve their slaves.[724] Such language fits Jesus's words that the one who leads should be a servant to all (Mark 10:41–45). At the very least,

---

719. On κομίζω see BDAG 557.

720. Patterson, *Slavery and Social Death*, 38.

721. Ilaria L. E. Ramelli, *Social Justice and the Legitimacy of Slavery: The Role of Philosophical Asceticism from Ancient Judaism to Late Antiquity* (Oxford: Oxford University Press, 2016), 102–3, 249, argues that Paul in Gal 3:28 overturned Aristotle's theory that men were by nature superior to women and free men superior by nature to slave men; however, she holds that Ephesians does not show this same conviction (a conclusion I do not share). She finds within Christian ascetic writers of the early centuries a strong aversion to slavery coupled with a conviction against social injustice, that is, the inequality of the numerous poor and the few wealthy.

722. Τὰ αὐτά. Fowl, 196. Lincoln, 423, insists that the focus is on masters having a "corresponding attitude to that required of the slaves."

723. Contra Best, 580, who suggest that the phrase should be "in some general way with *mutatis mutandis* understood."

724. Chrysostom, *Homilies on Ephesians* 6:9 in PG 62:157.

6:5–9 SLAVES AND MASTERS

Paul's injunction orders masters to follow the same principled behavior as enjoined for slaves, because the Lord tolerates no special treatment for the socially privileged. This includes owners presenting themselves as slaves of Christ, serving the Lord, doing good.

Not only are the masters to do the same things, but they are to cease threatening slaves. Paul connects the command "to do" with the participle "stopping" or "ceasing" the threats. It is possible the participle has the force of an imperative, which is captured in the English translation that begins a new sentence: "Do not threaten."[725] The threat need not be the use of the whip, but could be the threat to sell a child or "partner" or to deny food or drink or proper clothing. Taking away the owner's power to threaten violence (coupled with the power to make good on those threats) undermines the very ability of the master to control their slaves. Paul does not include a caveat that disobedient slaves can be threatened or that those who do wrong can be intimidated.[726] The domination that characterized the institution of slavery has no place within the church.

The second half of the verse begins with the conjunction "since" as Paul states the reason for his command to slave owners that they give up violent threats, namely, the impartiality of Christ, their Lord and master (see also Acts 10:34; Gal 2:6; Col 3:25). This verse develops a significant wordplay between the term for owner (*kyrios*) and the Lord (*Kyrios*) Jesus Christ. Paul is at pains to distinguish the two and thus emphasizes the title "Christ" in 6:5–6. What does it mean to call Christ "master" or "Lord" as Paul does here? Paul does not project the earthly characteristics of owners onto Christ, but rather invites believers to think differently about what "master" means. Who is this master in heaven? None other than Christ the Lord, the one who was crucified and raised and who now sits at God's right hand. This is the one who shows no favoritism, who does not count social status as determining a person's worth, who welcomes all into his family, his body.

Paul writes to slaves and masters; he does not write a treatise on the morality or immorality of the institution of slavery. In this sense, his work differs from many discussions in antebellum America, where debates had the power to change laws and social practices.[727] Proslavery arguments returned time and again to the biblical injunctions, such as our text, that seem

---

725. Thielman, 409n8, suggests that the participle is "probably an adverbial participle of result . . . , but the rhetorical effect is virtually the same as an imperative."

726. Contra Hoehner, 814, who assumes that Paul makes an implicit exception to the owner whose slave did wrong. He concludes that if the owner did not have some power to threaten, the slave might refuse to work.

727. For an excellent survey of the material, see Noll, *Civil War as a Theological Crisis*. See also Jennifer A. Glancy, *Slavery as Moral Problem: In the Early Church and Today* (Minneapolis: Fortress, 2011).

to allow slavery. Abolitionists recognized that neither Jesus nor Paul declared the institution a moral evil. Yet the abolitionists appealed to the broad sweep of canonical sentiment, which they argued put all people on equal footing and which required all Christians to treat others as they want to be treated themselves.[728]

Arguably, however, Harriet Beecher Stowe's *Uncle Tom's Cabin* did more to shift public sentiment against slavery. She revealed in narrative what the principled exegetical arguments could not muster, namely, the human at the center of it all. The human element is poignantly displayed when the runaway Eliza and her son arrive on the doorstep of John and Mary Bird. The couple had just finished a vigorous discussion about the appropriateness of the fugitive slave laws that required the return of any runaway. Mary Bird declares that God commands her to feed the hungry and clothe the naked, which would include runaway slaves. John, a senator in Ohio, falls back on principle and retorts that this could result in grave harm because of the general public unrest. Mrs. Bird has none of it and, even more, believes her husband would not turn away a shivering forlorn slave fleeing from her owner. The servant interrupts the debate to ask Mrs. Bird to come to the kitchen, and shortly afterward Mary calls to her husband to join her. There in the kitchen was the ragged and half-frozen Eliza with her little boy Henry. Suddenly, the couple's debate shifted from the abstract to the real flesh and blood mother and child who needed their help.[729] Suddenly it was personal.

For Paul and the early Christians, it was also personal. About 20 percent of the early gentile believing communities were slaves, perhaps more in Rome, given the larger slave population there. Each of these believers, including slaves, was coheir with their fellow believers (3:6). Each was a stone used in the Lord's temple (2:21). A slave might be a pastor, evangelist, or teacher, God's gift to the church (4:11). Tradition holds that Philemon's slave, Onesimus, became bishop of Ephesus.[730] The slave children and free born in the Ephesian church worshiped together alongside their slave, freed, and free caregivers. Paul identifies each believer as his brother or sister, which gives slaves a family. Paul establishes slaves as able to discern the will of God and model service to Christ, which gives slaves moral authority within the community (6:6–7). Paul warns masters publicly that the Lord watches them and is unmoved by their so-called higher social position. Slave and free are alike

---

728. Some abolitionists supported women's rights, including the right to vote; others spoke against women's rights and sought to distinguish the arguments for the abolition of slavery from women's suffrage.

729. Harriet Beecher Stowe, *Uncle Tom's Cabin* (Hartford, CT: Worthington, 1901), 88–99.

730. Ignatius, *To the Ephesians* 5.2–6.1.

before the throne of grace; even more, slaves seem better able to model the important role of "slave of Christ," a title connected to the apostolic leadership of the church. For the Lord Christ himself, though being in very nature God, yet took up the very nature of a slave—the humiliation that resulted in his exaltation (Phil 2:6-11).

D. ARMOR OF GOD (6:10-20)

With this final section before his concluding greetings, Paul draws the epistle to a close. Some suggest that Paul includes here a *peroratio*, the closing section of a rhetorically sophisticated speech that encapsulates and engages the listeners' emotions to move them toward particular actions.[731] The speaker hopes to rally his listeners to his side, discredit his enemies, and summarize his entire speech with an emotional climax. The typical context is a general's speech to his troops as they get ready for battle.[732] Others suggest that while Paul echoes specific terms and ideas found elsewhere in this epistle, nevertheless, the section is much shorter than the typical *peroratio*, and the enemy's power is magnified by Paul, not minimized.[733] As cautioned in the introduction, ancient rhetorical criticism focused on speeches, not epistles. Ancient listeners to Paul's letters would not be expecting a speechlike composition grounded in Greco-Roman conventions.[734] Thus this call to take up God's armor is best understood as restating and reemphasizing key themes expounded in the letter. Indeed, the emphasis on Christ's superiority to all other powers permeates Paul's argument in this epistle.[735] Is the victory of Christ over all authorities at odds with this passage's battle call? Not if we understand that Paul can speak both as a commander encouraging his troops to engage the enemy and as an incipient martyr ready to die for the noble cause.[736]

Does Paul intend to summarize the entire letter in these verses or only the second half that focuses on ethical and moral behaviors? Most likely, Paul's discussion about God's armor and believers standing firm provides a summary and action plan based on his thoughts throughout the epistle. Paul repeats in 6:10 the same phrase from 1:19, "in his mighty power," which serves

---

731. Lincoln, 432-33; Schüssler Fiorenza, 116.
732. For example, see Polybius, *History* 3.63-64; Cassius Dio, *Roman History* 38.36-46.
733. Thielman, 412-13.
734. Introduction, p. 48.
735. Gombis, *Drama of Ephesians*, 157, writes: "This passage is a rhetorical conclusion to the entire letter, in which Paul depicts the church as intimately identified with the exalted Lord Jesus."
736. Perkins, 141-42, points to 2 Cor 10:1-10 as an example of both images working in a single argument.

as an *inclusio* for the letter, stressing the mighty power revealed in the gospel of salvation. Paul's charge to put on God's whole armor connects with his description of the church and the powers in 3:7–13. God's wisdom expressed in Christ's salvation work is now made known to the spiritual powers in the heavenly realms. The church's mere existence displays God's surpassing generosity and grace to those spiritual forces that feed on evil and human suffering.[737] Human institutions that devastate and destroy are not absolved of responsibility, but the point Paul makes is that they do not act outside the realm of these dark forces.[738] When we factor in Paul's emphasis that the church is made up of Jews and gentiles who are now one body in Christ (2:14–15) and one temple for God in his Spirit (2:19–22), we see more clearly what Paul had in mind when he spoke about Christ bringing all things together under himself (1:10). The unity of humanity in Christ foreshadows the ultimate unity of the cosmos under the love of God (see also 1 Cor 15:24–28). This promise sounds the death knell for the powers and principalities that incite evil. The role of the faithful is to stand firm under the sure pledge and not give way to fear, even as Paul asks the Ephesians that they would pray that he has courage to preach the gospel (Eph 6:19–20).

While we see several connections with earlier sections of the epistle, Paul makes an abrupt shift in images as he moves from a discussion of the household to describing believers in military garb. This turn might have surprised the first readers, but perhaps not in the same way it shocks readers today.[739] For example, the Ephesians would be surprised by Paul's military metaphor that invites the listener to imagine slaves and their owners taking up a sword. The Ephesians might have paused at the notion of a slave holding a weapon, for slave uprisings were one of the great fears among Romans. Similarly, a Roman soldier's armor presented his rank and status, thus bringing him public honor. However, Paul encourages the lowly believer to put on what would be the highest of all social honors: God's armor. Finally, while we today might read this passage with a focus on an individual soldier, the ancient world would see in this military image an emphasis on a unit working as one for a common purpose.

What would likely not surprise the Jewish readers in the congregation are the images of warfare. In 167 BCE, the Jews threw off the Hellenistic rulers and established the Hasmonean Kingdom, which held power until Rome took

---

737. Fowl, 200.

738. Wright, *Paul and the Faithfulness of God*, 2:1287, writes: "That is why, in another relativizing move, he [Paul] insists that the real, ultimate enemy is not any human being or structure, but the dark anti-creational forces that stand behind them and use them as puppets in their nefarious purposes."

739. Best, 586, lists several places where this widely used image is found in ancient sources.

over in 63 BCE. Shortly after Paul's death, and again about seventy years later, the Jews revolted against Rome, with devastating consequences (66–70 CE and 132–35 CE).[740] But Paul's metaphorical use of military garb reframes the argument away from nationalistic goals, so as to line up with the crucified and resurrected Lord.[741]

Roman philosophers described their efforts with language of warfare, imagining their opponents as beasts and philosophical engagement as a battle in the arena of ideas.[742] Paul might have drawn on this metaphor in his description of his time in Ephesus, "facing wild beasts" (1 Cor 15:32).[743] Our passage in Ephesians might pick up on the notion of battling ideas, values, and ultimate good; however, believers face the enemy as a group, not as one individual against another individual.[744] In Ephesians, the warfare is real, but not literal; the armor is authentic, but not physical. The warfare is subversive, for it upends corruption, exploitation, and injustice, within both the church and the wider world.[745]

1. Be Strong in the Lord (6:10–13)

10Finally, be strong in the Lord and in his mighty power. 11Put on the full armor of God, so that you can take your stand against the devil's schemes. 12For our struggle is not against flesh and blood, but against the rulers, against the authorities, against the powers of this dark world and against the spiritual forces of evil in the heavenly realms. 13Therefore put on the full armor of God, so that when the day of evil comes, you may be able to stand your ground, and after you have done everything, to stand.

In these verses, Paul calls believers to stand firm, this in contrast to his earlier calls to "walk." Paul previously encouraged believers to exercise their new morality and to grow into maturity, to Christlikeness (4:15–16). When Paul

---

740. Perkins, 143, cites 1Q28b 5:21–26, as they bless the prince of the congregation that justice would be his belt. In the Qumran text, the enemies are the peoples who resist God and his anointed.

741. Wright, *Paul and the Faithfulness of God*, 2:1126.

742. Perkins, 142, lists Seneca, *On the Constancy of the Wise Man* 6.8; Dio Chrysostom, *Orations* 19.10–12.

743. David E. Garland, *1 Corinthians*, Baker Exegetical Commentary on the New Testament (Grand Rapids: Baker Academic, 2003), 720–21, lists several interpretative options, including that Paul referred to fighting his own passions as did Stoic and Cynic philosophers.

744. Schüssler Fiorenza, 117, writes: "Whereas the Stoic philosophers stress self-sufficiency and self-reliance as well as focusing on the solitary individual, Ephesians argues for mutual cooperation and interdependence."

745. Gombis, *Drama of Ephesians*, 159–60.

commands believers to stand in 6:10–13, this is hardly a passive posture; it is more akin to maintaining one's balance and remaining upright while knee deep in an angry sea.

10 Paul announces his change in focus from household imagery to military metaphor not only with the command "be strong" but also with the opening phrase of 6:10.[746] While some translations use "finally," a better rendering is "henceforth."[747] Paul presents a strategy for the church to prosper in the midst of heated battle with spiritual forces. Believers, individually and together, draw strength from the mighty power of the Lord. The passive voice of the imperative "be strong" points to the strength that comes from the Lord, not from the believer or from the church.[748] Less likely is the possibility that Paul intends the middle voice, which would stress the individual's actions.[749]

Earlier in the epistle, Paul spoke of the "mighty strength" that God used in raising Christ from the dead and seating him above all spiritual powers and dominion (1:19).[750] Paul uses the same terms in 6:10 to describe the "mighty power" that is more than capable of besting the spiritual authorities that work now in the sons of disobedience (2:2). Paul speaks of this strength as found in the Lord. Paul likely references Christ, as Paul commonly refers to Christ as Lord (2:21; 4:1; 5:8).[751] The strength of Christ is found in his sacrificial love demonstrated on the cross, which no mind can fully fathom (3:19) and which rises to the heights, plumbs the depths, and stretches across the vast universe and beyond (3:18). Readers do well to remember that the strength of Christ is measured in his love, because the military imagery of God's armor can sound a triumphal tone. Lest anyone think in this direction, at the close

---

746. The Greek phrase is most likely τοῦ λοιποῦ; however, the variant, τὸ λοιπόν, is widely attested. The latter phrase often means "finally" or "therefore." The former, genitive phrase is a shortened form of τοῦ λοιποῦ χρόνου, "henceforth" or "from now on." Thielman, 417, 430; Arnold, 442; Best, 589.

747. Thielman, 417; contra Barth, 759, who argues for "for the remaining time," that is, the current period that ends with the final judgment.

748. Arnold, 442; Best, 590.

749. Thomas R. Yoder Neufeld, *Put on the Armour of God: The Divine Warrior from Isaiah to Ephesians*, JSNTSup 140 (Sheffield: Sheffield Academic Press, 1997), 109–16, argues for the middle voice, stating that Paul fills out his earlier injunction to imitate God (5:1). However, in Eph 5, Paul makes clear that imitating God involves forgiving others and walking in Christlike love. The actions are directed to others in the church, and in the wider world, while in Eph 6 the focus is on spiritual forces.

750. On κράτος see BDAG 565. On ἰσχύς see BDAG 484.

751. Contra Yoder Neufeld, *Put on the Armour of God*, 117, who claims that Paul refers to God here and that "Christ disappears from the scene completely, or more accurately, the author of Ephesians applies Paul's ecclesiology radically by having the messianic warrior 'lose himself' in the corporate community that is now ordered to invest itself with the role and equipment of the Divine Warrior."

6:10–13 BE STRONG IN THE LORD

of this section, Paul reminds his readers of his chains (6:20; see also 3:1; 4:1). This is no victory lap for Paul, but a time to participate in the sufferings of Christ (Phil 3:10; Col 1:24).

11 In an echo of Eph 4:24, Paul commands believers "to put on" the whole armor of God (6:11, 13).[752] In Eph 4 Paul enjoined the Ephesians "to put on" the new self, having taken off their old self, corrupted by evil desires. The new self is created to be like God, being righteous and holy. Here in Eph 6 Paul has in mind the act of putting on armor, which results in the ability to stand fast.

We should not imagine the medieval suit of metal that encased knights. Paul's reference to armor included several protective pieces that shielded ancient foot soldiers from injuries as they engaged in hand-to-hand combat. Soldiers wore a breastplate, helmet, greaves (lower leg protection), and sturdy footwear. They held a shield and sword and perhaps a lance. Paul has spent the last three or four years in close company with Roman soldiers, so he is well aware of their gear. Yet he is also familiar with Isaiah's description of God's armor, his breastplate of righteousness and helmet of salvation (Isa 59:17). Isaiah stresses God's battle with injustice, as he sees that "justice is driven back, and righteousness stands at a distance; truth has stumbled in the streets, honesty cannot enter" (59:14). God acts to right wrongs and punish wrongdoers and will redeem those who repent (59:20). Paul will spell out the various pieces of armor and offer their symbolic spiritual meaning. His point here is that the armor is complete and fully capable of protecting believers.

The second half of Eph 6:11 offers a reason for putting on the armor: so as to stand.[753] Paul is quite clear that Christ accomplishes the victory and that the strength to stand comes from him.[754] Paul repeats the verb "to stand" two times in these verses (6:11, 13) and again in 6:14.[755] He speaks of being able to stand because God's armor enables believers to with*stand* or stand (your) ground against the devil (6:13).[756] James uses the same verb and noun in his command that believers resist the devil, and he assures them that the devil will run away (Jas 4:7). Likewise, Peter calls believers to flee the devil, which he likens to a roaring lion prowling about for prey (1 Pet 5:8–9). There is no talk among the apostles of defeating the devil or subduing the lion, for they

---

752. The verb ἐνδύω is used in both 6:11 and 4:24; another verb, ἀναλαμβάνω, correctly translated "put on," is used in 6:13.

753. Arnold, 444, explains that "the infinitive construction (πρὸς τό + infinitive) conveys purpose."

754. Thielman, 422–23.

755. On ἵστημι see BDAG 482–83.

756. On ἀνθίστημι see BDAG 80. Paul makes a similar injunction using different language in 4:27.

411

are well aware that this enemy can be conquered only by God.[757] Believers put on God's armor, which protects against the devil's schemes. The picture is one of indirect assault and trickery by the devil.[758] The same noun is used earlier to describe false teachers who cunningly scheme against young or immature believers (Eph 4:14).[759]

12 The armor provides protection against the devil's deception by enabling believers to be able to stand. Paul describes the situation as a "struggle," using a noun referring to a wrestling contest and by extension to a physical struggle with an opponent (6:12).[760] The struggle is not against humans—or, as Paul puts it, "flesh and blood"—but against spiritual rulers and authorities (6:12).[761] Paul speaks of "the rulers and the authorities," using terms found earlier in Ephesians (1:21; 3:10; see also 1 Cor 15:24; Col 1:16; 2:10, 15; Titus 3:1). He continues with a term found only here in the New Testament, "powers of [this dark] world," a combination of the terms "cosmos" and "power/strength."[762] The term is similar to an Old Testament title for God, *pantokratōr*, "all powerful" (2 Sam 5:10; 1 Kgs 19:10), but Paul might also have drawn from the broader culture that used the term for spirits.[763] We find the term in Jewish texts such as the Testament of Solomon in reference to demonic beings (8.2; 18.3), and Paul might be reflecting a general Jewish understanding of the evil spiritual world.[764] These malevolent superpowers rule "this dark world." Paul ends his list by pointing to "spiritual forces of evil." This final category catches all "classes of hostile spirits."[765] These four

---

757. Speyr, 257, writes: "One thing only is certain: no one will remain protected from temptation; but it is also certain that no believer will be refused God's weapons."

758. The New Testament uses the nouns "Satan" and the "devil" to describe the evil one. Paul uses "Satan" in Rom 16:20; 1 Cor 5:5; 7:5; 2 Cor 2:11; 11:14; 12:7; 1 Thess 2:18; 2 Thess 2:9. He uses the "devil" here in Ephesians. Some point to this variation as part of their argument against Pauline authorship of Ephesians. There is no reason, however, that Paul could not use either term, since the terms function as synonyms and "devil" is common in the Septuagint. In Eph 4:25 Paul quotes from Zech 8:16, and a few chapters earlier in this Old Testament book, the prophet uses the term "devil" in speaking about the evil one (3:1–2). Hoehner, 623, suggests that Paul recalled Zechariah's language.

759. On μεθοδεία see BDAG 625.

760. On πάλη see BDAG 752. The noun πάλη is used only here in the New Testament. Paul uses ἀγών (Phil 1:30; Col 2:1; 1 Thess 2:2; 1 Tim 6:12; 2 Tim 4:7) or μάχη (2 Cor 7:5) elsewhere.

761. The manuscript evidence is equally split between ἡμῖν and ὑμῖν. Thielman, 431, observes that ἡμῖν reflects the consensus among commentators.

762. On κοσμοκράτωρ see BDAG 561.

763. Arnold, 447, who remarks that "this same term was also used to magnify the omnipotence and universal power of various deities."

764. Arnold, 448.

765. Arnold, 448.

categories exist in the heavenly realm and desire nothing more than human faltering and failure.

What might such a struggle look like? Jesus faced Satan in the wilderness, experiencing the onslaught of his half-truths and shortcuts to power. Jesus shows his steadfast loyalty and faithfulness to God the Father through the testing. Jesus does not assert his power independent of God and thus rejects the devil's challenge to change stones to bread (Matt 4:1-4; Luke 4:3-4). Jesus rebuffs the devil's offer of the world's kingdoms in favor of the everlasting kingdom promised him by God (Matt 4:8-11; Luke 4:5-18, perhaps drawing on Ps 2:8).[766] Parenthetically, notice the unchallenged claim by Satan that he rules the human world (Luke 4:6), a conviction that Paul shares (Eph 2:2). Finally, Jesus repudiates the devil's interpretation of Scripture because it lacks understanding of God's true nature and no acknowledgement of sin's hold on the world (Matt 4:5-7; Luke 4:9-13). Satan sees Scripture as promising a way to demonstrate personal power and wow the crowds. Jesus understands that his ministry proceeds through the cross—there is no cheap grace or easy solution to the problem of sin.

13 Paul repeats his call to put on God's whole armor, having identified the terrible foe. He begins 6:13 with the conjunction "therefore" and follows with the aorist imperative "put on" God's armor. Paul explains that with this armor, believers can withstand the onslaught in "the day of evil" (6:13). Paul might be referring to the present time, which he earlier described with the phrase "the days are evil" (5:16).[767] If so, then believers must imagine themselves in a constant struggle with spiritual forces against which their only hope is standing firm in the Lord's strength and armor. Alternatively, it might refer to specific times in a believer's life that involve deep struggles with the deception of demonic forces. A ready example is Jesus's temptations. Finally, it is possible that Paul has in mind the end of this age, when Christ judges the world and the devil's schemes are forever destroyed.[768] It is most likely that Paul does not draw a sharp distinction between the current struggles of the faithful and the final cataclysm—it is a matter of degree, not kind.[769] Paul concludes 6:13 with the plural neuter adjective "all things" and the aorist participle "to do/work." The participle can also mean "to conquer/subdue," which leads some to suggest that Paul's emphasis is on the believer having survived the assault.[770] While it is true that Paul proclaims Christ's victory,

---

766. Joel B. Green, *The Gospel of Luke*, NICNT (Grand Rapids: Eerdmans, 1997), 194.
767. Hoehner, 833-34.
768. Muddiman, 290.
769. Best, 596-97; Arnold, 449-50.
770. Barth, 765-66, observes: "*Katergazomai* may mean 'to carry to victory,' 'to defeat,' 'to finish a job.'" He objects that this sense is not found in the New Testament and that the immediate passage speaks to preparation for the struggle. Muddiman, 290, asserts

his more limited point here is that, having put on God's armor, the believer is equipped to stand.

Several questions emerge from this overview as we seek to understand this passage in relation to the entire letter. First, how does this teaching about wearing God's armor fit with Paul's statement that believers are seated with Christ (2:6), who is himself seated at God's right hand in the heavenly realms? Second, are there evil forces in the heavenly realms, and if so, how does that shape our vision of the spiritual realm? Third, what does the term "heavenly realms" mean (6:12)?

We start with definitions for the phrase "in the heavenly realms." This phrase occurs five times in Ephesians, including our passage (6:12).[771] The noun "heaven" is found over 250 times in the New Testament, including four times in Ephesians (1:10; 3:15; 4:10; 6:9).[772] Jeff Brannon concludes that the noun and adjective are synonymous and both speak about a space that is not earth. In both cases, the terms point to the sky, firmament, or God's dwelling place.[773] Paul uses "heaven" as he distinguishes this space from that of earth in 3:15, where he highlights the scope of God's fatherly care. In 6:9 he contrasts the earth's hierarchical culture with heaven's lack of favoritism. He speaks of the heavenly realms as the place where Christ is seated at God's right hand, with believers there beside him. Again, the heavenly realms are where we find the spiritual forces of darkness from which believers need protection and so are provided with God's armor.

Are we seated in our armor? What can we make of these powerful, yet seemingly discordant images? The answer lies in Paul's eschatology, which is neatly summarized in the phrase "now/not yet." Christ's cross brings forgiveness of sins, his resurrection brings hope of inheritance, and his ascension opens the heavenly realms with their plethora of spiritual blessings (1:3). Yet there is more to come, as Christ will bring unity to all things in heaven and on earth (1:10). Paul declares that Christ is seated "now" in the heavenly realms, ascended to the greatest place of honor (1:20; 2:6). Yet Paul introduces the "not yet" component, that in these coming ages God's grace will be magnified in Christ Jesus. Paul applies this same principle to believers. They

---

that victory is gained only by Christ, but continues (with too much pessimism): "To be left standing at the end and not carried off the field as a casualty of war is all that one can reasonably hope for."

771. Ἐν τοῖς ἐπουρανίοις is found in Eph 1:3, 20; 2:6; 3:10; 6:12 (a close parallel is found in Heb 8:11: ἐν τοῖς οὐρανοῖς). The adjective is found five times in the Pauline corpus (1 Cor 15:40–49; Phil 2:10; 2 Tim 4:18).

772. On οὐρανός see BDAG 737–39.

773. M. Jeff Brannon, *The Heavenlies in Ephesians: A Lexical, Exegetical, and Conceptual Analysis* (London: T&T Clark, 2011), 80, summarizes "that these two 'heaven' words . . . refer to the same location and are references to that which is spatially distinct from the earth."

are now seated with Christ in the heavenly realms (2:6) and also must walk daily in the light (5:8–10). To walk safely, believers need God's protecting armor (6:11).

Yet this explanation leaves a final puzzle, namely, whether the heavenly realms include evil spiritual forces. If we take the definition of "heaven/heavenly realms" as that which is not earth, then we would expect that spiritual forces, good and bad, reside in the heavenly realm.[774] We tend to go further, however, and assume that heaven means only God's abode. However, in some Jewish literature, both evil and good reside in the heavenly realms. A familiar example comes from the beginning of Job, a scene wherein the Accuser (Satan) brings charges against humans before God's throne (Job 1:7; see also Dan 10:12–14; Zech 3:1). The book of Revelation depicts warring factions in heaven as angels battle the dragon and his forces (Rev 12:7–9; see Luke 10:17–19). The powers of darkness make accusations against God's faithful or devise schemes to deceive believers. In our passage, Paul views the situation from the perspective of the believer and recognizes the urgency in having proper protection against spiritual forces.[775] If we consider Paul's description of his visionary journey to the third heaven, we might have evidence that Paul saw levels of heaven, with the uppermost being that space reserved for the Godhead (2 Cor 12:1–4). If so, then perhaps Paul imagines the authorities and powers of darkness in the lower sections of the heavenly realms.[776] This could nuance Paul's note that Christ is seated "far above" all power and dominion (Eph 1:21). Therefore, these powers cannot dominate believers; nevertheless, these evil forces will seek to lead believers astray.

2. Put on God's Armor (6:14–17)

14 Stand firm then, with the belt of truth buckled around your waist, with the breastplate of righteousness in place, 15 and with your feet fitted with the readiness that comes from the gospel of peace. 16 In addition to all this, take up the shield of faith, with which you can extinguish all the flaming arrows of the evil

---

774. Thielman, 47, writes: "God and the ascended Christ dwell in the heavenly places in Ephesians, but so do 'the spiritual powers of evil.'"

775. Robert L. Foster, "Reoriented to the Cosmos: Cosmology and Theology in Ephesians through Philemon," in *Cosmology and New Testament Theology*, ed. Jonathan T. Pennington and Sean M. McDonough (London: T&T Clark, 2008), 108, writes about believers that "in the place where they receive every spiritual blessing they also struggle against spiritual forces of evil."

776. Brannon, *Heavenlies in Ephesians*, 218, writes: "From the evidence in Jewish literature and in Ephesians, it is also possible that the lower heavens serve as the location of the evil powers in Eph. 6.12."

one. ⁱ⁷ Take the helmet of salvation and the sword of the Spirit, which is the word of God.

In the previous verses, Paul commanded believers to put on the whole armor of God. In these verses, we discover more about this armor and how it protects believers. Throughout the epistle, Paul emphasizes the virtues expressed with the pieces of armor. He speaks of truth (1:13; 4:15–25; 5:9), righteousness (4:24; 5:9), peace (2:14–18; 4:3; 6:23), the gospel (1:13; 2:17; 3:6–8), and faith (1:15; 2:8; 3:12, 17; 4:5, 13). Paul presents these well-known virtues with vividness, drawing on Isaiah's presentation of God or his Messiah fighting injustice and establishing righteous peace.[777] In Isa 11:3–5, we read that the Messiah will judge the poor and needy with righteousness: "He will strike the earth with the rod of his mouth; and with the breath of his lips he will slay the wicked." He has righteousness as a belt about him, and in a parallel line, he has faithfulness as his sash about his waist. The virtues of righteousness and faithfulness are demonstrated by his powerful word going forth. In Isa 52, Isaiah celebrates the news of God's peace and salvation with the proclamation that beautiful are the feet of those who bring welcome reports to God's people (52:7; quoted in Rom 10:15). The poetic image draws on the perspective of the townspeople watching as a jubilant messenger comes near with news of God's victory. Finally, in Isa 59 we read of God's armor, his breastplate of righteousness and helmet of salvation, which represents his works of justice and salvation for his repentant people and his recompense to his enemies (59:14–20).[778]

While Paul's reference point is God's armor, derived from biblical images, he also drew on his first-century CE Roman culture. Roman society promoted military dress as a status indicator, much as a toga signaled an elite male citizen. Upper-class male and female civilians typically had rope belts, and those in the lower classes often wore their tunics without belts.[779] Off-duty Roman soldiers wore a tunic that reached to the thigh and a long cloak, just as would other well-to-do males. Soldiers were distinguished by their military belt and shoes/sandals.[780] The military belt could be decorated by the individual soldier, but its symbolic significance reflected troop solidary

---

777. Thielman, 424.

778. Similar language about the whole armor of God, including the breastplate, helmet, shield, and sword, is found in Wis 5:17–20. In this passage, creation is armed to fight God's enemies, and God's zeal is linked to his armor. See D. G. Reid, "Triumph," *DPL* 946–54.

779. Liza Cleland, Glenys Davies, and Lloyd Llewellyn-Jones, *Greek and Roman Dress from A to Z* (New York: Routledge, 2007), 19.

780. Apuleius's *Metamorphoses* (or *The Golden Ass*) offers an entertaining story of a soldier mixing with civilians and provides details about the off-duty attire of a Roman soldier (9.39–42; 10.1).

and unity.[781] To take away the soldier's belt was to humiliate him, and a commander might do this as a disciplinary measure.[782] It is precisely this identification that moved the newly baptized centurion, Marcellus, in 298 CE to throw off his belt (and sword), explaining to the officer that he swore an oath of service to the Lord Jesus Christ: "It is not proper for a Christian, who fears Christ the Lord, to fight for the troubles of this world." His stance cost him his head, literally.[783]

Paul's emphasis on armor, then, is not simply protection against the wicked spiritual forces that seek to bring down believers. The armor also testifies to the person's identity and loyalty. Jesus spoke of such loyalty in his call that believers acknowledge and confess him before others (Matt 10:32–33; Luke 12:8). Wearing the armor of God further distinguishes believers from those around them, as ones who seek holiness and justice, who practice kindness and forgiveness, and who humbly serve others above themselves. To draw a lighthearted analogy, as superfans wear clothing and hats with their team's insignia, so too wearing God's armor identifies believers as part of God's "team." Moreover, the virtues described serve to protect Paul's integrity in ministry. To the Corinthians he commends himself "in truthful speech and in the power of God; with *weapons* of righteousness in the right hand and in the left" (2 Cor 6:7).[784] Paul invites the Romans to imagine themselves as actual "instruments" (the Greek term is the same) of righteousness, tools that God uses to further his kingdom (Rom 6:13).

14 Paul begins 6:14 with the conjunction "then" and the imperative that believers "stand." This is similar to his command to the Philippians, for after he presents the powerful picture of Christ's return, Paul asks them to "stand" in the Lord (4:1). Paul follows with a description of the parts of armor that believers wear as they stand fast. Each item of the armor represents a virtue or an aspect of faithful discipleship. The overall picture is of a defensive posture, maintaining what has already been won in Christ. And it is a portrayal of corporate solidarity, as believers stand as one body clothed in God's armor. The several aorist participles that follow the imperative further describe how

---

781. Stefanie Hoss, "The Roman Military Belt," in *Wearing the Cloak: Dressing the Soldier in Roman Times*, ed. Marie-Louise Nosch, Ancient Textiles Series 10 (Oxford: Oxbow, 2012), 44, explains: "The Roman military belt was the outward manifestation of this [coordinated co-operation of many individuals] and a central part of the Roman soldier's identity."

782. Hoss, "Roman Military Belt," 29–30, citing Suetonius, *Octavian* 24, and Plutarch, *Lucullus* 15, among others.

783. John Helgeland, Robert J. Daly, and J. Patout Burns, eds., *Christians and the Military: The Early Experience* (Philadelphia: Fortress, 1985), 61, citing *The Acts of Marcellus* (Recension N).

784. On ὅπλον see BDAG 716. Paul uses ὅπλον in his encouragement to the Roman believers to put on armor of light (Rom 13:12).

believers prepare to withstand the attack from the evil spiritual forces—they wear God's armor.[785] Paul imagines believers fully dressed in the armor of God, now standing attentive and watchful, confident in the knowledge that they are strong in the Lord's might, not in their own strength or tactics.

First, Paul describes the belt.[786] The Roman military belt was composed of a leather strap that encircled the waist, and four to eight leather straps, decorated with metal studs (*bullae*), hung from the belt. It is unclear whether the straps were to protect the groin and thigh area or were a status symbol that was both seen and heard as the soldier moved.[787] The daily dress for men and women was loose fitting, draped clothing, not trousers. Such attire proved very impractical for military maneuvers. A belt gathered the material, enabling better movement. The old-fashioned phrase "gird up your loins" expresses the idea of being ready to fight by belting the loose clothing.[788]

Paul identifies the belt with truth, and he likely means both the objective truth that is the redemption story of Christ's work and a believer's subjective belief in the same (1:13; 4:21).[789] Paul advocates having truth as part of our protection against the deception of the devil. Truth is what believers speak to each other, because truth is the center of the gospel (4:25). Paul reminds the Ephesians that they are in Christ based on "the word of truth, the gospel of your salvation" (1:13). He reminds them that they learned Christ and were taught according to the truth that is in Jesus (4:21). For this reason, believers speak truth to each other (4:15) and refuse to lie (4:25). The popular phrase "speak truth to power" comes to mind. This phrase can carry a self-important overtone if the individual desires the limelight and attention. Thus, truth must also protect us from our selfish rationalizations that use "the truth" primarily for self-aggrandizement.

Believers also put on a breastplate.[790] This piece of equipment protects the wearer's vital organs, but also communicates his status.[791] One of the most famous examples is the breastplate of the Prima Porta Augustus

---

785. The aorist participles elaborate on the finite verb "to stand," and the aorist tense does not refer to the time at which the believer put on the armor. For another view, see Best, 597, who suggests that the aorist participles signal what was done before the imperative verb "to stand."

786. On περιζώννυμι see BDAG 801 (2).

787. An important general resource is M. C. Bishop and J. C. N. Coulston, *Roman Military Equipment from the Punic Wars to the Fall of Rome* (London: Batsford, 1993).

788. Barth, 766, argues that the "belt" is better understood as a sash indicating high office (Latin *cingulum*) that each believer now holds because they are members of the Messiah's army. This suggestion fails to fully account for the military context of Paul's imagery.

789. Thielman, 424; Best, 599.

790. On θώραξ see BDAG 463–64.

791. Thielman, 424–25, offers a description of a Roman soldier's breastplate.

statue (on display in the Vatican Museum) from the villa of his wife, Livia. This marble statue depicts a metal molded breastplate that highlights Augustus's military victories. Breastplates might be made of strips of metal placed horizontally and attached with leather strips; the more expensive option would be chain mail. Paul is less interested in describing the specific sort of breastplate, as he spotlights the virtue of righteousness. He likely has in mind both the righteousness that justifies believers in Christ and also the righteousness incumbent upon believers.[792] In each of the three places in this epistle where Paul mentions "righteousness," he pairs it with "truth." In 4:24 Paul explains that the new self that believers put on is created to be like God in "true righteousness and holiness." He explains that as children of the light, believers are to produce fruit of "goodness, righteousness and truth" (5:8). Paul might have in mind Isa 59:17 LXX, in which God put on a breastplate of righteousness to wage war against injustice and bring repentance to sinners.[793]

15 With loins girded and the breastplate attached, believers make ready their feet. Roman soldiers had heavy-soled, sandal-like shoes with hollow nail studs on the bottom, a bit like cleats on an athlete's shoes. Such protection allowed soldiers to march long distances and maneuver adroitly in battle. Paul may have had such shoes in mind; however, his primary reference is Isa 52:7, which refers to feet that bring good news of peace and deliverance, of salvation to God's people. Paul cites this verse as he argues that Israel heard God's message of salvation but has not embraced his Messiah, Jesus (Rom 10:15). In the passage in Romans, Paul emphasizes the act of bringing the good news, but here in Ephesians Paul underscores the content of the message brought, namely, peace and salvation.

Paul does not say that the believers put on the gospel as one puts on sandals, but rather that they put on the "readiness" of the gospel. Paul's focus on the message's content is evident by his use of the noun "readiness."[794] The noun is found only here in the New Testament; however, the cognate verb is used about forty times, always with the meaning "to prepare" or "to get ready."[795] Believers' feet are made ready through the gospel of peace because they prepared well in understanding the gospel message.[796] They know the true word of peace gained through Christ's work on the cross and can defend themselves against the devil's lies. The readiness is not related to the work

---

792. Arnold, 453. Thielman, 425, argues that the focus is on "an ethical quality—being just, fair, equitable."

793. Thielman, 425, suggests: "So here the warrior puts on a particular quality and does battle against evil."

794. On ἑτοιμασία see BDAG 401.

795. On ἑτοιμάζω see BDAG 400–401; Hoehner, 843; Arnold, 454.

796. Thielman, 426; Lincoln, 449.

of the evangelist preaching in the city's marketplace, but reflects the verbal defense of one's views to those who ask or challenge the believer's Christian convictions.[797] Paul asks the Ephesians to pray for him in just such circumstances so that when Roman magistrates confront him he might give a faithful testimony (6:19).[798]

The gospel is defined as peace, and this peace is found in the person and work of Christ. Paul speaks of Christ as "our peace" in bringing together all types and sorts of people under his redemptive care, creating a new fellowship of faithful followers (2:14–22). This is the peace that binds believers together in the Holy Spirit (4:3). Jesus brings peace, not as the world gives, but a peace that lives into eternity (John 14:27; 16:33).

16 Unlike the peace that Christ brings, the devil's warfare includes "flaming arrows" to inflict mortal wounds. Paul expands his listing of God's armor by asking believers to take up the "shield of faith."[799] He transitions to this item of armor with the phrase "in addition," which may draw attention to the shield's importance. We might think of the soldier receiving the shield from the Lord, taking hold of it, and using it to fend off the devil's deadly strikes.

The shield Paul refers to is approximately two feet wide and four feet long, semicylindrical in shape, with a handle in the center. The convex shape was made of two or three layers of wood glued together, over which could be put a layer of canvas and then of leather.[800] This leather might be painted.[801] Iron or bronze bands were wrapped around the top and bottom edges, and bronze decorations might adorn it. The ancient historian Polybius comments on the iron boss in the center of the shield that protects against missiles such as stones, spears, and arrows.[802] The shield might weigh about ten kilograms

---

797. Best, 599; contra Arnold, 454, who sees the phrase "of the gospel" as an objective genitive: "The preparation is for the gospel and speaks of an equipping to share the gospel."

798. Col 4:6 focuses on evangelism, speaking the gospel to the public.

799. Paul uses the term θυρεός (shield) in 6:16; God's shield (ὅπλον, a general term for armor found in Rom 6:13; 13:12; 2 Cor 6:7; 10:4; see also John 18:3) figures prominently in Ps 91, which speaks of God's faithfulness as the believer's shield (91:4) against which no force from the enemy will prevail. Specific mention is made of not fearing the enemy's arrows, for no harm will come to God's faithful (91:5, 10). The psalm continues with the promise that the faithful will tread on the lion and cobra and will trample on the great lion and the serpent (91:13), for God will deliver. In the temptation scene where Jesus faced Satan, the latter cites from this psalm that God's angels will keep the Lord's servant from striking his foot against a stone (Matt 4:6; Luke 4:10–11).

800. On θυρεός see BDAG 462; Bishop and Coulston, *Roman Military Equipment*, 61, 92.

801. Bishop and Coulston, *Roman Military Equipment*, 92, offer examples from Masada that indicated painted leather.

802. Polybius, *History* 6.23.2.

6:14–17 PUT ON GOD'S ARMOR

(about twenty-two pounds).[803] Roman soldiers used their shields not only to defend their person, but also in a maneuver known as the tortoise (Latin *testudo*) that enabled them to get close to a city's walls or gates without injury. The unit stood in a square, and those in the middle put their shields over their heads, while the men on the outside used the shields to guard their bodies. Now protected much as a turtle is by its shell, they moved close to their target without injury from missiles thrown at them. This common troop formation is etched on Trajan's Column in Rome. Josephus mentions this tactic in Rome's assault of the Jewish city of Jotapata.[804] In a clever tactical move, the Jews on the wall poured boiling oil on top of this formation, badly injuring the Roman soldiers as the oil ran between the shields and seeped under their armor. Josephus's men won the day, but lost within a few weeks to Rome's overpowering force. I mention this formation for two reasons. First, it required coordinated work on the soldiers' part. It would remind the Ephesians that they are stronger as a unit and that their unity is in Christ. Second, it leads us to consider Paul's statement about the enemy's artillery—flaming arrows.

Paul creates the terrifying picture of fiery assault raining down on believers and assures them that faith in the work of God in Christ dowses the flames. In ancient warfare, individual archers or a machine shot an arrow wrapped with combustible materials such as hemp and pitch in their efforts to take a city. They might also apply pitch to a javelin and launch that into the opponents' ranks. Livy writes of this horrible weapon, which included three feet of iron that was wrapped with tow (hemp) and covered with pitch, set on fire, and hurled at the enemy. The flame took life as it sailed through the air, and then it hit the shield in a ball of fire; the soldier often dropped the shield and became defenseless before the enemy.[805] Paul need not be familiar with this passage of Livy's *History* about the siege of Saguntum for us to read them together today and draw out the spiritual lesson of Paul's overall emphasis on faith. Without the shield, the soldier stands defenseless against the enemy, and it is only a matter of time before a second or third blow fells him. To drop the shield is to lose the battle. Thus, Paul enjoins believers to stand fast and to keep hold of their shields.

Paul notes that the shield protects by extinguishing the flames. Some commentators suggest that Roman soldiers soaked their shields in water to put out the flame. The ancient sources do not speak of this maneuver; instead, they describe the besieged army covering wooden structures within their city

---

803. Bishop and Coulston, *Roman Military Equipment*, 62.
804. Josephus, *Jewish War* 3.7.27 §270.
805. Livy, *History* 21.8. See also Herodotus, *Histories* 8.52; Ammianus Marcellinus, *The Later Roman Empire (A.D. 354–378)*, trans. Walter Hamilton, introduction and notes by Andrew Wallace-Hadrill (London: Penguin, 1986).

walls with soaked animal skins so that flaming arrows would be quenched.[806] Moreover, the glue that held together the wooden layers within the shield would be loosened if soaked in water, and the sodden shield would be much heavier and less easy to maneuver. Therefore, most likely Paul has in mind the shield's metal boss taking the arrow, rendering its flame useless against the metal guard.[807]

The shield represents faith, and Paul has in view both Christ's faithfulness as well as believers' response of faith to God's great work of redemption. Paul speaks of Christ's faithfulness in 3:12, granting believers boldness and freedom to access God. This faithfulness serves as the foundation of salvation, which is by grace from first to last (2:8). Paul speaks of "one faith" as that redemption story (4:5), established before time itself in the mysterious majesty of God (1:3–4). Paul prays that believers will allow Christ's love to take deep root in their hearts by faith (3:17), trusting God's promises and holding fast to their convictions. Believers exercise their convictions as a soldier moves his shield to prevent enemy weapons from killing him. The believer's task is to use what is given by God and watch as the enemy's fierce attack is brought to nothing through the surpassing power of God's armor.

17 Last to be put on is "the helmet of salvation," and then to pick up "the sword of the Spirit." Paul has been using participles to describe the action of putting on the various pieces of God's armor. Here he shifts to an imperative, "to take up," as he communicates the believer's reception of the final two items of armor.[808] Because the clause begins with "and" in the Greek, it seems unlikely that Paul intends a strong break in the flow of his description. Rather, the imperative reinforces the earlier imperative "to stand" (6:14) and reiterates the importance of using all the armor God provides.[809] The verb offers the picture of Christ handing to his faithful soldiers their sure deliverance and the soldiers receiving their helmets gladly.[810]

The helmet is identified as salvation, a term that carries the connotation of "deliverance" and has special impact in the context of a battle.[811] The

---

806. Josephus, *Jewish War* 3.7.10 §173; Thucydides 2.75.4.

807. Arnold, 458, argues that the Ephesians would have Artemis and her arrows in mind. While this cannot be ruled out, the image is not the dominant one as Paul is not focused primarily on establishing a connection between Artemis and the evil spiritual forces.

808. On δέχομαι see BDAG 221.

809. Arnold, 459–60; Salmond, 388. Contra Hoehner, 849.

810. MacDonald, 346. Lincoln, 450, writes that the shift from participles to an imperative indicates Paul moves from listing virtues that require human effort "to objects which are gifts in the purest sense, 'salvation' and 'the word of God.'" While this sentiment may be true theologically, it is not clear that the shift from participle to imperative in this case can bear the theological weight.

811. On σωτήριον see BDAG 986. Paul uses the neuter noun only here and the typical

6:14–17 Put on God's Armor

Ephesians are "saved" in the sense that they are seated with Christ, they have received the grace of God (2:6–8), and they are included in Christ (1:13). The salvation Paul speaks of here is that daily deliverance from the attacks of the evil one and the intense moments of spiritual assault that periodically threaten the church. Paul understands that the believers' future inheritance has important ramifications now as they live out their witness of God's salvation.[812] Paul expresses a similar theme to the Thessalonians, as he admonishes them to be alert as they put on "faith and love as a breastplate, and the hope of salvation as a helmet" (1 Thess 5:8). These three virtues are recognized and praised as characteristic of the Thessalonians' walk (1:3). Paul wants them to continue trusting in their sure hope of deliverance, for God has ordained such salvation through Christ (5:9). Here in Ephesians only, Paul uses the neuter adjective form of "salvation" rather than his typical choice of the feminine form. Paul probably draws on Isa 59:17 LXX, as the Septuagint commonly uses this form.[813] Isaiah speaks also of the breastplate of righteousness, as he describes God accomplishing salvation with his own arm and by his own righteous justice.

Believers receive not only the helmet of salvation but also the sword of the Spirit, that is, the sword that has the Holy Spirit as its source.[814] The sword itself is not the Spirit, but the sword is effective because it represents the Spirit's power. The Spirit of God can be described as breath, and Paul draws on the prophet Isaiah's evocative language. Isaiah describes the Messiah as bringing righteous judgement to bear through the breath of his lips (Isa 11:4; see also Rev 19:15). Isaiah paints the image of God's breath that brings wrath to his enemies and redemption to his people (Isa 59:19).

The sword is the word of God. The term "word" (*rhēma*) is found in only a few places in Paul, including earlier in 5:26, where Paul describes Christ's purifying actions that cleanse the church "by the washing with water through the word."[815] Commentators are split on whether the sword of the Spirit is an offensive or a defensive weapon. Some argue that the sword of the Spirit, the word of God, is the offensive weapon given to believers to attack the kingdom

---

feminine noun σωτηρία in 1:13 and in 1 Thess 5:8 ("helmet of salvation"); see L. Morris, "Salvation," *DPL* 858–62; Gerald G. O'Collins, "Salvation," *ABD* 5:907–14.

812. Hoehner, 850, contrasts this use of "salvation" with salvation "in the objective sense" and argues that here Paul intends "a conscious possession of it [salvation] in the midst of the onslaught of the evil one."

813. Hoehner, 850; Arnold, 460.

814. On μάχαιρα see BDAG 622.

815. On ῥῆμα see BDAG 905 (1). Paul uses the term λόγος in 1:13. MacDonald, 346, observes that the term ῥῆμα "refers to what is spoken" and points to Acts 6:13 where "*rēma* is used in the context of making threats against something." Arnold, 461, comments that the two terms are interchangeable.

of darkness by proclaiming the light of the gospel.[816] They highlight 6:15 with its reference to "the gospel of peace," and they point to its use in Romans, wherein Paul quotes Deut 30:14, "the word is near you," in his argument that Christ is the fulfillment of the law (Rom 10:8). Paul continues using "word" as he cites Ps 19:4, and the content of this message is "the word about Christ," namely, the gospel (Rom 10:17–18). Others see the sword of the Spirit as a defensive tool. Paul, they argue, imagines that Scripture is brought to mind as believers face the attacks of the evil powers and principalities.[817] An example of such is Jesus's temptations, as he drew on Scripture in battling Satan (Matt 4:1–11; Luke 4:1–13). A third option is to accept both positions, as believers defend themselves and advance the gospel.[818] The third view is the strongest, for it takes into account the dynamic metaphor Paul creates of Christian soldiers' response in the face of evil forces that seek their downfall.

The Ephesians have the sword of the Spirit, the promises of God made good in Christ and established in Scripture. The full story of redemption—from creation to fall to establishing God's people and giving the law, to the sacrifices and the tabernacle, the exile and the promise of the Messiah—this full story is captured in the gospel and is found in Christ. It is this sure truth that believers proclaim against the deception of the evil one. Paul envisions the believers standing fast, defending the territory won by their lord, Jesus Christ. As the evil spiritual forces mount their attack, the believers can cut and thrust against the ruses of the enemy. This is still a defensive posture, for the soldier is not advancing the line, but is protecting himself and the ground already acquired.

Paul presents a vivid image of a believer's situation. What does it mean to think of righteousness as a breastplate that shields the heart? Or truth that covers the midsection with protection and allows movement? Platitudes are no match for the onsite decisions and quick-thinking maneuvers necessary to block incoming fiery darts, often in the shape of slick sounding reports that favor the enemy. Paul knows the situation is ripe for self-deception, self-justification, rationalization, fear, despondency. Truth, righteousness, and faith—the gospel of redemption and peace—these form the story of Christ's work that should excite holy imagination to the possibilities of service to the kingdom of Christ and of God. Believers are to know this story, what righteousness looks like in action, what truth looks like in everyday expressions. Paul's dynamic image of armor moves away from thinking about discipleship as individualistic self-improvement techniques. It encourages believers to think about living holy lives in the midst of storms, chaos, confusion, and intrigue.

---

816. Lincoln, 451; Salmond, 388; Thielman, 429.

817. Hoehner, 853, although Hoehner himself identifies this as an "offensive weapon" because it is used against the devil.

818. Arnold, 462.

Readers today might be tempted to tame Paul's language to make it more amenable and comfortable, but there is nothing comfortable about being besieged. Modern militaries using powerful cannons and aircraft have made siege warfare a thing of the past, accessible now only through movies. But in Paul's day, everyone knew what it looked like for an enemy army to surround a city. And only a few decades after Paul wrote these words, Jerusalem itself is besieged by the general Titus, whose father, Vespasian, decimated Galilee. The great Arch of Titus in Rome celebrates Rome's victory over Jerusalem and records Titus's plunder of the temple. The iconic Colosseum of Rome was built and paid for by Jewish slaves from the Revolt of 70 CE. Jewish historian Josephus recounts the awful price paid by those living in Jerusalem, as Rome tightened its grip and squeezed the life out of its population.[819]

The second and third centuries were the age of the Christian martyrs, as a relatively small number of men and women succumbed to hideous torture and death in arenas around the empire. Their memory within the church shaped the vision of discipleship. As the early believers knew well, the armor of God does not protect against suffering, nor does it preserve a believer from a painful death. The armor is not a good luck charm that keeps sadness at bay or misfortune from entering a believer's life. The armor strengthens believers as they encounter the sorrow, pain, misfortune, and injustice that characterize the present evil age. By remembering what is true, by holding to what is just, by listening to the Savior's word of peace, believers together in the church can withstand the evil forces that seek to destroy all goodness and hope.

EXCURSUS: MILITARY IMAGES AND METAPHORS IN PAUL'S LETTERS

Several military allusions and analogies occur throughout Paul's letters. For example, the call to be faithful can be seen against the backdrop of soldiers' oath-taking. Each soldier gave an oath to the emperor when commissioned to serve, which in Latin is *sacramentum* and in Greek is *pistis*—faith or loyalty. This oath to be loyal or faithful was given to their lord, *kyrios*.[820] Paul's call to the Corinthians to stand firm in the faith (*pistis*) echoes this sentiment, and he calls them to be courageous using a verb related to military valor (*andrizomai*, 1 Cor

---

819. Josephus's works were among the most widely read throughout Western history. The Penguin Classics edition of his *Jewish War* is very readable and provides a front row seat to the events of the first century of the church's life; Josephus, *The Jewish War*, trans. G. A. Williamson, rev. E. Mary Smallwood (London: Penguin, 1981).

820. Raymond Hobbs, "The Language of Warfare in the New Testament," in *Modelling Early Christianity: Social Scientific Studies of the New Testament in Its Context*, ed. Philip F. Esler (London: Routledge, 1995), 260.

16:13). Moral philosophers spoke metaphorically of a student taking an oath of loyalty to a god, much as a soldier does.[821] The first-century philosopher Seneca compared life with a battle.[822] He advocated reason and a life of self-control as the way to master one's enemies, often defined as one's passions. Paul probably speaks with this sense of moral or spiritual battle in mind when he identifies Epaphroditus as a "fellow soldier" (Phil 2:25; see also Phlm 2). Paul enjoins Timothy to "fight the good fight" (1 Tim 1:18). Paul encourages the Philippians to follow his example and obey him, two qualities common for military officers to demand of their troops (Phil 2:12; 3:17). Paul also imagines believers as soldiers who conquer evil with good (Rom 12:21). He challenges the Romans to remain awake or be on guard, armed with weapons of light for their salvation or deliverance (Rom 13:11–14).[823] Paul charges believers to stand firm, as might an army defending a hard-won city (1 Cor 15:1; 16:13; Phil 1:27; 1 Thess 3:8; 2 Thess 2:15). Finally, Paul warns the Corinthians that, although they think they are standing strong, nevertheless they are in danger of falling (1 Cor 10:12).

Paul availed himself of the many military metaphors available in his culture. How do these metaphors advance his argument? As with any metaphor, the author draws attention to only certain aspects of the comparison. In our case, Paul stresses the loyalty of a soldier to his commander, even if that means suffering or death.[824] A soldier demonstrates loyalty by obeying commands, executing orders quickly, and remaining steadfast without fear in the midst of battle.[825] In contrast, a mercenary is in it for himself and the plunder he can acquire. He abandons his fellow soldiers if the going gets rough and runs when the battle turns against his side.

Especially when physical strength is the primary asset, men are judged to be better soldiers. However, women in the ancient world fought, and a few commanded armies. Usually, women took up arms to defend their walled city. From the height of the embattlements, they had tactical advantage that outweighed their lack of physical strength. And they certainly were motivated to protect the city, for if it fell, they knew they would likely be raped and sold into slavery, while their male family members would be put to death. Women were praised for their courage and ingenuity in this context. Less so were women praised as commanders of armies. Fulvia (wife of Marc Antony) and Marc Antony's brother, Lucius Antonius, led a rebellion

---

821. Epictetus, *Discourses* 1.14.13–17; Seneca, *Epistles* 59.7–8.

822. Seneca, *Epistles* 96.5; see also Epictetus, *Discourses* 3.24.

823. For a general discussion, see Edgar Krentz, "Paul, Games, and the Military," in *Paul in the Greco-Roman World: A Handbook*, ed. J. Paul Sampley (Harrisburg: Trinity, 2003), 344–83.

824. Hobbs, "Language of Warfare in the New Testament," 264.

825. Wansink, *Chained in Christ*, 169, explains: "Loyalty, perseverance and steadfastness are virtues which the ideal soldier was said to possess." See Seneca, *Epistles* 95.35.

against Octavian. They failed, and she died during her flight. Plutarch blames her as being meddlesome and headstrong, although earlier he praises her for defending Antony's interests in Rome while he was fighting elsewhere.[826] Cleopatra VII and Marc Antony led forces against Octavian in a disastrous attempt to secure rule over Rome. In Britain in 60-61 CE, Queen Boudicca of the Iceni rebelled against Roman rule, burning down three cities and the imperial cult temple in Camulodunum.[827] Her revolt was put down with as much violence as was the Jewish Revolt a few years later in Jerusalem. Perhaps the best-known female military commander is Queen Elizabeth I, who gave a rousing speech to her troops at Tilbury in 1588, wherein she declared: "I may have the body of a weak and feeble woman, but I have the heart and stomach of a king."[828]

Then and now, war and military service tends to be the purview of men. Does Paul wish to inscribe his Roman culture's masculinity on Christian men with his use of military metaphors? As we saw above, Paul turns many Roman values upside down, not the least in his claim that Christ the crucified one is also the world's savior (Eph 5:23, 25). It is Christ the crucified king who wins the battle against evil cosmic forces and the chaos that surrounds them (see also Col 1:12-14; 2:15). His ignoble death was, ironically, a triumph, over the spiritual forces (Col 2:15; see also 1 Cor 15:54-55).[829] Paul did not see the Messiah's work as primarily one of overthrowing Rome and restoring Jewish home rule over Judea and Galilee. Christ's work brought together Jews and gentiles, those near and far, as a new people in him (Eph 2:11-13). Christ's death on the cross breaks sin's hold on humanity, and his resurrection secures victory over death for his coheirs.

---

3. Pray in the Spirit (6:18-20)

¹⁸*And pray in the Spirit on all occasions with all kinds of prayers and requests. With this in mind, be alert and always keep on praying for all the Lord's*

---

826. Plutarch, *Antonius* 28-30.
827. Tacitus, *Annals* 14.31.6-7.
828. Carole Levin, *The Heart and Stomach of a King: Elizabeth I and the Politics of Sex and Power*, 2nd ed. (Philadelphia: University of Pennsylvania Press, 2013), 1.
829. Tremper Longman III and Daniel G. Reid, *God Is a Warrior* (Grand Rapids: Zondervan, 1995), 148, write: "Christ did not strip the powers, divesting them of their weaponry or clothing; in dying on the cross, he stripped off the principalities and powers from himself. In this way the cross was an instrument not of shame but of triumph."

people. ¹⁹*Pray also for me, that whenever I speak, words may be given me so that I will fearlessly make known the mystery of the gospel,* ²⁰*for which I am an ambassador in chains. Pray that I may declare it fearlessly, as I should.*

Often what makes a good soldier is the ability to anticipate the enemy's next move and to be prepared with a counteroffensive. If you know your enemy's playbook, you can develop your strategy to prevent their attacks or at least minimize the damage. Such thinking is behind Paul's remarks on prayer in these three verses. He knows that all the armor in the world will not aid a lazy, distracted, or overconfident soldier. The attitude is perhaps even more important than the equipment. That is why Paul insists that believers pray with all kinds of prayer, at all times, for all the saints. Only by having God's perspective will believers use his armor to full effect.

18 This passage has no finite verb, but two present participles that connect to the previous section. From a syntactical perspective, the participles "praying" and "being alert" link back to either the imperative "take/receive" in 6:17 or "stand" in 6:14. Usually the more proximate antecedent is the preferred choice, but in this case "stand fast" is the dominant claim made by Paul in this passage.[830] The grammatical link suggests to some that prayer is part of God's armor.[831] This is unlikely, however, because Paul does not figuratively compare prayer with a physical weapon or another piece of armor. Moreover, Paul begins 6:18 with the preposition "through" or "with," inadequately translated "and" in the NIV, which indicates Paul has turned his attention to another aspect of the struggle against spiritual forces.[832] Paul speaks generally now about how the armor is best used. It makes more sense, then, to translate the participles as imperatives, recognizing that they take their force from the previous discussion about the dangerous spiritual forces arraigned against believers.[833] We might think of prayer as the army supply line that brings bullets and butter to the soldiers on the front line. Without ammunition and food, the soldier has no strength or defense.

Paul uses the adjective "all" four times in 6:18, as he addresses "all kinds" of prayers given on "all occasions," urging them to "always" keep praying

---

830. Best, 604; Lincoln, 451.
831. Wink, *Naming the Powers*, 88.
832. Lincoln, 451–52. Fowl, 208n15, argues that the injunction to pray relies on the commands from 6:10, 11, 14 and, pointing to the repetition of "all" in 6:18, concludes that "prayer is presented as a comprehensive activity that covers and supports every aspect of the church's witness to the powers."
833. Thielman, 433, helpfully compares the syntax of this passage with that of 5:21: "The participles in both 5:21 and here are being used adverbially and are related to the imperative-mood verb that occurs before them, but these participles adopt an independent, imperatival quality of their own."

6:18–20 Pray in the Spirit

for "all the Lord's people." We have seen such linguistic flourish throughout Ephesians, but this is not mere rhetoric. Paul uses repetition as emphasis, much as we might use bold and italic type. He uses the noun "prayers" and its cognate participle, and twice he uses the noun "requests."[834] With great rhetorical force, Paul drives home the importance of prayer.

Paul invites believers to pray in the Spirit, as he stresses the power source of believers' petitions. Paul earlier urged the Ephesians to be filled with the Spirit in their community worship (5:18–20).[835] Paul modeled prayer twice in the epistle (1:15–23; 3:14–21). In these earlier prayers Paul prays for all the saints, consistent with his theme of unity. He emphasizes the power of the Holy Spirit, the indwelling of Christ in the believer's heart, and the capacity to know deep in one's bones the all-surpassing love that God has for his people. Elsewhere in Paul, it is the Spirit who aids believers in prayer (Rom 8:15; Gal 4:6) and who prays for them when their situation is beyond words (Rom 8:26; 1 Cor 14:14–17). Because of the Spirit's sustaining role in prayer, Paul commands the Thessalonians to "pray without ceasing" (1 Thess 5:17; see also Jude 20).

The verb "be alert" is used only four times in the New Testament and only here in Paul.[836] Jesus warns his followers about the coming day of the Lord (Mark 13:33), proclaiming that they must be alert and on guard, for no one knows when this great and terrible day will come. Jesus expresses a similar thought using a synonymous verb as he speaks to Peter, urging him to watch and pray so that he will not succumb to temptation, for the spirit is willing but the flesh is weak (Mark 14:38). The atmosphere of spiritual struggle is palpable in these Markan verses and pulsates through these passages in Ephesians as well (5:11, 15).

Paul emphasizes perseverance in his insistence that believers "keep on" praying. The noun translated here "keep on" is not found elsewhere in the New Testament, but the cognate verb is found in several places.[837] Paul calls on the Romans to be "faithful" in prayer (Rom 12:12), and he urges the Colossians to "devote" themselves to prayer (Col 4:2). The earliest believers modeled this faithfulness, as we find them together "constantly" in prayer (Acts 1:14), "devoting" themselves to each other in fellowship and prayer (Acts 2:42).

---

834. On προσευχή see BDAG 878 (1); on προσεύχομαι see BDAG 879; on δέησις see BDAG 213. NIV translates the second occurrence of the noun δέησις as "praying." Paul connects "prayers and requests" in his letter to the Philippians (Phil 4:6; see also 1 Tim 2:1; 5:5).

835. MacDonald, 347.

836. On ἀγρυπνέω see BDAG 16. Fowl, 209, notes that the verb ἀγρυπνέω is used in 6:18 and in some textual versions of Mark 13:33. The synonym γρηγορέω is used in Mark 14:34–38.

837. On προσκαρτέρησις see BDAG 881.

19–20 Paul requests that the Ephesians pray also for him and his current situation as he awaits an audience with the Roman magistrate. He asks the Ephesians to pray that he be given "words" from God.[838] Paul emphasizes that these words would come from God, not his own ingenuity, by using the divine passive voice of the verb "to give."[839] Paul indicates that when he speaks, God will shape the message. Paul draws on Old Testament imagery with his phrase "opening my mouth" (NIV reads "whenever I speak"). By using this figure of speech, Paul emphasizes the voice of God through the prophet. To Moses, God insists that he gives humans sight, hearing, and speech and will likewise give Moses the words he needs to say, specifically that he will open his mouth (Exod 4:11–12). God speaks prophetic words even through opening the mouth of a donkey (Num 22:28). And in a passage already on Paul's mind, Isaiah recounts the covenant God makes with his people, including his words that were put in their mouths (Isa 59:21; 59:17 speaks of God's armor). Jesus makes a similar promise to his followers that they will be given what to say when they are brought before officials (Matt 10:19–20).

Paul asks for "fearlessness in speaking."[840] The irony of a bold prisoner would not be lost on the Ephesians, for prisoners, like slaves, were often shamed into humiliating silence. Yet Paul speaks of boldness because his chains represent his commitment to Christ. The question is whether the phrase should be attached to what precedes it, thus describing bold words, or whether it belongs with what follows, explaining that Paul will fearlessly make known the mystery. The scales tip slightly in favor of the latter option.[841] Paul asks that God give him a word, but that he proclaims this word with boldness or fearlessly (see also 1 Thess 2:2). Paul reiterates his desire to be fearless in the next verse, using the cognate verb. Paul earlier noted that believers can boldly or freely approach God through Christ (Eph 3:12).

Paul describes the mystery "of the gospel"[842] as befits his emphasis throughout the epistle. This mystery has been revealed in Christ and includes the breathtaking truth that gentiles are united with Christ together with Jews as they make up one new humanity in the Lord (3:3–6, 9–10).

---

838. On λόγος see BDAG 598–601 (1).
839. On δίδωμι see BDAG 242 (2); Best, 607.
840. On παρρησία see BDAG 781–82 (3). On παρρησιάζομαι see BDAG 782.
841. Salmond, 390–91; Hoehner, 862; Lincoln, 454–55.
842. Thielman, 436, lists the few manuscripts, including Codex Vaticanus (B), that lack the phrase "of the gospel," but rightly concludes that the phrase should be included in our text due to strong external evidence and that a scribe would be more likely to add the phrase "of Christ" or "of God," as found in numerous places in Paul (cf. Eph 3:4). See also Hoehner, 860.

The mystery includes the union of Christ and the church, his body (5:32). The unity foreshadows the final union of all things under Christ (1:10, 21). He triumphed over all his enemies, who are under his feet (1:20-22). This picture draws on Ps 8:6 and 110:1, as Christ fulfills the Davidic promise that God's Messiah will reign over his people and will defeat humanity's enemies—sin and death (1 Cor 15:22-28; Eph 1:19-22; Col 3:1-11; Heb 1:3, 13; 2:8; 1 Pet 3:22).

Boldness is necessary due to the astounding content of the message, the mystery of the gospel, that challenges the Roman status quo. We rightly think of the gospel as "good news" and it is—for those who know they are broken people living in a sinful age. However, this picture of the times would sound blasphemous to imperial Roman ears that hear only the claim "peace and security" through their "savior" the emperor. Additionally, the gospel amounted to blasphemy against the gods and one's family, which is why Paul's message received so much negative attention (Acts 16:16-20; 17:6-9). Paul encouraged gentiles to embrace Christ, the Messiah of the Jews, and forsake their pagan gods and their ancestral and hearth gods. Undaunted by imperial power, Paul proclaims the gospel message throughout the empire to all gentiles, this mystery "which is Christ in you, the hope of glory" (Col 1:27; see also Rom 16:26).

As he writes this letter, Paul sits in chains, likely under guard under some sort of house arrest or physically handcuffed to a soldier. This treatment was painful and often included deprivation of food and sleep.[843] To be in chains was shameful and humiliating (Phil 1:20; 2 Tim 1:8).[844] Twice in Ephesians Paul stresses his prisoner status, that he is in chains because of his faithful proclamation of the gospel. He points to this reality that he might encourage believers to live a life worthy of their calling (4:1) and to explain that his imprisonment is their glory (3:13). Shifting the language from "prisoner" to "ambassador" reinforces the claim that his message is from God, the one whom Paul represents in the proclamation of the gospel. The image is ironic, even oxymoronic, for an ambassador typically has diplomatic immunity.[845] Paul identifies himself as an ambassador using a present indicative verb, meaning one who speaks on behalf of the government to a foreign sovereign (6:20).[846] Using the same verb, he describes his work as an ambassador of Christ to the Corinthians. Paul brings the message of his

---

843. Perkins, 148, writes: "Both the weight and manner of chaining prisoners made chains extremely painful." See also Rapske, *Book of Acts and Paul*, 206-9.

844. Rapske, *Book of Acts and Paul*, 288-98. He writes: "Whether convicted or not, those who became prisoners no longer possessed their former dignity in the public view" (291).

845. Lincoln, 454.

846. On πρεσβεύω see BDAG 861. See also Fowl, 209, and Thielman, 435.

king: be reconciled to God, be forgiven of your sins through the redemptive work of Christ (2 Cor 5:20).

Before leaving this section, a word must be said on how this passage fits with the broader conversation about this epistle's authorship. Some point to similarities with Col 4:3–4 and suggest that a pseudonymous author changed a few terms to create an ending in Ephesians that aligned with Paul's earlier letter to Colossae.[847] The similarities between the passages include the call to be watchful in prayer, the call to devote themselves to prayer, and the request by Paul that a door be open so as to speak the mystery of Christ (Colossians) or of the gospel (Ephesians). The differences include that Paul speaks of his coworkers ("us") in Colossians, but requests prayers for only himself in Ephesians. Paul speaks in both of his chains, although he uses different terms.[848]

The data need not indicate a pseudonymous author. First, Paul's request to the Romans that they pray for him, with no mention of coworkers (Rom 15:30–32; see also Phil 1:19–20), tallies with Paul's request here. Moreover, why would a pseudonymous author remove the request to pray for "us" and instead create a request from a posthumous Paul?[849] Second, Paul's flare for irony is displayed in the image of an ambassador in chains, similar to his celebration of his ignoble sufferings that confirm his apostolic calling (2 Cor 6:4–10; 11:21–33).[850] Third, this passage echoes several refrains found in Eph 3, including the themes of Paul's apostolic mission to make known the mystery of redemption to the church, which displays God's wisdom to the powers and principalities. Ephesians 6 picks up the focus on these powers and the church, in this case the latter's need for God's armor to stand fast against the spiritual authorities' hostility. The common threads suggest that 6:18–20 is not merely a "pseudonymous device."[851]

---

847. Lincoln, 452. Perkins, 148, remarks: "The formula has been appropriated from Col 4:2–4." She observes the similarities with Phil 1:14–20 and concludes that "the prayer formula at the conclusion to Ephesians has generalized this pattern."

848. On ἅλυσις in Eph 6:20 see BDAG 48; on δέω in Col 4:3 see BDAG 221 (1).

849. Best, 606, notes that if the author knew Paul was dead, then the prayer request "must be understood as part of the pseudepigraphic framework." Lincoln, 455, argues against Pauline authorship and suggests that "the writer considers himself a representative of Paul, [thus] the request can also be understood as his appeal for prayer for his own bold proclamation of the Pauline gospel."

850. Thielman, 413.

851. Fowl, 209; see also n16.

IV. FINAL GREETINGS (6:21–24)

21Tychicus, the dear brother and faithful servant in the Lord, will tell you everything, so that you also may know how I am and what I am doing. 22I am sending him to you for this very purpose, that you may know how we are, and that he may encourage you.

23Peace to the brothers and sisters, and love with faith from God the Father and the Lord Jesus Christ. 24Grace to all who love our Lord Jesus Christ with an undying love.

These last few verses of the epistle hold pearls of wisdom for pastors and church leaders (or leaders in any field): praise others, be transparent, encourage. Paul draws his letter to a close in ways that further reveal his pastor's heart and set an example for leaders today. First, he praises his coworker, Tychicus, as a faithful servant of the church who is one of his close friends. This empowers Tychicus and affirms him before the church. Second, Paul emphasizes his willingness to make his circumstances known to the Ephesians. Paul has nothing to hide about his conduct and was happy to have a coworker communicate to others about Paul's circumstances. Third, he believes his news will encourage them (3:13), and he wishes to comfort them. All three attributes point to Paul's outward-facing posture that puts others before himself.

21–22 Paul explains his actions in sending Tychicus to the Ephesians. Paul wants them to know his circumstances and how Paul and his companions are getting on.[1] Tychicus is to encourage the Ephesians as he informs them of Paul's situation. The verses empower Tychicus as a reliable witness and spokesperson for Paul. Paul repeats three times, in three different phrases, that Tychicus will inform them of his circumstances. This unusual redundancy likely serves to emphasize his point that Tychicus will be entirely forthcoming.[2]

What is the relationship between these two verses and Col 4:7–8? This question arises because Eph 6:21–22 and Col 4:7–8 share thirty-two words, written in the same order, making it most likely that one was copied from the other.[3] Some suggest that such copying points to a pseudonymous author

---

1. Lincoln, 462, comments that the first-person plural pronoun indicates borrowing from Colossians, specifically pointing to Col 4:8, which refers back to the prescript that names Paul and Timothy as cosenders.

2. Thielman, 440.

3. Perkins, 150–51, offers columns displaying the verses for comparison. Lincoln, 462, writes: "Ephesians reproduces in total thirty-two words found in the same sequence as in Colossians." Ephesians inserts the phrases ἵνα δὲ εἰδῆτε καὶ ὑμεῖς ("so that you also may know")

writing after Paul's death who had Colossians in front of him and wrote the verses verbatim into his Ephesians document. Those who argue this suggest that the details provide verisimilitude and that readers would be cognizant of such customs. But why would the author copy what he and his readers would know was impossible to provide, namely, current information about a man who is now dead? At one time, this question would be answered by pointing to the nature of pseudepigraphic literature. Recently the theory of pseudepigraphic material in the New Testament has been called into question. It is argued that the letters in Scripture have few commonalities with the known pseudepigraphic literature of the ancient world. I discuss pseudepigraphy at some length in the introduction, where I argue that the historical and textual evidence points to Paul as the author of the epistle.[4]

The most likely solution to the similar wording is that Paul's secretary had Colossians available and used that ending. This fits letter-writing patterns of Paul's day, with authors including similar material in different letters. Moreover, since Tychicus is taking both letters, and since Ephesus and Colossae are in the same region, it would make sense that they were written about the same time and might include similar information. The content of the shared material is not easily restated, for it describes Tychicus's character. Even more, why would Paul want to describe Tychicus in different terminology to the various churches? The same language might reinforce Paul's firm support of Tychicus.

Tychicus is a rather unfamiliar biblical figure today, but he was probably well-known to the first-century church. He was with Paul during his third missionary journey and is named with Trophimus as from Asia Minor (Acts 20:4). Trophimus is later mentioned on his own as coming from Ephesus (Acts 21:29; see also 2 Cor 8:18–24), and it is possible that Tychicus is a local from there as well. If so, it would mean he was involved in the collection Paul took from his gentile churches for the churches in Judea. Paul later uses him to deliver this letter, plus one addressed to Philemon, and two others, addressed to the Colossian and the Laodicean churches. In this critical role, not only would Tychicus read the letter and describe Paul's circumstances, but he would also be called on to explain the theology of Paul's teachings. One could say he was the first exegete of Paul's letter. Paul deputized Tychicus to present all the news concerning Paul with the goal of comforting and encouraging believers. This entails a theological and pastoral sensitivity. And Tychicus likely read the letter aloud to the congregation, fielding questions or offering explanations.[5] That the couriers shared information can be seen in

---

and τί πράσσω ("what I am doing"), while Colossians includes the description σύνδουλος ("fellow servant"). Additionally, Paul does not include greetings as he does in Col 4:10–18.

4. Introduction, pp. 15–19.

5. Richards, *Paul and First-Century Letter Writing*, 202.

Paul's response to the Corinthians. The letter carrier, "Chloe's people" (1 Cor 1:11), divulged to Paul that the community was torn into factions and was having moral problems related to lawsuits and sexual behavior (5:1). This bit of data was not part of the church's formal letter to Paul (7:1), and it might be that some in Corinth wished Paul had not discovered it.

Two additional times Paul refers to Tychicus, both after he is released from his Roman imprisonment. Paul writes to Titus that he considered sending either Artemas or Tychicus to Crete so that Titus could come to Nicopolis and help Paul (Titus 3:12). We do not know which one finally delivered the letter. In 2 Timothy, Paul's final letter, he indicates that Tychicus will stand in for Timothy in Ephesus (see 1 Tim 1:3) so that the latter can help Paul (2 Tim 4:12). Tychicus thus carried four or five letters for Paul and perhaps led the churches in Crete and Ephesus in the absence of Titus and Timothy.

Paul describes Tychicus as a dear or beloved brother and a faithful servant of the Lord. The early church spoke of fellow believers using kinship language, identifying them as brothers and sisters, for they were part of God's family in Christ. Paul identifies Tychicus as a servant, using the term from which we get the word "deacon."[6] This term has a wide sematic range, from one who does menial tasks, to one who assisted others, to a missional or congregational leader. Jesus speaks of the servant who does menial tasks (Luke 17:8; 22:26–27; see also Acts 6:2). Others are identified as "servants" who are leaders within the church, including Erastus (Acts 19:22), Phoebe (Rom 16:1), Apollos (1 Cor 3:5), Epaphras (Col 1:7), Timothy (Phil 1:1), and Paul himself (1 Cor 3:5; Phil 1:1; Eph 3:7; Col 1:23, 25). Paul speaks of Christ as a servant to the Jews (Rom 15:8).

23–24 As Paul closes the letter, he addresses the "brothers and sisters" rather than "you [plural]" as he wishes them "peace" and "love with faith."[7] All three nouns have played a crucial role in Paul's discussion of God's redemptive plan and the person of Christ. Paul declared that Christ is our "peace," for he brought together Jew and gentile, creating one new humanity through his work on the cross (2:14, 15, 17). This peace reconciled believers to God, and to each other. Moreover, this peace overthrew the hostility and division that characterized both relationships. Paul speaks of the gospel of peace that equips believers to stand fast against the schemes of the devil (6:15). The peace of Christ binds believers in unity (4:3), even as their love for each other causes them to support each other (1:15; 4:2, 15). Paul describes "love with

---

6. On διάκονος see BDAG 230 (1).

7. Lincoln, 463, 465. This departure from the expected second-person plural to the third-person plural has been used as evidence for non-Pauline authorship (yet see Gal 6:16). However, this theory raises the more difficult question, namely why would a pseudepigraphic author innovate here when convention would have him follow a traditional closing?

faith"; twice earlier he spoke of love and faith together (1:15; 3:17; see also Gal 5:6). Faith connects believers with Christ's work of redemption and is the shield of faith that protects believers from the devil's deceptions (6:11, 16). All is grounded in love. Paul emphasizes the love between Father and Son (1:6), extended to believers through Christ who gave himself for believers (5:2, 25). Such love has no boundaries, nor can it be comprehended by the human mind (3:18–19). Believers are made alive with Christ (2:4–5) and are being rooted in love (3:17).

These wishes for peace and love with faith are available to believers through God the Father and the Lord Jesus Christ. Paul characterizes God as father throughout the epistle, as one who blesses (1:3), who designed and implemented salvation (1:4–5; 2:4–5), who is the father of all peoples (3:15), and who is above all glorious (1:17). Christ is Lord, known through his death, resurrection, ascension, reign, and future kingdom that unites all things under him.

Paul offers a final wish that "grace" be with the believers, all who love the Lord Jesus Christ. Paul typically expresses a desire that grace be on those who read his letter. Here the blessing is broader to include those who love Christ. Paul finishes with a prepositional phrase, "with an undying love."[8] The meaning of "undying" can be ascertained by looking at its use in context. It is found seven times in the New Testament, only in Pauline letters. In his discussion about the resurrected body, Paul insists that it will be raised incorruptible (1 Cor 15:42, 50, 53, 54; see also Rom 2:7; 2 Tim 1:10). Paul uses the cognate adjective to describe the believer's crown that will last forever (1 Cor 9:25; see also 1 Pet 1:4, 23). The term also describes God (Rom 1:23; 1 Tim 1:17). Immortality prevents rot and decay, for it is incorruptible.[9]

Both the sentence's syntax and the term's meaning have generated several theories. Most likely the phrase links with the participle "love" in the phrase "those who love Christ."[10] This undying love speaks to its eternal nature or its purity. This love begins with God's love for believers, experienced now as the church is raised and seated with Christ (2:5–6) and will be established eternally as all things are united in Christ (1:10).[11] Some, however, suggest that the phrase best fits with the opening noun, "grace," such that Paul would be expressing the thought: grace and immortality be to those who love Christ.[12] The problem with this option is that the two terms are quite a dis-

---

8. Ἐν ἀφθαρσίᾳ. On ἀφθαρσία see BDAG 155.

9. Hoehner, 875–76, offers a discussion of the term in Paul.

10. Hoehner, 877; Salmond, 395.

11. Perkins, 152, writes: "The existence of the church, united in love with its head, is the sign of God's loving providence."

12. Lincoln, 467–68; Arnold, 482–83.

tance apart within the sentence.[13] A third option is that the noun describes the Lord Jesus Christ as the immortal one.[14] Yet if this was Paul's intention, it is likely that he would have included an article before the prepositional phrase.

Pulling the data together, Paul probably intends that believers love Christ with a love undying, reflecting both the believers' hope of immortality as well as their moral obligation to love with integrity, that is, without corruption.[15] The sense of moral obligation tied to the surety of salvation by grace through faith has been the burden of Paul's message in the final three chapters, resting on Paul's strong case for the triumph over sin and death that Christ's death and resurrection achieved. Now both Jew and gentile in Christ have been seated with him in the heavenly places and are becoming a mature church by growing in Christ. Paul speaks of God placing all things, including rulers and authorities, under Christ's feet and making him head over everything (1:22). Christ assumes a posture of victory by sitting at God the Father's right hand (2:5–6), having decisively defeated his enemies. Believers are sealed with the Holy Spirit, guaranteeing an inheritance (1:13–14). The kingdom of Christ and of God admits those who are holy through the work of Christ on the cross (5:5). With such great promises, believers can but pray with Paul that they might "grasp how wide and long and high and deep is the love of Christ" (3:18) and offer their voices to the unending chorus that praises the one who does immeasurably more than all they ask or imagine.

---

13. Hoehner, 877, adds that those who advocate this position often repeat "grace" in their translation, such that the last line reads "grace and immortality"; he adds: "However, this is not implicit from the text."

14. Snodgrass, 365.

15. Thielman, 447–48, points to a possible parallel passage in Ps Sol 6.6, arguing that the noun in Ephesians expresses a virtue, not an abstract state of being immortal. The love would be free from corruption, morally incorruptible.

Index of Subjects

Abraham, 57, 111, 221–22, 253, 318; children of, 6, 56, 171, 173, 300; promises to, 73n276, 229, 318
abuse, 225n613, 283, 304, 313, 401–2
Adam, 148, 307, 288n230, 356–57; new, Christ as, 124, 214n565, 356–57
Adam Christology, 58
adoption, 87, 88–91, 96–99, 148, 378, 386; inheritance, 85, 108–9, 212; redemption, 87, 103–4, 306–8, 386
adult children, 374, 377–78, 382, 383, 384
Aesop, 135
alienation from God, 141–42, 175–81, 196, 282–83, 313
alive in Christ, 154, 156–57
Ambrose, 21
American slavery, 342–43, 385, 390, 392, 399–400, 405–6
Ananias and Sapphira, 295–96, 298
Andronicus, 78n7, 268
angel of the Lord, 59
anger, 293–94, 302
Antinous, 380
anti-Semitism, 71, 168–71, 189–90
apocalyptic views, 4, 7, 55, 57; Jewish, 145–46, 168, 234
Apollos, 11–12, 209, 268, 297, 435
apostles, 77–78, 79, 116; authority, 29n114, 31, 79, 116, 208, 268; building church, 197–98, 267–69; Paul as, 77–78, 79, 116, 190, 204, 207–8, 224, 244, 268; revelation, 201, 202–3, 210–11
Apostles' Creed, 262
Aquinas, Thomas, 248n52
Aristotelians, 130
Aristotle, 247, 273, 316n332, 358, 404n721;

family, household codes, 197, 343–45, 366, 381, 383; slavery, 354, 389, 392–93, 394, 396, 399
armor of God, 31, 50, 407–9, 428; belt, 416–17, 418, 424; breastplate, 418–19, 423, 424; helmet, 416, 422–23; shield, 420–22; shoes, 419–20; sword of the Spirit, 422–24
arrows, flaming, 420–22
Artemis cult, 10, 34–36, 41n175, 44, 174, 278–79, 297
ascension, 258–61, 263–64, 309–10
Athanasian Creed, 262
Athanasius of Alexandria, 356
Athens, 392–93
Augustine of Hippo, 21, 97n59, 158n326, 378; grace, 102n77, 157; *imago Dei*, 310–11
Augustus, emperor, 37–38, 98, 183, 398, 418–19
authority, 21, 130; of apostles, 29n114, 31, 79, 116, 208, 268; of Christ, 42, 126; of Ephesians, 17–18, 23n83; of fathers, 130–31, 382, 384; headship, 130–32, 353; masculinity, 353, 361–62; of owners, masters, 389, 394, 399–400; of Paul, 29n114, 31, 79, 116, 208, 268; of ruler, 146–47

banquets, 316, 336–37
baptism, 32, 93, 102, 140, 249, 252, 363–64; early church, 286–87
Barnabas, 78n7, 254, 268, 298
barrier, Jerusalem temple, 184–85, 206
Basil of Caesarea, the Great, 27, 199n514
belt of truth, 416–17, 418, 424

439

Index of Subjects

Ben Sira, 336
bitterness, 301-2
blamelessness, 96, 241-42, 363
blessings, 89-90, 436
blood of Christ, 103-4, 112, 124-25, 180-81
boasting, 164-65, 363
body, Stoic view, 130, 134n224, 292n244, 387, 409n743
body metaphors, 129-30, 131-32, 133-36; feet, 65, 69, 115, 124, 127-28; head, 69, 114, 128-30; head/body, 353-58, 362-63, 366-67, 368; *kephalē*, 107, 130-32, 356-57; Plutarch, 136, 356n506
body of Christ, church as, 6, 69-70, 114-15, 133-34, 136-38; gentiles in, 142, 212-13; growth, 270-71, 275-77, 291; head, Christ as, 12-13, 69, 123, 128-29, 276-77, 354-57; joined, 276-77; as new entity, 181-89; unity, 249, 275-77, 368-69, 371-72
boldness, 220-21, 244, 430-31
Boudicca, 206-7, 427
breastplate of righteousness, 418-19, 423, 424
bride of Christ, 362-64
Britain, 206-7, 427
building church, 197-200, 267-69, 270-72, 277, 290, 298-300; cornerstone, 197-99, 270

Cain, 293
calling, 244-45; of Paul, 25, 167, 202, 213-14, 215-17, 387
Calvin, John, 94n44, 97n59, 248n52
Catullus, 316
celibacy, 367-68
children, 376-81; adult, 374, 377-78, 382, 383, 384; in church, 373, 378; education, 381-83; of light, 325-27, 331-33; obedience, 374-76, 377-78, 382; Roman art, 379, 380-81; sexual exploitation, 379-80; slave, 348, 373, 378-80, 383, 406; sons of disobedience, 146-48, 325-26; of wrath, 147-49
Christ. *See* Jesus Christ
Christology, 57-61, 136, 141n258, 260, 272, 341
church, the, 67-70, 132-33, 237; anti-Semitism, Judaism, 71, 168-71, 189-90; bride of Christ, 362-64; building, 197-200, 267-69, 270-72, 277, 290, 298-300; children in, 373, 378; cleansing, 363-65; equality, 136, 182, 344, 346, 351, 361, 367-68, 387-88; equipping, 265-71; false teaching, deception, 274-75, 277, 322, 363-64; hierarchy, structure, 165, 182, 213, 270-71; holiness, 363-66; as household, God's family, 195-97, 212, 214; identity, 11-12, 59-61, 63-66, 70; Israel and, 69-70, 79; marriage and, 7, 213; maturing, 265, 267, 273-74, 276; Old Testament and, 56-57; sin in, 293-94, 321; submission, 340-41; as temple, 176-77, 185, 195, 198-200; unity, 64-65, 66, 68, 136-37, 172, 179, 187-88, 245-46, 255, 271-72, 292-93; universal, 5-6, 68, 132-33; wisdom of God, 218-20. *See also* body of Christ; early church
Cicero, 17, 356n506, 377, 381n625, 396; letters, 9, 23, 24n88
circumcision, 57, 72, 164, 169, 176-77, 190
Claudius, emperor, 355
Clement of Alexandria, 21-22n78, 178n418, 199n514, 261n107
clothing metaphor, 20, 36, 87, 298, 417-18; new self, putting on, 87, 148, 242, 279, 285-87, 289
compassion, 303
Corinth, 12, 31-32
cosmic forces, 33, 67-68, 143-44
cosmic unity, 106-8, 243
creation, 55; Christ and, 129, 166-67; God and, 59-60, 67, 253-54, 288; human management of, 108, 123-24, 128; restoration, redemption, 113, 152n297, 166-67n371; time before, 1, 31, 95-96
creeds, 249, 262
crucifixion, 361-62
cruciformity, 93
Cynic philosophy, 166, 409n744
Cyril of Alexandria, 356-57

Daniel, prophet, 228
darkness, light and, metaphor, 325-33
darkness, powers of, 67, 146-47, 327, 415; age of, 2, 7, 55, 326-27, 413; deeds of, 329-31; sons of, 140n254, 146n272, 147, 168, 409n740
deception, lies, 294-95, 411-13, 418, 420n799, 424
Demetrius of Ephesus, 44, 279, 314
desires, of flesh, 144, 148-49, 395, 401

440

Index of Subjects

Dio Chrysostom, 199n514, 241, 360
Dionysius of Halicarnassus, 13n35, 49n206, 382
dispensationalism, 191
domestic violence, 225n613, 283, 401–2
Domitian, emperor, 39
drunkenness, 316, 334, 336–37

early church, 3–4, 298, 332, 435; Acts, book of, 43–44; baptism, 286–87; children, 373, 378; Christ's identity, 59–60; forgeries, 19–20; Judaism and, 170–71, 189, 190–91; slaves in, 136, 304, 345, 348–49, 378, 383, 387–88, 390, 397, 406; Trinity doctrine, 87, 124
Epaphroditus, 46, 426
Ephesians, letter of, 1–2; authorship, 3–5, 17–18, 21–22, 142, 216, 245, 412n758, 432, 433–34, 435n7; body, 50–52; Colossians and, 12–15, 17n56, 28–30, 116, 433–34; historical circumstances, 9–12, 30–32, 117; literary style, 8–9; purpose, 32–33; recipients, 3, 9–10, 25–30, 52, 140–41; structure, 47–54; theology, 5–7, 55, 115
Ephesus, 296–97; Artemis cult, 10, 34–36, 41n175, 44, 174, 278–79, 297; churches, 11–12; Jewish community, 25–26, 42–43, 177–78; paganism, magic, 22, 25–26, 36; Paul in, 11–12, 29, 43–44, 45–47
Epictetus, 49n207, 134n224, 246, 251
Epicurus, 17n55, 49
equality, 40; in church, 136, 182, 344, 346, 351, 361, 367–68, 387–88; kingdom of God, 403–6
Erasmus, 22
eschatology, 6, 10, 56–57, 191, 202, 251, 335; already/not yet, 69–70, 125, 414–15; judgment, final, 164n360, 269, 319, 410n747, 429; realized, 7, 92; return of Christ, 155, 319, 417
Essenes, 165, 217n579, 269n137, 290n236, 294n252; apocalyptic, 234, 325n371; grace, salvation, 73, 101; virtues, 316, 382
eternity, eternal, 60, 220, 414–15, 436; church, 132–33; grace, 154–55, 436–37; life, 112, 121, 140, 142, 152, 387, 403
evangelists, 268–69
Eve, 274–75, 307

evil, 149n286, 327, 331, 335–36; spiritual world, 146–47, 412–13, 415
Ezekiel, 309, 364

faith, 117, 223, 252, 258, 426, 436; in Christ, 161–63, 221–23; justification, 159–60; law and, 185–87; salvation by, 156–57, 161; shield of, 420–22, 436; standing firm in, 409–10, 411–12, 413–14, 417–18, 424–26
faithful, faithfulness, 79–80, 221–22, 223, 232, 416, 425–26; of Christ, 161–62, 221–23, 422
false teaching, 17, 274–75, 277, 322, 363–64
Father, God as, 37, 60–63, 65, 82, 87, 89–90, 118–19, 227–29, 253–54, 306–8, 436
fathers, 82, 197, 381; authority, 130–31, 382, 384; education of children, 381–83; God the Father and, 383–84; paterfamilias, 36–37, 98–99, 384, 398; and Zeus, 375, 383
fear, 105, 340–41, 401–2, 424
flesh, 368, 401; desires of, 144, 148–49, 395
fool, foolish, 335
forgery, 4, 17, 19–22
forgiveness, 13, 104–5, 108, 291, 303–4, 306, 309
Francis of Assisi, 330
freedom, 367–68, 394–95
freed slaves, 46, 160, 351, 367, 370, 391, 394, 396, 398–99
fruit, fruitful, 168, 325, 327–28, 419; fruitless, 280, 299, 322, 329, 331; of the Holy Spirit, 9n17, 247, 249n54, 327–28
fulfillment, 106–7, 114–15, 137–38, 192
fullness, 114–15, 137–38, 199; of God, 234–35, 236, 263–64
futile thinking, 279–83, 314

Gaius Caligula, 39n167, 355
Gaius Musonius Rufus, 346–47
Galen, 17, 130
Gamaliel, 300
gentiles, 25–26, 57, 110; alienation from God, 175–81, 196, 282–83, 313; ancestor worship, 229–30; in body of Christ, 142, 212–13; godless, 178–79; ignorance, 148, 178–79, 242, 278–79, 280–82, 287; inclusion, mystery of,

441

Index of Subjects

1–2, 172, 201–4, 209, 211, 212–14, 215, 217–18; Israel and, 5, 36, 70, 79; Jews, reconciliation with, 5, 68, 110, 171–74, 180–81, 188–89; Jews, unity with, 12, 32–33, 174–75, 388; uncircumcised, 144, 177–78, 388. *See also* paganism, polytheism
gentleness, 244, 247
gift giving, reciprocal, 100–102, 158–59, 164, 246, 369–70
gifts: *charismata*, 257–58; of Christ, 254–59, 261, 263, 264–70, 276–77; of God, 73, 99–102, 118, 264–66, 298; grace as, 73, 99–101, 157–60, 162–63, 205, 214, 218–19, 255–57; salvation as, 156, 223, 255–56; spiritual, 6, 264–65, 266
glory, 225, 231; of God, 83–84, 85–87, 88, 99, 112–13, 118–19, 236–37
Gnosticism, 33, 145–46n271, 183, 219n586, 231n633, 234, 332n412
God, 86, 149; access to, 194–95, 220–21; alienation from, 141–42, 175–81, 196, 282–83, 313; blessings, 89–90; choice, 88–89, 94–97; church as family, 195–97, 212, 214; as creator, 59–60, 253–54, 288; as Father, 37, 60–63, 65, 82, 87, 89–90, 118–19, 227–29, 253–54, 306–8, 436; fullness, 234–35, 236, 263–64; gifts, 73, 99–102, 118, 264–66, 298; glory, praise of, 83–84, 85–87, 88, 99, 112–13, 118–19, 236–37; image, humans made in, 287–88, 310–11; *imago Dei*, 287–88, 310–11; imitating, 306–11; justice, 225, 403, 411, 416; kindness, 155–56, 303, 306; love, 150–51, 174, 306, 308, 311, 323–24, 339; mercy, 150–51; pleasing, 328–29, 404; power, 114, 118, 121–25, 140, 214, 230–31, 236, 407–8, 410–11; riches, 104–5, 120–21, 150–51, 155, 217, 230–31; wisdom, 5, 62, 65, 87, 105, 114, 182, 204, 218–20, 334; work of, in Christ, 141–42, 151–53, 156–57, 303–4, 424; wrath, 145, 148–49, 313, 322–24, 423. *See also* armor of God; will of God
goodness, 327–28
good works, 157, 165–68, 297, 403–5
grace, 139–40, 299–300, 436; *charis*, 80–81, 99–101, 158; choice of God, 88–89, 94–96; definitions, 100–102; eternal, 154–55, 436–37; as gift, 73, 99–101, 157–60, 162–63, 205, 214, 218–19, 255–57; measure of, 257–58;

polyvalent, 100–101; riches of, 104–5; salvation, 153–55, 160–61, 163, 264–65
Greco-Roman culture, 68, 72, 164, 307; banquets, 316, 336–37; children, 376–81; gift giving, reciprocal, 100–102, 158–59, 164, 246, 369–70; Hades, 261–62; Hellenism, 72, 92; honor/shame, 165, 201–2, 203–4, 205, 315–16, 331, 361–62, 367, 391; household codes, 342–48; husbands, 345–48; marriage, 342, 351–52; morals, 51–52, 316; patron/client system, 131–32, 142, 219, 343, 355n503, 357, 369–70, 398; *polis, politeia*, 177–78; rhetoric, 20, 48, 407; submission, 349–50; values, 32, 302, 345; women, wives, 344–48, 354. *See also* hierarchy, social; Roman Empire; paganism, polytheism; slaves, slavery
greed, 31, 35–36, 282–83, 317–18, 328; as idolatry, 313, 314–15, 318, 325–36, 330
Gregory of Nazianzus, 66–67

Hades, hell, 261–62
Hadrian, emperor, 380
hapax legomena, 8, 182–83, 218n582
Hasmoneans, 408–9
head/body metaphor, 353–58, 362–63; focus of, on body, 366–67, 368
head, headship, 355–58; authority, 130–32, 353; Christ as, 12–13, 69, 123, 128–29, 276–77, 354–57; husbands as, 351–52; *kephalē*, 107, 130–32, 356–57; metaphor, 69, 114, 128–30
heart, 231–32, 281–82, 339, 402–3
heavenly realms, 90, 125–26, 153, 196, 414–15; air, kingdom of, 67–68, 143, 146–47, 150, 153, 219; beings, 229–30
Hebrew poetry, 331–33
Hermogenes, 382
hierarchy, social, 349; church, 165, 182, 213, 270–71; equality, 160, 182, 213, 239, 362, 387–88; family, household, 197, 343, 345, 381; gender, 354, 362, 392–93, 404n721; Greco-Roman, 128, 134–35, 159–60, 182, 197, 213, 342–48, 369–70, 391; marriage, 347–48, 352, 362, 366, 372–73, 389–90; overturning, 13–14, 182, 239, 246, 362, 370
Hippocrates, 130
holy, holiness, 96, 210, 241–42, 288–89, 312–13, 323–24, 417
Holy Spirit, 62–63, 250, 429; filling

442

with, 90, 333–34, 337–40; fruit of, 9n17, 247, 249n54, 327–28; grieving, 291, 300–301, 321; Pentecost, pouring out, 93, 263, 337n435; redemption, 112–13; revelation, 119–20; sealing by, 111–13, 250; strengthening, 231–32, 298; sword of, 422–24; unity, 247–49, 250; wisdom, 113–14, 115, 119–20; work of, 211, 236
honor/shame, 165, 201–2, 203–4, 205, 315–16, 331, 361–62, 367, 391
hope, 109–10, 120, 178–79, 251, 423
hostility, 184–86
household, family: of God, 195–97, 212, 214; hierarchy, 197, 343, 345, 381; mothers, 382–83, 384; slaves, 197, 342–43, 391–92. *See also* children; fathers
household codes, 13–14, 65, 342–48, 364, 385–90, 401; Greek, 197, 343–45, 366, 376, 381, 383; Jewish, 351n491, 379, 383; worship and, 341–42, 348–49
humans, humanity, 231–32; flourishing, 96, 146, 323–24, 375; new, 165–67, 171–72, 187–89, 201–2; plight, 141–47
humility, 239, 244, 246, 247, 290
husbands, 346–47; Greco-Roman view, 345–48; as head, 351–52; respect for, 340, 372, 401; sacrificial love, 347–48, 352, 359–62, 367–68, 372–73; submission, 352, 354
hymns, 32–33, 83–84, 101, 123–24, 126, 182–83, 332, 338–39

identity, 11, 160, 195, 287, 416–17; of Christ, 11–12, 59–61, 63–66, 70; of church, 11–12, 59–61, 63–66, 70; community and, 177–78; of God, 59, 67; of Jews, 25–26, 72, 74, 170, 172, 177, 190; new in Christ, 33n132, 33n133, 160, 172, 179, 195, 279; of Trinity, 59–63, 67, 87, 115
idolatry, 64, 110, 141, 278, 318–19, 323, 375–76; greed as, 313, 314–15, 318, 325–26, 330
Ignatius, 9n19
ignorance, 187, 241; futile thinking, 279–83, 314; gentiles, 148, 178–79, 242, 278–79, 280–82, 287
image of God, *imago Dei*, 287–88, 310–11; of Christ, conforming to, imitating, 244–45, 313–14, 328, 340–41, 402
imitating, 307–11

immoral behavior, 278–79, 282–83; drunkenness and, 336–37; of pagans, 35–36, 179, 278, 315. *See also* greed; sexual immorality
imperial cult, 10, 36–40, 42n178, 279, 354–55, 431
incarnation, 58, 94n39, 123, 260, 263, 311
individualism, 40, 99, 144, 343, 386
inheritance, 85, 108–9, 110, 212, 317–19, 423; of God, 120–21, 317; of slaves, 378, 390, 404
Irenaeus, 181n430, 261n107, 261n108
Isaiah, 10, 56–57, 66, 149, 430; armor, battle of God, 411, 416, 419, 423; on God, 228, 300; peace, 193–94; unity, 173–74, 187
Isocrates, 382
Israel, Israelites, 32n123, 62n248, 98, 253; church and, 69–70, 79; covenants, 178–79, 186; gentiles and, 5, 36, 70, 79; olive tree, 188–89; prophets, 93, 197–98; Shema, 59–60, 64, 253

James, brother of Jesus, 268
James, disciple, 125
Jerome, 16n51, 22, 375n588; grace, 256–57, 259; as scribe, 20–21
Jerusalem, 364, 388, 425
Jesus Christ, 102, 104; Adam, new, 124, 214n565, 356–57; ascension, 258–61, 263–64, 309–10; authority, 42, 126; blood, 103–4, 112, 124–25, 180–81; bride of, 362–64; captives, 258–59, 260–61; as Christ, 63–64, 65–66; in Christ, 2, 12, 53, 63, 79–80, 90–94, 103; as cornerstone, 197–99, 270; crucifixion, 361–62; descended, 261–63; divinity, 57–61; faithfulness, 161–62, 221–23, 422; fear, reverence, 340–41; gift, 254–59, 261, 263, 264–70, 276–77; as head, 12–13, 69, 123, 128–29, 276–77, 354–57; image, conforming to, 244–45, 313–14, 328, 340–41, 402; incarnation, 58, 94n39, 123, 260, 263, 311; Lord, *kyrios*, 59, 60–61, 64–66, 89–90, 251–52, 400, 405, 436–37; love of, 226–27, 232–34, 243–44, 308–9, 361–66, 367–69, 410–11, 436; Messiah, 82, 170, 177, 189, 191n483, 225, 284, 423, 431; name, 126–27; new in, 33nn132–33, 160, 172, 179, 195, 279; new life in, 165–67, 171–72, 279–81, 285–89;

443

Index of Subjects

peace of, 39–40, 66, 81–82, 181–84, 187, 193–94, 249, 420, 435; *pistis Christou*, 222–23; redeemer, 362–63; resurrection, 124–25, 136–37, 140–41, 151–52, 193; return of, 155, 319, 417; rule over all, kingship, 113–15, 122–25, 127–29, 320–22; sacrifice, 309–10; savior, 354–55, 358, 427; Son, 59, 60, 63, 89, 267, 272–73; spiritual forces, rule over, 31, 67–68, 122–23, 126–27, 143, 427; submission to, 352–53, 358; suffering, 224–25; temptation, 413, 424; as truth, 289–90; united, all things in, 86–87, 106–7, 174–75; work of God in, 141–42, 151–53, 156–57, 303–4, 424

Jews, 110, 396; anti-Jewish exegesis, 158, 168–71, 185n454, 189, 294–95; anti-Semitism, 71, 168–71, 189–90; gentile, reconciliation with, 5, 68, 110, 171–74, 180–81, 188–89; gentile, unity with, 12, 32–33, 174–75, 388; identity, 25–26, 72, 74, 170, 172, 177, 190; Roman Empire, 169, 206, 408–9, 421, 425. *See also* Israel, Israelites; Judaism

John, apostle, 125

John Chrysostom, 357

Josephus, 42n176, 223, 254, 284n209, 351, 379; Jews, 43, 169; Romans and, 421, 425; scribes, 20–21, 23; temple, 184n447, 240, 338n448

Joshua, 128

Judaism, 12, 42–43, 132; apocalyptic views, 145–46, 168, 234; circumcision, 57, 72, 164, 169, 176–77, 190; evil spiritual world, 412–13, 415; family life, 345–46, 351; grace, 102; Hellenism, 72, 92; laws, 185–87; monotheism, 57–60, 62–63, 74, 250; morals, 290, 312, 313; pesher, 260; proselytes, 169, 172–73, 179n423, 180n426, 188, 201; sacrifices, 180–81, 309–10; Second Temple, 71–74, 142, 168–71, 211, 307; supersessionism, 189–92; synagogue, 132; Targum, 259; works righteousness, 71–74, 102, 158

judgment, 31, 57, 149, 193–94, 302, 323, 404; final, 164n360, 269, 319, 410n747, 429

judgmental, 96, 189, 312, 315, 321–22, 363

Julian of Norwich, 311

Julius Caesar, 38–39, 98

Junia, 78n7, 268

justice, 225, 345, 397, 417; of God, 225, 403, 411, 416; social, 387, 389, 404n721

justification, 4, 5, 328, 386–87; by faith, 159–60; works righteousness and, 71–74

kephalē, 107, 130–32, 356–57

kindness, 155–56, 247, 302–3, 306

kingdoms: of air, 67–68, 143, 146–47, 150, 153, 219; of God, 318–22, 327, 387, 403–6

knowledge, understanding, 233–35; of Christ, 283–85; enlightenment, 119–20; *epignōsis*, 119–20; of Son of God, 265–67, 272; will of Lord, 335–36

kyriarchy, 220

Laodiceans, letter to, 9n20, 11n26, 14n38, 15n41, 19, 27, 28–29, 79n10, 434

Last Supper, 104

Lazarus, 145

letter forms, 48–52

lies, lying, 295–96; of Satan, devil, 294–95, 411–13, 418, 420n799, 424

life, 154, 156–57, 166, 251; eternal, 112, 121, 140, 142, 152, 387, 403; of God, 280–84, 290; new, in Christ, 165–67, 171–72, 279–81, 285–89

Livia, empress, 37, 38, 360, 418–19

Livy, 135, 421

Lois and Eunice, 383

Lord, *kyrios*, 59, 60–61, 64–66, 89–90, 251–52, 400, 405, 436–37

love, 13, 96, 117, 239, 277, 308–9, 435–37; of Christ, 226–27, 232–34, 243–44, 308–9, 361–66, 367–69, 410–11, 436; of God, 150–51, 174, 306, 308, 311, 323–24, 339; *ḥesed*, 151; of husbands, sacrificial, 347–48, 352, 359–62, 367–68, 372–73; speaking truth in, 275–76

lust, 283, 313, 314, 316

Luther, Martin, 94n44, 157–58

Lystra, 254

Maccabees, 31

magic, 41–42, 44, 127; paganism, 22, 25–26, 36, 146, 164

Marcion, 27–28, 29–30, 193n486

Marcus Aurelius, 376

marriage, 13–14, 342, 346–47, 351–53; as church unity metaphor, 7, 213; domestic violence, 225n613, 283, 401–2; har-

Index of Subjects

mony, 359–61, 367; hierarchy, 347–48, 352, 362, 366, 372–73, 389–90; unity, 362, 366–37, 368–69, 370–73. *See also* husbands; wives

Martial, 316

martyrs, martyrdom, 31, 196n495, 245, 252, 425; Paul, 10–11, 407; Perpetua, 377–78

Marx, Karl, 170–71n385

maturity, spiritual, 32–33, 265, 267, 273

measure, 257–58, 273

mercy, 150–51, 246–47

Messiah, 82, 170, 177, 189, 191n483, 225, 284, 423, 431

metaphors, 353, 408–10, 425–27; head/body metaphor, 353–58; military, 408–10, 425–27; soldiers, 411, 416–17, 418–22, 425–26. *See also* body metaphors

military, 131, 135, 259, 355, 357–58, 398; flaming arrows, 420–22

mind, attitude, 288

mission, missional, 93

morals, ethics, 51–52, 316, 343; instruction, 51–52, 240–41; Judaism, 290, 312, 313; Stoic, 290, 316, 395. *See also* immoral behavior; sexual immorality; vices; virtues

Moses, 57, 259, 263; God and, 126n183, 151, 253, 430; law, 169, 240

mothers, 382–83, 384

mystery, 5–6, 70–71, 87, 107; gentile inclusion, 172, 201–4, 209, 211, 212–14, 215, 217–18; of gospel, salvation, 162, 208–11, 430–31; of marital union, 209, 371–72; will of God, 105–6, 109; wisdom of God, 218–20

names, 126–27, 228–29

Nero, emperor, 31n122, 38, 39n167; Seneca and, 130, 246, 357–58, 395–96

new humanity, 165–67, 171–72, 187–89, 201–2

new in Christ, 33n132, 33n133, 160, 172, 179, 195, 279

New Perspective on Paul, 71–74, 164

new self, putting on, 87, 148, 242, 279, 285–87, 289

New Testament, early manuscripts, 26–28, 30, 80, 217n578

Noah, 309

old self, putting off, 279, 286–87, 291–92, 301

Old Testament, use of, 9, 55–57, 202–3, 251, 292, 371, 373–74, 430; Psalms, 56–57, 123–24, 258–62. *See also* Isaiah

Onesimus, 18n60, 45, 46–47, 387n651, 402, 406

Origen, 26–27, 28, 30, 116n138, 193n486, 199n514, 261n107, 375; and book of Hebrews, 21–22

owners, masters, 334, 395, 404–6; authority, 389, 394, 399–400; morality, character, 395, 399; Philemon, 45, 46–47, 434; tyranny, 345, 346, 392, 394, 396, 400–401, 405

paganism, polytheism, 142, 144, 172–73, 176, 188, 212, 242, 250, 278–81, 431; Hades, 261–62; immorality, 35–36, 179, 278, 315; magic, 22, 25–26, 36

paraenesis, 50–52, 238–41, 243–44

parents. *See* fathers; mothers

paterfamilias, 36–37, 98–99, 384, 398

patience, 247

patron/client system, 131–32, 142, 219, 343, 355n503, 357, 369–70, 398

Paul, apostle: as ambassador, 30, 202, 244, 431–32; anthropology, 93–94, 287n226; as apostle, 77–78, 79, 116, 190, 204, 207–8, 224, 244, 268; authority, 29n114, 31, 79, 116, 208, 268; calling, 25, 167, 202, 213–14, 215–17, 387; Christology, 57–61; cosenders, coworkers, 23–24, 44, 78–79, 432; imprisonment, 10–11, 30–31, 45–47, 201–2, 203–6, 224–25, 238–39, 244–45, 248–31; as martyr, 10–11, 407; New Perspective on, 71–74, 164; prayers, 31, 114–19, 120–22, 200, 226–29, 230–35, 429; undisputed letters, 3–4, 5–8, 17–18, 24

pax Romana, 38–40, 183; reconciliation, 186–87; shalom, 82, 171, 183

peace, 81–82, 183, 187, 193–94, 416, 435; bond of, 248–49; of Christ, 39–40, 66, 81–82, 181–84, 187, 193–94, 249, 420, 435; gospel of, 419–20, 435

Pentecost, 56, 93, 263, 337n435

Pergamum, 38

Perpetua, 377–78

Peter, apostle, 194–95, 198, 411–12, 429; Ananias and Sapphira, 295–96; Christ, power of, 127, 229; families, household

445

Index of Subjects

codes, 364, 401; Paul and, 3–4; Pentecost sermon, 56, 93, 337n435; redemption, 104, 194–95
Pharisees, 31, 165–66
Philemon, 45, 46–47, 434
Philo of Alexandria, 177n409, 184n444, 223, 307n299, 355; on God, 101n72, 158n330, 254, 307n299, 307n303; households, 351n491, 379, 383; Jewish meals, 336–37; laws of God, 345–46, 383, 404; slavery, 346, 394, 404
philosophy, 51–52. *See also individual philosophers*
Pilate, Pontius, 111
Plato, 15, 19n65, 343, 354; families, household codes, 344–45, 376, 381
Pliny the Younger, 316
pluralism, 189
Plutarch, 183, 426; body metaphor, 136, 356n506; marriage, 347, 351–52, 366, 377; morality, 316, 343
poetry, 234, 331–33
Porphyry, 16
power of God, 114, 118, 121–25, 140, 214, 230–31, 236, 407–8, 410–11
powers and authorities, 40–42, 126–27, 215–16, 219–20; battles against, 22, 145–46, 412–13, 428; Christ over, 10, 41–42, 121–22, 259; evil, 146–47; ruler of, 145–47, 219; wisdom of God, 218–19. *See also* darkness, powers of; spiritual forces, powers
prayer, 132, 428–32; kneeling, 227–28, 340; of Paul, 31, 114–19, 120–22, 200, 226–29, 230–35, 429
predestination, predetermining, 85, 88–89, 96–97, 108, 244–45
Priscilla, 295; and Aquila, 44, 68, 297
privilege, 136, 182, 225, 313, 361, 404; overturning of, 367, 369, 384, 388, 404–5; superordinate, 350, 362–63, 366–67, 369, 372–73, 384, 388, 400–401
prophets, 93, 197–98, 210, 268; revelation, 201, 202–3, 210–11, 430
Psalms, use of, 56–57, 123–24, 258–62
pseudepigraphy, 4, 10–11, 13, 15–19, 24–25, 49, 433–34, 435n7
Pseudo-Demetrius, 50n210
Pythagoras, 16

Quintilian, 17n55

Qumran community, 97n58, 119, 165, 192, 260, 300; darkness, sons of, 140n254, 146n272, 147, 168, 409n740; piety, virtue, 33, 246. *See also* Essenes

racism, 220, 298, 385, 390–91, 400
reciprocity, 344, 345–46, 357–58, 367, 394; gift giving, 100–102, 158–59, 164, 246, 369–70
reconciliation, 67, 90, 185–87, 188, 386–87; Jews and gentiles, 5, 68, 110, 171–74, 180–81, 188–89
redaction criticism, 13–14
redemption, 103–5, 140, 186–87, 386; as adoption, 87, 103–4, 306–8, 386; blood of Christ, 103–4, 112, 124–25; of creation, 113, 152n297, 166–67n371; forgiveness of sin, 13, 104–5, 306, 309; Holy Spirit and, 112–13; map, plan of, 84–87, 98–99, 202, 309–10, 424–25; Trinity and, 112–13, 124–25
repetition, 85–86, 227, 248, 269; for emphasis, 89, 97, 160, 236, 244, 331, 428–29, 433; textual structure, 215, 241n22, 256, 305, 350–51
resurrection, 140–41, 151–53, 371, 387–88, 436; of Christ, 124–25, 136–37, 140–41, 151–52, 193
rhetoric, rhetorical criticism, 20–21, 48–52, 407
riches of God, 104–5, 120–21, 150–51, 155, 217, 230–31
righteousness, 288–89, 416–17, 419
Roman Empire, 128, 225, 285, 316; army, military, 135, 259, 355, 357–58, 398; Britain, 206–7, 427; children, 379, 380–81; economy, 296–97; imperial cult, 10, 36–40, 42n178, 279, 354–55, 431; Jews and, 169, 206, 408–9, 421, 425; *pax Romana*, 38–40, 183; slaves, 387, 391, 395–97; soldiers, 411, 416–17, 418–22, 425–26
Rome, 45, 47, 135, 391, 406, 421
rulers and authorities. *See* powers and authorities

Sabbath, 43, 132, 144, 186–87, 394, 404
Sadducees, 165–66, 371
saints, 79–80, 96, 196, 265–71
salvation, 5, 110, 112; by faith, 156–57, 161; as gift, 156, 223, 255–56; by grace, 153–55, 160–61, 163, 264–65; helmet of,

446

Index of Subjects

416, 422–23; mystery of, 162, 208–11, 430–31; personal, 181–82; plan of, 1–2, 7, 31, 55–56; right living and, 304, 306, 317; universalism, 108; victory over spiritual forces, 67, 427; walk, 223, 240–43; works righteousness, 71–74, 102, 158

Satan, devil, 275–76, 304, 378, 412n758, 415; flaming arrows, 420–22; lies, deception, 294–95, 411–13, 418, 420n799, 424; resisting, 349, 411–12; temptation of Jesus, 413, 424

sealing by Holy Spirit, 111–13, 250

seals, 111–12

Second Temple Judaism, 71–74, 142, 168–71, 211, 307

secretaries, scribes, 3, 14, 15, 20–21, 22, 23–24, 29

self-control, 246–47, 293, 316, 346–47

Seneca, 16–17, 51, 158n330, 246; Nero and, 130, 357–58; slavery, 395–96

servant, 213, 216–17, 403, 435

service, ministry, 270–71

serving Christ, 13–14, 341, 352, 358, 387, 402–4

sexual immorality, 31, 35–36, 312–15, 317–19, 321, 325–26, 330, 336; children, exploitation of, 379–80; lust, 283, 313, 314, 316; sensuality, 282–83; slaves, exploitation of, 283, 314n322, 346, 379–80, 396–97

shalom, 82, 171, 183

shame, 165, 201–2, 203–4, 205, 315–16, 331, 361–62, 367, 391

Shema, 59–60, 64, 253

shepherd/pastors, 269, 433

shield of faith, 420–22

shoes, gospel, 419–20

sin, sinful, 146, 329–31; abuse, 304, 313; *aiōn*, age, 145–46; in church, 293–94, 321; dead in, 141–42, 143–46, 147–48, 153; forgiveness of, 13, 104–5, 306, 309; slavery to, 119, 171n385, 179, 387; wrath and, 323–24

slaves, slavery, 46–47, 160, 292, 304, 345–46, 348; children, 348, 373, 378–80, 383, 406; in early church, 136, 304, 345, 348–49, 378, 383, 387–88, 390, 397, 406; family, household, 197, 342–43, 391–92; freed, 46, 160, 351, 367, 370, 391, 394, 396, 398–99; inheritance, 378, 390, 404; manumission, 397–99; master, owner, relationship, 354, 397; obedience, 358, 374n583, 401–2; Onesimus, 18n60, 45, 46–47, 387n651, 402, 406; as property, tool, 344, 354, 389; serving Christ, 13–14, 341, 352, 358, 387, 402–4; sexual exploitation, 283, 314n322, 346, 379–80, 396–97; spiritual, 119, 171n385, 179, 387; submission, 340, 349–50; Western, American, 342–43, 385, 390, 392, 399–400, 405–6; will of God, doing, 402–3; worth, 160, 195, 246, 344, 346, 351, 368, 387, 389–91, 396, 398–99. *See also* owners, masters

Smyrna, 9n19, 38

social hierarchy. *See* hierarchy, social

social justice, 387, 389, 404n721

social memory, 11

soldiers, Roman, 68; belt, 416–17, 418; breastplate, 418–19; oath-taking, loyalty, 425–26; shoes, 419–20; shield, 420–22

Solomon, 228

Son of God, 59, 60, 63, 89, 267, 272–73

Sosthenes, 23–24, 278

speech, speaking, 430–31; truth, 275–76, 290–93, 294, 296, 301; unwholesome, 298–99, 313, 315–17

spiritual forces, powers, 42, 90, 123, 407–8; Christ's rule over, 31, 67–68, 122–23, 126–27, 143, 152, 427; world, 146–47, 412–13, 415. *See also* powers and authorities

spiritual gifts, 6, 264–65, 266

stand firm, 409–10, 411–12, 413–14, 417–18, 424–26, 428

stealing, 295–96

Stephen, 245, 300

Stoics, Stoicism, 164, 254, 347, 394, 409n744; body, 130, 134n224, 292n244, 387, 409n743; household codes, 344n465; life, 166, 251; morals, virtues, 290, 316, 395

Stowe, Harriet Beecher, 406

strengthening, 231–32, 233–34, 298

submission, 128, 340–41, 349–50, 362, 401; to Christ, 352–53, 358; church, 340–41; husbands, 352, 354; slaves, 340, 349–50; wives, 341, 351–53, 358, 359

Suetonius, 82

suffering, 375, 382, 425; participation in Christ's, 224–25, 411

447

Index of Subjects

superordinates, 350, 362–63, 366–67, 369, 372–73, 384, 388, 400–401
supersessionism, 189–92

Tacitus, 39, 41n175, 135
teachers, 269
temple, Jerusalem, 184n447, 240, 338n448, 199; barrier, 184–85, 206; church as, 176–77, 185, 195, 198–200
Ten Commandments, Decalogue, 56, 292, 394; fifth commandment, 375–76, 383
Tertullian, 27, 30, 261n107, 262n115
thanksgiving, 49–50, 83–84, 113–14, 116, 316–17, 339–40
Theodore of Mopsuestia, 11n26
Thessalonians, 17
Tiberius, emperor, 38–39, 135
Timothy, 24, 45, 78–79, 383, 426, 435
Titus, 435
Titus, emperor, 82, 425
Trinity, the, 60, 132; early church, 87, 124; identity, 59–63, 67, 87, 115; *imago Dei*, 310–11; redemption, 112–13, 124–25; reduplication, 66–67; relationships, 60–61; unity, 181–82, 250, 253, 254–55, 272–73
truth, 285, 289, 328; belt of, 418, 424; in Christ, 289–90; living, 290–91; seeing, 297–98; speaking, 275–76, 290–93, 294, 296, 301
Tychicus, 12, 79, 80, 433–35; Ephesians, Colossians, and, 14, 28–29, 45, 47, 80

union with Christ, 91–93, 151–52, 153
unity, 187, 239–40, 242; of body of Christ, 249, 275–77, 368–69, 371–72; in Christ, all things, 86–87, 106–7, 174–75; church, 64–65, 66, 68, 136–37, 172, 179, 187–88, 245–46, 255, 271–72, 292–93; cosmic, 106–8, 243; Holy Spirit and, 247–49, 250; Jews and gentiles, 12, 32–33, 174–75, 388; maintaining, 247–48; marriage, 362, 366–73; sameness and, 182, 187, 189; Trinity, 181–82, 250, 253, 254–55, 272–73

Valerius Maximus, 360–61
vices, 301–2, 313, 321, 322–23
virtue, 33, 246, 346–47
virtues, 290, 316, 382, 395

walk, live, 147–48, 166, 243–44, 278, 308–9, 334, 375; salvation and, 223, 240–43
will of God, 78, 86, 105–6, 268, 335–36, 402–4; doing, 402–3; knowledge of, 335–36; mystery of, 105–6, 109
wisdom, 100, 105, 115, 334–36; of God, 5, 62, 65, 87, 105, 114, 182, 204, 218–20, 334; Holy Spirit giving, 113–14, 115, 119–20; spiritual, 118
Wisdom, personified, 59, 218
wives, 345–46; freedom, 367–68; obedience, 351–52, 374; philosophy, 346–47; respect husband, 340, 372, 401; submission, 341, 351–53, 358, 359
women, 343, 364; in battle, 426–27; Greco-Roman view of, 344–45, 346–47, 354; virtue, 346–47
word of God, 365, 423–24
work, works, 160, 164–65; boasting, 164–65; of God in Christ, 141–42, 151–53, 156–57, 303–4, 424; good, 157, 165–68, 297, 403–5; handiwork, 166–68; Holy Spirit, 211, 236; of the law, 168, 222; manual labor, 296–97, 297–98; righteousness, 71–74, 102, 158; service, 270–71
worship, 32–33, 58–59, 333–34; household codes and, 341–42; hymns, 32–33, 83–84, 101, 123–24, 126, 182–83, 332, 338–39; praise, 83–84, 85–87, 88, 99, 112–13, 118–19, 236–37; Spirit-filled, 337–40; thanksgiving, 49–50, 83–84, 113–14, 116, 316–17, 339–40
wrath, children of, 147–49
wrath of God, 145, 148–49, 313, 322–24, 423

Xenophon of Ephesus, 35–36

Zechariah, prophet, 292
Zeus, 34, 37, 375, 383

Index of Authors

Abernethy, Andrew, 149
Allen, John A., 91
Anderson, Gary A., 101, 159, 298
Arnold, Clinton E., 4, 27, 33, 40, 41, 80,
   81, 85, 90, 95, 96, 103, 105, 107, 109,
   110, 112, 113, 114, 117, 119, 120, 123, 126,
   127, 137, 138, 141, 145, 146, 147, 148, 149,
   153, 155, 156, 160, 164, 166, 175, 176, 184,
   185, 186, 197, 199, 200, 202, 205, 207,
   208–9, 210, 215, 217, 218, 221, 226, 230,
   232, 235, 236, 245, 247, 249, 250, 256,
   257, 259, 261, 262, 266, 268, 269, 271,
   272, 273, 277, 322, 323, 324, 326, 327,
   329, 330, 331, 332, 333, 335, 338, 339, 363,
   364, 374, 376, 381, 382, 410, 411, 412,
   413, 419, 420, 422, 423, 424, 436
Aune, David E., 20, 41, 69, 338
Ayres, Lewis, 60, 310

Bachmann, Michael, 71
Bailey, Kenneth E., 355
Balch, David L., 343, 349, 352, 360
Bales, William, 261, 262
Banks, Robert, 243
Barclay, John M. G., 42, 73, 81, 99,
   100–101, 102, 157–60, 162, 164, 214, 219,
   222, 223, 369, 370, 390
Barth, Karl, 92
Barth, Markus, 4, 6, 53, 78, 116, 117, 123,
   129, 130, 133, 136, 137, 138, 144, 145, 147,
   151, 164, 165, 166, 171, 175, 182, 184, 188,
   189, 193, 211, 224, 226, 227, 228, 232,
   234, 235, 236, 238, 245, 248, 249, 263,
   265, 267, 269, 270, 273, 284, 306, 322,
   410, 413, 418
Barton, Carlin, 165

Bauckham, Richard, 59, 60
Baum, Armin D., 8, 16, 18, 22
Baur, Ferdinand Christian, 3, 16
Beard, Mary, 36
Beilby, James, 181
Bell, Richard H., 162
Berger, K., 238
Berrin, Shani, 260
Best, Ernest, 15, 19, 26, 27, 29, 30, 33, 51,
   78, 91, 94, 95, 96, 104, 105, 113, 116, 117,
   118, 120, 123, 124, 125, 126, 127, 128, 129,
   136, 137, 138, 139, 144, 145, 151, 152, 155,
   160, 161, 162, 163, 164, 166, 167, 173, 175,
   176, 177, 178, 179, 180, 181, 182, 183, 184,
   186, 196, 197, 198, 199, 205, 208, 210,
   214, 216, 223, 229, 230, 231, 232, 234,
   238, 239, 240, 241, 243, 244, 245, 248,
   249, 250, 261, 263, 269, 270, 271, 273,
   274, 275, 276, 277, 278, 281, 282, 283,
   284, 285, 286, 287, 288, 289, 290, 292,
   293, 295, 296, 297, 298, 302, 303, 305,
   307, 314, 315, 317, 321, 322, 325, 326, 327,
   328, 329, 331, 332, 333, 334, 335, 336, 337,
   338, 339, 340, 351, 365, 368, 370, 371,
   372, 374, 375, 376, 402, 404, 408, 410,
   413, 418, 420, 428, 430, 432
Betsworth, Sharon, 376, 384
Betz, Hans Dieter, 41, 52, 77
Billings, J. Todd, 91, 300
Bird, Michael F., 48, 58, 162, 178, 190, 222
Bishop, M. C., 418, 420, 421
Blaising, C. A., 191
Bock, Darrell L., 25, 388, 389
Boersma, Hans, 181
Bohak, Gideon, 41
Bonhoeffer, Dietrich, 225

Index of Authors

Braaten, Carl E., 188
Bradley, Keith R., 376, 378, 391
Brannon, M. Jeff, 414, 415
Braund, Susanna, 246
Braxton, Brad Ronnell, 388, 390, 391
Bruce, F. F., 4, 5, 33, 105, 106, 110, 210, 216, 219, 230, 231, 232, 236, 237, 241, 263, 319, 321, 332
Buell, Denise Kimber, 169–70, 173
Bultmann, Rudolf, 33, 55, 92, 170, 319, 332
Burke, Trevor J., 197
Burkert, Walter, 36
Burnette, Samuel D., 317
Burns, J. Patout, 417

Calvin, John, 94, 97, 248, 295
Campbell, Constantine R., 91, 92, 94, 207, 281, 287
Campbell, Douglas, 7, 9, 11, 15, 19, 23, 28, 79, 223
Canavan, Rosemary, 285
Capes, David B., 59, 63, 65
Carr, Wesley, 40, 126
Carroll, Maureen, 380
Carson, D. A., 72
Cartledge, Paul Anthony, 391, 392
Carver, W. O., 109, 168, 201, 207
Cassidy, Richard J., 11, 238
Casson, Lionel, 47
Cervin, Richard, 356
Chapman, Stephen B., 77
Chester, Stephen J., 71, 94
Childs, Brevard S., 18
Classen, Carl Joachim, 48
Cleland, Liza, 416
Cohen, Shaye J. D., 42, 74, 169
Cohick, Lynn H., 12, 15, 19, 41, 72, 116, 156, 190, 258, 295, 297, 336, 348, 376, 377, 383
Cole, Spencer, 37, 377
Conzelmann, Hans, 4, 33, 318
Cortez, Marc, 311
Couenhoven, Jesse, 97
Coulston, J. C. N., 418, 420, 421
Cranfield, C. E. B., 258
Crook, Zeba A., 370
Czajkowski, Kimberley, 342

Dahl, Nils A., 32
Daly, Robert, 417
Darko, Daniel K., 196, 197
Davies, Glenys, 416

Dawson, Gerrit Scott, 310
De Boer, Willis Peter, 307
Deissmann, Adolf, 41, 92
De Ste. Croix, G. E. M., 390
Dibelius, M., 51
Dickie, Matthew W., 41, 42
Donelson, Lewis R., 19, 20
Doty, William G., 50
Dunn, James D. G., 58, 59, 69, 72, 91, 93, 190, 258, 319
Dyer, Bryan R., 48
Dyson, Stephen L., 206

Eadie, John, 211
Eastman, Susan Grove, 93–94, 134, 287
Eddy, Paul R., 181
Ehrman, Bart D., 3, 16, 19–20, 57
Elliott, Neil, 37
Emery, Gilles, 67

Fant, Maureen B., 360
Fee, Gordon D., 17, 58, 62, 112, 130, 211, 253, 357
Feldman, Louis H., 144
Fitzmyer, Joseph A., 258
Foster, Paul, 162, 222
Foster, Robert L., 415
Fowl, Stephen E., 10, 256, 278, 281, 283, 284, 285, 288, 290, 293, 296, 304, 306, 317, 326, 327, 330, 331, 333, 335, 338, 361, 364, 374, 375, 402, 404, 408, 428, 429, 431, 432
Fredriksen, Paula, 170, 171, 189, 191
Frier, Bruce W., 295
Frymer-Kensky, Tikva, 192

Gager, John G., 160, 169, 191
Galinsky, Karl, 36, 39
Garland, David E., 409
Garnsey, Peter, 369, 378, 393
Gaston, Lloyd, 191
Gaventa, Beverly Roberts, 158, 192, 368
Gerdmar, Anders, 71
Glancy, Jennifer A., 385, 397, 405
Goguel, Maurice, 19
Gombis, Timothy G., 33, 127, 203, 220, 407, 409
Goodman, Martin, 178, 206–7
Goodspeed, Edgar J., 5, 18, 229
Gorman, Michael J., 12, 66, 67, 68, 92, 93, 181, 187, 347
Gradel, Ittai, 37

450

Index of Authors

Graf, Fritz, 41
Graves, Michael W., xvi, 21
Green, Joel B., xvi, 243, 297, 413
Grindheim, Sigurd, 6, 71
Grossman, Maxine, 168
Grubbs, Judith Evans, 373, 377, 379
Grudem, Wayne, 130
Gruen, Erich S., 42, 144
Gundry-Volf, Judith M., 384

Habinek, Thomas, 395
Harnack, Adolf von, 55
Harrill, J. Albert, 403
Harris, W. Hall, III, 263
Harrison, James R., 74
Harvey, Brian K., 361
Haufe, Günter, 319
Hays, Richard B., 56, 77, 92, 203, 222, 300, 321
Heffernan, Thomas J., 378
Heil, John Paul, 53, 337, 338, 395
Heim, Erin M., 97
Heine, Ronald E., 27, 28, 257, 259
Helgeland, John, 417
Hemer, Colin J., 43
Hengel, Martin, 42, 58
Hering, James P., 13, 14, 341, 343, 344, 346, 348, 352, 354, 376
Heschel, Susannah, 170, 190
Hezser, Catherine, 394, 396
Hill, Wesley, 59–61, 63, 64, 65, 67, 124, 272–73
Hoag, Gary G., 35, 36
Hobbes, Thomas, 401
Hobbs, Raymond, 425, 426
Hodge, Caroline Johnson, 173, 176, 190
Hoehner, Harold W., 3, 4, 8, 28, 29, 79, 84, 89, 91, 95, 96, 103, 104, 109, 111, 112, 119, 129, 137, 152, 153, 154, 199, 202, 205, 207, 210, 215, 221, 230, 232, 245, 258, 259, 262, 266, 271, 281, 283, 284, 285, 286, 288, 291, 292, 293, 294, 295, 302, 303, 334, 337, 368, 389, 405, 412, 413, 419, 422, 423, 424, 430, 436, 437
Hood, Jason B., 307
Horgan, Maurya P., 260
Hoss, Stefanie, 417
Hübner, Hans, 71
Hughes, Frank Witt, 17
Hüneburg, Martin, 20
Hurtado, Larry W., 58, 251, 253
Huskinson, Janet, 377

Isaac, Benjamin, 393, 396

Jeal, Roy R., 8, 32
Jenson, Robert W., 188
Johnson, Mark, 353
Joshel, Sandra R., 391

Karaman, Elif Hilal, 44
Käsemann, Ernst, 4, 32, 33, 52, 53, 192, 319
Keating, James F., 301
Keener, Craig S., 35, 43, 44, 348, 361
Kelly, J. N. D., 21
Kennedy, George A., 382
Kenny, Anthony, 8, 24
Klaiber, Walter, 69
Klauck, Hans-Josef, 18
Klawans, Jonathan, 240
Knox, John, 18
Kraemer, Ross S., 342
Kreitzer, Larry J., 133, 178, 321
Krentz, Edgar, 426

Laes, Christian, 378, 379, 380, 382
Lakoff, George, 353
Lang, T. J., 70, 208, 209, 372
Langmuir, Gavin L., 170
Larkin, William J., 30, 79, 84, 128, 138, 208, 217, 221, 224, 228, 241, 328, 334
Lau, Te-Li, 25, 82, 183, 248, 342, 344, 356
Lee, Chee-Chiew, 318
Lee-Barnewall, Michelle, 131, 357–58, 361
Lefkowitz, Mary R., 360
Levin, Carole, 427
Levine, Amy-Jill, 71, 168, 169, 171
Levinskaya, Irina, 43
Leyerle, Blake, 373
Lietzmann, H., 51
Lieu, Judith, 178
Lightfoot, J. B., 5
Lincoln, Andrew T., 8, 10, 12, 14, 15, 26, 27, 29, 32, 33, 48, 69, 78, 80, 83, 84, 85, 86, 90, 91, 95, 96, 97, 98, 99, 103, 104, 107, 109, 110, 111, 112, 116, 117, 119, 120, 121, 123, 137, 139, 141, 144, 147, 148, 151, 152, 154, 155, 157, 158, 160, 161, 164, 166, 167, 172, 173, 175, 180, 182, 183, 184, 185, 186, 193, 197, 198, 199, 200, 201, 208, 210, 211, 217, 221, 230, 239, 241, 242, 245, 246, 248, 249, 251, 254, 256, 259, 260, 261, 262, 263, 266, 267, 270, 271, 272, 277, 280, 285, 286, 288, 294, 301, 305, 307, 314, 315, 316, 322, 323, 325,

Index of Authors

326, 329, 331, 333, 334, 336, 337, 338, 339, 340, 363, 365, 368, 369, 371, 372, 374, 376, 381, 382, 401, 402, 404, 407, 419, 422, 424, 428, 430, 431, 432, 433, 435, 436
Lindemann, Andreas, 4
Linebaugh, Jonathan, 159
Llewellyn-Jones, Lloyd, 416
Longenecker, Bruce W., 269
Longenecker, Richard N., 260
Longman, Tremper, III, 427
Lyons, George, 130, 132

MacDonald, Margaret Y., 19, 32, 33, 80, 84, 90, 95, 97, 98, 99, 102, 103, 104, 105, 106, 107, 108, 109, 110, 114, 115, 116, 120, 123, 125, 126, 127, 128, 133, 136, 137, 138, 140, 143, 145, 146, 147, 151, 154, 156, 160, 164, 178, 180, 182, 196, 198, 200, 221, 224, 229, 239, 240, 254, 259, 263, 267, 269, 270, 271, 275, 305, 314, 322, 325, 350, 360, 362, 365, 373, 376, 378, 379, 380, 383, 385, 422, 423, 429
Maier, Harry O., 11, 16, 37, 38, 39
Malherbe, Abraham J., 46
Martin, Dale B., 135
Martin, Ralph P., 33, 183
Martín-Asensio, Gustavo, 53, 197
Mathewson, David L., 241, 288, 308, 323, 337, 338, 365
Matlock, R. Barry, 161, 222, 223
Mattingly, Harold, 355
McGinn, Thomas A. J., 295
McKnight, Scot, xvi, 15, 72, 93, 181, 187, 319, 399
McNeel, Jennifer Houston, 368
Merkle, Benjamin L., 153
Metzger, Bruce M., 17
Mickelsen, Alvera, 130
Mickelsen, Berkeley, 130
Mitton, C. Leslie, 14
Morris, Ian, 296
Morris, Leon L., 77, 79, 82, 103, 104, 149, 180, 252, 328, 423
Mott, Stephen Charles, 158
Moulton, J. H., 221
Mouritsen, Henrik, 392, 395, 396, 397, 398
Moxnes, Halvor, 197
Muddiman, John, 4, 13, 14, 15, 18, 19, 20, 27, 30, 80, 96, 102, 104, 110, 111, 112, 118,

119, 126, 128, 129, 139, 144, 145, 147, 196, 216, 217, 249, 413
Murray, John, 92, 252, 365

Nanos, Mark D., 191
Nasrallah, Laura Salah, 38
Nirenberg, David, 170
Noll, Mark, 385, 405
North, John, 36, 178, 385
Novak, David, 192
Novenson, Matthew V., 64
Nussbaum, Martha C., 346, 347

O'Brien, Peter T., 72, 132, 208
Ophir, Adi, 172
Orr, Peter, 92
Osgood, Josiah, 360
Osiek, Carolyn, 350, 360, 376, 379, 383
Overfield, P. D., 137

Patterson, Orlando, 386, 387, 391, 400, 401, 404
Perkins, Pheme, 5, 6, 33, 51, 97, 119, 126, 139, 141, 144, 146, 148, 151, 154, 164, 166, 167, 172, 177, 196, 197, 198, 200, 201, 210, 211, 216, 217, 219, 220, 225, 228, 231, 232, 234, 235, 236, 239, 241, 246, 247, 249, 260, 262, 263, 269, 290, 303, 305, 307, 312, 313, 316, 318, 320, 322, 325, 329, 407, 409, 431, 432, 433, 436
Pervo, Richard I., 44
Pitts, Andrew W., 51
Pokorný, Petr, 33
Pollard, Elizabeth Ann, 41
Porter, Stanley E., 2, 48, 79, 80, 183, 317, 363, 370
Preisendanz, Karl, 41, 146, 251
Price, Simon R. F., 36, 37, 38, 39

Rajak, Tessa, 178
Ramelli, Ilaria L. E., 404
Rapske, Brian M., 30–31, 238, 431
Reasoner, Mark, 37
Reece, Steve, 23, 49
Reid, Daniel G., 205, 238, 244, 416, 427
Rese, M., 5
Rhee, Helen, 296
Richards, E. Randolph, 6, 9, 23, 24, 49, 50, 434
Richardson, Neil, 59, 272

Index of Authors

Richlin, Amy, 316
Rist, M., 20
Roberts, J. H., 128
Roberts, Mark D., 15
Robertson, A. T., 258
Robertson, Paul M., 49
Robinson, John A. T., 134
Rogers, Guy MacLean, 34, 35, 36
Roon, A. van, 29
Rosenmeyer, Patricia A., 16
Rosen-Zvi, Ishay, 172
Rosner, Brian S., 314
Roth, Ulrike, 387
Rowe, C. Kavin, 60
Ruden, Sarah, 274, 314, 316, 367, 378, 390, 397
Ruether, Rosemary Radford, 170
Runge, Steven E., 338, 341
Russell, D. A., 20
Rutledge, Fleming, 323

Saller, Richard P., 296, 369, 384
Salmond, S. D. F., 96, 259, 272, 275, 302, 374, 375, 422, 424, 430, 436
Sanders, E. P., 71, 72, 73, 92, 93, 102
Scheidel, Walter, 296
Schenck, Kenneth, 222
Schlier, Heinrich, 85, 112, 210, 219, 231
Schnackenburg, Rudolf, 112
Schuller, Eileen, 101
Schüssler Fiorenza, Elisabeth, 20, 25, 82, 188, 190, 218, 219, 220, 225, 280, 284, 308, 390, 407, 409
Schweitzer, Albert, 92, 319
Schweizer, E., 133
Seierstad, Asne, 367
Seifrid, Mark A., 72, 91
Selderhuis, Herman J., 97
Sellin, Gerhard, 52
Severy, Beth, 384
Sharkey, Sarah Borden, 392
Sherwood, Aaron, 204
Shogren, Gary Steven, 80, 95, 103, 104, 318, 319
Sigismund-Nielsen, Hanne, 377
Smith, Julien, 239
Smith, Nicholas D., 393
Snodgrass, Klyne, 372, 437
Snowden, Frank M., 400
Son, Sang-Won (Aaron), 187
Soskice, Janet Martin, 310, 311

Soulen, R. Kendall, 191
Speyer, W., 16
Speyr, Adrienne von, 412
Sprinkle, Preston M., 162, 222
Stacey, Peter, 395
Starling, David, 174, 202, 203
Stec, David M., 259
Stegemann, Hartmut, 101
Stendahl, Krister, 71, 72
Stirewalt, M. Luther, Jr., 49, 52
Stowe, Harriet Beecher, 406
Stowers, Stanley K., 48, 49, 50, 191, 238, 240
Strelan, Rick, 35, 41
Strobel, Regula, 309
Suh, Robert H., 194
Swartley, Willard M., 183

Tanner, Kathryn, 272, 273, 291, 308
Taylor, Lily Ross, 37
Tellbe, Mikael, 42
Thate, Michael J., 92
Thielman, Frank, 4, 8, 9, 10, 11, 16, 26, 27, 30, 80, 91, 95, 96, 103, 104, 105, 109, 112, 113, 116, 120, 128, 138, 139, 148, 151, 152, 153, 186, 199, 202, 205, 208, 210, 211, 213, 216, 217, 225, 230, 242, 248, 254, 257, 258, 274, 275, 279, 281, 282, 284, 287, 288, 316, 320, 324, 326, 328, 329, 331, 332, 335, 337, 338, 339, 340, 364, 371, 372, 374, 375, 376, 401, 402, 405, 407, 410, 411, 412, 415, 416, 418, 419, 424, 428, 430, 431, 432, 433, 437
Thiselton, Anthony C., 124, 130, 131, 357
Thomas, Matthew J., 21
Thompson, James W., 69
Thompson, Marianne Meye, 253
Towner, Philip H., 35
Trebilco, Paul R., 11, 12, 28, 32, 34, 39, 43, 178, 279
Tulloch, Janet H., 350
Tutu, Desmond, 117

Uzzi, Jeannine Diddle, 380

Vanhoozer, Kevin J., 92
Vickers, Jason E., 97
Volf, Miroslav, 323, 324
Vout, Caroline, 380

Index of Authors

Wainwright, Arthur William, 58
Wallace, Daniel B., 89, 95, 154, 161, 221, 245, 267, 269, 293, 313
Wansink, Craig S., 45, 46, 238, 426
Wassen, Cecilia, 382
Watson, Francis, 59, 60, 72
Weima, Jeffrey A. D., 17, 24, 50
Westerholm, Stephen, 71, 102
Westfall, Cynthia Long, 131, 132, 343, 349, 354, 355, 357, 362, 364, 367
Wheatley, Alan B., 369
White, Thomas Joseph, 301
Wilder, Terry L., 17, 19
Williams, Margaret H., 144
Willitts, Joel, 192

Winer, G. B., 120
Wink, Walter, 40, 218, 219, 220, 428
Wistrand, E., 359
Witherington, Ben, III, 46, 48, 82, 132, 177, 319, 361, 366
Woyke, Johannes, 71
Wright, Christopher J. H., 307
Wright, N. T., 25, 43, 72–73, 189, 192, 252, 253, 343, 408, 409

Yinger, Kent L., 71
Yoder Neufeld, Thomas R., 259, 410
Yong, Amos, 40

Zetterholm, Magnus, 191

Index of Scripture and Other Ancient Texts

OLD TESTAMENT

Genesis
1:3	301
1:26	242n25, 279n194, 288
1:26–30	123
1:27	310, 371n564
1:27 LXX	388n654
2:23	368n554
2:24	56, 65, 69, 70, 134, 186, 209, 209n548, 348, 370, 371
3:5–6	307
4:5–7	293
6:1–4	126n181
6:1–8	262n116
8:20–22	309
8:21	309, 371
22:11–18	59
22:18	229
26:4	229

Exodus
3:14	27, 126n183
4:11–12	430
4:21	281–82n202
4:22–23	253
15:1–3	149
15:20–21	268
18:5	180n426
20:1–17	56
20:3–6	376
20:8	65n253
20:12	65, 375
20:12 LXX	375n585
20:15	292
20:16	292
22:31	79
29:18	309
30:12–13	104
34:6	247
34:6–7	151

Leviticus
11:45	79
17:6	309
17:11	180
19:1–2	65n253
19:2	307
19:18	371
26:1	177
26:30	177

Numbers
14:33 LXX	314
15:3–24	309
22:28	430
29:2–36	309

Deuteronomy
5:1–21	178
5:6–21	56
5:16	65, 375
5:19	292
5:20	292
6:4	59–60, 64, 253
6:4–6	250
7:6–8	95
8:17–18	314
9:5	289
10:9	108
10:16	177, 177n407
12:12	108
14:2	95
14:29	101n75
15:4–5	101n75
15:12–18	394
15:15	389
22:25–29	397
23:2	69–70n266
24:13–15	101n75
24:17–22	389
25:2	148
30:12–14	260
30:14	365, 424
32:4	289n233
32:21	381n623

Joshua
10:24–25	128

Judges
9:16	328

2 Samuel
5:10	412

1 Kings
8:15	84n3
8:39–49	199
8:54	228
8:56	84n3
19:10	412

Index of Scripture and Other Ancient Texts

2 Kings
22:8–20	268

2 Chronicles
6:30–39	199
7:1	137n239
24:16	328
30:27	199
34:14–28	268

Ezra
9:13	166

Nehemiah
6:14	166

Job
1:7	415
5:9	217
9:10	217
11:7–9	234

Psalms
2:8	413
4:2 MT	292n242
4:3 LXX	292n242
4:4	56, 293
4:5 LXX	293
8	123, 123n170, 127n190
8:6	113, 123, 127, 128, 320, 371, 431
8:6 LXX	56
8:7	56
8:7 LXX	123
12:4 LXX	119
18:9 LXX	119
18:13–14 LXX	145
19:4	424
19:13–14	145
23:4	243n29
24:8	118n149, 149
29	236n656
29:3	118n149
33:19 LXX	246
34:9	79
34:18	246
41:13	84n3
51:5 LXX	328
52:3	328
52:5 MT	328
61:4 LXX	184n446
62:3	184n446
67:19 LXX	255, 258
68	259, 260, 261, 263, 266, 310
68:18	56, 255, 258, 371
68:19 MT	255, 258
72:18–19	84n3
89:52	84n3
91	420n799
91:4	420n799
91:5	420n799
91:10	420n799
91:13	420n799
102:20	148
106:43 LXX	151
106:48	84n3
107:23–30	260
107:43	151
109:1 LXX	56
110	123, 123n170, 127n190
110:1	56, 59–60, 69, 113, 123, 125, 129, 320, 431
115:1	222n606
139:7–12	234

Proverbs
3:34	246, 258n89
8:12–31	59
8:27–30	218
25:15	247n45

Isaiah
2:18	177
5:7	187
6:1	137n239
6:8	268
6:10	282n202
9:2	326n376
9:5 LXX	82
9:5–6 MT, LXX	193
9:6	82
9:6–7	193
11:1–9	66
11:3–5	416
11:4	246, 423
24:17	260n101
26:19	332
28:16	198, 371
29:16	166
30:27–28	149
32:15	93
40–55	56
40:3	260n101
40:5	118n149
40:11	269
40:13	277
40:26	229
42:1–4	251
45:23	228
49:8	6
49:13	246
52	416
52:7	193n488, 194, 416, 419
52:10	66
56:7	132
57:14–19	174
57:19	56, 140, 172, 174, 180, 180n426, 193, 193n487, 371
57:19 LXX	193n486, 193n488
57:20	274
57:21	194
59	56, 416
59:2–8	149
59:11–13	149
59:14	411
59:14–20	416
59:14–21	66
59:16–17	149
59:17	411, 430
59:17 LXX	419, 423
59:19	423
59:20	411
59:21	430
60:1	332
60:1–2	326n376
60:19	326n376
61:1	268
63–64	300
63:1–6	149n287
63:3	149
63:4	149
63:8–64:12	149n287
63:10	62n248, 300
63:11	269
63:16	253
64:4	300n280
64:8	253, 300n280
66:2	246

Index of Scripture and Other Ancient Texts

Jeremiah
3:9	314
3:15	269
4:4	177, 177n407
7:26	282n202
9:24	165
10:16	109n112
15:15	247n45
22:16	246
23:3	269
31:9	253
31:10	269

Ezekiel
16:1–43	364
16:36	314
20:41	309, 371
30:5 LXX	147
34:2–10	269
36:25–27	364n536
36:26–27	111
37	194n489
37:1–14	93
43:5	137n239
44:4	137n239

Daniel
2:18 LXX	106n97
2:21 LXX	107n102
4:34 LXX	130n84
4:37	107n102
5:2	294n255
5:4	177
5:23	177
6:10	228
7:18–27	79
7:22	140
7:27	140
10:1	211n558
10:12–14	415
12	126n181
12:9	211n558

Hosea
1:2	314
11:1–3	253

Joel
2:28–29	111
2:28–32	93

Micah
1:7	314
6:6–8	389
6:8	382

Zechariah
3:1	415
3:1–2	294n256, 412n758
8:16	293, 294n256, 412n758
8:16 LXX	292, 292n243
8:23	292
9:9–10	82
11:15	269

NEW TESTAMENT

Matthew
3:17	102
4:1–4	413
4:1–11	424
4:5–7	413
4:6	420n799
4:8–11	413
5:9	184n441
5:21–24	293
5:23–24	163n355
5:32	314
5:43	368
5:43–48	254
5:44–48	307
5:48	273
6:9	228
7:11	261
7:17–18	299
9:36	303
10:19–20	430
10:32–33	417
11:25–26	106
11:29–30	247
11:30	375
12:15–21	251
12:31	210
12:33	299
13:17	210
13:22	322n359
13:48	299
14:27	126n183
16:9	210
16:11	210
16:24	375
16:24–26	358
17:5	102
18:15–17	329n397
19:3–6	371
19:4	371n564
19:9	314
19:16–23	298
19:16–30	159
19:30	361n528
20:16	361n528
20:21	125
20:28	104
21:4–5	82
21:13	132
21:33	184
22:23–33	371
22:43–45	125
22:44	123n169
23:15	148
25:31–32	269
26:27–28	104
26:64	123n169
27:66	111
28:18	199n514
28:19–20	211

Mark
1:11	102
1:17	306
1:41	303
3:5	282n202
3:28	210
4:19	322n359
5:1–20	126
6:50	126n183
6:52	282n202
6:55	274
8:35	127
9:7	102
9:35	361n528
10:17–23	298
10:17–31	159, 298n272
10:21	298n272
10:37	125
10:38	252
10:38–39	249
10:41–45	404
10:45	104, 309
11:17	132
12:1	184
12:35–37	123n169
13:33	429, 429n836

Index of Scripture and Other Ancient Texts

14:23–24	104	**John**		5:1–11	295
14:34–38	429n836	1:34	102	5:12–16	298
14:38	429	3:13	263	5:31	104n89, 123n169, 355
14:58	177	3:14	260		
		4:42	354	5:34	300
Luke		6:20	126n183	6:1–4	298
1:28	99n65	6:35	126n183	6:2	435
1:67–79	84n4	6:62	263	6:7	298
1:75	289n232	8:12	126n183	6:13	423n815
2:8–20	269	8:31–45	294	7	245
2:11	354–55	8:44	147, 292	7:2	118n151
2:36	268	8:58	126n183	7:22	199–200n514
2:51	349	10:1–30	269	7:48	177
3:22	102	10:2–14	269	7:51	300
4:1–13	424	10:11	126n183, 324	7:55–56	123n169
4:3–4	413	11:25	126n183	7:60	228, 228n620
4:5–18	413	11:39	145	9:1–6	208, 268
4:6	413	12:14–16	82	9:1–19	201
4:9–13	413	12:40	282n202	9:2	216
4:10–11	420n799	13	353	9:4	341
4:18–19	268	13:1–17	367	9:4–5	134
5:7	213	13:34–35	117	9:18	252
6:27	368	14:6	126n183	9:40	228
6:27–36	101	14:27	420	10	179n423, 194
6:35	303	15:1	126n183	10:34	68, 405
6:45	315	15:16	95	10:34–36	194
7:13	303	16:8	331n407	10:43	104n89
8:26–39	126	16:33	420	13:23	355
10:1–21	122	17:9	129	13:38	104n89
10:17	122, 349	18:3	420n799	14:4	78, 78n7, 268
10:17–19	415	19:30	301	14:14	78, 78n7, 268
10:20–21	122	20:17	273n163	14:15–17	254
10:21	106	21:16	269	15	388
11:13	261			15:5–6	190
12:8	417	**Acts**		15:5–29	144
12:20	335	1:8	211	15:21	253
12:50	249, 252	1:14	429	16	179n423
14:7	95	1:21	199n514	16:11–40	43
15:1–7	180	1:26	268	16:13	132
15:4–6	269	2:13–16	337n435	16:15	252
15:8–10	180	2:16–21	93	16:16	132
15:11–24	180	2:17	268	16:16–20	431
17:8	435	2:32–33	123n166	16:33	252
18:11	228	2:32–35	260	17:5–9	387
18:13	228	2:33	125	17:6–9	431
19:46	132	2:34–35	56, 123n169	17:24–26	199
20:41–44	123n169, 125	2:36	199n514	17:30	282n203
21:1–4	163n355	2:42	429	18:1–4	297
22:26–27	435	3:17	282n203	18:8	252
22:41	228, 228n620	3:25	229	18:18–19	297
24:27	203	4:32–35	298	18:19	43n184
24:47	21	4:36–5:11	298	18:19–21	44

Index of Scripture and Other Ancient Texts

18:24–26	11, 25–26	1:3–4	272	5:17	157n317, 163
18:26	43n184, 270	1:7	30, 79, 80	6:3–6	249
19	26, 279	1:8	116	6:4	151n294, 252, 286
19:1–7	11	1:9–10	116	6:4–5	252
19:1–10	208	1:13	106n100	6:5	151n294
19:1–20:1	44	1:15	30	6:6	151n294, 286, 287
19:5	252	1:18	324	6:8	151n294
19:8–9	43n184	1:18–32	148	6:11	286
19:8–10	9, 11, 26, 117	1:20	166, 210	6:11–14	141, 180n425
19:11–12	44	1:23	436	6:13	328, 417, 420n799
19:13–17	126	1:24–28	282	6:17	402
19:19	44, 146n276	1:26	148	6:17–18	386
19:19–20	127	1:30	374	6:17–20	387
19:22	435	2:4	247, 247n45, 303	7:22–23	231
19:24–27	314	2:7	296n265, 436	8:7	340, 349
19:27	44	2:8	302	8:11	285
19:31	44, 283	2:25–29	176–77	8:15	97, 119, 212, 228, 429
19:35	279	2:28–29	177		
19:40–41	45	3:1–2	178	8:17	109, 212, 225
20:4	434	3:3	221, 222n600	8:20	280
20:18–35	298	3:14	301	8:22–24	108
20:19	246	3:19	332n409	8:23	97, 104
20:28	104, 180, 269, 386	3:21–26	328	8:24	152n297, 153n301
20:28–30	322	3:22	117n146, 161, 161n347, 221n599, 222, 222n602	8:24–25	109
20:31	117			8:26	429
20:33	36n149			8:26–27	301
20:35	298	3:24–25	106n100	8:29	244, 273n163, 288
20:36	228	3:24–27	156n314	8:29–30	97
21:5	228	3:25	106n100	8:30	6, 152n297, 244
21:8	268	3:26	117n146, 161, 161n347, 221n599, 222, 222n602, 285	8:31–32	339
21:9	268, 270			8:32	162n351
21:20–26	174, 185			8:34	123n166, 123n169, 125, 152n297
21:27–29	185	3:27	165		
21:29	434	3:31	186	8:35–39	152n297
21:33	206	4:2	156n314	8:37–39	339
22:1–21	208	4:3	332n409	8:38	127
22:3	300	4:4	299	8:39	151
22:7–8	134	4:6	332n409	9–11	189, 189n468, 203n524
22:28	177n413	4:11	111		
23:1	199–200n514	4:12	221–22, 222n600	9:4	97, 212
26:1–23	208	4:13–14	7, 178	9:4–5	177n411, 178
26:18	104n89	5:1	184, 194	9:15	332n409
26:23	327	5:2	165, 194, 211	9:17	332n409
27:14–44	274	5:5	151, 157	9:20	166
28:16	238	5:8	151	9:21	300n280
28:20–30	30	5:8–11	180, 180n425	9:22	247, 247n45
28:30–31	47	5:10	188n465, 386n648	9:23	167
		5:11	165, 386n648	9:25	332n409
Romans		5:12–18	9	9:33	198
1–11	51	5:12–21	148n283	10:2–3	74n281
1:1	24n91, 77, 216, 267, 387n652, 403	5:15	105, 157n317, 163	10:3	340
		5:15–17	214n565	10:6–7	262

459

Index of Scripture and Other Ancient Texts

10:6–8	260, 264	13:12	287, 417n784, 420n799	2:1	5
10:7	262, 262n114			2:3	401
10:8	365, 424	13:12–14	287	2:6–8	218
10:9	9, 161, 252	13:13	282	2:7	5, 209
10:9–10	249, 330, 402	14	186	2:8	118
10:10	154n303	14:6	105n94	2:9	300n280
10:11	332n409	14:8–9	252	2:10–16	119
10:15	194, 416, 419	14:9	64, 320	2:16	277
10:16	332n409	14:10	321	3:5	213, 435
10:17–18	424	14:11	228	3:6	12
10:19	294, 332n409, 381n623	14:13–18	329	3:6–9	267
		14:17	7, 249n54, 320, 321	3:9	199
10:20	332n409			3:9–17	197n498
10:21	332n409	15:4	209	3:10	158n327
11:2	332n409	15:6	89	3:10–11	198n505
11:4	228	15:8	213, 435	3:16	7, 69
11:6	156n314	15:12	332n409	4:1	5, 209
11:9	332n409	15:13	249n54	4:6	268
11:12	137n232	15:14	271, 328	4:6–7	164n362
11:13–32	173n394	15:19	214	4:9	211, 268
11:15	386n648	15:26	329n392	4:9–13	78
11:17	329n392	15:29	137n232	4:15–16	197
11:22	303	15:30–32	432	4:16	307
11:25	71, 137n232	16:1	435	4:20	320
11:25–26	5	16:2–3	370	4:21	119
11:25–27	209n548	16:5	68	5–6	31
11:26	192	16:7	78n7, 268, 270	5:1	314, 331, 435
11:30	326n377	16:20	412n758	5:5	412n758
11:33	105, 121, 217, 219	16:21	24n91	5:7	309
11:36	236, 249	16:23	390n664	6:7	318
12	264, 267n128	16:25	236	6:9	7, 321
12:1	51, 51n215, 243, 243n27	16:25–26	6, 208, 211	6:9–11	180n425
		16:25–27	71	6:10	318
12:1–2	238n3, 328	16:26	431	6:11	319, 363, 365
12:2	127, 234	16:27	237	6:12	9
12:3	105n94, 165			6:12–20	314
12:3–6	69n261, 258	**1 Corinthians**		6:14	125
12:3–8	51n215, 69	1:1	77, 78, 267	7	5, 348
12:4–5	7, 134	1:2	6, 79	7:1	435
12:6	257	1:3	80	7:2–4	367, 372
12:12	429	1:4	116, 339	7:4	68
12:15	286n221	1:4–8	9	7:5	412n758
12:16	105n94	1:9	273n163, 329n392	7:7	266–67
12:19	332n409	1:11	435	7:11	188n465, 386n648
12:21	426	1:12	332n409	7:22	398
13:1	128, 340, 349	1:14–17	252	7:40	367
13:5	340, 349	1:17	198	8:6	64, 90, 249, 249n56, 250, 251
13:8–10	293	1:18–2:16	389n658		
13:9	107	1:20	127, 146	9:1	78
13:10	137n232	1:27–28	95	9:5–7	268
13:11–14	426	1:30	7, 105, 218	9:21	320
		1:31	165	9:23	329n392

9:25	436	15:9	68, 204, 216, 216n572	3:10	155n310
10:1–4	69–70			3:18	245, 288
10:12	426	15:10	158n327, 167	4:2	147n281, 275
10:16	329n392	15:14–23	125	4:5	387n652
10:16–17	134	15:17	280	4:6	331n407
10:23	9	15:19	109	4:7	214
10:26	137n232	15:20	134n225, 136	4:10	274
11:1	307	15:22–28	431	4:13	222n606
11:3	69n264, 131n213, 357	15:24	412	4:16	231
		15:24–27	123, 123n170	5:1	8
11:4–5	268	15:24–28	65, 320, 408	5:2–4	6
11:5	268	15:25	56	5:5	112
11:14	148	15:25–26	320	5:9	328
11:22	132	15:25–27	128	5:10	404
11:27	134	15:27	123, 124, 127, 349	5:17	167n371
11:29	134	15:28	124, 138	5:18	386n648
12	264, 267n128	15:32	29, 45, 46, 409	5:18–20	188n465, 386n648
12:2	56	15:36	335		
12:4	257	15:40–49	414n771	5:19	92, 324, 386n648
12:4–6	254	15:42	436	5:20	432
12:6	138	15:50	318, 321, 436	6:2	6, 332n409
12:7–11	264	15:51	5, 71n268	6:4–10	78, 432
12:7–14	6	15:51–57	209n548	6:6	247n45
12:12–13	249	15:52	6	6:7	214, 417, 420n799
12:12–27	7, 134, 292	15:53	436	6:14	329n392
12:12–28	69n261	15:53–58	287	6:16	7, 69
12:13	250, 252, 332n409, 364	15:54	436	7:5	412n760
		15:54–55	427	7:9–10	296n265
12:18–25	136	16:2	132	7:15	401
12:22–23	361n528	16:8	29	8:4	299, 329n392
12:27	69	16:12	12	8:9	81
12:27–31	6	16:13	230, 426	8:13–15	298
13:4	324n370	16:15–16	349	8:18–24	434
13:11	273	16:16	340, 340n454	8:23	78, 268
13:12	235n649	16:19	28	9:8	105, 157
14:1–4	268	16:21	23	9:9–10	328
14:3	299			9:11–13	370
14:5	299	**2 Corinthians**		9:13	329n392
14:12	299	1:1	77, 78, 79, 267	9:14	155n310
14:14–17	429	1:2	80	9:15	157n317, 162n351, 163
14:15	339n450	1:3	89, 228		
14:24–25	331n407	1:3–7	83	10:1	243, 247
14:26	271, 299, 339n450	1:8	78	10:1–10	407n736
14:32	349	1:19	272	10:4	420n799
15:1	426	1:22	111, 112	10:17	165
15:1–8	9, 330	2:1–5	304	11:1–21	335
15:3–5	64	2:5–11	295	11:3	274
15:3–8	309	2:11	304, 412n758	11:14	412n758
15:5	268	2:12–7:7	9	11:21–33	432
15:7	78, 268	2:15	309	11:23	45
15:8	78	3:6	213	11:23–28	10, 78
		3:9	105	11:25	274

Index of Scripture and Other Ancient Texts

12:1–4	415		161n347, 221n599,		88, 89, 89n14,
12:2	208		222, 222n602		91n21, 93, 103, 111,
12:6–9	335	3:26	117n146		118, 125, 228n621,
12:6–11	335	3:26–27	388		327, 350, 414,
12:7	208, 412n758	3:27	249, 252, 286		414n771, 436
12:9	214	3:28	371n564, 388,	1:3–4	85, 85n9, 272n161,
12:9–10	198		404n721		422
12:12	78, 267n131	3:29–4:7	7	1:3–6	53, 86, 88–91
12:21	282, 296, 313, 314	4:1–7	390	1:3–7	306
13:13	329n392	4:3–9	180n425	1:3–14	8, 53, 83–87, 95,
		4:5	97, 212, 335		95n52, 113n128,
Galatians		4:6	228, 429		218, 241, 339
1:1	61, 77, 267, 268	4:8	179	1:3–23	53
1:2	68, 78	4:30	318, 318n347,	1:3–3:21	53
1:3	63, 80		332n409	1:4	62, 63, 79, 84, 85,
1:4	7, 9n17, 127,	5:1	12		85n8, 88, 95–96,
	162n351	5:4	158n327		102, 105, 106, 120,
1:5	236	5:6	117n146, 177, 223,		122, 133, 141, 167,
1:10	216, 403		233, 436		173, 186, 238, 241,
1:12	208	5:9	314		311, 363, 366
1:13	68, 216	5:13	246	1:4–5	61, 94–99, 105,
1:13–14	31	5:14	293		308, 436
1:13–24	201	5:16	12	1:4–6	85n10
1:15	158n327	5:17	368	1:4–7	244
1:16	78	5:19	282, 313, 314	1:4–10	85n8, 217–18
1:17	78	5:21	7, 318, 318n347,	1:5	63, 70, 85, 85n11,
1:19	78, 268		321		88, 89n14, 90, 96,
1:23	326n377	5:22	9n17, 247,		97, 104, 105, 106,
2:1–10	190, 388		247n45, 327–28		108, 109, 113, 136,
2:4	203	5:23	247		148, 151, 212, 336,
2:6	405	6:2	320		342, 403
2:7	78	6:8	368	1:5–6	85n9, 151–54
2:9	158n327, 329n392	6:10	196, 335	1:5–8	85
2:11–18	144	6:11	23	1:6	61, 84, 85n8,
2:15	148	6:14	165		85n11, 86, 88,
2:16	117n146, 156n314,	6:15	167n371, 177		88n13, 96,
	161, 161n347,	6:16	6, 435n7		99–102, 103, 109,
	221n599, 222,	6:17	9n17, 285		118, 151, 158n329,
	222n602				225n615, 231, 237,
2:20	117n146, 161,	**Ephesians**			436
	161n347, 221n599,	1	52n220, 99, 140,	1:6–7	99
	222, 222n602, 272		154, 172, 200, 226,	1:7	10, 85, 85n11,
2:21	158n327		250		102–3, 104–5,
3:1	209	1–2	8n15		108, 109, 111, 112,
3:1–6	349	1–3	32n128, 51, 53, 238		113, 120, 122, 125,
3:2–5	156n314	1:1	26, 28, 30, 62,		141, 151, 154, 155,
3:13	335		267, 289n231		162, 180, 216, 299,
3:16	332n409	1:1–2	53, 77–82		309, 386
3:17–19	178	1:2	61, 63, 65, 100	1:7–8	85n9, 103–6, 151
3:18	318, 318n347	1:2–3	61, 65, 251, 252,	1:7–9	106n100
3:19	205n527		253	1:7–10	85
3:22	117n146, 161,	1:3	8, 63, 82, 84, 87,	1:7–12	53, 86, 102–10

462

1:8	84, 85n8, 105, 334	1:15–2:22	53n223	1:23	31, 62, 69, 107, 114, 115, 118, 133–34, 133n220, 137, 140, 188, 212, 226, 250, 264, 273, 292
1:9	84, 85–86n11, 89n14, 103, 105–6, 108, 109, 372, 403	1:16	113, 116		
		1:17	62, 63, 82, 105, 118, 119, 119n158, 120n159, 225n615, 228, 230, 237, 251, 252, 253, 308, 334, 436		
1:9–10	70, 85n9, 209, 209n547, 254				
1:9–14	85			2	139, 140–41, 143, 210, 212, 227, 250, 267
1:10	7, 69, 70, 86, 103, 106–8, 107n106, 107n108, 122, 126, 139, 168, 172, 174, 182, 207, 239, 243, 251, 254, 264, 276, 284, 324, 335, 408, 414, 431, 436	1:17–18	272		
		1:17–19	118–22	2:1	103n83, 141, 143–45, 143n261, 144, 150, 153, 166, 281
		1:17–23	143		
		1:18	31, 70, 105, 110, 118, 119, 119n158, 151, 168, 179, 217, 225n615, 237, 251, 402	2:1–2	148, 168, 179, 215
				2:1–3	54, 140, 142–50, 143n263, 150, 350
1:11	85, 85–86n11, 97, 103, 108–9, 111, 112n122, 113, 141, 212, 220, 336, 403			2:1–5	287
		1:18–19	118, 228, 327	2:1–7	8, 139n253, 141
		1:19	69, 113n129, 114, 120, 121, 124, 148, 149, 155n310, 407, 410	2:1–10	53, 139n252, 140–42, 180
1:11–12	85, 85nn9–10			2:1–22	53, 139–40
1:11–14	85			2:2	25, 68, 70, 97n58, 126, 144, 145–48, 145n269, 146, 166, 179, 219, 242, 251, 261, 274n169, 275, 280, 282, 291, 301, 322, 327, 331, 410, 413
1:12	86, 88, 99, 103, 109–10, 118, 141, 148, 225n615, 231, 237	1:19–20	140, 236, 431		
		1:20	8, 59, 65, 90, 113, 113n129, 113n130, 114n133, 115, 123, 124–25, 136, 140, 143, 151, 153, 183, 187n462, 261n110, 324, 414, 414n771		
1:12–14	67				
1:13	85, 87, 103, 108, 109–10, 119, 121, 161, 162, 211, 252, 275, 283, 284, 288n231, 301, 324, 328, 337, 416, 418, 423, 423n815				
				2:2–3	167–68, 323
		1:20–21	115, 118, 259, 284, 310, 320	2:3	141, 144, 145, 148–50, 280n197, 281, 401
		1:20–22	60, 87, 320, 431		
		1:20–23	13, 53, 121, 122–29, 123n168, 198n504, 234, 272n161	2:4	141, 143, 150–51, 154, 155, 232
1:13–14	53, 62, 70, 85, 85n9, 86, 87–91, 111–13, 120, 120n160, 225, 250, 291, 299, 437			2:4–5	141, 281, 324, 436
				2:4–6	272n161
		1:21	7, 114, 115, 125–27, 128, 146, 168, 219, 229, 263, 315n327, 412, 415, 431	2:4–7	54, 150–56
				2:5	5, 81, 99, 139, 141, 141n260, 143, 151, 152, 153, 154, 160, 165, 299, 303, 324
1:14	7, 62, 85n11, 86, 86n11, 88, 99, 104, 109, 110, 112, 113, 118, 121, 212, 225n615, 231, 237, 309, 318				
		1:21–22	10, 139, 153, 294, 320		
		1:21–23	251	2:5–6	5, 6, 70, 139, 140, 143, 143n263, 437
1:15	11, 79, 232n640, 233, 416, 435, 436	1:22	9, 56, 67, 69, 107, 113n129, 114n133, 115, 118, 123, 125, 127–29, 129n200, 137, 204, 254, 349, 371, 437		
				2:5–8	252
1:15–16	116–17			2:6	8, 60, 61, 65, 90, 91n21, 94, 94n42, 125, 133, 140, 151, 151n294, 153, 154, 198n504, 200, 225, 235, 237, 263, 265, 284, 307,
1:15–19	53, 115–22, 140, 143, 226				
1:15–23	8, 32, 53, 84, 113–14, 136n231, 429	1:22–23	7, 69, 70, 80, 113, 113n129, 142, 143, 237, 242, 276, 284, 354, 368		

463

2:6–8	310, 320, 324, 355, 414, 414n771, 415, 423		193, 194, 206, 227, 248n51, 249, 284, 355, 368, 386, 435		198, 225, 232, 237, 248, 250, 252, 284, 299, 337
2:7	7, 99, 105, 120, 146, 151, 154–56, 155n310, 156, 162, 168, 217, 274, 303, 435	2:14–15	68, 87, 132, 139, 172, 250, 292, 408	3	99–100, 106, 118, 172, 182, 201, 202n521, 203, 210n549, 219, 226, 254, 267, 278
		2:14–16	183–89, 239		
		2:14–17	61, 187n462		
		2:14–18	54, 171–72, 175, 181–89, 281, 416	3:1	78, 116, 205–6, 223, 224, 227, 244, 375, 411, 432
2:8	5, 61, 81, 99, 139, 141, 154, 156, 157, 160–63, 160n342, 162n352, 214, 232n638, 256, 257, 264, 299, 303, 416, 422	2:14–19	373		
		2:14–22	420	3:1–2	412n758
		2:15	7, 10, 25n94, 66, 69, 94n42, 167, 179, 184, 185, 185n450, 186, 187, 188, 188n464, 193, 201, 237, 259n95, 273, 307, 309, 435	3:1–5	54, 204–11
				3:1–7	8, 202, 204
				3:1–10	253
				3:1–13	54, 201–4, 201n518
2:8–9	163n357, 205			3:1–21	54, 200–201
2:8–10	54, 81n27, 140, 156–60, 156n315			3:1–4:24	53n223
2:9	5, 144, 157, 163–65	2:16	69, 114, 185–86, 187, 188, 194, 221, 294	3:2	11, 81, 100, 117, 204, 207–8, 208n543, 213, 215, 217, 224, 256, 257n86, 283
2:9–10	167				
2:9–11	65				
2:10	62, 80, 139, 141, 147, 151, 165–68, 237, 242, 265, 266, 279, 280, 288, 297, 307, 327, 375, 403	2:16–18	187		
		2:17	56, 66, 140, 172, 187, 193, 248n51, 416, 435	3:2–7	215
				3:2–13	84, 202n523, 208n545, 244
		2:17–18	25		
		2:17–19	180		
2:11	25, 50, 144, 368, 401	2:18	62, 63, 87, 187, 194, 195, 197n498, 211, 221, 250, 337	3:3	103, 106, 208, 208n543, 209, 210
				3:3–4	208, 372
2:11–12	172, 175, 176–79, 220n589	2:18–19	62	3:3–5	208–11, 315, 328
		2:19	56, 70, 87, 132, 139, 172, 196–97, 225, 278, 288, 309, 342	3:3–6	70, 430
2:11–13	54, 110, 171, 175–81, 215, 427			3:3–9	6
				3:4	103, 106, 209, 210, 430n842
2:11–15	280n197				
2:11–18	68, 69				
2:11–22	12, 32n124, 54, 74, 139n252, 171–75, 189, 205, 209–10, 209n546	2:19–22	54, 172, 175, 195–200, 251, 408	3:4–5	119
		2:20	64, 78, 193, 197–98, 197n497, 242, 267, 269, 299, 371	3:5	78, 187n461, 193, 198, 210, 211, 224, 242, 267, 289n231, 337
2:12	110, 178, 193, 195–96, 203, 212, 251, 281				
				3:5–7	286
		2:20–22	6, 270	3:6	62, 66, 69, 70, 134, 172, 205, 209, 212–13, 217, 224, 278, 292, 325–26, 373, 401, 406
2:12–13	87	2:21	7, 65, 79, 94n42, 132, 198, 199, 199n513, 200, 276, 277, 289n231, 374n580, 406, 410		
2:13	56, 94n42, 175, 176, 179–81, 183, 188, 193, 204, 371				
				3:6–7	54, 61, 212–14
2:13–14	142			3:6–8	416
2:14	2, 12n30, 64, 66, 81, 93, 134, 136–37, 171, 172, 181, 184, 184n441, 185, 185n450, 187,	2:21–22	69, 139, 198–200, 299	3:6–11	87
		2:22	61, 62, 63, 69, 140, 142, 197n497,	3:7	62, 81, 100, 157n317, 163, 204, 213–14, 215, 224,

Index of Scripture and Other Ancient Texts

	257, 257n86, 265, 277		230–31, 233, 236, 237, 288n227	4:2–3	62, 182, 245–49
3:7–13	408	3:16–17	226, 284	4:2–5	365
3:8	79, 100, 105, 120, 151, 162, 209, 214, 215, 216–17, 216n572, 221, 231, 256, 257n86, 265, 266, 299, 339	3:16–18	384	4:3	12, 62, 63, 66, 68, 81–82, 187n462, 239, 245, 248, 250, 272, 328, 416, 420, 435
		3:16–19	31, 54, 62, 230–35		
		3:16–20	308		
		3:17	96n54, 162n352, 199, 230, 231–33, 250, 339, 402, 416, 422, 436		
				4:3–4	211
				4:4	69, 110, 114–15, 120, 134, 222, 248, 250, 250n60, 292
3:8–9	215				
3:8–10	237	3:17–18	31		
3:8–12	202	3:17–19	172, 308	4:4–6	9, 60, 64, 67, 84n7, 182, 194, 240, 248, 249–54, 266, 275
3:8–13	54, 214–21	3:18	79, 226, 232, 233–34, 263, 410, 437		
3:9	103, 106, 107, 207, 209, 211, 216, 217–18, 254, 276, 372				
				4.4–16	51n215
		3:18–19	230, 266, 277, 436	4:5	93, 250, 250n60, 251, 365, 416, 422
		3:19	107, 114, 119, 139n250, 155, 155n310, 175, 226, 233, 234–35, 263, 264, 273, 334, 410		
3:9–10	87, 172, 430			4:6	37, 82, 87, 228, 251, 252, 253, 384
3:10	8, 90, 105, 114, 123, 125, 126, 146, 168, 172, 182, 209, 218–20, 234, 239, 259, 279, 334, 412, 414n771			4:7	56, 64, 81, 100, 157n317, 163, 184, 214, 239, 255–58, 260, 261, 264, 265–66, 267, 273
		3:20	121, 133, 210, 236, 374n578		
		3:20–21	51, 54, 335–37, 374		
		3:21	118, 225n615, 236–37	4:7–10	54, 255–64
3:10–11	119			4:7–16	54, 242, 248n50, 249, 254–55
3:11	65, 162				
3:11–12	161–62, 220–21	4	100, 137, 194, 238, 240, 252, 255, 276, 289, 292	4:8	9, 68, 163, 187n461, 255, 258–61, 332, 371
3:12	62, 118, 152, 162, 162n348, 162n352, 194, 215, 220, 221, 222, 232n638, 327, 416, 422, 430				
		4–5	341n458		
		4–6	51, 53, 84n7, 145, 167, 238, 241, 275n179	4:8–10	198n504, 255, 310
				4:9	184, 261–63
				4:9–10	64, 255, 260, 261
3:13	11, 25, 30, 205, 207, 223–25, 231, 237, 243n27, 339, 431, 433	4:1	31, 50, 51, 51n215, 65, 70, 78, 116, 120, 147, 166, 222, 238, 240, 242, 243–45, 248, 251, 265, 266, 280, 308, 327, 334, 374n580, 375, 410, 411, 417, 431	4:10	138, 263–64, 265, 276, 414
				4:11	64, 70, 78, 197n499, 239, 242, 255, 257, 258, 260, 261, 265, 266, 271, 406
3:13–17	401				
3:14	205, 206, 227–28, 230, 308, 340				
3:14–15	37, 54, 82, 87, 226, 227–30, 253, 370, 384			4:11–12	265–71
				4:11–13	328, 336
3:14–18	67	4:1–2	12n31, 238n3	4:11–16	8, 54, 84, 200, 255, 264–65
3:14–19	14, 50–51, 272	4:1–6	54, 68, 84, 242, 243		
3:14–21	54, 226–27, 429			4:12	69, 79, 114–15, 134, 167, 197, 199, 213, 255, 266, 281n153, 275, 284, 299, 375
3:15	62, 228–30, 228n621, 254, 279, 315n327, 414, 436	4:1–16	241		
		4:1–32	54, 241–42		
		4:1–6:20	54, 238–41		
		4:2	51n215, 245, 275, 277, 278, 294, 340, 375, 435		
3:16	62, 63, 105, 118, 120, 121, 151, 187n461, 211, 217, 225n615, 226,			4:12–16	242
				4:13	63, 82, 107, 114,

465

	119, 132, 137, 167, 239, 248, 252, 271–73, 276, 355, 416		336, 353, 366, 411, 411n752, 416, 419	5:3	65, 282, 305, 313, 317, 366
		4:25	87, 133, 267, 279, 286, 290, 291–93, 292nn241–42, 294n256, 297, 301, 340, 412n758, 418	5:3–5	280n197
4:13–14	267			5:3–6	54, 312–13
4:14	187n461, 265, 273, 274–75, 322			5:3–7	306
4:14–16	69			5:4	315–17, 339
4:15	64, 69, 132, 137, 167, 265, 267, 275–76, 292, 328, 418, 435			5:5	7, 31, 63, 67, 70, 133, 142, 212, 251, 313, 317–22, 327, 366, 397, 404, 437
		4:25–32	54, 242, 279, 289–91, 321n357		
		4:25–5:2	302	5:5–8	240, 252
		4:25–6:20	53n223	5:6	26, 31, 97n58, 145, 147, 313, 322–24, 331
4:15–16	6, 134, 239, 341, 354, 409	4:26	56, 247, 293, 381		
		4:26–27	290, 293–95		
4:15–17	31	4:27	70, 411n756	5:6–14	241
4:15–25	416	4:28	84n7, 291, 295–98, 303, 310	5:7	212, 213, 241n22, 325–26, 329
4:16	87, 114–15, 138, 197, 199, 200, 256n78, 276–77, 299				
		4:28–29	403	5:7–14	54, 324–25
		4:29	81, 84n7, 87, 100, 197, 199, 267, 291, 303, 310, 313	5:8	65, 87, 147, 166, 242, 243, 280, 319, 326, 327, 328, 331, 334, 339, 350, 374n580, 410, 419
4:16–17	200				
4:17	36, 56, 65, 147, 166, 212, 240, 242, 243, 274n169, 278, 279, 280, 281, 284, 288, 292n242, 308, 313, 327, 334, 374n580				
		4:29–30	298–301		
		4:29–32	340		
		4:30	7, 62, 84n7, 87, 111–12, 239, 250, 288n231, 291, 300, 306, 337	5:8–9	326–28
				5:8–10	415
				5:8–14	168
		4:31	84n7, 247, 293, 301–2	5:8–16	36
				5:9	416
		4:32	94, 133, 241n22, 296n265, 302–4, 305, 306, 340	5:10	336
4:17–18	25, 68			5:10–11	328–30
4:17–19	242, 278, 279, 280–83			5:11	331, 429
				5:12	315–16, 330
4:17–24	54, 277–80	4:32–5:2	312	5:12–13	329
4:17–32	241	5	106, 240	5:12–14	330–33
4:18	281, 313, 402	5:1	62, 68, 87, 197, 241n22, 305, 306, 324, 327, 342, 410n749	5:13	331, 332
4:19	281, 282, 313, 314			5:13–14	331
4:20	279, 283			5:14	9, 145, 258, 261n110, 331, 331n408
4:20–21	64, 242, 279				
4:20–24	242, 279, 283–89, 328	5:1–2	54, 239, 291, 305–10, 320, 339		
				5:15	147, 166, 242, 243, 280, 327, 334, 429
4:21	117, 283, 284, 286, 289, 290, 328, 336, 418	5:1–5	241		
		5:1–6	238	5:15–16	334–35
		5:1–8	149	5:15–20	330
4:22	148, 187n461, 289, 291–92, 292n241, 322	5:1–21	54, 305	5:15–21	54, 333–34
		5:2	64, 68, 117, 129n202, 147, 166, 242, 243, 275, 280, 284, 308, 313, 327, 334, 358, 361, 362, 363, 371, 384, 436	5:15–6:9	241
				5:16	126, 413
4:22–24	252, 272, 285, 286			5:17	335–36
				5:17–20	333–34n418
4:23	119			5:18	62, 63, 114, 138, 175, 235, 239, 240, 334, 337, 338, 341, 349, 362
4:24	87, 167, 187n461, 231, 239, 288, 290, 303, 307, 328,				

5:18–19	90	5:32	14, 69, 87, 103, 106, 371–72, 431	6:14	328, 411, 417–19, 422, 428, 428n832
5:18–20	32, 67, 429	5:33	340, 352, 371, 372–73, 401	6:14–17	54, 415–17
5:18–21	182, 316, 336–42			6:14–20	8
5:19	271, 338, 402	6	115, 240, 249, 251, 295n261, 410n749, 411, 432	6:15	66, 81, 187n462, 248n51, 249, 419–20, 424, 435
5:19–6:9	12n31				
5:20	65, 82, 87, 253, 339–40			6:16	259, 294, 420–22, 420n799, 436
5:20–32	131n211	6:1	401		
5:21	68, 128, 239, 334, 341, 348–50, 351, 352, 372, 400, 401, 428n833	6:1–3	374–76	6:17	62, 365, 422–25, 428
		6:1–4	54, 56, 197, 373, 392	6:18	79, 233, 337, 428–29
		6:2	9, 186	6:18–20	54, 427–28, 432
5:21–22	374	6:4	247, 294, 368, 381–84	6:19	6, 30, 70, 103, 106, 209, 220, 372, 420
5:21–24	54, 350–51				
5:21–33	54, 134, 348–50, 372n574	6:5	14, 251, 340, 368, 402		
		6:5–6	405	6:19–20	116, 408, 430–32
5:21–6:9	54, 348, 402n714	6:5–7	401–3	6:20	78, 202, 238, 244, 411, 431
		6:5–9	54, 347, 385–91		
5:22	128, 334, 341, 341n457, 348–50, 351–53	6:6	14, 400, 402, 403	6:21	79, 342, 374n580
		6:6–7	406	6:21–22	12, 433–35
		6:7	187n461, 346, 400, 402, 403, 404	6:21–24	50, 54, 117, 433
5:22–24	132			6:23	187n462, 253, 416
5:22–6:9	239, 334n420			6:23–24	82, 435–37
5:23	14, 64, 69, 87, 107, 115, 239, 276, 353–58, 427	6:7–8	401	6:24	100
		6:8	70, 400, 403–4		
		6:9	68, 182, 229, 246, 251, 344, 350, 404–7, 414	**Philippians**	
5:24	14, 128, 358–59			1:1	78, 79, 216, 265, 387n652, 403, 435
5:25	14, 117, 129n202, 138, 341, 352, 359–62, 363, 365, 366, 371, 372, 427, 436				
		6:10	66n255, 114, 123, 133, 374n580, 407, 410–11, 428n832	1:2	80
				1:3	116, 116n140
				1:3–7	9
		6:10–12	115	1:3–11	113n129
5:25–27	252	6:10–13	54, 68, 240, 375, 409–10	1:5	329n392
5:25–33	7, 54, 359			1:6	167
5:26	363, 364, 423	6:10–17	149, 324	1:7	105n94, 329n392
5:26–27	69, 79, 289n231, 362–66	6:10–20	54, 407–9	1:11	327
		6:11	66n255, 275, 294, 350, 411–12, 415, 428n832, 436	1:13	10
5:27	96, 364, 365			1:14–20	432n847
5:28	115, 347, 352, 354, 366–68			1:15	271
		6:11–12	275	1:15–17	203
5:28–29	68	6:11–13	239	1:17	283
5:29	14, 276, 368, 381, 401	6:12	8, 90, 114, 125, 126, 127n184, 146, 219, 259, 261, 327, 401, 412–13, 414, 414n771, 415n776	1:17–18	293
				1:19–20	432
5:29–30	69, 250, 368–69			1:20	431
5:29–32	70			1:27	196, 426
5:30	7, 87, 115, 188, 213, 276, 292, 365, 368			1:30	412n760
		6:12–13	70, 218	2:1	329n392
5:30–32	186, 292–93	6:12–14	204	2:2	105n94
5:31	9, 69, 129n202, 187n461, 370–71	6:13	66n255, 335, 411, 411n752, 413–15	2:3	246
				2:5	246
5:31–32	56, 209				

467

Index of Scripture and Other Ancient Texts

2:5–8	367	1:10	157, 244, 327	2:12	252
2:6–11	9, 123, 123n168, 260, 263, 407	1:11–13	247	2:12–13	151
		1:12	108, 108n110	2:13	143n263, 152
2:8	246	1:12–13	321	2:14	159n334, 187
2:9	126	1:12–14	327, 427	2:15	259, 412, 427
2:9–11	58, 65, 252, 340	1:13	102, 103, 146, 317	2:16–19	276
2:10	228, 263, 285, 414n771	1:14	103, 104	2:19	69, 129, 134, 200n517, 264, 277, 354
		1:15	200n514, 311		
2:12	401, 426	1:15–20	13, 14, 103, 107, 123n168, 182	3:1	123
2:12–13	168			3:1–11	431
2:13	106	1:16	8, 59, 126, 412	3:2	105n94
2:15	331n407	1:18	68, 69, 129, 251, 276	3:3	314
2:25	46, 78, 268, 426			3:3–5	315
3:3	177	1:19	105n91, 137, 199, 232, 235	3:5	11n25, 313, 314, 315n328
3:5–6	74n281				
3:6	31	1:19–20	324	3:5–7	286
3:9	117n146, 161, 161n347, 221n599, 222, 222n602	1:20	8, 180, 181, 183, 184n441, 188, 193, 229	3:5–8	313, 316
				3:6	148
				3:8	301
3:10	119, 125, 283, 329n392, 411	1:21	281	3:8–10	302
		1:21–23	180n425	3:8–12	287
3:10–11	119	1:22	96, 188, 363, 368	3:9	252
3:10–12	224	1:23	193, 200n514, 213, 233, 252, 435	3:10	167n371, 287n223, 288
3:11	271				
3:16	286n221	1:23–25	205		
3:17	307, 426	1:23–27	201	3:12	12n31, 247, 252, 303
3:20	8, 133, 196, 229	1:23–28	201n518		
3:20–21	152, 319n349, 354	1:23–29	204	3:13	246
		1:24	68, 129, 134, 137, 204, 224, 411	3:15	134, 194
3:21	128, 349			3:16	90, 271
4:1	417	1:25	213, 435	3:16–25	12n31
4:6	429n834	1:25–27	210n549, 217	3:17	339
4:7	184	1:26	209, 211, 217	3:17–18	350
4:7–9	194	1:26–27	71, 217n580	3:19	14
4:9	184, 285	1:27	5, 151, 204, 209, 431	3:20	358, 373n575, 374
4:10	105n94			3:20–21	374
4:10–19	298	1:28	217n578, 273	3:22	341, 358, 368, 400, 402
4:13	233	1:29	214		
4:14	329	2:1	412n760	3:23	352
4:14–18	329	2:1–3:4	14	3:24–25	404
4:17	261	2:2	5, 151, 209	3:25	405
4:20	236	2:6	283	4:1	404
		2:7	197, 233, 252	4:2	429
Colossians		2:8	322	4:2–4	432n847
1:1	77, 78, 267	2:8–23	275	4:2–6	333
1:2	68, 79, 80	2:9	137, 199, 232	4:3	10, 432n848
1:3	102, 339	2:9–10	235	4:3–4	5, 209, 432
1:3–14	113n129	2:10	412	4:5	147n280, 335
1:4	117n146	2:10–13	141	4:6	300n277, 420n798
1:7	435	2:11	177, 281		
1:9	90, 116, 118	2:11–12	249, 286	4:7–8	12, 433
1:9–20	84	2:11–13	140	4:7–14	47

468

Index of Scripture and Other Ancient Texts

4:8	433n1
4:10–18	434n3
4:12	200n514
4:15	68
4:15–16	28
4:16	9n20, 18, 19, 23n87, 27, 29n115
4:17	167
4:18	23

1 Thessalonians

1:1	78, 80
1:2	116, 339
1:3	157, 423
1:6	307
2:2	412n760, 430
2:6	78n7
2:7	197, 368
2:10	289n232
2:12	147n280
2:14	68, 307
2:18	412n758
3:5	116
3:8	426
3:10	236
4:1	243
4:1–12	147n280
4:3	314, 336
4:6	314
4:10	243n27
4:11–12	297
4:13	178, 375
5:4–8	333, 333n416
5:8	7, 423, 423n811
5:9	112n124, 423
5:11	271
5:13	236
5:17	429
5:18	339
5:23	363

2 Thessalonians

1:1	78
1:2	80
1:11	157, 328
2:2	17
2:3	14
2:9	412n758
2:10	322
2:14	112n124
2:15	14, 426

3:6–13	297
3:17	23

1 Timothy

1:1	267
1:3	435
1:5	383
1:7	210
1:10	355n499
1:16	247, 247n45
1:17	436
1:18	426
1:20	294n256
2:1	429
2:2	35n143
2:7	269
2:8	227
2:9	35n147
2:9–10	364
2:11	349
3:1–13	265
3:4	349
3:15	383
3:16	123n168
4:1	332n409
5:5	429
5:8	377
5:14	205n527
5:15	294n256
5:20	329n397
6:12	412n760

2 Timothy

1:1	77, 267
1:8	431
1:9	153n301, 244
1:10	436
1:11	269
2:10	224
2:25	296n265
4:2	329n397
4:5	268
4:7	412n760
4:12	435
4:18	414n771

Titus

1:1	267, 387n652
1:4	80, 355n499
1:5	205n527
1:6	336

1:8	289n232
1:9	329n397
1:11	205n527
1:13	329n397
2:9	340, 349, 352
2:13	355n499
3:1	340, 349, 412
3:4	303
3:5	153n301, 164n360, 365
3:6	355n499
3:12	435

Philemon

1	10, 78, 205n529
2	426
3	80
4	339
4–6	113n129
6	329n392
9	10, 205n529
11	402
12	47n197
12–14	46–47
13	402
19	23

Hebrews

1:3	123n169, 431
1:13	125, 431
2:5–8	123, 127
2:6–8	56
2:6–9	349
2:7–8	128
2:8	431
3:1	78, 213
3:14	213
5:1	163n355
5:8	285, 382, 382n632
6:4	163, 231
7:5–6	267
8:1	107, 414n771
8:3–4	163n355
9:5	106n100
9:9	163n355
9:11	177
9:13	363
9:22	104, 180
9:24	177
10:10	363
10:12	123n169

10:18	104	4:4	336	**DEUTEROCANONICAL**	
10:19–23	152	4:11	237	**WORKS**	
10:39	112n124	4:17	196n491		
11:4	163n355	5:2	269	**Tobit**	
11:9	212	5:4	269	4:11	159n334
12:2	361	5:5	246, 349	14:5	107n102
12:5–11	382	5:8–9	411		
12:8	213			**Wisdom of Solomon**	
12:9	349	**2 Peter**		5:17–20	416n778
13:12	363	1:1	216, 355n499,	8:5	158n330
13:20	269		387n652	9:18	158n330
13:21	237	1:11	355n499	14:12	312n315, 313n317
		2:13	365		
James		2:18	280	**Sirach**	106
1:1	80n22, 216,	2:20	355n499	2:4	166
	387n652	3:2	355n499	3:17	166
1:6	274	3:9	324n370	9:9	336
1:9–10	246	3:15	247	31:12–32:13	336
1:17	101n72, 118n151,	3:18	355n499		
	228			**2 Maccabees**	
1:19–21	247	**1 John**		2:21	169n377
1:26	322n359	4:14	355n499	6–7	245
3:13	247	4:16	324	6:10	177n409
3:14–15	301			8:17	178
4:6	258n89	**Jude**			
4:7	411	1	216, 387n652		
5:10	247	3	252	**PSEUDEPIGRAPHA**	
		4	209		
1 Peter		12	274	**2 Baruch**	
1:3	89	20	429	40.3	107n102
1:3–9	83	24	236, 363		
1:4	436			**1 Enoch**	
1:15	200n514, 307	**Revelation**		1–36	262n116
1:18–19	104	1:6	236n656	6–9	126n181
1:23	436	1:18	262n114	10.16–22	168
2:3	303	3:19	329n397	11	168
2:4–6	196n491, 198	5:13	236n656	15	126n181
2:5	199, 199n509	7:12	236n656	45.3–6	168
2:9	112, 112n124	11:18	293n247	108.12	140
2:10	326n377	12:7–9	415		
2:11	196n492	12:17	293	**4 Ezra**	
2:13	349	14:10	302	4.37	107n102
2:18	349	18:4	329n392		
2:25	269	19:1	236n656	**Jubilees**	
3:3–6	364	19:15	423	1.23	177n407
3:6	400	21:1–5	133	1.29	168
3:7	212	21:2	364	23.26–29	168
3:8	303	21:9–11	364		
3:18	195, 262n114			**Psalms of Solomon**	
3:19–22	262n116			6.6	437n15
3:20	247, 247n45				
3:22	123n169, 127, 128,				
	349, 431				

Index of Scripture and Other Ancient Texts

Testaments of the Twelve Patriarchs
18.2–14   168

Testament of Dan
5.2   294n255

Testament of Judah
19.1   313n317
23.1   313n317

Testament of Solomon
8.2   412
18.3   412

QUMRAN LITERATURE

CD
4:13–15   260n101
7:2–3   290n236, 294n252
13:7–11   269n137
13:7–19   382n633

1Q28b
5:21–26   409n740

1QH
3:19–22   140
5:7   140n254
5:20   84n3
10:14   84n3
11:27–33   84n3
15:15–17   97n58
16:8   84n3
18:20   177

1QHa   73, 159
11:19–22   332n411
12:5–6   332n411
12:23   332n411

1QM
1:7   140n254
1:16   140n254
14:14   107n102

1QpHab
7:1–4   106n97
7:2   107n102
7:13   107n102
7:13–14   106n97
8:1–3   106n97
11:13   177n407

1QpPs = 1Q16   260

1QS
1:10   140n254, 147
2:3   119
3:13–4:14   168
3:15–23   97n58
3:21   140n254
4:2   246
4:9–10   312n315
4:17–19   146n272
4:18   107n12
5:5   177, 177n407
5:18–19   318n344
7:2–11   290n236
7:16   312n315, 316n335
8:13–16   260n101
10:7–8   318n344
10:21–24   312n315, 316n335
11:15   84n3

JEWISH LITERATURE

Josephus

Against Apion
1.9 §50   20–21n72
2.15–18 §§151–78   169n377
2.23 §193   169n376, 240n13
2.24 §§202–3   379n609
2.25 §204   351n491
2.28 §210   169n379, 178n418
2.37 §§273–75   379n611
2.179–87   240n13

Jewish Antiquities
1.1–26   240n13
1.10.5 §192   177n408
1.11.3 §§200–201   379n611
4.3.2 §45   178n414
4.8.5 §§200–201   240n13
4.9.2 §494   246n42
6.9.4 §293   47n197
8.2.5 §§42–49   42n176
12.3.4 §§148–53   42n179
12.8.7 §323   338n448
13.8.3 §245   178n414
14.10.11 §§223–27   43n182
14.10.12 §227   43n184
14.10.13–19 §§228–30, 234, 240   43n183
14.10.25 §§262–64   43n182
15.11.5 §§417–18   184n447
16.6.2 §§162–73   43n182
18.1.6 §§23–25   240n12
18.3.4 §79   361n529
20.5.1 §§97–99   284n209
20.8.6 §§167–72   284n209

Jewish War   425n819
2.8.12 §159   382n634
2.11.2 §207   47n197
2.13.4–5 §§258–63   284n209
2.17.10 §451   47n197
3.7.10 §173   422n806
3.7.27 §270   421n804
5.5.2 §§193–94   184n447
7.5.4–6 §§123–57   355n500

Philo of Alexandria

Against Flaccus
74   355n501

Allegorical Interpretation
1.33–34   158n330
3.77   158n330
3.79   158n330
3.83   158n330
3.95   158n330
3.166   158n330
3.315–16   43n182

Hypothetica
7.3   346n471

On God
106   158n330

On the Contemplative Life
40   336–37n433
60–62   379n611

On the Embassy to Gaius
148   355n501

On the Life of Abraham
268   101n72
133   379n611

Index of Scripture and Other Ancient Texts

On the Life of Joseph
43–44   312n315

On the Sacrifice of Cain and Abel
121–25   158n330

On the Special Laws
1.4–7   177n409
1.23   312n315, 313n317
1.25   312n315, 313n317
1.305   177n407
2.66–67   394n686
2.69   394n683
2.85   394n684
2.224–36   383n639
3.110–19   379n609
3.137   394n683
3.137–43   394n685
3.169–71   351n491
4.34   307n299
4.73   307n299
4.186–87   307n299

APOSTOLIC FATHERS

Barnabas
10:8   379n611
19:5   379n609

1 Clement
65:1   47n197

2 Clement
7:6   111n120

Didache
2:2   379n609, 379n611

Hermas
8.6.3 [= 72:3]   111n120

CLASSICAL AND HELLENISTIC LITERATURE

Antipater
Greek Anthology
9.58   34n138

Apuleius
Metamorphoses (or The Golden Ass)
9.39–42   416n780
10.1   416n780

Aristotle
Eudemian Ethics
3.7.1234a.4–23   316n332
7.3.4   358n515

History of Animals
2.3.501b19–21   392n673

Magna moralia
1.22.2–3   247n46

Nicomachean Ethics
1.13.20   247n46
4.8.1128a.14–15   316n332
8.10.4   383n638
8.10.1160b29–31   392n671
8.11.3   381n621
8.11.6–7   345n470

Parts of Animals
2.7.653a28–29   392n673

Politics
1252a30–34   393n676
1252b5–9   393n678
1255a28   393n679
1255b   354n496
1259b   381n620
1260a   345n469
1278b32–37   392n671
5.2.10 (1303a25)   183n439

Callimachus
Hymn
Suda 3.302   35n142
Suda 3.859   35n142

Cassius Dio
Roman History
38.36–46   407n732
51.20.6–7   38n162

Cicero
Letters to Atticus
3.9   23n86
11.5.1   24n88

Letters to Family
7.25.1   23n85
10.28.1   9n19
12.4.1   9n19

Letters to Quintus
2.12.4   23n84
3.1.3   377n598

On Duty
2.26   396n694
3.5.22   135n226

On the Consular Provinces
5.10   396n696

Stoic Paradoxes
5.33–34   396n695

Diogenes Laertius
Lives of the Philosophers
10.3   17n55
10.35–83   49n206
10.84–116   49n206
10.122–35   49n206

Dionysius of Halicarnassus
Roman Antiquities
2.26.1–4   13n35
2.27.1   382n631
2.27.1–2   384n641
3.10.6   183n439

Epictetus
Discourses
1.9.10   246nn42
1.14.13–17   426n821
3.24   426n822
3.24.56   246n40, 246n42

Index of Scripture and Other Ancient Texts

Epistles
52.8   316n334

Fragment
30 (89)   251n63

Galen of Pergamum

De libris propriis in *Scripta Minora*
2.91.1–93.16   17n54

Hermogenes

Preliminary Exercises
3.7   382n629

Herodotus

Histories
2.158.2   393n680
8.52   421n805

Juvenal

Satire
7.230–31   21n74

Livy

History
2.32.7–11   135n226
21.8   421n805

Marcus Aurelius

Meditations
4.23   254n76, 376n594
7.13   292n244

Nicolaus of Damascus

Die Fragmente der griechischen Historiker
90 F 125   38

Ovid

Calendar
6.637–40   360n523

Plato

Laws
3.690a–b   381n619

3.776d–777e   344n468
7.808d   376n593

Republic
5.455c–e   344n467

Plautus

Curculio
389   165

Pliny the Younger

Letters
4.19   360n519
7.5   360n522

Plutarch

Advice to Bride and Groom
8   357n512
11   347n481, 352n493
19   347n482
33   352n493

Antonius
28–30   427n826

Cicero
14.6–7   356n506

Consolation to His Wife   377n597

Lucullus
15   417n782

Moralia
37.1   285n219
329A–B   183n438
439A–523B   136n229
452E–464D   290n236
479A–B   136n229
488C   294n252
504A–C   316n331

Numa
2.4–5   183n439

On the Fortune of Alexander
1.6   183n438

Polybius

History
3.63–64   407n732
6.23.2   420n802

Quintilian

Institutio oratoria
2.3.137–42   285n218
7.2.24   17n55

Seneca

Epistles
4.2   285n218
31.11   396n695
47.5   395n690
47.11   395n691
47.16   395n692
47.17   395n689
59.7–8   426n821
70.20–23   386n649
80.9   391n669
89.13   51n217
94.1   51n217
95   292n244
95.1   51n217
95.35   426n825
96.5   426n822
101.13   386n649
123.1–4   395n688

Epistulae ad Atticum
5.20.9   285n218

On Benefits
1.1.1–2   158n330
1.3.2   100n70
1.15.6   101n73, 158n330
3.20.1–2   395n687
3.28.1   396n695
4.18.1   369n559
4.28   158n330

On Clemency
2.2.1   130n207, 358n514

On the Constancy of the Wise Man
6.8   409n742

473

Index of Scripture and Other Ancient Texts

Strabo

Geography

14.1.4–38	34n136
14.1.20	34n139

Suetonius

Augustus

31.1	41n173
74	398n702

Octavian

24	417n782

Tiberius

61.5	46n195

Titus

8.3	82n32

Tacitus

Annals

1.12	135n228
1.13	135n228
2.85	41n175
4.15.37	38n163
14.31.6–7	206n532, 427n827

Histories

5.5.1–2	169n378
5.5.2	177n408

Thucydides

2.75.4	422n806

Valerius Maximus

Memorable Deeds and Sayings

2.1.6	361n525
6.3.11	398n703

Xenophon of Ephesus

Ephesiaca

1.2.2–4	35n146
1.2.24	35n146
1.3.1–2	36n148

EARLY CHRISTIAN LITERATURE

Ambrose

Epistles

21	21n75

Ambrosiaster

Ephesians

4	262n115

Athanasius

Against the Arians

1.29	60n242

De synodis

2.27	356n507

Augustine of Hippo

Exposition on Romans

60.13	158n326

Sermons

281.2	378n602

Basil of Caesarea, the Great

Against Eunomius

2.19	27n100

Refutation of the Apology of the Impious Eunomius

2.4	60n242

Clement of Alexandria

Exhortation to the Greeks

2.17–21	178n418

Miscellanies

1.42.2	170n384

Cyril of Alexandria

De recta fide ad Arcadiam et Marinam

5.6	357n508

Dio Chrysostom

Ephesians

1:15–20	129n201

Homilies on Ephesians

11	262n115

Homilies on First Corinthians

40	46n194

On Covetousness

17.2	241n17

Orations

19.10–12	409n742

To the Nicomedians

38.14–16	360n524

Eusebius

Ecclesiastical History

2.22.2	31n122
6.14.2–3	22n78
6.25.11–14	21n76

Gregory of Nazianzus

Orations

31.9	66–67

Ignatius

To the Ephesians

4.2	248n49
5.1	248n49
5.2–6.1	406n730
14.1	248n49

To the Philadelphians

2.2	248n49
3.2	248n49
5.2	248n49
8.1	248n49
9.1	248n49
11.2	9n19

To the Smyrnaeans

12.1	9n19

Irenaeus

Against Heresies

4.22.1	107n106, 262n115
5.2.3	27n104
8.1	27n104
14.3	27n104
24.4	27n104

474

Index of Scripture and Other Ancient Texts

Jerome

Apology
2 — 21n73
20 — 21n73

Commentary on Ephesians — 257n81, 259n96
preface, book 1 — 22n80
2.4 — 262n115

Epistle
57.5.1 — 22n79

Letters
45.3 — 21n73

John Chrysostom

Homilies on Ephesians
6:9 — 404n724

Homilies on First Corinthians
26.3 — 357n509

Justin Martyr

Dialogue with Trypho
119.4 — 170n384

Origen

Against Celsus
7.29 — 21n77

Commentary on Job
2.6 — 21n77
10.11 — 21n77

First Principles
3.1.10 — 21n7
3.2.4 — 21n7
3.2.5 — 21n7
3.5.4 — 27n104
4.1.24 — 21n7

Polycarp

To the Philippians
1.3 — 163n357

Tertullian

Against Marcion
5.17.1 — 27nn101–2

The Soul
55.2 — 262n115